The 6th International Conference on Communications, Information, Electronic and Energy Systems

The 6th International Conference on Communications, Information, Electronic and Energy Systems

Volume Editors

Teodor Iliev
Ivaylo Stoyanov
Grigor Mihaylov

MDPI

Basel • Beijing • Wuhan • Barcelona • Belgrade • Novi Sad • Cluj • Manchester

Volume Editors
Teodor Iliev
University of Ruse
Ruse
Bulgaria

Ivaylo Stoyanov
University of Ruse
Ruse
Bulgaria

Grigor Mihaylov
University of
Telecommunications and Post
Sofia
Bulgaria

Editorial Office
MDPI AG
Grosspeteranlage 5
4052 Basel, Switzerland

This is a reprint of the Proceedings, published open access by the journal *Engineering Proceedings* (ISSN 2673-4591), freely accessible at: https://www.mdpi.com/2673-4591/122/1.

For citation purposes, cite each article independently as indicated on the article page online and as indicated below:

Lastname, A.A.; Lastname, B.B. Article Title. *Journal Name* **Year**, *Volume Number*, Page Range.

ISBN 978-3-7258-7967-0 (Hbk)
ISBN 978-3-7258-7968-7 (PDF)
https://doi.org/10.3390/books978-3-7258-7968-7

Contents

About the Editors

Teodor Iliev

Teodor Iliev received his M.Sc. and Ph.D. degrees in Telecommunication Engineering from the University of Ruse "Angel Kanchev," Ruse, Bulgaria, in 1999 and 2007, respectively. He is currently a Full Professor within the Department of Telecommunication, the University of Ruse "Angel Kanchev." He has qualifications and experience in electronics and telecommunications engineering from/at institutions, including the University of Ruse "Angel Kanchev" and the University of Telecommunications and Post. He has authored or co-authored over 170 papers in refereed academic journals and international conferences in the areas of telecommunications, electronics, and energy. His research interests include mobile communications networks, signal processing, wireless technologies, and satellite navigation. Prof. Iliev currently serves as a conference chair for the International Scientific Conference on Communications, Information, Electronic and Energy Systems (CIEES) and the International Conference on Electronics, Engineering Physics and Earth Science (EEPES); he is also Editor-in-Chief of *The Journal of CIEES*.

Ivaylo Stoyanov

Ivaylo Stoyanov received his M.Sc. and Ph.D. degrees from the University of Ruse "Angel Kanchev," Ruse, Bulgaria, in 1995 and 2005, respectively. He is currently an electrical engineer and a full professor within the Department of Electrical Power Engineering, the University of Ruse "Angel Kanchev." He has qualifications and experience related to smart grids, electronics, and communications engineering. He has authored or co-authored more than 110 papers in refereed academic journals and at international conferences in the area of communications. His research interests include D2D communication, wireless technologies, and smart grids. He currently serves as a conference chair for the International Scientific Conference on Communications, Information, Electronic and Energy Systems (CIEES) and the International Conference on Electronics, Engineering Physics and Earth Science (EEPES); he is also Editor-in-Chief of *The Journal of CIEES*.

Grigor Mihaylov

Grigor Mihaylov studied communication technologies at the University of Ruse "Angel Kanchev", Bulgaria. He received his BSc and MSc degrees in 2004 and 2005, respectively. In 2015, he received a PhD/doctoral degree in Communication Networks from the University of Ruse "Angel Kanchev", Bulgaria, and subsequently received a post-doctoral degree (Habilitation) from the University of Telecommunications and Post, Sofia, Bulgaria, in 2018. Since 2018, he has taught and conducted research as an associate professor at the University of Telecommunications and Post, Sofia, in the Department of Telecommunications. In 2023, he received his full professor degree at the University of Telecommunications and Post, Sofia. His research is dedicated to radio transmission, wireless networks, and next-generation mobile networks. This research area covers the design of radio transmission systems, modulation and coding techniques, and contemporary mobile networks architecture designing, including interdisciplinary simulations and technological backgrounds. He has published more than 120 journal and conference papers and several books, he acts as a reviewer and a Guest Editor for several international journals, and he is a member of various international conference programs and organizing committees.

engineering proceedings

MDPI

Editorial

Preface and Statement of Peer-Review: The 6th International Conference on Communications, Information, Electronic and Energy Systems (CIEES 2025) †

Teodor Iliev [1,*], Ivaylo Stoyanov [2] and Grigor Mihaylov [3]

1 Department of Telecommunication, University of Ruse, 7004 Ruse, Bulgaria
2 Department of Electrical Power Engineering, University of Ruse, 7004 Ruse, Bulgaria; stoyanov@uni-ruse.bg
3 Department of Telecommunications, University of Telecommunications and Post, 1700 Sofia, Bulgaria; gregmihaylov@gmail.com
* Correspondence: tiliev@uni-ruse.bg
† Proceeding papers in this volume were presented at the 6th International Conference on Communications, Information, Electronic and Energy Systems (CIEES 2025), Ruse, Bulgaria, 26–28 November 2025.

Abstract

The conference is aimed to provide an international forum for researchers, academics, people in industry, and students to address recent research results and to present and discuss their ideas, theories, technologies, systems, tools, applications, works in progress and experiences on all theoretical and practical issues arising in telecommunications, electronics, signal processing and applications, information technologies, energy, automotive and industrial engineering.

Keywords: telecommunication; ICT; AI; RES; industrial engineering; electronics; thermodynamics; automotive engineering

1. Introduction

The sixth edition of the International Conference on Communications, Information, Electronic and Energy Systems (CIEES 2025) was held in hybrid mode at the University of Ruse "Angel Kanchev", Ruse, Bulgaria, from 26 to 28 November 2025.

The CIEES 2025 Conference is the premier international forum dedicated to advancing the understanding of the current state and future evolution of science and technology through the lens of telecommunications, information technologies and artificial intelligence, power systems & smart cities, energy and renewable sources, automotive and industrial engineering, smart telecommunications, industry and services, electronics, power electronics and EMC, and many other related disciplines. It is a venue where researchers, academics, industry professionals, and students come together to present and discuss progress in research, development, standards, and applications across these diverse areas.

2. Program and Speakers

The technical program of this year's edition of the conference features two distinguished keynote speakers, both world-renowned experts in their fields, with their plenary lectures as follows:

- **Prof. Dimiter Ialnazov, PhD**, Kyoto University, Japan, the title of the lecture "The Energy Transition in Japan: Current Situation and Future Prospects";

- **Assoc. Prof. Kuanish Alipbayev, PhD**, Almaty University of Power Engineering and Telecommunications, Almaty, Kazakhstan, the title of the lecture "Multifunctional Robotic System for Sequential Assignment";

In addition, we have prepared an engaging plenary program not only with presentations by respected university professors and academic speakers on visionary topics, but with an outstanding technical contribution from our Golden Sponsor, SUNOTEC Group, Bulgaria:

- **Vladimir Zinoviev, PhD**, SUNOTEC Group, Bulgaria, the title of the lecture "Innovative Approach for BESS-based PV Power Integration".

The technical program of the conference includes the plenary session as well as in-person and online technical sessions for research papers. The authors of the accepted papers who were unable to attend the conference in person were allowed to present their papers online and participate in an interactive virtual conference. Online presentations were conducted via the Zoom Meeting platform and were available for the opening ceremony, all conference sessions, and meetings.

3. Statement of Peer-Review

In submitting conference proceedings to *Engineering Proceedings*, the volume editors of the proceedings certify to the publisher that all papers published in this volume have been subjected to peer review administered by the volume editors. Reviews were conducted by expert referees to the professional and scientific standards expected of a proceedings journal.

- Type of peer review: single-blind;
- Conference submission management system: Microsoft CMT;
- Number of submissions received: 230;
- Number of submissions sent for review: 214;
- Number of submissions accepted: 136;
- Number of submissions published in this volume: 29;
- Acceptance rate (number of submissions accepted/number of submissions received): 59%;
- Average number of reviews per paper: 0.53;
- Total number of reviewers involved: 114;
- Additional information on the review process: All submitted manuscripts to the CIEES 2025 conference were single-blind peer-reviewed and were carried out to meet the scientific criteria of novelty and academic excellence.

4. Sponsorship

We would like to express our sincere gratitude to SUNOTEC Group, Bulgaria for becoming an official sponsor of the CIEES 2025, and to the Project "Scientific University of Ruse", funded by the European Union NextGenerationEU through the National Plan for Recovery and Resilience of the Republic of Bulgaria, BG-RRP-2.013-0001, for supporting this event. Our thanks also go to our Institutional partner, the University of Ruse "Angel Kanchev", Bulgaria, as well as to the TPC members, conference chairs, and reviewers for their dedicated efforts in creating a successful and rigorous technical program. Without their contributions, this event would not have been possible.

We extend our heartfelt gratitude and appreciation to our esteemed Media Partner—MDPI's *Electronics* journal.

Conflicts of Interest: The authors declare no conflicts of interest.

engineering proceedings

MDPI

Proceeding Paper

Non-Parametric Model for Curvature Classification of Departure Flight Trajectory Segments †

Lucija Žužić [1,2,*], Ivan Štajduhar [1,2], Jonatan Lerga [1,2] and Renato Filjar [1,2,3]

[1] Department of Computer Engineering, Faculty of Engineering, University of Rijeka, Vukovarska 58, 51000 Rijeka, Croatia; ivan.stajduhar@uniri.hr (I.Š.); jonatan.lerga@riteh.uniri.hr (J.L.); renato.filjar@gmail.com (R.F.)

[2] Center for Artificial Intelligence and Cybersecurity, University of Rijeka, Radmile Matejcic 2, 51000 Rijeka, Croatia

[3] Laboratory for Spatial Intelligence, Hrvatsko Zagorje Krapina University of Applied Sciences, Šetalište Hrvatskog Narodnog Preporoda 6, 49000 Krapina, Croatia

* Correspondence: lucija.zuzic@uniri.hr

† Presented at the 6th International Conference on Communications, Information, Electronic and Energy Systems, Ruse, Bulgaria, 26–28 November 2025.

Abstract

This study introduces a novel approach for classifying flight trajectory curvature, focusing on early-stage flight characteristics to detect anomalies and deviations. The method intentionally avoids direct coordinate data and instead leverages a combination of trajectory-derived and meteorological features. This research analysed 9849 departure flight trajectories originating from 14 different airports. Two distinct trajectory classes were established through manual visual inspection, differentiated by curvature patterns. This categorisation formed the ground truth for evaluating trained machine learning (ML) classifiers from different families. The comparative analysis demonstrates that the Random Forest (RF) algorithm provides the most effective classification model. RF excels at summarising complex trajectory information and identifying non-linear relationships within the early-flight data. A key contribution of this work is the validation of specific predictors. The theoretical definitions of direction change (using vector values to capture dynamic movement) and diffusion distance (using scalar values to represent static displacement) proved highly effective. Their selection as primary predictors is supported by their ability to represent the essential static and dynamic properties of the trajectory, enabling the model to accurately classify flight paths and potential deviations before the flight is complete. This approach offers significant potential for enhancing real-time air traffic monitoring and safety systems.

Keywords: aircraft; trajectory; classification; machine learning

1. Introduction

Aircraft trajectory classification to define flight characteristics is crucial in air traffic management, flight safety analysis, and operational planning. Accurately categorising flight trajectories can help optimise airspace usage, improve predictive modelling, and enhance aviation safety. The classification of aircraft trajectories is a task of great importance for multiple applications, including air traffic management where identifying trajectory patterns can help improve flight scheduling and congestion prediction, aviation safety and security where anomaly detection and detecting deviations from expected trajectories is crucial, and the automation of trajectory analysis since efficient machine learning (ML) classification eliminates the need for human labelling.

Existing studies have focused on trajectory prediction using statistical models, clustering, and deep learning (DL) methods. However, a significant research gap is evident, and additional studies remain to be conducted in feature selection for efficient real-time classification of aircraft departure trajectories. This study explores how trajectory and meteorological characteristics in early flight contribute to the classification of flight curvature.

Existing approaches to aircraft trajectory classification often rely on high-dimensional representations of flight paths, requiring significant computational resources. However, for real-time applications and deployment in environments with limited processing power, such as onboard systems and embedded devices, it is essential to develop lightweight models that use minimal but highly discriminative features.

This paper proposes a classification model based on ML that does not require direct input of geospatial coordinates. Instead, it evaluates and explores the effectiveness of selected trajectory-derived metrics, particularly diffusion distance and the arithmetic average of direction change, used as key trajectory features to differentiate trajectory segments effectively and achieve accurate classification.

Prior research has analysed trajectory patterns using Mode S messages and Automatic Dependent Surveillance-Broadcast (ADS-B) data [1]. Deep learning (DL) models have also been used for trajectory classification. Jiménez-Campfens et al. [2] applied DL to air traffic trajectory classification based on meteorological reports, showing that weather conditions impact aircraft movement deviations, supporting the choice to include these variables in the conducted experiment described in this paper. Zhang and Liu [3] extended this work by combining DL and clustering techniques for four-dimensional trajectory prediction. This highlights the need for temporal and spatial data integration to improve generalisation across different aircraft types. Conflict and anomaly detection using machine learning remains a crucial air traffic management component. Pérez-Castán et al. [4] explored the application of probabilistic ML classification techniques to air traffic conflict management and detection in free-route airspace for better risk assessment of flight paths, demonstrating how predictive models can enhance Air Traffic Control (ATC) decision-making and improve predictive conflict resolution. Aircraft manoeuvre classification is essential for detecting anomalies, violations, and operational inefficiencies. Jouaber et al. [5] developed a real-time aircraft manoeuvre classification system, enabling automated monitoring of pilot actions.

Despite these advances, limited research is focused on aircraft departure trajectory classification using minimal feature sets. Few studies address classification and flight type definition based solely on extracted trajectory metrics rather than direct geospatial coordinates. Most existing approaches rely on complete trajectory sequences, which can be computationally intensive. Several other works have successfully explored different techniques for trajectory feature extraction, and the R trajr library [6] has been widely used across various domains, including the analysis of trajectories representing animal movement, such as griffon vultures [7], and different kinds of traffic, including aerial transport [8].

This paper aims to expand the application of these features by evaluating ML models. We investigate whether departure flights from 14 airports can be classified based on trajectory and meteorological features, without relying on direct coordinate-based classification to assign flights to the appropriate human-defined curvature categories using minimal predictors while maintaining a high accuracy.

The k-Nearest Neighbours (k-NN), Linear and Radial Basis Function (RBF) Support Vector Machine (SVM), Gaussian Process (GP), Decision Tree (DT), Random Forest (RF), Multilayer Perceptron (MLP), Naive Bayes (NB), Quadratic Discriminant Analysis (QDA) and Adaptive Boosting (AdaBoost, AB) algorithms were used for classification in this paper. The listed classifiers have solved various problems, including behaviour analysis [9].

 https://doi.org/10.3390/engproc2026122001

Bosson and Nikoleris [10] use some of these classifiers and additional methods to predict the runway on which airplanes land, while this paper focuses on take-off direction.

We hypothesise that trajectory-derived geometric features such as diffusion distance and the arithmetic average of direction change provide sufficient information for classification without requiring full trajectory input. ML classifiers, particularly the MLP method, and ensemble methods like RF, outperformed simple probabilistic models in the experiment due to their ability to capture complex trajectory variations. Meteorological factors are secondary in departure trajectory classification since adverse weather effects are already reflected in trajectory features. This study examines whether departure flight trajectories can be effectively classified using only diffusion distance and the arithmetic average of direction change as key predictive features.

2. Materials and Methods

The experiment was conducted using the R statistical computing software [11]. Machine learning models were trained and evaluated using the R package caret version 4.5.1 2025 [12], which facilitates processes like cross-validation and hyperparameter tuning. The selection and application of various machine learning classifiers [13] were informed by established methodologies [14]. The R trajr library [6] was also used because of its applicability for trajectory feature extraction across various domains, including animal movement analysis [7]. Additionally, the inclusion of meteorological features as model inputs was supported by prior research, including the review by Gultepe et al. [15], which confirms the significant impact of weather conditions on aviation.

We used a sequential data processing and modelling pipeline, as depicted in Figure 1. The process begins with two parallel data inputs (raw trajectory data (ADS-B messages) and Meteorological Aerodrome Report (METAR) data). Both sets of raw data are fed into this stage for cleaning and preparation. The pre-processed data moves to the feature extraction stage, where relevant predictors (such as direction change and diffusion distance) are calculated. The trajectories are manually inspected, and at his stage, the two distinct trajectory classes (the labels) are defined. The output of the inspection stage is the final, labelled dataset, which now includes the features and the assigned curvature class for each trajectory. This labelled dataset is used to begin the machine learning phase, starting with the selection of candidate models. The selected models are trained on the labelled dataset. The trained models are validated and evaluated to determine their performance and accuracy. The process concludes with the final output representing the optimised classification model (identified in the experiment as the Random Forest (RF) model) for classifying flight trajectory curvature.

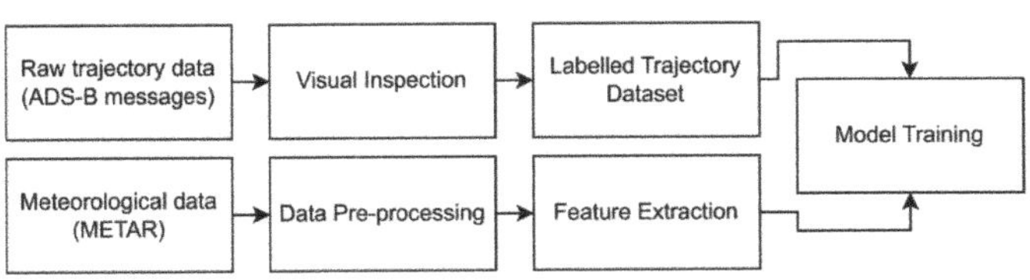

Figure 1. Schematic diagram of the experimental setup.

2.1. Materials

This paper uses different trajectory and meteorological features as classifier input in the statistical computing software R [11] to determine the take-off curvature of aircraft flights from the selected point of departure to the destination airport. The previously manually labelled flight trajectories are classified without directly using the coordinates as input for the This paper uses different trajectory and meteorological features as classifier input in the

 https://doi.org/10.3390/engproc2026122001

statistical computing software R [11] to determine the take-off curvature of aircraft flights from the selected point of departure to the destination airport. The previously manually labelled flight trajectories are classified without directly using the coordinates as input for the model. Such an analysis confirms the significance of trajectory features and enables performance comparison of different classifiers.

The results also provide insight into the influence of different meteorological factors on aircraft movement. Publicly available data on meteorological features was used as model input because meteorological conditions influence the frequency of incidents, as confirmed by reports on airplane accidents [15].

2.1.1. Trajectory Features

OpenSkyNetwork is a non-profit network collecting air traffic data using state vector information from ADS-B receivers. This dataset is public and available for free.

The authors assembled 9849 flight trajectories from 14 origin airports using data gathered from 5 June 2017 to 27 June 2022. for each full hour on Mondays. Only an area of 0.4° longitude and latitude around the origin airport was used for further trajectory processing, approximately equal to 44.4 km at the latitude and longitude of this airport. The observed area is limited to the initial phase of the flight near the airport since the research goal was to determine a take-off flight class for each trajectory. The 11 trajectory features generated using the trajr library are: (1) diffusion distance (the Euclidean distance of the start and end), (2) length (the total length of the curve representing the trajectory), (3) duration (the time in s elapsed between the trajectory start and end), (4) speed (the mean value of the speed in each trajectory segment), (5) acceleration (the mean value of the acceleration in each segment), (6) straightness, (7) sinuosity, (8) maximum expected displacement, (9) the arithmetic average and (10) standard deviation of direction change, and (11) fractal dimension.

The calculation methods for straightness, sinuosity, maximum expected displacement, the arithmetic average and standard deviation of direction change, and the fractal dimension are given in the continuation of the text.

The straightness is calculated using the formula defined by Benhamou [6], where D is the Euclidean distance of the beginning and end points of the trajectory, and L is the length of the trajectory:

$$\frac{D}{L}. \tag{1}$$

The sinuosity index defined by Benhamou [6] and used in this experiment is a function of the mean cosine of the turning angles. This is a corrected form of the original sinuosity index defined by Bovet and Benhamou [6].

The corrected sinuosity index S is formulated in:

$$S = 2\left[p\left(\frac{1+c}{1-c} + b^2\right)\right]^{-0.5}, \tag{2}$$

with p denoting the mean step size, c the mean cosine of the turning angles, and b the step size variation coefficient. A sinuosity index closer to 1 represents linear movement because the cosine of turning angles approaches 1 as the turning angle decreases.

The maximum expected displacement is calculated according to:

$$\frac{b}{1-b}, \tag{3}$$

https://doi.org/10.3390/engproc2026122001

where b represents the mean value of the cosine of the turning angles, is a dimensionless estimate calculated from the beginning to the end of the trajectory, and larger values represent linear movement [6].

Direction change is a vector containing the change in angle (in °) between each pair of consecutive steps in a trajectory, divided by the time difference between the two steps. The arithmetic mean of direction change represents the non-linearity index, and the standard deviation measures irregularity, so both values were used as model input.

In mathematics, fractal dimension is a term used in geometry to give a rational statistical index of the complexity of detail in a pattern. A fractal pattern changes with the scale at which it is measured, which is the step size for trajectories. The fractal dimension is also a measure of the space occupied by the pattern and describes how the fractal scales differently in the non-integer fractal dimension.

The fractal dimension calculation uses the modified "dividers" method to account for rounding errors [6]. This function compensates for overestimating the trajectory length by going through "splits" representing trajectory segments forward and backward and returning the arithmetic mean of the calculated fractal dimension values. After the last step, the length of the remaining trajectory is estimated. The formula for calculating fractal dimension is given in:

$$D_0 = \lim_{\varepsilon \to 0} \frac{log N(\varepsilon)}{log \frac{1}{\varepsilon}}, \tag{4}$$

where ε is the step size, $N(\varepsilon)$ is the number of trajectory segments, and D_0 is the fractal dimension.

The range of step sizes used to calculate the fractal dimension must be predefined. A thousand values uniformly spaced between 1 km and 2 km on the logarithmic axis were used to estimate the fractal dimension of the aircraft's trajectory. The arithmetic average of these fractal dimensions was used as model input. Linear regression confirms that the relationship between step size and trajectory length is linear for the chosen range of step sizes. This means that the trajectory is a fractal curve for these step sizes.

2.1.2. Meteorological Features

Publicly available meteorological data from Meteorological Aerodrome Report (METAR) reports on the website https://rp5.ru (accessed on 3 September 2025), was used along with aircraft trajectory features to train classifiers in this paper using manually marked trajectories.

The 5 meteorological features used as model input are: (1) temperature and dew point in °C, (2) relative humidity between 0% and 100%, air pressure in mmHg (3) at the altitude of the measuring station and (4) at sea level, and (5) wind speed in m/s.

Measurements of meteorological features are added every 30 min or every 60 min, and state vectors every 10 s. The value from the meteorological report with the smallest time gap was used for each aircraft state vector. The arithmetic mean for each meteorological feature across a trajectory is used as model input.

2.1.3. Training and Testing Dataset

A total of 9849 trajectories from 14 airports are used for training and testing: 9 airports from Croatia were processed (Zagreb Pleso (LDZA), Dubrovnik Čilipi (LDDU), Osijek/Klisa (LDOS), Rijeka/Omišalj (LDRI), Mali Lošinj (LDLO), Pula (LDPL), Split (LDSP), Brač (LDSB), and Zadar (LDZD)), 3 from Slovenia (Ljubljana/Brnik (LJLJ), Maribor/Slivnica (LJMB), and Portorož/Sečovlje (LJPZ)), and 2 from Bosnia and Herzegovina (Tuzla (LQTZ) and Banja Luka (LQBK)).

https://doi.org/10.3390/engproc2026122001

Table 1 lists the total number of samples in each class or aggregated, the number of samples used for testing and training, and presents these numbers combined for all 14 airports. The trajectories were randomly divided into training and testing datasets by sampling from a normal distribution with a 70/30 probability. The split was done separately for each airport and class to maintain a similar ratio of data from each airport and class in the training and testing datasets.

Table 1. The total number of samples and the number of samples used for testing and training combined for 14 airports. The values are listed for each class separately and aggregated.

Class	All	Test	Train
All	9849	2967	6882
−1	870	263	607
1	8979	2704	6275

The original set of observations has been split into training and testing subsets while sustaining proportions of data relating to classes of trajectories representing flight curvature categories.

It is evident from Table 1 that class 1 is almost ten times more common than class −1, impacting model performance.

2.1.4. Data Pre-Processing

Before the data was used as input to classification models, each feature, or each column of the matrix, was scaled. When scaling, the arithmetic mean of all feature values (matrix column) is subtracted from the feature value for a given sample (trajectory), and the result is then divided by the standard deviation of the feature value (matrix column).

2.2. Methods

Multiple machine learning (ML) models are compared in this study to classify aircraft departure trajectories by assigning them to a flight curvature class based on geometric and meteorological features. The selected models belong to different families of classification approaches, each with unique strengths and limitations. Understanding these families helps justify their selection and interpret their performance in trajectory classification. Classification methods can be broadly categorised into different families based on underlying principles. These families include: (1) maximum margin methods (Support Vector Machine (SVM)), (2) Bayesian non-parametric methods (Naive Bayes (NB), Quadratic Discriminant Analysis (QDA)), (3) ensemble learning methods (RF and Adaptive Boosting (AdaBoost, AB), utilising Decision Tree (DT) classifiers), (4) Neural Network (NN) methods (Multilayer Perceptron (MLP)), and (5) instance-based learning methods (k-Nearest Neighbours (k-NN)). Each of these families offers different strengths. Our study evaluates them to determine the most effective approach for trajectory classification. Hyperparameters were tuned in repeated cross-validation for all models across 10 folds, and 10 complete sets of folds were computed.

2.2.1. Maximum Margin Methods

Maximum margin methods, such as the SVM method, aim to find a decision boundary that maximises the margin between different classes. The SVM method creates a hyperplane that maximises the margin between trajectory classes and can use kernel functions, such as a Linear or Radial Basis Function (RBF), to handle non-linearly separable data. This approach is relevant to our study because trajectory data may exhibit complex, non-linear separability, requiring an effective boundary to distinguish classes.

https://doi.org/10.3390/engproc2026122001

2.2.2. Probabilistic Methods

Probabilistic methods such as Naive Bayes (NB) estimate class probabilities based on feature distributions. The NB method assumes independence between features and applies Bayes' theorem to compute probabilities. Quadratic Discriminant Analysis (QDA) extends linear classifiers to implement quadratic decision boundaries. These models provide probabilistic interpretations but might be less suitable for trajectory classification since several features are theoretically connected by their calculation methods.

2.2.3. Bayesian Non-Parametric Methods

Bayesian non-parametric methods are probabilistic but do not use a fixed number of parameters like the Naive Bayes (NB) and Quadratic Discriminant Analysis (QDA) methods. The Gaussian Process (GP) method is kernel-based and probabilistic, generalising well to small datasets by defining distributions over functions. The GP method can capture non-linear relationships in trajectory data but may require more training time than simpler models.

2.2.4. Ensemble Learning Methods

Ensemble learning methods combine multiple weak classifiers to improve accuracy and robustness. Random Forest (RF) is a bagging-based ensemble of Decision Tree (DT) classifiers that reduces overfitting by aggregating and averaging multiple tree predictions. Instead of relying on a single DT, the RF method uses stochastic discrimination to introduce randomness and generates multiple trees using different feature subsets and training samples. The final classification is based on the majority vote of these trees. This process prevents overfitting, which includes memorising specific details and the noise present in individual trajectories, instead focusing on generalizable patterns. The number of randomly selected predictors for RF is a tuneable hyperparameter, adjusted in repeated 10-fold cross-validation for this study.

Adaptive Boosting (AdaBoost, AB) is a boosting algorithm that sequentially trains weak classifiers instead of averaging multiple outputs, extending the model training time and assigning more weight to misclassified instances in each iteration. Ensemble methods like RF and AB help smooth out inconsistencies and noise, improving classification performance. This is useful in our study because aircraft trajectories contain noise due to sensor inaccuracies or environmental factors such as wind, and a single classifier may struggle to capture this complexity. The AB algorithm is often called the best classifier using initial settings without adjustment, so it is hypothesised to be more successful than other classifiers.

2.2.5. Neural Network Methods

Neural Network (NN) methods simulate the structure of biological neurons and are particularly suited for learning complex patterns. The Multilayer Perceptron (MLP) method is a feedforward NN that learns through backpropagation. The MLP method performed well in our study, likely due to its ability to effectively model uncertainty in trajectory data. The tuneable hyperparameters for the MLP determining the layer size (the number of hidden units) and the weight decay were adjusted by computing 10 complete sets of folds in 10-fold cross-validation.

2.2.6. Instance-Based Learning Methods

Instance-based learning methods classify new instances based on similarity to stored examples. The k-Nearest Neighbours (k-NN) method assigns a class based on the majority vote of the k nearest training samples. While simple, k-NN may be sensitive to noise and

https://doi.org/10.3390/engproc2026122001

computationally expensive for large datasets. A good k can be chosen via the bootstrap method or using different heuristic techniques, such as hyperparameter optimisation. In binary classification, k is often an odd number to avoid ties. Integers from one to twenty, including the range limits, were tested as k values in this experiment.

3. Results

Results present model performance, and the combined training and inference time. McNemar's test compares models using the optimal set of predictors and different methods.

Balanced Accuracy (BA) accurately assesses model performance for unbalanced classes since accuracy does not consider them individually. The BA is the arithmetic mean of the True Positive Rate (TPR), focused on the positive class, and the True Negative Rate (TNR), focused on the negative class. BA can provide valuable insights into this study since only 870 samples (8.83%) out of 9849 trajectories belong to the negative class, and linear trajectories are uncommon. Another metric used to evaluate each class separately is the F1 score. The F1 is the harmonic mean of the TPR and Precision, also called the Positive Predictive Value (PPV).

The experiment was conducted on the AMD Ryzen 5 PRO 4650G Central Processing Unit (CPU) with 6 cores, which should be considered when interpreting training and inference time.

3.1. Model Comparison

Candidate models were assessed to determine the optimal method and set of predictors to be used in the final model for application in real settings. The accuracy (number of correct classifications, abbreviated as Acc), Balanced Accuracy (BA), and F1 score of the candidate models are listed in Figures 2–5. Candidate models have been developed using: (1) all available trajectory and meteorological features (Figure 2) (2) exclusively trajectory features (Figure 3) (3) exclusively meteorological features (Figure 4), and (4) exclusively diffusion distance and the arithmetic average of direction change (Figure 5).

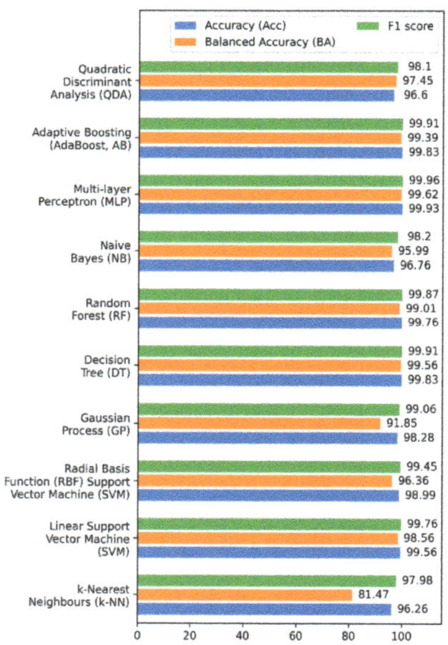

Figure 2. The Accuracy (Acc), Balanced Accuracy (BA), and F1 score (from bottom to top, respectively) as a percentage (%) for each candidate model developed using different methods with trajectory and meteorological features as predictors.

 https://doi.org/10.3390/engproc2026122001

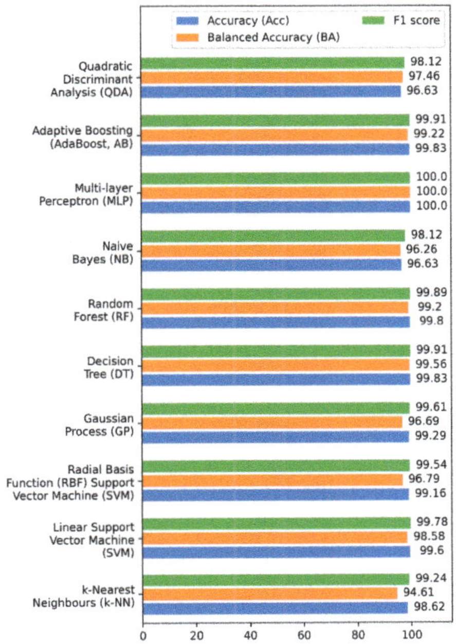

Figure 3. The Accuracy (Acc), Balanced Accuracy (BA), and F1 score (from bottom to top, respectively) as a percentage (%) for each candidate model developed using different methods with trajectory features as predictors.

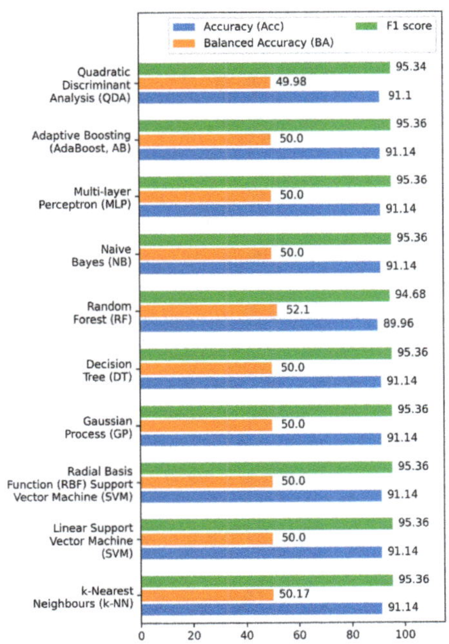

Figure 4. The Accuracy (Acc), Balanced Accuracy (BA), and F1 score (from bottom to top, respectively) as a percentage (%) for each candidate model developed using different methods with meteorological features as predictors.

https://doi.org/10.3390/engproc2026122001

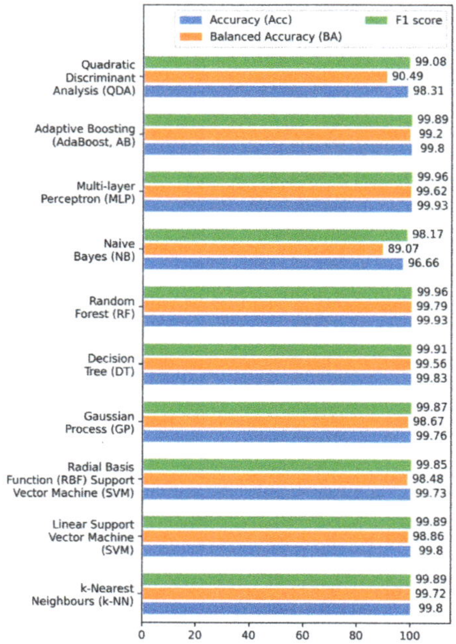

Figure 5. The Accuracy (Acc), Balanced Accuracy (BA), and F1 score (from bottom to top, respectively) as a percentage (%) for each candidate model developed using different methods with the diffusion distance and the arithmetic average of direction change as predictors.

The highest accuracy using diffusion distance and the arithmetic average of direction change as predictors in Figure 5 was achieved with the Multilayer Perceptron (MLP) classifier method. This supports the hypothesis that meteorological features and trajectory features other than diffusion distance and the arithmetic average of direction change should be removed from the set of predictors. The MLP method also yielded the model with the highest accuracy in Figures 2–4, leading to the decision that it should be used in the final model. Diffusion distance and the arithmetic average of direction change were chosen to establish a model with a minimal predictor set since they describe the static and dynamic aspects of the trajectory expressed as a scalar and vector variable, in that order. This pair of predictors was also used in the final model.

The reasoning behind this approach was the assumption that reducing the set of predictors would reduce model complexity and computation time. It is theoretically sound that the impact of changes in meteorological features is reflected in the movement of the aircraft and the trajectory features describing it, so adding additional data is redundant.

With trajectory and meteorological features used as predictors, MLP was the most successful classifier in Figure 2. It had the highest accuracy, BA, and F1 score values of 99.93%, 99.62%, and 99.96%, respectively.

The MLP method was the most successful classifier with the highest accuracy, BA, and F1 score values of 100% when trajectory features were provided as the only model input, as presented in Figure 3.

All models except Random Forest (RF) and Quadratic Discriminant Analysis (QDA) had the highest accuracy of 91.14% when using exclusively meteorological predictors, as listed in Figure 4. Similarly, all models except k-Nearest Neighbours (k-NN), RF, and QDA had the highest F1 score of 95.36%, as listed in Figure 4. However, the RF method has the highest BA of 52.1%. The low BA compared to the accuracy and the F1 score with this set of predictors indicates that the minority class was not predicted accurately, and all the samples were classified into the majority class.

The diffusion distance and the arithmetic average of direction change as predictors lead to the MLP method as the best overall performer once again in Figure 5, with the highest accuracy and F1 score of 99.93% and 99.96%, respectively. Additionally, the RF method had the same accuracy and a higher BA of 99.79%.

The combined model training and inference time in seconds utilising the R system.time function for all candidate models is displayed in Table 2. Training takes much longer than testing, so the values were combined to provide a more realistic overview of the total demand for the full process. The training and inference time is relevant in all use cases, especially for real-time applications and devices with low computational capabilities.

Table 2. The combined training and inference time in seconds for each candidate model developed using different methods and sets of predictors. Predictor set 1 covers all features, set 2 contains exclusively trajectory features, set 3 utilises meteorological features, and set 4 leverages diffusion distance and the arithmetic average of direction change. The longest inference time for each set of predictors is marked in bold.

Method	1	2	3	4
k-NN	0.93	0.66	0.43	**1.47**
Linear SVM	0.24	0.14	0.36	<0.01
RBF SVM	1	0.66	2.32	<0.01
GP	**12,849.66**	**8890.4**	**612.23**	0.08
DT	0.11	0.06	0.02	<0.01
RF	53.12	52.79	31.07	0.05
NB	2.56	0.04	0.02	<0.01
MLP	23.5	20.04	20.64	0.38
AB	6.68	5.2	3.75	0.59
QDA	0.08	0.06	0.01	<0.01

The candidate models using the Gaussian Process (GP) method in Table 2 have the highest combined training and inference time when using all predictors, exclusively trajectory data, or exclusively meteorological data. This is due to automatic sigma estimation for the Laplace or Radial Basis Function (RBF) kernel in GP training. When using only diffusion distance and the arithmetic average of direction change as predictors, the k-NN method has the longest combined training and inference time. It should be noted that the training time was evaluated for a single k-value for the k-NN method, and hyperparameter tuning will lengthen the training time depending on the number of possibilities tested.

RF is the classifier with the second-highest training and inference time when using any set of predictors except exclusively diffusion distance and the arithmetic average of direction change. The increase in the RF training time is due to the ensemble approach in training multiple trees. The Adaptive Boosting (AdaBoost, AB) method has the second-largest combined training and inference time with the diffusion distance and the arithmetic average of direction change as predictors. The MLP method has the third-largest combined training and inference time with any predictor set. This occurs because of the iterative approach in AB and complex Neural Network (NN) training for the MLP method.

3.2. Results of McNemar's Test

McNemar's test with continuity correction is applied to paired classification results to test model differences. This helps assess if a candidate model performs significantly worse or better than others in a more detailed and robust manner than using a simple sensitivity and specificity comparison.

https://doi.org/10.3390/engproc2026122001

Figure 6 contains p-values of McNemar's test when comparing candidate models using either exclusively trajectory features or diffusion distance and the arithmetic average of direction change as predictor variables and various classification methods. The Bonferroni correction was applied and the significance level α was divided by the number of tests to account for the increased likelihood of incorrectly rejecting a null hypothesis when conducting multiple tests, equal to making a Type I error. The p-values larger than the significance level of 1.11×10^{-3} which was adjusted from an alpha value of 0.05 with the Bonferroni correction, indicate the compared models show similar results and could be used to infer trajectory class.

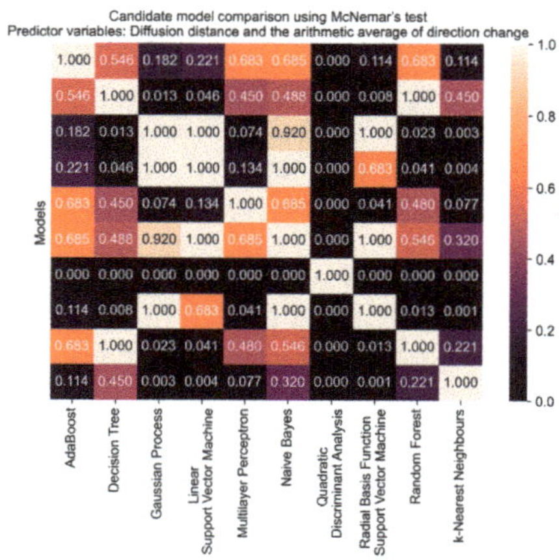

Figure 6. Candidate model comparison using p-values of McNemar's test with various classification methods combined with trajectory features or diffusion distance and the arithmetic average of direction change as predictor variables.

In Figure 6 the black represents a low p-value near 0, white represents a high p-value near 1, and red represents a p-value near 0.5 between the two extremes. Each candidate model is equal to itself, so values on the primary diagonal equal 1. The matrix is symmetrical concerning the primary diagonal because the same result is achieved when swapping the order of the first and second compared candidate models. The only pairs of models in Figure 6 that are statistically significantly different according to the p-values and the Bonferroni correction are Random Forest (RF) and Multi-layer Perceptron (MLP) compared with Quadratic Discriminant Analysis (QDA), with p-values of 4.22×10^{-12} and 1.17×10^{-11}, respectively. The QDA method had the lowest accuracy of 98.31% among all the candidate models using diffusion distance and the arithmetic average of direction change as predictor variables. This supports the conclusion that all other methods achieved superior results with this reduced set of predictors.

4. Discussion

The presented study aims to classify trajectories originating from a chosen origin airport and heading for a target destination airport by determining the flight curvature category. Classification models were applied to multiple trajectory-derived and meteorological features representing independent variables to predict the dependent variable representing the trajectory class. The trajectories were labelled with two categories according to visible flight curvature. Statistical analysis confirmed that trajectory features change distribution based on trajectory class.

https://doi.org/10.3390/engproc2026122001

The k-Nearest Neighbour (k-NN), Linear and Radial Basis Function (RBF) Support Vector Machine (SVM), Gaussian Process (GP), Decision Tree (DT), Random Forest (RF), Multi-layer Perceptron (MLP), Naive Bayes (NB), Quadratic Discriminant Analysis (QDA), and Adaptive Boosting (AdaBoost, AB) methods created a trajectory classification from multiple combinations of input variables. The MLP method using the arithmetic average of direction change and diffusion distance as predictors achieved a 99.93% testing accuracy. The total execution time is much longer when using all tested trajectory features, making a smaller predictor set more suitable for compact, low-performance, and low-cost portable devices installed on board an aircraft.

However, the study's limitations must be acknowledged. The model was trained and validated using 9849 trajectories from 14 specific airports located in Croatia, Slovenia, and Bosnia and Herzegovina. This limited dataset diversity means the model's generalizability to other geographical regions, larger international airports with different departure procedures, or more varied meteorological conditions is not yet confirmed. Future work should therefore focus on validating this model against a larger, more diverse global dataset. Despite this limitation, this research confirms the viability of a computationally efficient method for early-stage flight path classification, offering a promising tool for enhancing air traffic monitoring and safety.

Author Contributions: Conceptualization, L.Ž., I.Š., J.L. and R.F.; methodology, L.Ž., I.Š., J.L. and R.F.; software, L.Ž. and R.F.; validation, L.Ž., I.Š., J.L. and R.F.; formal analysis, L.Ž., I.Š., J.L. and R.F.; investigation, L.Ž.; resources, R.F.; data curation, L.Ž.; writing—original draft preparation, L.Ž.; writing—review and editing, L.Ž., I.Š., J.L. and R.F.; visualization, L.Ž.; supervision, R.F.; project administration, R.F.; funding acquisition. All authors have read and agreed to the published version of the manuscript.

Funding: This research received no external funding.

Institutional Review Board Statement: Not applicable.

Informed Consent Statement: Not applicable.

Data Availability Statement: The original data used in this study was obtained through the OpenSkyNetwork service and the website https://rp5.ru (accessed on 3 September 2025). The original data and the scripts used to produce the presented results are available at https://github.com/LucijaZuzic/JOAS_R_planes_Classification (accessed on 3 September 2025).

Conflicts of Interest: The authors declare no conflicts of interest.

References

1. Sun, J. *The 1090 Megahertz Riddle: A Guide to Decoding Mode S and ADS-B Signals*; Technische Universiteit (TU) Delft OPEN Publishing: Delft, The Netherlands, 2021. [CrossRef]
2. Jiménez-Campfens, N.; Colomer, A.; Núñez, J.; Mogollón, J.M.; Rodríguez, A.L.; Naranjo, V. Deep learning in aeronautics: Air traffic trajectory classification based on weather reports. In *Intelligent Data Engineering and Automated Learning–IDEAL 2020: 21st International Conference, Guimaraes, Portugal, 4–6 November 2020, Proceedings, Part II 21*; Springer Nature: London, UK, 2020; pp. 148–155. [CrossRef]
3. Zhang, H.; Liu, Z. Four-Dimensional Aircraft Trajectory Prediction with a Generative Deep Learning and Clustering Approach. *J. Aerosp. Inf. Syst.* **2025**, *22*, 90–102. [CrossRef]
4. Pérez-Castàn, J.A.; Pérez-Sanz, L.; Bowen-Varela, J.; Serrano-Mira, L.; Radišić, T.; Feuerle, T. Machine Learning classification techniques applied to static air traffic conflict detection. In *IOP Conference Series: Materials Science and Engineering*; Institute of Physics (IOP) Publishing: London, UK, 2022; p. 012019. [CrossRef]
5. Jouaber, S.; Bonnabel, S.; Santiago, V.-F.; Pilté, M.; Angulo, J. Real-time classification of aircrafts manoeuvers. *J. Signal Process. Syst.* **2023**, *95*, 425–434. [CrossRef]
6. McLean, D.J.; Skowron Volponi, M. Trajr: An R package for characterisation of animal trajectories. *Ethology* **2018**, *124*, 440–448. [CrossRef]

 https://doi.org/10.3390/engproc2026122001

7. Dumenčić, S.; Žužić, L.; Breš, B. Trajectory analysis of griffon vulture in Kvarner bay. *J. Commun. Inf. Electron. Energy Syst. (CIEES)* **2022**, *2*, 36–42. [CrossRef]
8. Makar, D. Analiza putanja zrakoplova korištenjem opažanja iz mreže OpenSky Network [Analysis of Aircraft Trajectories Using Observations from the OpenSky Network]. Master's Thesis, University of Rijeka, Rijeka, Croatia, 2022. Available online: https://urn.nsk.hr/urn:nbn:hr:190:547850 (accessed on 3 September 2025).
9. Garcia Ceja, E. *Behavior Analysis with Machine Learning Using R*; Chapman & Hall/CRC Books: Philadelphia, PA, USA, 2021. [CrossRef]
10. Bosson, C.; Nikoleris, T. Supervised learning applied to air traffic trajectory classification. In *2018 AIAA Information Systems-AIAA Infotech*; The American Institute of Aeronautics and Astronautics (AIAA): Reston, VA, USA, 2018; p. 1637. [CrossRef]
11. R Core Team. *R: A Language and Environment for Statistical Computing*, Version 4.5.1. 2025. Available online: https://www.r-project.org (accessed on 3 September 2025).
12. Kuhn, M. The Caret Package. Available online: https://topepo.github.io/caret (accessed on 3 September 2025).
13. Boehmke, B.; Greenwell, B.M. *Hands-On Machine Learning with R*, 1st ed.; CRC Press: Boca Raton, FL, USA, 2019. [CrossRef]
14. James, G.; Witten, D.; Hastie, T.; Tibshrani, R.; Taylor, J. *An Introduction to Statistical Learning: With Applications in R*, 2nd ed.; Springer: New York, NY, USA, 2023. [CrossRef]
15. Gultepe, I.; Sharman, R.; Williams, P.D.; Zhou, B.; Ellrod, G.; Minnis, P.; Trier, S.; Griffin, S.; Yum, S.S.; Gharabaghi, B.; et al. A review of high impact weather for aviation meteorology. *Pure Appl. Geophys.* **2019**, *176*, 1869–1921. [CrossRef]

 https://doi.org/10.3390/engproc2026122001

engineering proceedings

MDPI

Proceeding Paper

A Study on Fuzzy PID Controllers with a Parallel Structure for Electro-Hydraulic Servo System Control †

Georgi Mihalev [1,*], Stanimir Yordanov [1], Krasimir Ormandzhiev [2], Stefan Ivanov [1] and Hristina Stoycheva [3]

1 Department of Automation, Information and Control Systems, Faculty of Electronics and Engineering, Technical University of Gabrovo, 5300 Gabrovo, Bulgaria; sjjordanov@mail.bg (S.Y.); st_ivanov@abv.bg (S.I.)
2 Department of Power Engineering, Faculty of Mechanical and Precision Engineering, Technical University of Gabrovo, 5300 Gabrovo, Bulgaria; khormandzhiev@abv.bg
3 Department of Communication Technique and Technologies, Faculty of Electronics and Engineering, Technical University of Gabrovo, 5300 Gabrovo, Bulgaria; hsstoycheva@tugab.bg
* Correspondence: gmihalev@tugab.bg

† Presented at the 6th International Conference on Communications, Information, Electronic and Energy Systems, 26–28 November 2025, Ruse, Bulgaria.

Abstract

This paper presents the design of a fuzzy PID controller with a parallel structure for controlling an electro-hydraulic servo system. The main factors affecting control performance in electro-hydraulic systems are discussed in detail. The proposed fuzzy controller features a specific structure obtained through a coefficient transfer approach from a classical PID controller, enabling seamless integration of the fuzzy logic component and simplifying the tuning process. Relevant mathematical equations and dependencies are provided. The closed-loop system's stability is analyzed using the BIBO (Bounded Input, Bounded Output) criterion. The designed controller is implemented in the MATLAB/Simulink 2019 environment and tested using a real-time measurement and control system. Graphical results are presented, illustrating the performance of the closed-loop system under step and sinusoidal reference signals. The obtained results confirm the qualities and proper tuning of the implemented controller.

Keywords: electro-hydraulic servo system; fuzzy-PID; real-time control; BIBO stability

1. Introduction

Electro-hydraulic systems are widely used in industrial automation and manufacturing, as well as in actuating mechanisms for machines and equipment operating in harsh environments with high levels of dust, humidity, chemical exposure, and radiation. The advantages of this type of actuators have been repeatedly emphasized in the literature, including their high power-to-weight ratio, self-lubricating properties, good controllability, reliability, and low positioning error.

This type of actuating systems also poses significant challenges to control and automation engineers. Factors such as fluid compressibility, temperature dependence, and pressure-flow characteristics introduce strong nonlinearities, while the presence of hysteresis due to piston friction and dead zones further complicate system behavior. These are just some of the difficulties that modern control systems have to deal with.

Consequently, the modern trend in controlling such systems is based on a combined control approach that integrates more than one type of control law. These hybrid structures aim to achieve improved dynamic performance and enhanced robustness of the control system.

 https://doi.org/10.3390/engproc2026122002

Within the broad category of intelligent control methods [1–5], a significant portion includes controllers based on fuzzy logic. Fuzzy controllers, as well as their hybrid forms with classical linear control laws, fulfill the conceptual criteria for designing controllers in electro-hydraulic systems and are essential to consider when evaluating tracking performance. Although, at first glance, controlling systems with unstructured parametric uncertainties may not appear to be the primary domain of fuzzy logic controllers, they have demonstrated potential in enhancing both the robustness and the overall performance of closed-loop systems.

In the contemporary overview of electro-hydraulic system control using fuzzy regulators, several key directions can be identified, each addressing the specific challenges associated with this class of systems.

Based on conducted analyses [6] regarding the characteristics of electro-hydraulic systems, the improved techniques for PID control, in terms of tuning, can be classified as: parametric tuning of PID controllers, online PID tuning, and combined strategies. In the presented modifications implementing standard FPID [7,8], HFPID [9], and FPID(BLT) [10], the application of fuzzy logic aims to compensate for the disadvantages of linear PID controllers, achieving high accuracy, robustness, and fast response.

Depending on the type of membership functions, fuzzy PID controllers are classified as type-1 and type-2. In relation to electro-hydraulic systems, ref. [11] presents a study in which IT2FPID provides better results under highly noisy signals.

The combination of fuzzy logic and PID controllers also enables the implementation of another type of hybrid controllers, known as adaptive Fuzzy-PID or self-tuning Fuzzy-PID [12–14]. In these controllers, by using various algorithms (primarily the "centroid" defuzzification method), fuzzy logic modifies the coefficients of the linear controller, thus realizing the property of adaptiveness, which is of great benefit in the control of electro-hydraulic systems.

Due to its stability and ability to effectively suppress disturbances, the sliding mode control approach (SMC) is often combined with fuzzy logic [15,16]. Fuzzy logic complements SMC control ideally by addressing the issues of uncertainties and the need for an accurate model of the controlled system, while also allowing the use of various optimization mechanisms [17,18]. FLSMCPID controllers demonstrate increased accuracy in tracking systems and high robustness across different trajectories.

Fuzzy PID controllers are also successfully combined with other methods used in control system design, such as system identification [19], ontological/semantic representation [20], artificial neural networks [21], prediction [22], and fault diagnosis [23].

In the current paper, a fuzzy PID controller with parallel structure and coefficient transfer is proposed for the control of an electro-hydraulic servo system. The approach to implementing this type of control device follows the conceptual requirement for the use of intelligent control methods within the overall structure of the control system, aiming to achieve improved performance. The designed controller is implemented and tested in real time on a laboratory electro-hydraulic test bench.

2. Materials and Methods

The control configuration is introduced, along with the general structure of the proposed control approach, the tuning methodology, and the stability analysis.

2.1. *Influence of Some Key Factors*

In practice, it is necessary to take into account the actual capabilities and characteristics of control systems. Due to manufacturing limitations and imperfections in real components, industrial control systems exhibit behaviors and performance that differ from those

https://doi.org/10.3390/engproc2026122002

obtained through simulation. In electro-hydraulic systems, this discrepancy is primarily caused by three key factors: the influence of the dead zone, the influence of friction and backlash, and the influence of saturation.

Influence of the dead zone—In real systems, a dead zone typically appears due to the actuator or the control element. In the electro-hydraulic systems under consideration, this factor arises in the servo valve. This insensitivity introduces a fundamental change in the behavior of the control system, manifesting at low input signal levels and leading to significant steady-state errors. This means that the control characteristic will not be linear but will generally be bounded by curved lines. The magnitude describing this phenomenon is referred to as the degree of insensitivity and depends on the arithmetic mean of the minimum and maximum values of the limiting curves.

Influence of friction and backlash—Many components used in automation exhibit friction and backlash, which significantly affect the control behavior. Friction and backlash often introduce a dead zone, meaning these factors are interrelated. As a result, the system's characteristics become non-unique, since frictional forces oppose the motion forces. Consequently, the characteristic of the controlled object will not pass through zero, because a minimum force is required to initiate movement. From here, the formation of the dead zone is also evident. The clearances will also have a similar influence, and then the dead zone will be determined by them.

Influence of saturation—The effect of saturation can lead to undesirable outcomes and, in almost all cases, degrades control quality by increasing dynamic errors and regulation time. It is important that the structural design of the controller accounts for the possibility of reaching the saturation zone and considers the potential consequences of this condition.

2.2. Control Configuration

The issues described above, along with the presence of strong nonlinearities and parametric uncertainties in the controlled object, lead to the conclusion that the use of a fuzzy structure within the control configuration would result in improved performance.

Control devices based on fuzzy logic have emerged as one of the most extensively studied areas within fuzzy set theory and have been successfully applied to the control of complex technological systems. The methodology of fuzzy controllers is based on expressing the control actions of the system not through mathematical equations, but by means of linguistic rules. The situation is defined as a combination of the values of all inputs, while the action involves generating an output response based on the predefined rules.

A conventional fuzzy controller typically operates using the input signals of the system error e and its instantaneous change Δe, while the output variable is the control signal (the signal to the servo valve).

On the other hand, in the classical PID control law, the output of the controller $u(t)$ can be defined by the following expression:

$$u(t) = K_p e(t) + K_i \int e(t)dt + K_d \frac{de(t)}{dt}, \quad (1)$$

where $e(t) = y(t) - r(t)$ is the error, K_p is the proportional gain, K_i is the integral gain, and K_d is the derivative gain.

In the case under consideration, where the electro-hydraulic system has a complex mathematical model and is subject to all the aforementioned challenges, it is necessary to design a feedforward control strategy consisting of a linear and a fuzzy controller integrated within a unified structure.

https://doi.org/10.3390/engproc2026122002

A key task is how exactly to transfer the coefficients of the PID controller to the linear fuzzy controller. When implementing a fuzzy PID controller, three main types of structures are possible: fuzzy PD + I control, fuzzy PI + D control, and fuzzy PI + fuzzy PD controller. Each of these three structures has its own advantages and disadvantages, and it is important to note that there is no analytical tuning method available for any of them.

The third structural type is selected, namely fuzzy PI control with parallel fuzzy PD control. An advantage of this structure is that it does not rely on conventional elements and allows for the avoidance of complex design of logical rules and membership functions. It is particularly beneficial in terms of design that both the PI and PD components use the same set of logical rules and membership functions. The final control action is obtained as the sum of the output signals from both controllers:

$$u(k) = u_{\mathrm{PI}}(k) + u_{\mathrm{PD}}(k) = u_{PI}(k-1) + \Delta u_{PI}(k) + u_{\mathrm{PD}}(k). \quad (2)$$

The main structural diagram of this type of control is shown in Figure 1. Figure 2 presents its implemented equivalent in the MATLAB/Simulink environment.

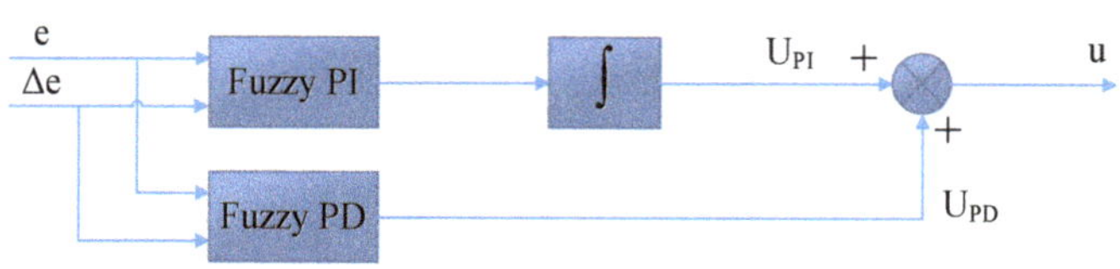

Figure 1. Typical structure of fuzzy PI control with parallel fuzzy PD control.

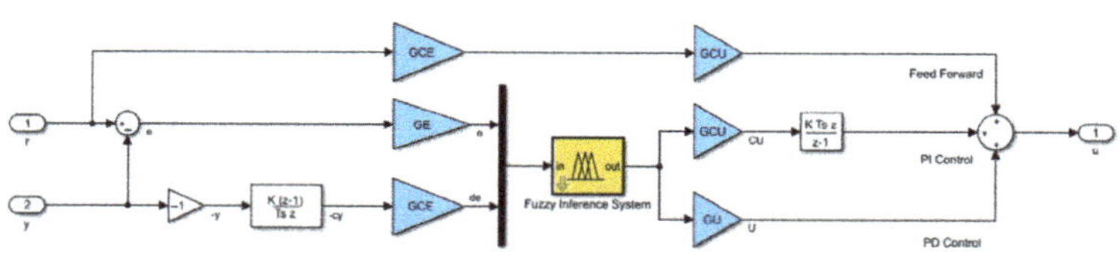

Figure 2. Simulation diagram of fuzzy PI control with parallel fuzzy PD control in the MATLAB/Simulink environment.

In the implementation of the fuzzy PID controller, an FIS structure is used, based on the Sugeno model with a fuzzy implication method that relies on scaling the consequent membership function using the previous output value.

Figure 3 shows the membership functions for the two outputs, while Table 1 presents the logical rules that form the fuzzy FIS structure.

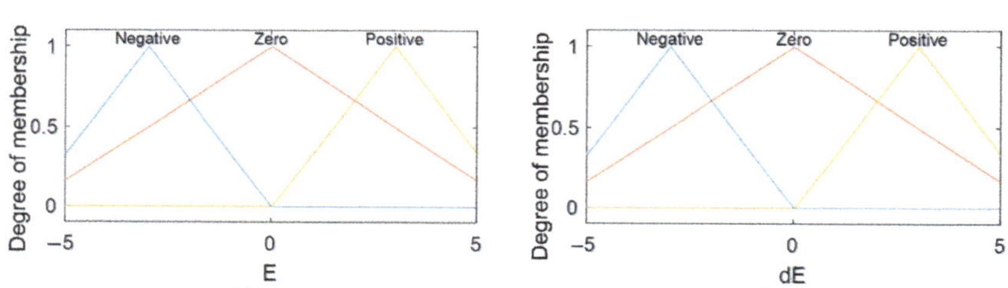

(a) (b)

Figure 3. Functions of membership of fuzzy sets of input quantities: (**a**) for error—E; (**b**) for change in error—dE.

https://doi.org/10.3390/engproc2026122002

Table 1. Rules for formulating a fuzzy controller.

u		dE		
		Negative	**Zero**	**Positive**
E	Negative	LN	SN	Z
	Zero	SN	Z	SP
	Positive	Z	SP	LP

In the rule aggregation method, the defined fuzzy sets are summed sequentially. For the defuzzification block, the real values are obtained using one of the well-known methods for the Sugeno model—specifically, the weighted average of all rule outputs.

Figure 4 presents a three-dimensional control surface plot, illustrating the relationship between the two inputs—the error e and the change in error Δe—on the one hand, and the output of the fuzzy structure u on the other, for a set of 9 logical rules.

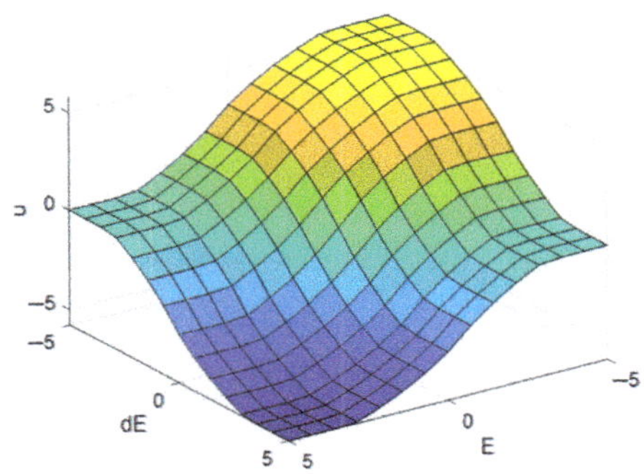

Figure 4. Control surface.

The inputs are described by the terms Negative, Zero, and Positive, while the output is characterized by the terms LN (Large Negative), SN (Small Negative), Z (Zero), SP (Small Positive), and LP (Large Positive). Table 1 provides information about the set of logical rules used.

In the presented block diagram, the change in measurement $(y(k) - y(k-1))$ is used instead of the change in error $(e(k) - e(k-1))$ as the second input signal to the fuzzy structure. In this way, step changes in the reference signal—caused by the direct action of the derivative block—are avoided. However, this modification also requires changes in the controller's structure in order to preserve its functional behavior. The three main coefficients (proportional, integral, and derivative) of the conventional PID controller are transformed into four new coefficients denoted as GCE, GCU, GE, and GU. This approach is known as coefficient transfer of the PID controller and is described in detail in [24]. To ensure that the error e is fully utilized, the two gain coefficients GCE and GCU are added in the feedforward path. The values of the new coefficients are functionally dependent on the standard ones and can be calculated using the following formulas:

$$\begin{gathered} GE = 6 \\ GCE = \frac{GE\left(K_p - \sqrt{K_p^2 - 4K_iK_d}\right)}{2K_i} \\ GCU = \frac{K_i}{GE} \\ GU = \frac{K_d}{GCE} \end{gathered} \tag{3}$$

https://doi.org/10.3390/engproc2026122002

When calculating the new coefficients, only GE is defined in advance and depends on the predefined limits of the error input to the fuzzy structure. For example, if the input error range is $[-6;6]$, then GE is first set to 6, and the remaining coefficients—GCE, GCU, and GU—are calculated using the formulas described above.

2.3. Tunnig of Controller

The presented parallel structure of the fuzzy PID controller has several advantages, one of which is the tuning process. The coefficient transfer approach allows the implementation of the fuzzy FIS structure to occur after the linear controller has already been tuned, or even to build upon an existing PID controller. Thus, the tuning procedure for this type of controller follows these steps:

1. **Tuning the PID controller**—most commonly, the Ziegler–Nichols method is used. In the current implementation, the method is applied experimentally.
2. **Design of the linear fuzzy controller**—a linear control surface is designed.
3. **Coefficient transfer**—the standard PID controller coefficients are replaced with gain coefficients using the relationships defined in (3).
4. **Modification of the fuzzy structure into a nonlinear one**—typically achieved by altering the shape of the surface and selecting appropriate linguistic rules, as in most cases, heuristic approaches are used.
5. **Fine tuning**—once the fuzzy structure has been modified into a nonlinear one, the adjustment of the coefficients is traditionally based on experience and intuition.

Overall, the tuning process is essentially the design procedure itself, and the simplest approach is to begin with designing a PID or even a P controller to stabilize the system, and then to add the fuzzy structure afterward.

2.4. BIBO Stability of the Fuzzy Control System

When controlling a nonlinear system with a nonlinear controller, it is essential to evaluate the global stability of the system. This also contributes to the investigation of the quantitative relationship between the conventional PID controller and the fuzzy structure.

To achieve this, the so-called BIBO stability of the system is examined. When analyzing the interconnection of two nonlinear systems, BIBO stability generally implies that a bounded input results in a bounded output, which is also the case in the scenario under consideration. A suitable tool for this analysis is the application of the Small-Gain Theorem [25] and the theorem presented in [26], according to which a sufficient condition for stability is that the product of the gain coefficients of the two systems is less than 1. When implementing control using a fuzzy PID controller, this condition is expressed as:

$$K_c(k)\left(1+\frac{T_d}{T_i}+\frac{\Delta t}{T_i}+\frac{T_d}{\Delta t}\right)\cdot\|G\|<1 \tag{4}$$

where $K_c(k)$, T_d and T_i are the parameters of the fuzzy PID controller, and $\|G\|$ denotes the gain of the nonlinear system under consideration.

To compute the first part of condition (4), by converting the time constants into gain coefficients for the PID controller, Equations (3) are transformed into:

$$\begin{aligned} K_c(k) &= GU\cdot GE+GCE\cdot GCU \\ K_i &= GCU\cdot GE \\ K_d &= GU\cdot GCE \end{aligned} \tag{5}$$

Using (5), the gain coefficient of the fuzzy PID controller is obtained as:

 https://doi.org/10.3390/engproc2026122002

$$GU \cdot GE + GCE \cdot GCU + \frac{GU \cdot GCE \cdot GCU \cdot GE}{GU \cdot GE + GCE \cdot GCU} + \frac{\Delta t(GU \cdot GE + GCE \cdot GCU)^2}{GCU \cdot GE} + \frac{GU \cdot GCE}{\Delta t}. \quad (6)$$

With the selected coefficients after tuning, $K_c(k) = 0.26, T_i = 0.1116, T_d = 0.003$ and $\Delta t = 0.003$, the gain coefficient of the proposed controller is calculated to be 0.5306.

The gain coefficient of the system is typically defined as:

$$||G|| = sup_{\nu_1 \neq \nu_2, k \geq 0} \frac{|G(\nu_1(k)) - G(\nu_2(k))|}{|\nu_1(k) - \nu_2(k)|} \quad (7)$$

This value is determined experimentally. According to definition (7), two output values are recorded for two different input values after the transient responses have settled. For the electro-hydraulic system under consideration, data from the open-loop response is recorded by applying input commands ranging from 3 V to 4.5 V. The resulting output values of the variable ω are shown in Figure 5. Based on Equation (7), the largest observed gain $||G||$ is calculated to be 1.51 over the entire operating range.

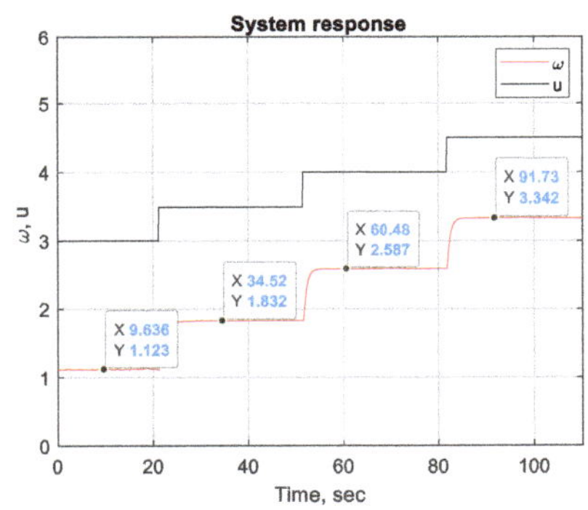

Figure 5. Open loop system response for input commands from 3 V to 4.5 V.

According to the calculations presented above, condition (4) is satisfied, and the closed-loop system is BIBO stable. If the nonlinear system is stably controlled by a conventional PID controller, then, according to (4), the linear control can always be replaced by a fuzzy PID controller that ensures the same stability margin. Moreover, since the stability condition (6) is independent of the weighting coefficients of the error and its change, the use of this parallel fuzzy PID structure provides additional freedom in the design process, allowing for improved performance without affecting system stability.

3. Experimental Results and Analysis

The system under study has been extensively examined in other authors publications as well [27,28] and is presented with the generalized block diagram shown in Figure 6, while the key parameters of the system are provided in [29]. The controlled variable is the rotational speed (ω) of the hydraulic motor shaft, while the movement of the servo-valve plunger (x_{sv}) is the system input.

 https://doi.org/10.3390/engproc2026122002

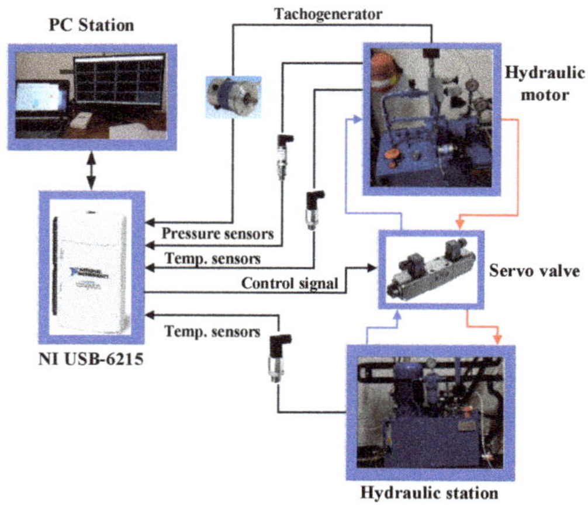

Figure 6. Generalized block diagram of the electro-hydraulic system under consideration.

The system under consideration is a laboratory test bench consisting of several main modules: a hydraulic station, an NI measurement module USB-6215, a PC station with specialized software operating in the MATLAB/Simulink environment, and an electro-hydraulic module. Thanks to the presence of multiple sensors for temperature, pressure, and a sensor measuring the rotational speed of the hydraulic motor, the PC-based system allows for the implementation and analysis of various control schemes within the MATLAB/Simulink environment.

To test the system, a model representing an integrated control system was developed in the MATLAB/Simulink environment. The model includes a complete functional chain for data acquisition, filtering, digital processing, control, and real-time visualization.

The architecture of the software system is based on a hierarchical principle and consists of five main subsystems:

1. ADC (Analog-to-Digital Conversion)—conversion and filtering of analog input signals;
2. Automatic Processes 1 and 2—generators of test signals in the form of step functions;
3. FuzzyPID Regulator—the investigated controller combining PID and fuzzy logic;
4. PID Temperature—a classical PID controller for the temperature channel;
5. DAC (Digital-to-Analog Conversion)—generation and transmission of analog control outputs.

Additional subsystems, such as *Step Up Signal*, *Step Down Signal*, and *RTFM*, perform auxiliary functions related to system testing and tuning.

Figure 7 shows the Simulink model of the system, which serves as a software platform for measurement and control. The system is suitable for both scientific experiments and for training and demonstration of adaptive and intelligent control methods.".

The ADC subsystem implements the interface between the external hardware and the Simulink model. The *Analog Input (Single Sample)* block is used, configured to operate with the NI USB-6215 device, which provides up to 12 analog input channels. Each channel passes through an individual low-pass Butterworth filter, implemented using *Analog Filter Design* blocks 1–12 (State-Space realization, order N = 1). The filters provide frequency selectivity with a lower cutoff frequency of 0.04–0.06 Hz and a high-frequency attenuation of 50 dB, ensuring noise suppression and elimination of parasitic signals.

https://doi.org/10.3390/engproc2026122002

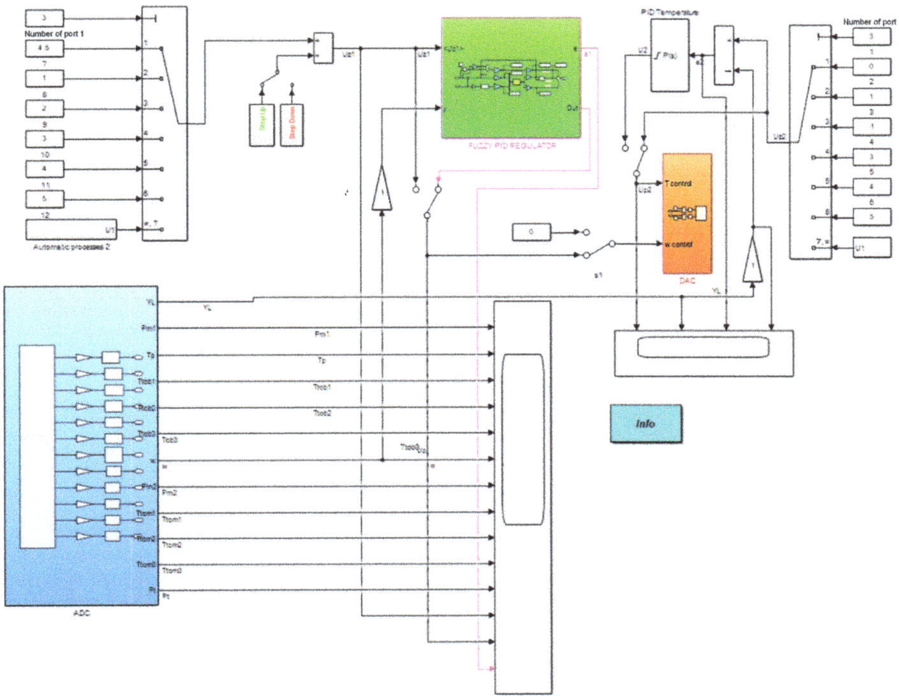

Figure 7. Model of the studied system developed in the MATLAB/Simulink environment. * denotes automatic reference sequence (not static) coming from functional block.

After filtering, the signals are scaled using *Gain* blocks (*Gain1–Gain12*), enabling normalization to a suitable range for digital processing. The combination of filters and amplifiers forms a reliable real-time data acquisition and preprocessing module.

The task modeling for the system is implemented through the subsystems *Automatic Processes 1* and *Automatic Processes 2*. Each contains multiple Step blocks that generate sequences of step changes in the input variables. In this way, the model can simulate typical changes in the reference input or process disturbances.

The additional subsystems *Step Up Signal* and *Step Down Signal* enable independent control of the rising and falling transitions of the signal, which are used for analyzing transient characteristics and system stability.

The PID Temperature subsystem represents a continuous-time PID controller (Form = Parallel) with parameters P = 1, I = 0.04, and D = 0. The controller is configured with output limits between 0 and 6 V and includes an anti-windup mechanism (*AntiWindupMode = back-calculation*). This module is designed to control the thermal regime of the test stand, where smooth response and protection against saturation are required.

The DAC subsystem performs the digital-to-analog conversion using the *Analog Output (Single Sample)* block connected to the NI USB-6251 device. This block provides two analog output channels through which the computed control signals are delivered to external actuators. The DAC inputs pass through Saturation blocks that limit the voltage within permissible ranges and Sum blocks that adjust the control components. This approach prevents signal saturation and ensures proper reproduction of the analog outputs.

The model also contains multiple *Display* and *Scope* blocks, enabling real-time monitoring of the time dependencies of the main variables: reference value, output, error, and

https://doi.org/10.3390/engproc2026122002

control signal. The inclusion of *Manual Switch* and *Multiport Switch* blocks allows switching between different control modes (e.g., manual, PID, or Fuzzy).

During system operation, data are recorded at a sampling rate of 50 Hz. The following measurements are collected: reference input—u, rotational speed—ω, control error—ε, controller output—μ_p, oil pressure in the pump—P_t, pressure before the proportional distributor—P_{m1}, pressure after the proportional distributor—P_{m2}, and oil temperature in the tank—T_p. Measuring parameters such as fluid temperature and pressure is essential for analyzing the performance of hydraulic systems [29].

When studying the designed fuzzy controller, data was recorded under sinusoidal variation in the reference signal and under increasing step changes. The graphical results are presented in Figure 8.

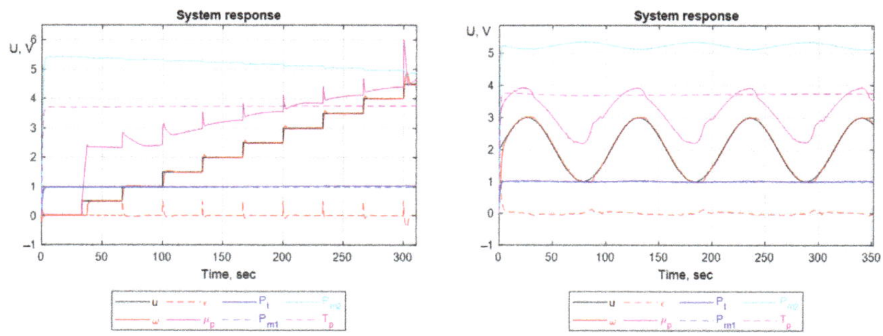

(a) (b)

Figure 8. Closed-loop system response: (**a**) to an increasing step input; (**b**) to a sinusoidal reference input.

In Figure 8a, under stepwise changes in the reference signal, i.e., transitioning through multiple target positions or tracking multi-step signals, the closed-loop system demonstrates very good technical performance. The amplitude of the reference signal varies from 1 to 5.5 in increments of 0.5 every 30 s. No steady-state error is observed, the settling time does not exceed 3.5 s, and the overshoot remains below 10% across the entire range of variation. The small error and fast settling time indicate that the controller is well-tuned.

Figure 8b presents the graphical results of system performance in dynamic mode for the main variables during the tracking of a periodic (sinusoidal) reference signal. The control signal and output variable exhibit a stable periodic regime with constant amplitude and period, without signs of saturation or distortion. The error oscillates around zero with a small amplitude throughout the interval, indicating effective tracking and a well-tuned control loop. Slight peak values are observed when the reference signal reaches its lower levels, which is due to the system entering the dead zone of the control element. Practically no phase shift is observed between the reference and the system output. The control signal remains within technically acceptable limits, with no indication of saturation.

Table 2 presents a comparison between the studied fuzzy controller and a conventional PI, PID controller. From the data, it can be seen that the fuzzy controller shows better results. Despite the good results and well-tuned controller, the use of electro-hydraulic components in automation leads to a deterioration in control quality within the dead zone of the proportional valve, which spans approximately 10% of the lower end of the operating range. Additionally, a saturation zone is observed beyond a reference input of 4.5 V, where the steady-state error increases.

https://doi.org/10.3390/engproc2026122002

Table 2. Comparative analysis with a conventional PID controller.

Criterion	Fuzzy PID	PI, PID
entry 1 Settling time t_s	Up to 3.5 s	2 s–13 s
Overshot σ	<10%	Up to 11.6%
Static error ε_{st}	0	0
Oscillations	No	Yes

The use of a fuzzy PID controller with a parallel structure is a very effective option for implementing a compensation mechanism to eliminate this system deficiency. The designed controller enables the realization of an additional level of adaptability by incorporating supplementary fuzzy structures or neuro-fuzzy structures, which can be easily integrated into the overall controller architecture. The coefficient transfer approach would also be beneficial when applying more conventional methods such as functional or scaling compensators. Addressing this issue remains a subject for future research.

4. Conclusions

In the present study, the control of an electro-hydraulic actuator system with a rotary actuator was investigated using a fuzzy PID controller with a parallel structure and coefficient transfer. In accordance with the described challenges associated with controlling such systems, a tuning methodology for the controller was applied as reported in the literature. The designed controller demonstrated very good results in terms of transient response duration and smoothness of control. The stability of the closed loop system was evaluated through the calculation of the BIBO stability condition. The system's operability was demonstrated under the application of various reference signals. The closed-loop system's response to a sinusoidal input demonstrated stable behavior with acceptable dynamic performance, taking into account the characteristics of the controlled system. The experimental results obtained under both step and sinusoidal reference inputs revealed good system dynamics and absence of oscillations.

Author Contributions: Conceptualization, S.I., H.S. and K.O.; Methodology G.M. and S.Y.; Software, S.I., H.S. and K.O.; Validation, G.M., S.Y., S.I., H.S. and K.O.; Formal analysis, G.M., S.Y., S.I., H.S. and K.O.; Investigation, G.M., S.Y. and S.I.; Resources, S.Y., H.S. and K.O.; Writing—Original Draft Preparation, H.S. and S.Y.; Writing—Review & Editing, G.M. and H.S. All authors have read and agreed to the published version of the manuscript.

Funding: This research is funded by University Center for Research and Technology at the Technical University of Gabrovo, project SRP 2025-12 (НИП 2025-12) "Intelligent IoT-Based Sensors and Sensor Systems".

Institutional Review Board Statement: Not applicable.

Informed Consent Statement: Not applicable.

Data Availability Statement: The data presented in this study is available on request from the corresponding authors.

Conflicts of Interest: The authors declare no conflicts of interest.

References

1. Chandrasekaran, E.; Anandan, R.; Suseendran, G.; Balamurugan, S.; Hachimi, H. *Fuzzy Intelligent Systems: Methodologies, Techniques, and Applications*; John Wiley & Sons: Hoboken, NJ, USA, 2021.
2. De Silva, C.W. *Intelligent Control: Fuzzy Logic Applications*; CRC Press: Boca Raton, FL, USA, 2018.
3. Lu, H.; Wang, H.; Zhao, D.; Meng, Z.; Wang, M.; Zhan, S.; Guo, W.Q. An Intelligent Fuzzy PI Hybrid Control Strategy for Energy Optimization and N_2O Mitigation in WWTPs: A Model-Based Study. *J. Clean. Prod.* **2025**, *513*, 145681. [CrossRef]

 https://doi.org/10.3390/engproc2026122002

4. Wei, H.; Zhu, N.; Sun, Z.; Tan, S.; Tian, R. Research on the intelligent control strategy of pressurizer pressure in PWRs based on a fuzzy neural network PID controller. *Nucl. Eng. Des.* **2025**, *433*, 113875. [CrossRef]
5. Lee, M.-F.R. A Review on Intelligent Control Theory and Applications in Process Optimization and Smart Manufacturing. *Processes* **2023**, *11*, 3171. [CrossRef]
6. Li, J.; Li, W.; Liang, H.; Kong, L. Review of research on improved PID control in electro-hydraulic servo system. *Recent Pat. Eng.* **2024**, *18*, 54–68. [CrossRef]
7. Ren, X.Y.; Du, F.S.; Huang, H.G.; Zhang, S.B. Application of improved fuzzy immune PID controller to bending control system. *J. Iron Steel Res. Int.* **2011**, *18*, 28–33. [CrossRef]
8. Kumar, G.; Mandal, N.P. Position Control of Electrohydraulic Positioning System Using PID and Fuzzy-PID Controller. In *Advances in Thermo-Fluid Engineering*; Springer Nature: Singapore, 2024; pp. 113–126.
9. Ali, N.H.M.; Ghazali, R.; Tahir, A.W.; Jaafar, H.I.; Ghani, M.F.; Soon, C.C.; Has, Z. Enhanced hybrid robust fuzzy-PID controller for precise trajectory tracking electro-hydraulic actuator system. *Int. J. Robot. Control Syst.* **2024**, *4*, 795–813. [CrossRef]
10. Kumar, V.; Rana, K.P.S. A novel fuzzy PID controller for nonlinear active suspension system with an electro-hydraulic actuator. *J. Braz. Soc. Mech. Sci. Eng.* **2023**, *45*, 189. [CrossRef]
11. Haq, J.A.K.; Wahyunggoro, O.; Firmansyah, E. Implementation of interval type-2 fuzzy PID controller on electro-hydraulic servo valve system with noise. *AIP Conf. Proc.* **2024**, *3069*, 020121. [CrossRef]
12. Ormandzhiev, K.; Yordanov, S. Design of Adaptive Fuzzy PID Controller for Electropneumatic System. *E3S Web Conf.* **2020**, *207*, 04002. [CrossRef]
13. Ghosh, B.B.; Sarkar, B.K.; Saha, R. Realtime performance analysis of different combinations of fuzzy–PID and bias controllers for a two degree of freedom electrohydraulic parallel manipulator. *Robot. Comput.-Integr. Manuf.* **2015**, *34*, 62–69. [CrossRef]
14. Truong, D.Q.; Kwan, A.K.; Hung, H.T.; Yoon, J., II. A study on hydraulic load simulator using self tuning grey predictor–fuzzy PID. *IFAC Proc.* **2008**, *41*, 13791–13796. [CrossRef]
15. Feng, H.; Jiang, J.; Chang, X.; Yin, C.; Cao, D.; Yu, H.; Xie, J. Adaptive sliding mode controller based on fuzzy rules for a typical excavator electro-hydraulic position control system. *Eng. Appl. Artif. Intell.* **2023**, *126*, 107008. [CrossRef]
16. Ghani, M.F.; Faudzi, A.A.M.; Ghazali, R.; Mohamaddan, S. Application of Fuzzy Logic Sliding Mode Control Approach with PID Structure for Electro-Hydraulic Actuator Tracking System. *IEEE Access* **2025**, *13*, 97818–97834. [CrossRef]
17. Mandal, P.; Sarkar, B.K.; Saha, R.; Chatterjee, A.; Mookherjee, S.; Sanyal, D. Real-time fuzzy-feedforward controller design by bacterial foraging optimization for an electrohydraulic system. *Eng. Appl. Artif. Intell.* **2015**, *45*, 168–179. [CrossRef]
18. Mu, H.; Luo, Y.; Luo, Y.; Chen, L. Numerical Analysis of Energy Recovery of Hybrid Loader Actuators Based on Parameters Optimization. *Actuators* **2022**, *11*, 260. [CrossRef]
19. Vinod, J.; Sarkar, B.K.; Sanyal, D. Flow control in a small Francis turbine by system identification and fuzzy adaptation of PID and deadband controllers. *Renew. Energy* **2022**, *201*, 87–99. [CrossRef]
20. Benić, J.; Pender, A.; Kasać, J.; Stipančić, T. Sugeno-type fuzzy ontology PI controller for proportional electrohydraulic system. *IFAC-PapersOnLine* **2023**, *56*, 8732–8737. [CrossRef]
21. Li, J.; Li, W.; Du, X. Research on the characteristics of electro-hydraulic position servo system of RBF neural network under fuzzy rules. *Sci. Rep.* **2024**, *14*, 15332. [CrossRef]
22. Zhong, J.; Wu, H.; Jiang, W. Fuzzy Predictive PID Control of a 7-Dofs Electro-Hydraulic Driven Manipulator. *SSRN* **2025**. [CrossRef]
23. Schwung, A.; Beck, M.; Adamy, J. Fault diagnosis of dynamical systems using recurrent fuzzy systems with application to an electrohydraulic servo axis. *Fuzzy Sets Syst.* **2015**, *277*, 138–153. [CrossRef]
24. Jantzen, J. *Tuning of Fuzzy PID Controllers*; Technical University of Denmark, Department of Automation: Kongens Lyngby, Demark, 1998; p. 326.
25. Vidyasagar, M. *Nonlinear Systems Analysis*; Society for Industrial and Applied Mathematics: Philadelphia, PA, USA, 2002.
26. Xu, J.X.; Hang, C.C.; Liu, C. Parallel structure and tuning of a fuzzy PID controller. *Automatica* **2000**, *36*, 673–684. [CrossRef]
27. Mihalev, G.; Yordanov, S.; Ormandzhiev, K. Switching Multi-regulator Control of Electro-Hydraulic Servo System. In Proceedings of the 2024 International Conference Automatics and Informatics (ICAI), Varna, Bulgaria, 10–12 October 2024; pp. 592–597.
28. Yordanov, S.; Mihalev, G.; Ormandzhiev, K.; Ivanov, S. Application of a Modified Multiparametric PID Controller for Control of an Electrohydraulic Servo System. In Proceedings of the 2024 International Conference Automatics and Informatics (ICAI), Varna, Bulgaria, 10–12 October 2024; pp. 598–603. [CrossRef]
29. Nikolaev, I.N.; Raeva, E.R.; Mihova, V.A. Mathematical Modeling of the Operation of a Hydrophoric Installation. *J. Phys. Conf. Ser.* **2024**, *2910*, 012019. [CrossRef]

 https://doi.org/10.3390/engproc2026122002

engineering proceedings

MDPI

Proceeding Paper

A Low-Cost and Reliable IoT-Based NFT Hydroponics System Using ESP32 and MING Stack †

Tolga Demir and İhsan Çiçek *

Δ-Laboratory, Department of Electronics Engineering, Gebze Technical University, 41400 Kocaeli, Türkiye; t.demir2023@gtu.edu.tr

* Correspondence: ihsancicek@gtu.edu.tr

† Presented at the 6th International Conference on Communications, Information, Electronic and Energy Systems, 26–28 November 2025, Ruse, Bulgaria.

Abstract

This paper presents the design and implementation of an IoT-based automation system for indoor hydroponic plant cultivation using the Nutrient Film Technique. The system employs an ESP32-based controller with multiple sensors and actuators. These enable real-time monitoring and control of pH, TDS, temperature, humidity, light, tank level, and flow conditions. A modular five-layer architecture was developed. It combines the MING stack, which includes MQTT communication, InfluxDB time-series storage, Node-RED flow processing, and Grafana visualization. The system also includes a Flutter-based mobile app for remote access. Key features include temperature-compensated calibration, hysteresis-based control algorithms, dual-mode operation, TLS/ACL security, and automated alarm mechanisms. These features enhance reliability and safety. Experimental results showed stable pH/TDS regulation, dependable actuator and alarm responses, and secure long-term data logging. The proposed open-source and low-cost platform is scalable. It provides a solution for small-scale producers and urban farming, bridging the gap between academic prototypes and production-grade smart agriculture systems. In comparison to related works that mainly focus on monitoring, this study advances the state of the art. It combines continuous time-series logging, secure communication, flow verification, and integrated safety mechanisms to provide a reproducible testbed for future smart agriculture research.

Keywords: ESP32; hydroponics; IoT; NFT; smart agriculture

1. Introduction

The growing global population, climate change, and geopolitical risks pose serious threats to food security. The United Nations projects the world population to reach 9.7 billion by 2050, intensifying pressure on agricultural production [1]. Geopolitical events, such as the Russia–Ukraine war, have exposed vulnerabilities in grain and fertilizer supply chains. Meanwhile, the COVID-19 pandemic has further disrupted global logistics, exacerbating food insecurity in developing countries [2].

Traditional farming is limited by soil fertility, climate, and practices like fallowing, which, while restoring soil health, reduce continuous production. Intensive pesticide use boosts yields in the short term but poses long-term risks. Glyphosate has been classified as "probably carcinogenic" (Group 2A), and organophosphates such as malathion and diazinon as "possibly carcinogenic" (Group 2B) [3]. Beyond health hazards, chemical reliance leads to soil and water pollution, loss of beneficial microorganisms, and a decline in biodiversity. Therefore, reducing pesticide dependence is essential for sustainable farming.

E-agriculture approaches—such as IoT, sensor networks, and data analytics—offer valuable options when combined with controlled-environment agriculture. Hydroponic systems, particularly the Nutrient Film Technique (NFT), facilitate soil-free growing through nutrient solutions, which reduces the need for pesticides while improving water and fertilizer efficiency [4]. NFT keeps plant roots in a thin film of nutrients that supplies both oxygen and water efficiently, and its low-cost infrastructure is suitable for IoT-based sensing and actuation. It is commonly used for leafy vegetables like lettuce but requires continuous flow, making real-time monitoring and control essential [5].

Unlike traditional farming's high-water use, pesticide dependence, and climate vulnerability, IoT-enabled hydroponics encourages sustainable, year-round growth with efficient resource management. These factors make NFT systems ideal for IoT automation, where continuous flow demands real-time sensing, control, and reliability through features like alarms, data storage, and mobile notifications.

1.1. Related Work and Research Gap

In recent years, a considerable number of studies have focused on IoT-based hydroponic systems, as summarized in Table 1. These works have utilized various sensors, microcontrollers, and IoT platforms to enable remote monitoring and control of hydroponic cultivation, often emphasizing user-friendly interfaces through mobile applications.

Table 1. Summary of IoT-based hydroponic system studies.

Paper	Components	Features	Limitations
[6]	Arduino Mega, ESP8266, DHT22, NPK, water-level & light sensors; Azure–Flutter interface	Smart home hydroponics for urban use; real-time monitoring and nutrient adjustment	Small-scale only; needs continuous power/internet; no industrial-grade sensors
[7]	NodeMCU, pH & EC sensors, DHT11; ThingSpeak, IoT MQTT Panel	Automated pH/EC control and water circulation; mobile visualization	No long-term data logging or security; lacks calibration; limited scalability
[8]	Arduino–ESP8266, pH/EC & color sensors; Blynk IoT	Fuzzy-logic control for pH and nutrient regulation; mobile access	No cloud storage or calibration; lacks security; energy optimization not addressed
[9]	Raspberry Pi & ESP-12E, pH/TDS/T-H/flow sensors; MQTT app	Dual controller for nutrient and climate control; live camera feedback	No TLS/ACL security or calibration; risk of water contamination
[10]	ESP32, pH, T/H, air-quality sensors; Blynk platform	Autonomous control of pump, fan, and lighting with alerts	Power- and internet-dependent; lacks security and full calibration
[11]	NodeMCU, pH, T/H, water-temp sensors; MQTT app	Real-time monitoring and alerting via mobile interface and buzzer	Monitoring-only; no actuator control; lacks calibration and data security

IoT-based hydroponic systems primarily address real-time monitoring but often fall short of production-grade reliability due to architectural and feature limitations.

Kushawaha et al. [6] developed a compact system for NPK and environmental monitoring with Azure–Flutter visualization, yet reported limitations such as small-scale applicability, lack of industrial-grade sensors, and dependency on constant connectivity.

Patil et al. [7] designed a NodeMCU-based automated system for pH and EC control using ThingSpeak and an MQTT mobile app, but it lacked robust data logging, calibration, and security protocols.

https://doi.org/10.3390/engproc2026122003

Blancaflor et al. [8] implemented pH and EC regulation with fuzzy logic through a Blynk interface, incorporating additional parameters such as color sensing; however, their system lacked long-term cloud storage, detailed calibration, and adequate security.

Vineeth and Ananthan [9] employed a master–slave (Raspberry Pi/ESP-12E) architecture using MQTT for remote monitoring, threshold customization, and live video streaming, yet omitted TLS/ACL security and showed vulnerability to water-borne contamination.

Lal [10] implemented autonomous actuator control (fan, light, pump) via ESP32 and Blynk, but required continuous power and internet, while lacking data security and full calibration.

Finally, Waghmare et al. [11] focused solely on MQTT-based monitoring and alerting (NodeMCU with buzzer), omitting actuator control, calibration, and security mechanisms necessary for autonomous operation.

Although these studies have advanced IoT use in hydroponics, most remain focused on monitoring and do not meet production-level needs such as continuous time-series logging, secure communication (TLS/ACL/LWT), dual control modes, sensor calibration, and reliability validation through flow and level monitoring. As shown in Table 1, works [6–11] mainly address short-term visualization and lack redundancy, alarm handling, and operational fault detection. These limitations reveal a gap between prototype IoT systems and reliable, field-ready hydroponic automation platforms.

1.2. Contributions

To address these gaps, this study proposes an IoT-enabled NFT hydroponic system for indoor lettuce cultivation with the following contributions:

- Design of a new NFT architecture integrating ESP32 with multiple sensors and actuators.
- Modular hardware–software design with IoT integration using MQTT, InfluxDB, Node-RED, Grafana (MING) stack, and a Flutter-based mobile app.
- Advanced control mechanisms, including hysteresis-based algorithms, multi-mode operation, and threshold-triggered alarms with preventive actions.
- A low-cost, open-source platform accessible for small-scale producers and urban farming.

The remainder of this paper is structured as follows: Section 2 explains the NFT system design and implementation; Section 3 provides measurement results and assesses performance; and Section 4 concludes with future research directions, including plant growth experiments, ML-based nutrient optimization, energy efficiency, and Over-The-Air (OTA) updates.

2. A New NFT Hydroponic Automation System

2.1. System Architecture

In this study, we present a new NFT hydroponic automation system built on a five-layer modular architecture—sensor, control, actuator, communication, and visualization layers—shown in Figure 1. This design enhances modularity, scalability, and ease of maintenance.

- Sensor Layer: pH and TDS sensors monitor nutrient solution chemistry, while DS18B20 measures solution temperature. AHT10 records ambient temperature and humidity. BH1750 tracks light intensity. HC-SR04 determines tank level. YF-S201 validates circulation flow. Analog probes are read via the ADS1115 ADC using MOSFET-controlled time-division sampling, whereas digital sensors use I^2C or 1-Wire protocols.
- Control Layer: An ESP32-S board serves as the core, processing sensor data, comparing them against thresholds, and executing algorithms in automatic, manual, or calibration modes. It also activates actuators and manages cloud communication via MQTT.

https://doi.org/10.3390/engproc2026122003

- Actuator Layer: Includes the circulation pump, nutrient dosing pump, pH up/down pumps, LED grow lights, and intake/exhaust fans, which perform irrigation, lighting, and ventilation based on control commands.
- Communication Layer: Communication is conducted via the MQTT protocol, well-known in IoT applications for its lightweight and scalable design [6,11]. In this layer, Node-RED handles data streams, InfluxDB maintains long-term time-series logs, and MQTT features such as LWT and retained messages improve resilience against network disruptions.
- Visualization Layer: Grafana dashboards enable real-time and historical monitoring, while a Flutter-based mobile app supports remote access, manual control, and alarm notifications, thereby strengthening decision support and user interaction.

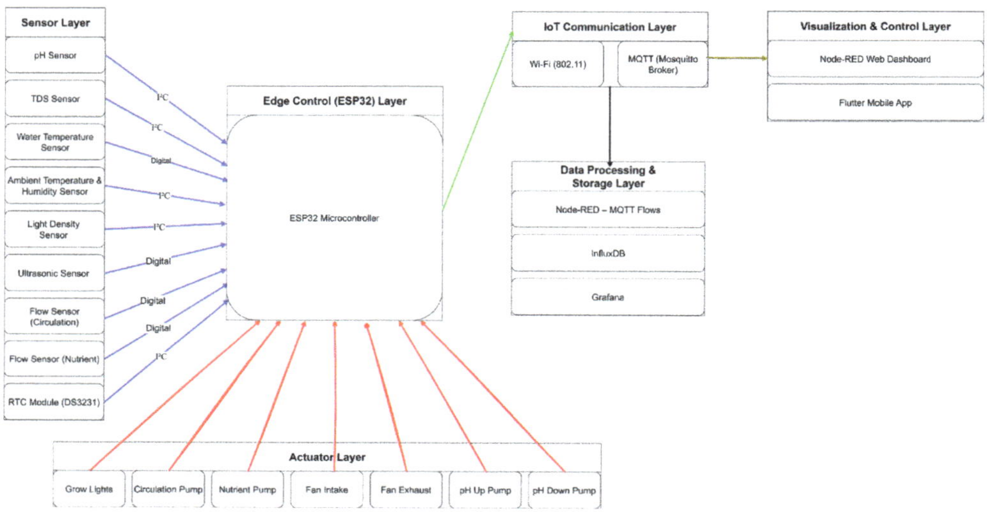

Figure 1. Proposed NFT hydroponics automation system architecture.

2.2. Mechanical Enclosure Design

The chamber shown in Figure 2 was built as a sealed growing environment focused on energy efficiency and sustainability. Upcycled steel rack profiles formed the frame, while discarded roller blinds were repurposed for side panels and the front cover, reducing the carbon footprint and demonstrating the potential of recycled materials in agriculture [4].

The structure measures 200 × 170 × 120 cm and features three parallel NFT channels made of 115 cm × 7.5 cm PVC pipes, each with six planting holes, supporting up to 18 plants. The NFT system keeps roots in continuous contact with a thin nutrient film, ensuring low water usage, oxygen supply, and easy automation integration [5]. A 40 × 38 × 60 cm plastic tank holds the nutrient solution, which circulates in a closed loop with a pump, promoting water conservation and continuous renewal.

The internal components of the system, as shown in Figure 2, are organized logically. The primary hardware is distributed across two dedicated enclosures:

- Power Box (1): This unit contains the 12 V power supply that drives the actuators (pumps and fans) and the 5 V adapter which provides power to the control electronics and sensors.
- Control Box (2): This enclosure houses the main control logic, including the ESP32-based microcontroller and the 8-channel Relay Board responsible for switching and managing the high-power actuators based on signals from the ESP32.

https://doi.org/10.3390/engproc2026122003

The system incorporates comprehensive sensing and actuation devices:

- Nutrient and Solution Management: The solution chemistry is monitored by the pH Sensor (8) and TDS Sensor (9). The solution temperature is tracked by the Water Temperature Sensor (DS18B20) (10). The tank volume is measured by the Ultrasonic Level Sensor (HC-SR04) (5).
- Flow and Circulation: Circulation effectiveness is confirmed by the Circulation Flow Sensor (YF-S201) (6), and nutrient addition is monitored by the Nutrient Flow Sensor (YF-S402) (7). The solution is kept in the Nutrient Tank (17).
- Environmental Control: Ambient conditions are tracked using the Ambient Temperature and Humidity Sensor (AHT10) (13) and the Light Intensity Sensor (BH1750) (4).
- Actuators (Pumps and Climate Control): The system maintains parameters using the Nutrient Pump (14), pH Up Pump (15), and pH Down Pump (16). Environmental stability is ensured by the Air Intake Fan (11), Air Exhaust Fan (12), and LED Grow Lights (3).

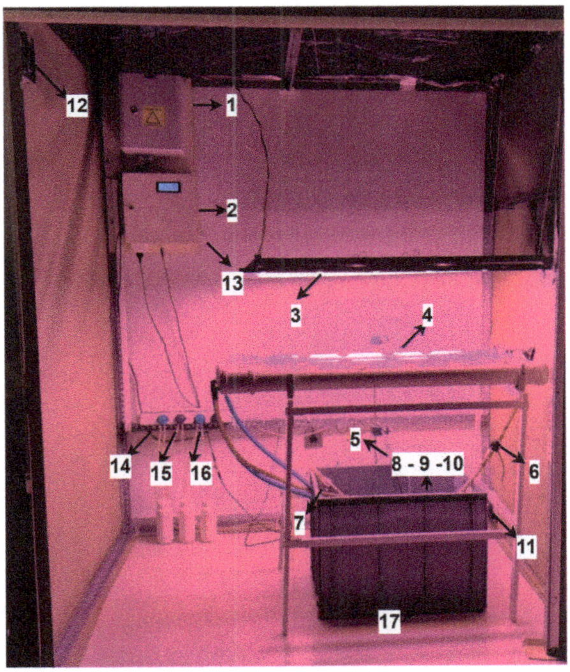

Figure 2. Internal view of the NFT hydroponic automation system developed in a closed environment.

2.3. Electronic Controller Design

The controller design is centered around the ESP32-S development board, as shown in Figures 1 and 3, which acts as the core of the automation layer. The ESP32, with its dual-core architecture, up to 240 MHz clock speed, extensive GPIO capacity, integrated Wi-Fi/Bluetooth connectivity, and low cost, offers one of the most affordable solutions for IoT-based agricultural automation.

These features ensure reliable sensor data collection and quick actuation of components within the NFT hydroponic system. The technical specifications of the sensors used in the system, including their measurement ranges, supply voltages, output types, and functions, are summarized in Table 2. The technical specifications of the actuators are listed in Table 3, covering their operating ranges, supply voltages, control types, and specific functions. All

 https://doi.org/10.3390/engproc2026122003

actuators are controlled through an 8-channel relay module, which communicates with the ESP32 and operates based on simple ON/OFF commands.

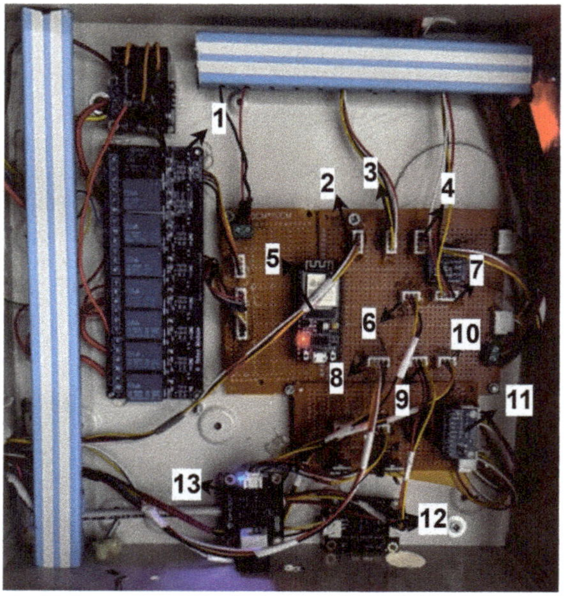

Figure 3. Internal view of the ESP32-based controller hardware developed for the NFT hydroponic system.

Table 2. Specifications of sensors.

Sensors	Measurement Range	Output Type	Supply Voltage	Function
pH Sensor	pH 0–14	Analog	3.3–5.5 V	Nutrient solution pH monitoring
TDS Sensor	0–1000 ppm	Analog	3.3–5.5 V	Solution conductivity monitoring
DS18B20	−55–125 °C	Digital (1-Wire)	3–5.5 V	Solution temperature measurement
AHT10	0–100%RH, −40–85 °C	I^2C	1.8–3.6 V	Ambient temperature & humidity
BH1750	0–65 klux	I^2C	3–5 V	Light intensity monitoring
YF-S201	1–30 L/min	Digital (Pulse)	5–24 V	Circulation flow monitoring
YF-S402	0.3–6 L/min	Digital (Pulse)	5–24 V	Nutrient dosing flow monitoring
DS3231	-	I^2C	3.3–5 V	Real-time clock (RTC)
LCD 20 × 4	-	I^2C	5 V	Data visualization

The internal structure of the ESP32-based controller hardware, as detailed and numbered in Figure 3, is carefully organized for reliable and modular operation. The core control unit is the ESP32 Microcontroller Board (5), which executes all control logic and

https://doi.org/10.3390/engproc2026122003

data processing. Actuators are controlled via the Relay Board (8-channel, 12 V DC) (1), which is essential for managing high-power components. Because high-resolution measurement from analog sensors is needed, the Analog-to-Digital Converter Module (ADS1115) (11) is used to ensure accurate data collection. The controller integrates a comprehensive array of sensors and interface components:

- Nutrient and Solution Sensing: Solution chemistry is monitored using the specialized pH Module (DFRobot SEN0161-V2) (13) and TDS Module (DFRobot SEN0244) (12). Solution temperature is tracked by the Solution Temperature Sensor (DS18B20) (6).
- Flow and Level: Fluid circulation is monitored by the Circulation Flow Sensor (YF-S201) (10), while nutrient addition is tracked by the Nutrient Flow Sensor (YF-S402) (9). The tank level is measured by the Ultrasonic Level Sensor (HC-SR04) (8).
- Environmental and Timing: Ambient conditions are captured by the Ambient Temperature and Humidity Sensor (AHT10) (4), and light intensity is measured by the Light Intensity Sensor (BH1750) (2). Accurate timekeeping is ensured by the Real-Time Clock Module (DS3231) (3).
- Local Interface: An LCD display (20 × 4 I^2C) (7) provides immediate local status feedback to the user.

Table 3. Specifications of actuators.

Actuators	Operating Range	Control Type	Supply Voltage	Function
Nutrient Pump	0.5–2 L/min	Relay (ON/OFF)	12 V	TDS low → nutrient dosing
pH ↑ Pump	0.5–2 L/min	Relay (ON/OFF)	12 V	pH < threshold → pH increase
pH ↓ Pump	0.5–2 L/min	Relay (ON/OFF)	12 V	pH > threshold → pH decrease
Circulation Pump	3000 L/h	Relay (ON/OFF)	12 V	Maintain NFT solution circulation
LED Lighting	14.4 W/m, R:B = 3:1	Relay (ON/OFF)	12 V	Photoperiod-based illumination
Intake Fan	12 V, 0.2–0.3 A	Relay (ON/OFF)	12 V	Climate control (air intake)
Exhaust Fan	12 V, 0.2–0.3 A	Relay (ON/OFF)	12 V	Climate control (air exhaust)

2.4. *Software Design*

The system software was developed in C++ using the Arduino IDE, featuring a modular architecture that separates sensor acquisition, actuator control, communication, data logging, and user interface layers. It offers three modes: automatic, manual, and calibration. The automatic mode, shown in Figure 4, compares sensor readings with predefined thresholds and activates the appropriate actuators, including nutrient and pH pumps, fans, and LED grow lights. In manual mode, actuators can be controlled directly through the mobile application or web dashboard.

A hysteresis-based algorithm stabilizes control actions. The pH down pump activates when pH exceeds the upper threshold, while the pH up pump triggers if it falls below the lower limit. Nutrient dosing starts when TDS drops below the specified range, fans respond to changes in temperature or humidity, and LEDs follow a photoperiod schedule to ensure consistent growth conditions.

https://doi.org/10.3390/engproc2026122003

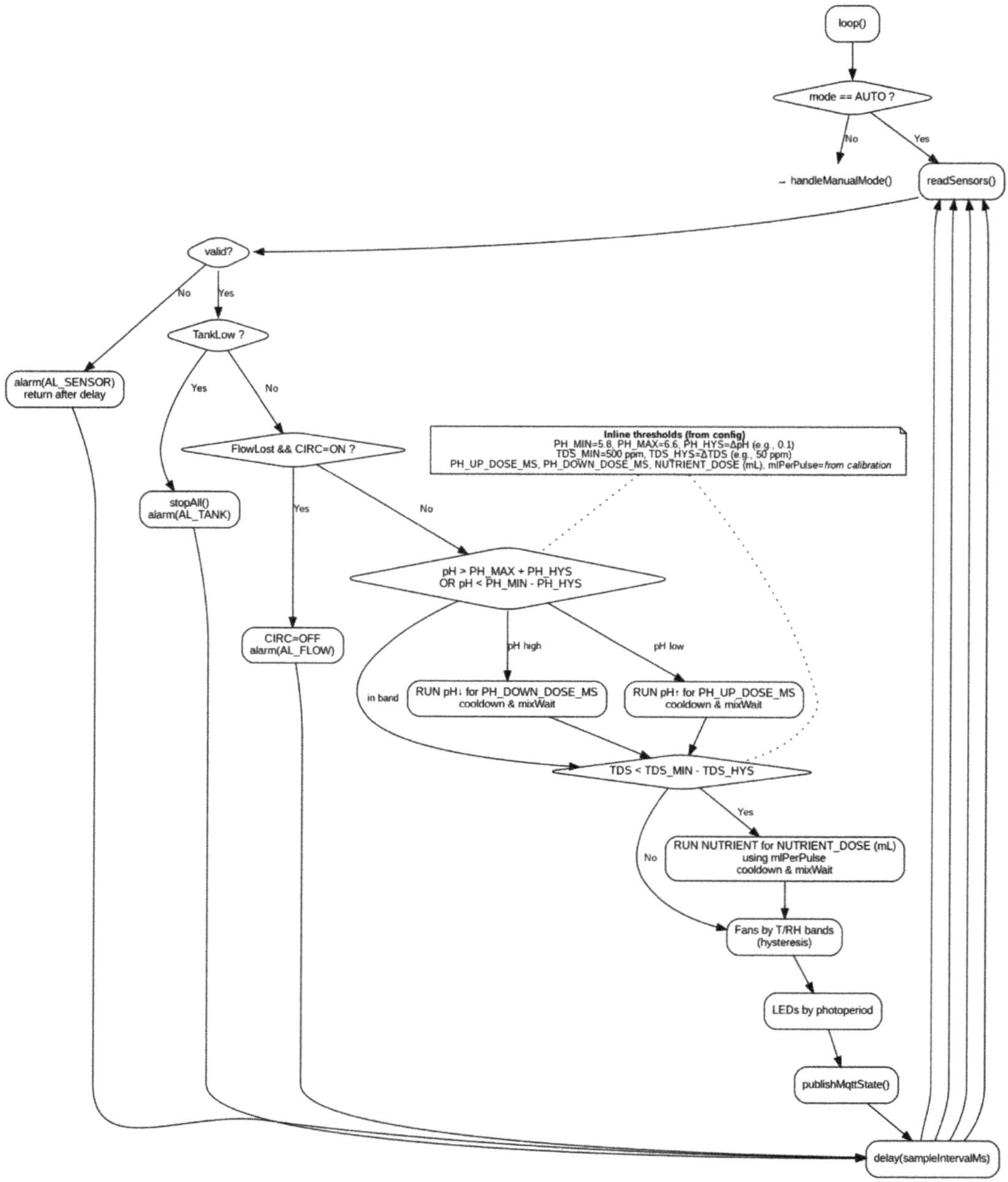

Figure 4. Flow diagram of the automatic mode operation in the IoT-based NFT hydroponic system.

Data transmission uses the MQTT protocol. The Node-RED platform receives these messages and forwards them to InfluxDB for continuous storage of time-series data and to Grafana for real-time visualization, as shown in Figure 5. Additionally, Node-RED keeps a CSV backup of all sensor readings, creating a dual-layer data logging system. To improve communication resilience, LWT and retained messages are employed, allowing fault-tolerant operation during network disconnections [10,11].

https://doi.org/10.3390/engproc2026122003

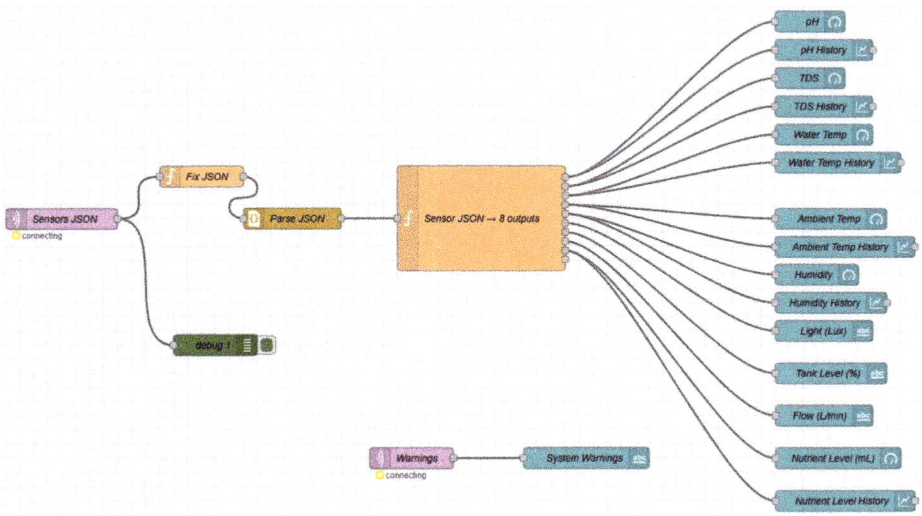

Figure 5. IoT software architecture based on the MING stack.

Two separate user interfaces were developed for system interaction. First, the Node-RED-based web dashboard shown in Figure 6a provides real-time, continuous monitoring of sensor data, observation of threshold limits, and control of actuator states. Second, the system was integrated with a Flutter-based mobile app, deployed on an Android tablet as shown in Figure 6b. This app allows sensor monitoring, mode switching, and manual actuator control. Additionally, push notifications are sent to users for critical events, improving system reliability and user engagement.

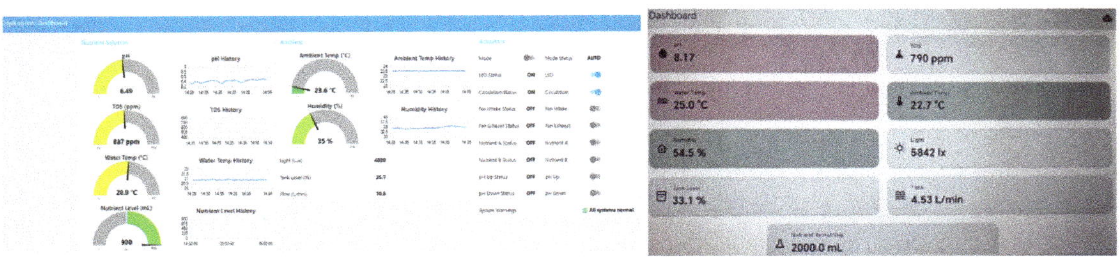

(**a**) (**b**)

Figure 6. System user interfaces: (**a**) Node-RED dashboard; (**b**) Flutter mobile app.

2.5. Data Logging, Security and Alarms

The software architecture integrates data logging, security, and alarm systems. All sensor data are timestamped with the DS3231 RTC and stored locally as CSV files and in InfluxDB as time-series data, supporting both redundancy and long-term analysis. Data are visualized on Grafana dashboards, providing real-time and historical insights. Unlike previous works [6–11], which mainly focus on monitoring, our system offers production-grade security with TLS encryption, ACL-based access control, and LWT/retained messaging. These features ensure synchronization after disconnections and protect data confidentiality and integrity. The alarm subsystem also enhances reliability. Critical conditions—such as low tank levels, circulation failures, or persistent pH/TDS deviations—initiate automatic pump shutdowns and notify users via both the web dashboard and mobile app.

 https://doi.org/10.3390/engproc2026122003

This integration demonstrates that the system emphasizes not only automation but also operational safety.

3. Measurement Results and Evaluation

3.1. Measurement System Structure and Sensors

In the advanced indoor NFT hydroponic system, pH, TDS/EC, nutrient solution temperature, ambient temperature, humidity, light intensity, tank level, and both circulation and dosing flows were constantly monitored. These data supported both closed-loop control and long-term analysis.

The pH and TDS probes were connected through the ADS1115 ADC using MOSFET-based time-sharing, while digital sensors such as DS18B20 for solution temperature, AHT10 for ambient temperature and humidity, and BH1750 for light were linked via standard protocols. Tank level was calculated as percentage fullness using temperature-compensated HC-SR04 measurements, and flow rates were determined from YF-S201 and YF-S402 Hall-effect sensors using pulse-counting methods.

For data collection, the ESP32 sent MQTT messages time-stamped by the DS3231 RTC. Node-RED processed these messages and stored them in InfluxDB as time-series data while creating CSV backups, ensuring both persistence and redundancy. Each record included: timestamp, pH, TDS, solution and ambient temperatures, humidity, light, tank level, and flow rate.

Control depended on hysteresis-based thresholds. Nutrient dosing was turned off when tank levels were low. Fans activated when temperature or humidity went beyond set limits. LED lights followed a photoperiod schedule. Alarms sounded during circulation interruptions to ensure safe shutdown. These thresholds and logic rules were clearly defined in the software configuration and finite state machine.

3.2. Data Presentation

To illustrate the recording structure, Table 4 presents the sensor measurement format used in the system. Figure 7 shows the Grafana dashboard visualization of a 10-min time-series segment, highlighting pH, TDS, and nutrient solution temperature. These results demonstrate the system's dynamic response to control actions.

Table 4. Sample sensor measurements recording format.

Time	pH	TDS (ppm)	Sol. Temp (°C)	Amb. Temp (°C)	Humidity (%)	Light (lux)	Tank Level (%)	Flow (L/min)
15:35	8.27	620	25	23.4	53.5	5216	30.2	4.4

3.3. Evaluation

The two-point calibration of pH and TDS sensors, along with temperature compensation, ensured consistent in situ measurements. Flow rates from YF-S201 sensors (approximately 7.5 pulses, about 1 L/min) enabled reliable monitoring of circulation and dosing, while temperature-based sound velocity correction reduced noise in ultrasonic tank readings. Combined with alarm systems and safe-state strategies, these measures enhanced operational reliability and data integrity.

Table 5 offers a comparative overview with related works, revealing that most studies [6–11] focused on basic monitoring but neglected production-grade needs such as long-term data logging, secure communication, flexible control, flow verification, and safety features.

https://doi.org/10.3390/engproc2026122003

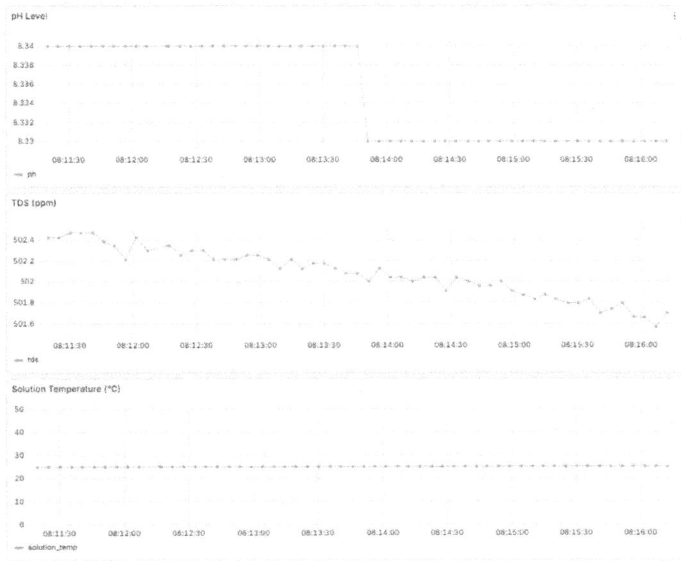

Figure 7. Grafana dashboard visualization of a 10-min time-series excerpt showing pH, TDS, and nutrient solution temperature from InfluxDB data.

Table 5. Comparison of features with the literature.

Study/Feature	Continuous Data Logging	Data Security	Manual/ Automatic Control Modes	Remote Monitoring	Flow Monitoring	Alarm & Safety Mechanisms
[6]	X	X	X	X	X	X
[7]	X	X	X	Mobile	X	X
[8]	X	X	Semi-Auto	Mobile	X	Partial (pH/EC)
[9]	X	X	X	X	X	X
[10]	X	X	X	Mobile	X	X
[11]	X	X	X	X	X	X
This Work	√	√	√	√	√	√

√ indicates that the feature is available in the study, whereas X indicates that the feature is not reported or not implemented.

For instance, TLS/ACL/LWT security, manual and automatic mode switching, and integrated alarms were rarely implemented, while mobile apps (e.g., Blynk, Firebase) lacked robustness for long-term deployment. Conversely, our proposed system features continuous logging, data security, flow validation, and alarm mechanisms, establishing a dependable and scalable testbed for smart hydroponic automation.

4. Conclusions and Future Work

In this study, we developed and deployed an IoT-based monitoring and automation system for NFT hydroponics in enclosed environments. The automation system integrates temperature-compensated pH/TDS measurement, dual flow sensing for circulation and dosing verification, manual and automatic modes, and continuous data logging through an MQTT–InfluxDB–Node-RED–Grafana pipeline. Unlike monitoring-only solutions found in the literature, it also provides alarm mechanisms, data security, and operational reliability.

https://doi.org/10.3390/engproc2026122003

Experimental results showed consistent pH/TDS regulation with hysteresis control, reliable fan and LED operation, and accurate flow-based verification of pump activity and nutrient dosing. Safety features such as alarms and shutdowns in critical conditions enhanced system reliability.

Future work will focus on (i) experimentally validating with different plant species (e.g., lettuce, spinach) to assess biomass growth, yield, and agronomic results; (ii) integrating energy consumption monitoring to derive efficiency metrics such as kWh per kilogram of produce; (iii) implementing advanced control strategies like PID/MPC or machine learning-based dosing algorithms to improve control precision; and (iv) enhancing communication and security layers with mutual TLS (mTLS) and over-the-air (OTA) software updates to increase scalability and maintainability in field deployments.

Author Contributions: Conceptualization, T.D. and İ.Ç.; methodology, T.D. and İ.Ç.; software, T.D.; validation, T.D. and İ.Ç.; formal analysis, İ.Ç.; investigation, İ.Ç.; resources, T.D.; data curation, T.D.; writing—original draft preparation, T.D.; writing—review and editing, T.D. and İ.Ç.; visualization, T.D.; supervision, İ.Ç.; project administration, İ.Ç. All authors have read and agreed to the published version of the manuscript.

Funding: This research received no external funding.

Institutional Review Board Statement: Not applicable.

Informed Consent Statement: Not applicable.

Data Availability Statement: The original contributions presented in this study are included in the article. Further inquiries can be directed to the corresponding author.

Conflicts of Interest: The authors declare no conflicts of interest.

References

1. UN DESA. *World Population Prospects 2022: Summary of Results*; United Nations: New York, NY, USA, 2022.
2. FAO. *The Importance of Ukraine and the Russian Federation for Global Agricultural Markets and the Risks Associated with the Current Conflict*; FAO: Rome, Italy, 2022.
3. UN. *Black Sea Grain Initiative—Update*; United Nations: New York, NY, USA, 2023.
4. FAO. *COVID-19 and the Risk to Food Supply Chains: How to Respond?* FAO: Rome, Italy, 2020.
5. IARC/WHO. *Monographs on the Evaluation of Carcinogenic Risks to Humans, Vol. 112: Glyphosate*; IARC: Lyon, France, 2015.
6. Kushawaha, A.; Shah, D.; Vora, D.; Zade, N.; Iyer, K. Urban small-scale hydroponics: A compact, smart home-based hydroponics system. *MethodsX* **2024**, *13*, 102998. [CrossRef] [PubMed]
7. Patil, N.; Patil, S.; Uttekar, A.; Suryawanshi, A.R. Monitoring of hydroponics system using IoT technology. *Int. Res. J. Eng. Technol. (IRJET)* **2020**, *7*, 1873–1877.
8. Blancaflor, E.; Jamena, J.N.D.; Banganay, K.N.U.; Rabanal, R.S.C.; Fernandez, K.E.; Zamora, S.L.G. An IoT monitoring system designed for hydroponics plant cultivation. In Proceedings of the 2022 5th International Conference on Computing and Big Data (ICCBD), Shanghai, China, 16–18 December 2022; pp. 1–6.
9. Vineeth, V.P.; Ananthan, T. Automated hydroponic system using IoT for indoor farming. In Proceedings of the 4th International Conference on Electronics and Sustainable Communication Systems (ICESC 2023), Coimbatore, India, 6–8 July 2023; pp. 369–373.
10. Lal, R. Autonomous hydroponic farming using internet of things. In Proceedings of the 1st IEEE International Conference on Cognitive, Green and Ubiquitous Computing (IC-CGU 2024), Bhubaneswar, India, 1–2 March 2024; pp. 1–6.
11. Waghmare, V.; Rakte, P.; Gadalkar, M.; Bhaleghare, S.; Sakhare, D.; Goudar, M. Real time monitoring of hydroponic system using IoT. In Proceedings of the 2024 IEEE International Conference on Intelligent Systems and Advanced Applications (ICISAA 2024), Pune, India, 25–26 October 2024; pp. 1–6.

https://doi.org/10.3390/engproc2026122003

engineering proceedings

Proceeding Paper

Integrated Potential for Wind and Solar Energy in the Context of Sustainable Development of the Coastal Regions of Bulgaria †

Rositsa Velichkova [1,*], Iskra Simova [1], Elitsa Gieva [2], Angel Aleksandrov [3] and Aleksandar Stanilov [1]

1 Department of Hydroaerodynamics and Hydraulic Machines, Technical University of Sofia, 1000 Sofia, Bulgaria; isimova@tu-sofia.bg (I.S.); astanilov@tu-sofia.bg (A.S.)
2 Department of Microelectronics, Technical University of Sofia, 1000 Sofia, Bulgaria; gieva@tu-sofia.bg
3 Department of Machine Elements and Non-Metallic Constructions, Technical University of Sofia, 1000 Sofia, Bulgaria; alexandrov.angel1@gmail.com
* Correspondence: rvelichkova@tu-sofia.bg

† Presented at the 6th International Conference on Communications, Information, Electronic and Energy Systems, 26–28 November 2025, Ruse, Bulgaria.

Abstract

This study presents a comparative analysis of the potential for combined use of wind and solar energy in nine key coastal settlements on the Bulgarian Black Sea coast—Shabla, Balchik, Varna, Byala, Obzor, Nesebar, Burgas, Primorsko, and Tsarevo—selected for their diverse geographical and meteorological characteristics. The study evaluates the feasibility of implementing hybrid renewable energy systems by analyzing the average annual solar radiation and wind velocity for each location. A methodology based on physical and technical parameters is applied to determine the required installed capacity of photovoltaic systems to meet the average annual household electricity consumption of 6000 kWh. Concurrently, wind energy potential is assessed through theoretical and practical models using two turbine sizes (3 m and 6 m in diameter), which represent small-scale residential wind applications.

Keywords: hybrid system; Black Sea coast; energy efficiency; return on investment

1. Introduction

With the accelerated depletion of fossil fuels and the need to limit carbon emissions, renewable energy sources (RES) are becoming a strategic priority for the sustainable development of the energy sector. Among them, wind and solar energy are the most affordable and technically mature technologies, suitable for both centralized energy and decentralized systems with local application [1].

Small wind turbines, especially those with a capacity of less than 10–20 kW, are used in the domestic sector, rural areas and off-grid systems. They offer the opportunity to reduce dependence on the electricity grid and ensure partial or complete energy independence. However, a major challenge in their use is the variability of the wind, which limits production in some periods [2–4].

To overcome these limitations, hybrid solutions combining wind and solar (photovoltaic) energy are increasingly being applied. Solar energy is particularly suitable for areas with seasonal activity—such as the Bulgarian Black Sea coast—where in the summer months, when the wind is weaker, solar panels compensate for the energy deficit [5–7]. This achieves a more even and predictable energy supply throughout the year.

The Bulgarian Black Sea Coast has favorable natural and climatic conditions for the development of renewable energy sources, especially wind and solar energy. The geographical location, proximity to the sea and open terrain create good conditions for constant air flow, while high levels of insolation guarantee stable solar radiation throughout most of the year [8–10].

Combining wind and solar energy in hybrid systems offers an optimal balance between the seasonal variability of the two sources. In winter, when sunlight decreases, wind activity along the Black Sea coast increases, and vice versa—in summer, solar production dominates. This allows the construction of energy-autonomous sites that can cover a large part of their own consumption without the need for expensive storage or backup generators.

This study performs a comparative analysis of the efficiency of wind turbines with a diameter of 3 m and 6 m in nine coastal settlements in Bulgaria. The annual electricity production, economic savings and the return on investment period are assessed. While many studies look at large RES parks or general regional indicators, this article focuses on an "average household" with consumption of ~6000 kWh/year and shows what sizing a ~4–5 kWp system in a coastal location would look like—a practical approach that is more accessible to households or small businesses.

2. Methodology of the Study

2.1. Methodology

The calculation of wind energy is based on the estimation of the kinetic energy of air masses passing through the area covered by the rotor blades of the wind turbine. The quantitative analysis process includes several stages related to physical dependencies, meteorological data, and technical characteristics of the facility.

The theoretical power P that can be extracted from the wind is calculated using the following formula:

$$P = \frac{1}{2}\rho V^3 A \quad (1)$$

where P—theoretical wind power (W), ρ—air density (kg/m^3), A—the area through which the air passes (m^2), i.e., the rotor area, V—wind speed (m/s).

According to Betz's law, no more than 59.3% of the kinetic energy of the wind can be converted into mechanical energy by a wind turbine. This leads to the introduction of a coefficient of efficiency:

$$P_{\max} = 0.593\frac{1}{2}\rho V^3 A \quad (2)$$

However, in practice, the actual efficiency of modern turbines is around 35–45% of the total kinetic energy of the wind, due to technological and aerodynamic limitations.

The actual electrical power is obtained by multiplying the theoretical power by the overall efficiency coefficient C_p:

$$P_e = C_p\frac{1}{2}\rho V^3 A \quad (3)$$

where C_p—overall efficiency coefficient (usually between 0.3 and 0.45).

To calculate the total amount of electricity produced for a certain period, the following formula is used:

$$E = P_e.t \quad (4)$$

where E—electricity produced (Wh or kWh), t—operating time (in hours).

The calculation of solar energy follows the following methodology.

https://doi.org/10.3390/engproc2026122004

For each location, the required installed capacity (in kWp) is determined to ensure that the system's annual production covers a consumption of 6000 kWh. The calculation is performed using the following equation:

$$P_{req} = \frac{E_{year}}{H\eta},\ kWp \tag{5}$$

where P_{req}—required installed power (kWp), H—average annual solar radiation (kWh/m^2/year), η—system efficiency (≈0.75–0.90, depending on losses).

2.2. Experimental Data

For the practical application of the methodology, the following input data are required:

- Temperature and pressure (Figures 1 and 2).
- Average wind speed at a certain height; in our case, 10 m (Figure 3).
- Geographical location and altitude (affect air density) (Figure 4).
- Rotor diameter (or radius)—most often, turbines with a power of 1–5 kW are used for a single-family house, which corresponds to a rotor diameter between 2.5 and 7 m, depending on the specific conditions.
- Average annual electricity consumption—it is assumed that an average household on the Black Sea coast consumes about 6000 kWh/year.
- Solar radiation—for each of the selected locations, approximate values of the average annual global solar radiation on a horizontal surface (kWh/m^2) are used, obtained from public climate databases and literature (Table 1).
- System Efficiency Coefficient—the actual system output is assumed to be 90% of the theoretical maximum, taking into account losses from temperature, contamination, cable resistances, and non-ideal orientation.

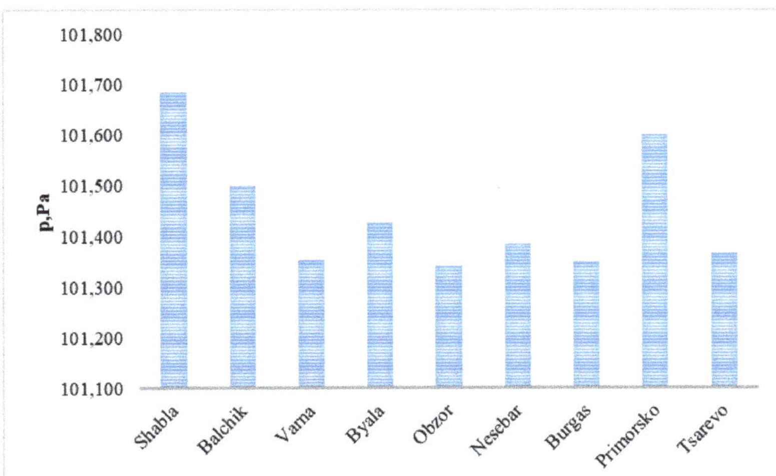

Figure 1. Average atmospheric pressure for each point.

Table 1. Solar radiation at each point.

Town	Solar Radiation kWh/m^2/year
Shabla	1450–1550
Balchik	1450–1550

https://doi.org/10.3390/engproc2026122004

Table 1. *Cont.*

Town	Solar Radiation kWh/m²/year
Varna	1250–1350
Byala	1450–1550
Obzor	1450–1550
Nesebar	1450–1550
Burgas	1500–1600
Primorsko	1450–1600
Tsarevo	1450

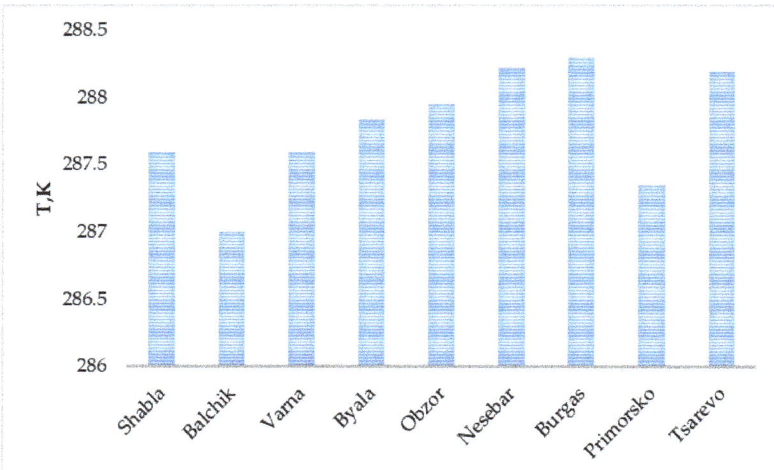

Figure 2. Average temperature for each point.

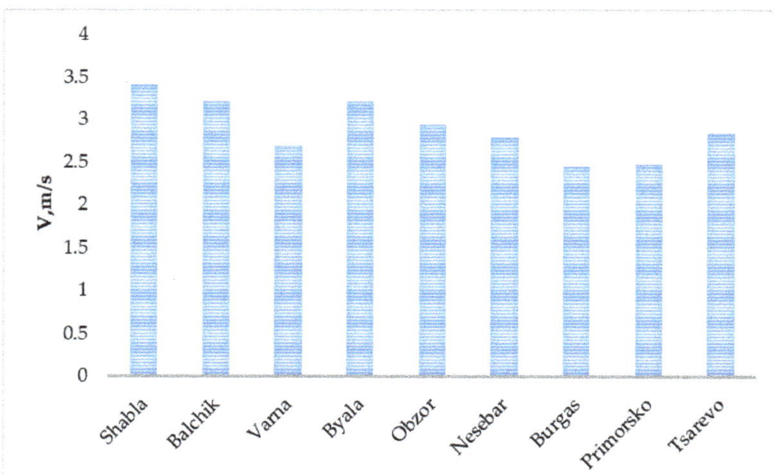

Figure 3. Average wind velocity for each point.

https://doi.org/10.3390/engproc2026122004

Figure 4. Geographical location for each point.

3. Results and Discussion

3.1. Analysis of the Results

Based on the methodologies described in Section 2, an assessment of the possibilities for using wind and solar energy for domestic use for a single-family house has been made.

Figures 5–8 present the results of the calculations of the theoretical and actual electrical power of wind turbines with diameters of 3 m and 6 m in nine coastal Bulgarian cities. The data are based on average annual wind speeds for each location and reflect both ideal conditions (without losses) and a realistic scenario with the efficiency factor included.

With a small rotor diameter (3 m), the theoretical power reaches maximum values in the northern part of the Black Sea coast—Shabla, Balchik, Varna and Byala—where it varies between 130 and 180 W. In the southern regions such as Burgas, Primorsko and Nessebar, the power drops below 80 W, which indicates a relatively weak wind energy potential in these areas.

After taking into account the real efficiency of the turbine (in this case 58%), the power values drop, as expected, by about 60–65%. However, the trend between cities remains the same—the northeastern regions retain their advantage. The actual power in Shabla and Balchik reaches approximately 100–120 W, while in Burgas and Primorsko it is below 50 W.

Increasing the rotor diameter to 6 m leads to a fourfold increase in the rotor area, which also drastically increases the theoretical power. In Shabla, Balchik and Byala, the values exceed 600–700 W. Even in less windy areas such as Obzor and Nessebar, a twofold increase is observed compared to the previous scenario.

Under realistic conditions and D = 6 m, the wind turbine could provide 400–500 W in cities with an average wind speed above 3.2 m/s. This makes the project for partial

https://doi.org/10.3390/engproc2026122004

household electricity supply technically feasible with a suitable location. At the same time, in the southern Black Sea cities, the values remain low and unjustified from an economic point of view.

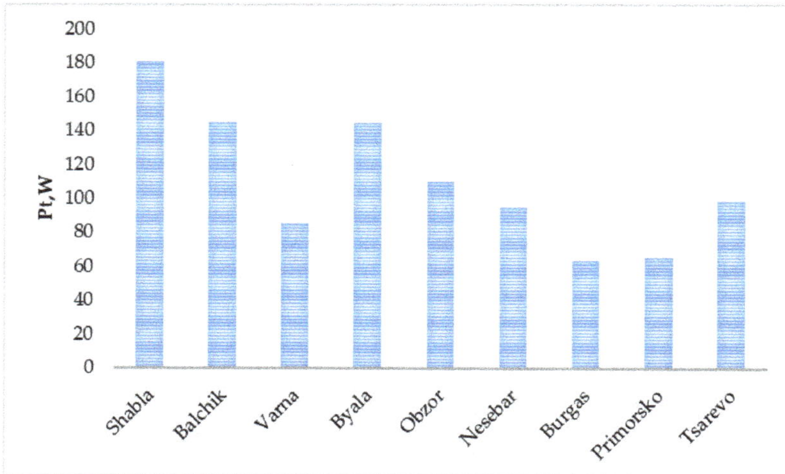

Figure 5. Theoretical power at D = 3 m.

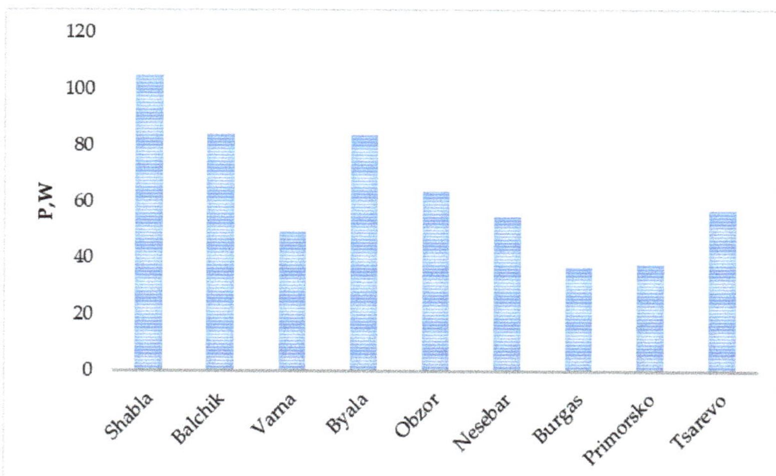

Figure 6. Power at D = 3 m.

The required installed capacity of a photovoltaic system to cover the average annual electricity consumption of a household is calculated using the following data. Average consumption of a household: 6000 kWh/year. Average efficiency of a photovoltaic system: 90% (0.9).

Figures 9 and 10 present the results for the annual energy of each of the considered systems, including a small photovoltaic power plant with a capacity of 6000 kWh/year.

All locations show energy yields in the range of 6000 to 6900 kWh/year, which suggests that cumulative production from several turbines is being considered or extrapolation has been made. Shabla, Balchik and Varna again stand out with the highest values (~6900 kWh),

https://doi.org/10.3390/engproc2026122004

which is in line with their higher average annual wind speeds. Burgas, Primorsko and Nessebar remain at the bottom of the ranking (~6200 kWh/year).

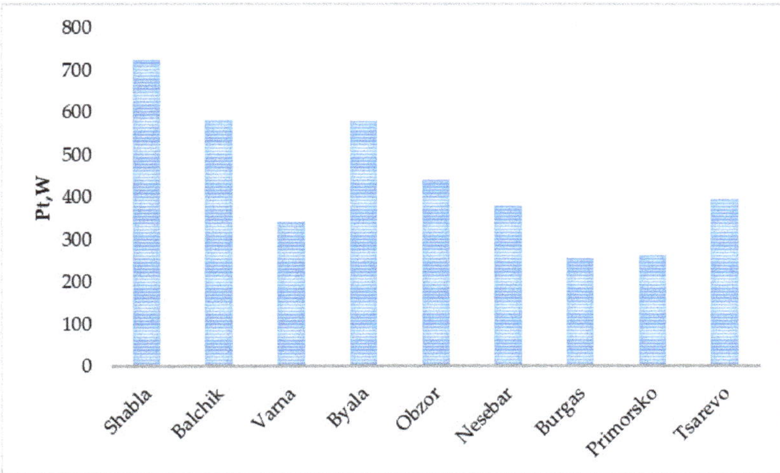

Figure 7. Theoretical power at D = 6 m.

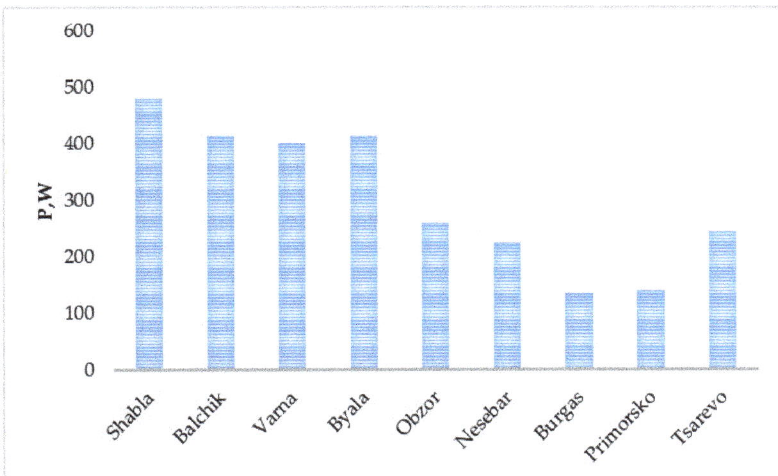

Figure 8. Power at D = 6 m.

Even with a smaller rotor diameter, location has a significant impact on the annual energy yield. The difference between the best and the weakest places is about 700–800 kWh per year, which is significant in long-term investment planning.

With a larger rotor (6 m), all annual production values increase significantly—in the range of 9000 to almost 12,000 kWh/year. The leaders are again Shabla, Balchik and Varna, where the yield exceeds 11,500 kWh per year. In the southern part of the Black Sea coast (Burgas, Primorsko, Nessebar), it reached below 10,000 kWh/year, which again indicates the lower local potential.

Increasing the diameter from 3 m to 6 m leads to an almost twofold increase in annual electricity production, which is logical due to the quadratic dependence of the area on the

 https://doi.org/10.3390/engproc2026122004

radius. This makes the investment in larger rotors economically more expedient—especially in areas with good wind conditions.

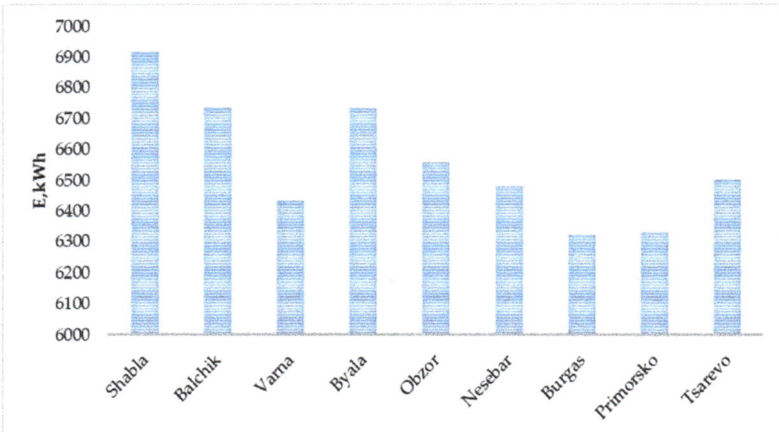

Figure 9. Combined annual electricity at D = 3 m.

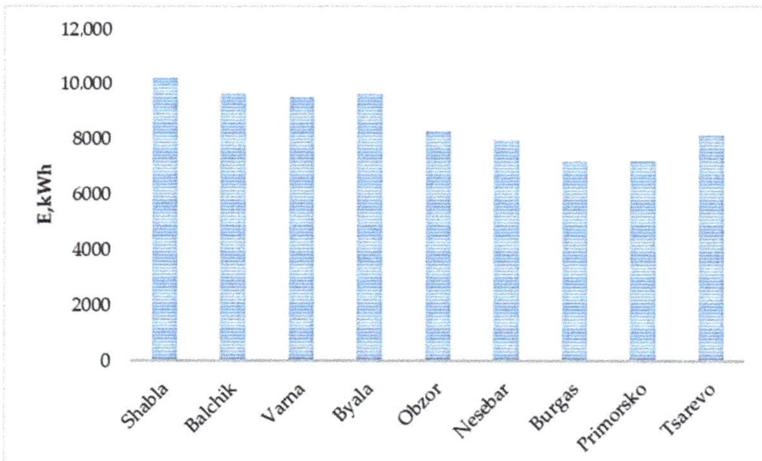

Figure 10. Combined annual electricity at D = 6 m.

3.2. Economic Efficiency Analysis

Tables 2 and 3 present the results of calculating the annual savings and the payback period, taking into account the following values: electricity price of 0.25 BGN/kWh; an investment of BGN 10,000 for 3 m; and BGN 25,000 for 6 m.

The results show that the annual savings from using a wind turbine are directly related to the local wind characteristics. In the most favorable areas—Shabla, Balchik, Varna and Byala—savings between BGN 2380 and 2551 per year are achieved, while in less windy areas such as Burgas and Primorsko the value drops to around BGN 1800.

The time required to recover the initial investment shows significant differences between the two cases:

- at D = 3 m: best return: Shabla—9.80 years; weakest: Burgas—13.92 years;
- at D = 6 m: best return: Shabla—8.67 years; weakest: Burgas—9.49 years.

https://doi.org/10.3390/engproc2026122004

Table 2. Annual savings and payback period at D = 3 m.

Location	Annual Saving BGN	Payback Period Year
Shabla	2551.2	9.79931
Balchik	2408.85	10.3784
Varna	2380.38	10.50252
Byala	2408.85	10.3784
Obzor	2069.4	12.0808
Nesebar	1992.75	12.54548
Burgas	1795.65	13.92254
Primorsko	1806.6	13.83815
Tsarevo	2036.55	12.27566

Table 3. Annual savings and payback period at D = 6 m.

Location	Annual Saving BGN	Payback Period Year
Shabla	2551.2	8.669225805
Balchik	2408,85	8.904898459
Varna	2380.38	9.326213486
Byala	2408.85	8.908445029
Obzor	2069.4	9.147866112
Nesebar	1992.75	9.255607049
Burgas	1795.65	9.489055188
Primorsko	1806.6	9.474235568
Tsarevo	2036.55	9.22580455

4. Conclusions

The analysis shows that combining wind and solar energy offers an effective solution for sustainable power supply in the coastal regions of Bulgaria. With a rotor diameter of 6 m, an almost double increase in annual electricity production is observed compared to 3 m, which significantly improves the economic return. The best results are achieved in the northeastern regions, where wind speed and solar radiation are optimal. Calculations for annual savings and payback period show that such an investment is profitable in the long term, especially when implementing a hybrid system. The study supports the need for strategic development of decentralized energy solutions in coastal regions and demonstrates their applicability in the context of energy transformation and climate sustainability. The results show that the northeastern part of the coast (Shabla, Balchik, Byala) has the highest potential for electricity production, as well as the best economic parameters for return on investment. The combined use of wind and sun is an optimal solution for sustainable and independent energy supply to households in the region. The results can serve as a basis for energy planning in small settlements and municipalities along the Black Sea coast, which aim for sustainable development and energy independence. The study can be used by home users, designers and RES installers for realistic sizing of autonomous or semi-autonomous systems.

Author Contributions: Conceptualization, R.V. and I.S.; methodology, R.V.; software, A.S. and A.A.; validation, E.G.; investigation, R.V. and I.S.; writing—original draft preparation, R.V.; writing—review and editing, I.S.; visualization, E.G. All authors have read and agreed to the published version of the manuscript.

Funding: This research received no external funding.

Institutional Review Board Statement: Not applicable.

 https://doi.org/10.3390/engproc2026122004

Informed Consent Statement: Not applicable.

Data Availability Statement: The data presented in this study are available upon request from the corresponding author.

Acknowledgments: The research in this work was carried out within the project "Integrated system for energy production from renewable energy sources for environmentally friendly residential houses", КП-06-Н77/2 от 04.12.2023г, funded by the Bulgarian Science Fund of the Ministry of Education and Science, and the infrastructure of Operational Programme "Research, Innovation and Digitalisation for Smart Transformation 2021–2027" under Project NoBG16RFPR002-1.014-0006-C01 "National center of excellence for mechatronics and clean technologies" was used to process the results.

Conflicts of Interest: The authors declare no conflicts of interest.

References

1. Ackermann, T.; Soder, L. An overview of wind energy-status 2002. *Renew. Sustain. Energy Rev.* **2002**, *6*, 67–127. [CrossRef]
2. Terziev, A.; Panteleev, Y.; Ivanov, M. Wind energy assessment for low complex terrain using reference meteorological mast. In Proceedings of the International Scientific Conference of Communications, Information, Electronic and Energy Systems (CIEES 2020), Borovets, Bulgaria, 26–29 November 2020.
3. Rohit, R.V.; Vipin, R.R.; Veena, R.; Kumar, K.S.; Mathew, S. Realization of Small Wind Turbines for Low-Speed Wind Regions. In Proceedings of the 7th International Conference on Trends in Electronics and Informatics (ICOEI), Tirunelveli, India, 11–13 April 2023.
4. Moreira, R.; Sousa, J.; Camus, C. Challenges and Opportunities in the Integration of Wind Turbines in Urban Areas: A Technical and Economic Analysis. In Proceedings of the 21st International Conference on the European Energy Market (EEM), Lisbon, Portugal, 27–29 May 2025.
5. Rahman, M.W.; Velmurugan, K.; Mahmud, M.S.; Al Mamun, A.; Ravindran, P. Modeling of a stand-alone Wind-PV Hybrid Generation System Using (MATLAB/SIMULINK). In Proceedings of the International Conference on Computing, Communication, and Intelligent Systems (ICCCIS), Greater Noida, India, 19–20 February 2021; pp. 1000–1006. [CrossRef]
6. Kumar, A.; Sood, Y.R.; Mahia, R.N. Hybrid Energy System Simulation and Modelling Incorporating Wind and Solar Power. In Proceedings of the 2024 IEEE International Students' Conference on Electrical, Electronics and Computer Science (SCEECS), Bhopal, India, 24–25 February 2024.
7. Rana, A.; Pfeiffer, T.; Rafajlovski, G. Wind and Solar Integration with Pumped Hydro Energy Storage: A Tool to Optimize Hybrid Renewable Energy System. In Proceedings of the International Conference on Communications, Information, Electronic and Energy Systems (CIEES2022), Veliko Tarnovo, Bulgaria, 24–26 November, 2022.
8. Galabov, V. On the Wave Energy Potential of the Bulgarian Black Sea Coast. In Proceedings of the 13th SGEM GeoConference on Water Resources, Forest, Marine and Ocean Ecosystems: SGEM2013 Conference Proceedings, Albena, Bulgaria, 16–22 June 2013. Available online: https://arxiv.org/pdf/1304.7806 (accessed on 1 September 2025).
9. Silion, A.; Rusu, L. A Review Concerning the Offshore Wind and Wave Energy Potential in the Black Sea. *J. Mar. Sci. Eng.* **2025**, *13*, 1643. [CrossRef]
10. Belev, G.; Obrenovic, B. Regional Disparities and Features of Solar and Wind EnergyPotential of Bulgaria. *Int. J. Oper. Manag.* **2021**, *2*, 7–11. [CrossRef]

https://doi.org/10.3390/engproc2026122004

engineering proceedings

MDPI

Proceeding Paper

Simple Experimental Evaluation of a Quantum Computer via Tomography and GHz States †

Darin Peev * and Yordan Sivkov

Department of Electronics, Nikola Vaptsarov Naval Academy, 9002 Varna, Bulgaria; jsivkov@naval-acad.bg
* Correspondence: d.peev@naval-acad.bg; Tel.: +359-882-412-447

† Presented at the 6th International Conference on Communications, Information, Electronic and Energy Systems, 26–28 November 2025, Ruse, Bulgaria.

Abstract

This paper presents a simple experimental method for evaluating a superconducting quantum processor through two-qubit quantum state tomography and generalized GHZ-state benchmarking. The goal is to provide an accessible procedure for assessing hardware fidelity and entanglement capability. The method was demonstrated using IBM's 127-qubit ibm_brisbane device, where each Bell state was prepared and reconstructed from 10,000 shots, and the resulting fidelities were compared to Qiskit Aer simulations. The method further examines multi-qubit GHZ states to gauge scalability. The main advantages are its simplicity, reproducibility on free IBM Quantum hardware, and its suitability for entry-level experimentation and performance evaluation.

Keywords: quantum computing; quantum state tomography; Qiskit; IBM Quantum; density matrix; quantum state fidelity; bell states

1. Introduction

Although quantum computers are still in their infancy today, they possess a number of unique properties that distinguish them from their classical counterparts. In 2019, Google announced that it had executed a quantum algorithm which would take a classical computer an estimated 10,000 years to complete [1]. The advantage of the quantum computer does not lie in component miniaturization necessarily or access speed. In fact, in terms of these two factors, the current hardware implementation of a quantum computer is significantly less efficient than that of traditional classical computers.

What makes the superiority of quantum computing possible is its access to quantum properties of information, which are radically different from those in the macroscopic world. Like a classical computer, a quantum computer can process information in binary form. However, while a classical bit exists as either a 0 or a 1 at any given moment, depending on the voltage of the signal encoding it, a qubit can occupy a superposed state combining 0 and 1, with different probabilities and a specific phase associated with each component. The phase arises from the fact that quantum systems also exhibit wave-like behavior. There are various methods for encoding a quantum state, such as the polarization of photons or the quantum spin of electrons [2].

Quantum computing is rapidly evolving, driven by foundational breakthroughs like Shor's factoring algorithm to recent advances in certified randomness and quantum sampling. Central to this progress is the ability to accurately prepare, manipulate, and measure quantum states—a capability that underpins tasks such as quantum cryptography,

 https://doi.org/10.3390/engproc2026122005

and quantum machine learning. The Bell states are among the most fundamental quantum configurations. They exhibit maximal entanglement and are critical for demonstrating quantum nonlocality, teleportation, and superdense coding [3,4].

By enabling the generation and distribution of entanglement across many interconnected nodes, quantum communication networks—realized through optical interactions involving single photons—offer a means to detect eavesdropping through Bell's theorem [5]. The possibility for a free-space quantum communication based on entanglement has been shown, even in daylight rain conditions in urban areas.

Future quantum internet could utilize a variety of photonic technologies, such as quantum repeaters and satellite-based entanglement. Satellite-based quantum key distribution on entanglement has already been successfully demonstrated and utilized.

Various architectures can link high-precision quantum sensors with a quantum computer for data processing. In an example scenario, each quantum sensor is paired with a small local quantum module that performs limited quantum pre-processing and converts the result into classical data, which is then sent to a remote quantum computer or cloud for further analysis.

This paper explores quantum state tomography for characterizing entanglement on an IBM quantum computer. State tomography, which involves reconstructing the complete state of a quantum system from measurement data, is essential for assessing the accuracy and guiding the development of quantum technologies [6–8]. With advances in quantum processor architectures, tomography is an important tool for analyzing coherence properties, evaluating gate performance, and characterizing entanglement within the system [6].

The IBM Quantum platform used in this work offers free cloud-based access to actual quantum processors, enabling users to run experiments on physical quantum hardware [9]. It is seamlessly integrated with Qiskit, an open-source quantum programming framework developed by IBM for building, simulating, and executing quantum programs in Python. In this work, Python version 3.12.4 and Qiskit versions 1.2.4 and 1.3.1 were used [10–12]. Together, IBM Quantum and Qiskit form a user-friendly environment for developing, testing, and deploying quantum algorithms.

In this work, we used ibm_brisbane, belonging to the IBM's Quantum Eagle r3 series of processors.

The quantum state fidelities reported in this work were obtained directly from the quantum hardware, and, for simulations, from the Aer simulator.

2. Materials and Methods

2.1. Basic Theory

In general, the state vector for a two-qubit system according to Dirak notation [13] is

$$|\psi\rangle = \alpha_{00}|00\rangle + \alpha_{01}|01\rangle + \alpha_{10}|10\rangle + \alpha_{11}|11\rangle, \tag{1}$$

with the normalization condition concerning the probability amplitudes

$$|\alpha_{00}|^2 + |\alpha_{01}|^2 + |\alpha_{10}|^2 + |\alpha_{11}|^2 = 1. \tag{2}$$

The four maximally entangled pure states are

$$|\Phi^+\rangle = (1/\sqrt{2}) \begin{pmatrix} 1 \\ 0 \\ 0 \\ 1 \end{pmatrix}, \tag{3}$$

https://doi.org/10.3390/engproc2026122005

$$|\Phi^-\rangle = (1/\sqrt{2})\begin{pmatrix}1\\0\\0\\-1\end{pmatrix}, \quad (4)$$

$$|\Psi^+\rangle = (1/\sqrt{2})\begin{pmatrix}0\\1\\1\\0\end{pmatrix}, \quad (5)$$

$$|\Psi^-\rangle = (1/\sqrt{2})\begin{pmatrix}0\\1\\-1\\0\end{pmatrix}. \quad (6)$$

They are known as Bell states, named after the renowned physicist John Bell. A generalized state involving n entangled qubits is [14]

$$|GHZ_n\rangle = \left(1/\sqrt{2}\right)\left(|0\rangle^{\otimes n} + |1\rangle^{\otimes n}\right) \quad (7)$$

Entangled qubits are successfully used for establishing secure communications and they are widely used in quantum cryptography [14].

2.2. Quantum State Tomography, Density Matrix and State Fidelity

The application of state vectors in describing quantum states does not extend beyond states termed pure states. In cases when a state vector $|\psi\rangle$ does not occur with probability 1, i.e., the state is not pure, a generalized description is provided through the so-called density matrix. If the actual state is unknown, but several pure states $|\psi_i\rangle$ are candidates instead, each with its corresponding probability of occurring p_i, the system's state is described by the following density matrix ρ [6–8]:

$$\rho = \sum_{i=1}^{N} p_i|\psi_i\rangle\langle\psi_i| \quad (8)$$

with N being the number of possible pure states in the list. Several types of measurements are required to form a complete picture of a quantum state. Each type of measurement then serves as a "different observation angle" to reconstruct the "object in its entirety". That process is called quantum state tomography, from the Greek word tomos—section. Exactly in this capacity of encompassing the complete description that is accessible, quantum tomography is indispensable. It uses a sufficient basis of measurement operators and multiple shots to reconstruct the quantum state.

By introducing a type of distance measure, the closeness of two quantum states can be evaluated for the purpose of quantifying the quality of a quantum algorithm implementation. It relates to the overlap between a pure desired state and an arbitrary state. The general formulation [6] is as follows:

$$F(\rho,\sigma) = \left(Tr\left\{\sqrt{\sqrt{\rho}\sigma\sqrt{\rho}}\right\}\right)^2 \quad (9)$$

where for either matrix being a pure state it works out as $Tr\{\rho\sigma\}$ [6].

A significant contributor to the loss of performance in a quantum system is decoherence due to undesired influences, incl. environmental [15].

 https://doi.org/10.3390/engproc2026122005

3. Results of Two-Qubit Quantum State Tomography on IBM Quantum Computer for the Four Bell States

The preparation of the four Bell states follows distinct gate sequences, while the measurement and analysis procedure remains identical. To generate $|\Phi^+\rangle$, qubit q_0 is subjected to a Hadamard gate, after which a controlled-NOT gate with q_0 being the control and q_1 the target is applied. The state $|\Phi^-\rangle$ is obtained by applying an X gate and a Hadamard gate to q_0, followed by the same CNOT operation. For $|\Psi^+\rangle$, a Hadamard gate is applied to q_0 and an X gate to q_1. The last circuit stage is an identical CNOT gate. Finally, $|\Psi^-\rangle$ is prepared by applying a Hadamard on q_0, an X gate on q_1, and Z gates on both qubits, before completing the circuit with analagous CNOT.

In all cases, the density matrix $\rho = |\psi\rangle\langle\psi|$ of the target state is reconstructed through quantum state tomography on the ibm_brisbane device using 10,000 shots. The experimentally measured fidelities, listed in Table 1, are compared with ideal states simulated using Qiskit Aer (see the description of Table 1).

Table 1. Measured quantum fidelities (Fidelity_M) executed on the ibm_brisbane quantum computer and fidelities from the Qiskit Aer simulator (Fidelity_S) for the four Bell states.

Index	Fidelity_M	Fidelity_S
$\|\Phi^+\rangle$	0.8735	0.9972
$\|\Phi^-\rangle$	0.8513	0.9983
$\|\Psi^+\rangle$	0.8688	0.9954
$\|\Psi^-\rangle$	0.8625	0.9918

The graphical representation of these results is presented in Figure 1. The differences between the experimentally obtained density matrix and the one acquired by simulation are shown in Figure 2 element by element. The discrepancies reflect the effect of noise and device imperfections, providing a more realistic estimate of hardware performance than gate-level fidelity values alone. The maximum absolute differences in the density matrix elements between real hardware measurements and Aer simulation were evaluated separately for the real and imaginary parts. For the first Bell state $|\Phi^+\rangle$, the real and imaginary parts are 0.0824 and 0.0174, respectively; for the second Bell state $|\Phi^-\rangle$, 0.1013 and 0.0128; for the third Bell state $|\Psi^+\rangle$, 0.0842 and 0.0223; and for the fourth Bell state $|\Psi^-\rangle$, 0.0870 and 0.0265. The values for the real part align with the measured fidelities—the larger the differences, the lower the fidelity. The imaginary parts do not exhibit a clear trend; in this case they mainly reflect noise. That is expected since the ideal density matrices of the Bell states have zero imaginary entries.

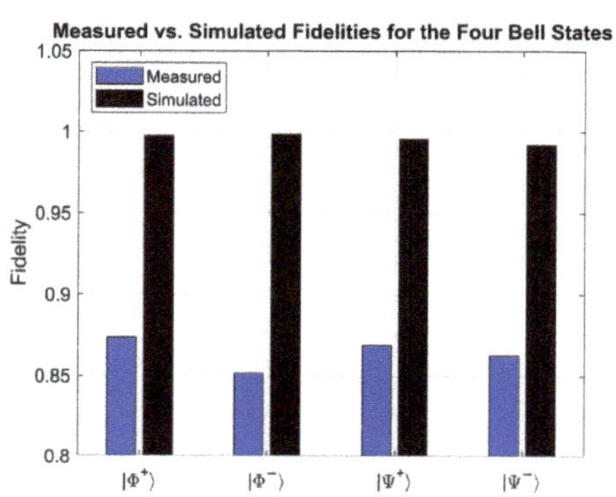

Figure 1. Fidelities of the four Bell states obtained experimentally (blue) for the ibm_brisbane quantum computer and from Qiskit Aer simulation (black).

 https://doi.org/10.3390/engproc2026122005

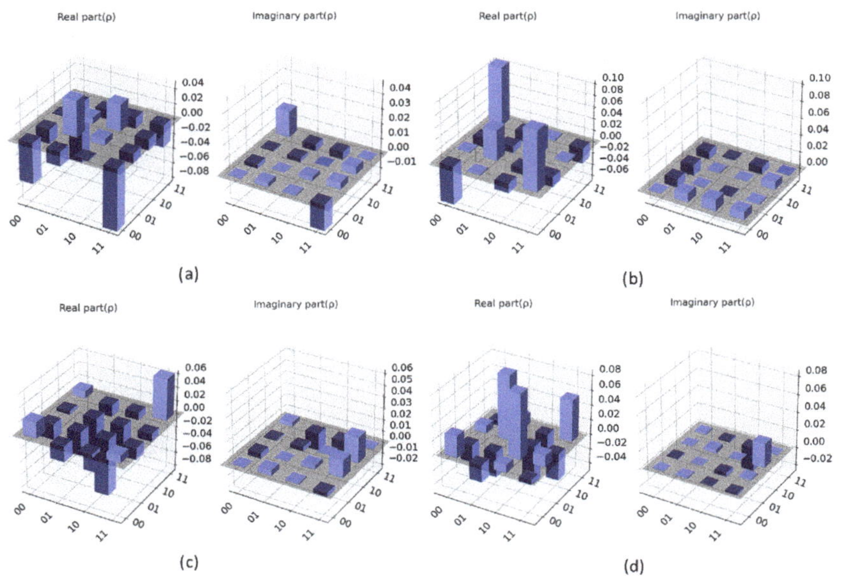

Figure 2. Differences between the density matrix measured by real quantum hardware ibm_brisbane and the density matrix from the Aer quantum simulator for the Bell set: (**a**) $|\Phi^+\rangle$; (**b**) $|\Phi^-\rangle$; (**c**) $|\Psi^+\rangle$; (**d**) $|\Psi^-\rangle$.

4. Results of Generalized n-Qubit GHZ States Preparation and Measurement

Experiments to measure the generalized GHZ states from Equation (7) on the default (Z) basis with a varied number of qubits involved in the state n = [3,5,8–10] were conducted on ibm_brisbane quantum machine. The number of shots in every experiment was 2000. Based on the counts N_0 revealing all zeros in the measurement $\left(|0\rangle^{\otimes n}\right)$ and counts N_1 yielding all ones from measurement $\left(|1\rangle^{\otimes n}\right)$, the probability $p\left(|0\rangle^{\otimes n}\right) + \left(p|1\rangle^{\otimes n}\right)$ was estimated as

$$p_{GHZ}(n) = p\left(|0\rangle^{\otimes n}\right) + p\left(|1\rangle^{\otimes n}\right) = \frac{N_0 + N_1}{N_{sh}} \tag{10}$$

with N_{sh} referring to the total shot count of 2000. The results are reported in Table 2 and plotted in Figure 3.

Table 2. Measured $p_{GHZ}(n)$ for different numbers of qubits. The n = 10 experiments were performed twice.

Qubits n	$p_{GHZ}(n)$
3	0.9600
5	0.8230
8	0.5395
9	0.0665
10	0.2490
10	0.1195

https://doi.org/10.3390/engproc2026122005

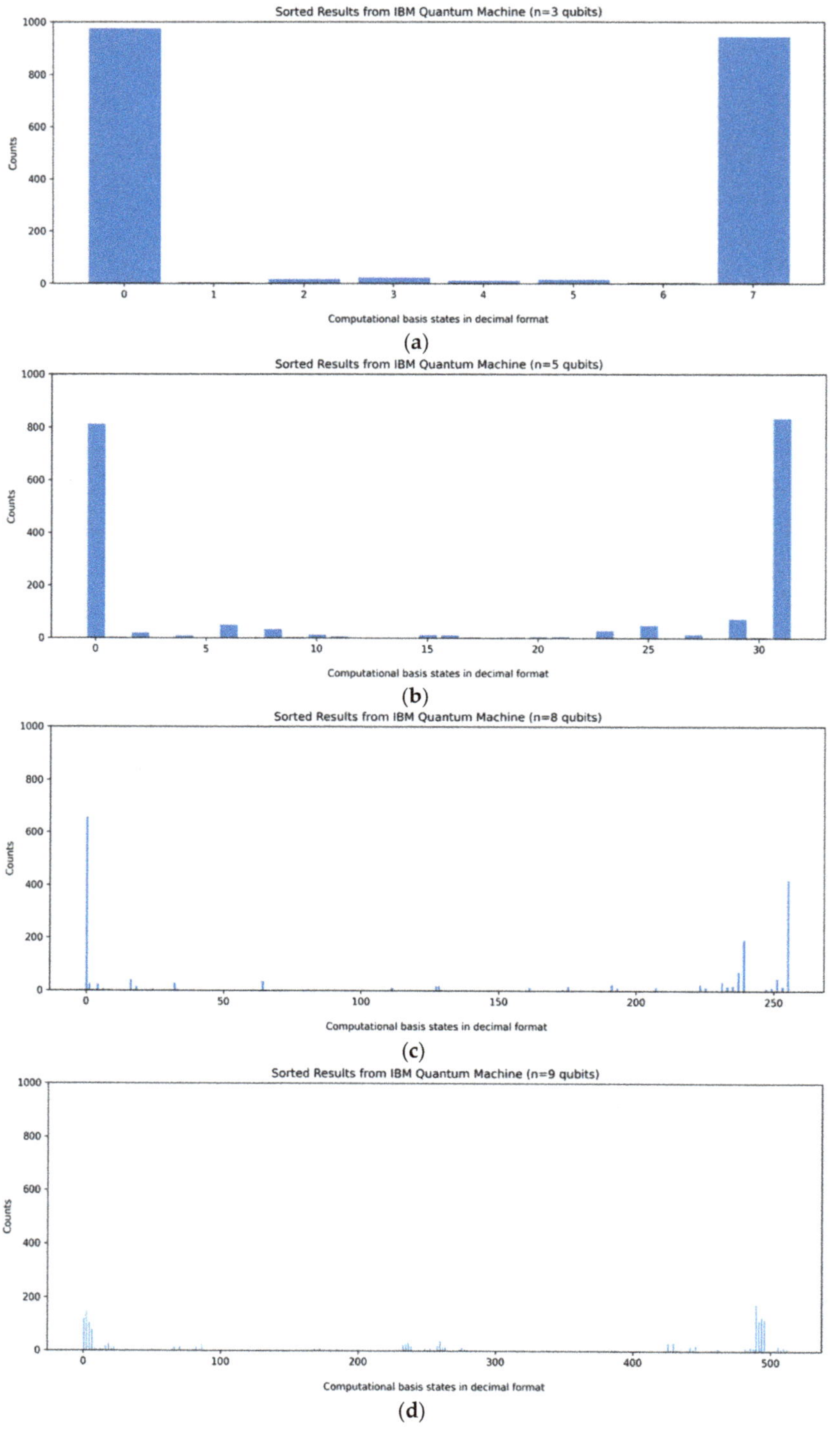

Figure 3. Measurement counts for GHZ states executed on ibm_brisbane: (**a**) results from IBM Quantum Machine at n = 3 qubits; (**b**) results from IBM Quantum Machine at n = 5 qubits; (**c**) results from IBM Quantum Machine at n = 8 qubits; (**d**) results from IBM Quantum Machine at n = 9 qubits.

https://doi.org/10.3390/engproc2026122005

Ideally, for the generalized GHZ state in Equation (7), $p_{GHZ} = 100\%$. In practice, even at $n = 3$ false counts were observed, corresponding to states other than the two expected outcomes $\left(|0\rangle^{\otimes n}\right)$ and $\left(|1\rangle^{\otimes n}\right)$. Nevertheless, the observed probability remained close to the ideal, with $p_{GHZ}(3) = 96\%$. At $n = 5$, the total counts for the two exclusive states dropped to 1646, giving $p_{GHZ}(5) = 82.3\%$. The probability continued to decrease approximately linearly with n, with the notable exception of $n = 9$, where $p_{GHZ}(9) = 6.65\%$ marked a sharp drop that deviated from the general trend. Probability $p_{GHZ}(n)$ versus the number of qubits is plotted in Figure 4. For n = 10, the plotted value corresponds to the mean of two experimental runs.

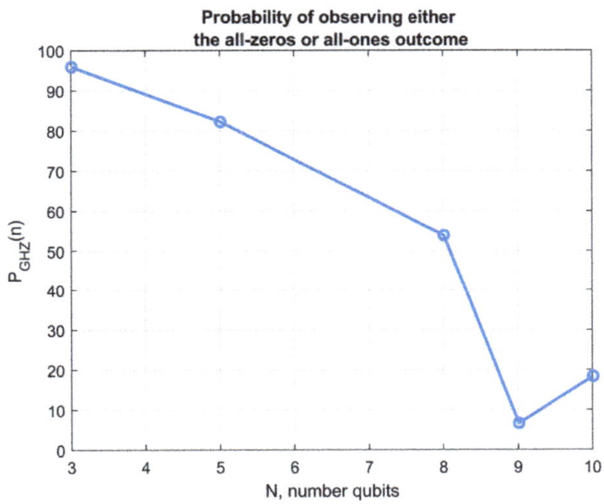

Figure 4. Probability $p_{GHZ}(n)$ vs. number of qubits.

The Qiskit program to generate and measure n-qubit GHZ states on IBM Quantum hardware was initialized with n qubits and an equal number of classical bits. A Hadamard gate was applied to the first qubit, followed by a chain of CNOT gates from the first to all the remaining qubits, creating the entangled GHZ state. All qubits were then measured within the computational basis and stored in the conventional bits. The circuit was transpiled for the selected IBM backend (here ibm_brisbane) and executed using 2000 shots. The output provides the empirical probabilities of the two GHZ basis states $|0\rangle^{\otimes n}$ and $|1\rangle^{\otimes n}$, together with the additional noise-induced outcomes.

States $|\Phi^+\rangle$, $|\Phi^-\rangle$, and $|\Psi^+\rangle$ as well as the generalized GHZ states were executed using an earlier Qiskit version [11], while the fourth Bell state $|\Psi^-\rangle$ was executed using an updated Qiskit release [12]. Ideally, only the two states to the extreme left $\left(|0\rangle^{\otimes n}\right)$ and to the extreme right $\left(|1\rangle^{\otimes n}\right)$ should be present.

The Jupyter notebooks implementing the quantum algorithms are provided in the Supplementary Materials.

5. Conclusions

This work demonstrated the preparation and quantum state tomography of the four standard Bell configurations on IBM's ibm_brisbane quantum computer as well as an assessment of performance with generalized GHZ states with up to 10 qubits.

The element-wise comparison between the experimentally reconstructed and the simulated density matrices for the four Bell states represents the discrepancies arising from

https://doi.org/10.3390/engproc2026122005

noise and device imperfections. These differences provide a more realistic assessment of hardware performance than quantum state fidelity values alone.

As the density matrix scales up, the entry count grows as 4^n, and its size quickly becomes unmanageable with the volume of qubits. The simplified procedure of observing the correct counts when the state detection is made in the default computational frame provides a straightforward way to assess the device's performance. The generalized GHZ-states experiment demonstrated that although the quantum processor ibm_brisbane has 127 qubits, a reliable entangled state involving a significant number of qubits (beyond 8) could not be achieved at the time of the experiment (October 2024), under the criterion that the "leakage" into incorrect measurement outcomes should not exceed 50%.

Supplementary Materials: The Jupyter notebooks implementing the quantum algorithms using Qiskit are openly available at https://github.com/quantum-tomography/quantum-tomography-GHZ (accessed on 13 January 2026) under the MIT License.

Author Contributions: Conceptualization, D.P.; methodology, D.P.; software, D.P.; validation, D.P.; formal analysis, D.P.; investigation, D.P.; resources, Y.S.; data curation, D.P.; writing—original draft preparation, Y.S.; writing—review and editing, Y.S.; visualization, Y.S.; supervision, Y.S.; project administration, Y.S.; funding acquisition, Y.S. All authors have read and agreed to the published version of the manuscript.

Funding: This study is co-financed by the European Union through the Program "Research, innovation and digitalization for smart transformation 2021–2027", project Center of Competence "Blue Coastal Marine and Riverine Innovative & Sustainable Management of Environments and Resources (Blue Cristal)", contract #BG16RFPR002-1.014-0016-C01.

Institutional Review Board Statement: Not applicable.

Informed Consent Statement: Not applicable.

Data Availability Statement: The experimental data presented in this study are openly available in the GitHub repository "quantum-tomography-GHZ" at https://github.com/quantum-tomography/quantum-tomography-GHZ (accessed on 13 January 2026). The repository includes all Jupyter notebooks implementing the quantum experiments, including Bell and GHZ-state preparation and tomography. Raw measurement data produced on the IBM ibm_brisbane quantum device are available within the corresponding notebook cells.

Acknowledgments: We acknowledge the use of IBM Quantum services for this work. The views expressed are those of the authors, and do not reflect the official policy or position of IBM or the IBM Quantum team.

Conflicts of Interest: The authors declare no conflicts of interest. The funders had no role in the design of the study; in the collection, analyses, or interpretation of data; in the writing of the manuscript; or in the decision to publish the results.

References

1. Arute, F.; Arya, K.; Babbush, R.; Bacon, D.; Bardin, J.C.; Barends, R.; Biswas, R.; Boixo, S.; Brandão, F.G.S.L.; Buell, D.A.; et al. Quantum supremacy using a programmable superconducting processor. *Nature* **2019**, *574*, 505–510. [CrossRef] [PubMed]
2. Upadhyay, S.; Alam, M.; Ghosh, S. Architectures for quantum information processing. *arXiv* **2022**, arXiv:2211.06449. Available online: https://arxiv.org/abs/2211.06449 (accessed on 21 January 2025).
3. Macchiavello, C. On the role of entanglement in quantum information. *Phys. A* **2004**, *338*, 68–75. [CrossRef]
4. Hauser, N.; Bayerbach, M.J.; D'Aurelio, S.E.; Weber, R.; Santandrea, M.; Kumar, S.P.; Dhand, I.; Barz, S. Boosted Bell-state measurements for photonic quantum computation. *NPJ Quantum Inf.* **2025**, *11*, 41. [CrossRef]
5. Ekert, A.K. Quantum cryptography based on Bell's theorem. *Phys. Rev. Lett.* **1991**, *67*, 661–663. [CrossRef] [PubMed]
6. Altepeter, J.B.; James, D.F.; Kwiat, P.G. 4 Qubit Quantum State Tomography. In *Quantum State Estimation*; Paris, M.G.A., Řeháček, J., Eds.; Springer: Berlin/Heidelberg, Germany, 2004; pp. 113–145.

 https://doi.org/10.3390/engproc2026122005

7. Patel, A.D. The quantum density matrix and its many uses: From quantum structure to quantum chaos and noisy simulators. *J. Indian Inst. Sci.* **2023**, *103*, 401–417. [CrossRef]
8. Sisodia, M. Comparison the performance of five-qubit IBM quantum computers in terms of Bell states preparation. *Quantum Inf. Process.* **2020**, *19*, 215. [CrossRef]
9. IBM Quantum. Available online: https://quantum.cloud.ibm.com/ (accessed on 21 January 2025).
10. Javadi-Abhari, A.; Treinish, M.; Krsulich, K.; Wood, C.J.; Lishman, J.; Gacon, J.; Martiel, S.; Nation, P.D.; Bishop, L.S.; Cross, A.W.; et al. Quantum computing with Qiskit. *arXiv* **2024**, arXiv:2405.08810. [CrossRef]
11. IBM Quantum. Qiskit and IBM Runtime Tools (Versions: Qiskit 1.2.4, Qiskit Aer 0.15.1, Qiskit Experiments 0.7.0, Qiskit IBM Runtime 0.28.0) [Computer Software]. Available online: https://quantum.cloud.ibm.com/docs/en/api/qiskit/1.2 (accessed on 7 January 2025).
12. IBM Quantum. Qiskit and IBM Runtime Tools (Versions: Qiskit 1.3.1, Qiskit Aer 0.16.0, Qiskit Experiments 0.8.1, Qiskit IBM Runtime 0.34.0) [Computer Software]. Available online: https://quantum.cloud.ibm.com/docs/en/api/qiskit/1.3 (accessed on 21 January 2025).
13. Nielsen, M.A.; Chuang, I.L. *Quantum Computation and Quantum Information*; 10th Anniversary ed.; Cambridge University Press: Cambridge, UK, 2010. Available online: https://www.cambridge.org/core/product/01E10196D0A682A6AEFFEA52D53BE9AE (accessed on 21 January 2025).
14. Broadbent, A.; Chouha, P.R.; Tapp, A. The GHZ state in secret sharing and entanglement simulation. In Proceedings of the 2009 Third International Conference on Quantum, Nano and Micro Technologies (ICQNM), Cancun, Mexico, 1–7 February 2009; IEEE: Los Alamitos, CA, USA, 2009; pp. 59–62.
15. Adedoyin, A.; Ambrosiano, J.; Anisimov, P.; Casper, W.; Chennupati, G.; Coffrin, C.; Djidjev, H.; Gunter, D.; Karra, S.; Lemons, N.; et al. Quantum algorithm implementations for beginners. *ACM Trans. Quantum Comput.* **2022**, *3*, 1–92. [CrossRef]

https://doi.org/10.3390/engproc2026122005

engineering proceedings

MDPI

Proceeding Paper

Methodology for Selecting an Electric Pump and Battery Pack for a Low-Thrust LRE: Computational Simulation Study †

Kenzhebek Myrzabekov [1,*], Kuanysh Alipbayev [2], Akylbek Bapyshev [3], Zhandos Kozhabek [1], Nazgul Kaliyeva [2] and Makpal Nogaibayeva [2]

1 Department of Aerospace and Electronic Engineering, Almaty University of Power Engineering and Telecommunications, Almaty 050013, Kazakhstan; z.kozhabek@aues.kz
2 Department of Sciences, Almaty University of Power Engineering and Telecommunications, Almaty 050013, Kazakhstan; k.alipbayev@aues.kz (K.A.); n.kaliyeva@aues.kz (N.K.); m.nogaibaeva@aues.kz (M.N.)
3 Department of Science and Innovation, ALT University, Almaty 050012, Kazakhstan; a.bapyshev@alt.edu.kz
* Correspondence: k.myrzabekov@aues.kz; Tel.: +7-(776)-929-0000
† Presented at the 6th International Conference on Communications, Information, Electronic and Energy Systems, 26–28 November 2025, Ruse, Bulgaria.

Abstract

The paper offers a practical method for selecting an electric pump and battery pack for low-thrust liquid rocket engines. The approach combines 0D/1D modeling of hydraulic, electromechanical, and thermal subsystems in a single environment and is supplemented by sensitivity analysis, correlation analysis, and Monte Carlo simulation with N = 3000 iterations to verify the stability of the estimates. The methodology has been tested on mission profiles in the 5–50 kN thrust range and shows that the electric pump scheme is most effective at low thrusts, while an increase in thrust leads to a disproportionate increase in energy and thermal loads and narrows the scope of applicability. The determining factors remain the hydraulic efficiency of the pump η_pump and the oxidizer pressure; electrical parameters such as bus voltage and internal battery resistance have less influence and become noticeable at high power levels. Modeling confirms the stability of the obtained estimates; at a thrust of 20 kN, the spread of the battery block mass is close to ±10%. The proposed methodology provides quantitative guidelines in the early stages of design and helps to justify the scope of application of electric pump liquid rocket engines; expansion beyond low thrust requires progress in battery technologies.

Keywords: liquid rocket engine; electric pump circuit; battery pack; low thrust; simulation modeling

1. Introduction

In recent years, light and ultra-light rockets have been attracting increasing interest. The reason is simple: the number of launches of small satellites and CubeSats is growing, and with it, the demand for affordable and frequent launches. In such systems, cost, technological feasibility, and ease of operation remain key factors.

Traditional liquid rocket engines (LREs) operate on a gas generator or closed cycle. They provide high specific impulse and are based on proven technology. However, such systems are complex in design, expensive to manufacture, and require lengthy fine-tuning.

An alternative is electric pump (EPS) LREs. Fuel is supplied by a pump with an electric motor powered by batteries. This system eliminates the gas generator and turbine, simplifies the design, and reduces costs. The practical feasibility of this approach has been demonstrated by Rocket Lab's Rutherford engine [1]. It has been confirmed by European projects for thrusts of 20–30 kN [2] and research for engines in the 5–6 kN range [3].

Three main fuel supply schemes are used in rocket technology. The gas generator scheme is simple and reliable, but it loses part of its specific impulse due to gas discharge [4]. Closed schemes provide maximum efficiency but require complex turbomachinery and increase development costs. Electric pump systems eliminate the gas generator and turbine, simplify the system, and improve fuel supply control [5]. Comparative studies show that EPS systems are most competitive in the low and medium thrust ranges [6].

The use of electric pumps has already been proven in practice. Rutherford's serial EPS engines are installed on Rocket Lab Electron, projects for 20–30 kN are underway in Europe, and a LOX/CH_4 engine with a thrust of 5.4 kN has been demonstrated in South Korea. Cavitation in methane pumps is being studied in China [7], and hybrid EPS schemes are being researched in Italy and Switzerland [8,9]. These projects show that EPS are moving from theory to practice.

EPS LREs also has limitations. The energy density of batteries remains a bottleneck. Modern lithium-ion systems provide 180–250 Wh/kg, which limits the duration of operation at thrusts above 20 kN [9]. High C-ratings increase heat dissipation, requiring separate cooling circuits [10,11]. Cavitation in pumps reduces service life, so inductors are used and NPSH reserves are maintained [7,12]. The reliability of power electronics depends on resistance to vibrations and thermal cycles; cryogenically cooled SiC inverters remain a promising solution [13].

The range of 5–50 kN is typical for suborbital vehicles and small launch vehicles. EPS engines are particularly promising in this area. For light and ultra-light launch vehicles, environmental and flight safety requirements for landing areas are becoming more stringent. Information-analytical and information-prognostic systems at spaceports, including Baikonur, require controlled descent, narrowing of the landing ellipse, and rapid trajectory correction. This affects the thrust profile of the liquid-propellant rocket engine, as well as modulation, duration, and number of pulses. The result is an increase in the requirements for pump pressure and battery power [14,15]. Taking this circuit into account sets the criteria for selecting an electric pump and battery. The paper proposes a selection method based on computational simulation modeling.

2. Materials and Methods

At the beginning of the work, we set requirements for electric pumps and batteries, taking into account the mission profiles of light and ultra-light launch vehicles. We considered three options: suborbital flights with short ignition of 5–10 kN engines, orbital missions with long operation at 20–30 kN thrust, and booster blocks or upper stages with multiple ignitions at up to 50 kN thrust. Input data was specified for each option, including chamber pressure of 5–20 MPa, mixture ratio of 2.5–3.5 for LOX/kerosene and LOX/methane pairs, operating time of 30–600 s, and firing frequency from single-pulse to multi-pulse mode. These parameters were used as boundary conditions in the design of the pump system and battery.

We considered several fuel pairs. LOX/kerosene is dense and well-established, but requires a larger cavitation margin. LOX/methane burns cleaner and is suitable for reusable engines, although its density is lower [7]. N_2O/ethanol and H_2O_2/kerosene were analyzed as "green" alternatives [16]. The properties of the components dictate the requirements for the pumps. Density and viscosity determine the operating speed and geometry of the impeller, phase properties determine the risk of cavitation, and thermal stability determines

 https://doi.org/10.3390/engproc2026122006

the need for cooling. In the calculations, LOX/methane was selected as the base pair as the most promising for engines with a thrust of 5–50 kN [2].

The method for determining the mass flow rate of components was based on the classic thrust equation:

$$\left(\dot{m} = \frac{F}{I_{sp}\, g_0}\right). \tag{1}$$

where F is the engine thrust, I_{sp} is the specific impulse and g_0 is the acceleration due to gravity.

In the thrust range of 5–50 kN at I_{sp} = 300–340, the mass flow rate was 15–150 kg/s. The oxidizer accounted for 70–75%. These data were used as input parameters for the hydraulic model of the pumps.

The pump head was determined from the pressure balance:

$$H = \frac{p_c + \Delta p_f + \Delta p_i - p_t}{\rho g}. \tag{2}$$

where p_c is the pressure in the chamber, Δp_f is the loss in the pipelines, Δp_i is the resistance of the nozzle head, p_t is the pressure in the tank, and ρ is the density of the component.

For a comprehensive assessment of the electric pump circuit, we developed a multi-level simulation model consisting of three interconnected subsystems.

2.1. Hydraulic Subsystem

The model describes the dynamics of flows in the pump, pipelines, and combustion chamber nozzles. The calculation is based on the pressure balance equation:

$$\Delta p = f(Q, n) - \Delta p_{losses} \tag{3}$$

where Δp is the pump head, Q is the mass flow rate, n is the rotational speed, and Δp_{losses} are the hydraulic losses in the system.

The cavitation margin (NPSH) was calculated using the method [12], taking into account the latest data from modern studies of cryogenic cavitation [7].

2.2. Electromechanical Subsystem

The model simulates the operation of an electric drive consisting of a motor (BLDC or PMSM), an inverter, and a control system. The interaction between the electrical and mechanical parts of the system is described as follows:

$$T = \frac{P}{\omega} = \frac{U \cdot I \cdot \eta}{\omega} \tag{4}$$

where T is torque, P is power, U is voltage, I is current, η is efficiency, and ω is angular shaft speed.

The model takes into account commutation losses, electromagnetic oscillations, and thermal limitations of the inverter [13].

2.3. Thermal Subsystem

The subsystem describes heat dissipation in the battery pack and electric motor. Heat generation in the battery cells was specified by the equation:

$$Q_{heat} = I^2 \cdot R_{in} \tag{5}$$

where I is the discharge current, R_{in} is the internal resistance of the battery.

The model takes into account the thermal resistance of the elements and heat dissipation in a vacuum, where there is no convection.

https://doi.org/10.3390/engproc2026122006

To assess uncertainties, we applied the Monte Carlo method based on random sampling of parameters:

$$X_i = f(\theta) + \in_i, \qquad i = 1 \ldots N, \tag{6}$$

where θ is the parameter vector (e.g., pump efficiency, battery current, thermal resistance), $\in_i$ is random variation, and N is the number of iterations.

The model was implemented in MATLAB/Simulink R2022b using a 0D/1D approach. This provided a balance between accuracy and computational costs. System modeling combined hydraulics, electromechanics, and thermal processes into a single simulation platform and allowed the stability of the system to be evaluated at thrusts of 5–50 kN.

3. Results

The main results of calculations performed for three characteristic thrust levels (5, 20, and 50 kN) are presented in Table 1. This table contains information on the mass flow rates of components, pump pressures, power consumption ranges, as well as energy requirements and the mass of the battery pack (BP).

Table 1. Calculation parameters for modes 5–50 kN.

Thrust, kN	Σ Flow Rate, kg/s	LOX, kg/s	CH_4, kg/s	H_{LOX}, MPa	H_{CH4}, MPa	Power, kW	Energy, kWh	Battery Mass, kg
5	1.6	1.2	0.4	8.0	3.0	80–100	5.5	25
20	6.4	4.8	1.6	10.0	4.0	250–300	19	95
50	16.0	12.0	4.0	12.5	5.5	600–750	42	210

As summarized in Table 1, the total propellant mass flow rate increases from 1.6 kg/s at 5 kN to 16.0 kg/s at 50 kN, while the LOX: CH_4 ratio remains approximately 3:1.

Figure 1 shows the required pump pressures. The oxidizer pump (LOX) operates in the range of 8–13 MPa, and the fuel pump (CH_4) operates in the range of 3–5.5 MPa. This makes the oxidizer pump the most energy-intensive component of the system. Our values correlate well with the results presented in [2], where a pressure of 10–12 MPa was recorded for an engine with a thrust of 25 kN.

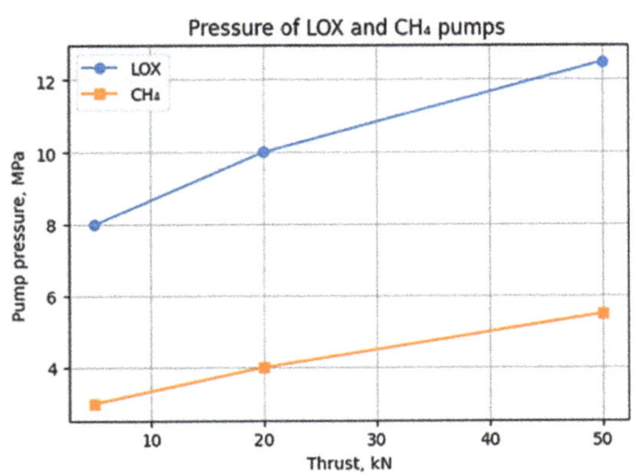

Figure 1. LOX and CH_4 pump pressure in the range of 5–50 kN.

According to Figure 2, the power consumption of the electric drive shows a clear tendency to increase with increasing thrust. Average power values range from 80–100 kW at a thrust of 5 kN to 600–750 kW at a thrust of 50 kN. The noted variations in power are due to fluctuations in the total efficiency of the system in the range of 0.6–0.7. These results

https://doi.org/10.3390/engproc2026122006

confirm the data presented in study [17], where for a motor with a thrust of about 30 kN, the power consumption was 400–500 kW.

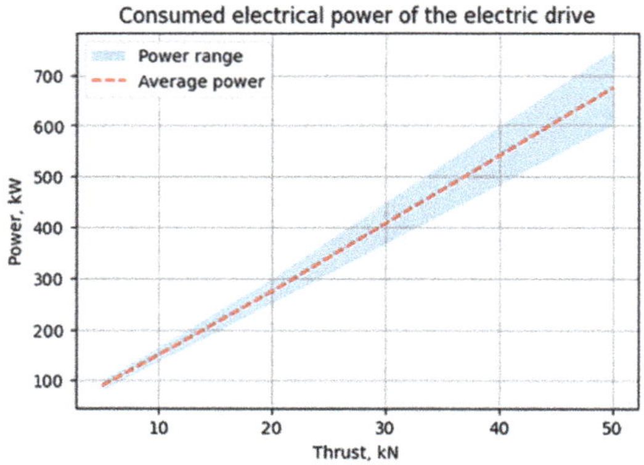

Figure 2. Power consumption of the electric drive depending on thrust.

The energy requirements and mass of the battery pack are shown in Figure 3. With an operating time of 200 s, the total energy consumption increases from 5.5 to 42 kWh for thrusts of 5–50 kN. Accordingly, the mass of the batteries at a specific energy of 200 Wh/kg is 25–210 kg. These estimates are comparable to [9], where the battery pack mass was approximately 10–20% of the electric drive mass.

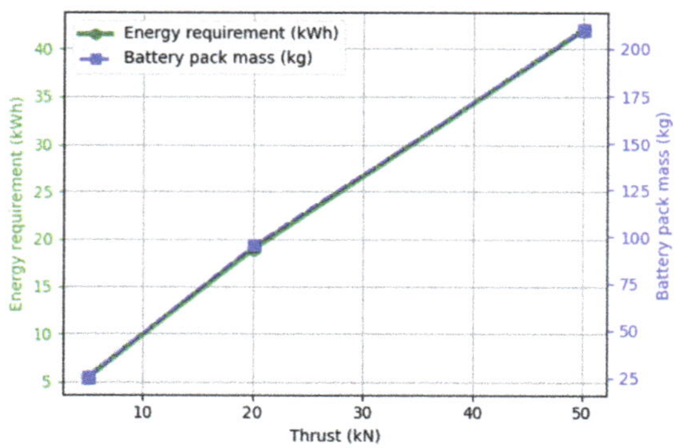

Figure 3. Energy requirement and battery pack mass versus thrust for t = 200 s and E_{sp} = 200 Wh/kg.

Sensitivity analysis showed that the battery pack mass strongly depends on the hydraulic efficiency of the pumps and the oxidizer pressure level. Figure 4 shows that when η_{pump} decreases from 0.80 to 0.50, the battery pack mass increases by more than 60%. A 20% increase in Δp_{ox} adds another 8–10 kg.

The effect of fuel pressure is less significant. According to Figure 5, a change in Δp_{fuel} within $\pm$20% changes the mass of the battery pack by only 3–5 kg.

The results for electrical parameters are shown in Figures 6 and 7. At a bus voltage of 600 V, the battery pack mass decreases by approximately 25%. When the internal resistance increases to 0.020 ohms, it increases by 5–7 kg.

To evaluate the stability of the results, the Monte Carlo method with N = 3000 iterations was used. Changes in pump parameters, component density, specific impulse, bus voltage, and internal battery resistance were randomly incorporated into the model.

Figure 8 illustrates the distribution of battery pack mass and total power. The median mass was 24.9 kg with a range of 22.6–27.6 kg. The median power value is 86 kW, with a range of 78–96 kW. The spread of characteristics is mainly due to changes in pump efficiency and hydraulic losses.

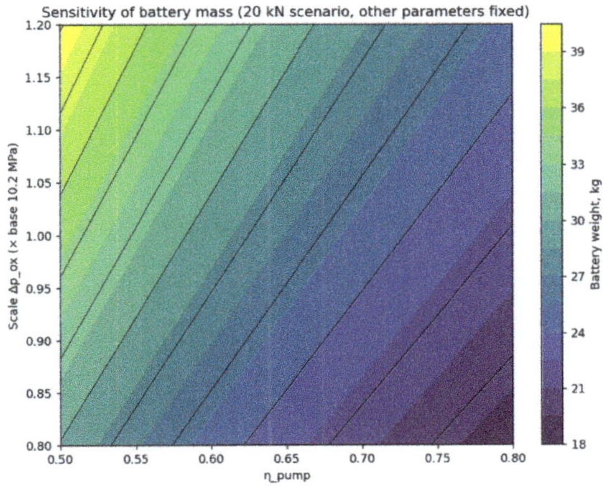

Figure 4. Sensitivity of battery mass to η_{pump} and Δp_{ox}.

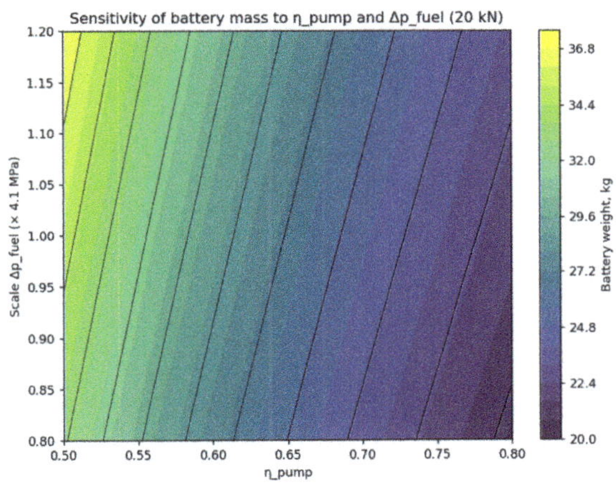

Figure 5. Sensitivity of battery mass to η_{pump} and Δp_{fuel}.

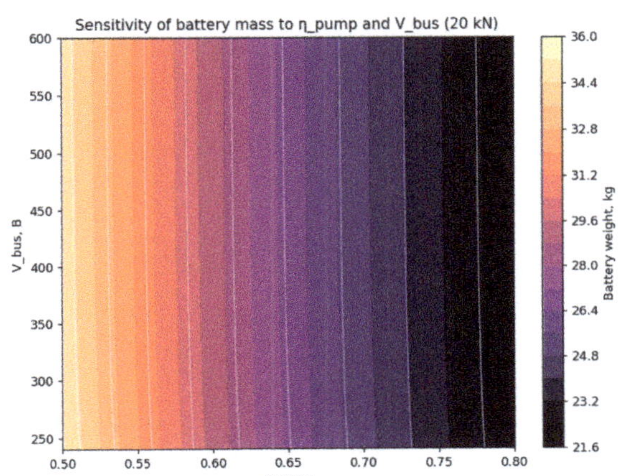

Figure 6. Sensitivity of battery mass to η_{pump} and bus voltage.

 https://doi.org/10.3390/engproc2026122006

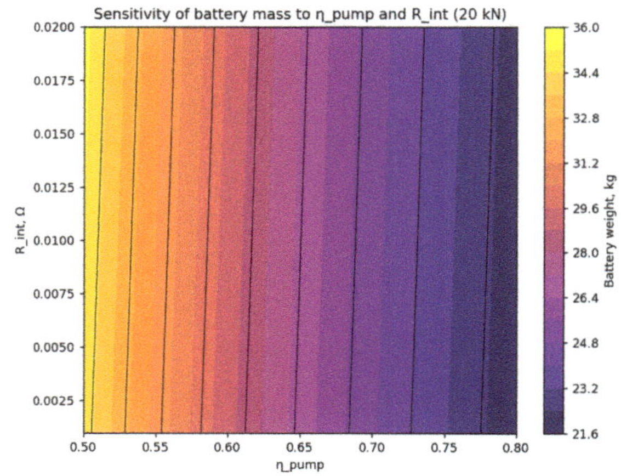

Figure 7. Sensitivity of battery mass to η_{pump} and battery resistance.

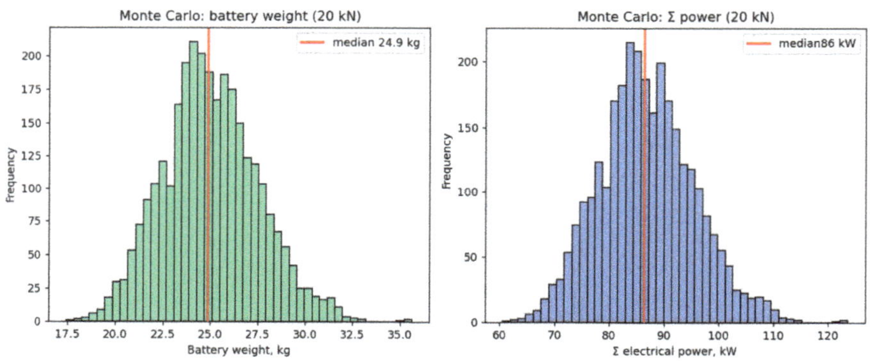

(a) (b)

Figure 8. Distribution of battery pack mass (**a**) and total power (**b**) based on Monte Carlo simulation results (thrust 20 kN).

According to the results of Monte Carlo simulation presented in Figure 9, there is a clear negative correlation between the hydraulic efficiency of the pump (η_{pump}) and the mass of the battery pack. An increase in η_{pump} leads to a decrease in battery mass and a reduction in its variability. Analysis of the color scale shows that low pump efficiency ($\eta_{pump} < 0.6$) results in high energy consumption (over 110–120 kW), while high efficiency ($\eta_{pump} > 0.75$) allows power consumption to be kept within the range of 70–80 kW. These data clearly indicate that improving pump efficiency is a critical area for optimizing the energy system, allowing for a reduction in both the battery pack mass and the required power of the electric drives.

To quantitatively assess the influence of the parameters, a correlation analysis was performed, and the results are summarized in Table 2.

The battery pack mass is most strongly influenced by the hydraulic efficiency of the pump η_{pump}. The correlation coefficients were −0.705 according to Pearson and −0.685 according to Spearman. The oxidizer pressure drop Δp_{ox} is also significant. The correlation is positive, +0.608. The influence of the fuel pressure drop is moderate, +0.216. Other factors, such as specific impulse, component densities, bus voltage, and internal battery resistance, show a weak or statistically insignificant correlation, with a modulus below 0.2.

https://doi.org/10.3390/engproc2026122006

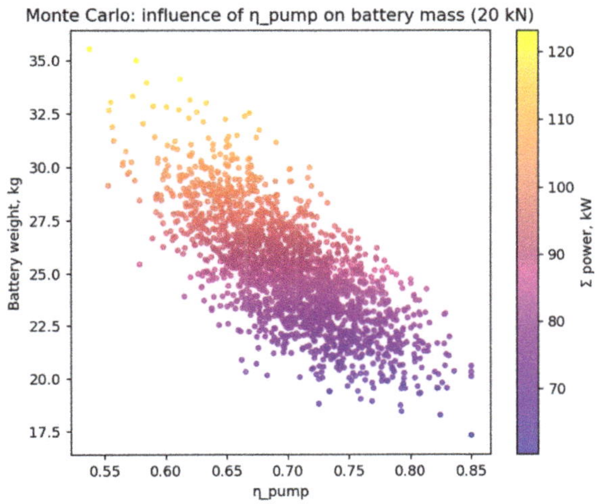

Figure 9. Monte Carlo simulation results (thrust 20 kN): dependence of battery pack mass on pump hydraulic efficiency η_{pump}.

Table 2. Correlation coefficients of factors with battery pack mass (20 kN).

Factor	Pearson	Spearman
η_{pump}	−0.705	−0.685
Δp_{ox}	+0.608	+0.590
Δp_{fuel}	+0.216	+0.216
I_{sp}	−0.208	−0.203
p_{ox}	−0.204	−0.199
p_{fuel}	−0.038	−0.036
V_{bus}	−0.015	−0.015
R_{int}	+0.027	+0.029

4. Discussion

Modeling has shown that the electric pump scheme of the liquid rocket engine is most effective in the range of low thrusts of 5–10 kN. In this mode, the mass of the battery pack remains within 25–30 kg, and the power consumption is limited to 80–120 kW. When the thrust is increased to 20 kN, the mass of the batteries increases to approximately 95 kg, and the power to 300 kW. These parameters remain feasible provided that high-efficiency pumps ($\eta_{pump} >$ 0.7) and a bus voltage of at least 400 V are used. In the 50 kN range, the situation changes: the battery pack mass exceeds 200 kg, and the power reaches 0.7 MW. This significantly limits the practical application of the scheme. The critical factor is the scaling of thrust, which leads to a sharp increase in energy and thermal loads.

The key factors determining the characteristics of the battery pack are the hydraulic efficiency of the pumps and the pressure drop in the oxygen line. Their significance has been confirmed by both sensitivity analysis and correlation analysis results. Electrical parameters—bus voltage and internal battery resistance—have a secondary effect but become critical at power levels above 300 kW. Monte Carlo simulation confirmed the stability of the obtained estimates: at a thrust of 20 kN, the spread of the battery mass was only ±10%, which indicates the reliability of the model.

https://doi.org/10.3390/engproc2026122006

The conclusions of this work are consistent with foreign studies [16,17] and the practice of Rocket Lab and Astra. These sources show that electric pump circuits are justified for low-thrust liquid rocket engines, up to 20 kN, when the mass of the batteries remains at an acceptable level. With further increases in thrust, energy requirements increase disproportionately, as confirmed by the results obtained. A comparison with modern lithium-ion batteries with a specific energy of 200–250 Wh/kg indicates the limits of current technology. For thrusts above 50 kN, a transition to new-generation batteries, such as Li-S or solid-state batteries, is required.

The study has limitations. The use of 0D/1D models of pumps and accumulators does not reflect transient modes and degradation of elements. Thermal management and integration of cooling circuits were not considered, which can significantly affect the results during long-term operation. The thrust range of 5–50 kN narrows the scope of applicability of the conclusions. Despite this, the estimates obtained are useful for preliminary engineering calculations and serve as a basis for recommendations on optimizing small and medium thrust electric pump liquid rocket engines.

5. Conclusions

A method for selecting an electric pump and battery pack for a low-thrust liquid rocket engine is proposed. It is based on joint modeling of hydraulic, electromechanical, and thermal subsystems in a single environment and is supplemented by statistical analysis. Sensitivity and correlations show the leading role of the hydraulic efficiency of the pump and the pressure drop in the oxygen path. Monte Carlo simulation confirms the stability of the estimates and allows the working ranges to be outlined. The scheme is most effective at thrusts of 5–10 kN, remains feasible at around 20 kN with high pump efficiency and bus voltage not lower than 400 V, and at 50 kN, its applicability is limited by the increase in energy and thermal loads. The practical value of the method is its applicability to the design of engines for light launch vehicles and small spacecraft with strict restrictions on mass and energy consumption. The limitations of the work are related to simplified 0D/1D models and the lack of experimental verification, as well as incomplete development of the thermal circuit and battery degradation. Further steps include refining thermal regimes, accounting for cyclic battery aging, and expanding the set of scenarios, which will improve the accuracy of forecasts and the reliability of design recommendations.

Author Contributions: Conceptualization, K.M. and K.A.; methodology, M.N.; software, K.M.; validation, A.B., Z.K. and N.K.; formal analysis, M.N.; investigation, K.M.; resources, M.N.; data curation, Z.K.; writing—original draft preparation, K.M.; writing—review and editing, K.M.; visualization, A.B.; supervision, K.A.; project administration, K.A.; funding acquisition, K.A. All authors have read and agreed to the published version of the manuscript.

Funding: This research was funded by the Science Committee and Higher Education of the Republic of Kazakhstan, grant number BR27195331.

Institutional Review Board Statement: Not applicable.

Informed Consent Statement: Not applicable.

Data Availability Statement: The data generated in this study are presented in the article. For any clarifications, please contact the corresponding author.

Conflicts of Interest: The authors declare no conflicts of interest.

https://doi.org/10.3390/engproc2026122006

Abbreviations

The following abbreviations are used in this manuscript:

LRE	Liquid rocket engines
EPS	Electric pump systems
LOX	Liquid Oxygen
CH_4	Methane
NPSH	Net Positive Suction Head
N_2O	Nitrous Oxide
H_2O_2	Hydrogen peroxide

References

1. Rocket Lab. *Rutherford Engine—State-of-the-Art Oxygen and Kerosene Pump-Fed Engine with High-Performance Electric Propellant Pumps*; DARPA R3D2 Press Kit; Rocket Lab: Long Beach, CA, USA, 2019.
2. Danescu, S.; Ifrim, D.; Cancescu, A.; Andreescu, T. Exploring the potential of electropump feed systems for extending high thrust and deep throttle performance for CH_4/LOX rocket engines. In Proceedings of the Aerospace Europe Conference—EUCASS—CEAS 2023, Lausanne, Switzerland, 9–13 July 2023. [CrossRef]
3. Park, Y.-K.; Yoon, J.; Kim, D.; Yoon, Y. Design and Verification of Electric Pump for Small LOX/Methane Rocket Engine. *Int. J. Aeronaut. Space Sci.* **2023**, *24*, 955–969. [CrossRef]
4. Kwak, H.-D.; Kwon, S.; Choi, C.-H. Performance assessment of electrically driven pump-fed LOX/kerosene cycle rocket engine: Comparison with gas generator cycle. *Aerosp. Sci. Technol.* **2018**, *77*, 67–82. [CrossRef]
5. Fujii, G.; Gaiser, N.; Gernoth, A.; Perigo, D. Modelling of Electrical Pump-Fed Propulsion Systems for Trade-Off Assessments. *Trans. Jpn. Soc. Aeronaut. Space Sci. Aerosp. Technol. Jpn.* **2020**, *18*, 375–383. [CrossRef]
6. Shoyama, T.; Wada, Y.; Shimagaki, M.; Hashimoto, T.; Takada, S. Liquid propellant rocket engine cycles partially using electric turbopump. *Acta Astronaut.* **2024**, *224*, 138–147. [CrossRef]
7. Lin, Y.; Wang, L.; Zhang, F.; Li, X.; Zhu, Z. Study on cryogenic cavitation and its temperature-pressure correlated characteristics of methane pump in rocket engine. *Aerosp. Sci. Technol.* **2024**, *155*, 109679. [CrossRef]
8. Casalino, L.; Masseni, F.; Pastrone, D. Viability of an Electrically Driven Pump-Fed Hybrid Rocket for Small Launcher Upper Stages. *Aerospace* **2019**, *6*, 36. [CrossRef]
9. Masseni, F. Optimal battery selection for hybrid rocket engine. *Adv. Aircr. Spacecr. Sci.* **2022**, *9*, 401–414. [CrossRef]
10. Hwang, F.S.; Confrey, T.; Reidy, C.; Picovici, D.; Callaghan, D.; Culliton, D.; Nolan, C. Review of battery thermal management systems in electric vehicles. *Renew. Sustain. Energy Rev.* **2024**, *192*, 114171. [CrossRef]
11. Afzal, A.; Abdul Razak, R.K.; Mohammed Samee, A.D.; Kumar, R.; Ağbulut, Ü.; Park, S.G. A critical review on renewable battery thermal management system using heat pipes. *J. Therm. Anal. Calorim.* **2023**, *148*, 8403–8442. [CrossRef] [PubMed]
12. Kumar, P.R.; Kumar, B.P.; Harikumar, K.; Panigrahi, S.; Nair, P.U.; Jayan, N. Cavitation Performance of a Cryogenic Upper Stage Liquid Rocket Engine Pump Operating in Liquid Hydrogen. In Proceedings of the 26th National & 4th International ISHMT-ASTFE Heat and Mass Transfer Conference, Chennai, India, 17–20 December 2021; pp. 1437–1442. [CrossRef]
13. Chen, R.; Niu, J.; Ren, R.; Gui, H.; Wang, F.; Tolbert, L.; Choi, B.; Brown, G. A Cryogenically Cooled MW Inverter for Electrified Aircraft Propulsion. In Proceedings of the AIAA Propulsion and Energy 2020 Forum, Virtual Event, 24–28 August 2020. [CrossRef]
14. Alipbayev, K.A.; Yermoldina, G.T.; Bapishev, A.M.; Aden, A.E. Modernization of the Information and Analytical System of the Crash Areas of the Baikonur Cosmodrome during the Controlled Descent of the Spent Stage of the Launch Vehicle. In Proceedings of the 2021 International Conference on Electrical, Communication, and Computer Engineering (ICECCE), Kuala Lumpur, Malaysia, 12–13 June 2021; pp. 1–7. [CrossRef]
15. Yermoldina, G.T.; Trushlyakov, V.I.; Alipbayev, K.A.; Utegenova, A.U. Information and Forecasting System for Determining the Launch and Impact Areas of Ultralight Launch Vehicles, Taking into Account the Requirements of Environmental Safety. *J. Theor. Appl. Inf. Technol.* **2022**, *100*, 52–60.
16. Ordonez Valles, L.; Apel, U.; Tajmar, M. Monte Carlo analysis of a 400 N electric pump-fed engine powered by green propellants: Key trends towards an optimal subsystem design. *Acta Astronaut.* **2024**, *225*, 234–242. [CrossRef]
17. Bai, X.; Xu, M.; Li, Q.; Yu, L. Trajectory-battery integrated design and its application to orbital maneuvers with electric pump-fed engines. *Adv. Space Res.* **2022**, *70*, 825–841. [CrossRef]

https://doi.org/10.3390/engproc2026122006

engineering proceedings

MDPI

Proceeding Paper

Precision Localization of Autonomous Vehicles in Urban Environments: An Experimental Study with RFID Markers †

Svetozar Stefanov [1], Valentina Markova [1,*] and Miroslav Markov [2]

1 Department of Communication Engineering and Technologies, Technical University Varna, Varna 9000, Bulgaria; svetozar.stefanov@tu-varna.bg

2 Department of Software and Internet Technologies, Technical University Varna, Varna 9000, Bulgaria; m.markov@tu-varna.bg

* Correspondence: via@tu-varna.bg

† Presented at the 6th International Conference on Communications, Information, Electronic and Energy Systems, Ruse, Bulgaria, 26–28 November 2025.

Abstract

This paper presents an experimental study validating the feasibility of Radio Frequency Identification (RFID) marker systems as a complementary solution for autonomous vehicle (AV) localization in Global Navigation Satellite System (GNSS)-degraded urban environments. A novel synchronized dynamic testbed featuring hardware-level integration with wheel revolution tracking enables precise correlation of RFID marker reads with vehicle angular position. Experimental results demonstrate that multi-antenna configurations achieve consistently high read success rates (up to 99.6% at 0.5 m distance), sub-meter localization accuracy (~55 cm marker spacing), and reliable performance at average urban speeds (36 km/h simulated velocity). Spatial diversity from four strategically positioned antennas overcomes multipath interference and orientation challenges inherent to high-speed RFID reading. Processing latency remains well within the 58 ms time budget critical for autonomous navigation. These findings validate RFID's potential for smart road infrastructure integration and demonstrate a scalable, cost-effective solution for enhancing AV safety and decision-making capabilities through contextual information transmission.

Keywords: RFID localization; autonomous vehicles; UHF RFID markers; multi-antenna systems; GNSS-denied navigation; smart infrastructure

1. Introduction

Autonomous vehicles (AVs) face significant localization challenges in urban environments where Global Navigation Satellite System (GNSS) signals are degraded or unavailable due to signal blockage, reflection from buildings, and multipath propagation. While GNSS remains the primary localization method for AVs, it exhibits considerable limitations in dense urban canyons, tunnels, and indoor environments, with potential lateral position errors exceeding several meters [1]. This necessitates complementary or alternative localization technologies [2].

Radio Frequency Identification (RFID) technology offers a promising solution such as a localization aid and contextual information channel for AVs. Unlike GNSS, RFID operates independently of external satellite signals [3] and can function reliably indoors and in obstructed environments [4]. Existing research demonstrates that RFID can provide localization accuracy comparable to or exceeding GNSS in challenging scenarios [5].

However, the transition from passive RFID applications (access control, inventory management) to active automotive localization at vehicle speeds requires rigorous validation of reading reliability, processing latency, and accuracy under dynamic conditions [6]. This paper addresses a critical research gap by introducing a synchronized dynamic testbed that enables high-fidelity experimental validation of UHF RFID marker systems under realistic operational parameters. The key novelty of this work is the hardware-level synchronization between RFID reads and wheel revolution tracking, eliminating timing discrepancies and providing precise spatial correlation [7]. Additionally, this study demonstrates that multi-antenna configurations significantly enhance system robustness, achieving near-ideal read success rates through spatial diversity and orientation agnosticism.

The objectives of this research are as follows:

- Validation of UHF RFID feasibility for urban speed AV localization;
- To quantify the impact of multi-antenna configurations on read success and processing latency;
- Assessment of sub-meter localization accuracy and real-time processing capability;
- To identify limiting factors and practical deployment considerations.

2. Materials and Methods

The technical equipment required to conduct this test analysis comprises two integrated parts: a hardware platform for RFID signal acquisition and rotational sensing and software modules for temporal correlation and data validation. Together with the measurement parameters defined in Section 2.3, these components form the complete experimental system.

2.1. Hardware Architecture

UHF RFID Reader: A high-performance reader (Impinj R2000, Hopeland Technologies Co, Ltd., Shenzhen, China) [8] capable of autonomous operation with USB interface connectivity. Configured to operate at 865–867.6 MHz (ETSI European regulation). Supports multiple antenna connections with integrated anti-collision protocol (EPC Gen2).

UHF RFID Antennas: Four circularly polarized UHF RFID antennas with SMA connectors, providing omnidirectional coverage and reduced orientation sensitivity [9].

RFID Markers: Ten weather-resistant UHF RFID markers (ISO 18000-6C passive tags) [10]. Four were deployed in each experiment with the remainder serving as spares.

Urban Speed Simulator: A 29-inch mountain bike wheel (diameter $\approx$ 0.75 m, perimeter $\approx$ 2.356 m) mounted on an electric motor with precise RPM control. Four RFID markers fixed at 90 degrees intervals around the tire's periphery. By rotating at controlled speeds, the wheel simulates a vehicle traveling at 36 km/h over RFID markers positioned on the ground.

Revolution Trigger Sensor: The RPM sensor is a Hall-effect sensor detecting a magnet affixed to the wheel rim, generating timestamped pulses at each complete revolution. Connected to Raspberry Pi, it records timestamps and revolution numbers. This allowed precise correlation between the start time of each new revolution and the timestamp of each marker reading from the reader module, eliminating the need for separate time synchronization, as both measurements were linked to a hardware device with a common timer.

Data Acquisition Unit: A Raspberry Pi 4 (2 GB RAM, the Sony UK Technology Centre, Pencoed, UK) with USB and serial interfaces was used for receiving reader and sensor data. Python-based 3.12 data logging modules executed parallel processes for RPM monitoring and RFID read timestamping.

https://doi.org/10.3390/engproc2026122007

Figure 1 presents the complete experimental apparatus, consisting of a 29-inch wheel equipped with four circularly polarized UHF RFID tags rotating at controlled speed to deliver markers systematically to multiple RFID readers. An electric motor provides precise rotation control, while an RPM sensor ensures synchronization with the data acquisition system. Multiple RFID readers are positioned at distances of 0.5 m, 1 m, and 2 m from the marker zone, enabling systematic evaluation of reader sensitivity degradation and validation of multi-antenna performance enhancement strategies. The dashed lines denote distinct measurement configurations, representing two independent experimental protocols executed at varying operational distances. This controlled test environment enables rigorous assessment of RFID reading accuracy—a capability fundamental to autonomous vehicle localization applications requiring three essential functions: local navigation relative to infrastructure, precise trajectory planning, and reliable collision avoidance. Figure 1 also depicts a schematic representation of an urban deployment scenario with strategically positioned RFID markers. The East-North-Up (ENU) coordinate system, established locally at each marker position, provides a reference frame wherein static RFID markers function as known spatial reference points, enabling precise vehicle localization and path planning in GNSS-denied environments.

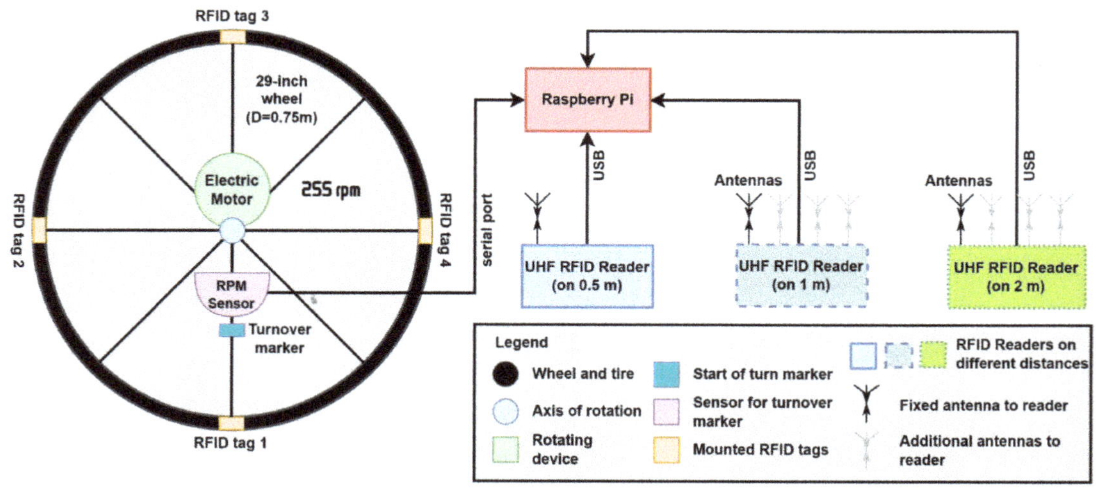

Figure 1. Rotating wheel platform for testing UHF RFID tag reading performance across variable distances at constant speed (36 km/h equivalent).

2.2. Software Components

Software modules were installed on the Raspberry Pi 4 Rev 1.5, consisting of Python scripts and libraries for serial and USB port communication, which recorded the timestamp of each read and the data read. One application was launched, simultaneously executing two processes: the first monitored RPMs and recorded a timestamp in a text file at each new revolution, while the second monitored the time interval from the start of each new revolution to the expected new data from the reader, also recording it with a timestamp in the text file. If the reader did not provide data within this time window, the marker was considered not successfully read.

2.3. Parameters for Measurement in Each Test

To ensure a thorough and consistent evaluation of the system, the following critical parameters were meticulously defined for measurement in each test:

 https://doi.org/10.3390/engproc2026122007

Reaction and Processing Time: The system was designed to operate within the following time budget for reaction and processing [11]: Marker reading: ~5 ms; data processing: ~5 ms; decision-making: ~5 ms; execution of process based on data: ~10 ms; total: ~25 ms. Possible reading omissions at high speeds can be compensated by duplicating the same RFID marker at a close distance [12], as well as by placing other control RFID markers nearby. The switching time of the RFID readers transmit/receive mode (Tx-to-Rx and Rx-to-Tx) is in order of a few microseconds, as modern readers must adhere to the strict timing requirements of the EPC Gen2 protocol, which defines communication intervals in the microsecond range, and no delay is expected from this component [13].

Number of Markers: If, in real conditions, markers are spaced 50 cm apart and a vehicle passes over them at 36 km/h, then 20 markers should be successfully read sequentially per second. In the experimental setup, a similar accuracy, corresponding to approximately 55 cm distance between markers, was sought. A high success rate was defined as reading 17 markers within 1 s, which would indicate precise positioning. If tests confirm this is possible, localization with an approximate accuracy of 0.5 m would be achieved [7]. This number of markers corresponds to a time window of ~58 ms per marker.

Sensitivity of the Marked Zone: The distance from which markers are successfully read is particularly important for accurate UHF RFID readings. Test values for this distance were 0.5 m, 1 m, and 2 m. The reader's power was not changed during the tests. To improve sensitivity for the more distant reader, the addition of antennas was evaluated in a second series of experiments.

2.4. Tests Specifications for Hardware and Software Setup

The software applications were started after the tachometer readings reached 255 revolutions, which took an average of 10 to 15 s. For each specific setup of the experimental rig with the reader at a fixed distance from the wheel's periphery (0.5 m, 1 m, and 2 m), three analogous tests were conducted to confirm the data, especially for calculating the average data processing time. After each individual test, the text files were renamed for the specific scenario. All data from the text files were analyzed with the hardware test environment and application stopped. Figure 2 shows the timing diagram for data processing. A unique aspect of the timing diagram is the initiation of a time cycle of 17 equal intervals of 58.82 ms at each new revolution reading. This time constant is calculated based on the presumption that 4 readings are made within 1 revolution, and 4.25 revolutions are made within 1 s. That is, for a unit time of 1 s, 17 readings are expected at equal intervals of 58.82 ms, which are monitored from the start of each new revolution (marked with a red rectangle in the diagram).

This temporal synchronization diagram shows hardware-level timing correlation. The timeline should show sequence of events during the whole wheel revolution divided into 17 equal intervals of 58.82 ms, but after the first two cycles, the rest are equal, that is why not all of them are shown. Revolutionary trigger events (red), RFID reader responses (blue), and software processing windows (green) are precisely time-correlated, enabling accurate marker position determination.

It is observed that the processing time decreases with greater deviation (i.e., with a larger number of missed markers), which is a predictable consequence of fewer processing operations by the reader and the Raspberry Pi processor. Crucially, however, the processing time consistently remained well within the allocated 58 ms time window.

To mitigate the reduced system sensitivity observed at greater reader distances, a series of additional tests were conducted. These involved progressively adding 2, 3, and finally all 4 available antennas at distances of 1 and 2 m, consistently yielding significant improvements in reading results. Although the RFID reader was intrinsically configured

https://doi.org/10.3390/engproc2026122007

with an algorithm to prevent re-reading the same marker, experiments utilizing multiple antennas revealed instances of data duplication in the raw output files.

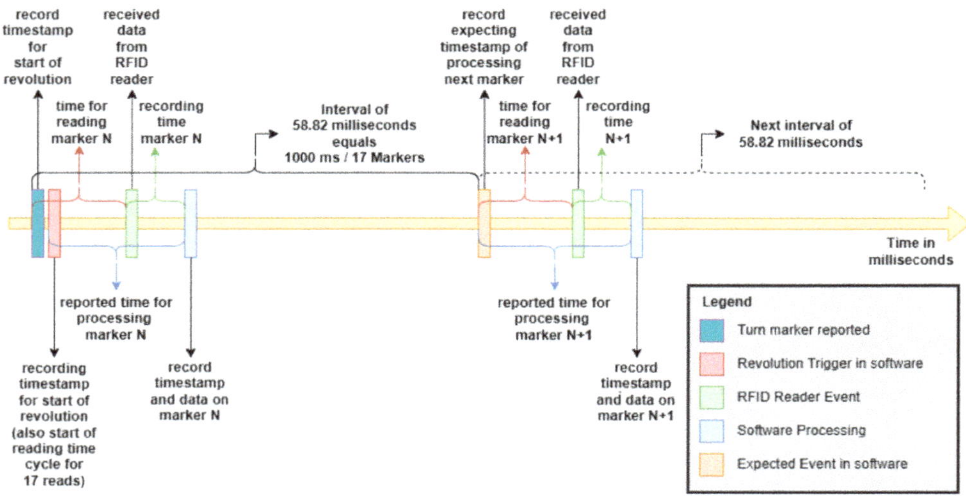

Figure 2. Timing diagram for monitoring successfully read markers.

To effectively manage this data turnover and ensure accurate measurement despite potential redundant reads, a specialized software mechanism was implemented. This mechanism functioned as a logical "data turnover marker," ensuring that each physical marker was counted only once, irrespective of detection by multiple antennas. The software was modified to consider the timestamp from the first antenna to successfully read a specific marker as the definitive event. Subsequent detections of the same marker by other antennas within a defined timeframe were effectively filtered out. This was achieved through a time-based software buffer, specifically a FIFO (First-In, First-Out) queue, which stored unique read markers within the last 200 ms, thereby efficiently identifying and discarding duplicate reads. In all multi-antenna experiments, the antennas were initially mounted in a flat plane, equidistant from the markers. Subsequent experiments, however, explored configurations where some antennas were moved out of this plane and positioned closer to the wheel, achieving even higher success rates. While these advanced configurations are not reflected in the current tables, they highlight promising avenues for further investigation.

3. Results

3.1. Single-Antenna Configuration Performance

Table 1 presents the test data from the experiments conducted with a single-antenna configuration, together with read success rates and processing times across three reader distances. The performance at 0.5 m returned success rates ranging from 98.9% to 99.6%, which is an excellent result. However, some omissions still occurred. This is likely due to the high peripheral speed of the markers. Although 0.5 m is a proficient reading distance, the time the marker spends in the optimal "golden" reading zone of the antenna is noticeably short (only a few milliseconds) [6]. The reader must successfully power the marker, receive a response, and decode it within this brief time window.

 https://doi.org/10.3390/engproc2026122007

Table 1. Experimental data of RFID markers reading from three different distances.

Test No.	Read Markers (Count)	Parameters [1] Difference (Count)	Avg Deviation (%)	Avg Success Rate (%)	Avg Reading Time (ms)
		Reader at 0.5 m distance			
1	1690	10	0.6	99.4	21.1
2	1681	19	1.1	98.9	21.3
3	1693	7	0.4	99.6	20.7
		Reader at 1 m. distance			
4	1508	170	11.3	88.7	19.3
5	1584	116	6.82	93.18	20.1
6	1641	59	3.47	96.53	20.5
		Reader at 2 m. distance			
7	879	821	48.3	51.7	15.6
8	1066	634	37.3	62.7	17.3
9	1209	491	28.9	71.1	18.9

[1] The reader is equipped with only one antenna.

At optimal distance (0.5 m), success rates exceed 99%, indicating excellent system performance. However, at 2.0 m, performance degrades significantly to ~51%, demonstrating the critical importance of reader-to-tag distance in UHF RFID systems.

3.2. Multi-Antenna Configuration Performance

Table 2 shows the results of using multiple antennas during the tests. The addition of a second antenna at 2.0 m distance increased the success rate from 50.7% to 78.4%, a 54.6% relative improvement [14]. With four antennas, performance reaches 94.2%, nearly matching the single-antenna performance at 0.5 m distance.

Table 2. Data from additional experiments for improving accuracy at greater reader distances.

Num of Antennas	Read Markers (Count) [1]	Parameters Difference (Count)	Avg Deviation (%)	Avg Success Rate (%)	Avg Reading Time (ms)
		Reader at 1 m. distance			
2	1678	22	1.29	98.71	26.1
3	1690	10	0.59	99.41	25.7
4	1695	5	0.29	99.71	28.8
		Reader at 2 m. distance			
2	1335	365	21.47	78.53	25.2
3	1516	184	10.82	89.18	27.5
4	1601	99	5.82	94.18	29.75

[1] Only unique identification numbers of markers (no duplicates).

3.3. Spatial Diversity and Orientation Agnosticism

Analysis of read failures reveals that multi-antenna spatial diversity effectively mitigates multipath induced "dead zones" in the radio frequency field. At any given moment, at least one of the four strategically positioned antennas maintains optimal polarization alignment with the rotating markers.

https://doi.org/10.3390/engproc2026122007

3.4. Processing Latency and Time Budget Compliance

Despite the increased processing load from multi-antenna inputs, processing times remain well within the critical 58 ms time window. At 2.0 m with four antennas, the mean processing time was 19.6 $\pm$ 2.0 ms, representing only 34% of the allocated time budget.

4. Discussion

4.1. Multi-Antenna Configuration as a Critical Design Parameter

The experimental results unambiguously demonstrate that the number and placement of antennas constitute the single most influential design parameter for UHF RFID-based AV localization systems. The 85.8% improvement in success rate at 2.0 m. distance through the addition of three antennas provides compelling evidence that spatial diversity directly addresses the fundamental limitations of single-antenna systems in high-speed, high-dynamic environments.

This finding has profound implications for smart road infrastructure design. Rather than relying on a single powerful reader with expensive amplification, deploying multiple economical antennas provides superior performance at lower cost and complexity [15].

4.2. Root Causes of Remaining Read Failures

Even with an optimal antenna configuration, ~5.8% of reads fail at 2.0 m distance. Analysis identifies several contributing factors:

High-Speed Dynamics: At 255 RPM and 0.75 m diameter, markers transit the optimal "golden reading zone" in only a few milliseconds. The reader must energize the tag, receive modulated backscatter response, and decode the message within this brief window.

Multipath Propagation: Metal surfaces (wheel frame, facility walls) create constructive and destructive interference patterns. Although circular polarization mitigates this, deep nulls remain unavoidable in uncontrolled environments [9].

Tag Collision Resolution: With four tags and 17 theoretical reads per second, the EPC Gen2 anti-collision protocol must resolve tag responses within microsecond time windows [12]. Occasional frame collisions remain inevitable despite the protocol's efficiency.

System Latency Accumulation: While individual component latencies are minimal (marker: <1 ms, reader Tx-Rx switching microseconds, processor: <5 ms), accumulated jitter can occasionally exceed the time window when a tag occupies the optimal reading zone.

4.3. Practical Deployment Considerations

Road Marker Spacing and Installation: At 36 km/h, markers should be placed at 50–55 cm intervals. In actual deployment, this requirement is achievable using embedded road markers or surface-mounted tags within painted road markings.

Reader Mounting Strategy: Single-point mounting is insufficient. Multi-reader redundancy with overlapping coverage zones provides both localization accuracy and fault tolerance. Vehicle-mounted antennas positioned around the perimeter [16] (as simulated in this work) optimize orientation diversity.

Environmental Robustness: The present work used weather-resistant markers; however, their long-term durability in automotive environments (thermal cycling, road salt, mechanical vibration) requires further validation. Marker mounting technique significantly influenced antenna efficiency in preliminary trials.

Cost–Benefit Analysis: Multi-antenna passive RFID systems cost approximately 5–10 times less than automotive-grade GNSS + INS hybrid systems [15], while providing complementary localization in GNSS-denied environments.

https://doi.org/10.3390/engproc2026122007

4.4. Limitations and Future Validation Requirements

Current Study Limitations:

1. Controlled Laboratory Environment: Experiments were conducted indoors without realistic road materials (asphalt) or multi-story building interference.
2. Simplified Vehicle Dynamics: The tire-based simulator provides longitudinal velocity profile but does not capture lateral dynamics, acceleration, or realistic urban driving patterns.
3. Static Infrastructure: Road markers were fixed on the test platform; real-world deployment requires weatherized, permanently installed markers.
4. Single-Speed Testing: Validation was conducted at 36 km/h only; higher-speed performance (highway scenarios > 100 km/h) requires additional testing.

Critical Future Research Directions:

- Validation with embedded road markers in asphalt and plastic roadway materials.
- Real-world testing in actual urban environments with multipath-rich scenarios.
- Integration with vehicular-grade GNSS and INS to demonstrate hybrid localization performance.
- Evaluation of active RFID tags (self-powered, extended range, higher data rates);
- Comprehensive cost–benefit analysis comparing RFID + GNSS hybrid versus standalone GNSS + INS systems.

5. Conclusions

This experimental study rigorously validates the technical feasibility of UHF RFID marker systems for autonomous vehicle localization in GNSS-degraded urban environments. The novel synchronized dynamic testbed enables precise correlation of RFID reads with vehicle position, demonstrating consistently high success rates (>94% at 2 m distance with multi-antenna configuration), sub-meter accuracy capability, and compliant real-time processing latency.

The critical finding—that multi-antenna spatial diversity provides disproportionate performance gains—establishes a clear design principle for RFID-based localization systems. Four strategically positioned antennas overcome multipath interference and tag orientation challenges inherent to high-speed automotive environments.

Beyond localization, RFID systems provide a robust vehicle-to-infrastructure (V2I) communication channel for transmitting contextual data (speed limits, traffic signals, road conditions) directly to autonomous vehicles, enhancing safety and decision-making capabilities.

Primary limitations of the present work include controlled laboratory conditions, simplified vehicle dynamics, and operation at a single speed (36 km/h). Real-world deployment requires validation in actual urban environments, integration with deployed road infrastructure, and evaluation across the full operational speed range of autonomous vehicles.

This work establishes the technical foundation for RFID-based smart road infrastructure and demonstrates a cost-effective, complementary localization solution scalable to large-scale autonomous transportation systems.

Author Contributions: Conceptualization, S.S. and V.M.; methodology, V.M.; formal analysis, S.S. and M.M.; investigation, S.S.; resources, M.M. and S.S.; data curation, S.S.; writing—original draft preparation, S.S.; writing—review and editing, V.M. and M.M.; visualization, S.S.; supervision, V.M. and M.M. All authors have read and agreed to the published version of the manuscript.

Funding: This research received no external funding.

https://doi.org/10.3390/engproc2026122007

Institutional Review Board Statement: Not applicable.

Informed Consent Statement: Not applicable.

Data Availability Statement: Raw experimental data including timestamped RFID read logs, wheel revolution events, and processed success rate calculations are available upon request from the corresponding author.

Acknowledgments: The authors acknowledge the technical support provided by the laboratory staff in equipment configuration and data acquisition.

Conflicts of Interest: The authors declare no conflicts of interest.

Abbreviations

The following abbreviations are used in this manuscript:

AV	Autonomous Vehicle
GNSS	Global Navigation Satellite System
RFID	Radio Frequency Identification
UHF	Ultra-High Frequency
EPC	Electronic Product Code
ETSI	European Telecommunications Standards Institute
SMA	Subminiature version A
RPM	Revolutions Per Minute
FIFO	First-In-First-Out
V2I	Vehicle-to-Infrastructure
INS	Inertial Navigation System
ENU	East-North-Up (coordinate system)

References

1. Groves, P.D. Shadow matching: A new GNSS positioning technique for urban canyon navigation. *J. Navig.* **2011**, *64*, 417–430. [CrossRef]
2. Dissanayake, M.W.M.G.; Newman, P.; Clark, S.; Durrant-Whyte, H.F.; Csobra, M.M. A solution to the simultaneous localization and map building (SLAM) problem. *IEEE Trans. Robot. Autom.* **2001**, *17*, 229–241. [CrossRef]
3. Costa, F.; Genovesi, S.; Borgese, M.; Michel, A.; Dicandia, F.A.; Manara, G. A Review of RFID Sensors, the New Frontier of Internet of Things. *Sensors* **2021**, *21*, 3138. [CrossRef] [PubMed]
4. Finkenzeller, K. *RFID Handbook: Fundamentals and Applications in Contactless Smart Cards, Radio Frequency Identification and Near-Field Communication*, 3rd ed.; John Wiley & Sons: Hoboken, NJ, USA, 2010. [CrossRef]
5. Ni, L.M.; Liu, Y.; Lau, Y.C.; Patil, A.P. LANDMARC: Indoor location sensing using active RFID. In Proceedings of the 1st IEEE International Conference on Pervasive Computing and Communications (PerCom 2003), Fort Worth, TX, USA, 26 March 2003; pp. 407–415. [CrossRef]
6. Dobkin, D.M. *The RF in RFID: Passive UHF RFID in Practice*; Newnes: Oxford, UK, 2007; ISBN 978-0750682091.
7. Deshmukh, R.A.; Hasamnis, M.A.; Kulkarni, M.B.; Bhaiyya, M. Advancing indoor positioning systems: Innovations, challenges, and applications in mobile robotics. *Robotica* **2025**, *43*, 2710–2750. [CrossRef]
8. Wang, Y.; Zhang, N.; Jin, L. The hardware design and implementation of four-channel UHF RFID reader based on Impinj R2000. In Proceedings of the 2015 6th IEEE International Conference on Software Engineering and Service Science (ICSESS), Beijing, China, 23–25 September 2015; pp. 565–568. [CrossRef]
9. Kaplan, E.D.; Hegarty, C.J. (Eds.) *Understanding GPS/GNSS: Principles and Applications*, 3rd ed.; Artech House: Boston, MA, USA, 2017; ISBN 978-1-63081-050-1.
10. *ISO-IEC-18000-6*; Information Technology—Radio Frequency Identification for Item Management—Part 6: Parameters for Air Interface Communications at 860 MHz to 960 MHz. ISO: Geneva, Switzerland, 2004.
11. Campbell, M.; Egerstedt, M.; How, J.P.; Murray, R.M. Autonomous driving in urban environments: Approaches, lessons and challenges. *Philos. Trans. A Math. Phys. Eng. Sci.* **2010**, *368*, 4649–4672. [CrossRef] [PubMed]
12. Savage, P.G. *Strapdown Inertial Navigation Integration Strategy and Computations*; Strapdown Associates Inc.: Maple Plain, MN, USA, 2007; ISBN 978-0-9765070-0-9.

 https://doi.org/10.3390/engproc2026122007

13. Luh, Y.-P.; Liu, Y.-C. Reading Rate Improvement for UHF RFID Systems with Massive Tags by the Q Parameter. *Wireless Pers. Commun.* **2011**, *59*, 147–157. [CrossRef]
14. Choi, J.W.; Lee, J.H.; Lee, G.H. Broadband RFID tag antenna with quasi-isotropic radiation pattern. *Electron. Lett.* **2005**, *41*, 1091–1092. [CrossRef]
15. EPCglobal. *Class-1 Generation-2 UHF Air Interface Protocol Standard*; Version 2.0.1; EPCglobal Inc.: Brussels, Belgium, 2015. Available online: https://www.gs1.org/sites/default/files/docs/epc/Gen2_Protocol_Standard.pdf (accessed on 14 September 2025).
16. Gezici, S.; Tian, Z.; Giannakis, G.B.; Kobayashi, H.; Molisch, A.F.; Poor, H.V.; Sahinoglu, Z. Localization via ultra-wideband radios. *IEEE Signal Process. Mag.* **2005**, *22*, 70–84. [CrossRef]

https://doi.org/10.3390/engproc2026122007

engineering proceedings

MDPI

Proceeding Paper

LiDAR-Based 3D Mapping Approach for Estimating Tree Carbon Stock: A University Campus Case Study †

Abdul Samed Kaya *, Aybuke Buksur, Yasemin Burcak and Hidir Duzkaya

Department of Electrical-Electronics Engineering, Faculty of Engineering, Gazi University, 06570 Ankara, Türkiye; buksur.aybuke@gmail.com (A.B.); yaseminburcak61@gmail.com (Y.B.); hduzkaya@gazi.edu.tr (H.D.)

* Correspondence: aasamedkaya06@gmail.com; Tel.: +90-312-582-3313

† Presented at the 6th International Conference on Communications, Information, Electronic and Energy Systems, 26–28 November 2025, Ruse, Bulgaria.

Abstract

This study aims to develop and demonstrate a low-cost LiDAR-based 3D mapping approach for estimating tree carbon stock in university campuses. Unlike conventional field-based measurements, which are labor-intensive and error-prone, the proposed system integrates a 2D LiDAR sensor with a servo motor and odometry data to generate three-dimensional point clouds of trees. From these data, key biometric parameters such as diameter at breast height (DBH) and total height are automatically extracted and incorporated into species-specific and generalized allometric equations, in line with IPCC 2006/2019 guidelines, to estimate above-ground biomass, below-ground biomass, and total carbon storage. The experimental study is conducted over approximately 70,000 m^2 of green space at Gazi University, Ankara, where six dominant species have been identified, including Cedrus libani, Pinus nigra, Platanus orientalis, and Ailanthus altissima. Results revealed a total carbon stock of 16.82 t C, corresponding to 61.66 t CO_2eq. Among species, Cedrus libani (29,468.86 kg C) and Ailanthus altissima (13,544.83 kg C) showed the highest contributions, while Picea orientalis accounted for the lowest. The findings confirm that the proposed system offers a reliable, portable, cost-effective alternative to professional LiDAR scanners. This approach supports sustainable campus management and highlights the broader applicability of low-cost LiDAR technologies for urban carbon accounting and climate change mitigation strategies.

Keywords: LiDAR-based 3D mapping; carbon stock; biomass estimation; urban green areas; sustainable campus management

1. Introduction

Global climate change has become one of the most critical challenges of the 21st century, primarily driven by increasing atmospheric carbon dioxide (CO_2) concentrations. Urban green spaces, especially trees, are vital in mitigating these impacts by storing atmospheric carbon and acting as natural carbon sinks [1]. University campuses, often characterized by dense vegetation, provide a unique opportunity to quantify and monitor carbon stock potential locally, supporting sustainability initiatives and climate change mitigation strategies [1].

Traditional methods for estimating tree biomass and carbon stock rely on manual field measurements, such as diameter at breast height (DBH) and tree height (H), which are time-consuming and prone to human error [2]. Light Detection and Ranging (LiDAR)

technology has emerged as a powerful alternative, offering non-destructive, accurate, and efficient measurement of tree parameters. LiDAR-based systems have been successfully applied to assess tree volume, biomass, and carbon storage in diverse environments, including university campuses [1–3]. However, high costs associated with commercial LiDAR scanners often limit their accessibility for small-scale research and educational institutions [3].

Several campus-based studies have demonstrated the effectiveness of combining allometric models with LiDAR data for assessing carbon stock. For instance, Sharma et al. [1] quantified the carbon sequestration of 1997 trees at Amity University, India, estimating a sequestration potential of approximately 139.9 tons of CO_2. Similarly, Canadian and European campus studies have highlighted the potential of LiDAR to provide reliable estimations of tree metrics at reduced costs [3]. In Turkey, research on forest ecosystems has also highlighted the importance of temporal carbon and oxygen dynamics for sustainable land-use planning [4].

In addition to these efforts, recent advances in low-cost LiDAR and sensor fusion techniques have enabled the development of portable mobile mapping systems. Tantrairatn et al. [2] confirm that LiDAR-based DBH and H measurements can achieve high accuracy, with error margins as low as 1.734% for DBH and 1.572% for H, supporting their application in carbon assessment workflows.

Durkaya et al. [5] conducted a study on pure cedar stands in Antalya, using 36 sample trees to estimate biomass and carbon content for all tree components. They reported that approximately 51% of fresh biomass corresponds to dry Biomass, with carbon content ranging from 49.5% to 52.8%. The results showed that 100 m^3 of stem volume corresponds to 70.27 tons of biomass and 35.56 tons of stored carbon, underlining the high storage capacity of Cedrus libani [5]. Similarly, Durkaya et al. [6] developed equations for aboveground biomass in pure Pinus nigra stands in Zonguldak, demonstrating that models incorporating both DBH and H achieve strong correlations ($R^2 > 0.95$) and provide reliable estimates for carbon sequestration and biomass energy potential [6]. In the context of urban ecosystems, Shadman et al. [7] investigated a park in Dhaka, Bangladesh, finding a total lifetime storage of 660.8 t CO_2eq with an annual sequestration of 33.24 t CO_2eq. They also emphasized the role of species selection in maximizing urban carbon sinks [7].

Building upon these developments, this study proposes a low-cost LiDAR-based 3D mapping system designed to estimate the carbon stock potential of trees within the Gazi University campus. By integrating a 2D LiDAR sensor with a servo motor and odometry data, the system generates 3D point clouds of individual trees. DBH and H values are extracted from these point clouds, and biomass equations are applied to compute the stored carbon and CO_2 equivalents. This work aims to demonstrate that affordable LiDAR-based systems can provide reliable estimations of campus-level carbon stock, supporting sustainable urban planning and climate-focused decision-making.

2. Methods and Materials

2.1. System Design

Today, 3D LiDAR systems are widely preferred for high-precision environmental scanning; however, they remain expensive hardware solutions. This high cost poses a significant barrier to their widespread use, particularly in research, education, and prototyping applications. In this context, the present system combines low-cost components to provide an accessible and flexible solution that addresses the need for 3D mapping.

This system architecture represents a modular 3D mapping solution mounted on a mobile robotic platform as shown in Figure 1. A YDLidar G2 sensor, installed on a platform rotated by a Tower Pro MG996R servo motor, enables 3D environmental scanning

 https://doi.org/10.3390/engproc2026122008

by generating slices of 2D scans [8]. Each scan is captured at 0.5-degree intervals and sequentially added to the previous one, constructing a 3D scan from 2D data. Additionally, odometry data is generated through DC motors driven by an L298N module, controlled by an Arduino Mega 2560, based on motion commands received via an HC-06 Bluetooth module from a mobile application [9,10]. These odometry-based movements allow the system to perform scans over larger areas.

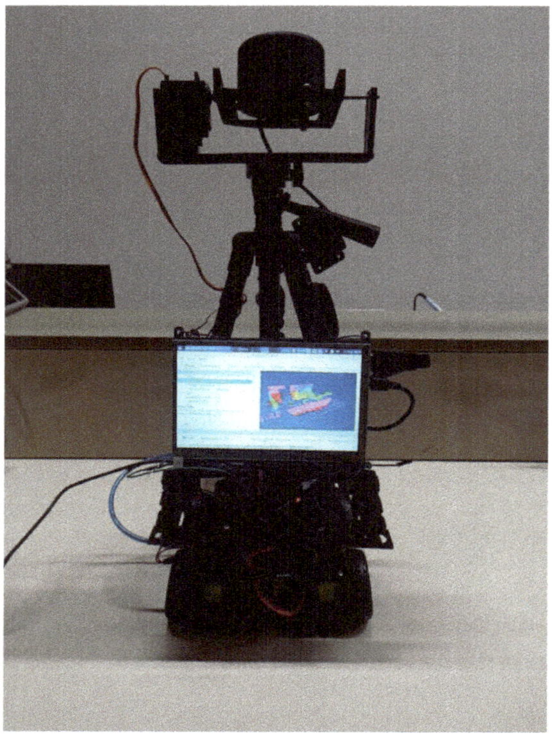

Figure 1. LiDAR-based outdoor 3D mapping system.

The control of the LiDAR and servo motor and the processing of acquired data is handled by a Raspberry Pi 4 (8 GB), which also communicates with the Arduino Mega 2560 to receive odometry data. The system incorporates a 7-inch WaveShare HDMI capacitive touchscreen display for real-time outdoor mapping and visualization. Processed maps and records are stored on a 128 GB SD card, ensuring long-term data storage. The entire software stack is built on the Robot Operating System (ROS) [11], which provides a flexible framework for sensor integration, data handling, and visualization. This integrated architecture supports real-time mapping, data visualization, and system control in outdoor environments.

The scans are saved as bag files for further analysis. These bag files can be replayed in the RViz application, allowing users to generate a 3D map that can be observed from different perspectives. On this map, essential measurements can be performed, such as determining tree heights and diameters. Additionally, the tf transformation library is utilized to perform sensor fusion, ensuring accurate alignment between LiDAR scans, servo rotation angles, and odometry data, which yields consistent and reliable 3D maps [12].

https://doi.org/10.3390/engproc2026122008

2.2. Tree Inventory and Carbon Estimation

The study is conducted in the green areas of Gazi University campus. To assess the carbon stock capacity of the study area, the campus map is divided into three zones based on the spatial distribution of vegetation density and land use characteristics. A map view of the campus and its zones is shown in Figure 2. Tree inventories are prepared within each zone by identifying the dominant species present. The principal species included Cedrus libani (Lebanon cedar), Pinus nigra (Black pine), Platanus orientalis (Oriental. plane), Picea orientalis (Oriental spruce), Ailanthus altissima (Tree-of-heaven), and Cupressus arizonica (Arizona cypress).

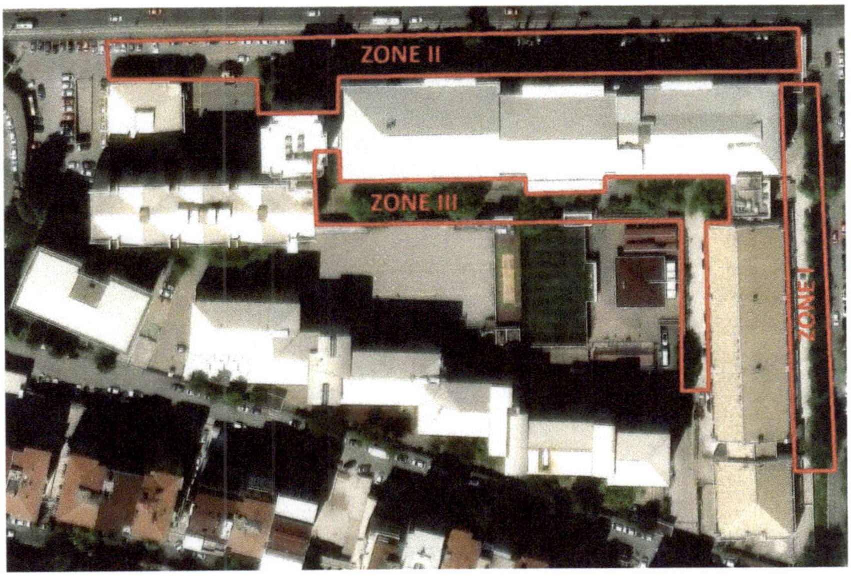

Figure 2. Zones of the campus.

From the LiDAR-derived point cloud, diameter at breast height (DBH) and tree height (H) are extracted as the fundamental biometric parameters. These measurements served as inputs to species-specific or allometric equations widely used for estimating biomass and carbon.

The calculation steps are summarized as follows:

Individual trees' above-ground biomass (AGB) is estimated using species-specific or generalized allometric equations. A widely used pantropical model developed by Chave et al. [13] is expressed as:

$$AGB = 0.0673 \times (\rho D^2 H)^{0.976} \quad (1)$$

where D is the DBH (cm), H is the total tree height (m), and ρ is the wood density (g/cm^3), obtained from published wood density values [14,15].

Root biomass (Below-Ground Biomass (BGB)) is estimated as a fraction of AGB, following the IPCC 2006/2019 Guidelines [16,17]. The relationship is:

$$BGB = R \times AGB \quad (2)$$

where R is the root-to-shoot ratio, for planted coniferous stands with low-to-medium biomass ($\leq$125 t ha^{-1}), a value of R = 0.34 is recommended (IPCC, 2019 [17]).

https://doi.org/10.3390/engproc2026122008

Total Biomass (TB) equation is:

$$TB = AGB + BGB \quad (3)$$

Biomass is converted to carbon stock using dry biomass's carbon fraction (CF). According to IPCC 2006/2019 Guidelines [16,17], the default value is CF = 0.47–0.50. Carbon Stock equation is (C):

$$C = CF \times TB \quad (4)$$

Finally, the amount of sequestered CO_2 is obtained by converting carbon mass into CO_2 equivalent using the molecular weight ratio:

$$CO_{2eq} = C_{total} \times 44/12 \quad (5)$$

For Cedrus libani (Lebanon cedar), biomass estimation is carried out using a species-specific equation developed by Durkaya et al. [5], which employs Diameter at Breast Height (DBH, $d_{1.30}$) and tree height (H) as independent variables in the Above-Ground Biomass (AGB) equation. Here, D is expressed in centimeters, H in meters, and AGB in kilograms (oven-dry AGB).

$$AGB = 51.38543 - 12.2998 \times d_{1.30} - 2.75361 \times H + 0.543984 \times {d_{1.30}}^2 + 0.896138 \times H^2 \quad (6)$$

This equation, with a high coefficient of determination (R^2 = 0.97), provides reliable results, and the estimated biomass values are subsequently converted into carbon and CO_2 equivalents using carbon conversion factors. The remainder of the Cedrus libani calculations is carried out the same way as for allometric equations.

Biomass estimation for Pinus Nigra (Black Pine) is performed using the Above Ground Biomass (AGB) equation developed by Durkaya et al. [6], which incorporates DBH ($d_{1.30}$) and tree height (H) as independent variables. Here, D is expressed in cm, H m, and AGB is expressed in kg (oven-dry AGB).

$$AGB = 106.6611 - 11.5098 \times d_{1.30} - 11.481 \times H + 0.5972 \times {d_{1.30}}^2 + 0.7758 \times H^2 \quad (7)$$

This equation, with a high coefficient of determination (R^2 = 0.86), provides reliable results, and the estimated biomass values are subsequently converted into carbon and CO_2 equivalents using carbon conversion factors. The remainder of the calculations for Pinus Nigra are carried out in the same way as for allometric equations.

3. Results and Discussion

This study analyzed the green areas of Gazi University campus using a LiDAR-based scanning system. The study area covered approximately 70,000 m^2 [18] within the Faculty of Engineering region of Gazi University, located at coordinates 39°55′54.4″ N and 32°50′47.6″ E. Trees within the campus are scanned using the developed system, as illustrated in Figure 1, and the acquired data are subsequently processed to generate three-dimensional point clouds, as shown in Figure 3. The coloring applied to the point clouds enabled a more distinct distinction of tree stems and crowns from surrounding objects, thereby facilitating more precise measurements of diameter at breast height (DBH) and total tree height (H). Example visualizations representing three different study zones (Zone I, Zone II, and Zone III) provide evidence of the methodology's effectiveness in characterizing campus vegetation.

https://doi.org/10.3390/engproc2026122008

Figure 3. Three-dimensional visualization of trees in the campus samples. (a) Zone III scan example 1; (b) Zone I scan example 1; (c) Zone III scan example 2; (d) Zone I scan example 2.

The extracted DBH and H values are classified by species using RViz, and the results are summarized in Table 1. The table reports average DBH and height, the number of individuals per species across the zones, carbon stock per tree, and total carbon stock.

Table 1. Carbon stock and CO_2 equivalent results by tree species in the campus.

Tree Spices	Average DBH (cm)	Average Height (m)	N Zone Number I	II	III	Carbon Stock per Tree (kg)	Total Carbon Stock (kg)	CO_2 Equivalent per Tree (kg)	Total CO_2 Equivalent (kg)
Cedrus Libani	23.61	14.81	35	22	1	138.57	8036.96	508.08	29,468.86
Pinus Nigra	26.73	12.15	6	0	3	126.42	1137.78	463.54	4171.87
Platanus Orientalis	26.04	21.31	0	0	13	237.79	3091.30	871.90	11,334.76
Picea Orientalis	14.61	5.04	0	0	8	14.61	116.91	53.58	428.66
Ailanthus Altissima	52.52	19.42	2	0	2	923.51	3694.04	3386.21	13,544.83
Cupressus Arizonica	17.19	9.75	0	12	4	46.28	740.53	169.71	2715.29

The results demonstrate distinct variations in carbon storage capacity among species. Cedrus libani emerged as the most significant contributor, storing 29,468.86 kg C across 58 individuals, primarily due to its abundance and robust size. Despite consisting of only 13 individuals, Platanus orientalis achieved a total of 11,334.76 kg C, owing to its high per-tree carbon stock (871.90 kg). Similarly, Ailanthus altissima, represented by only four individuals, contributed 13,544.83 kg C due to its large DBH and height values. In contrast,

https://doi.org/10.3390/engproc2026122008

Pinus nigra (9 individuals) accounted for 4171.87 kg C, Cupressus arizonica (16 individuals) for 2715.29 kg C, and Picea orientalis (8 individuals) stored only 428.66 kg C, marking the lowest contribution.

Overall, the cumulative carbon stock of campus trees is approximately 16.82 t C, equivalent to 61.66 t CO_2eq when applying the conversion factor (44/12). These findings highlight that species-specific traits and their distribution within the campus directly affect total carbon stock. Dominant and fast-growing broadleaf species (e.g., Platanus orientalis, Ailanthus altissima) exhibited disproportionately higher storage capacity. In contrast, coniferous species (Picea orientalis, Cupressus arizonica) contributed less due to smaller sizes and lower abundance.

In comparison with previous studies, the results are consistent with the literature reporting the role of urban green spaces as local carbon sinks. For instance, Nowak and Crane [19] emphasized that urban trees significantly mitigate CO_2 emissions, while Durkaya et al. [5,6] demonstrated that Cedrus libani and Pinus nigra are effective carbon-sequestering species in Turkish forests. Chave et al. [13] also confirmed the importance of integrating wood density and tree height in allometric models to minimize uncertainties, a practice adopted in this study. Finally, applying IPCC guidelines [16,17] ensured methodological consistency in biomass-to-carbon conversion and the estimation of below-ground biomass.

These results underscore the dual contribution of both species richness and measurement technology: while the species composition of the campus ecosystem determines the magnitude of stored carbon, the LiDAR-based, low-cost scanning system has proven to be an efficient, scalable, and non-destructive method for monitoring urban vegetation and assessing carbon sequestration potential at a local scale.

4. Conclusions

This study demonstrated the potential of a low-cost LiDAR-based 3D mapping system to estimate carbon stock in university campuses. By integrating a 2D LiDAR sensor with a servo motor and odometry data, three-dimensional point clouds of trees are generated and used to extract fundamental biometric parameters such as DBH and total height. Combined with species-specific and generalized allometric equations, these parameters enabled reliable estimation of above-ground biomass, below-ground biomass, and total carbon stock.

The experimental results from the Gazi University campus revealed a total carbon stock of approximately 16.82 t C, equivalent to 61.66 t CO_2eq, highlighting the role of campus vegetation as a significant local carbon sink. Species such as Cedrus libani, Platanus orientalis, and Ailanthus altissima exhibited disproportionately high contributions due to their size and growth characteristics. In contrast, species like Picea orientalis and Cupressus arizonica contributed less. These findings underline that species composition and distribution strongly influence urban green areas' overall carbon sequestration capacity.

Compared with previous literature, the results are consistent with international studies emphasizing the importance of urban trees in mitigating carbon emissions. Moreover, the application of IPCC guidelines ensured methodological robustness in biomass-to-carbon conversion. The proposed system thus provides a scalable, affordable, and non-destructive alternative to high-cost professional LiDAR systems, making it especially suitable for educational institutions and local-scale sustainability projects.

Future work can focus on expanding the system with sensor fusion techniques and integration with Geographic Information Systems (GIS) to enhance urban carbon management strategies. Overall, the developed approach contributes to advancing sustainable campus

https://doi.org/10.3390/engproc2026122008

management and demonstrates the broader applicability of low-cost LiDAR technologies in climate change mitigation efforts.

Author Contributions: Conceptualization, H.D. and A.S.K.; methodology, A.S.K., A.B. and Y.B.; software, A.S.K., A.B. and Y.B.; validation, A.B. and Y.B.; formal analysis, A.S.K. and A.B.; investigation, A.S.K., A.B., Y.B. and H.D.; resources, A.S.K., A.B. and Y.B.; data curation, A.S.K., A.B. and Y.B.; writing—original draft preparation, A.S.K., A.B. and Y.B.; writing—review and editing, H.D.; visualization, A.S.K. and H.D.; supervision, H.D.; project administration, H.D.; funding acquisition, A.S.K., A.B. and Y.B. All authors have read and agreed to the published version of the manuscript.

Funding: This research was funded by the Scientific and Technological Research Council of Turkey (TUBITAK) grant program 2209-A-Research Project Support Program for Undergraduate Students with grant number 1919B012446214.

Institutional Review Board Statement: Not applicable.

Informed Consent Statement: Not applicable.

Data Availability Statement: The data supporting the findings of this study are available from the corresponding author upon reasonable request.

Conflicts of Interest: The authors declare no conflicts of interest.

References

1. Sharma, R.; Pradhan, L.; Kumari, M.; Bhattacharya, P. Assessment of carbon sequestration potential of tree species in Amity University campus Noida. *Environ. Sci. Proc.* **2021**, *3*, 52.
2. Tantrairatn, S.; Pichitkul, A.; Petcharat, N.; Karaked, P.; Ariyarit, A. Evaluating LiDAR technology for accurate measurement of tree metrics and carbon sequestration. *MethodsX* **2025**, *14*, 103237. [CrossRef] [PubMed]
3. Huai, J.; Shao, Y.; Zhang, Y.; Yilmaz, A. A low-cost portable LiDAR-based mobile mapping system on an Android smartphone. *arXiv* **2025**, arXiv:2506.15983. [CrossRef]
4. Suryawanshi, M.; Patel, A.; Kale, T.S.; Patil, P.R. Carbon sequestration potential of tree species in the environment of North Maharashtra University Campus, Jalgaon (MS), India. *Biosci. Discov.* **2014**, *5*, 175–179.
5. Durkaya, B.; Durkaya, A.; Makineci, E.; Ülküdür, M. Estimation of above-ground biomass and sequestered carbon of Taurus Cedar (*Cedrus libani* L.) in Antalya, Turkey. *iForest* **2013**, *6*, 278–284. [CrossRef]
6. Durkaya, B.; Durkaya, A.; Yağcı, H. Biomass equations in natural black pines. *Fresenius Environ. Bull.* **2019**, *28*, 1132–1139.
7. Shadman, S.; Khalid, P.; Hanafiah, M.M.; Koyande, A.; Islam, A.; Bhuiyan, S.; Woon, K.S.; Show, P.-L. The carbon sequestration potential of urban public parks of densely populated cities to improve environmental sustainability. *Sustain. Energy Technol. Assess.* **2022**, *52*, 102064. [CrossRef]
8. Ocando, M.G.; Certad, N.; Alvarado, S.; Terrones, Á. Autonomous 2D SLAM and 3D mapping of an environment using a single 2D LIDAR and ROS. In Proceedings of the 2017 Latin American Robotics Symposium (LARS) and 2017 Brazilian Symposium on Robotics (SBR), Curitiba, Brazil, 8–11 November 2017.
9. Oprea, M.; Mocanu, M. Bluetooth communications in educational robotics. In Proceedings of the 2021 23rd International Conference on Control Systems and Computer Science (CSCS), Bucharest, Romania, 26–28 May 2021.
10. Chen, L.; Zhang, J.; Wang, Y. Wireless Car control system based on Arduino Uno R3. In Proceedings of the 2018 2nd IEEE Advanced Information Management, Communicates, Electronic and Automation Control Conference (IMCEC), Xi'an, China, 25–27 May 2018.
11. Quigley, M.; Gerkey, B.; Conley, K.; Faust, J.; Foote, T.; Leibs, J.; Berger, E.; Wheeler, R.; Ng, A. ROS: An open-source Robot Operating System. In Proceedings of the IEEE International Conference on Robotics and Automation (ICRA), Workshop on Open Source Software, Kobe, Japan, 12–17 May 2009.
12. Foote, T. Tf: The transform library. In Proceedings of the 2013 IEEE Conference on Technologies for Practical Robot Applications (TePRA), Woburn, MA, USA, 22–23 April 2013.
13. Chave, J.; Réjou-Méchain, M.; Búrquez, A.; Chidumayo, E.; Colgan, M.S.; Delitti, W.B.; Duque, A.; Eid, T.; Fearnside, P.M.; Goodman, R.C.; et al. Improved allometric models to estimate the aboveground biomass of tropical trees. *Glob. Change Biol.* **2014**, *20*, 3177–3190. [CrossRef]
14. Nowak, D.J. *Understanding i-Tree: 2021 Summary of Programs and Methods*; General Technical Report NRS-200-2021; U.S. Department of Agriculture, Forest Service, Northern Research Station: Madison, WI, USA, December 2021; pp. 23–24.

https://doi.org/10.3390/engproc2026122008

15. Zanne, S.A.; Lopez-Gonzalez, G.; Coomes, D.A.; Ilic, J.; Jansen, S.; Lewis, S.L.; Miller, R.B.; Swenson, N.G.; Wiemann, M.C.; Chave, J. Data from: Towards a worldwide wood economics spectrum. *Ecol. Lett.* **2009**, *12*, 351–366.
16. IPCC. *2006 IPCC Guidelines for National Greenhouse Gas Inventories, Volume 4: Agriculture, Forestry and Other Land Use*; Eggleston, H.S., Buendia, L., Miwa, K., Ngara, T., Tanabe, K., Eds.; Institute for Global Environmental Strategies (IGES): Hayama, Japan, 2006.
17. IPCC. *2019 Refinement to the 2006 IPCC Guidelines for National Greenhouse Gas Inventories, Volume 4: Agriculture, Forestry and Other Land Use*; Calvo Buendia, E., Tanabe, K., Kranjc, A., Baasansuren, J., Fukuda, M., Ngarize, S., Osako, A., Pyrozhenko, Y., Shermanau, P., Federici, S., Eds.; IPCC: Geneva, Switzerland, 2019.
18. Gazi Üniversitesi Mühendislik Fakültesi. Tanıtım; Gazi Üniversitesi. Available online: https://mf.gazi.edu.tr/view/page/150945 (accessed on 1 September 2025).
19. Nowak, D.J.; Crane, D.E. Carbon storage and sequestration by urban trees in the USA. *Environ. Pollut.* **2002**, *116*, 381–389. [CrossRef]

https://doi.org/10.3390/engproc2026122008

engineering proceedings

MDPI

Proceeding Paper

Computation of Conduction and Displacement Current Densities in Modelled Human Organs near an Overhead Transmission Line †

Cvetanka Bilbiloska, Elena Todorova, Bojan Glushica * and Andrijana Kuhar

Institute of Electronics, Faculty of Electrical Engineering and Information Technologies, "Ss. Cyril and Methodius" University in Skopje, 1000 Skopje, North Macedonia; kuhar@feit.ukim.edu.mk (A.K.)

* Correspondence: glushica@feit.ukim.edu.mk

† Presented at the 6th International Conference on Communications, Information, Electronic and Energy Systems, 26–28 November 2025, Ruse, Bulgaria.

Abstract

This study employs numerical simulations to analyse current densities in modelled human organs originating from extremely low frequency (ELF) electromagnetic fields emanating from a 110 kV single-circuit high-voltage transmission line. Exposure to these ELF fields gives rise to both conduction and displacement currents within the human body, potentially perturbing endogenous bioelectric currents and raising concerns of health risks. Using CST Studio Suite 2018 software, a three-dimensional multipart ellipsoidal anatomical model is developed to analyse these phenomena. Although displacement currents have lower magnitudes than conduction currents, they contribute significantly to the total current density and must therefore be included in rigorous safety assessments. Simulation results indicate that the current density values remain below the basic restrictions of the International Commission on Non-Ionizing Radiation Protection.

Keywords: current density; electromagnetic exposure; ELF fields; endogenous currents; transmission lines

1. Introduction

Humans are constantly exposed to electromagnetic fields, both natural and man-made. Extremely low frequency (ELF) electromagnetic fields (EMFs), such as those produced by high-voltage transmission lines, can give rise to current densities within the human body, in addition to the endogenous currents that are essential for physiological functions. As recognised by the World Health Organization, the externally caused current densities may pose potential health risks.

The distribution and intensity of these currents depend on several factors, including the geometry of the human body, as well as the properties of different tissues. To address various challenges regarding safety, numerous standards and protocols have been established, outlining methods for assessing and protecting against the effects of electromagnetic fields and induced currents. The International Commission on Non-Ionizing Radiation Protection (ICNIRP) provides guidelines that recommend limiting human exposure to fields that give rise to current densities below 10 $\mathrm{mA/m^2}$ for occupational exposure and 2 $\mathrm{mA/m^2}$ for general public exposure, particularly in critical regions such as the head, neck, and torso [1]. These basic restrictions are based on studies that have been conducted mostly through experimental measurements on animals, phantom scale models of humans, or theoretical analyses using simplified human models.

Additional studies have been conducted using numerical simulations. Since the internal electric field can be represented as a vectorial sum of the emerging electric fields caused by external electric and magnetic fields at ELF, it is often sufficient to describe the same system with only an electric or magnetic field source [2,3]. The impact of external electric fields [4–6] and external magnetic fields [7–9] on a modelled human body has been studied in various scenarios. However, given the large scale of the systems considered, various trade-offs have been implemented in order to provide reliable results. Some of the modelling compromises include the following: considering only the electric field or only the magnetic field; not taking into account field perturbations introduced by the presence of the human body when applying a previously computed external electric field (without the body); omitting the electric permittivity of biological tissues; employing overly simplified human models and field sources.

Despite the potential health risks posed by high-voltage overhead transmission lines (OTLs), there is a notable gap in modelling studies that integrate external field distributions originating from the OTL with human models. In this paper, the gap is addressed by employing a computational approach to investigate induced currents in human organs due to ELF EMF exposure originating from an OTL.

A numerical simulation of a three-dimensional multipart ellipsoidal model, consisting of multiple ellipsoids representing distinct anatomical regions, is conducted, implementing a widely used commercial EM simulation platform, CST Studio Suite 2018 [10]. This simulation enables a detailed analysis of field distributions within human tissues when exposed to a three-phase transmission line system, offering a more precise understanding of electromagnetic field interactions and their potential implications for human health.

The aim of this study is to determine how ELF exposure from a 110 kV OTL affects the externally caused current densities within the human body. The displacement current densities [11,12] are also taken into account because of their analogous role to conduction currents in generating magnetic fields and influencing the overall electromagnetic field distribution within the surrounding medium. Compliance with ICNIRP basic restrictions is determined by verifying that these current densities stay below 10 mA/m^2 for occupational and 2 mA/m^2 for public ELF exposure.

2. Methodology

2.1. Theoretical Foundations

Considering the quasistatic frequency range, the electric field inside the human body can be represented as two separate electric fields $\vec{E}_i$ and $\vec{E}_{ind}$, originating from the external electric and from the magnetic field, respectively [13].

The internal electric field $\vec{E}_i$ (originating from the external electric field) depends on multiple parameters, including the following: geometry of the body, tissue properties, boundary conditions at the air-tissue and tissue–tissue interfaces. In addition to specifying boundary conditions, the field distribution can be determined by applying Gauss' law for an arbitrary electric field $\vec{E}$

$$\nabla \cdot \varepsilon \vec{E} = \rho, \tag{1}$$

and the continuity equation, expressed in the frequency domain:

$$\nabla \cdot \vec{J} = \nabla \cdot \sigma \vec{E} = -j\omega\rho \tag{2}$$

https://doi.org/10.3390/engproc2026122009

where ρ is the free charge density, ω the angular velocity, $\vec{J}$ the current density, ε the electric permittivity of the medium, and σ the specific electric conductivity of the medium. Combining Equations (1) and (2) results in

$$\nabla \cdot (\sigma + j\omega\varepsilon)\vec{E} = 0 \tag{3}$$

satisfying the charge conservation law. Using Equation (3), the total current density $\vec{J}_{E,tot}$, originating from $\vec{E}_i$, can be represented as the sum of the conduction and displacement current densities, $\vec{J}_{E,C}$ and $\vec{J}_{E,D}$, respectively:

$$\vec{J}_{E,tot} = \vec{J}_{E,C} + \vec{J}_{E,D} = \sigma\vec{E}_i + j\omega\varepsilon\vec{E}_i. \tag{4}$$

The displacement current density $\vec{J}_{E,D}$ inside the human body originates mainly from the polarisation current density $\vec{J}_P = j\omega\vec{P}$, which depends on the polarisation vector $\vec{P}$. Since $\vec{P}$ can be expressed by the electric field $\vec{E}_i$ as

$$\vec{P} = \varepsilon_0(\varepsilon_r - 1)\vec{E}_i, \tag{5}$$

and taking into account that $\varepsilon_r \gg 1$ in our case, it follows that $\vec{P} \cong \varepsilon\vec{E}_i$, or $\vec{J}_{E,D} \cong \vec{J}_P$. This means that the polarisation current density $\vec{J}_P$ can be described by the displacement current density $\vec{J}_{E,D}$ through the same internal electric field $\vec{E}_i$, and the medium properties.

The internally induced electric field $\vec{E}_{ind}$, originates from the temporal variation in the magnetic field inside the body. The ELF magnetic field in biological tissues generates eddy currents flowing along pathways within a plane perpendicular to the field's direction of incidence. This is described by the local form of Faraday's law, expressed in the frequency domain:

$$\nabla \times \vec{E}_{ind} = -j\omega\vec{B} \tag{6}$$

where $\vec{B}$ is the magnetic induction vector. Taking into account boundary conditions and medium properties, the induced electric field $\vec{E}_{ind}$ can be obtained. Finally, applying the charge conservation law (Equation (3)), the total current density $\vec{J}_{B,tot}$ originating from the induced electric field $\vec{E}_{ind}$ is represented as follows:

$$\vec{J}_{B,tot} = \vec{J}_{B,C} + \vec{J}_{B,D} = \sigma\vec{E}_{ind} + j\omega\varepsilon\vec{E}_{ind}. \tag{7}$$

The same conclusions about the polarisation current density and Equation (5) apply here.

The total current density inside the body can be computed by summing the current densities $\vec{J}_{E,tot}$, and $\vec{J}_{B,tot}$ from Equations (4) and (7). Because $\vec{E}_i$ and $\vec{E}_{ind}$ originate from different physical mechanisms, the associated current densities are not in phase, and will be analysed separately.

2.2. Model of the System

The simulation in CST Studio Suite 2018, which employs the three-dimensional finite element method, is conducted in two stages: first, the Fullwave solver is used to compute the magnetic field and the induced current densities; followed by the implementation of the Electroquasistatic solver to compute the electric field and the resulting current densities.

https://doi.org/10.3390/engproc2026122009

2.2.1. System Properties

The study focuses on a three-phase 110 kV single-circuit OTL at a frequency of 50 Hz, consisting of three-phase conductors (Phase A, B, and C) and a ground wire (GW), with a minimal conductor height of 15 m. Each phase conductor is based on a composite Al/Fe strand with a cross-sectional area of 360/57 mm^2. For the computations, the phase conductors are modelled as cylinders with an outer diameter of 26.6 mm, and the GW as a cylinder with an outer diameter of 16 mm. The conductor positions of the OTL, relative to the coordinate origin, are provided in Table 1. The OTL properties were taken from a prior project investigating the impact of OTL's EMFs on nearby systems. The ground is modelled with a specific electric conductivity of 0.01 S/m, and the rest of the domain is modelled as air.

Table 1. Conductor positions of the single-circuit OTL.

Conductor	Horizontal Position (m)	Vertical Position (m)
Phase A	4.8	15
Phase B	−4.1	17.4
Phase C	3.4	19.8
GW	0	26

In the Fullwave simulation, a current of 800 A is forced in each phase conductor as the theoretical maximum that the OTL can handle. It is also assumed that current does not flow in the ground wire. As for the Electroquasistatic simulation, a Perfect Electric Conductor (PEC) is used to model the phase conductors and the ground wire. A line-to-neutral voltage of 63.5 kV is forced.

An ungrounded and three-dimensional multipart ellipsoidal human model with a height of 1.8 m is placed directly below the OTL, at ground level, representing the subject for the simulation analysis of the influence of electromagnetic fields originating from the transmission line. Figure 1 illustrates the multipart ellipsoidal human model along with the organs in which the analysis is conducted: brain, heart, lungs, and kidneys.

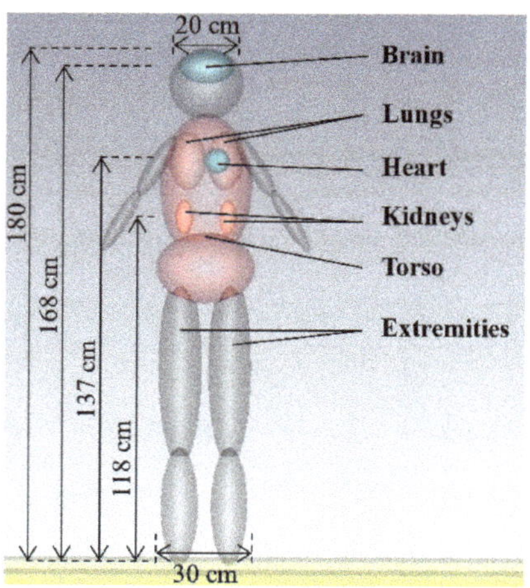

Figure 1. Three-dimensional and multipart ellipsoidal human model with a height of 1.8 m.

The specific electric conductivity and relative electric permittivity of each part of the body are given in Table 2, as provided by [14]. For all materials used in this simulation, the relative magnetic permeability is set to one.

https://doi.org/10.3390/engproc2026122009

Table 2. Specific electric conductivity and relative electric permittivity of each organ/tissue.

Organ/Tissue	σ (S/m)	ε_r
Brain	0.06	1.21×10^7
Heart	0.1	8.66×10^6
Lungs	0.08	5.76×10^6
Kidneys	0.1	1.01×10^7
Head	0.02	8.87×10^3
Torso	0.223	1.77×10^7
Extremities	0.196	7.89×10^5

2.2.2. Domain Boundary Conditions and Domain Discretisation

For both the Fullwave and Electroquasistatic simulations, a zero tangential electric field is forced at domain boundaries. This ensures that the electric field is pointing away from the system at the domain boundary. In order to minimise the influence of the boundary on the system, it is modelled as a cylinder with a radius of 200 m and a height of 200 m, placed at the coordinate origin. The OTL extends along a path parallel to the height of the cylinder (z-axis).

Due to system complexity, it is necessary to divide the system into several regions with varying discretisation levels. The system with its different discretisation regions is shown in Figure 2.

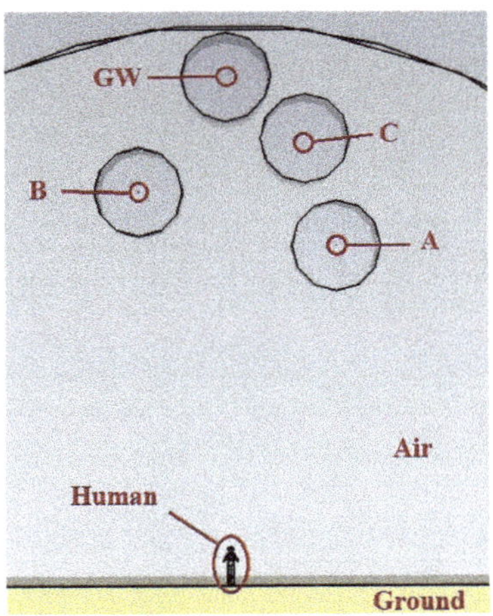

Figure 2. Section of the system showing the modelled components with the different discretisation regions.

Each object in the simulation has its own local discretisation, with the highest level of discretisation applied to the human model shown in Figure 3.

As the distance from the human model increases, the level of local discretisation decreases. The only exceptions are the OTL conductors and the area around them, where finer local discretisation is necessary in order to minimise errors in field distribution.

https://doi.org/10.3390/engproc2026122009

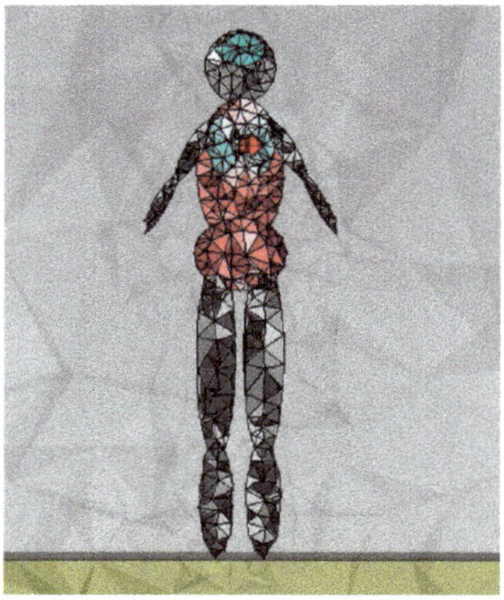

Figure 3. Discretisation of the modelled human body.

3. Results and Discussion

In this section, the computed values for the internal electric fields originating from the external electric and magnetic fields, and the associated current densities at different regions of the modelled human body are presented.

Figure 4 illustrates the spatial distribution of the magnitude of the internal electric field in the body, originating from electric and magnetic field sources. The results are presented on a cross-sectional area perpendicular to the OTL, located at $z = 0$ (XOY plane).

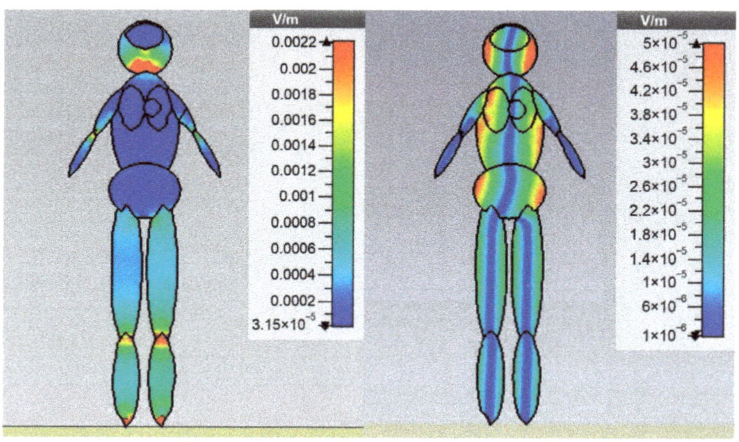

(**a**) (**b**)

Figure 4. Computed magnitude of the internal electric field distribution at $z = 0$ (XOY plane), (**a**) originating from the electric field sources, and (**b**) originating from the magnetic field sources.

Because of the geometry of the body and tissue properties, the electric field in Figure 4a exhibits its highest values around the neck area. Higher values of the electric field are also observed in the extremities. These areas exhibit proportionally higher current densities, reaching around 440 $\mu A/m^2$ in the legs, which is 4.5 times lower than the ICNIRP established restrictions for general public exposure. The electric field in Figure 4b demonstrates a more peripheral distribution across the head and torso, resulting from the formation of circular pathways. The observed asymmetry in the distribution of the field is a result of the positioning of the body relative to the OTL, specifically the closer

https://doi.org/10.3390/engproc2026122009

position to the phase conductor A. The induced electric field values in this case are lower compared to those in Figure 4a. However, changing the position and orientation of the body has an impact on the magnitude of the induced electric field. The greatest difference in magnitude would appear in the case of rotating the body by 90° (on the XOZ plane), and changing its position in order to create an almost perpendicular angle between the body and the magnetic field. It should be noted that the EMF maxima occur at different positions at ground level, depending on the OTL geometry. At horizontal distance x = 0, the magnitude of the magnetic field is almost at its maximum; however, the magnitude of the external electric field is not. This indicates that the magnitude of the internal electric field, originating from the electric field sources, can exhibit higher values for the same system.

The corresponding magnitudes of the total current densities around the organs of interest are shown in Figures 5 and 6. The current densities are shown as a planar distribution on cross-sections containing the organs, perpendicular to the body at heights as depicted in Figure 1: 1.68 m, 1.37 m, and 1.18 m. The total current density is calculated as a Euclidean norm of the conduction and displacement currents. The total current originating from the electric field sources (Figure 5) exhibits high values at regions with high electric conductivity, and at interfaces with small areas. The total current originating from the magnetic field sources (Figure 6) exhibits high values at the periphery of the body, with values about five times lower than those of the electric field sources at the organs of interest. While the neck area is not depicted in the figure, it should be noted that the magnitude of the total current density due to electric field sources is 265 $\mu A/m^2$, a substantially higher value than any other area in the head and torso. From a safety perspective, this magnitude is approximately 7.5 times lower than the ICNIRP-established restrictions for general public exposure.

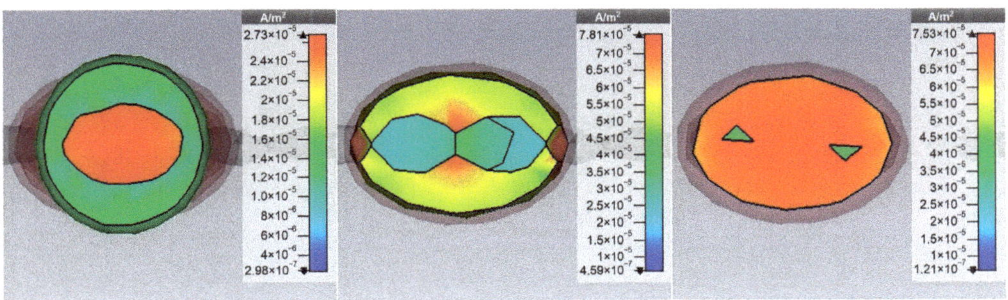

(a) (b) (c)

Figure 5. Computed magnitudes of the total current densities $\vec{J}_{E,tot}$ on cross-sections perpendicular to the body, at heights: (**a**) 1.68 m, (**b**) 1.37 m, and (**c**) 1.18 m.

To provide a more detailed representation of the current densities, an analysis of the distribution is conducted along profiles at specific heights across the organs of interest depicted in Figure 1. The magnitudes of the conduction current density $\vec{J}_{E,C}$, and displacement current density $\vec{J}_{E,D}$, originating from the electric field sources, are shown in Figure 7. The highest values of $\vec{J}_{E,C}$ appear around the kidney area. This is due to the higher specific conductivity of the torso. The currents in the heart, lungs, and brain are comparably lower because of the properties of the surrounding tissue. The displacement currents $\vec{J}_{E,D}$ are notably lower in value; however, they still have an impact on the total current density in the organs, especially in the brain.

https://doi.org/10.3390/engproc2026122009

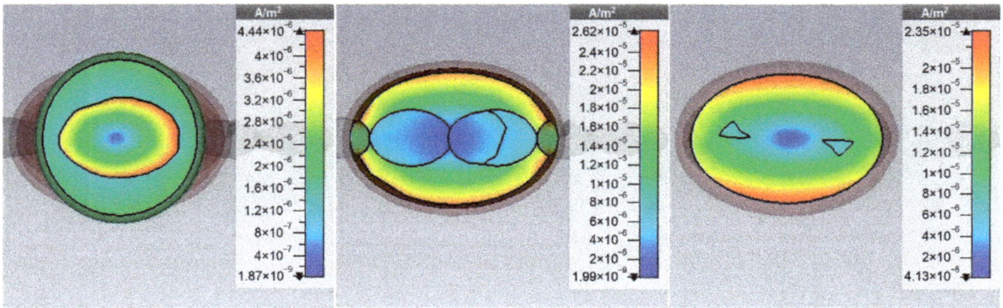

(a) (b) (c)

Figure 6. Computed magnitudes of the total current densities $\vec{J}_{B,tot}$ on cross-sections perpendicular to the body, at heights: (**a**) 1.68 m, (**b**) 1.37 m, and (**c**) 1.18 m.

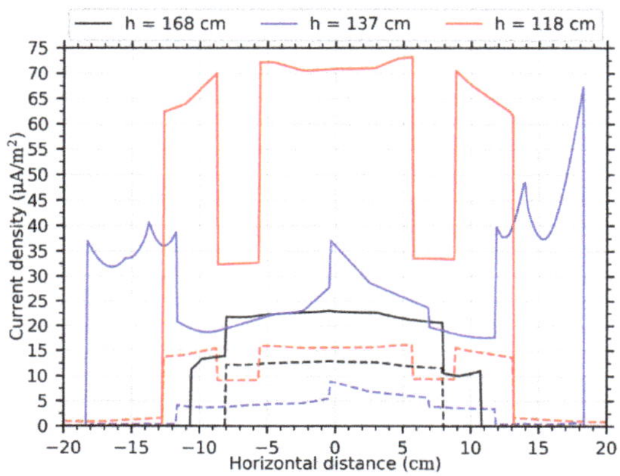

Figure 7. Computed magnitudes of the conduction current densities $\vec{J}_{E,C}$ (solid lines) and the displacement current densities $\vec{J}_{E,D}$ (dashed lines) at different heights in the body, originating from the electric field sources. The abrupt changes in values occur at tissue boundaries.

The magnitudes of the conduction current density $\vec{J}_{B,C}$, and displacement current density $\vec{J}_{B,D}$, originating from the magnetic field sources, are shown in Figure 8. The highest values of $\vec{J}_{B,C}$ again appear around the kidney area because of the specific conductivity. However, the highest values appear at the periphery of the body, where the electric field is highest. As a result, the currents that are induced inside the heart and parts of the brain exhibit lower magnitudes than those in other organs. The displacement currents $\vec{J}_{B,D}$ are lower in value, but still comparable to the conduction currents $\vec{J}_{B,C}$, notably to those in the brain.

The endogenous current density of the brain is estimated at a minimal value of 1 mA/m^2 [15]. The current densities presented in Figures 7 and 8 are more than 40 times lower than the endogenous current. Compared to the restrictions established by ICNIRP for general public exposure, the computed currents are more than 25 times lower around the analysed organs, and more than 55 times lower within the organs.

While the presented results point to magnitudes lower than the ICNIRP established restrictions, certain factors are not taken into account in the modelled system, such as the following: complex tissue layering, soil inhomogeneity, atmospheric conditions, or transient field components. A grounded human body has a further impact on the field

https://doi.org/10.3390/engproc2026122009

distribution compared to the modelled ungrounded body. A complete analysis requires evaluating the impact of these factors, combined with the discretisation of the system.

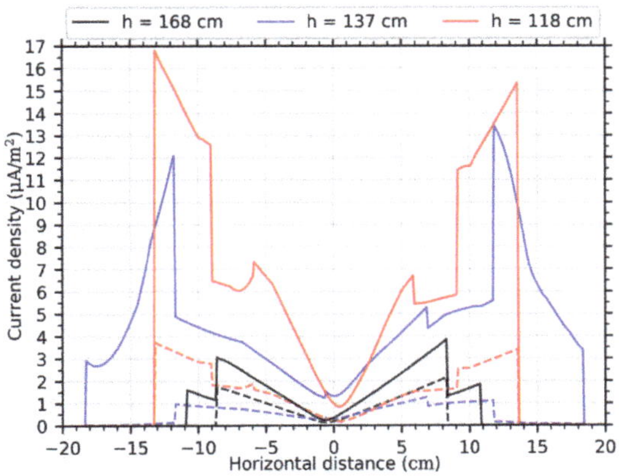

Figure 8. Computed magnitudes of the conduction current densities $\vec{J}_{B,C}$ (solid lines) and the displacement current densities $\vec{J}_{B,D}$ (dashed lines) at different heights in the body, originating from the magnetic field sources. The abrupt changes in values occur at tissue boundaries.

4. Conclusions

In this paper, a numerical simulation was conducted to compute the internal electric field, the conduction, and the displacement current densities in key human organs—specifically the brain, lungs, heart, and kidneys—using a three-dimensional multipart ellipsoidal model composed of multiple ellipsoids representing distinct anatomical regions. The internal electric field originates from a 110 kV single-circuit OTL with typical conductor geometry, each phase conductor carrying 800 A.

The internal electric field distribution, originating from the electric field sources, reflects the geometry of the body and tissue properties. The resulting current densities exhibit the highest magnitudes around the neck and kidney area. The induced electric field distribution, originating from the magnetic field sources, is more peripherally distributed. This leads to a more peripheral distribution of the resulting current densities, with their maxima appearing outside of the analysed organs. While the displacement current densities are lower in magnitude compared to the conduction current densities, they have a non-negligible impact.

According to the World Health Organization, elevated values of these currents may pose potential health risks. In this case, notably, the computed current densities are at least an order of magnitude below ICNIRP's basic restrictions on induced current density in body tissues at ELF, specifically 10 mA/m^2 for occupational exposure and 2 mA/m^2 for general public exposure. This considerable safety margin confirms that, under the considered conditions, exposure to EMF from the OTL does not constitute a significant risk. However, considering the variations in positions of the human body relative to the OTL, and the occurrence of the EMF maxima at ground level, the internal electric field may exhibit a different distribution. Therefore, there is a possibility that the current density magnitudes and the related potential health risk will increase in regions that already exhibit high values, such as the neck area. Future work would include current density analysis under various human body positions, OTL conductor configurations, and applied voltages.

 https://doi.org/10.3390/engproc2026122009

Author Contributions: Conceptualisation, B.G. and A.K.; methodology, C.B., E.T., B.G. and A.K.; software, C.B. and E.T.; validation, C.B., E.T. and B.G.; writing—original draft preparation, C.B. and E.T.; writing—review and editing, B.G. and A.K.; visualisation, C.B., E.T. and B.G.; supervision, B.G.; project administration, A.K.; funding acquisition, A.K. All authors have read and agreed to the published version of the manuscript.

Funding: This research has been supported by the EMP-INT project financed by the Faculty of Electrical Engineering and Information Technologies, "Ss. Cyril and Methodius" University in Skopje, North Macedonia.

Institutional Review Board Statement: Not applicable.

Informed Consent Statement: Not applicable.

Data Availability Statement: The data presented in this study are available from the corresponding author upon request.

Conflicts of Interest: The authors declare no conflicts of interest.

Abbreviations

The following abbreviations are used in this manuscript:

ELF	Extremely low frequency
EM	Electromagnetic
EMF	Electromagnetic field
GW	Ground wire
INCIRP	International Commission on Non-Ionizing Radiation Protection
OTL	Overhead transmission line
PEC	Perfect Electric Conductor

References

1. International Commission on Non-Ionizing Radiation Protection. Use of the ICNIRP EMF Guidelines. 1999. Available online: https://www.icnirp.org/cms/upload/publications/ICNIRPUseEMFgdl.pdf (accessed on 14 September 2025).
2. Sekiba, Y.; Kodera, S.; Yamazaki, K.; Hirata, A. Calculation of Electric Field Induced in the Human Body for Simultaneous Exposure to Spatially Uniform ELF Electric and Magnetic Fields With a Phase Difference. *IEEE Access* **2023**, *11*, 95455–95466. [CrossRef]
3. Glushica, B.; Markovski, B.; Kuhar, A.; Arnautovski Toseva, V. Assessment of human exposure to electric and magnetic fields near transmission lines using FEMM. *J. Energy Technol.* **2023**, *16*, 41–50. [CrossRef]
4. Peratta, A.; Gonzalez, M.; Poljak, D. Current Density Induced in the Human Body due to Power Distributions Lines using the Boundary Element Method. *J. Commun. Softw. Syst.* **2007**, *3*, 11–16. [CrossRef]
5. Bidi, M. Biological Risk Assessment of High-Voltage Transmission Lines on Worker's Health of Electric Society. *Arch. Electr. Eng.* **2020**, *69*, 57–68. [CrossRef]
6. El-Makkawy, S.M. Numerical determination of electric field induced currents on human body standing under a high voltage transmission line. In Proceedings of the Conference on Electrical Insulation and Dielectric Phenomena, Vancouver, BC, Canada, 14–17 October 2007; pp. 802–806. [CrossRef]
7. Barchanski, A.; Clemens, M.; De Gersem, H.; Weiland, T. Efficient calculation of current densities in the human body induced by arbitrarily shaped, low-frequency magnetic field sources. *J. Comput. Phys.* **2006**, *214*, 81–95. [CrossRef]
8. Li, Y.; Hand, J.W.; Wills, T.; Hajnal, J.V. Numerically-simulated induced electric field and current density within a human model located close to a z-gradient coil. *J. Magn. Reson. Imaging* **2007**, *26*, 1286–1295. [CrossRef] [PubMed]
9. Scorretti, R.; Burais, N.; Fabregue, O.; Nicolas, A.; Nicolas, L. Computation of the induced current density into the human body due to relative LF magnetic field generated by realistic devices. *IEEE Trans. Magn.* **2004**, *40*, 643–646. [CrossRef]
10. *Dassault Systèmes, CST Studio Suite*, Version 2018; Dassault Systèmes: Darmstadt, Germany, 2018.
11. Barchanski, A.; De Gersem, H.; Gjonaj, E.; Weiland, T. Impact of the displacement current on low-frequency electromagnetic fields computed using high-resolution anatomy models. *Phys. Med. Biol.* **2005**, *50*, N243–N249. [CrossRef]
12. De Santis, V.; Douglas, M.; Kuster, N.; Chen, X.L. Impact of the skin conductivity and displacement currents on LF numerical dosimetry. In Proceedings of the International Symposium on Electromagnetic Compatibility—EMC EUROPE, Rome, Italy, 17–21 September 2012. [CrossRef]

 https://doi.org/10.3390/engproc2026122009

13. Griffiths, D.J. *Introduction to Electrodynamics*, 4th ed.; Pearson Education, Inc.: Hoboken, NJ, USA, 2013; pp. 312–342.
14. Gabriel, C. *Compilation of the Dielectric Properties of Body Tissues at RF and Microwave Frequencies*; Report N.AL/OE-TR-1996-0037; Occupational and environmental health directorate, Radiofrequency Radiation Division: Brooks Air Force Base, TX, USA, 1996. Available online: https://apps.dtic.mil/sti/citations/ADA309764 (accessed on 14 September 2025).
15. Nathan, S.S.; Sinha, S.R.; Gordon, B.; Lesser, R.P.; Thakor, N.V. Determination of current density distributions generated by electrical stimulation of the human cerebral cortex. *Electroencephalogr. Clin. Neurophysiol.* **1993**, *86*, 183–192. [CrossRef] [PubMed]

https://doi.org/10.3390/engproc2026122009

engineering proceedings

MDPI

Proceeding Paper

Artificial Neural Network Model for Predicting the Characteristics of a Solar Vacuum Tube System for Domestic Hot Water Heating †

Mariyana Sestrimska [1], Nikolay Komitov [1] and Margarita Terziyska [2,*]

[1] Department of Electrical Engineering, Electronics and Automation, University of Food Technologies, 4002 Plovdiv, Bulgaria; m_sestrimska@uft-plovdiv.bg (M.S.); nkomitov@uft-plovdiv.bg (N.K.)

[2] Department of Mathematics, Physics and Information Technologies, University of Food Technologies, 4002 Plovdiv, Bulgaria

* Correspondence: mterziyska@uft-plovdiv.bg

† Presented at the 6th International Conference on Communications, Information, Electronic and Energy Systems, 26–28 November 2025, Ruse, Bulgaria.

Abstract

The use of different energy sources for heating and year-round domestic water heating is driven by the European Union's increasingly strict environmental and climate requirements. For this reason, consumers are seeking alternatives and show growing interest in implementing installations that utilize solar energy. Modern households typically employ at least two different energy sources for this purpose. In practice, these are hybrid installations that, depending on the season, can operate with one, two, or more energy sources. The system examined in this paper is of this type, comprising a pellet boiler, solar vacuum tubes, and electric heaters. Managing such a system is complex, and based on the conducted studies, process optimization can be pursued. This report presents an artificial neural network (ANN) model developed to predict the behavior of a real solar installation for domestic hot water heating during the summer season. This study aims, through the obtained model, to forecast the system's performance during transitional periods such as autumn and spring, thereby enabling more efficient control.

Keywords: artificial neural network; predictive model; solar vacuum tubes; hot water

1. Introduction

The growing requirements of the European Union regarding the use of conventional heating methods, along with the promotion of new technologies, have led to a boom in the commissioning of systems employing diverse energy sources. This study is directly related to the current energy policies of the European Union, which aim to accelerate the deployment of renewable energy sources and improve overall energy efficiency. The European Green Deal and the 'Fit for 55' package set the ambitious target of achieving climate neutrality by 2050 and reducing greenhouse gas emissions by at least 55% by 2030. In this context, the use of solar systems for domestic hot water, combined with intelligent control methods based on artificial neural networks, represents a practical contribution to the implementation of the Energy Efficiency Directive (Directive (EU) 2023/1791) and the Renewable Energy Directive (RED III, Directive (EU) 2023/2413). On one side are boilers using biofuels, natural gas, or heat pumps that rely on various media as heat-transfer agents. These systems may produce some combustion by-products, albeit minimal, and they require periodic maintenance, while the initial investment is significant. Regardless of the energy source, electrical power is always used to control the overall system. On the other side are systems utilizing free solar energy, where the investment costs are lower, maintenance is cheaper, and they can operate year-round in practice.

Most heating and domestic hot water systems do not rely on a single energy source. By their nature, these systems are hybrid, allowing the use of multiple energy sources, which provides flexibility in operation. Various methods are applied to achieve higher system efficiency. The heating season is particularly important, with the greatest challenge occurring in the spring and autumn transitional periods, where process optimization can be realized. Data collected from a real system helps to develop accurate models capable of predicting system behavior in specific situations.

One effective approach for building predictive models is using an artificial neural network (ANN). This method can reveal trends in the variation of a given parameter quite well, but it requires a large amount of data. Many studies employ artificial neural networks to develop models for different purposes.

In [1], an ANN model adapted for a small 8 kW CO_2 heat pump. A detailed understanding of the heat pump's behavior under varying input conditions provided users with information necessary for effective management and the construction of a stable energy system.

A comprehensive review of ANN applications and machine-learning methods for modeling various manufacturing processes and optimizing their parameters was presented in [2]. The study provides a broad perspective on research aimed at improving production efficiency through the combined use of different computational tools and artificial neural networks.

In [3], an ANN was used to predict various temperature loads in a domestic hot water system.

Continuous learning in forecasting domestic hot water consumption has been examined in [4], where established continuous-learning methods were compared on both real and synthetic consumption data. The results demonstrated that continuous learning improves forecasting performance.

A brief overview in [5] discusses the current state of applying artificial neural networks to complex thermal problems that cannot easily be solved with traditional approaches.

In [6], an experimental investigation of heat transfer in a tube immersed in a gas–solid fluidized bed using an ANN. The performance results show that ANNs can be successfully applied in many heat-transfer applications.

Machine learning techniques using custom MATLAB code are proposed in [7] for analyzing energy-consumption data from two different buildings in Spain. The predictive performance of artificial neural networks and Random Forests (RFs) is compared to evaluate their suitability for forecasting energy demand based on the unique characteristics of each algorithm.

A method for the automatic selection of boundary-condition parameters, enabling preliminary evaluation during different operations, was introduced in [8]. The same study presented an ANN model designed to predict heat-source parameters during welding. During the training process, an analysis was performed to examine how the network topology and the number of training vectors influence the root mean square error (RMSE). The authors also compared the ANN implementation with conventional optimization approaches, emphasizing the advantages of systems that incorporate artificial intelligence.

The approach proposed in [9], based on artificial intelligence, evaluates and synthesizes models for predictive analysis using Markov chains. Regression models were created using generalized regression neural networks (GRNNs) and cascaded-forward neural

https://doi.org/10.3390/engproc2026122010

networks (CFNNs). The study achieved satisfactorily low total RMSE levels, emphasizing the strong predictive capability of the developed models.

An ANN model for convective heat transfer at a stagnation point in a non-Newtonian fluid flow over flat and cylindrical surfaces was developed in [10]. The model was constructed as a multilayer perceptron network with both feedforward and feedback connections, using various input parameters. During the training phase, 80% of the dataset was applied for model learning, while the remaining 20% was reserved for testing and validation.

The conducted research shows that an ANN can accurately predict changes in a desired variable based on previously obtained data. In the present study, an ANN is used to develop a model for optimizing the control of a system composed of different energy sources. The model will help improve the energy efficiency of the system during the spring and autumn transitional periods.

2. Materials and Methods

2.1. Solar System Description

The heating and domestic hot water system is installed in a three-story building in Plovdiv, Bulgaria. It consists of a pellet boiler, radiators, a water storage tank, end users (consumers), and a vacuum solar panel(KIT Engineering, Plovdiv, Bulgaria). The heated floor area of the building is 510 m^2, and the heated volume is 1280 m^3. The system operates in two modes—winter and summer—where the solar panel is connected year-round, while the boiler is used only during the winter season. A block diagram of the system is shown in Figure 1. Water circulation is provided by pumps P1 and P2. The biofuel boiler has a capacity of 15 kW. The storage tank has a volume of 300 L and contains two coils forming two independent water-circulation loops. Because the solar panel is integrated year-round, it is possible under certain conditions during the spring and autumn transitional periods for both the boiler and the solar panel to operate simultaneously.

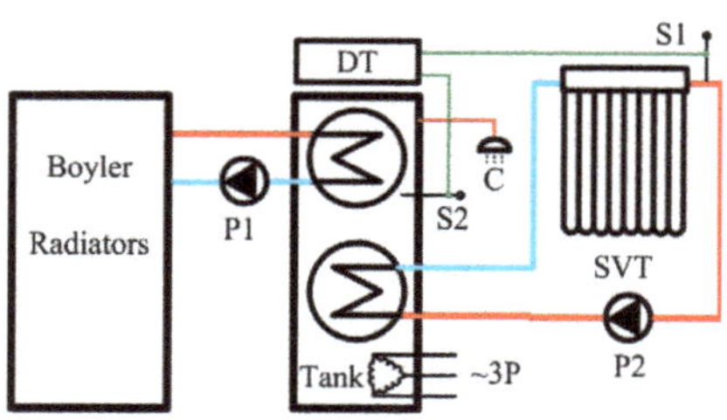

Figure 1. Heating system diagram.

The report focuses on the summer operating stage. The solar panel consists of a collector and 30 vacuum tubes connected to it, with a total surface area of 2.5 m^2. The panel is installed on top of a garage and is not continuously exposed to sunlight, as it is shaded by a neighboring building in the morning. Full sun exposure begins after 10:20 a.m. The distance from the panel to the storage tank is approximately 7 m.

The operation of pump P2 is controlled by a differential thermostat, which receives data from two sensors—S1 located at the collector outlet and S2 positioned in the middle of the storage tank. The thermostat switches on under specific conditions: the temperature in the collector must be higher than 40 °C plus a temperature difference ΔT. This ΔT is the temperature difference between the storage tank and the solar panel, set by the user within the range of 4–20 °C.

If the water temperature in the storage tank is not sufficient for end users, it is heated by electric heaters with a total power of 9 kW supplied from the three-phase network.

https://doi.org/10.3390/engproc2026122010

Measurements were recorded over a 10-day period at the end of August and the beginning of September 2025. The temperature sensors recorded data at regular intervals of one minute (Δt = 1 min) throughout the entire measurement campaign, providing a time-synchronized dataset for both collectors (S1 and S2).

2.2. *Artificial Neural Network*

The data are based on artificial neural network models whose primary goal is to emulate the functional and structural characteristics of the biological nervous system. This approach is increasingly applied for modeling, simulation, optimization, and prediction of the behavior of various technological objects or processes. An artificial neural network essentially represents a multilayer structure composed of neurons that possess a set of properties adapting to the information-processing workflow.

This flexible architecture offers several advantages, such as the ability to learn and self-organize, the capacity for prediction, and the capability to find optimal solutions for specific tasks. Figure 2 presents a basic structure of an artificial neural network.

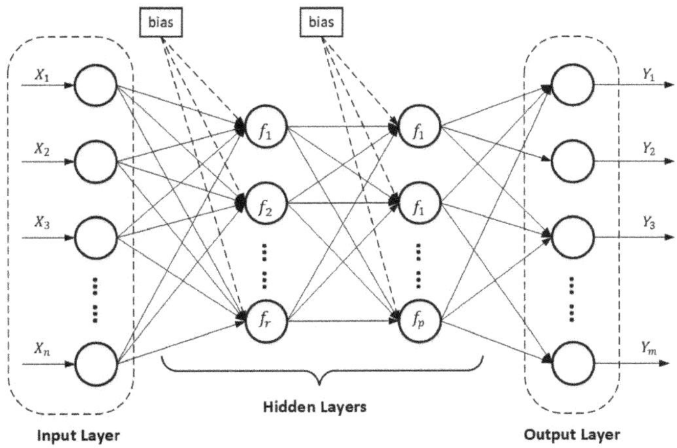

Figure 2. Schematic diagram of a multilayer artificial neural network.

The tasks that can be solved using artificial neural networks are diverse in nature, most commonly serving as data-archiving structures, simulators, approximators, or classifiers.

The artificial neural network model consists of layers of neurons whose purpose is to transform the input variables into output variables with the highest possible accuracy. Each output from one layer is connected to every neuron in the next layer through weight coefficients. The input/output variables may be represented as binary combinations (from 0 to 1) or as experimental values in either real or normalized form.

The data entering the network are transformed by a discriminant function of the following form:

$$X = \sum_{i=1}^{n} w_{ij} \cdot x_i + b_j, \quad (j = 1,\ 2,\ \ldots, n), \tag{1}$$

where w_{ij} is the weight vector representing the connection between the individual layers of the network, b_j is the bias for the neuron, and n is the number of input data points.

In the hidden layers of the artificial neural network, the discriminant function (1) is transformed through a transfer (activation) function.

In this study, the hidden layers use the hyperbolic tangent (tansig) and the logistic sigmoid (logsig) activation functions, respectively, which are standard in MATLAB's Neural Network Toolbox for nonlinear regression using the Levenberg–Marquardt training

 https://doi.org/10.3390/engproc2026122010

algorithm. These functions provide smooth nonlinear mappings and stable gradients, ensuring reliable convergence during training.

The mathematical expressions of these two activation functions, commonly used in artificial neural network models [11], are as follows:

- Sigmoid transfer function:

$$f(X) = \frac{1}{1+e^{-\lambda x}}, \quad 0 \leq f(X) \leq 1 \tag{2}$$

where λ is a parameter that determines the slope of the transfer function.

- Hyperbolic tansig transfer function:

$$f(X) = \frac{1-e^{-\lambda x}}{1+e^{-\lambda x}} \quad -1 \leq f(X) \leq 1 \tag{3}$$

This artificial neural network model forms the basis for developing structures such as multi-layer perceptrons (MLP), adaptive neuro-fuzzy inference systems (ANFIS), self-organizing neural networks (SOM), and others.

When synthesizing a predictive model, it is necessary to introduce criteria for evaluating its performance. The most commonly used accuracy metrics include [12]:

- Mean square error (MSE):

$$MSE = \frac{1}{n} \cdot \sum_{i=1}^{n} (X_i - X_{i,\ mod})^2 \tag{4}$$

where the following definitions are used:

X_i—experimental input values;
$X_{i,\ mod}$—values predicted by the artificial neural network (model);
n—number of input values.

- Root mean square error (RMSE):

$$RMSE = \sqrt{\frac{\sum_{i=1}^{n} (X_i - X_{imod})^2}{n}} \tag{5}$$

- Coefficient of determination:

$$R^2 = 1 - \frac{\sum_{i=1}^{n} (X_i - X_{i,\ mod})^2}{\sum_{i=1}^{n} X_{i,\ mod}^2} \tag{6}$$

The coefficient of determination is the squared form of the correlation coefficient and explains the dispersion of the predicted values relative to the experimental data.

3. Results and Discussion

To predict the performance of solar collectors or other types of systems using artificial neural network (ANN) methods, a large set of experimental data is required. For the purposes of the present study, the temperatures of the tank, as well as at the inlet and outlet of the solar collector, were measured over a period of 10 days.

Figure 3 shows the temperature curves of the storage tank and the inlet and outlet of the collector. During the ten-day measurement period, a total of 13,622 temperature samples were collected at a fixed sampling interval of one minute, covering the storage tank and both inlet and outlet points of the solar collector.

The collected data were implemented as input training vectors for the artificial neural network model. Figure 4 presents the selected network architecture in the MATLAB R2024b software environment (MathWorks, Natick, MA, USA).

https://doi.org/10.3390/engproc2026122010

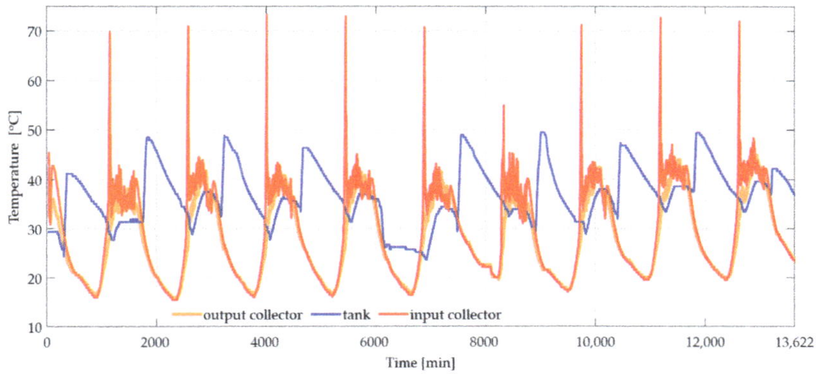

Figure 3. The temperature curves of the storage tank and the inlet and outlet of the collector.

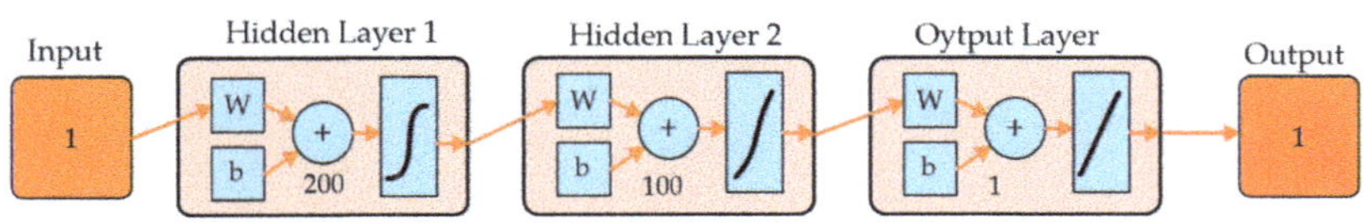

Figure 4. Artificial neural network topology.

The implemented artificial neural network model consists of one input layer with several neurons corresponding to the length of the input experimental vectors, two hidden layers, and one output layer.

The number of neurons in the hidden layers was determined experimentally to enable training to be performed in a relatively short time while achieving satisfactory accuracy.

During the simulations, it was found that increasing the number of neurons in the hidden layers led to a slowdown in the network's performance.

The neural network was trained using the Levenberg–Marquardt (trainlm) algorithm. This algorithm offers a relatively high network training speed and is well-suited for solving nonlinear problems.

The activation functions used in the two hidden layers are the hyperbolic tangent (tansig) and the logarithmic sigmoid (logsig) functions, respectively.

Figures 5–7 present simulations of the artificial neural network output for the temperature at the tank, as well as the inlet and outlet temperatures of the solar collector, compared to the measured data.

To avoid the risk of overfitting, the input data were divided into three sets (using the *divider and* function). Seventy percent of the experimental data points were used for training, 15% for validation—so that the network would stop before overfitting occurred—and 15% for independent testing.

In the MATLAB environment, these parameters can be adjusted according to the operator's (user's) preference.

As the graphs show, the neural network predicts the discussed variables with relatively high accuracy. The training time is also short, specifically in the order of a few minutes.

To evaluate the model's performance, Table 1 provides data on the root mean square error (RMSE) and the coefficient of determination (R^2) of the network output.

The low RMSE values, together with R^2 values close to one, demonstrate the strong predictive capability of the synthesized artificial neural network in this case.

https://doi.org/10.3390/engproc2026122010

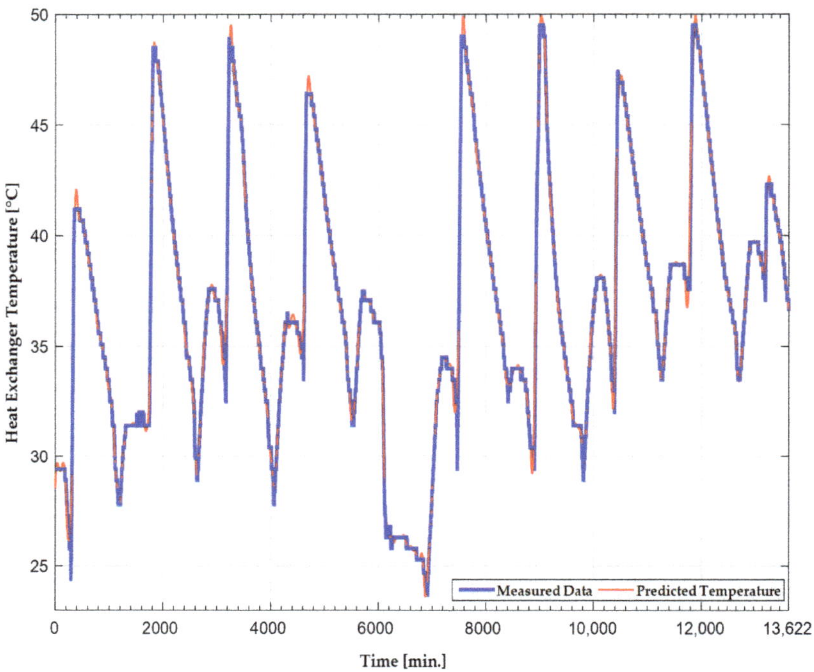

Figure 5. Predicted and measured values of the storage tank.

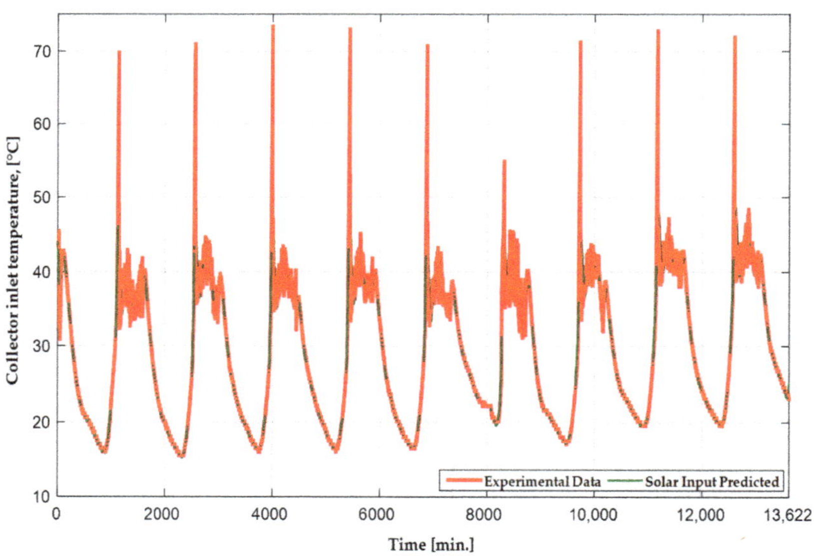

Figure 6. Predicted and measured values at the collector inlet.

https://doi.org/10.3390/engproc2026122010

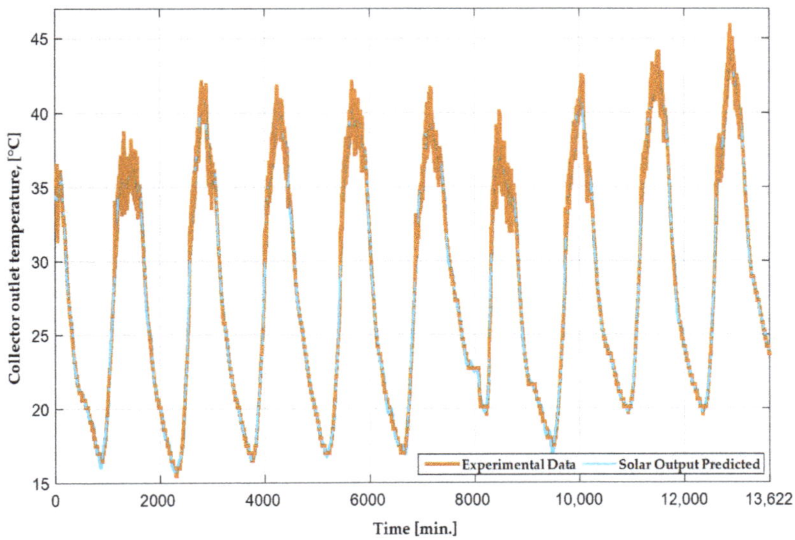

Figure 7. Predicted and measured values of the collector outlet.

Table 1. Artificial neural network parameters.

Network Parameters	Heat Exchanger	Solar Collector Inlet	Solar Collector Output
Number of neurons in hidden layer 1	200	200	200
Number of neurons in hidden layer 2	100	100	100
Number of epochs	10,000	20,000	5000
Training time, [min.]	8.5	17.5	4.45
Learning Rate	2.7×10^{-4}	6.9×10^{-5}	5.4×10^{-4}
Gradient	14.26	3.16	0.47
RMSE	0.473	2.31	0.630
R^2	0.9998	0.9995	0.9944

4. Conclusions

This publication presents an approach for modeling artificial neural networks (ANNs) to predict the performance of a solar system with vacuum tubes. The controlled system was analyzed during the summer season over a 10-day period, when the highest amount of solar energy is observed in this geographical region. The authors do not exclude the possibility of extending the study over a longer period to achieve greater reliability of the results.

Based on the collected experimental data, an artificial neural network model was implemented using the Levenberg–Marquardt training algorithm. Through simulations in the MATLAB environment, a suitable network architecture was selected to minimize the mean square error at the output of the ANN model.

The favorable results indicate that the proposed application of artificial neural networks is a promising approach for the development of intelligent automated heating systems for both residential and industrial purposes.

Future research will focus on extending the observation period to the transitional seasons—spring and autumn—to increase the reliability and generalizability of the developed models. Additional efforts will be directed toward comparing different machine learning algorithms, including Random Forest, XGBoost, and deep neural networks, to evaluate their predictive accuracy relative to ANN. Furthermore, the integration of adap-

 https://doi.org/10.3390/engproc2026122010

tive strategies for intelligent control of hybrid energy systems is planned, which is expected to contribute to higher energy efficiency and sustainability in both residential and industrial applications.

These results also align with the current European Union energy policies, including the European Green Deal, the 'Fit for 55' package, the Energy Efficiency Directive (Directive (EU) 2023/1791), and the Renewable Energy Directive (RED III, Directive (EU) 2023/2413). The developed ANN-based approach can therefore be regarded not only as a contribution to intelligent energy management but also as practical support for achieving the EU's long-term goals of climate neutrality, improved energy efficiency, and accelerated deployment of renewable energy technologies.

Author Contributions: Conceptualization, N.K., M.S. and M.T.; Methodology, N.K. and M.S.; software, M.S.; validation, M.S.; formal analysis, N.K. and M.T.; investigation, N.K.; resources, N.K.; writing—original draft preparation, M.T.; writing—review and editing, M.T.; supervision, M.T.; project administration, M.T. All authors have read and agreed to the published version of the manuscript.

Funding: This research was supported by project "Robotic System with Artificial Intelligence Elements for the Management of Technological Objects and Processes in the Food Industry," Contract No. 09/25-N, dated 23 July 2025.

Institutional Review Board Statement: Not applicable.

Informed Consent Statement: Not applicable.

Data Availability Statement: The data supporting the findings of this study are available from the authors upon reasonable request.

Conflicts of Interest: The authors declare no conflict of interest.

References

1. Fadnes, F.S.; Banihabib, R.; Assadi, M. Artificial neural network model for predicting CO_2 heat pump behaviour in domestic hot water and space heating systems. *IOP Conf. Ser. Mater. Sci. Eng.* **2023**, *1294*, 012054. [CrossRef]
2. Rathi, N.K.; Rathi, N. An application of ANN for modeling and optimisation of process parameters of manufacturing process: A review. *Int. J. Eng. Appl. Sci. Technol.* **2020**, *4*, 127–134. [CrossRef]
3. Barteczko-Hibbert, C.; Gillott, M.; Kendall, G. An artificial neural network for predicting domestic hot water characteristics. *Int. J. Low-Carbon Technol.* **2009**, *4*, 112–119. [CrossRef]
4. Bayle, R.; Reyboz, M.; Lomet, A.; Cook, V.; Mermillod, M. Continuously Learning Prediction Models for Smart Domestic Hot Water Management. *Energies* **2024**, *17*, 4734. [CrossRef]
5. Yang, K.T. Artificial Neural Networks (ANNs): A New Paradigm for Thermal Science and Engineering. *J. Heat Transf.* **2008**, *130*, 093001. [CrossRef]
6. Kamble, L.V.; Pangavhane, D.R.; Singh, T.P. Heat Transfer Studies using Artificial Neural Network—A Review. *IEJ* **2014**, *14*, 25–42.
7. Salem, K.M.; Rey-Hernández, J.M.; Elgharib, A.O.; Rey-Martínez, F.J. Optimizing Energy Forecasting Using ANN and RF Models for HVAC and Heating Predictions. *Appl. Sci.* **2025**, *15*, 6806. [CrossRef]
8. Wróbel, J.; Kulawik, A. Calculations of the heat source parameters on the basis of temperature fields with the use of ANN. *Neural Comput. Appl.* **2019**, *31*, 7583–7593. [CrossRef]
9. Balabanova, I.; Georgiev, G. Traffic Load Prediction in Markov Chains using Artificial Intelligence Techniques. In Proceedings of the International Conference on Communications, Information, Electronic and Energy Systems (CIEES), Veliko Tarnovo, Bulgaria, 24–26 November 2022; pp. 1–6. [CrossRef]
10. Rehman, K.U.; Çolak, A.B.; Shatanawi, W. Artificial Neural Networking (ANN) Model for Convective Heat Transfer in Thermally Magnetized Multiple Flow Regimes with Temperature Stratification Effects. *Mathematics* **2022**, *10*, 2394. [CrossRef]

https://doi.org/10.3390/engproc2026122010

11. Nasr, M.S.; Moustafa, M.E.; Seif, H.E.; El Kobrosy, G. Application of Artificial Neural Network (ANN) for the prediction of EL-AGAMY waste water treatment plant performance-EGYPT. *Alex. Eng. J.* **2012**, *51*, 37–43. [CrossRef]
12. Ghritlahre, H.K.; Prasad, R.K. Application of ANN technique to predict the performance of solar collector systems—A review. *Renew. Sustain. Energy Rev.* **2018**, *84*, 75–88. [CrossRef]

 https://doi.org/10.3390/engproc2026122010

engineering proceedings

MDPI

Proceeding Paper

Study of the Effect of Higher-Order Harmonics on the Frequency Response Analysis of Series Resonant Converter †

Dimitar Spirov [1], Angel Lichev [2], Vasil Mihov [1,*], Yasen Madankov [1] and Hristo Vargov [1]

1 Department of Electrical, Electronics and Automation, University of Food Technologies, 4002 Plovdiv, Bulgaria; d_spirov@uft-plovdiv.bg (D.S.); y_madankov@uft-plovdiv.bg (Y.M.); h.vargov@gmail.com (H.V.)
2 Department of Electronics, Technical University of Sofia—Branch Plovdiv, 4000 Plovdiv, Bulgaria; alichev@tu-plovdiv.bg
* Correspondence: v_mihov@uft-plovdiv.bg
† Presented at the 6th International Conference on Communications, Information, Electronic and Energy Systems, 26–28 November 2025, Ruse, Bulgaria.

Abstract

This paper presents an investigation of the influence of higher-order harmonics on the frequency-response characteristics of a full-bridge series-resonant DC-DC converter. A Fourier series-based analytical method is developed to include these harmonics, providing a more accurate representation of voltage and current waveforms within the resonant tank, as well as in the converter input and output. The frequency characteristics, total harmonic distortion (THD) and ripple factors of the converter are derived for various quality factors and normalized frequencies using GNU Octave for computational modeling. The results reveal that the higher-order harmonics considerably affect the shape and amplitude of the resonant current, especially below the resonant frequency. Experimental validation using a laboratory prototype demonstrates good correlation with the theoretical predictions obtained by the Fourier series analysis, whereas the FHA method shows noticeable deviations. The proposed approach offers improved precision and can serve as a practical tool for the filter design and performance optimization of resonant power converters.

Keywords: Fourier analysis; resonant power converters; first harmonic approximation

1. Introduction

The First Harmonic Approximation (FHA) is a well-known and widely used approach for analyzing resonant converters. This method considers only the fundamental (first) harmonic of periodic signals [1,2]. This approach significantly simplifies the mathematical analysis and facilitates the study of converter behavior under various operating conditions. One of the main drawbacks of this method is the neglect of the higher-order harmonics effect, which could be significant in applications where the signals are not purely sinusoidal [3].

Studies considering the influence of higher-order harmonics can be found in the literature. For instance, in [4], a multi-harmonic analysis is employed to develop an AC small-signal equivalent circuit for dynamic control design. However, that work does not focus on the representation of THD, RMS current, ripple factor, or harmonic spectra.

This article examines a full-bridge series-resonant converter. In addition to providing high efficiency and enabling soft switching capability, an advantage of this topology is its inherent protection against short circuits. This behavior results from the converter's

https://doi.org/10.3390/engproc2026122011

inductance, which prevents a sudden rise in the current even when the output is shorted. In this way, a built-in current limiter is provided, protecting the switching elements and transformer from overload and potential damage [5–7].

The objective of this study is to emphasize the importance of expanded harmonic analysis in modeling series resonant converters and to demonstrate that highly accurate results could be achieved through simple computations, surpassing the accuracy of classical simplified models.

2. Fourier Series Analysis of the Series Resonant Converter

A circuit of a full-bridge voltage-switching series resonant converter is depicted in Figure 1. It consists of an inverter with four controllable switches, a series-resonant tank, a high-frequency rectifier and a load. The harmonic analysis of the circuit assumes operation without input and output filters, which allows the influence of different harmonics to be assessed. After performing the harmonic analysis of the input and output currents and voltages, suitable filters can be selected to attenuate the undesired harmonics that exhibit significant amplitudes.

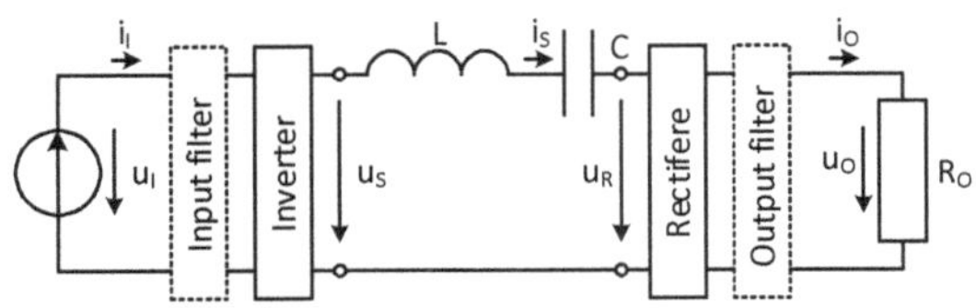

Figure 1. Series resonant DC-DC converter block diagram.

2.1. Resonant Current of Series-Resonant Circuit

The input voltage of the series-resonant circuit is a square wave described in [1]. In the case of the square wave signal, the Fourier series includes the odd harmonics (k), and the input voltage of the resonant tank (u_S) can be expressed with the equations shown in [1]. The Fourier series has a fundamental frequency ω_f. The phasor voltage for the n-th consecutive element is expressed by (1). We restrict the analysis to odd-order harmonics by replacing the harmonic index k with $k = 2n - 1$. This keeps the series indexed by successive integers in the calculating procedure.

The analysis of the converter of Figure 1 is based on the equivalent circuit with the following assumptions [1]:

- The transistor and diode form a resistive switch whose on-resistance is linear; the parasitic capacitances of the switch are neglected, and with zero switching time.
- The series-resonant tank elements are passive, linear, and time-invariant and do not have parasitic reactive components.

The parameters of the series-resonant circuit are [1]: $\omega_0 = 1/(LC)^{1/2}$—resonant frequency; $Z_0 = (L/C)^{1/2} = \omega_0 L = 1/(\omega_0 C)$—characteristic impedance; $Q_L = Z_0/R$—loaded quality factor; $\nu = \omega_f/\omega_0$—normalized frequency. The impedance of the inductor and capacitor for the n-th consecutive element could be represented as $Z_{L(n)} = j(2n - 1)\nu Z_0$; $Z_{C(n)} = -jZ_0/((2n - 1)\nu)$, and the impedance of the resonant tank in Equation (1):

$$Z_{(n)} = R + Z_{L(n)} + Z_{C(n)} = R + jZ_0 \frac{(2n-1)^2\nu^2 - 1}{(2n-1)\nu} \quad (1)$$

https://doi.org/10.3390/engproc2026122011

The phasor current for the n-th element expressed in Equation (2), and its time domain transformation is presented in Equation (3).

$$\dot{U}_{Sm(n)} = \frac{4U_I}{(2n-1)\pi};\ \dot{I}_{Sm(n)} = \dot{U}_{Sm(n)} e^{j\psi_{I_S(n)}} \tag{2}$$

$$i_S(t) = \sum_{n=1}^{\infty} I_{Sm(n)} \sin\left[(2n-1)\omega_f t + \psi_{I_S(n)}\right] \tag{3}$$

Figure 2 presents waveforms of u_S, i_S and $i_{S(1)}$ in relative units, using the base values $U_b = U_{Sm(1)}$; $I_b = I_{sm(1)}$. The total RMS current can be determined by the RMS current at each component in the Fourier series, as expressed in [2].

$$I_S = \sqrt{\sum_{n=1}^{\infty} I_{S(n)}^2} = \sqrt{\sum_{n=1}^{\infty} \left(\frac{I_{Sm(n)}}{\sqrt{2}}\right)^2}, \tag{4}$$

where $I_{Sm(n)} = U_{Sm(n)}/z_{(n)}$.

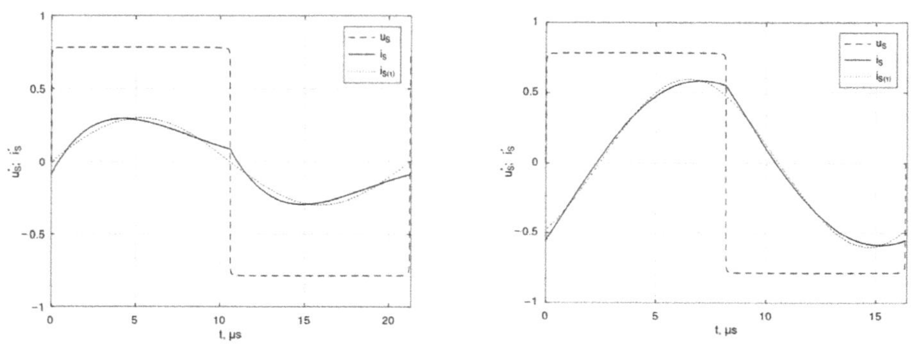

Figure 2. Resonant voltage and current waveforms for: (**a**) Q_L = 0.8 and ν = 0.7; (**b**) Q_L = 2.5 and ν = 1.3.

The resonant tank input impedance for the n-th consecutive element is given by the following:

$$z_{(n)} = \sqrt{R^2 + Z_0^2\left[\frac{(2n-1)^2\nu^2 - 1}{(2n-1)\nu}\right]^2} \tag{5}$$

Using the proposed analysis the normalized frequency characteristics of the total re-sonant current for different values of Q_L are presented in Figure 3.

Calculation of THD for the resonant current is made using the proposed analysis. The results for different values of Q_L and ν are presented in Table 1. Based on the results, the higher-order harmonics effect is more significant under resonant frequency (ν < 1). The converter load influences the THD results as well.

https://doi.org/10.3390/engproc2026122011

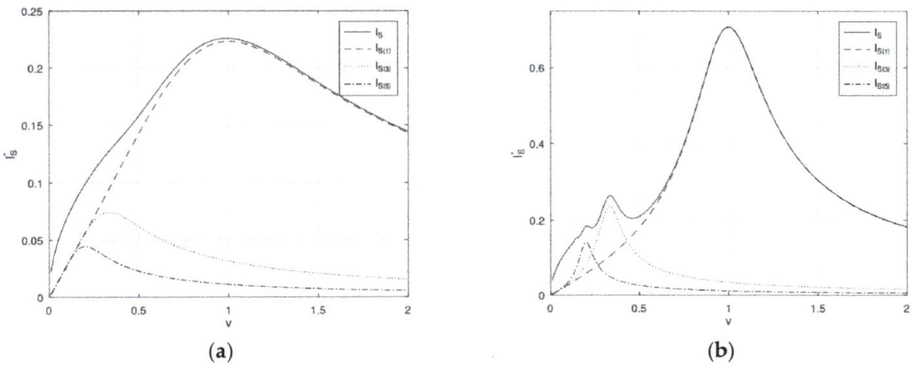

Figure 3. Frequency characteristics of the resonant current and 1st, 3rd and 5th harmonics for: (**a**) $Q_L = 0.8$; (**b**) $Q_L = 2.5$.

Table 1. THD of the resonant current.

$\mathbf{THD_{Is}}$	$\boldsymbol{\nu = 0.7}$	$\boldsymbol{\nu = 1}$	$\boldsymbol{\nu = 1.3}$
$Q_L = 0.8$	26.20%	16.12%	13.34%
$Q_L = 1$	23.35%	12.69%	10.86%
$Q_L = 2.5$	17.62%	5.28%	6.52%

2.2. Input and Output Currents

The input and output currents of the converter could be determined by the resonant current, with the periodic switching of the inverter's switches and rectifier's diodes, respectively, reversing the current polarity [2]. The cycle of these currents is twice the operating frequency [1]: $T_{fI} = T_f/2$; $\omega_{fI} = 2\omega f$.

Fourier series analysis of the resultant waveform is performed, and the following parameters could be obtained for the input, as well as the output current: DC component I, amplitude $I_{m(n)}$ and phase shift $\Psi_{I(n)}$ of the fundamental component and high-order harmonics. The plot between $I_{Im(n)}$ and $I_{Om(n)}$ versus harmonic sequence number n for different values of Q_L and ν are presented in Figure 4.

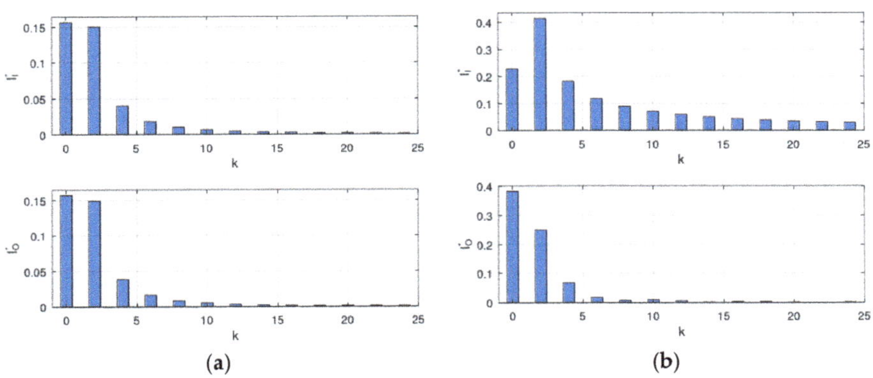

Figure 4. Harmonic spectra of the input and output currents for: (**a**) $Q_L = 0.8$ and $\nu = 0.7$; (**b**) $Q_L = 2.5$ and $\nu = 1.3$.

Based on the harmonic spectra obtained for the desired nominal operating mode of the resonant converter, a decision can be made on whether to employ input and/or output

https://doi.org/10.3390/engproc2026122011

filters. This decision should consider the magnitude of the higher-order harmonics and the specific requirements of the intended application. Appropriate filters can then be selected to attenuate the frequencies of the specific harmonics.

Calculation of the ripple factor (RF) for the input and output currents are made using the proposed analysis. It is defined as the ratio of the RMS value of the AC component to the average DC component. The results for different values of Q_L and ν are presented in Table 2.

Table 2. Ripple Factor of the input and output current.

$RF_{Ii/o}$		$\nu = 0.7$	$\nu = 1$	$\nu = 1.3$
Input current RF	$Q_L = 0.8$	71.10%	45.24%	64.43%
	$Q_L = 1$	88.84%	46.46%	75.64%
	$Q_L = 2.5$	205.52%	48.05%	157.29%
Output current RF	$Q_L = 0.8$	69.99%	40.05%	37.84%
	$Q_L = 1$	70.74%	42.63%	40.55%
	$Q_L = 2.5$	50.72%	47.05%	48.30%

It can be observed that for frequencies away from the resonant, the RF of the input current is significantly higher than that of the output current, especially under near no-load operating conditions. The primary cause of this behavior is the presence of negative input current during part of the period. The Fourier series of the total input and output currents can be obtained by the amplitude and phase shift in each harmonic.

Waveforms of u_I, i_I and $i_{I(1)}$ in relative units as dependency of time are shown in Figure 5a and for u_O, i_O and $i_{O(1)}$ in Figure 5b.

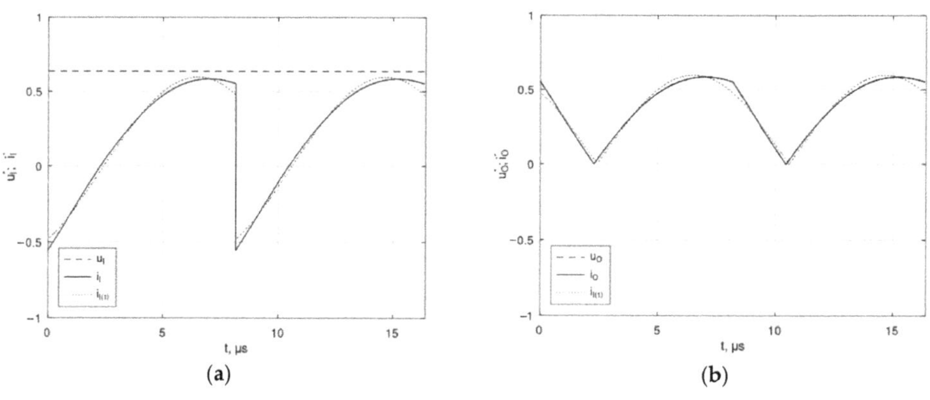

Figure 5. Voltage and current waveforms for $Q_L = 2.5$ and $\nu = 1.3$: (**a**) input; (**b**) output.

3. Experimental Results

Test circuit of a series resonant DC-DC converter with frequency control has been developed. It consists of a signal logic board and a gate driver board, which controls the operation of a full-bridge transistor inverter. The operating mode of the converter is generated via a computer interface and subsequently stored in the signal board for execution. It generates a control sequence for the power switches. Output of the inverter is connected to a series resonant LC-circuit with a resonant frequency of 44 kHz. The converter supply voltage is 32 VDC. A full-bridge uncontrollable rectifier is used, as well as a resistive load with values between 6 Ω and 20 Ω. Test circuit parameters are given in Table 3:

https://doi.org/10.3390/engproc2026122011

Table 3. Circuit parameters.

L, µH	C, nF	f_0, kHz	Z_0, Ω
60	220	44	16.4

Figure 6 shows the waveforms of the resonant circuit voltage and current at quality factor Q_L = 2.5, corresponding to a load resistance R_O = 5 Ω and normalized frequency ν = 1 (switching frequency of 44.13 kHz) and ν = 1.3, respectively. The experimental data in Figure 6b confirm the results of the theoretical analysis shown in Figure 2b.

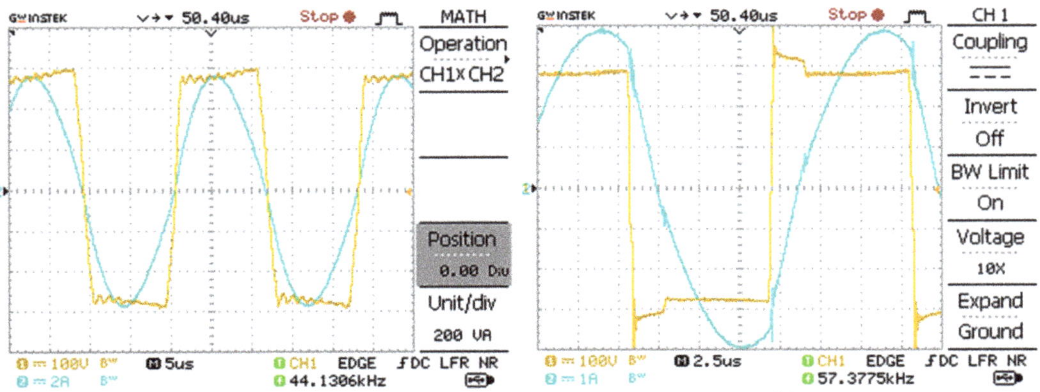

(**a**) (**b**)

Figure 6. Resonant voltage and current waveforms for: (**a**) Q_L = 2.5 and ν = 1; (**b**) Q_L = 2.5 and ν = 1.3.

4. Conclusions

This study demonstrated the effectiveness of Fourier series analysis in analyzing resonant converters with higher accuracy than the classical First Harmonic Approximation (FHA). By including higher-order harmonics in the analysis, a more precise representation of circuit behavior has been achieved, especially under non-sinusoidal conditions. The quantitative evaluations of resonant-current THD and input/output ripple factor highlight the operating modes where FHA has significant deviations from the Fourier series analysis results, mainly for frequencies under the resonant and at relatively low-quality factor. Harmonic spectra of the converter's input and output currents can be obtained using the proposed analysis. The results can be used for filter topology choice and sizing.

Experimental validation of the analytical results has been presented using a laboratory prototype of a full-bridge series resonant DC-DC converter. The experimental waveforms of input, resonant and output currents and voltages under various operating modes showed close compliance with the theoretical predictions derived using the Fourier method.

Author Contributions: Conceptualization, D.S., A.L., V.M. and Y.M.; Methodology Y.M. and H.V.; Software, H.V.; Validation, D.S., A.L., V.M., Y.M. and H.V.; Formal analysis, V.M. and Y.M.; Investigation, D.S., V.M., Y.M. and H.V.; Resources, A.L., H.V.; Writing—Original Draft Preparation, D.S., Y.M. and H.V.; Writing—Review and Editing, Y.M. and H.V. All authors have read and agreed to the published version of the manuscript.

Funding: This research has been funded by "Science" Fund at University of Food Technologies—Plovdiv, Bulgaria.

Institutional Review Board Statement: Not applicable.

https://doi.org/10.3390/engproc2026122011

Informed Consent Statement: Informed Consent Statement: Informed consent was obtained from all subjects involved in the study.

Data Availability Statement: The data presented in this study is available on request from the corresponding authors.

Conflicts of Interest: The authors declare no conflicts of interest.

References

1. Kazimierczuk, M.K.; Czarkowski, D. *Resonant Power Converters*, 2nd ed.; Wiley: Hoboken, NJ, USA, 2011.
2. Hart, D. *Power Electronics*; McGraw-Hill: Columbus, OH, USA, 2011.
3. Rossetto, L.; Sipazzi, G. Series Resonant Converter with Wide Load Range. In *Industry Applications Conference, Thirty-Third IAS Annual Meeting*; IEEE: Piscataway, NJ, USA, 1998; Volume 2, pp. 1326–1331.
4. Corti, F.; Bertolini, V.; Reatti, A.; Faba, A.; Cardelli, E. Advanced Modeling Approach for LLC Resonant Converters: From Multiharmonic Analysis to Small Signal Model. *IEEE Trans. Power Electron.* **2025**, *40*, 3899–3915. [CrossRef]
5. Mukherjee, S.; Barbosa, P. Design and Optimization of an Integrated Resonant Inductor with High-Frequency Transformer for Wide Gain Range DC–DC Resonant Converters in Electric Vehicle Charging Applications. *IEEE Trans. Power Electron.* **2023**, *38*, 6380–6394. [CrossRef]
6. Kasiran, M.A.N.; Ponniran, A.; Siam, N.N.M.; Yatim, M.H.; Che Ibrahim, N.A.; Md Yunos, A. DC-DC converter with 50 kHz-500 kHz range of switching frequency for passive component volume reduction. *IJECE* **2021**, *11*, 1114–1122. [CrossRef]
7. M'barki, Z.; Senhaji Rhazi, K.; Mejdoub, Y. A novel fuzzy logic control for a zero current switching-based buck converter to mitigate conducted electromagnetic interference. *IJECE* **2023**, *13*, 1423–1436. [CrossRef]

https://doi.org/10.3390/engproc2026122011

engineering proceedings

MDPI

Proceeding Paper

Study of the Influence of the Geometric Shape of Structural Elements on the Hydrodynamic Pattern in a Radial Precipitator †

Aleksandrina Bankova [1,*], Anastas Yangyozov [2], Stefan Tenev [1] and Asparuh Atanasov [1]

[1] Department of Mechanics and Machine Elements, Faculty of Manufacturing and Technologies, Technical University—Varna, Studentska 1, 9000 Varna, Bulgaria; stefo_83@tu-varna.bg (S.T.); asparuh.atanasov@tu-varna.bg (A.A.)
[2] Department of Thermal Engineering, Faculty of Shipbuilding, Technical University—Varna, Studentska 1, 9000 Varna, Bulgaria; yangyozovtu@tu-varna.bg
* Correspondence: ina_bankova@tu-varna.bg; Tel.: +359-89666131

† Presented at the 6th International Conference on Communications, Information, Electronic and Energy Systems, Ruse, Bulgaria, 26–28 November 2025.

Abstract

Wastewater treatment facilities of a diameter of approximately 15 m or more provide the opportunity to process large volumes of stormwater. The current report investigates the operation of a stormwater radial precipitator, without an impeller, working with particles of various sizes. A distinguishing feature is that the two-phase flow is solely gravity-driven, which leads to reduced energy requirements. This entails the necessity of a facility in which the linear and the local losses are minimized as much as possible. Linear losses can be reduced by decreasing the precipitator's size. The initially proposed 15 m diameter proved to be ineffective since the sand only reached a certain zone and could not flow further to the outlet due to the insufficient energy. Therefore, it was necessary to reduce the size of the radial precipitator, which resulted in a shorter path for the sand particles and the water, which, in turn, reduced the linear resistance. As for the local losses, it turned out that many areas of the precipitator construction could be geometrically modified to significantly reduce the energy loss of the sand–water mixture. The boundary layer cannot be removed. However, it is possible the size and the number of vortex structures inside the settler to be reduced in order to create an optimal working environment.

Keywords: water; sand particles; purification settler; hydrodynamics; construction

1. Introduction

In the recent decades, with the rapid development of computer technology, computational fluid dynamics (CFD) software and techniques have become powerful and effective tools for studying complex flows. Many researchers [1–6] have proven that CFD can predict the flow field accurately and reliably in many mixing tanks.

Previous research related to hydrodynamic analysis has proposed mathematical models that can predict the solid content and the particle size distribution in tanks (often quite different from the feed material) [7]. In their study, the authors Schmid et al. theoretically and numerically explored electrohydrodynamic (EHD) flows and presented the results in model electrostatic filters (EF). They show the effect of the flow on the resulting secondary flows through mathematical dependencies in laminar and "RANS" models of study. According to them, the high accuracy, and the correct computation of the entire channel,

 https://doi.org/10.3390/engproc2026122012

with proper boundary conditions at the inlet and outlet, are critical for the accurate flow field calculations [8]. According to another study, by the same authors, secondary flows have only a minor impact on the overall particle sedimentation, although they cause some local sedimentation modelling. They argue that the heterogeneity of turbulence has a stronger effect on particle dynamics [9]. Recently, Soldati [10] published a systematic study on the influence of secondary flow on particle dynamics, calculating their trajectories in a highly detailed flow field obtained through a direct numerical simulation, with and without coupling to an electric field. However, this study was limited to the effect of an electrochemical–diffusion flow, using a simplified distribution of the electric field.

Research and various sources on particle transport, whether denser (e.g., mineral sediments) or less dense (e.g., air bubbles) than the surrounding fluid, show that if the settling velocity of the particles is much lower than the flow's friction velocity, turbulence will be strong enough to keep the particles in suspension. Small particles closely follow the flow of the fluid with components of velocity u, v, and w along the respective X, Y, and Z axes, so their movement is described by the equation used for chemical solutions considering concentration C. In some cases, in the particle transport equations, it is more convenient to use the particle concentration n (particles/m^3) instead of concentration C (kg/m^3). Then, the equation for particle motion is the following:

$$\begin{aligned}&\frac{\partial n}{\partial t}+u\frac{\partial n}{\partial x}+v\frac{\partial n}{\partial y}+\left(w+w_p\right)\frac{\partial n}{\partial z}\\&=D_x\frac{\partial^2 n}{\partial x^2}+D_y\frac{\partial^2 n}{\partial y^2}+D_z\frac{\partial^2 n}{\partial z^2}\end{aligned} \quad (1)$$

In turbulent flow, the diffusion coefficients D_x, D_y, D_z for the respective particles can be assumed to be the same as those for the dissolved particles. In laminar flows, the particle diffusion will be a function of their size.

Particles whose density differs from the fluid's, whether higher (e.g., sand grains or metal spheres) or lower (e.g., air bubbles), will have a vertical velocity relative to the fluid w_p, which is accounted for with an additional component in the advection term. Equation (1) is valid for particles with density close to the surrounding fluid. If the particle size d and their density ρ_p are higher than those of the surrounding fluid ρ_F, then additional equations should be introduced, but this is not addressed in this report. In the simplified case, a particle, surrounded by fluid, is considered to be acted upon by gravitational, lift, and drag forces. In Equation (1), in the fourth term, the movement velocity along the vertical axis z, can be determined according to:

$$w_p=\left[\frac{4}{3}\frac{gd\left(\rho_p-\rho_F\right)}{\rho_F C_D}\right]^{1/2} \quad (2)$$

where C_D is the drag coefficient, g = 9.81 m/s^2—the gravitational acceleration [11].

2. Materials and Methods

2.1. Numerical Model

The current paper describes some stages in the development of a three-dimensional CFD model of a radial precipitator working with a mixture of stormwater and particles of different sizes. When using Ansys CFX 2021 is a computational fluid dynamics (CFD) software product, the rules for operation described in [12,13] were followed.

Figure 1 shows the three-dimensional cross-section of one of the models under consideration. Table 1 presents the geometric dimensions of the precipitator.

https://doi.org/10.3390/engproc2026122012

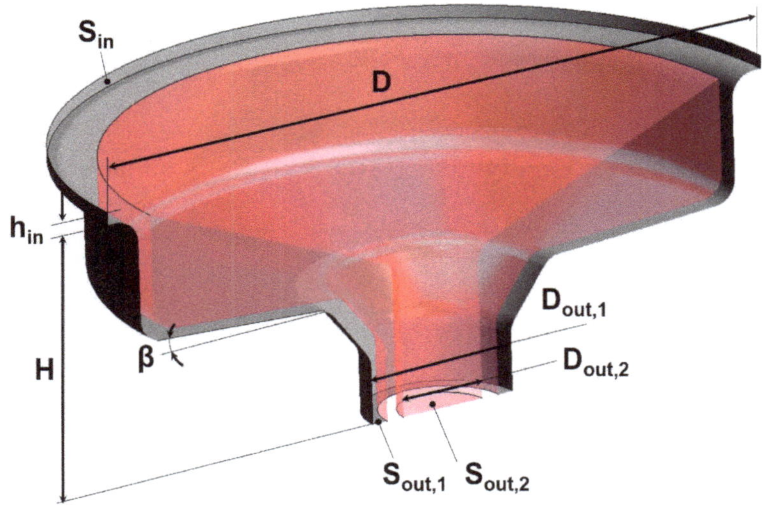

Figure 1. General view of the radial precipitator in cross section.

Table 1. Geometric Dimensions of The Precipitator.

Name	Value
Height, H	1 m
Diameter, D	2 m
Volume, V	1.32–0.52 m^3
Height of the inlet channel, h_{in}	0.034 m
Output area 1, $S_{out,1}$	0.0502062 m^2
Output area 2, $S_{out,2}$	0.0430629 m^2
Slope, β	86.8°
Entrance area S_{in}	0.206857 m^2
Outlet outer diameter 1 water, $D_{out,2}$	0.236 m
Outer diameter. outlet 2 water and sand, $D_{out,1}$	0.418 m

The so-called Control Volume Method is used in the software product. The sand particles' behavior in the fluid area is described by the Lagrangian method [14].

During the initial modeling, a model with periodic boundary conditions was created, but the fluid pattern was proved to be not symmetric. The interaction between the particles of various sizes and the water, along with phenomena such as Turbulent Dispersion and Particle Collision, which were considered and included, contributed to the asymmetry. A CFD model with periodic boundaries would have significantly reduced the computation time, but in the end, the possibility to study the complex processes occurring in the facility led to the decision to model the entire volume and to conduct a detailed analysis. A three-dimensional shape of the precipitator was created by the geometric module of ANSYS Design Modeler. The dimensions were clarified and the parameters were introduced. The latter would be modified during the research process. In this module, the solid body part and the fluid volume were separated. The surfaces on which boundary conditions would be applied were labeled. These data were passed to the next module, Mesh, to create a mesh for the fluid region. It is unstructured with 286,771 nodes and 656,111 elements, consisting of tetrahedra, pyramids, and prisms. After the first calculation, the Yplus value was checked, and it turned out to be around 25.

https://doi.org/10.3390/engproc2026122012

According to Patankar [15], this mesh has appropriate size and density in the vicinity of the walls, and the next stage of modelling can be initiated, namely the boundary conditions setting. This is achieved by the CFX-Pre-module. Some of the settings are shown in Table 2.

Table 2. Physical properties of sand and water. Modelling conditions.

Name	Value	Condition
Sand density	2300 kg/m^3	constant
Size	1–10 mm	constant
Water density	997 kg/m^3	constant
Mass flow rate "water"	62 kg/s	constant
Mass flow rate "sand"	1–10 kg/s	variable
Number of particles	200; 5000; 12,000	variable
Turbulence model	k-eps; SST	variable
Water velocity inlet	0.3 m/s	constant
Outlet pressure 1	0 Pa	constant
Outlet pressure 2	0 Pa	constant

The number of the particles and the mass flow rate "sand" change during the investigation, while their size and the mass flow rate "water" remain constant, as described in Table 2. The hydrostatic pressure is modelled, and for this purpose, the settings of the CFD model are adjusted. The vector of gravitational acceleration is set with a magnitude of g = 9.81 m/s^2 and a sign "-" along the Y-axis. The settings for the Particle Collision–Turbulent Dispersion and the Sommerfeld Collision Model are included.

The parameters for the computational process are set in the CFX-Solver module, and for better visualization, the same parameters are shown in Table 3.

Table 3. Parameters of the computational process.

Name	Value
Advection scheme	High resolution
Max iterations	150
Convergence criteria RMS residual target	1×10^5
Max. Particle Intg. Time Step	1×10^{10} s
Particle Termination Control Maximum Tracking Time	10 s
Maximum Tracking Distance	10 m
Max.num. Integration steps	1000

The created model allows for changes both in the construction and in the boundary conditions, which define the outflow mode of the water and sand mixture. The results obtained in the CFX-Post module are described in the report below.

2.2. Construction Modification

In this stage of the precipitator internal space creation, several constructions are analysed, which were modified after initial analysis. CFD modelling allows for quick detection of inefficient designs and helps focus efforts on improving the variants with better performance. Models that do not show convergence during the computational process are not considered for further analysis.

Constructions of precipitators used in treatment plants were taken into account when creating the model. These served as prototypes for creating the baseline version and the subsequent modifications.

In the baseline version BASE, the sand and water mixture is fed radially through the incoming ring in the upper half of the facility—see Figure 2. The sand, as the denser

https://doi.org/10.3390/engproc2026122012

component, moves along the outer wall. Two outlets are provided: one for sand (with a ring-shaped section with a radius of 0.209 m) and one for water (with a radius of 0.118 m). It is observed that in the base version, there are numerous vortices that consume part of the fluid's energy. This energy dissipates due to the high losses from the high velocity at the precipitator's outlet. This shows that the BASE design is unsuitable, as the sand particles encounter a wall of rotating water (the vortex in the lower half is visible). In reality, these particles cannot exit through the precipitator's outlet.

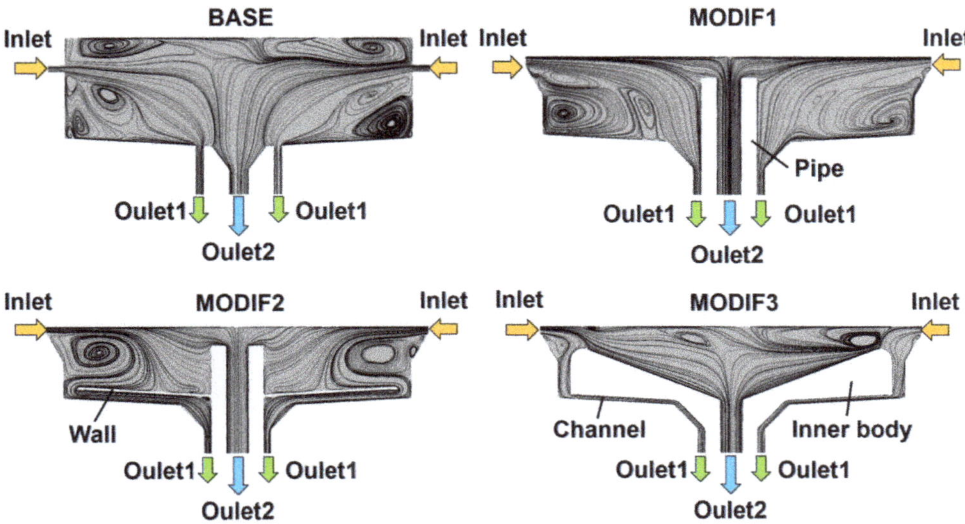

Figure 2. Surface streamlines designed in a plane for variants BASE, MODIF1, MODIF2, MODIF3.

In *Modification 1 (MODIF1)*, a pipe-in-pipe element is used. Water flows from the central part, which is larger in diameter, while the water–sand mixture flows from the ring-shaped cross-section pipe. In this configuration, numerous vortices are still observed. They consume the fluid's energy in order to exist within the volume of the precipitator. When the water–sand mixture is introduced, a conical shape is created to help direct the sand mass toward the outer wall. Ultimately, the sand fails to exit through the ring-shaped section outlet in the lowest part of the precipitator due to the vortices that are generated. This configuration also turned out to be ineffective.

In *Modification 2 (MODIF2)*, an additional wall (a double bottom) was introduced under which the sand can flow and be directed toward the outlet. The height of this channel should not be too small because it is necessary to allow enough water to pass through along with the sand. These aids pushing the solid particles toward the outlet. However, the presence of vortices once again indicates an inefficient design from a hydrodynamic perspective. This configuration also fails to meet the requirements for an efficient precipitator.

From the presented design options so far, it is clear that the structure needs to be modified in such a way that the vortices are either removed or weakened. One of the approaches suggested in this study is to introduce an additional body inside the structure. What shape should it have? The process of searching for the appropriate shape is not presented in the report. The idea being implemented is to direct the water–sand mixture toward channels of a specific size and shape, while taking into account the specifics of the two-phase flow.

In *Modification 3 (MODIF3)*, an additional body is introduced inside the precipitator. This body is hollow and its purpose is to direct the water–sand mixture toward the

https://doi.org/10.3390/engproc2026122012

two outlets in the lowest part of the system. This body should have the simplest possible shape to avoid complicating the assembly and increasing manufacturing costs; thus, it should not raise the cost of the precipitator. The sand, which has a smaller mass flow rate than the water, is directed toward a vertical ring-shaped channel along the outer wall, allowing it to move in a straight line with minimal resistance. At the end of the vertical channel, a large inlet area (1.108 m^2) is provided, resulting in low local losses. The sand–water mixture then curves and is directed into a conical-shaped channel towards the bottom of the precipitator. In this case, the movement is centripetal, and the channel has a decreasing cross-section toward the outlet. Capturing the sand at the beginning, at the inlet of the precipitator, is a critical moment that requires special attention (the influence of the radius R and the slope of the inlet section is discussed below). Sufficient volume is provided in the central part of the construction to drain the water without the sand. The absence of obstacles, i.e., resistance, during the movement of water in the core of the system, ensures a continuous flow of purified water.

The next goal is to analyse the impact of adding a rounding, R = 0.06 m, at the highest part of the internal body. Figure 2 shows that after the rounding a relatively small vortex is formed. It should be investigated how the size of the geometric parameter R helps improve the hydrodynamic behaviour in the settler. This configuration ensures successful sand drainage through the outlet with a ring-shaped cross-section. The precipitator is functional, but further improvements are needed for the flow around the internal body.

The calculations were carried out with a water mass flow rate of Gw = 62 kg/s and a sand mass flow rate of Gs = 1 kg/s.

- Effect of the inlet slope γ—MODIFG:

In the version with $\gamma = 90^\circ$, vortices are formed in the upper part of the precipitator, above the inner body, which makes this design inefficient. In the versions with $\gamma = 14.9^\circ$ and $\gamma = 26.7^\circ$, vortices are present near the inlet path where the sand descends. These vortices are shown in blue. These designs are ineffective because they slow down the sand particles and make the sedimentation process impossible.

Among the presented variants in Figure 2, the vortices in *MODIF3* prove to be the smallest Comparative analysis shows that *MODIF3* is the most promising for optimization in the next stage. In this configuration, the velocity of the water–sand mixture does not exceed 1 m/s, which meets the requirements for the operation of such a system [16–21]. The next question that needs to be addressed is whether it is possible to improve this configuration by eliminating the vortices in the zone above the internal body. This issue will be discussed in the next section.

2.3. Model Optimization

The next task is to develop a MODIF3 filter design, in which minimal modifications can positively affect the hydrodynamic behavior in the facility. In the created geometric model of the MODIF3 variant, the parameters of the geometric shape of the filter are introduced, such as: radius R and angle γ. The first parameter R is changed for three new designs with a rounding of the upper edge of the inner body: R = 0; 0.03 m; 0.06 m; and 0.09 m. The second parameter γ is changed in the range $\gamma = 90^\circ; 68^\circ; 26.7^\circ$; and 14.9°. At the next stage, it is necessary to determine the optimal values of angle γ and radius R, at which the existing vortices are weakened. These values were introduced and the result is shown in Figure 3 for the MODIF3 variant.

https://doi.org/10.3390/engproc2026122012

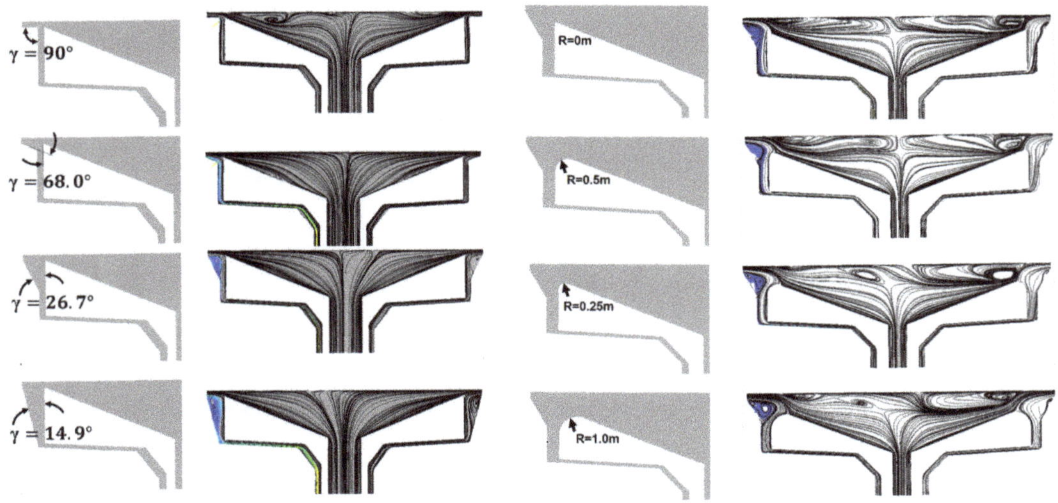

Figure 3. Changes in the geometric shape of elements of the precipitator and the influence it has on the formation of vortices.

Calculations show that in the design with an angle of γ = 68°, there is a significant change in the size of the vortices in the facility, and the sand flows vertically downward with an average velocity of 0.6 m/s.

- Effect of the radius R—MODIFR:

It turns out that changing the rounding radius—or its absence—does not positively influence or eliminate the vortices in the precipitator. Vortices appear both in the inlet section and above the wall of the inner body. Their location changes. The reason is the low water velocity (around 0.2 m/s) in the diffused section. Due to the low kinetic energy and the increasing cross-sectional area, the fluid separates or forms recirculating flows, which create the conditions for the vortex formation.

In the design variants with the optimal values—radius R = 0 m and, in the second set of calculations, with an inlet slope of γ = 68°—the large vortex structures are weakened and reduced in size.

3. Results and Discussion

3.1. Optimized Design

From the options examined above, two designs stood out with noticeably improved hydrodynamic flow characteristics. These were combined into the FINAL design by introducing the following modification: rounding is added at the inlet of the water–sand mixture, and the rounding at the highest part of the inner body is removed. In this way, the beneficial effect of the inlet slope angle γ = 68° is taken into account. The presence of a sharp edge (R = 0 m) in the FINAL design is a more suitable option compared to the MODIF3R modification with a variable rounding radius R. The reason is that under the given outflow conditions in the FINAL design, the vortex is pressed against the wall of the inner body and is very small in size, which improves the flow pattern in the precipitator—see Figure 4b FINAL. The same figure also shows the additionally introduced rounding's with R = 0.06 m (at all sharp edges), which form channels where the sand can run. This further reduces local flow resistances.

https://doi.org/10.3390/engproc2026122012

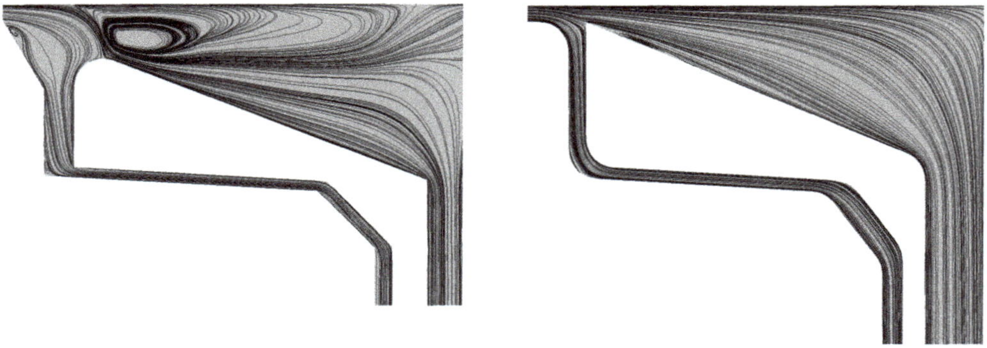

(**a**) (**b**)

Figure 4. Streamlines picture in a structure with modification MODIF3R (**a**), compared to the final version FINAL (**b**).

In summary, in the FINAL version, the inlet is shaped so that the top of the inner body is designed with a sharp edge, slope $\gamma = 68°$, and with a rounded inlet. In this configuration, no vortex is generated that would consume the energy of the moving fluid. The FINAL design, as modelled, is now ready to be tested with varying quantities of water and sand.

Figure 5 presents streamlines showing the changes in the water flow velocities. In the CFX-Pre-module, the mass flow rate of the water was set to Gw = 62 kg/s, and for the sand: Gs = 1 kg/s, and in another simulation—Gw = 62 kg/s and Gs = 3 kg/s.

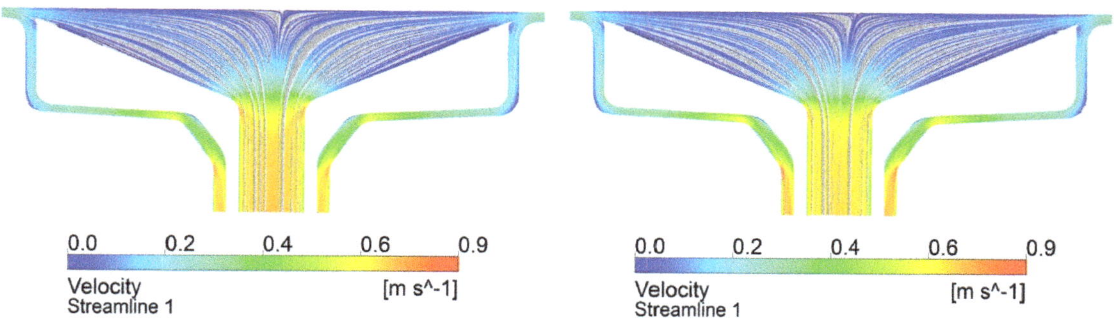

(**a**) (**b**)

Figure 5. Streamlines pattern with changing water velocity MODIF3R (**a**), compared to the final version FINAL (**b**).

Additionally, flow velocities lower than 1 m/s were achieved, and there was unification in the following: the velocity field of the sand in the outlet section of the settler, and the purity of the water exiting through the central outlet.

3.2. Testing in Different Operation Modes

When a sand flow rate above 5 kg/s is set, a deterioration in the convergence of the computational process is observed, which leads to a blockage of the process within the facility. Under these conditions, the water flow rate is not changed in order to meet the requirement for maintaining low velocities in the precipitator. The water content in the channel filled with sand is of particular importance for ensuring proper drainage [22,23]. The model represents a plane with 250 streamlines projected within it. This method of visualization allows for an analysis of the influence of the proposed shape of the inner body

https://doi.org/10.3390/engproc2026122012

on the vortex formation in the two-phase mixture. The analysis of the flow surrounding the inner body with the proposed shape shows that the water flow does not separate from the walls, and consequently, no vortices are formed. It is evident from the figure that the flow velocities do not exceed 0.9 m/s.

So far, a qualitative representation of the movement of the two-component mixture has been presented. With the developed model, it is also possible to perform a quantitative assessment by extracting the data of interest. As long as the fluid is concerned, the trajectory of all sand particles can be calculated, but this would complicate the analysis. Therefore, two randomly selected particles with sizes of 1 mm and 7 mm are chosen, and their motion within the fluid is visualized. In the CFX-Post module, the trajectory is displayed using a single monochrome colour. The module also allows for visualization of how the static pressure acting on the particles mentioned above changes during their movement from the inlet to the outlet of the precipitator.

Figure 6 shows the change in the average velocity of the sand particles with sizes of 1 mm and 7 mm.

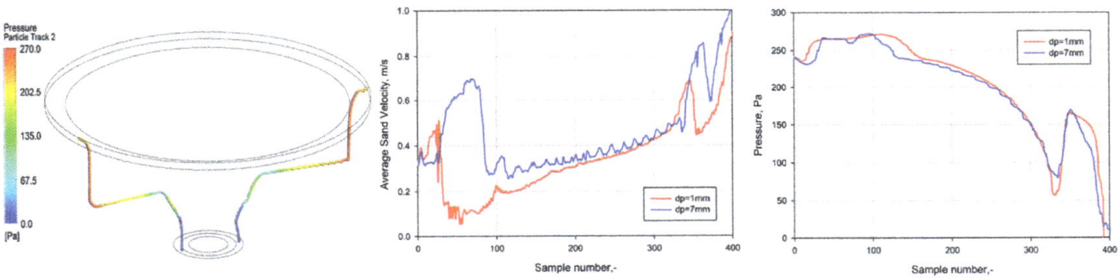

Figure 6. Trajectory of a 1 mm and 7 mm sand particle with visualization of static pressure and sand velocity—(**a**,**b**) decrease in the static pressure, (**c**) the average velocity of the sand.

In addition to the effects described above, the sand particles are also influenced by the action of inertial forces, collisions with the walls, turbulent dispersion force, rotation system force, added mass force, etc. However, the simulation does not take into account the buoyancy force, since the temperature of the mixture in the facility is assumed to remain constant during operation—that is, no heat is added to or removed from the precipitator.

Additionally, the data obtained using the SST (Shear Stress Transport) turbulence model for pressure and sand velocity were analysed and compared.

As the sand-and-water particles move toward the outlet of the facility, the cross-sectional area decreases, which leads to an increase in the velocity of both water and sand (Figures 5 and 6b). On the other hand, this results in a decrease in the static pressure (Figure 6a,b). The transition from the inclined bottom to the final vertical section is accompanied by a pressure increase through the curvature, which we modelled with a rounded shape.

The average velocity of the sand is higher for the 7 mm particle compared to the 1 mm particle (Figure 6c). This aligns with relation (2), according to which larger and heavier particles will have a higher settling velocity w_p.

4. Conclusions

For large precipitator dimensions, the sand particles must travel long distances, which, due to high friction forces, leads to a reduction in their kinetic energy and eventually to

https://doi.org/10.3390/engproc2026122012

their stoppage. Therefore, reducing the size of the precipitator could allow for operation without the need for additional pumps.

In the present study, no external energy is supplied to the precipitator to drive or accelerate the sedimentation process. The system relies solely on gravitational force to move the sand toward the outlet. Any linear and/or local resistances are undesirable.

The water vortex in the baseline (BASE) design obstructs the movement of sand toward the outlet, and therefore it must be eliminated. This is achieved by designing an appropriate shape of the walls of the precipitator.

The introduction of an internal body with a carefully selected shape leads to an improved flow pattern within the facility. The vortex structures are reduced in size, and in some areas of the fluid, they disappear entirely. Adding such a hollow body inside the settler reduces the overall weight of the structure, although it is more complex to manufacture. The reduced water volume during operation also lessens the load on the supporting structure.

Adding an inlet slope when introducing the water–sand mixture into the facility is a positive modification, as it directs the sand vertically and facilitates its discharge.

The shape and the position of the internal body ensure a mass flow rate of the exiting clean water that corresponds to half of the mass flow entering the precipitator. This configuration allows for an even distribution of water into the core of the precipitator, while also providing sufficient water to transport the sand toward the outlet via a separate channel, in which flow resistance is overcome.

The addition of a rounded edge is not a good design solution for this type of precipitator configuration. It results in the generation of vortices, which hinder the separation and discharge of sand.

The motion of the sand particles is centripetal, meaning that the cross-sectional area of the channel in the direction of the precipitator outlet decreases. This leads to an increase in the velocity of the water–sand mixture. The increasing kinetic energy of the mixture provides the necessary energy to overcome resistance in the outlet section. However, excessively high velocity would increase the resistance in the outlet channel. An average discharge velocity of around 0.35 m/s is considered optimal for these dimensions and for a mass flow rate of Gw = 62 kg/s and Gp = 1 kg/s.

The cross-sectional area in the radial channel beneath the internal body decreases from 1.108 m^2 to 0.058 m^2. As a result:

- the velocity of the water increases from 0.26 to 0.58 m/s;
- the pressure decreases from 240 to 90 Pa;
- the velocity of the sand increases from 0.15 to 0.43 m/s.

The analysis presented in this report allows the recommendations above to be applied, but only for a precipitator with the specified dimensions and design. When scaling up, the flow pattern changes, and new recommended values for sand flow rate must be determined.

Author Contributions: Conceptualization, A.B. and A.Y.; methodology, A.Y.; software, S.T.; validation, A.Y.; formal analysis, A.Y.; investigation, A.B.; resources, A.A.; data curation, A.Y.; writing—original draft preparation, A.B.; writing—review and editing, A.Y.; visualization, S.T.; supervision, A.B.; project administration, A.A.; funding acquisition, A.B. and S.T. All authors have read and agreed to the published version of the manuscript.

Funding: The study was partially funded by the scientific research project NP7/2025 "Research and comparative analysis of power/working machines with elements of complex three-dimensional shape" at the Technical University of Varna, funded specifically by the state budget. We thank the entire project team and its leader for the data processing and visualization activities. The authors thank their university colleagues for their assistance.

 https://doi.org/10.3390/engproc2026122012

Institutional Review Board Statement: Not applicable.

Informed Consent Statement: Informed Consent Statement: Informed consent was obtained from all subjects involved in the study.

Data Availability Statement: The data presented in this study is available on request from the corresponding authors.

Conflicts of Interest: The authors declare no conflicts of interest.

References

1. Hoseini, S.; Najafi, G.; Ghobadian, B.; Akbarzadeh, A. Impeller shape-optimization of stirred-tank reactor: CFD and fluid structure interaction analyses. *Chem. Eng. J.* **2021**, *413*, 127497. [CrossRef]
2. Tamburini, A.; Gagliano, G.; Micale, G.; Brucato, A.; Scargiali, F.; Ciofalo, M. Direct numerical simulations of creeping to early turbulent flow in unbaffled and baffled stirred tanks. *Chem. Eng. Sci.* **2018**, *192*, 161–175. [CrossRef]
3. Neria, I.; Alonzo-Garcia, A.; Martínez-Delgadillo, S.; Mendoza-Escamilla, V.; Yáñez-Varela, J.; Verdin, P.; Rivadeneyra-Romero, G. PIV and dynamic LES of the turbulent stream and mixing induced by a V-grooved blade axial agitator. *Chem. Eng. J.* **2019**, *374*, 1138–1152. [CrossRef]
4. Saikali, E.; Rodil, M.; Bois, G.; Bieder, U.; Leterrier, N.; Bertrand, M.; Dolias, Y. Validation of the hydrodynamics in a turbulent un-baffled stirred tank: A necessity for vortex-reactor precipitation studies. *Chem. Eng. Sci.* **2020**, *214*, 115426. [CrossRef]
5. Zhao, Z.; Chen, F.; Liu, J.; Liu, Q.; Hou, Y.; Yang, N.; Xie, G. Numerical Simulation Study of Gas-Liquid Two-Phase Flow in a Pressurized Leaching Stirred Tank. *Processes* **2024**, *12*, 896. [CrossRef]
6. Li, L.; Xu, B. CFD simulation of hydrodynamics characteristics in a tank with forward-reverse rotating impeller. *J. Taiwan Inst. Chem. Eng.* **2022**, *131*, 104174. [CrossRef]
7. Perret, Y. Hydrodynamics of Hydrate Slurries in Prepicipators Application to Precipitators Design. In *Essential Readings in Light Metals*; Donaldson, D., Raahauge, B.E., Eds.; Springer: Cham, Switzerland, 2016; pp. 559–562. [CrossRef]
8. Schmid, H.J.; Stolz, S.; Buggisch, H. On the Modelling of the Electro-Hydrodynamic Flow Field in Electrostatic Precipitators. *Flow Turbul. Combust.* **2002**, *68*, 63–89. [CrossRef]
9. Schmid, H.J. On the modelling of the particle dynamics in electro-hydrodynamic flow fields: II. Influences of inhomogeneities on electrostatic precipitation. *Powder Technol.* **2003**, *135–136*, 136–149. [CrossRef]
10. Soldati, A. On the effects of the electrohydrodynamic flows and turbulence on aerosol transport and collection in wire-plate electrostatic precipitators. *J. Aerosol Sci.* **2000**, *31*, 293–305. [CrossRef]
11. Nepf, H. Conceptual Model of Diffusion. Transport Processes in the Environment, Lecture Notes MIT OpenCourseWare: 2008. Available online: https://ocw.mit.edu/courses/1-061-transport-processes-in-the-environment-fall-2008/pages/lecture-notes/1-anim/ (accessed on 30 September 2025).
12. *Ansys CFX-Solver Manager User's Guide*; Simulate the Future; ANSYS, Inc.: Canonsburg, PA, USA, 2021; pp. 1–209.
13. *ANSYS CFX Tutorials, Release 18.0*; Ansys CFX, Computational Fluid Dynamics (CFD) Software: Canonsburg, PA, USA, 2017; pp. 1–1052.
14. Patankar, N.A.; Joseph, D.D. Modeling and numerical simulation of particulate flows by the Eulerian–Lagrangian approach. *Int. J. Multiph. Flow* **2001**, *27*, 1659–1684. [CrossRef]
15. Ebrahimi, M.; Tamer, M.; Villegas, R.; Chiappetta, A.; Mozaffari, F. Application of CFD to Analyze the Hydrodynamic Behaviour of a Bioreactor with a Double Impeller. *Processes* **2019**, *7*, 694. [CrossRef]
16. Liu, X.; García, M. Computational fluid dynamics modeling for the design of large primary settling tanks. *J. Hydraul. Eng.* **2011**, *137*. [CrossRef]
17. Georgieva, V. *Generalized Network Modeling of Water Purification Processes*; Bulgarian Academy of Sciences, Institute of Biophysics and Biomedical Engineering: Sofia, Bulgaria, 2017; pp. 1–46.
18. Arsov, R.; Draganov, D.; Kostova, I.; Koleva-Simeonova, M. *Design of Wastewater Treatment Plants*; Tehnika Publishing House: Sofia, Bulgaria, 2017; pp. 1–840.
19. Bankova, A.; Yangyozov, A.; Tenev, S.; Atanasov, A. Simulation of a Two-Phase Fluid Flow in a Design Solution of a Secondary Radial Settling Tank for Wastewater Treatment. *Eng. Proc.* **2025**, *104*, 21. [CrossRef]
20. Toneva, D.; Dimitrova, D. Some Aspects of the Water Crisis in Bulgaria. In *Environment. Technology. Resources. Rezekne, Latvia, Proceedings of the 15th International Scientific and Practical Conference*; Rezekne Academy of Technologies: Rēzekne, Lettland, 2024; Volume I, pp. 373–377. [CrossRef]
21. Nikolova, N.; Toneva, D.; Tsonev, Y.; Burgess, B.; Tenekedjiev, K. Novel Methods to Construct Empirical CDF for Continuous Random Variables using Censor Data. In Proceedings of the 2020 IEEE 10th International Conference on Intelligent Systems (IS), Varna, Bulgaria, 28–30 August 2020; pp. 61–68. [CrossRef]

 https://doi.org/10.3390/engproc2026122012

22. Song, S.; Le-Clech, P.; Shen, Y. Microscale fluid and particle dynamics in filtration processes in water treatment: A review. *Water Res.* **2023**, *233*, 119746. [CrossRef] [PubMed]
23. Allam, A.N.; Ben-Mansour, R.; Habib, M.A. Computational Fluid Dynamics of Wastewater Treatment Using Sand Filter. In Proceedings of the 2024 IEEE Sustainable Power and Energy Conference (iSPEC), Kuching, Sarawak, Malaysia, 24–27 November 2024; pp. 309–314. [CrossRef]

https://doi.org/10.3390/engproc2026122012

engineering proceedings

Proceeding Paper

Numerical Modelling of the Thermal State of a Cylinder Head †

Delyan Petkov [1] and Simeon Iliev [2,*]

1 Department of Transport Engineering and Technologies, Technical University of Varna, 9000 Varna, Bulgaria; delyan.petkov@tu-varna.bg
2 Department of Engines and Vehicles, University of Ruse, 7012 Ruse, Bulgaria
* Correspondence: spi@uni-ruse.bg; Tel.: +359-82888331
† Presented at the 6th International Conference on Communications, Information, Electronic and Energy Systems, 26–28 November 2025, Ruse, Bulgaria.

Abstract

The presented work is part of a comprehensive study exploring the feasibility of spark-ignited engines operating on fuels enhanced with additives derived from renewable sources. The investigation focuses on understanding how these alternative fuel mixtures influence engine performance and durability. In particular, attention was given to the thermal behavior of the cylinder head during engine operation with gasoline–ethanol blends. The cylinder head was selected for detailed analysis because it is one of the most thermally stressed components in the engine, directly exposed to combustion heat and pressure. Understanding its thermal state is crucial for assessing the impact of renewable fuel additives on engine reliability, efficiency, and emission characteristics. This study aims to provide insights into optimizing engine design and fuel formulation to accommodate sustainable fuel alternatives while maintaining or improving engine operation under varying conditions.

Keywords: gasoline engine; FEM; alternative fuels; engine simulation; heat transfer

1. Introduction

Understanding the thermal state of internal combustion engine components is crucial, particularly when there are alterations in the operational parameters or modifications to the engine design. This is especially relevant in the context of utilizing alternative fuels, such as gasoline–ethanol blends. If that is the case, it is the thermal condition of the cylinder head that serves as the key indicator for determining the necessary adjustments to the engine design in response to the changes in the type of the fuel.

Conducting purely experimental research to ascertain the temperature distribution across the cylinder head is inherently complex and often yields limited results. Proposed, therefore, in the present paper is a theoretical–experimental approach that leverages experimentally obtained temperature measurements at specific points to construct a comprehensive temperature field for the entire cylinder head. This is achieved through the utilization of a numerical model that simulates the thermal state of the cylinder head.

The numerical modelling draws upon data derived from a laboratory study examining the thermal conditions of cylinder heads, conducted by the Department of Transport Engineering and Technologies at the Technical University of Varna, as previously outlined in an earlier publication [1].

The 3D modelling was performed within the SolidWorks 2024 environment, which provides robust capabilities for analyzing mechanical and thermal stresses [2]. This platform features an extensive library of basic machine elements and a diverse array of materials, each with specific properties. The volumetric representation of the shape of the cylinder head encompasses all intricacies of its design, as even tiniest geometric alterations can have a dramatic effect on the outcomes of stress and deformation analyses.

A widely accepted method for addressing problems related to stress and deformation is the Finite Element Method (FEM), a numerical network technique. The FEM involves approximating the solution of the continuously varying within the volume of the body quantity (temperature, displacement) to its discrete model [3]. The model is constructed through the use of an interpolating polynomial, capturing the variation in the target function within the confines of a finite element's volume, which is based on the function's values at the notes along the element's edges [4]. To achieve this, the body must be fragmented into a sufficiently small set of elements, each with distinct geometric shapes -finite elements. In the context of heat conduction problems, the finite element method is employed [5]. Grounded in four years [6]. Law of heat conduction [7]. In addressing heat conduction issues, the FEM is employed, founded on Fourier's law of heat transfer.

2. Experimental Results

Numerical modelling is one of the effective approaches to extend the results of experimentally measured temperatures and gain a comprehensive view of the temperature field within the cylinder head.

The accuracy of the results is dependent upon the precision of the three-dimensional representation and the appropriate specification of the thermal boundary conditions. Implemented, in the proposed numerical model, are the first-kind boundary conditions (temperature values) and third-kind boundary conditions (parameters governing the convective heat exchange between the gas medium and the surfaces of the cylinder head: (αg.avg [W/(m^2.deg)], and the resultant temperature tg.res [°C]).

The temperatures measured during laboratory experiments are directly incorporated into the numerical model as boundary conditions of the first kind.

Determining the third-kind boundary conditions directly can be quite challenging. An indirect approach is, therefore, adopted for their estimation. The initial values for these parameters are derived from the existing literature, and the subsequent adjustments are made based on the temperature readings at designated control points. It is at these specific locations, where the temperatures obtained from the numerical simulations are compared with those measured experimentally. Modifications to the boundary conditions are implemented until the temperature values from the experimental data and the numerical model converge or are sufficiently close.

To establish the variable parameters for the current study, a load characteristic mode was selected at 3000 min^{-1}, based on laboratory tests, with an open throttle position of 30%. Subject to these conditions, the engine Daewoo Lanos 1,4 cc (Daewoo Motor, Bupyeong, Republic of Korea) under examination demonstrates an effective power output of 25.2 kW. The fuel utilized in this experiment is standard gasoline blended with 20% ethanol. This specific operational mode is among the most frequently employed in automotive applications, where issues related to the thermal state of various engine components are commonly observed.

For each of the operational regimes under study, first-kind boundary conditions are applied to both external and internal surfaces, utilizing values obtained from laboratory measurements. These values are detailed in Tables 1 and 2.

The points, where temperatures t1 through t5 were recorded, are shown in Figure 1.

In the numerical model, the temperature readings correspond to the positions of the thermocouples used in the laboratory experiments. To ensure precision in measurements,

 https://doi.org/10.3390/engproc2026122013

openings are "drilled" in the model at the exact locations of the thermocouples, allowing the samples to capture temperatures at the bottom of these holes (Figure 2).

Table 1. First-kind boundary conditions.

Pe, (KW)	t1, (°C)	t2, (°C)	t3, (°C)	t4, (°C)	t5, (°C)
19.20	55	94	89	85	79
25.20	60	95	90	86	82
33.90	64	101	95	90	88
38.40	71	104	99	92	90

Table 2. First-kind boundary conditions.

Cooling Space, (°C)	Intake Runners, (°C)	Exhaust Runners, (°C)
85	28	417
85	29	509
85	29	562
85	31	584

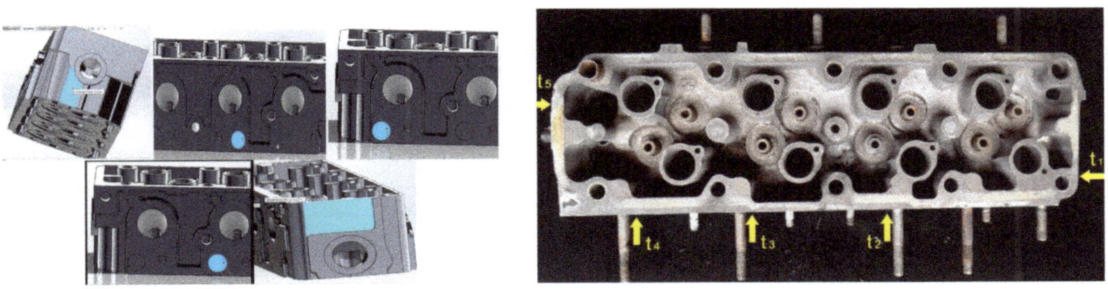

(a) (b)

Figure 1. Points, where temperatures t1 through t5 were recorded: (**a**) SolidWorks model; (**b**) Cylinder Head.

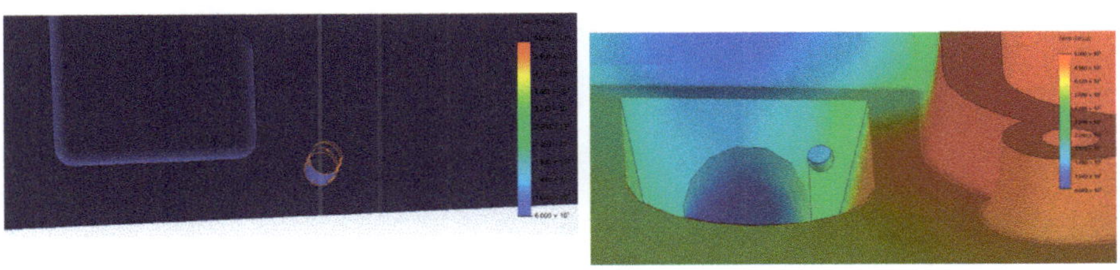

(a) (b)

Figure 2. Locations of the thermocouples: (**a**) Thermocouple hole 4; (**b**) Thermocouple hole 1.

The material selected for the model is cast aluminium alloy containing 13% silicon, alloyed with copper and magnesium, as specified in the material catalogue of the SolidWorks 2024 software [6]. This choice of material closely matches that of the actual component used in the experimental study.

The parameters for convective heat transfer (αg.avg [W/(m^2.deg)] and the resultant temperature tg.res [°C]), which serve as boundary conditions of the third kind, are determined through an iterative process, involving successive approximations during the numerical experiment until the temperature values at the specified points of the calculated temperature field aligned closely with those measured by the thermocouples in the con-

https://doi.org/10.3390/engproc2026122013

tinuous monitoring system. The resulting parameters, thus obtained, in direct correlation with the effective power are presented in Tables 3 and 4.

Table 3. Correlation with the effective power.

Pe, (KW)	Pe, (MPa)	α, (W/m²K)	Res t°	α, (W/m²K)
19.20	0.55	249	900	85
25.20	0.72	285	1045	86
33.90	0.97	374	1395	90
38.40	1.10	392	1450	92

Table 4. Correlation with the effective power.

Res t°	Pe, (KW)	Pe, (MPa)	α, (W/m²K)
800	19.20	0.55	249
850	25.20	0.72	285
1000	33.90	0.97	374
1030	38.40	1.10	392

The results acquired from the experiments have been compared with the measured temperatures obtained from the laboratory experiment, as presented in Tables 5–8. Displayed in that table is also the percentage difference between the measured and calculated temperature values. The iterative process of refining the boundary conditions can be continued to achieve even greater accuracy.

Table 5. Comparison of data from numerical and laboratory experiments.

Pe, (MPa)	Pe, (KW)	tc1	tc1 NE
0.549	19.20	149.2	151.2
0.720	25.20	152.1	154.5
0.969	33.90	172.3	173.8
1.097	38.40	176.6	177.2

Table 6. First-kind boundary conditions: NE-numerical experiment.

Δ [%]	tc2	tc2 NE	Δ (%)
1.32	146.3	145.5	0.55
1.55	149.8	148.8	0.67
0.86	168.2	166.4	1.07
0.34	172.5	171.3	0.70

Table 7. First-kind boundary conditions: NE-numerical experiment.

Pe, (Mpa)	Pe, (KW)	tc3	tc3 NE
0.549	19.20	91.8	93.2
0.720	25.20	95.8	96.4
0.969	33.90	104.7	105.7
1.097	38.40	106.1	107.7

The boundary conditions of the third kind, which pertained to the surfaces of the combustion chamber, are determined by the engine load.

One of the significant benefits of extending the laboratory results with numerical standards is the ability to evaluate the impact of the engine's mean effective pressure on the third-kind boundary conditions.

https://doi.org/10.3390/engproc2026122013

Table 8. First-kind boundary conditions: NE-numerical experiment.

Δ (%)	tc4	tc4 NE	Δ (%)
1.50	94.1	93.4	0.74
0.62	103.9	96.6	7.03
0.95	105.3	105.2	0.09
1.49	106.9	107.2	0.28

The graphical representations visualized in Figures 3–6 are constructed using the data provided in Tables 7 and 8. Figures 3 and 4 reveal the influence of the mean effective pressure on the predetermined boundary conditions for the thermally stressed surface of the combustion chamber (S1) (Figure 7a), while Figures 5 and 6 provide the corresponding graph for the surface that experiences less thermal load (S2) (Figure 7b).

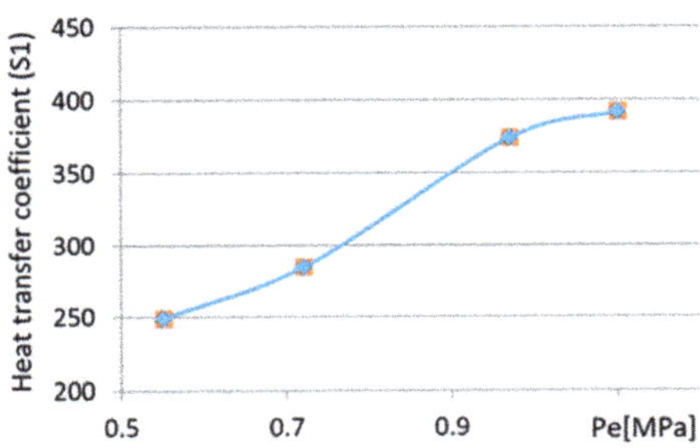

Figure 3. Influence of the mean effective pressure on the predetermined boundary conditions (Heat transfer) for the thermally stressed surface of the combustion chamber (S1).

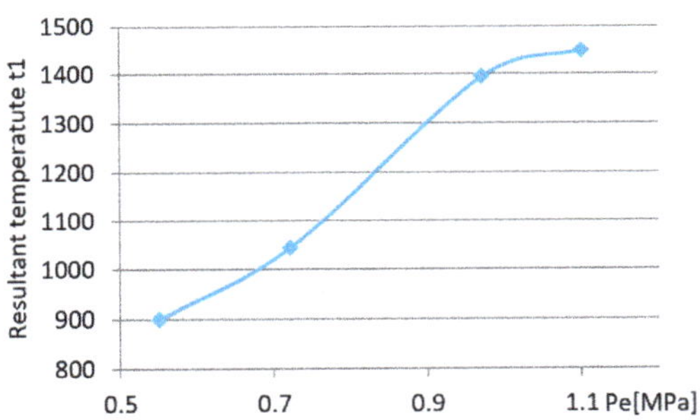

Figure 4. Influence of the mean effective pressure on the predetermined boundary (Resultant temperature) conditions for the thermally stressed surface of the combustion chamber (S1).

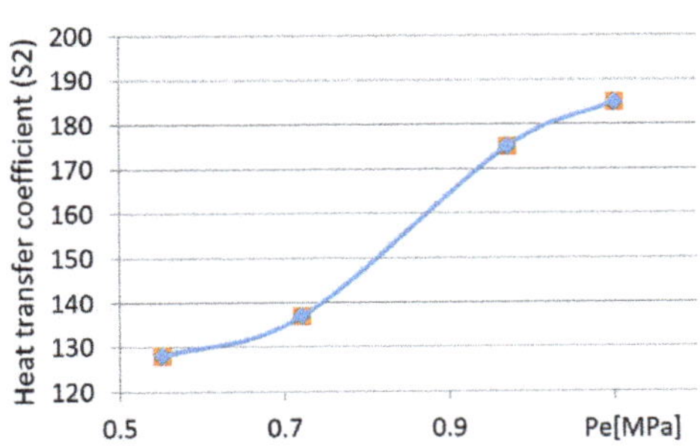

Figure 5. Influence of the mean effective pressure on the predetermined boundary conditions (Heat transfer) for the thermally stressed surface of the combustion chamber (S2).

https://doi.org/10.3390/engproc2026122013

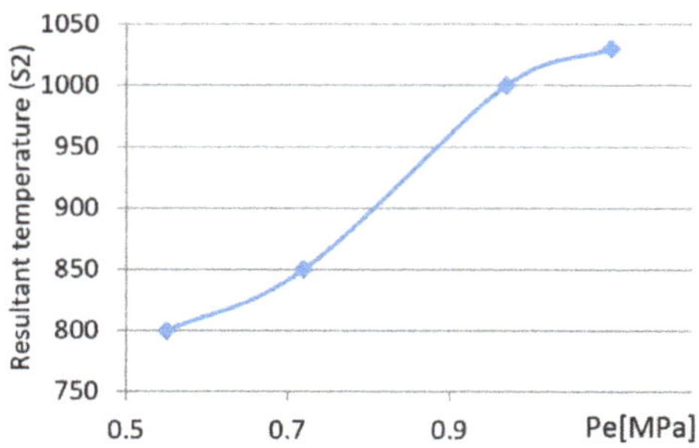

Figure 6. Influence of the mean effective pressure on the predetermined boundary conditions (Resultant temperature) for the thermally stressed surface of the combustion chamber (S2).

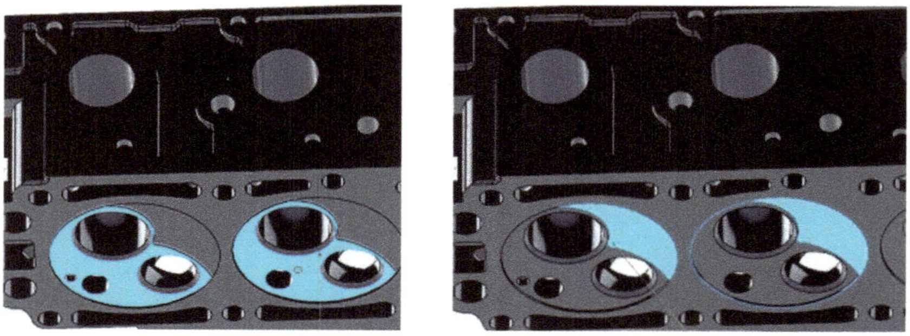

(**a**) (**b**)

Figure 7. Setting boundary conditions across the combustion chamber surface area: (**a**) Surface 1; (**b**) Surface 2.

The temperature distribution within the cylinder head is easily affected by the heat exchange parameters across the combustion chamber surfaces. The heat exchange is defined by the average resultant temperature of the hot gases and the heat transfer coefficient, both of which serve as third-kind boundary conditions [7]. The impact of the engine load on the boundary condition values is clearly illustrated in Figures 3 and 4. It appears that the trends observed in the curves for the two parameters (temperature and heat transfer coefficient) demonstrate a consistent pattern across different surfaces.

The temperature field generated from the numerical analysis, based on the experimental research, yields an extensive temperature distribution that enables the calculation of temperatures at any selected point. The variations in temperature throughout the volume of the component are depicted in Figures 8 and 9.

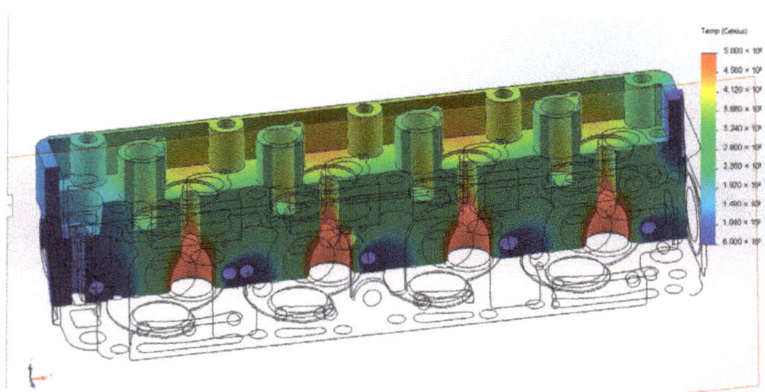

Figure 8. Cut through the exhaust channels in the valve area.

 https://doi.org/10.3390/engproc2026122013

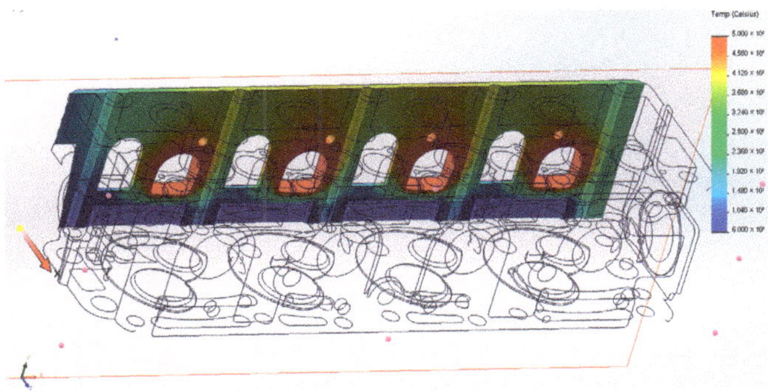

Figure 9. Section of the exit of the exhaust channels.

3. Conclusions

This study presents a novel hybrid theoretical–experimental methodology for comprehensive thermal analysis of cylinder heads operating on gasoline–ethanol blends, addressing the critical challenge of predicting temperature distributions in engines using alternative renewable fuels. The primary scientific contribution lies in developing and validating a systematic approach that combines limited experimental temperature measurements with finite element modeling to generate complete three-dimensional temperature fields, thereby overcoming the inherent limitations of purely experimental investigations.

The methodology demonstrates exceptional accuracy, with numerical predictions deviating from experimental measurements by only 0.09% to 7.03%, and most deviations remaining below 1.5%. For the tested gasoline–E20 blend at 3000 min^{-1} and 30% throttle opening (effective power range of 19.20–38.40 kW), the iterative determination of third-kind boundary conditions successfully established quantitative relationships between engine load and thermal parameters. Specifically, the heat transfer coefficient ranged from 249 to 392 W/m^2K, while resultant gas temperatures varied between 800 °C and 1450 °C, both correlating strongly with mean effective pressure (0.55–1.10 MPa).

The validated model enables prediction of temperatures at any location within the cylinder head, providing critical insights for thermal management when transitioning to renewable fuel blends. The integration of experimentally measured temperatures as first-kind boundary conditions, combined with the iterative refinement of convective heat transfer parameters as third-kind boundary conditions, establishes a robust and reproducible framework applicable to various engine configurations and operating conditions.

Future research should focus on extending this methodology to higher ethanol concentrations and other biofuel blends to establish comprehensive design guidelines for alternative fuel engines. Investigation of transient thermal behavior during dynamic load variations would provide valuable insights into thermal fatigue mechanisms. Additionally, coupling the thermal model with mechanical stress analysis would enable holistic assessment of component durability under combined thermo-mechanical loading. Experimental validation across multiple engine types and geometries would further enhance the generalizability of the approach, while integration with real-time combustion simulation could enable predictive optimization of cooling systems for next-generation sustainable powertrains.

Author Contributions: Conceptualization, D.P. and S.I.; methodology, D.P. and S.I.; software, S.I.; validation, D.P. and S.I.; formal analysis, D.P.; investigation, D.P. and S.I.; resources, D.P.; data curation, D.P. and S.I.; writing—original draft preparation, D.P. and S.I.; writing—review and editing,

https://doi.org/10.3390/engproc2026122013

S.I.; visualization, D.P. and S.I. All authors have read and agreed to the published version of the manuscript.

Funding: The present document was supported with the financial assistance of the Project 2025-RU-02 funded by the Scientific Research Fund of the University of Ruse.

Institutional Review Board Statement: Not applicable.

Informed Consent Statement: Not applicable.

Data Availability Statement: The original contributions presented in this study are included in the article. Further inquiries can be directed to the corresponding authors.

Conflicts of Interest: The authors declare no conflict of interest.

References

1. Petkov, D.; Belchev, S.; Yordanov, K. Experimental study into the effect of the addition of fuels from renewable sources on the thermal state of body parts in spark ignition engines, Transport, ecology, sustainable development. *AIP Conf. Proc.* **2024**, *3104*, 020016.
2. Iliev, S. A Comparison of Ethanol, Methanol, and Butanol Blending with Gasoline and Its Effect on Engine Performance and Emissions Using Engine Simulation. *Processes* **2021**, *9*, 1322. [CrossRef]
3. Zhang, Y.; Yan, Y.; Yang, R.; Wang, Q.; Zhang, B.; Gan, Q.; Liu, Z.; Fu, J. Study of in-cylinder heat transfer boundary conditions for diesel engines under variable altitudes based on the CHT model. *Front. Energy Res.* **2022**, *10*, 828215. [CrossRef]
4. Li, Y.; Kong, S.C. Coupling conjugate heat transfer with in-cylinder combustion modeling for engine simulation. *Int. J. Heat Mass Transf.* **2011**, *54*, 2467–2478. [CrossRef]
5. Wróbel, R.; Łoza, Ł.; Haller, P.; Włostowski, R. The effect of fuel mixture on engine vibrations. *Combust. Engines* **2019**, *177*, 136–138. [CrossRef]
6. Hu, L.; Yang, J.; Yu, Y.; Dong, F. Analysis and Optimisation of Thermo-Mechanical Coupling Load of Cylinder Head Considering Fluid-Structure Interaction for a Marine High-Power Diesel Engine. *Energies* **2020**, *13*, 3597. [CrossRef]
7. Zhao, P.C.; Li, Z.; Shang, Z.; Wang, J.F. Experimental study on surface roughness of fused deposition based on Taguchi method. *Exp. Technol. Manag.* **2020**, *3*, 162–164. (In Chinese)

https://doi.org/10.3390/engproc2026122013

engineering proceedings

MDPI

Correction

Correction: Petkov, D.; Iliev, S. Numerical Modelling of the Thermal State of a Cylinder Head. *Eng. Proc.* 2026, *122*, 13

Delyan Petkov [1] and Simeon Iliev [2,*]

1 Department of Transport Engineering and Technologies, Technical University of Varna, 9000 Varna, Bulgaria; delyan.petkov@tu-varna.bg
2 Department of Engines and Vehicles, University of Ruse, 7012 Ruse, Bulgaria
* Correspondence: spi@uni-ruse.bg

Error in Figure

In the original publication [1], there was a mistake in Figures 5 and 6 as published. The wrong images were used for Figure 5 (duplicated with Figure 3; the correct Figure 5 was incorrectly placed in Figure 6) and Figure 6 (needs be added). The authors stated that it was caused by shapes being in a different order; when formatting the template, these shapes were rearranged. The corrected Figures 5 and 6 appear below.

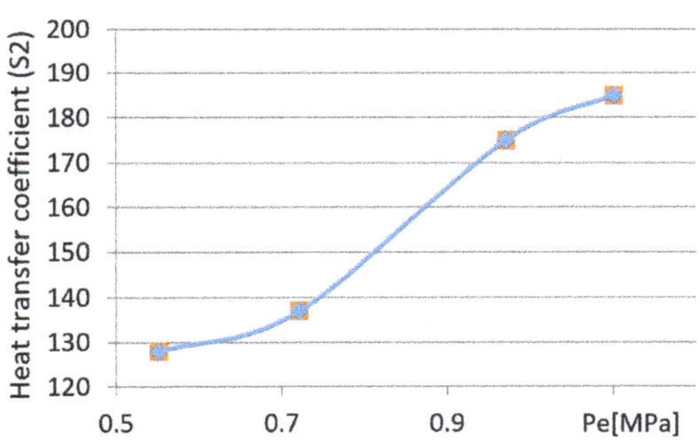

Figure 5. Influence of the mean effective pressure on the predetermined boundary conditions (Heat transfer) for the thermally stressed surface of the combustion chamber (S2).

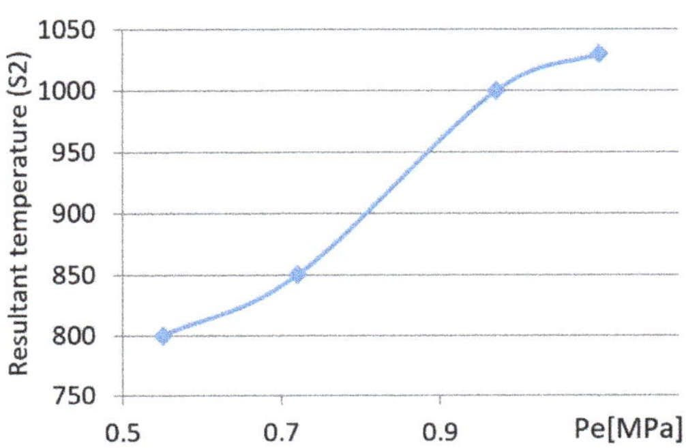

Figure 6. Influence of the mean effective pressure on the predetermined boundary conditions (Resultant temperature) for the thermally stressed surface of the combustion chamber (S2).

https://doi.org/10.3390/engproc2026122031

Text Correction

There was an error in the original publication. The description regarding Figures 3–7 is unclear.

A correction has been made to 2. Experimental Results, Paragraph 14:

"The graphical representations visualized in Figures 3–6 are constructed using the data provided in Tables 7 and 8. Figures 3 and 4 reveal the influence of the mean effective pressure on the predetermined boundary conditions for the thermally stressed surface of the combustion chamber (S1) (Figure 7a), while Figures 5 and 6 provide the corresponding graph for the surface that experiences less thermal load (S2) (Figure 7b)."

The authors state that the scientific conclusions are unaffected. This correction was approved by the Academic Editor. The original publication has also been updated.

Reference

1. Petkov, D.; Iliev, S. Numerical Modelling of the Thermal State of a Cylinder Head. *Eng. Proc.* **2026**, *122*, 13. [CrossRef]

https://doi.org/10.3390/engproc2026122031

engineering proceedings

MDPI

Proceeding Paper

Aerodynamic Analysis of Small-Scale Turbines with Complex 3D Blade Shape †

Anastas Yangyozov [1], Aleksandrina Bankova [2,*], Stefan Tenev [2] and Asparuh Atanasov [2]

1 Faculty of Shipbuilding, Department of Thermal Engineering, Technical University—Varna, Studentska 1, 9000 Varna, Bulgaria; yangyozovtu@tu-varna.bg

2 Faculty of Manufacturing and Technologies, Department of Mechanics and Machine Elements, Technical University—Varna, Studentska 1, 9000 Varna, Bulgaria; stefo_83@tu-varna.bg (S.T.); asparuh.atanasov@tu-varna.bg (A.A.)

* Correspondence: ina_bankova@tu-varna.bg; Tel.: +359-8966-6131

† Presented at the 6th International Conference on Communications, Information, Electronic and Energy Systems, Ruse, Bulgaria, 26–28 November 2025.

Abstract

The paper presents a comprehensive aerodynamic analysis of toroidal blade turbines, proposing them as a novel approach to enhance efficiency in the conversion of airflow kinetic energy. The unique toroidal blade geometry allows for reduced vortex-induced losses and improved aerodynamic performance relative to conventional blade configuration. The study encompasses crucial performance parameters, including the airflow velocity at the outlet of the aerodynamic channel, rotational speed of the turbine model, electrical current and voltage output, the electrical power produced by the generator, and the power coefficient. Explored are strategies for optimizing structure design to minimize losses and maximize the power coefficient. The findings reveal that toroidal blade designs can significantly increase the effectiveness of low-power turbines, establishing them as a promising alternative for renewable energy applications in both urban and rural environments.

Keywords: turbines; toroidal blades; efficiency; CFD; ANSYS CFX; experiment; sustainability

1. Introduction

The originality of the present study lies in the investigation of toroidal turbines, which, to the best of our knowledge, have not been previously examined in the scientific literature. While toroidal propellers have been explored in several unofficial studies, these investigations have not been formally published. In contrast, this work focuses on the aerodynamic and energy conversion characteristics of toroidal turbines, representing a novel application of the toroidal geometry concept.

The development of unconventional air turbine geometry shapes has been greatly facilitated by the advent of computational fluid dynamics (CFD). The recent literature underscores the potential of the CFD design approach, which, in recent decades, has emerged as an adequate substitute for conventional design methods [1–3].

Before starting to model the operation of an air turbine, an analysis of structures of similar dimensions was made and an assessment was made of what power can be realized from such units. Products such as axial wind turbines "Shine" [4,5] with a power of 40 W and "Waterlily" [6] with 15 W, respectively, were considered. These turbines are specifically engineered for deployment in remote locations, integrating mobile energy generation unit with battery storage solutions. The "Waterlily" turbine, in particular, demonstrates high versatility by functioning in both air and water environments. The diameter of the first configuration is 600 mm, and that of the second is 180 mm. Manufacturer data for these types of turbines indicate that substantial electrical power output is inherently limited by the physical constraints of the size of the turbine's wheel.

The principal focus of the present study is on the development of a turbine's wheel with an approximate diameter of 200 mm to be affixed at the outlet of an existing aerodynamic channel. The company "FRIENDSHIP SYSTEMS" has developed a powerful geometry shape optimization software CAESES, which offers extensive capabilities for parametric description of complex three-dimensional blade geometries. This platform enables advanced modeling of advanced blade profiles, as exemplified in the configurations displayed in [7]. Performed, in collaboration with AirShaper, are performance analyses of these toroidal blade geometries, particularly in the context of ship propellers, i.e., the models serve as work machines. The findings, as documented in [8], include both computational analyses and references to experimental validation. A critical inquiry emerging from this research pertains to the operational efficiency of unconventional, paired-blade geometries when implemented as part of the air turbine unit, i.e., as a power machine.

Selected, for the initial phase of this investigation, are prototype models with toroidal blade geometries that are known within the expert community. The baseline power machine geometries were adopted from [7,8], which are openly accessible datasets. Figure 1 presents the computational meshes generated in the Mesh module for the three modified turbine configurations evaluated in this research: Model 1—conventional blade design (a), Model 2—toroidal configuration with three paired blades (b), and Model 3—toroidal configuration with two paired blades (c).

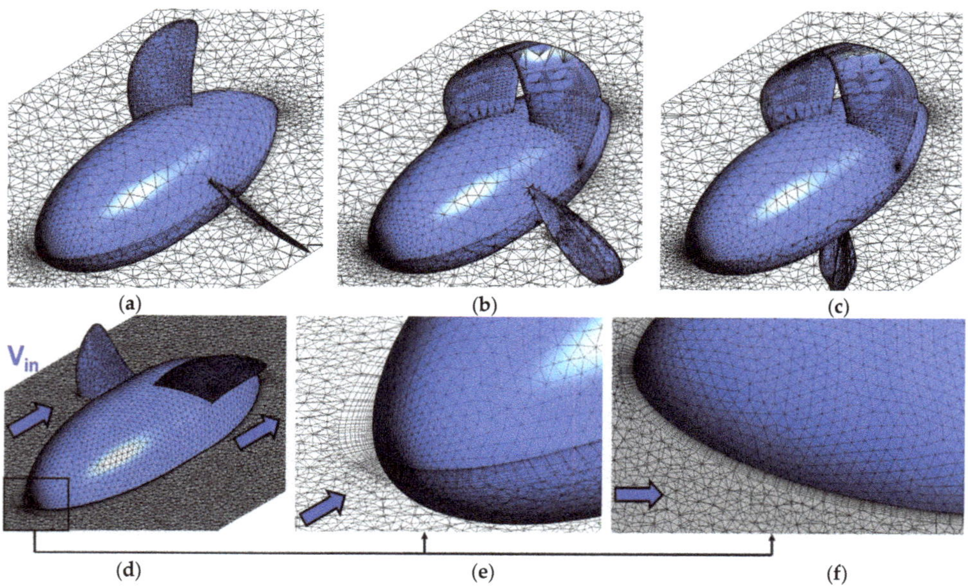

Figure 1. Fluid domain mesh around the three turbine variants (**a**) Model 1 (Conventional), (**b**) Model 2 (Toroidal3blades), (**c**) Model 3 (Toroidal2blades), (**d–f**) fine mesh around hub.

Additionally, Figure 1d,e,f illustrate a fine mesh generated for Model 1, with special emphasis on increased mesh density near the wall boundaries (Figure 1e,f). These unconventional blade designs are compared to the turbine wheel designated as conventional

https://doi.org/10.3390/engproc2026122014

(Model 1). It is similar in shape to the blade shapes commonly employed in standard axial-flow turbines.

The complex toroidal blade shapes of the models are adapted using ANSYS Workbench, via DesignModeler, SpaceClaim for geometric modifications, with final visualization conducted in CFX-Post [9,10]. This procedure is needed due to the fact that the FRIENDSHIPSYSTEMS models were designed for applications where the blade profiles impart energy to the fluid (propeller as work machine). In contrast, the present study requires an inversion of the energy cascade, whereby the blade profiles are reconfigured to deflect the air and extract energy from the airflow (turbine as power machine). The ultimate goal is to modify the model constructions (referenced in [8]) so that Models 1, 2, and 3 are optimized for turbine operation, i.e., enabling their effective use as power-generating machines.

The selected dimensions for the three air turbine models are as follows: diameter D = 192 mm, and model length L = 200 mm. Detailed view of the unconventional geometries (Models 2 and 3) reveals that they represent paired blades at the periphery, whose profiles in one section for a given radius form a tandem configuration. The blade roots are connected to the hub wall. Although the tandem blade concept is well established, its practical application has been limited due to the inherent complexity of the turbine wheel geometry. The tandem configuration offers several aerodynamic advantages. Applying such a combination of two profiles to the flow between the two blades delivers a portion of high kinetic energy to an area of low kinetic energy and avoids flow separation. Moreover, the tandem arrangement enhances overall lift generation. Another notable benefit is the suppression of secondary flows at the blade tip, which contributes to improved aerodynamic efficiency.

2. Materials and Methods

Computational Fluid Dynamics (CFD)

Numerical simulations are realized using the CFX software. The turbine geometric models are initially constructed in DesignModeler, followed by surface refinement in SpaceClaim. Subsequently, the geometry is exported to ideaMaker software for preparation of 3D printing files compatible with the Raise3D printer.

A fluid domain is then established around the three-dimensional turbine models. Mesh generation for the extracted fluid volume is performed in the Mesh module. Due to the complex geometry shape of the toroidal turbine designs (Model 2 and Model 3), an unstructured mesh was employed, comprising 792457 nodes and 4425037 elements, of which 4358172 are tetrahedra, 65022 are wedges, and 1843 are pyramids. To model the boundary layer, a refined mesh layer is implemented adjacent to the blade and hub surfaces (Figure 1f). A "Yplus" assessment is conducted, with wall-adjacent cell values varied up to a maximum of 160. Evaluated, further, is the impact of the mesh on key performance indicators-including the power coefficient C_p, the torque M, the inflow energy, velocity profiles, and other relevant quantities.

In the CFX-Pre module, the boundary conditions and parameters of the computational process are set. Physical timescale is determined following the recommendation outlined in [11], in accordance with the relation:

$$\Delta t = \frac{60}{2\pi \times n_R}, s \tag{1}$$

Incorporating the calculated value of Δt with Equation (1) into the solver settings enhances simulation convergence. This characteristic is applied to all simulations herein adjusted for the model's angular velocity n_R. The boundary conditions and CFX-Solver settings are detailed, for clarity, in Table 1.

 https://doi.org/10.3390/engproc2026122014

Table 1. Boundary conditions and parameters of the computational process.

Name	Value
Boundary conditions:	
Inlet velocity Vin, m/s	5–23
Outlet average static pressure	0 Pa
Angular velocity nR, tr/min	37–1855
Turbulence model	SST
Fluid	Air
Rotating walls	Yes
Solver settings:	
Advection scheme	High resolution
Physical timescale, s	Var acc. nR Equation (1)
Max iterations	100
Convergence criteria RMS residual target	1×10^{-4}

Upon completion of the solution in CFX-Solver, a results file is generated, from which data required for subsequent structural (FSI) analysis are extracted. The computed pressure data (Figure 2) is transmitted to the solution of the fluid–structure interaction problem, as described in [12]. Throughout the simulation, convergence is rigorously monitored; in the event of divergence, the results file is discarded, and the relevant data is excluded from the analysis. Post processing in CFX-Post module involves detailed examination of the velocity field data, determination of pressure distributions around the model, assessment of vortex structures, and calculation of the fluid-induced torque M.

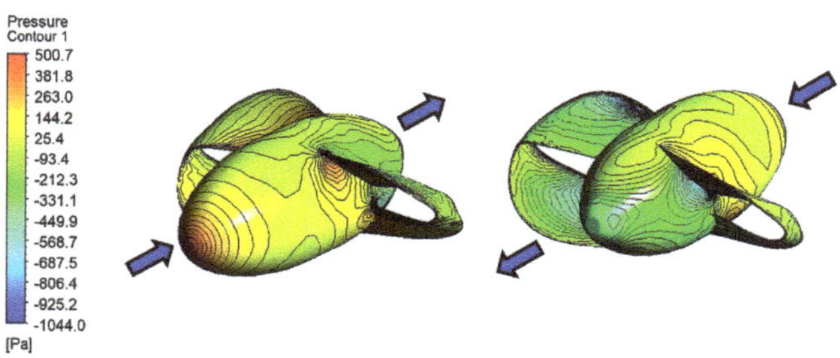

Figure 2. Static pressure distribution contours on Model 3 surface in CFX-Post.

3. Results and Discussion

To visualize the flow in the rotating part of the stand, the CFD model developed above is used, and more specifically, CFX-Post. The module helps to analyze the air movement between the paired blades, to make a comparison with the conventional model and to determine some parameters characterizing the operation of the turbines. Boundary conditions for the numerical simulations are derived from data obtained through experiments conducted on the custom-built test stand, as referenced in [12].

The torque M is computed in CFX-Post [11] by integrating the pressure distribution over the entire surface of the turbine wheel. The circumferential component of the pressure is extracted, multiplied by the corresponding surface area, and then by the radial distance to the axis of rotation. The resistive torque due to frictional forces is also accounted for, although with a sign opposite to that of the useful torque M. The mechanical power output is later computed as the product of the net torque and the angular velocity.

The angular velocity of the model, measured during the experimental trials with the help of a UNI-T UT372 tachometer and a Pitot tube in conjunction with a Testo400 [12], are in the range n_R = 37–1855 tr/min at inlet velocities V_{in} = 5.7–22.9 m/s. The experimental

 https://doi.org/10.3390/engproc2026122014

results are depicted in Figure 3, where the ordinate represents the calculated electrical power output Pel determined by

$$P_{el} = 3 \times U \times I \quad (2)$$

where (2) I, U represent the current and voltage values measured using the UNI-T UT210E instrument, multiplied by a factor of 3 to account for the three-phase configuration of the electrical generator.

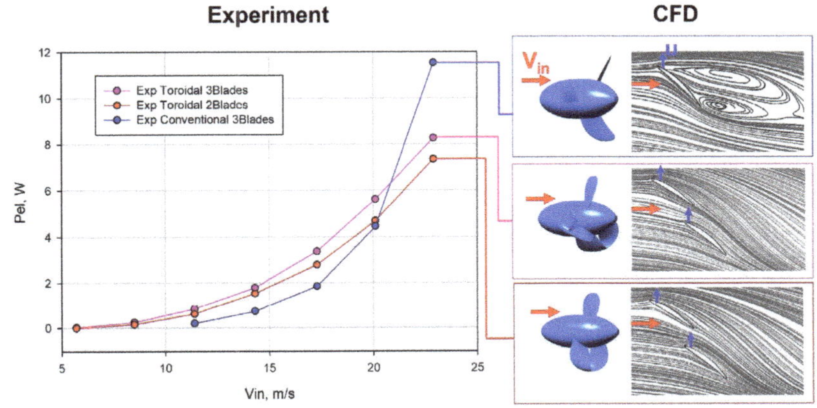

Figure 3. Experimentally obtained data on the bench for the three turbines at constant air velocities at the inlet with the same electricity load and streamline visualization in CFX-Post module.

The power curves presented in Figure 3 demonstrate a clear positive correlation between electrical power outputs and increased inlet air velocity Vin. This trend is characteristic of axial-flow turbines and aligns with the performance curves reported in [4] for similar devices, such as the Shine turbine. Among the tested configurations, the turbine equipped with conventional blade geometry (Model 1) achieves the highest power output. However, this does not necessarily imply superior efficiency (C_p) relative to the toroidal blade models.

Notably, the conventional turbine failed to initiate rotation at air velocity 10 m/s, resulting in the absence of data for the initial portion of Model 1 curve depicted in Figure 3. Such a limitation arises because at reduced kinetic energy, the pressure difference generated across the blades is insufficient to produce the torque required to overcome system resistances and initiate rotor motion. Operation of the conventional turbine begins after Vin reaches 11.4 m/s. In contrast, Models 2 and 3 commence rotation at V_{in} = 5.7 m/s, which is explained by the larger blade surface area, enabling greater lift and more effective energy transfer from the airflow, as opposed to Model 1. All experimental data for the three turbine models, depicted in Figure 3, are collected under constant and the same electrical load implemented as three resistors connected in parallel.

Provided to the right of Figure 3 are the computed streamlines for each turbine model at the same radial position (R = const). Red arrows denote the inlet velocity V_{in}, while blue arrows indicate the tangential velocity of the profiles u. Numerical simulations are performed using boundary conditions corresponding to the V_{in}, n_R, pair derived from the experimental setup [12]. This approach ensures a comprehensive analysis of all the three turbines, facilitating a comparative evaluation of their performance indicators. In wind turbine studies, the parameters C_p, M, and TSR are used to compare various design

 https://doi.org/10.3390/engproc2026122014

modifications and turbine types. Detailed methodologies and considerations for their application are extensively discussed in the specialized literature [13,14].

The power coefficient is defined by the relation as follows:

$$C_{p,mech} = \frac{M \times \omega}{\frac{1}{2} \times \rho \times A \times V^3}, \quad (3)$$

where

$$A = \frac{\pi \times D^2}{4} \quad (4)$$

is the swept area of the turbine disk, with a calculated diameter of D = 0.192 m.

The ratio of the circumferential speed, determined at the maximum radius ($R_{max} = \frac{D}{2} = 0.096$ m), relative to the incoming flow velocity, i.e., the tip–speed ratio (TSR), is given by

$$TSR = \frac{u_{max}}{V_{in}}, \quad (5)$$

where $u_{max} = R_{max}.\omega$; ω is angular speed, rad/s.

These parameters are calculated from both experimental measurements and corresponding numerical simulations. The resulting values are used to determine the power coefficients across different operational regimes for all the three turbine models (encompassing both experimentally tested configurations and those yielding the maximum C_p values).

Two numerical models with two test regimes TSR = 2.4 and TSR = 1.8 are set up. Illustrated in Figure 4 is a comparative analysis of the power coefficient for the three turbine configurations, with values derived from both CFD simulations and experimental measurements of inlet velocity V_{in} and angular velocity n_R. Noticeably, the maximum computed C_P remains below the Betz limit of 0.59 [13], thereby confirming the physical validity of the model and its suitability for integration with the experimental test stand.

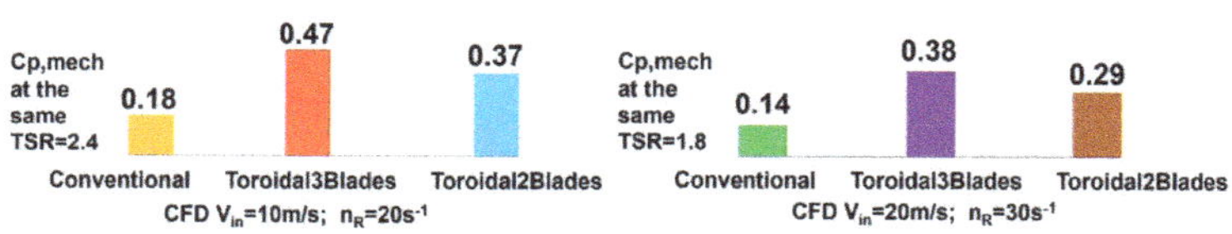

Figure 4. Comparison of the power coefficient calculated for the three turbine models under different operating conditions.

The conventional turbine design exhibits the lowest power coefficients, with C_P values of 0.18 in the first test regime (TSR = 2.4) and 0.14 in the second (TSR = 1.8), despite achieving the highest absolute power output at highest inlet velocity Vin = 22.9 m/s (Figure 3).

Analysis of the streamlines in Figure 3 reveals that the paired-blade configurations (Models 2 and 3) effectively suppress flow separation at the airfoils' walls. In contrast, the conventional single-blade design (Model 1) is characterized by the formation of a vortex pair downstream of the blade, which explains the low C_P values in the current investigation. The enhanced C_P values observed in Models 2 and 3 are indicative of superior aerodynamic performance and more efficient energy conversion.

4. Conclusions

For the two toroidal blade configurations, the flow remains smoothly attached across the tandem airfoils, with no evidence of flow separation. This phenomenon explains the attainment of higher power coefficients C_p. Specifically, the toroidal turbine, featuring three

https://doi.org/10.3390/engproc2026122014

paired blades, achieves a peak C_p of 0.47 within the tested range of velocities, whereas the conventional turbine Model 1 exhibits the lowest power coefficient C_p, reaching only 0.14.

The conventional turbine Model 1 initiates operation exclusively at air speeds exceeding 11.4 m/s. This threshold is primarily due to the smaller blade surface area available for aerodynamic interaction, resulting in diminished lift generation compared to the toroidal blade models 2 and 3. Additionally, significant energy losses result from secondary flows at the blade tip, which preclude the generation of a useful circumferential force necessary for torque production at the maximum radius cross-sections. In contrast, models 2 and 3 benefit from a continuous blade-to-blade transition at the periphery, effectively minimizing tip vortex size and associated losses. For models 2 and 3, their rotation starts after reaching an input speed V_{in} = 5.7 m/s.

Although Model 1 realizes the lowest C_p values, this does not necessarily mean that its design is inefficient. Optimization of the blade profile—specifically adjusting the blade stagger angle—should be explored to avoid flow separation on the airfoil suction side. Such refinements have the potential to improve the aerodynamic airfoil performance and overall efficiency of the conventional turbine configuration.

The attainable TSR values are limited by both the maximum air speed provided by the aerodynamic test channel and the structural strength of the stand components. The objective of this work is to evaluate which of the developed turbine models perform most efficiently within this realizable range. The maximum air velocity at the nozzle exit of the wind tunnel is approximately 25 m/s. Indeed, there is difference between the C_p values. This is because C_p, as defined by Equation (3), is based on mechanical power (torque and angular velocity), whereas Figure 3 presents electrical power. Naturally, there is always a difference between generated mechanical and electrical power, which depends on the efficiency of the generator. We are currently working on improving the electrical testing circuitry to better quantify this efficiency. Mathematically, this relationship can be expressed as $C_{p,mech} > C_{p,\ el}$, $C_{p,\ mech} = \frac{M.\omega}{0.5.A.V^3}$, $C_{p,\ el} = \frac{P_{el}}{0.5.A.V^3}$.

Here, Pel is determined experimentally (as the product of voltage and current), while torque M is obtained from CFD simulations. The streamlines shown in Figure 3 correspond to a flow velocity of 22.9 m/s, with measured rotational frequencies of n_R = 30.9 s^{-1} (conventional turbine), n_R = 24.2 s^{-1} (three-bladed toroidal), and n_R = 22.8 s^{-1} (two-bladed toroidal).

It is clarified that the improved performance of the toroidal blades is primarily attributed to the pressure redistribution resulting from the tandem arrangement of two airfoil sections, which helps to prevent flow separation along the blade surfaces. In future work, we plan to perform a detailed investigation of the vortex structures formed near the periphery of the toroidal blades, as these are expected to differ significantly from those observed in conventional geometries.

In this study, the team combined experimental and CFD data to address the research objectives within the existing constraints. Specifically, the experimentally obtained average flow velocity and rotational speed were used as input parameters in the CFD simulations, from which the torque values were subsequently derived. In the next phase of the project, focusing on toroidal turbines, more advanced measuring instruments will be implemented to enable detailed comparison between the experimental and numerical results, including uncertainty and error analysis.

Author Contributions: Conceptualization, S.T. and A.Y.; methodology, A.Y.; software, S.T.; validation, A.Y., formal analysis, A.Y.; investigation, A.B.; resources, A.A.; data curation, A.B.; writing—original draft preparation, A.B.; writing—review and editing, A.Y.; visualization, S.T.; supervision, A.B.; project administration, A.A.; funding acquisition, A.B. and S.T. All authors have read and agreed to the published version of the manuscript.

https://doi.org/10.3390/engproc2026122014

Funding: The study was partially funded by the scientific research project NP7/2025 "Research and comparative analysis of power/working machines with elements of complex three-dimensional shape" at the Technical University of Varna, funded specifically by the state budget. We thank the entire project team and its leader for the data processing and visualization activities. The authors thank their university colleagues for their assistance.

Institutional Review Board Statement: Not applicable.

Informed Consent Statement: Informed consent was obtained from all subjects involved in the study.

Data Availability Statement: The data presented in this study is available on request from the corresponding authors.

Conflicts of Interest: The authors declare no conflicts of interest.

References

1. Rosato, A.; Perrotta, A.; Maffei, L. Commercial Small-Scale Horizontal and Vertical Wind Turbines: A Comprehensive Review of Geometry, Materials, Costs and Performance. *Energies* **2024**, *17*, 3125. [CrossRef]
2. Chong, W.; Muzammil, W.; Wong, K.; Wang, C.; Gwani, M.; Chu, Y.C.; Poh, S. Cross axis wind turbine: Pushing the limit of wind turbine technology with complementary design. *Appl. Energy* **2017**, *207*, 78–97. [CrossRef]
3. Tang, X.; Huang, X.; Peng, R.; Liu, X. A Direct Approach of Design Optimization for Small Horizontal Axis Wind Turbine Blades. *Procedia CIRP* **2015**, *36*, 12–16. [CrossRef]
4. Shine Portable Wind Turbine. Specs. 5 May 2025. Available online: https://shineturbine.com/products/shinewindturbine (accessed on 12 September 2025).
5. Shine Turbine Quick Start User Guide & Instructions 2024 Aurea Technologies Inc. Available online: https://cdn.shopify.com/s/files/1/0742/2715/5220/files/Shine_QSG_PDF_May1_2024.pdf?v=1715609412/ (accessed on 13 August 2025).
6. Fazylova, A.; Alipbayev, K.; Aden, A.; Oraz, F.; Iliev, T.; Stoyanov, I. A Comparative Review of Vertical Axis Wind Turbine Designs: Savonius Rotor vs. Darrieus Rotor. *Inventions* **2025**, *10*, 95. [CrossRef]
7. Tadros, M.; Boulougouris, E. Performance Assessment of B-Series Marine Propellers with Cupping and Face Camber Ratio Using Machine Learning Techniques. *J. Mar. Sci. Eng.* **2025**, *13*, 1345. [CrossRef]
8. Propeller, A.I. Design Optimization using CAESES and AirShaper. Available online: https://airshaper.com/blog/ai-propeller-design (accessed on 4 September 2025).
9. *ANSYS CFX-Solver Manager User's Guide; Simulate the Future*; ANSYS, Inc.: Canonsburg, PA, USA, 2021; pp. 1–214. Available online: https://ansyshelp.ansys.com/public/Views/Secured/corp/v251/en/pdf/Ansys_CFX-Solver_Manager_Users_Guide.pdf (accessed on 15 April 2025).
10. *ANSYS CFX Tutorials*; ANSYS, Release 18.0 January 2017. pp. 1–892. Available online: https://www.scribd.com/document/406467578/ANSYS-CFX-Tutorials-R180-pdf (accessed on 1 July 2025).
11. *ANSYS CFX-Solver Theory Guide*; Release 2025 R1; Published in U.S.A.; 2025. pp. 1–392. Available online: https://ansyshelp.ansys.com/public/Views/Secured/corp/v251/en/pdf/Ansys_CFX-Solver_Theory_Guide.pdf (accessed on 28 August 2025).
12. Yangyozov, A.; Bankova, A.; Tenev, S.; Atanasov, A. Developing a Functional Test Stand for Advanced Air Turbine Models. In Proceedings of the 6th International Conference on Communications, Information, Electronic and Energy Systems (CIEES 2025), Ruse, Bulgaria, 26–28 November 2025.
13. Bankova, A.; Yangyozov, A.; Tenev, S.; Atanasov, A. Simulation of a Two-Phase Fluid Flow in a Design Solution of a Secondary Radial Settling Tank for Wastewater Treatment. *Eng. Proc.* **2025**, *104*, 21. [CrossRef]
14. Mannwell, J.; Mcgowan, J.; Rogers, A. *Wind Energy Explained: Theory, Design and Application*, 2nd ed.; John Wiley & Sons Ltd.: London, UK, 2009; pp. 1–705.

https://doi.org/10.3390/engproc2026122014

engineering proceedings

MDPI

Proceeding Paper

Progress on Developing a Sustainable BESS Technical–Economic Model by Mapping the Latest Grid-Connected Installations in Bulgaria †

Dimitrina Koeva [1,*], Metodi Dimitrov [1] and Vladimir Zinoviev [2]

1 Department of Electric Power Distribution and Electrical Equipment, Center of Competence "Smart Mechatronic, Eco- and Energy-Saving Systems and Technologies", Technical University of Gabrovo, 5300 Gabrovo, Bulgaria; m.dimitrov@tugab.bg

2 Department Economics of Transport and Energy, University of National and World Economy, 1700 Sofia, Bulgaria; vzinoviev@unwe.bg

* Correspondence: dkoeva@tugab.bg

† Presented at the 6th International Conference on Communications, Information, Electronic and Energy Systems, 26–28 November 2025, Ruse, Bulgaria.

Abstract

The rapid construction and commissioning of battery energy storage system (BESS) installations, both standalone and combined with photovoltaic power plants (PVPPs), is rapidly reshaping the energy market. Mapping these latest iterations in the energy infrastructure allows for a detailed analysis of the effects they have on the grid, in correlation with the already abundant operational PPV. This paper will provide a list of all BESS installations commissioned between 1 January and 30 September 2025. Taking into consideration their grid-connection power, and respective battery capacity, along with their geographical location and co-located (or lack thereof) PVPPs, the following-up analysis aims to answer several key questions: how do these installations compare to one another in terms of power, capacity and distribution across Bulgaria; how do they affect the availability of electric power from PVPP, co-located or not, to the end consumers; and how does that shift in availability affect the profits, both for the BESS and PVPP owners, based on the shifting price of electricity?

Keywords: energy storage; energy storage system; battery energy storage system; economics; photovoltaic power plants

1. Introduction

This study profiles grid-connected energy storage systems (ESSs), both standalone and co-located with PVPPs, based on a curated project list and an accompanying dataset [1]. All reviewed installations were commissioned before 30 September 2025. Methodologically, the workflow provides a reproducible pipeline for location normalization and unit harmonization suited to regulatory and planning analyses. Standardized location descriptors (region -> municipality -> settlement; parcel identifiers) and harmonized technical parameters add to the reproducibility. Eight nominally separate PVPP + ESS projects labeled 1 through 8 were aggregated into a single composite site, since they are located at the same site [2]. When ESS power is reported in kVA, values are converted to MW, assuming a power factor PF = 1; missing power and/or capacity are set to zero. These constraints notwithstanding, the dataset offers a transparent baseline for follow-on geospatial, techno-economic, and grid-impact assessments.

This publication explores the current state of the integration process regarding battery energy storage systems (later referred to as BESSs or ESSs) in Bulgaria's electrical grid. There is an interactive map of the country with the location, power, and capacity of these systems. The objectives are threefold. First, to characterize the techno-geographic profile of the current project portfolio, including the distribution of ESS power and capacity across administrative units and by project type (PVPP + ESS vs. standalone ESS). Second, to quantify storage "duration" (hours), defined as the ratio of usable capacity to connection power (MWh/MW), for projects with complete metrics, thereby illuminating typical operational envelopes relevant to PV integration and peak management. Third, to identify patterns of scale—for example, the prevalence of repeated mid-scale configurations versus singular large installations—that may reflect permitting practices, interconnection constraints, or developer strategies.

Across N = 19 unique projects, the portfolio comprises a total ESS connection power of 379.73 MW and a total storage capacity of 981.35 MWh. Projects with both metrics explicitly available exhibit a capacity-weighted mean storage duration of around 3.53 h (range 2.05 to 4.00 h; median 2.70 h). The sample mixes PVPP + ESS (9/19) and standalone ESS (10/19), including one large two-stage installation (124 MW/496 MWh) and a repeated "mid-scale" motif around 5 MW/13.4 MWh and 10 MW/27 MWh. Geographically, the projects are distributed across multiple municipalities and regions, with cadastral parcel identifiers enabling precise spatial traceability for subsequent mapping and regional aggregation (Figure 1). Each site is represented with a number, referenced in Table 1.

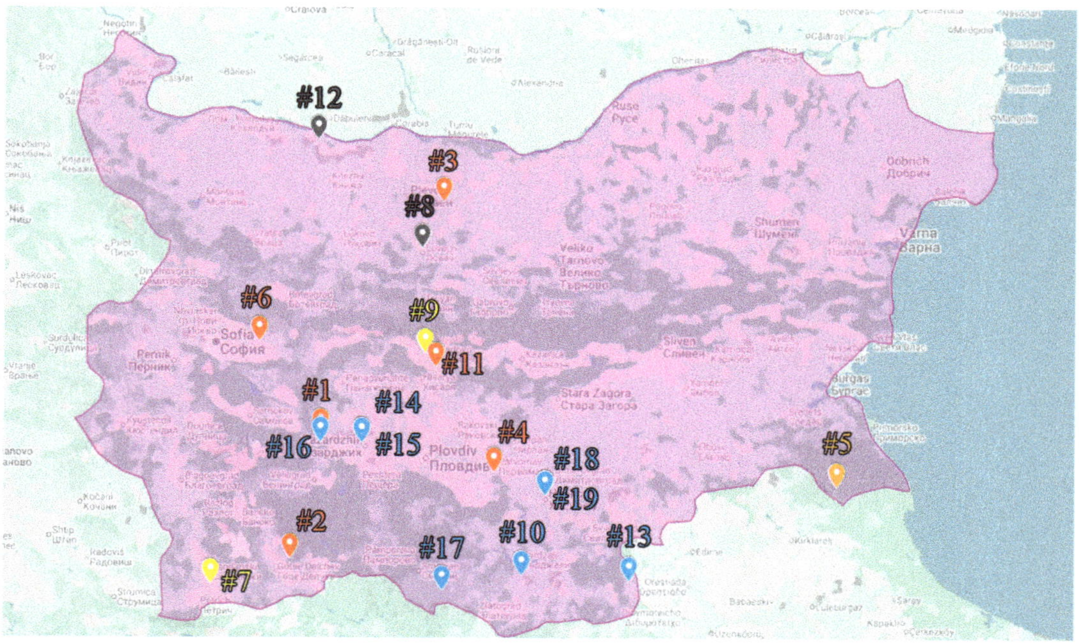

Figure 1. Interactive map of Bulgaria with all of the sites marked on it. Sites in red represent missing values (power, storage, or both). Sites in gray are the large-scale installations. Sites in blue are the later discussed 10 MW/27 MWh motif and sites in yellow and orange fall in none of the above categories.

 https://doi.org/10.3390/engproc2026122015

Table 1. A list of all the BESS sites commissioned in Bulgaria between 1 January and 30 September 2025.

Site	Town, Province	Power	Storage	Type
#1	Akandzhievo, Pazardzhik	3 MW	N/A	PVPP + BESS
#2	Leshten, Blagoevgrad	N/A	N/A	PVPP + BESS
#3	Pordim, Pleven	N/A	N/A	PVPP + BESS
#4	Debar, Plovdiv	10 MW	N/A	PVPP + BESS
#5	Malko Tarnovo, Burgas	110 MW	130 MWh	PVPP + BESS
#6	Stolnik, Sofia-Province	N/A	N/A	PVPP + BESS
#7	Novo Delchevo, Blagoevgrad	1.25 MW	3.7 MWh	BESS
#8	Lovech, Lovech	124 MW	496 MWh	BESS
#9	Sopot, Plovdiv	1.48 MW	1.65 MWh	PVPP + BESS
#10	Momchilgrad, Kardzhali	10 MW	27 MWh	BESS
#11	Dabene, Plovdiv	N/A	N/A	PVPP + BESS
#12	Selanovtsi, Vratsa	40 MW	107 MWh	PVPP + BESS
#13	Ivaylovgrad, Haskovo	10 MW	27 MWh	BESS
#14	Pazardzhik, Pazardzhik	10 MW	27 MWh	BESS
#15	Pazardzhik, Pazardzhik	10 MW	27 MWh	BESS
#16	Belovo, Pazardzhik	10 MW	27 MWh	BESS
#17	Rudozem, Smolyan	10 MW	27 MWh	BESS
#18	Haskovo, Haskovo	10 MW	27 MWh	BESS
#19	Haskovo, Haskovo	10 MW	27 MWh	BESS

The rapid expansion of photovoltaic generation amplifies the need for flexible resources capable of mitigating variability, aligning supply with demand, and supporting distribution and transmission-level reliability. Grid-connected energy storage systems (ESSs) address these needs by providing short-to-mid-duration services such as peak shaving, intra-day energy shifting, ramp-rate control, and reserve provision [3,4]. When co-located with PVPPs (PVPP + ESS), storage can also enable higher self-consumption and improve the economic efficiency of interconnection assets. Against this backdrop, a transparent, location-aware inventory of ESS projects is essential for planning studies, regulatory oversight, and investment appraisal. In Bulgaria, as in many European power systems, the accelerating deployment of PPV and the emergence of battery storage projects heighten the importance of consistent siting, permitting, and compliance practices. Publicly available project descriptions—often prepared for administrative and regulatory processes—contain rich but heterogeneous information on technical parameters and geography (for example, installed or connection power, usable capacity, cadastral parcel identifiers, municipality and region). Converting these narrative records into a harmonized analytical dataset enables reproducible assessments of technology mix, scale, and spatial distribution. It also facilitates traceability from aggregate statistics back to the underlying projects, a prerequisite for robust policy and grid-impact analysis [5,6].

This study develops such a dataset by systematizing a curated list of ESS projects, comprising both standalone installations and systems co-located with PVPPs. We standardize these descriptors into an administrative path (region -> municipality -> settlement) and extract cadastral identifiers (parcel numbers, RPI/PI) where available, supporting precise spatial referencing. On the technical side, we harmonize ESS connection power (MW) and energy capacity (MWh); when power is reported in kVA, we convert to MW, assuming power factor PF = 1 in the absence of explicit specifications. Missing power or capacity values are retained as zeros to preserve the completeness of the project list while transparently signaling data gaps. Eight nominally separate PV projects labeled 1 through 8, located at the same site, are aggregated into a single composite site for analysis.

https://doi.org/10.3390/engproc2026122015

2. Regulatory and Institutional Framework

2.1. Construction and Siting

In Bulgaria, the design, construction, and lawful use of PVPPs and energy storage systems (ESSs) are governed by the Spatial Development Act (SDA) and overseen by the National Construction Control Directorate (NCCD). The NCCD exercises legality control over construction, may suspend or order removal of unlawful works, and supervises compliance at commissioning and use stages—functions explicitly framed as SDA enforcement.

2.2. Energy-Sector Definition

The Energy Act recognizes storage facilities as part of the electricity system and (via its Additional Provisions) provides a legal definition of an "energy storage facility," clarifying the distinction between grid-oriented storage and assets used solely for self-consumption that do not inject to the grid. The NCCD has circulated guidance reflecting this definition; more recent amendments also define "co-located storage" with generation. These definitional elements matter for permitting pathways and market roles.

2.3. Grid Connection

Technical and procedural rules for connecting consumption, generation, and storage to electricity networks are set by Ordinance №6 of 28 March 2024 [2], which superseded the earlier 2014 ordinance and was promulgated in State Gazette №28 on 2 April 2024. The ordinance expressly covers storage connections and amendments to existing connections. Sector commentary notes a concurrent alignment of connection thresholds (projects over 10 MW to the transmission grid operated by ESO; under or up to 10 MW to distribution grids) and transitional arrangements for projects holding pre-13 October 2023 grid agreements.

2.4. EU Context

Bulgaria's framework is shaped by the EU Clean Energy Package. Directive (EU) 2019/944 establishes market rules and restricts DSO/TSO ownership of storage, allowing narrowly tailored exceptions subject to regulatory approval; Regulation (EU) 2019/943 sets internal-market principles affecting dispatch, balancing, and capacity mechanisms. The revised Renewable Energy Directive (EU) 2023/2413 (RED III) raises the 2030 RES target (min. 42.5%), reinforcing the system's need for storage to integrate variable renewables [2,7]. These instruments provide the backdrop against which national definitions, ownership restrictions, and connection procedures are transposed and applied.

3. Materials and Methods

3.1. Data Sources and Scope

The analysis draws on two inputs:

- A curated project list describing PVPPs co-located with ESSs and standalone ESSs.
- A companion dataset (Table 2), containing project names and location descriptors. The unit of observation is the site. Per the research brief, eight nominally separate PV projects labeled 1 through 8 are aggregated into a single composite site, based on their location.

https://doi.org/10.3390/engproc2026122015

Table 2. Cosine profile of the hourly production of PV generation, based on which we have the hourly real PV + BESS generation (MW), proxy PV generation (MW), and total PVPP generation (MW), starting at 05:00 and ending at 19:00.

Hour	Cosine Profile	PV + ESS (MW)	Proxy PV (MW)	Total (MW)
05:00	0.000	0.000	0.000	0.000
06:00	0.000	0.000	0.000	0.000
07:00	0.067	14.420	11.020	25.442
08:00	0.250	53.810	41.120	94.933
09:00	0.500	107.620	82.240	189.865
10:00	0.750	161.440	123.360	284.798
11:00	0.933	200.830	153.460	354.288
12:00	1.000	215.250	164.480	379.730
13:00	0.933	200.830	153.460	354.288
14:00	0.750	161.440	123.360	284.798
15:00	0.500	107.620	82.240	189.865
16:00	0.250	53.810	41.120	94.933
17:00	0.067	14.420	11.020	25.442
18:00	0.000	0.000	0.000	0.000
19:00	0.000	0.000	0.000	0.000

3.2. Inclusion Criteria and Unit Conventions

Projects are included if they (a) contain an ESS (standalone or PVPP + ESS) and (b) report at least one of ESS connection power (kW/kVA/MW) or usable capacity (kWh/MWh). Power is expressed in MW, capacity in MWh. PV installed power (kWp) is recorded only for context and is not used in ESS power/capacity metrics.

3.3. Variable Definitions

- ESS connection power (MW): the rated AC power at the point of connection;
- ESS capacity (MWh): usable energy at the AC side (when ambiguous, the stated capacity is taken verbatim);
- Storage duration (h): h = MWh/MW, calculated only where both metrics are present;
- Project type: PVPP + ESS vs. standalone ESS;
- Administrative path: region -> municipality -> settlement; supplemented with parcel identifiers (PI/RPI) when present.

3.4. Data Standardization

Unit harmonization: kW to MW; kWh to MWh; kVA to MW, using PF = 1 when power factor is not provided (conservative, transparent assumption).

- Inverter-based power statements: When power is specified via inverter counts (for example—48 inverters x 110 kW per stage, two stages), the site power is the sum of inverter ratings across stages, converted to MW;
- Staged projects: If stages are additive and explicitly quantified, stage values are summed; otherwise, the clearly reported stage is retained and the remainder is documented as missing;
- Missing values: Absent power and/or capacity are set to 0 by design to signal data gaps while preserving the site in aggregates. Zeros therefore denote "unknown," not physical zero.

3.5. Aggregations and Derived Indicators

- Site-level: original records are consolidated at site level; for the 1–8 group, entries are collapsed into one composite site and their location descriptors concatenated (deduplicated);

https://doi.org/10.3390/engproc2026122015

- Portfolio-level: totals of ESS power (MW) and capacity (MWh); counts by project type; and distributions of storage duration (h) for sites with complete metrics;
- Geographic: sums of MW and MWh by municipality and region using the standardized administrative path.

3.6. Statistical Treatment and Presentation

We report descriptive statistics (count, min-max, median) for MW, MWh, and duration (h); portfolio totals; and type shares (PVPP + ESS vs. standalone ESS). Where visualizations are used (bar charts by region, histograms of MW/MWh, duration distributions), axes and units are explicitly labeled, and one metric is shown per figure to avoid overplotting. All rounding is to two decimals unless transparency requires full precision (for example, cumulative totals)

3.7. Limitations and Sensitivity

Results are constrained by incomplete reporting (zeros as placeholders), the PF = 1 assumption for kVA -> MW, and ambiguity in whether stated capacities are usable AC values. Sensitivity checks can be performed by varying PF (0.9–1.0) and recalculating totals and durations; staged builds can be bracketed by "as-built" vs. "fully built" scenarios when documentation becomes available.

3.8. Reproducibility

The standardized location table is provided in Table 1, enabling re-calculation of all portfolio and geographic aggregates and straightforward revision if improved site specifications are supplied.

3.9. Proxy PV Capacity

To reflect the reality that numerous PV plants are already in operation but fall outside this study's empirical dataset due to unknown counts and ratings, we introduce a proxy PV capacity used solely for scenario and balance checks. The proxy assumes that the aggregate AC capacity of the out-of-sample PV fleet equals the aggregate AC connection power of the standalone ESS—for example, those not co-located with PV plants within our dataset. The purpose of this construct is to provide a transparent, conservative baseline for counterfactual reasoning (e.g., PV-backstopping thought experiments) without altering the primary, observation-based results. It serves as a balancing proxy—a placeholder for the "background" solar generation plausibly available in the real system, while avoiding double-counting with the PVPP + ESS sites already present in the dataset. The scope and constraints of it include aggregation and no spatial redistribution across regions or municipalities. It also represents power only (MW), not energy (MWh), and does not encode seasonal/diurnal variability, availability, or export limits. Finally, it does not modify site-level metrics, type shares, or duration statistics derived from observed data. Results derived with this proxy should be read as illustrative system-level bounds rather than as an inventory of specific PVPPs, where improved information on the existing operating PV fleet becomes available with specific counts, AC ratings, and geography. The proxy can be replaced by empirically grounded PV aggregates and, if desired, distributed geographically to enable network-aware analyses.

4. Results

4.1. Portfolio Overview

The consolidated sample comprises N = 19 sites (including the aggregated PV projects 1–8 as a single site). Across the portfolio, the total ESS connection power is 379.73 MW

 https://doi.org/10.3390/engproc2026122015

and the total storage capacity is 981.35 MWh. The mix includes PV + ESS (9/19 sites) and standalone ESS (10/19 sites). Standalone ESS accounts for 215.25 MW (56.7%) and 742.70 MWh (75.7%), while PVPP + ESS accounts for 164.48 MW (43.3%) and 238.65 MWh (24.8%). Several PV + ESS entries report ESS association without complete metrics; per protocol, missing values are retained as zeros and excluded from calculations. The portfolio is dominated by one large, two-stage installation (124 MW/496 MWh), which contributes 32.7% of total power and 50.5% of total capacity. The aggregated PV 1–8 composite site (40 MW/107.2 MWh) contributes 10.5% of power and 10.9% of capacity. Two mid-scale patterns are visible: 10 MW/27 MWh (23.7%/24.8%) and around 10.56 MW/21.672 MWh (2.8%/2.2%). A smaller standalone unit (1 MW/3.7 MWh) contributes 0.39%/0.17%.

4.2. Storage Duration

For the thirteen sites with both metrics reported, the fleet-average duration (calculated as total MWh divided by total MW) is around 2.68 h. The median duration is 2.70 h, with a range from around 2.04 h (21.672 MWh/10.56 MW) to 4.00 h (496.392 MWh/124.098 MW). The aggregated PV 1–8 site exhibits around 2.68 h (107.2 MWh/40 MW), and the 10 MW/27 MWh site exhibits 2.70 h. Overall, durations cluster in the 2 to 4 h band, consistent with short-to-mid-duration applications (intra-day shifting, peak shaving, ramp-rate control).

4.3. Composition by Project Type

- PVPP + ESS (9 sites):

Contribute 164.48 MW/238.65 MWh, largely driven by the aggregated 1–8 composite (40 MW/107.2 MWh). Several PV-co-located entries lack explicit ESS capacity and therefore do not affect duration statistics. One PV + ESS entry contributes around 4.8 MW based on AC equipment (3 × 1600 kVA, PF = 1), with no stated energy capacity.

- Standalone ESS (10 sites):

Contribute 215.25 MW/742.7 MWh, including the large two-stage installation (124 MW/496 MWh) and two mid-scale motifs (10 MW/27 MWh; around 10.56 MW/21.672 MWh).

4.4. Proxy PV Capacity

To reflect solar generation that exists in reality but lies outside the empirical dataset, we adopt a proxy PV capacity set equal to the aggregate AC connection power of the standalone ESS subset—215.25 MW.

4.5. Data Completeness and Traceability

Zeros mark missing power/capacity by design and are excluded from duration aggregates. Location standardization yields an administrative path (region -> municipality -> settlement) and captures parcel identifiers (RPI/PI) where present; each standardized record preserves the original location text to maintain auditability. These features enable direct roll-ups by administrative unit and straightforward verification against source descriptions.

5. Analysis

5.1. Portfolio Structure and Concentration

The sample exhibits a heavy-tailed size distribution: one two-stage standalone installation (124 MW/496 MWh) supplies around 33% of total ESS power and around 50% of total capacity. This concentration shapes portfolio indicators and suggests that incremental additions to this large node (for example staging and augmentation) would materially shift system-level statistics. The aggregated PV composite (1–8; 40 MW/107.2 MWh) accounts for a further 10% of power and nearly 11% of capacity, indicating a secondary pole of influence. Excluding the largest

 https://doi.org/10.3390/engproc2026122015

installation yields a portfolio-average duration of around 1.9 h (485 MWh/255 MW), while excluding instead the aggregated PV composite yields around 2.57 h (874 MWh/339 MW). Excluding both produces around 1.75 h (378 MWh/216 MW). These sensitivity checks underline how a few high-impact sites drive apparent "system averages."

5.2. Storage Duration and Operational Envelope

Among sites with complete metrics (thirteen cases), durations cluster in the 2 to 4 h band, with a median of 2.7 h and a capacity-weighted mean of around 3.53 h. This range is consistent with short-to-mid-duration use cases such as PV ramp-rate smoothing, midday-to-evening shifting, and peak shaving at distribution level. The repeated 5 MW/near 13.4 MWh motif (1–8 composite) and the 10 MW/27 MWh configuration point to templated designs, likely aligned to interconnection, equipment sizing, and site-specific load or market objectives. The large standalone system at around 4 h suggests a strategy oriented toward deeper intra-day arbitrage, reserve stacking, or more stringent ramp control.

5.3. Type Mix and Data Completeness

While standalone ESS entries outnumber PVPP + ESS, the latter contribute a smaller share of aggregate MWh due to incomplete reporting for several PV-co-located sites.

5.4. Geographic Traceability and Planning Implications

The standardized administrative paths (region -> municipality -> settlement) and extracted parcel identifiers (RPI/PI) enable reproducible roll-ups by jurisdiction and straightforward cross-checking with permitting records. Even without coordinates, parcel-level references provide sufficient precision for follow-on geocoding, proximity analysis to substations, and assessment of likely interconnection voltage levels. From a planning perspective, the observed clustering around 5–10 MW and around 2–3 h suggests designs tailored to distribution-level constraints, PV self-consumption/curtailment mitigation, and peak management. The dominance of an over 100 MW asset indicates parallel activity at transmission-relevant scales and underscores the need to consider both DSO and TSO interfaces in scenario work.

5.5. Interpreting the Proxy PV Capacity

We use the proxy PV capacity—set equal to the aggregate AC connection power of the standalone ESS subset (215.25 MW)—as an interpretive device for power sufficiency, without altering observation-based metrics. Analytically, the proxy benchmarks whether a background fleet of operating, yet unobserved PV plants could meet the charging-power constraint of the standalone batteries. As a sanity check, applying the previously established capacity-weighted mean duration of around 3.53 h to 215.25 MW implies around 759.83 MWh of energy for a full daily cycle. This is close to, but not a substitute for, the observed standalone aggregate of 742.7 MWh. The 2.3% gap reflects rounding and compositional differences and is purely a consistency check. Actual energy adequacy still depends on realized PV energy, including PR, DC/AC ratio, irradiance, and seasonality, and on operational limits like the battery C-rate, interconnection and export constraints, and round-trip efficiency. The proxy avoids double-counting with PVPP + ESS sites and serves as a system-level benchmark and not as an inventory claim, nor a guarantee of seasonal adequacy.

5.6. Cosine-Bell PV Variants with vs. Without ESS

In Table 2 and Figure 2 below we establish a simple cosine profile of the hourly production of PV generation, based on which we will run scenarios for real PVPP + BESS generation (excl. the BESS component) and imaginary proxy PV generation, before

 https://doi.org/10.3390/engproc2026122015

introducing ESS installations into the mix. We will also establish a constant value for the demand for power in order to explore particular cases of wasted generation of PV power plants due to over-generation during the early afternoon and how ESS installations can be used to correct that.

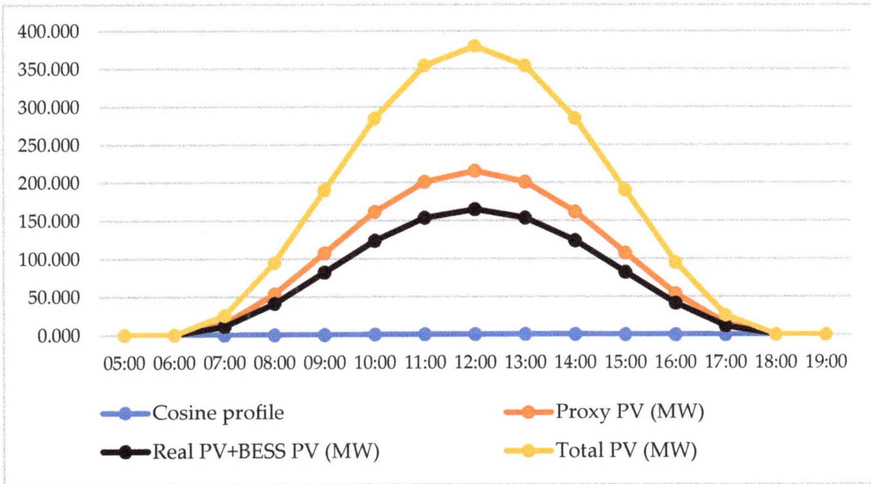

Figure 2. The graph visualizes the established in Table 2 cosine profile the hourly (between 05:00 and 19:00) production of PV generation, along with PVPP + BESS generation, proxy PV generation, and total PVPP generation.

If we export this to the grid as produced and establish the aforementioned constant value for the demand for power at 200 MW across the entire grid, we can see that between 09:00 and 15:00, the PVPPs generate electricity that we cannot utilize. That equals to a little over 1.6 GWh of unutilized energy daily or over 605 GWh wasted on a yearly basis. The demand can no longer be met solely by PV generation for the next 18 h, between 15:00 and 09:00. In the case (Table 3 and Figure 3) we will look at the total PV generation (MW), this time with the newly installed ESS sites in Bulgaria, meant to even-out the curve by gathering the electrical energy unutilized during peak hours. For that, we will need to visually introduce constant energy consumption and establish the state-of-charge (SOC) of the ESS and the energy output to the grid (MW).

Table 3. The hour of the day, total consumption (MW), total generation from PV power plants (MW), and the state-of-charge (SOC) of all grid-connected ESS installations and the availability of energy on the grid (MW).

Hour	Consumption (MW)	PV Generation (MW)	SOC (MWh)	Grid (MW)
05:00	200.000	0.000	0.000	0.000
06:00	200.000	0.000	0.000	0.000
07:00	200.000	25.442	0.000	25.442
08:00	200.000	94.933	0.000	94.933
09:00	200.000	189.865	0.000	189.865
10:00	200.000	284.798	84.798	200.000
11:00	200.000	354.288	239.086	200.000
12:00	200.000	379.730	418.816	200.000
13:00	200.000	354.288	573.104	200.000
14:00	200.000	284.798	657.901	200.000
15:00	200.000	189.865	647.766	200.000
16:00	200.000	94.933	542.699	200.000

https://doi.org/10.3390/engproc2026122015

Table 3. *Cont.*

Hour	Consumption (MW)	PV Generation (MW)	SOC (MWh)	Grid (MW)
17:00	200.000	25.442	368.141	200.000
18:00	200.000	0.000	168.141	168.141
19:00	200.000	0.000	0.000	0.000

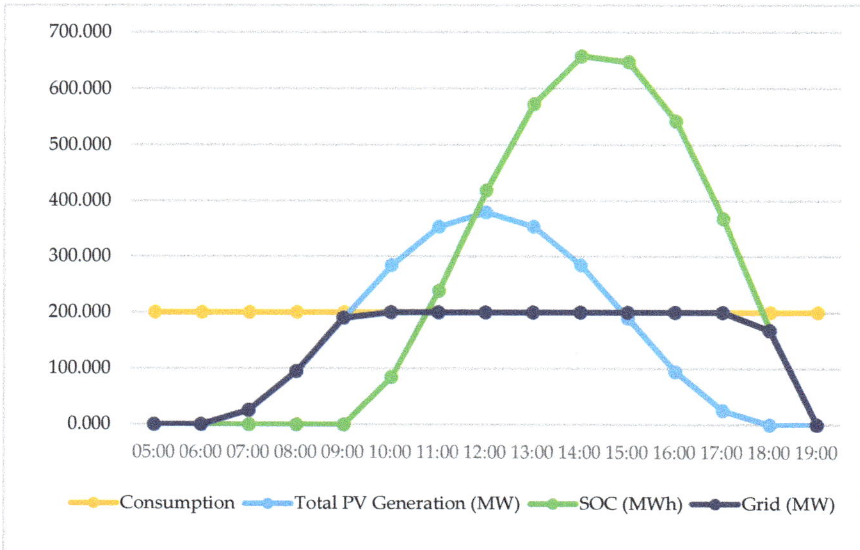

Figure 3. The graph visualizes the cosine profile established in Table 3 of the hourly (between 05:00 and 19:00) production of PV generation, along with PV + BESS generation, proxy PV generation, and total PV power generation.

As we can see, the introduced ESS installations significantly expand the availability of renewable energy to the grid throughout the day by flattening the curve. This case in particular revolves around the immediate discharge of energy stored within the same day. In order to compare the grid availability of PV energy with and without ESS installations, we will study a case where the excess energy generated from PV plants the previous day (657.901 MWh) is retained within the ESS and discharged evenly throughout the next day, meeting the demand for consumption as best as possible. On top, we will overlay the curve of PV generation without any ESS installations.

As we can see from Table 4 and Figure 4, the ESS installation significantly spreads-out the available renewable energy generated by PV plants that would otherwise be wasted. An interesting thing to note is that the ESS installations can never reach a fully charged state, because the constant consumption outweighs generation significantly.

Table 4. The hour of the day, total grid consumption (MW), total grid availability from PV power plants without ESSs (MW), total grid availability from PVPPs with ESS installations charged the day before, and the state-of-charge (SOC) of ESS installations paired with PVPPs (MWh).

Hour	Consumption (MW)	PV Only (MW)	PV + ESS (MW)	ESS SOC (MWh)
03:00	200.000	0.000	0.000	657.901
04:00	200.000	0.000	0.000	657.901
05:00	200.000	0.000	168.141	489.761
06:00	200.000	0.000	200.000	289.761

https://doi.org/10.3390/engproc2026122015

Table 4. *Cont.*

Hour	Consumption (MW)	PV Only (MW)	PV + ESS (MW)	ESS SOC (MWh)
07:00	200.000	25.442	200.000	115.202
08:00	200.000	94.933	200.000	10.135
09:00	200.000	189.865	200.000	0.000
10:00	200.000	284.798	200.000	84.797
11:00	200.000	354.288	200.000	239.086
12:00	200.000	379.730	200.000	418.816
13:00	200.000	354.288	200.000	573.104
14:00	200.000	284.798	200.000	657.901
15:00	200.000	189.865	200.000	647.766
16:00	200.000	94.933	200.000	542.699
17:00	200.000	25.442	200.000	368.141
18:00	200.000	0.000	168.141	168.141
19:00	200.000	0.000	0.000	0.000
20:00	200.000	0.000	0.000	0.000
21:00	200.000	0.000	0.000	0.000

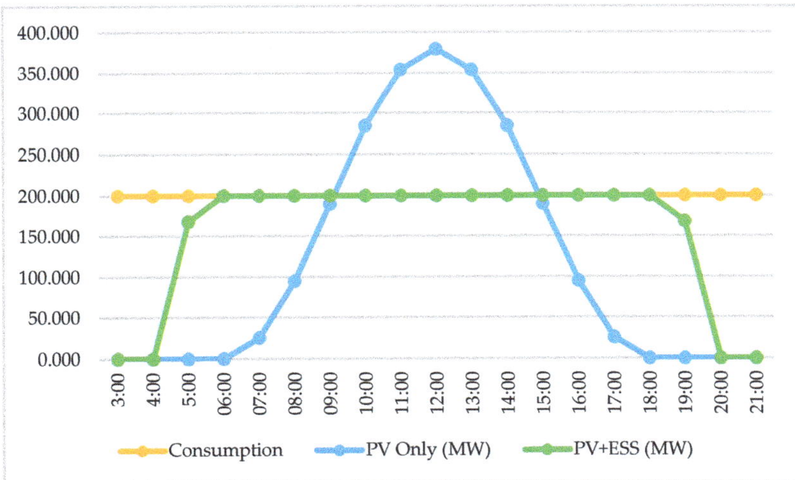

Figure 4. The graph visualizes the cosine profile established in Table 4 of the hourly grid availability in MW of PV generation without and with ESS installations, with the ESS installations having already been charged the day before (the SOC from Table 4 excluded).

The next case we look at is if PV production were to remain the same (379.73 MWp). The ESS matches the grid-connection AC power of the PV production (379.73 MW—both real and aux.), the total installed ESS capacity remains at 981.35 MWh, but the consumption is cut by 50%, being at a constant 150 MW. This will generate a total excess of 947,766 MWh from the day prior to the studied time interval, as evident in Table 5.

Table 5. Spans across two days' worth of PV generation and respective ESS storage, taking into consideration the hour of the day, total grid consumption (MW), total grid availability from PV power plants without ESSs (MW), total grid availability from PV power plants with ESS installations charged the day before, and the state-of-charge (SOC) of ESS installations paired with PVPPs (MWh).

Hour	Consumption (MW)	PV Only (MW)	PV + ESS (MW)	ESS SOC (MWh)
05:00	150.000	0.000	0.000	0.000
06:00	150.000	0.000	0.000	0.000
07:00	150.000	25.442	25.442	0.000
08:00	150.000	94.933	94.933	0.000

 https://doi.org/10.3390/engproc2026122015

Table 5. *Cont.*

Hour	Consumption (MW)	PV Only (MW)	PV + ESS (MW)	ESS SOC (MWh)
09:00	150.000	189.865	189.865	0.000
10:00	150.000	284.798	284.798	134.798
11:00	150.000	354.288	354.288	339.086
12:00	150.000	379.730	379.730	568.816
13:00	150.000	354.288	354.288	773.104
14:00	150.000	284.798	284.798	907.901
15:00	150.000	189.865	189.865	947.766
16:00	150.000	94.933	94.933	947.766
17:00	150.000	25.442	25.442	947.766
18:00	150.000	0.000	0.000	947.766
19:00	150.000	0.000	0.000	947.766
20:00	150.000	0.000	0.000	947.766
21:00	150.000	0.000	0.000	947.766
22:00	150.000	0.000	0.000	947.766
23:00	150.000	0.000	0.000	947.766
00:00	150.000	0.000	0.000	947.766
01:00	150.000	0.000	18.141	929.625
02:00	150.000	0.000	150.000	779.625
03:00	150.000	0.000	150.000	629.625
04:00	150.000	0.000	150.000	479.625
05:00	150.000	0.000	150.000	329.625
06:00	150.000	0.000	150.000	179.625
07:00	150.000	25.442	150.000	55.067
08:00	150.000	94.933	150.000	0.000
09:00	150.000	189.865	150.000	39.865
10:00	150.000	284.798	150.000	174.662
11:00	150.000	354.288	150.000	378.950
12:00	150.000	379.730	150.000	608.680
13:00	150.000	354.288	150.000	812.968
14:00	150.000	284.798	150.000	947.766
15:00	150.000	189.865	150.000	987.631
16:00	150.000	94.933	150.000	932.563
17:00	150.000	25.442	150.000	808.005
18:00	150.000	0.000	150.000	658.005
19:00	150.000	0.000	150.000	508.005
20:00	150.000	0.000	150.000	358.005
21:00	150.000	0.000	150.000	208.005
22:00	150.000	0.000	150.000	58.005
23:00	150.000	0.000	18.141	39.864
00:00	150.000	0.000	0.000	39.864

With the concept proven, we will pair it with real data taken from the Bulgaria's state-owned grid operator, ESO. The following chart is generated based on open-source data taken from their website and represents the real energy consumption in Bulgaria on 30 September 2025. With the real consumption data at hand, spreading across an entire day, we will overlay the PV generation and BESS storage data from Figure 5 over the data from Figure 6, visualizing the rift between the currently installed BESS capacity, charged by PV generation, and the real demand for electric power. As we can see, the installed ESS capacity within the scope of this study (~380 MW) can barely account for 10.6% of the lowest consumption (3582 MW) at 01:00 and even less, 7.5%, of the peak consumption (5054 MW) at 19:00 (Figure 7).

 https://doi.org/10.3390/engproc2026122015

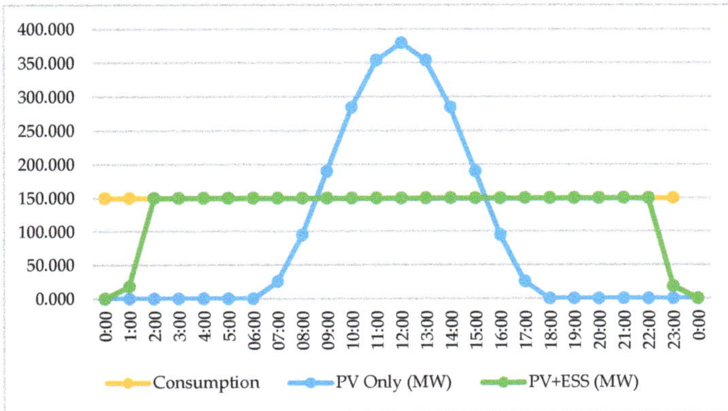

Figure 5. The graph visualizes the interval after 00:00 of the second day of the cosine profile established in Table 5 of the hourly grid availability in MW of PV generation without (PV only) and with ESS installations, with the ESS installations having already been charged the day before (the SOC from Table 5 excluded).

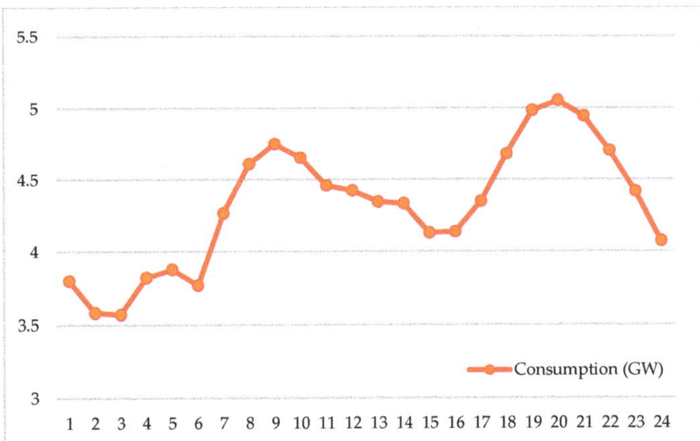

Figure 6. The graph visualizes the real measured grid consumption on 30 September 2025 across the entire grid in Bulgaria, represented in GW.

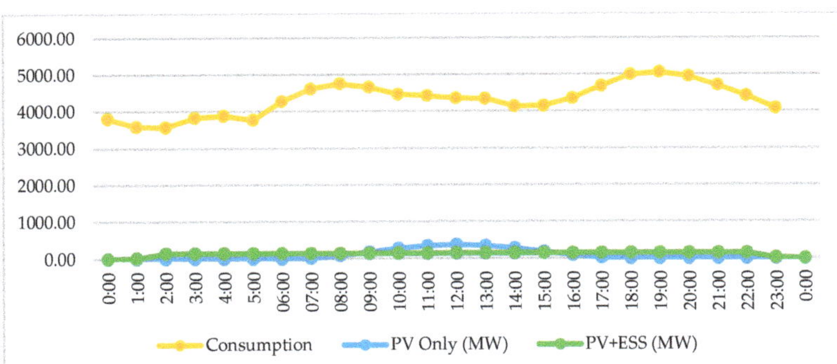

Figure 7. The graph visualizes the real measured consumption on 30 September 2025, across the entire grid in Bulgaria, represented in MW. Below we can see the data from Figure 5.

https://doi.org/10.3390/engproc2026122015

5.7. Uncertainties and Paths to Refinement

Based on the case examined in Figure 5, we can conclude that as a concept, matching PV generation with ESS installations of identical AC power can help match demand and extend the availability of almost 2.3 GWh, all of which would otherwise be wasted, by a total of 12 h, significantly before (and beyond) the time the sun is no longer shining.

The main uncertainties arise from missing ESS metrics for several PV-co-located projects, reliance on PF = 1 for kVA -> MW conversion in the absence of specified power factors, and occasional ambiguity over whether reported capacities are usable (AC-side) values. These can be progressively reduced by requesting explicit ESS AC connection power, usable MWh, and power factor (or inverter apparent-power ratings with PF) data. Where projects are staged, distinguishing "as-built" versus "fully built" states would clarify temporal comparability. Finally, adding coordinates (centroids or parcel vertices) would enable spatial accessibility analyses (for example, distance to 20/110 kV nodes) and loss modeling, improving the fidelity of geospatial and grid-impact assessments.

5.8. Economic Model

The data provided shows that during periods of high solar generation, particularly between 10:00 and 16:00 when excess energy is produced, the BESS can capture and store this surplus. For instance, if excess energy is estimated to reach over 1.6 GWh daily, this would otherwise be wasted without storage. By smoothing out the output and discharging the stored energy during peak consumption periods (like 18:00 to 20:00 when generation declines), the ESS effectively flattens the energy generation curve, meeting grid demand more consistently and reducing reliance on fossil fuels during these high-demand hours. Operationally, the observed characteristics such as storage duration clustering around 2 to 4 h imply that these systems are well-suited for applications like intraday shifting and peak shaving—qualities that can be monetized through improved market participation. However, potential misattributions of generation between PV and ESS subsystems, along with incomplete reporting for certain co-located projects, underscore the need for refinement in the metrics used to assess performance and economic returns.

The financial metrics show a net presented value as a function of the benefits minus costs in a year divided by the discount rate (assuming usually 8–10% depending on the risk assessment). This perspective makes it difficult to structure a transparent sensitivity and scenario analysis due to the significant deviation of crucial parameters such as electricity prices and the charge/discharge approach based on them. The model could become more simplified if the storage systems use pre-defined prices based on long-term agreements, providing additional services for coordination and balance of the national grid that could improve stability and reliability by maintaining the technical parameters. ENTSO-E is providing additional possibilities in this direction in the context of the 2026 TYNDP [8,9].

We now look at the leveled cost of storage delivered (LCOS), representing long-run average cost per MWh discharged by including capital recovery, O&M, and the cost of buying charging energy. Taking 30 September 2025 as a sample, we are looking at data from IBEX, including the prices and volume of energy being traded.

As stated above, the drop in price is noticeable between 10:00 and 16:00, when PVPPs are generating an abundance of electrical power. The price ranges between EUR 54.20 and 146.80/MWh, or at an average of EUR 89.82 /MWh. On the contrary, between 07:00 and 09:00, as well as in the interval between 18:00 and 21:00, the price of electricity rises to the range between EUR 92.03 and 367.91/MWh, or EUR 232.62/MWh on average.

This price difference allows us to charge the entire 981.35 MWh portfolio for an average of EUR 88,144.86 while selling it at both peak times for an average of EUR 228,281.64,

https://doi.org/10.3390/engproc2026122015

reaching a profit margin of up to EUR 140,136.78, or the equivalent of 61%. This excludes any transmission and distribution fees, taxes, and other expenses (Figure 8).

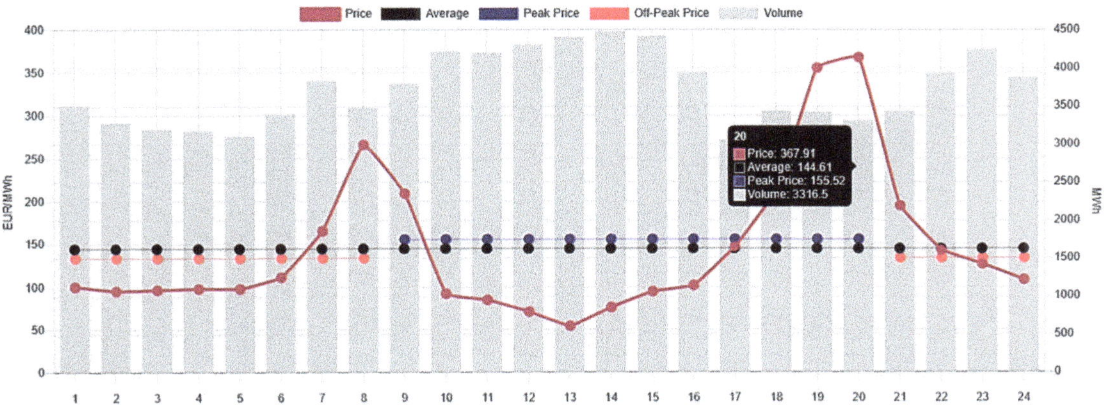

Figure 8. The graph represents the volume (MWh) and price (EUR/MWh) of traded electrical energy on 30 September 2025 over at IBEX.

In order for the LCOS to be properly calculated, we must first take into consideration the round-trip efficiency η rt = 0.88, the CAPEX of EUR 250 per MW and additional EUR 250 per MWh duration, the fixed operations and maintenance FOM = 1.5% of CAPEX per year with a lifetime of 15 years, a discount of 8% (CRF), 95% availability of the system, and one full discharge per day. This results in three possible outcomes, considering the 2–4 h motif of the overviewed BESS installations. At a 2 h rate, the LCOS lays at 244.64/MWh, losing 12.02/MWh. Keeping to the one cycle per day and 95% availability, the entire portfolio's loss is nearly EUR 4,100,000 per year. At the 3 and 4 h rate, the LCOS is priced at EUR 228.80 and 220.88/MWh, respectively, earning a margin of EUR 3.82 and 11.74/MWh. With a single cycle per day, the portfolio-level gross margin is at EUR 1,300,000 per year for the 3 h and the much more impressive EUR 4,000,000 per year for the 4 h.

The LCOS changes drastically when we utilize the BESS installations twice per day, however. The 2 h LCOS rate is at EUR 173.35/MWh, leaving a margin of EUR 59.27/MWh or a EUR 40,340,000/year portfolio gross margin. The 3 and 4 h LCOS is EUR 165.43 and 161.47/MWh, with a margin of 67.19 and 71.15/MWh, respectively. On a yearly basis, the gross margin goes up to EUR 45,730,000 yearly for the 3 h, and 48,420,000 gross margin for the 4 h LCOS, since doubling the cycles halves the CAPEX/FOM component per MWh, dropping LCOS materially, while the energy-cost term stays at the average price paid to charge over the round-trip efficiency (Pcharge/η).

6. Limitations of the Study

6.1. Data Completeness and Representativeness

The dataset comprises N = 19 sites assembled from project descriptions and an accompanying spreadsheet. It is not a statistically sampled frame; therefore, results should be interpreted as descriptive for this portfolio rather than inferential for all ESS/PVPP + ESS projects in Bulgaria. Several entries lack either ESS power or capacity; by protocol, these are retained as zeros (placeholders), which preserves coverage but reduces the number of records eligible for duration analysis and may bias type-level shares.

 https://doi.org/10.3390/engproc2026122015

6.2. Assumptions in Unit Harmonization

Where power is reported in kVA, conversion to MW assumes PF = 1 in the absence of an explicit power factor. Actual PF values (0.9–0.98) would scale the corresponding MW downward, altering aggregate indicators and duration (MWh/MW). Similarly, power derived from inverter counts may overstate interconnection-limited AC power if grid constraints, clipping, or control setpoints are binding.

6.3. Ambiguity in Capacity Definitions

Reported "capacity" is taken at face value; however, sources may alternately refer to DC nameplate, energy content at the battery terminals, or usable AC-side MWh after conversion and control limits. If values are DC or nominal rather than usable AC, duration estimates may be upwardly biased.

6.4. Treatment of Staged and Composite Projects

Staged projects are included as reported; where both stages are quantified, totals are summed, but where only one stage is explicit, the remainder is effectively missing. The deliberate aggregation of the eight PV-labeled projects (1–8) into a single composite site masks intra-group heterogeneity in siting and configuration.

6.5. Temporal Scope and Status Uncertainty

The analysis is a snapshot of project specifications at the time of data compilation. Project statuses (permitting, under construction, commissioned), equipment revisions, or grid-connection amendments that occur prior to 01 January 2025 and after 30 September 2025 are not reflected. For staged assets, "as-built" versus "fully built" distinctions may shift totals over time.

6.6. System Boundaries and Omitted Variables

The study focuses on nameplate MW and MWh. It does not model degradation, usable state-of-charge windows, round-trip efficiency, availability, or operational strategies (for example reserve stacking), all of which affect effective deliverable energy and system services. Cost metrics, market revenues, and network constraints are outside scope and thus not used to contextualize techno-economic viability.

6.7. Sensitivity of Portfolio Indicators to Large Sites

Aggregate metrics are sensitive to a small number of high-capacity entries (notably a 124.098 MW/496.392 MWh installation). While sensitivity checks are provided in Section 5, any changes in the specification or status of these sites would materially shift portfolio averages and duration statistics.

6.8. Potential Misattribution Between PV and ESS Subsystems

For co-located assets, some AC ratings (for example, transformer MVA) may pertain primarily to the PV subsystem rather than the ESS. Where documentation is ambiguous, this can inflate apparent ESS connection power and depress computed duration.

6.9. Implications for Interpretation

Given these limitations, results should be read as a transparent baseline for the current portfolio, suitable for scoping, benchmarking, and planning dialog. Refinements should prioritize explicit ESS AC power and usable MWh, power factor specifications for kVA-reported entries, clear "as-built vs. planned" staging, and geocoded locations to enable network-aware analysis.

https://doi.org/10.3390/engproc2026122015

7. Conclusions

This study systematized a portfolio of 19 ESS sites—both standalone and co-located with PV—into a harmonized, traceable dataset. After standardizing location descriptors and technical metrics, the portfolio totals 379.73 MW of connection power and 981.35 MWh of storage capacity. Where both metrics are reported, storage durations cluster in the 2 to 4 h range (median 2.70 h; capacity-weighted mean around 3.53 h), consistent with short-to-mid-duration applications such as intra-day shifting, peak shaving, and ramp-rate control. The distribution is markedly heavy-tailed, with a single 124 MW/496 MWh installation driving most aggregate indicators and an aggregated PV composite (1–8, 40 MW/107.2 MWh) forming a secondary concentration. Repeated mid-scale templates (for example 10 MW/27 MWh, around 10.56 MW/21.672 MWh) further suggest standardized design and interconnection strategies.

Methodologically, the work delivers a reproducible pipeline for location normalization down to parcel identifiers (PI/RPI), unit harmonization (including transparent kVA to MW conversion with PF = 1 when unspecified), and principled handling of staged and composite projects. Retaining zeros for missing values preserves coverage while signaling data gaps, and keeping the original text fields ensures auditability from aggregate statistics back to source descriptions. The findings provide a transparent baseline for planning and policy dialog: the observed duration band aligns with current grid needs for PV integration, while the coexistence of distribution-scale clusters and a transmission-relevant outlier highlights the need to consider both DSO and TSO interfaces. Key priorities for refinement include explicit ESS AC connection power and usable MWh, stated power factor for kVA-reported sites, clear as-built vs. planned staging, and geocoded locations to enable network-aware assessments. With these enhancements, the dataset can underpin geospatial analyses, techno-economic appraisal, and grid-impact studies, supporting the evidence-based development of storage-enabled PV plants across regions and municipalities.

Finally, to acknowledge the existing but unobserved operating PV fleet, we report a proxy PV capacity equal to the aggregate AC connection power of the standalone ESS subset (215.25 MW). This proxy serves solely as a system-level benchmark for charging-power sufficiency—without modifying observation-based site metrics or portfolio totals—and should be replaced by empirically grounded PV aggregates when available to enable fuller, network-aware adequacy assessments. This volume of synthetic data allowed us to analyze scenarios that are beyond the currently available data, while still remaining grounded in reality. Matching existing PV generation with appropriate ESS installations extends the availability of renewable energy to consumers on the grid significantly beyond the point in which the sun has already set beyond the horizon.

Author Contributions: Conceptualization, D.K. and M.D.; methodology, D.K. and V.Z.; software, M.D.; validation, D.K., M.D., and V.Z.; formal analysis, M.D.; investigation, M.D.; resources, M.D.; data curation, M.D.; writing—original draft preparation, M.D.; writing—review and editing, D.K.; visualization, M.D.; supervision, D.K. All authors have read and agreed to the published version of the manuscript.

Funding: This research was funded by the European Regional Development Fund within the OP "Research, Innovation and Digitalization Programme for Intelligent Transformation 2021–2027", Project No. BG16RFPR002-1.014-0005, Center of competence "Smart Mechatronics, Eco- and Energy Saving Systems and Technologies".

Institutional Review Board Statement: Not applicable.

Informed Consent Statement: Not applicable.

https://doi.org/10.3390/engproc2026122015

Data Availability Statement: The data generated in this study are presented in the article. For any clarifications, please contact the corresponding author.

Conflicts of Interest: The authors declare no conflict of interest.

Abbreviations

The following abbreviations are used in this manuscript:

BESS	Battery energy storage system
PVPP	Photovoltaic power plant
EES	Energy storage system
RPI/PI	Regulated Parcel Identifier/Parcel Identifier
ENTSO-E	European Network of Transmission System Operators for Electricity
ESO	Electricity System Operator
NCCD	National Construction Control Directorate
SDA	Spatial Development Act
DSO/TSO	Distribution System Operator/Transmission System Operator
AC	Alternating current
DC	Direct current
PF	Power factor
LCOS	Levelized Cost of Storage
IBEX	Independent Bulgarian Energy Exchange
O&M	Operation and maintenance
CAPEX	Capital expenditures

References

1. Republic of Bulgaria's National Construction Control Directorate (DNSK). *Public Register of Usage Permits Issued by the National Construction Control Directorate—2025*; NCCD: Sofia, Bulgaria, 2025.
2. Republic of Bulgaria's Energy and Water Regulatory Commission. Available online: https://dv.parliament.bg/DVWeb/showMaterialDV.jsp;jsessionid=59932B0C6EBF25EA318CB2D16CF88672?idMat=211280 (accessed on 30 September 2025).
3. Sigrist, L.; Lobato, E.; Rouco, L. Energy storage systems providing primary reserve and peak shaving in small isolated power systems: An economic assessment. *Int. J. Electr. Power Energy Syst.* **2013**, *53*, 675–683. [CrossRef]
4. Kloess, M.; Zach, K. Bulk electricity storage technologies for load-leveling operation—An economic assessment for the Austrian and German power market. *Int. J. Electr. Power Energy Syst.* **2014**, *59*, 111–122. [CrossRef]
5. Beaudin, M.; Zareipour, H.; Schellenbergalbe, A.; Rosehart, W. Energy storage for mitigating the variability of renewable electricity sources: An updated review. *Energy Sustain. Dev.* **2010**, *14*, 302–314. [CrossRef]
6. Loisel, R. Power system flexibility with electricity storage technologies: A technical–economic assessment of a large-scale storage facility. *Int. J. Electr. Power Energy Syst.* **2012**, *42*, 542–552. [CrossRef]
7. Regulation (EU) 2019/943 of the European Parliament and of the Council of 5 June 2019 on the Internal Market for Electricity. Available online: https://eur-lex.europa.eu/eli/reg/2019/943/oj/eng (accessed on 30 September 2025).
8. European Network of Transmission System Operators for Electricity. *TYNDP 2026 Guidance for applicants—Transmission and Storage Project Promoters, Criteria for Applications and Their Treatment*; ENTSO-E: Brussels, Belgium, 2025.
9. Locatelli, G.; Palerma, E.; Mancini, M. Assessing the economics of large Energy Storage Plants with an optimization methodology. *Energy* **2015**, *83*, 15–28. [CrossRef]

https://doi.org/10.3390/engproc2026122015

engineering proceedings

MDPI

Proceeding Paper

A Low-Cost 3D Printed Piezoresistive Airflow Sensor for Biomedical and Industrial Applications †

Utkucan Tek, Mehmet Akif Nişancı and İhsan Çiçek *

Δ-Laboratory, Department of Electronics Engineering, Gebze Technical University, 41400 Kocaeli, Türkiye; utkucantek@gtu.edu.tr (U.T.); m.nisanci2021@gtu.edu.tr (M.A.N.)

* Correspondence: ihsancicek@gtu.edu.tr

† Presented at the 6th International Conference on Communications, Information, Electronic and Energy Systems, 26–28 November 2025, Ruse, Bulgaria.

Abstract

Flow sensing is essential in biomedical engineering, industrial process control, and environmental monitoring. Conventional sensors, while accurate, are often constrained by high fabrication costs, complex processes, and limited design flexibility, restricting their use in disposable or rapidly customizable applications. This paper presents a novel ultra-low-cost airflow sensor fabricated entirely through fused deposition modeling 3D printing. The device employs a cantilever-based structure printed with PETg filament, followed by the deposition of a conductive ABS piezoresistive layer in a two-step process requiring no curing or post-processing. Experimental characterization reveals that the sensor operates in an ultra-low pressure range of 0.88–26.68 Pa, corresponding to flow velocities of 1.2–6.6 m/s. The sensor achieves a sensitivity of 967 Ω/Pa, a resolution of 9.27 Pa, and a detection limit of 83.27 Pa, with a total resistance change of approximately 51.5 kΩ. This kilo-ohm-scale response enables direct readout via a digital multimeter without requiring Wheatstone bridges or instrumentation amplifiers. The minimalist design, combined with sub-5 min fabrication time and material cost below $0.05, positions this sensor as an accessible platform for disposable, scalable, and resource-constrained flow monitoring applications in both biomedical and industrial contexts.

Keywords: airflow sensor; additive manufacturing; 3D printing; printed electronics; piezoresistive sensing

1. Introduction

Flow sensing plays a vital role in diverse fields, including biomedical engineering (e.g., respiratory monitoring [1]), industrial process control, and environmental monitoring. Conventional flow sensors, while accurate, are often constrained by high production costs, complex fabrication requirements, and limited design flexibility [2]. These limitations restrict their use in applications that demand disposable devices, rapid customization, or low-volume production. As a result, there is a growing demand for cost-effective sensing solutions that reduce manufacturing complexity while maintaining essential performance. Additive manufacturing, particularly 3D printing, has emerged as a promising approach to address these challenges by enabling rapid prototyping and the fabrication of complex geometries with minimal resources [3]. This technology allows for the creation of functional composite systems, such as triboelectric energy harvesters for biomechanical applications or highly personalized devices like 3D-printed insoles for gait analysis [4].

When combined with printed electronics, this approach allows conductive materials to be directly integrated into sensor structures. The ongoing trend in this domain is the advancement of next-generation smart carbon–polymer nanocomposites [5], which are key to improving the performance of flexible sensing devices. Among various sensing mechanisms, piezoresistive sensors [6]—which exploit resistance changes under mechanical deformation—have demonstrated strong potential for low-cost, scalable sensing applications [7]. However, while the field is rapidly advancing towards complex multi-modal sensors featuring piezoelectric and ionic coupling mechanisms [8], these cutting-edge designs often necessitate sophisticated readout electronics. Our work is motivated by the objective of developing an extremely economical and accessible flow sensor that entirely bypasses this complexity-cost trade-off.

In this work, we present a novel 3D-printed piezoresistive airflow sensor designed to overcome the cost–complexity trade-off. The sensor body is fabricated entirely via Fused Deposition Modeling (FDM) using polyethylene terephthalate (PET) filament, followed by the deposition of the sensing element using a conductive Acrylonitrile Butadiene Styrene (ABS) filament on the same substrate. This two-step process results in a highly economical and rapidly fabricated device. The sensor's operation is modeled using cantilever beam mechanics, and experimental results confirm a nearly linear relationship between airflow velocity and resistance change. Our work establishes an accessible and practical solution for applications in biomedical and industrial monitoring where simplicity and cost-efficiency are paramount. The main contributions of this study are:

- The design of a low-cost and customizable airflow sensor fabricated solely through 3D printing,
- Experimental validation of its performance in biomedical and industrial contexts, and
- Demonstration of its suitability for disposable and resource-constrained applications, including direct resistance readout without external signal conditioning.

The remainder of this paper is organized as follows: Section 2 reviews related work; Section 3 details the sensor design and fabrication process; Section 4 presents and discusses the experimental results; Section 5 concludes the paper with future research directions.

2. Related Work

Current research on disposable flow sensors based on the piezoresistive principle faces persistent limitations related to structural design and electronic readout requirements. This section critically reviews these challenges, establishing the motivation for the proposed sensor and its structural and electronic advantages. The rising demand for cost-effective, disposable sensors in biomedical [1] and environmental applications has driven research into printed electronics and flexible substrates. Paper-based sensors, in particular, have gained traction due to their low material cost and inherent flexibility [2], supporting both thermal flow sensors [6,9] and piezoresistive configurations [10].

However, two major limitations restrict their effectiveness. First, thermal sensing approaches are highly sensitive to ambient temperature fluctuations and require continuous power, complicating deployment in field environments [9,11]. Second, most paper-based and printed electronics are confined to two-dimensional substrates [2,6,10]. This restriction prevents the integration of sensing elements into robust, customized three-dimensional geometries that are essential for effective aerodynamic interaction and mechanical amplification of airflow forces. Without such structural optimization, achieving high sensitivity in flow measurements remains difficult. The piezoresistivity principle is widely adopted for low-cost sensing, as resistance changes induced by strain can be modeled with structural mechanics such as cantilever beam theory [12,13]. Despite this advantage, the practical implementation of piezoresistive sensors often involves significant system-level complexity.

 https://doi.org/10.3390/engproc2026122016

The resistance variations (ΔR) are typically small (micro- to milliohm range), requiring precision Wheatstone bridge circuits combined with high-gain instrumentation amplifiers (e.g., Texas Instruments INA series [14]) for readout. This increases power consumption, cost, and circuit footprint, undermining the "low-cost" advantage of the sensing element itself. Furthermore, ink- or paste-based sensors often require curing or drying, introducing extra fabrication delays and additional processing steps that hinder rapid prototyping [15]. While prior studies have successfully reduced material costs, two critical gaps remain: limited structural customization and reliance on complex readout signal conditioning. The sensor presented in this work addresses both issues. First, the use of 3D printing enables the fabrication of a single-piece structural body optimized for aerodynamic coupling, overcoming the inherent limitations of 2D substrates. Second, the sensor's response can be directly measured as a resistance change, eliminating the need for Wheatstone bridges or amplification stages. This approach minimizes component count, reduces manufacturing complexity to only two steps, and enables immediate usability without curing or drying. Through this combination of structural freedom and electronic simplicity, the proposed work establishes a novel, low-cost paradigm for disposable and rapidly deployable airflow sensors.

3. Design of the Airflow Sensor

3.1. Mechanical Design Based on Cantilever Beam Model

The proposed airflow sensor employs a cantilever beam mechanism as shown in Figure 1, chosen for its ability to maximize deflection and strain under applied force—an essential requirement for piezoresistive sensing. The airflow-induced dynamic pressure is directed perpendicularly onto the beam's free end surface, generating measurable strain at the fixed support where the sensing element is printed for maximum sensitivity. The tip deflection δ of the cantilever under an external force F is expressed as:

$$\delta = \frac{FL^3}{3EI}. \tag{1}$$

where L is the beam length, E is the Young's modulus of the structural material, and I is the area moment of inertia. The applied force is derived from the dynamic pressure acting over the sensor's effective area A, $F \approx Pd \cdot A$ and $Pd = \frac{1}{2}\rho v^{2}$ where v is the airflow velocity and ρ is the air density. This deflection induces strain ϵ concentrated near the beam's fixed support, resulting in a resistance change in the piezoresistive layer. The piezoresistive effect is given by:

$$\frac{\Delta R}{R} = GF\epsilon, \tag{2}$$

where $\frac{\Delta R}{R}$ is the normalized resistance change and GF is the material's gauge factor and ϵ is the induced strain. This theoretical foundation directly correlates airflow velocity V with the experimentally measured resistance change ΔR.

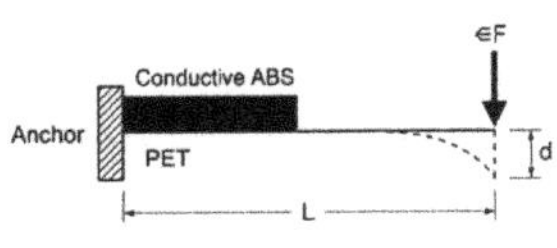

Figure 1. Cantilever beam model of the proposed airflow sensor.

3.2. Practical Sensor Design and Structural Choices

Sensor Design: The sensor design in Figure 2a is fabricated as a monolithic structure via the FDM 3D printing method, as shown in Figure 2b, eliminating assembly requirements and ensuring seamless integration into the airflow channel. The design prioritizes rapid

https://doi.org/10.3390/engproc2026122016

manufacturability, structural robustness, and direct adaptability to standard ducts. The structural body is fabricated using readily available PETg filament due to the optimal balance of structural strength and printability, along with its reliability and flexibility.

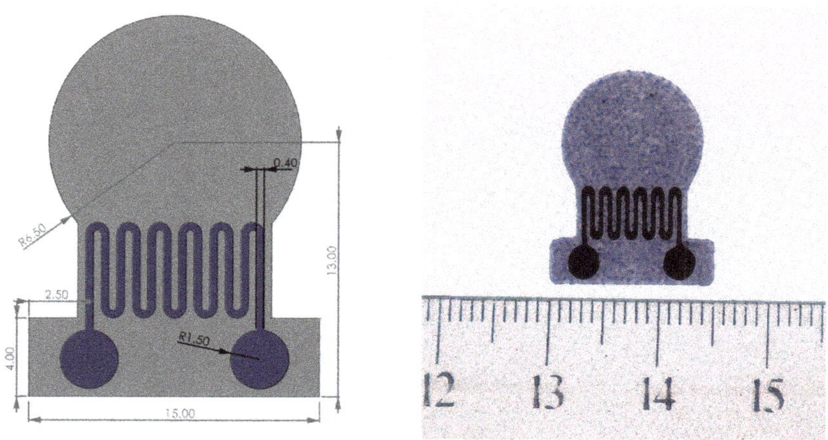

(**a**) (**b**)

Figure 2. CAD drawing (**a**) and photo (**b**) of the proposed 3D printed airflow sensor.

The piezoresistive layer uses a low-cost, Frosch ABS-based conductive filament [14]. This material choice is pivotal, as its ease of application and zero required curing time circumvent the need for time-consuming conventional microfabrication processes. The piezoresistive layer is strategically placed near the fixed support of the cantilever—the zone where the theoretical strain ϵ is maximized as shown in Figure 2a. This placement ensures that even minor deformations caused by the airflow are efficiently converted into the largest possible change in electrical resistance. A summary of the materials and parameters is presented in Table 1.

Table 1. FDM filament material properties.

Material	Type/Form	Key Properties (Typical)
Non-Conductive PET Filament (1.75 mm)	Substrate/Base film	Thickness: ~250 µm (adjustable) Density: ~1.38 g/cm^3 Tensile Strength: 55–75 MPa Electrical Resistivity: >10^{15} Ω·cm (insulator)
Conductive ABS Filament (1.75 mm)	Piezoresistive/Sensing Element	Resistivity: ~0.6–1.0 Ω·cm (depends on grade)

Sensor Testbed Design: The 3D CAD design in Figure 3a acts as the testbed tailored to the specific inner diameter of the air duct generated by the motor of a repurposed hair dryer. The design in Figure 3b is an adapter for the UNI-T UT363BT inline anemometer used as the golden reference for airflow measurements. This configuration ensures that all airflow is channeled directly over the sensing element. The primary sensing element is a single cantilever beam anchored to a central plate. The beam is strategically designed to present a surface area perpendicular to the flow, thereby maximizing the aerodynamic force F applied to the structure. Aerodynamic force F is applied to the structure.

 https://doi.org/10.3390/engproc2026122016

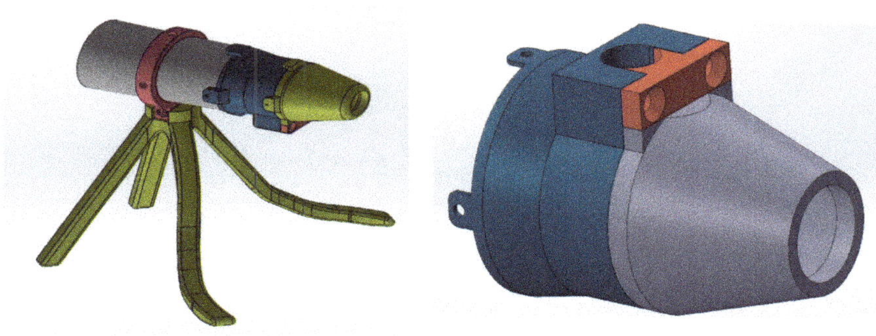

(**a**) (**b**)

Figure 3. 3D CAD drawing of the 3D fabricated sensor testbed (**a**) and the mounting adapter for UNI-T 363BT anemometer (**b**).

3.3. Measurement and Readout Approach

A key novelty of this work is the deliberate exclusion of complex, off-the-shelf analog conditioning circuits such as Wheatstone bridges and instrumentation amplifiers [13]. Instead, the sensor's performance is validated by measuring the direct change in resistance (ΔR) using a standard digital multimeter. This minimalist approach drastically reduces the total system cost and power consumption, making the sensor platform exceptionally simple and economically viable for field deployment. The performance of the proposed piezoresistive flow sensor was rigorously characterized using a special test setup that facilitates accurate data measurements.

4. Experimental Results

4.1. Experimental Setup

The proposed piezoresistive airflow sensor was characterized using a purpose-built testbed designed for accurate correlation between airflow velocity and resistance response. The airflow source was provided by a repurposed direct current (DC) fan motor (salvaged from a hair dryer), with velocity controlled via the input voltage V_{motor} supplied by a GW Instek GPC-3303A DC power supply (Good Will Instrument Co., Ltd., New Taipei City, Taiwan).

A 3D-printed adapter (see Figure 3b) was mounted to the fan outlet of the testbed, ensuring that the entire airflow was directed over the cantilever beam structure. Reference velocity v_{flow} was measured using a UNI-T UT363BT digital anemometer (Uni-Trend Technology Co., Ltd., Dongguan, China), placed immediately downstream of the sensor inside the adapter channel. The UT363BT supports a range of 0.5–30 m/s, with logging of minimum and maximum velocities. Its integrated Bluetooth module enabled continuous real-time data transfer and visualization via the UNI-T iENV mobile application, ensuring reliable acquisition.

The sensor resistance R_{sensor} was measured directly using a precision benchtop digital multimeter, Fluke 8808A (Fluke Corporation, Everett, WA, USA), consistent with the simplified testbed architecture introduced in Section 3. A schematic and a photograph of the experimental setup are shown in Figures 4 and 5, respectively.

https://doi.org/10.3390/engproc2026122016

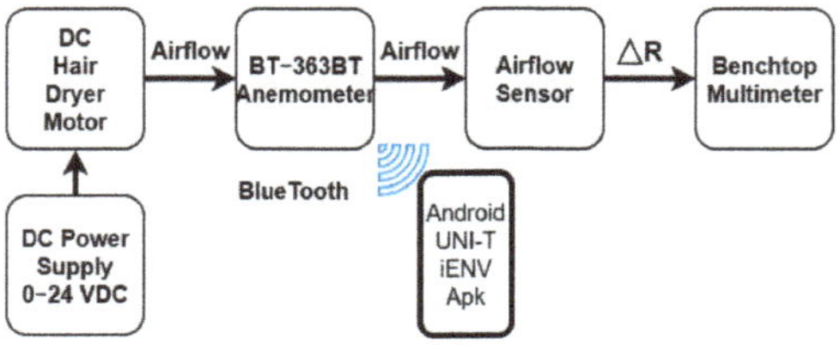

Figure 4. Test setup schematic for sensor characterization.

Figure 5. Photograph of the experimental test setup.

4.2. Sensor Characterization

Measurements were taken across the fan's operational range, corresponding to flow velocities between 0.5 m/s and 15.0 m/s. Each reported point represents the average of multiple steady-state readings to minimize noise. Experimental results confirmed the theoretical prediction from Section 3: since dynamic pressure is proportional to v^2, the resulting force and strain also scale quadratically with airflow velocity, as shown in Figure 6. Accordingly, the measured resistance response was best fit by a second-order polynomial:

$$R_{sensor} = c_0 + c_1 v + c_2 v^2, \quad (3)$$

where R_{sensor} is resistance in Ω, and v is velocity in m/s. The fitted coefficients were: $c_0 = 1.9657$, $c_1 = -1.031 \times 10^{-2}$, $c_2 = 7.46 \times 10^4$. The polynomial model achieved an excellent fit, with RMSE = 1.709 kΩ. A practical quasi-linear region in Figure 6 was also identified between 1.2 m/s and 7 m/s, where the sensor response can be approximated by a first-order model:

$$R_{sensor} = c_0 + c_1 v, \quad (4)$$

with coefficients: $c_0 = 1.956$, $c_1 = -4.428 \times 10^{-3}$, RMSE = 1.164 kΩ. This region, shown in Figure 7, is particularly useful for applications requiring simplified calibration. To visualize the statistical reliability of the polynomial fit, a 95% confidence band (red-shaded region) was added around the fitted curve in Figures 6 and 7. This band represents the range within which 95% of the experimental data points are expected to fall, thereby indicating the model's uncertainty and credibility.

https://doi.org/10.3390/engproc2026122016

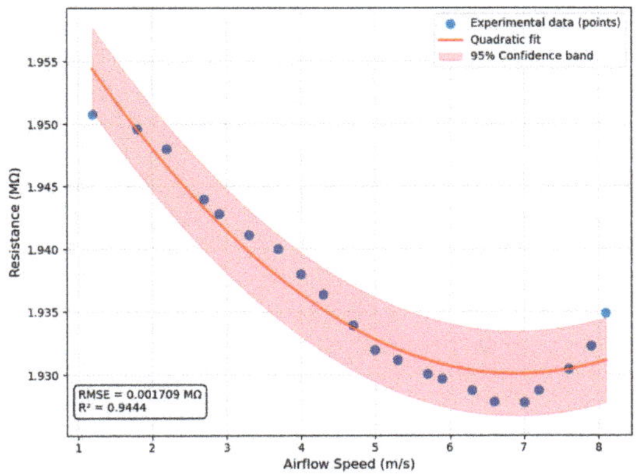

Figure 6. Experimental resistance response and polynomial fitting results.

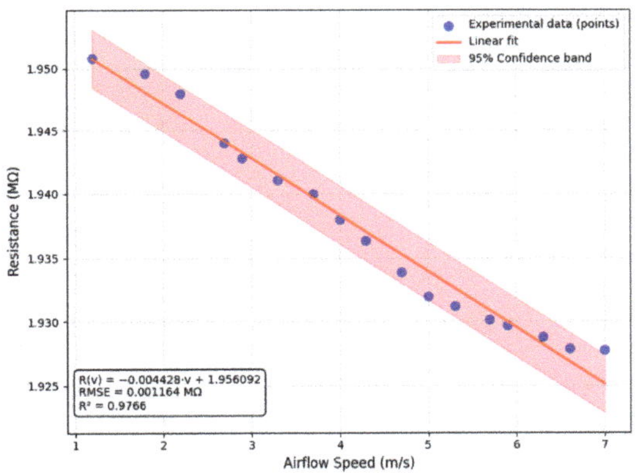

Figure 7. Quasi-linear operation region and first-order fitting results.

4.3. Extracted Characteristics

From the fitted model, the following operating characteristics were derived:

Minimum detectable speed v_{min}: 1.2 m/s, corresponding to $\Delta R \approx 400\ \Omega$.

Maximum tested speed v_{max}: 7.0 m/s, with $\Delta R \approx 16\ k\Omega$.

Resolution: 9.27 Pa equivalent, enabled by the large-scale resistance changes measured directly on a DMM.

Dynamic Range: up to ~51.5 kΩ across the tested range.

4.4. Comparative Analysis

For a broader context, the proposed sensor was benchmarked against similar low-cost piezoresistive flow and pressure sensors from the literature [10,14]. Since many studies report sensitivity in terms of pressure, airflow velocity values were converted to dynamic pressure P_d using:

$$P_d = \frac{1}{2}\rho v^2, \tag{5}$$

where ρ is the density of air is taken as 1.225 kg per cubic meter (kg/m^3) at standard conditions. This conversion allows for direct, physically sound comparison with other studies in the literature, as presented in Table 2.

https://doi.org/10.3390/engproc2026122016

Table 2. Comparison of the proposed 3D-Printed airflow sensor with the literature.

Specification	Our Work	Ref. [14]	Ref. [10]
Sensing material	Conductive ABS	Carbon nanotubes	Graphite pencil
Substrate material	PETg	polyimide	A4 paper
Fabrication technique	FDM 3D printed	Direct-writing	Hand-drawing
Fabrication duration	1 min	>8 h	<30 min
Sensitivity	967 Ω/Pa	1.00537 kPa^{-1}	0.9 Mv/mV
Resolution	9.27 Pa	NA	500 μN
Detection Limit	83.27 Pa	153 Pa	NA
Operation Range	0.88–26.68 Pa	0–3 kPa	0–50 mN
Bill of Material	<$0.05	NA	<$0.01

The comparison in Table 2 demonstrates that, while the sensitivity of 967 Ω/Pa is competitive with established low-cost solutions, the key advantage of the proposed sensor lies in its readout simplicity and manufacturing efficiency. Unlike prior works that require Wheatstone bridges and instrumentation amplifiers to resolve milliohm-scale changes, the present design produces resistance shifts on the order of kiloohms, enabling direct digital multimeter readout. Furthermore, the two-step fabrication (3D printing of substrate and sensor deposition) eliminates curing/drying steps, allowing near-instantaneous prototyping and deployment.

5. Conclusions

This work presented the design and characterization of an ultra-low-cost piezoresistive airflow sensor fabricated via FDM 3D printing and conductive paint deposition. Operating over a dynamic pressure range of 0.88–26.68 Pa, the device achieved a sensitivity of 967 Ω/Pa with a resolution of 9.27 Pa. A key outcome is its kΩ-scale resistance response (≈51.5 kΩ total change), which enables direct resistance readout and eliminates the need for complex analog front-end circuits such as Wheatstone bridges and instrumentation amplifiers. This simplification reduces cost, size, and power consumption, positioning the sensor as a practical solution for scalable, disposable, and cost-sensitive flow monitoring applications. Future work will address two directions: (i) integration of a passive reference resistor for thermal drift compensation to ensure long-term stability, and (ii) dynamic response and frequency characterization to establish suitability for time-varying flows in biomedical domains such as respiratory monitoring.

Author Contributions: Conceptualization, U.T., M.A.N. and İ.Ç.; methodology, U.T., M.A.N. and İ.Ç.; software, U.T. and M.A.N.; validation, U.T. and İ.Ç.; formal analysis, İ.Ç.; investigation, U.T. and İ.Ç.; resources, U.T. and M.A.N.; data curation, U.T.; writing—original draft preparation, U.T.; writing—review and editing, U.T. and İ.Ç.; visualization, U.T. and M.A.N.; supervision, İ.Ç.; project administration, İ.Ç. All authors have read and agreed to the published version of the manuscript.

Funding: This research received no external funding.

Institutional Review Board Statement: Not applicable.

Informed Consent Statement: Not applicable.

Data Availability Statement: The original contributions presented in this study are included in the article. Further inquiries can be directed to the corresponding author.

Conflicts of Interest: The authors declare no conflicts of interest.

https://doi.org/10.3390/engproc2026122016

References

1. Malik, S.; Ahmad, M.; Punjiya, M.; Sadeqi, A.; Baghini, M.S.; Sonkusale, S. Respiration Monitoring Using a Flexible Paper-Based Capacitive Sensor. In Proceedings of the IEEE Sensors, New Delhi, India, 28–31 October 2018; pp. 1–4.
2. Liu, X.; Mwangi, M.; Li, X.; O'Brien, M.; Whitesides, G.M. Based Piezoresistive MEMS Sensors. *Lab Chip* **2011**, *11*, 2189–2196. [CrossRef] [PubMed]
3. Abdalla, O.; Azami, M.; Ameli, A.; Salman, E.; Stanacevic, M.; Willing, R.; Towfighian, S. Experimental Investigation of 3D-Printed TPU Triboelectric Composites for Biomechanical Energy Conversion in Knee Implants. *Sensors* **2025**, *25*, 6454. [CrossRef] [PubMed]
4. Vu, L.T.; Bottin-Noonan, J.; Armitage, L.; Alici, G.; Sreenivasa, M. 3D-Printed Insole for Measuring Ground Reaction Force and Center of Pressure During Walking. *Sensors* **2025**, *25*, 2524. [CrossRef] [PubMed]
5. Mubasshira, N.; Rahman, M.; Uddin, N.; Rhaman, M.; Roy, S.; Sarker, S. Next-Generation Smart Carbon–Polymer Nanocomposites: Advances in Sensing and Actuation Technologies. *Processes* **2025**, *13*, 2991. [CrossRef]
6. Ren, T.-L.; Tian, H.; Xie, D.; Yang, Y. Flexible Graphite-on-Paper Piezoresistive Sensors. *Sensors* **2012**, *12*, 6685–6694. [CrossRef] [PubMed]
7. Huang, J.; Xu, Z.; Zhang, J.; Wei, Y.; Peng, B.; Liang, G.; Yu, S. Recent Advances in Porous Polymer-Based Flexible Piezoresistive Pressure Sensors. *Polymers* **2025**, *17*, 2584. [CrossRef] [PubMed]
8. Ouyang, Y.; Huang, S.; Huang, Z.; Wu, S.; Wang, X.; Chen, S.; Zhang, H.; Yang, Z.; Liu, M.; Gao, L. Dual-Mode Flexible Pressure Sensor Based on Ionic Electronic and Piezoelectric Coupling Mechanism Enables Dynamic and Static Full-Domain Stress Response. *Micromachines* **2025**, *16*, 1018. [CrossRef] [PubMed]
9. Dinh, T.; Phan, H.-P.; Dao, D.V.; Woodfield, P.; Qamar, A.; Nguyen, N.-T. Graphite on Paper as Material for Sensitive Thermoresistive Sensors. *J. Mater. Chem. C* **2015**, *3*, 8776–8779. [CrossRef]
10. Lim, W.Y.; Goh, C.-H.; Yap, K.Z.; Ramakrishnan, N. One-Step Fabrication of Paper-Based Inkjet-Printed Graphene for Breath Monitor Sensors. *Biosensors* **2023**, *13*, 209. [CrossRef] [PubMed]
11. Lu, R.; Arifuzzman, A.K.M.; Hossain, K.; Gardner, S.; Eliza, S.A.; Alexander, J.I.D.; Massoud, Y.; Haider, M.R. A Low-Power Sensitive Integrated Sensor System for Thermal Flow Monitoring. *IEEE Trans. Very Large Scale Integr. (VLSI) Syst.* **2019**, *27*, 2949–2953. [CrossRef]
12. Young, W.C.; Budynas, R.G.; Sadegh, A.M. *Roark's Formulas for Stress and Strain*, 7th ed.; McGraw-Hill: New York, NY, USA, 2002.
13. Chen, J.; Tran, V.-T.; Du, H.; Wang, J.; Chen, C. A Direct-Writing Approach for Fabrication of CNT/Paper-Based Piezoresistive Pressure Sensors for Airflow Sensing. *Micromachines* **2021**, *12*, 504. [CrossRef] [PubMed]
14. 3DYazdiralim.com. Frosch Conductive ABS Filament Specifications. Available online: https://www.3dyazdiralim.com/frosch-iletken-abs-filament (accessed on 4 October 2025).
15. Anuar, A.F.M.; Johari, S.; Wahab, Y.; Zainol, M.; Fazmir, H.; Mazalan, M.; Arshad, M. Development of a Read-Out Circuitry for Piezoresistive Microcantilever Electrical Properties Measurement. In Proceedings of the IEEE Regional Symposium on Micro and Nanoelectronics (RSM), Penang, Malaysia, 19–21 August 2015; pp. 1–4.

https://doi.org/10.3390/engproc2026122016

engineering proceedings

Proceeding Paper

Analysis of the Two-Stage Phenomenon and Construction of the Theoretical Model for Metal Hydride Reactors †

Jing Wang [1], Fusheng Yang [1,*], Xinlong Zhao [1], Zaoxiao Zhang [1], Jasmina Grbović Novaković [2] and Zhen Wu [1]

1 Department of Process Equipment and Control Engineering, Xi'an Jiaotong University, Xi'an 710000, China; duijingwuxinjing@163.com (J.W.); xlzhao2024@163.com (X.Z.); zhangzx@mail.xjtu.edu.cn (Z.Z.); wuz2015@mail.xjtu.edu.cn (Z.W.)
2 Center of Excellence for Hydrogen and Renewable Energy, "Vinča" Institute of Nuclear Sciences—National Institute of Republic of Serbia, University of Belgrade, 11351 Belgrade, Serbia; jasnagn@gmail.com
* Correspondence: yang.fs@mail.xjtu.edu.cn
† Presented at the 6th International Conference on Communications, Information, Electronic and Energy Systems, 26–28 November 2025, Ruse, Bulgaria.

Abstract

The metal hydride (MH) reactor serves as the core unit of hydrogen storage systems, with its reaction performance limited by heat transfer rates. Effective enhancement of reactor heat transfer performance can only be achieved through a fundamental understanding of the reactor's hydrogen–thermal coupling mechanism. The reaction process within the reactor typically exhibits two distinct stages, a characteristic frequently disregarded in previous theoretical models. Through numerical simulation and analysis, the two-stage phenomenon and its associated hydrogen–thermal coupling mechanism were first quantitatively investigated. Based on the assumptions of neglecting the first-stage reaction time and maintaining bed thermal equilibrium, a novel two-stage theoretical model (a quantitative analytical model) was developed. This model successfully characterizes the internal hydrogen–thermal coupling and reaction progress. Having been numerically validated, the new model achieves a prediction accuracy of 2% for reaction rates, significantly outperforming the original reaction front model's 25.5% error margin.

Keywords: hydrogen storage reactor; hydrogen energy; theoretical model; thermal-hydrogen coupling

1. Introduction

Theoretical models of metal hydride (MH) reactors can predict the reaction completion time for specific bed thicknesses, serving as practical tools for designing reactor dimensions under given operating conditions [1,2]. Understanding the internal thermal–hydrogen coupling mechanism is crucial for effective thermal management in reactor design. Previous studies have analyzed the reaction front phenomenon and confirmed the existence of a two-stage process in MH reactors [3,4]. Furthermore, the heat transfer rate has been identified as the rate-limiting factor for the reaction kinetics, leading to the development of analytical theoretical models based on this finding. However, the specific mechanisms underlying the bidirectional thermal–hydrogen coupling in MH reactors remain unclear. Existing analytical models, such as the reaction front model [5,6] and thermal diffusion model [7,8], primarily describe the heat transfer controlled second stage of the reaction, while lacking quantitative characterization of the first stage involving uniform reaction and temperature rise. Therefore, it is essential to investigate and quantitatively analyze these stages to develop corresponding quantitative theoretical models for a more systematic understanding of reactor performance.

2. Numerical Model

2.1. Geometric Model

To facilitate the analysis of the internal thermal–hydrogen coupling characteristics within the reactor, a numerical model of a simple rectangular MH reactor was constructed. The geometric model of the reactor has a length of 0.06 m and a height of 0.012 m. The reactor is filled with an MH bed layer with a height of 0.02 m, while a free space of 0.005 m in height is maintained at the top to serve as a hydrogen flow channel, as illustrated in Figure 1. The commonly used LaNi5 material was selected as the MH material, and 1060 aluminum alloy was used for the reactor wall. The main parameters used in the simulation can be found in our group's prior work [9].

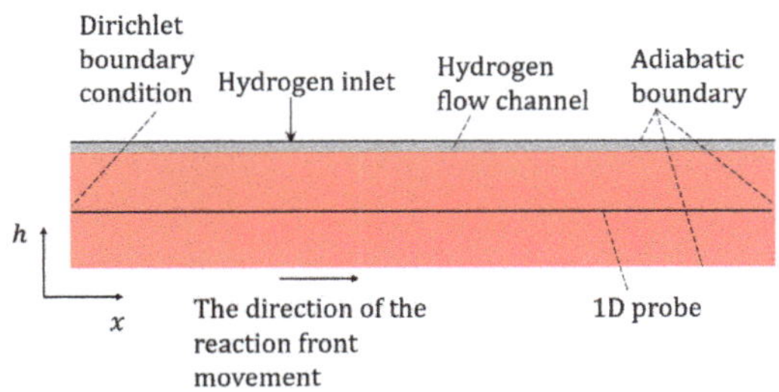

Figure 1. Schematic diagram of the geometric model.

2.2. Model Assumptions

1. Heat conduction is the dominant mode of thermal transfer in the reactor model, with zero contact thermal resistance between the bed and the wall.
2. The thermophysical properties of the metal hydride (MH) and hydrogen remain constant and isotropic.
3. Local thermal equilibrium is maintained between hydrogen and the MH bed (porous medium).
4. Pressure drop induced by hydrogen flow is neglected.
5. Heat dissipation from the outer wall to the environment is ignored.

2.3. Basic Setup

As shown in Figure 1, the thermal boundary conditions for the MH reactor are defined as follows: the left wall is subjected to a Dirichlet boundary condition with a constant temperature of 283 K, while the remaining boundaries are adiabatic. The initial temperature of the MH bed is set to 294 K (ambient temperature), at which the equilibrium reaction pressure is 0.15 MPa. The hydrogen charging pressure of the reactor is 2 MPa.

The numerical model was implemented using the finite element analysis software COMSOL Multiphysics 5.6. The backward differentiation formula (BDF) method was employed for equation discretization, with key equations discretized to second-order accuracy. Experimental data from a water-cooled reactor [10] were used to validate the model's accuracy, and the results [9] confirmed the reliability of the model.

3. Simulation Results and Discussion

3.1. Variation of the [H/M] Ratio over Time

The key hydrogen absorption characteristics of the MH reactor in practical applications were first considered, with analysis focused on the temporal evolution of the

 https://doi.org/10.3390/engproc2026122017

hydrogen-to-metal atom ratio [H/M] (hereinafter referred to as the hydrogen ratio), as shown in Figure 2. Previous studies [4] have found that during the first reaction stage, the [H/M] ratio increases rapidly throughout the reactor, indicating highly efficient hydrogen absorption/desorption in the early reaction period. At this stage, the reaction is governed by the initial temperature and pressure, with heat transfer exhibiting negligible influence on the process. The simulation results in this work also show that in the early reaction phase, the [H/M] ratio in most regions of the bed quickly rises to 0.84 and then stabilizes, corresponding to the first reaction stage. The hydrogen ratio of 0.84 at the end of the first stage is marked in Figure 2, clearly illustrating the two-stage phenomenon reported by researchers [3,11]. The reaction curve exhibits two stages: in the first stage, the MH material reacts rapidly, and the [H/M] ratio increases to approximately 0.84; in the second stage, the reaction rate gradually decreases, and the growth of the [H/M] ratio slows down, following a power-law function with an exponent less than 1.

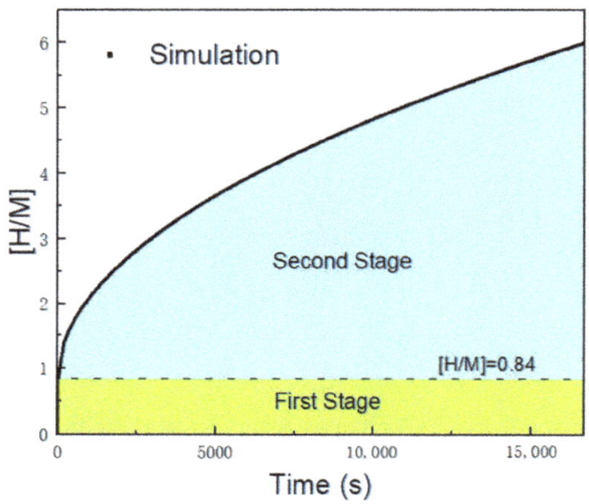

Figure 2. Variation of the hydrogen-to-metal atom ratio [H/M].

3.2. *Variation of the Volumetric Reaction Rate over Time*

Figures 3–6 show the variation of the volumetric reaction rate within the bed of the MH reactor. At t = 1 s, the bed exhibits a clearly uniform and rapid reaction state, with the reaction occurring throughout the entire bed.

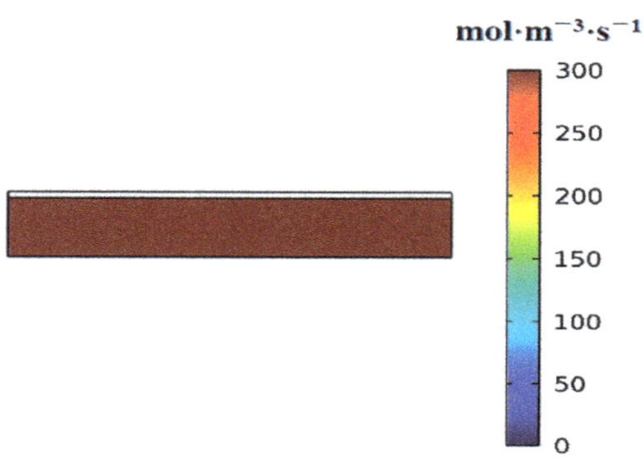

Figure 3. Volumetric reaction rate at 1 second in the MH reactor.

https://doi.org/10.3390/engproc2026122017

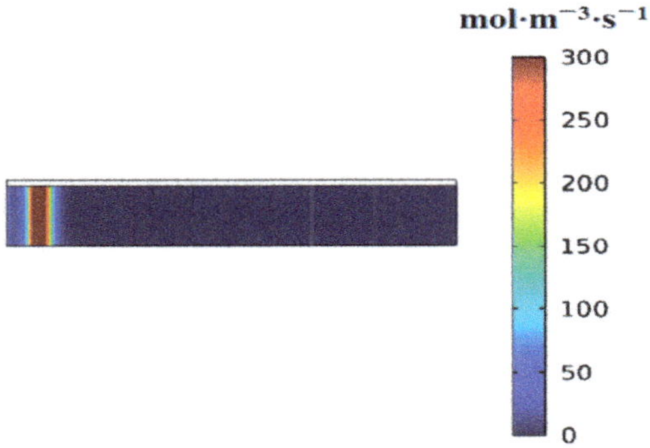

Figure 4. Volumetric reaction rate at 100 seconds in the MH reactor.

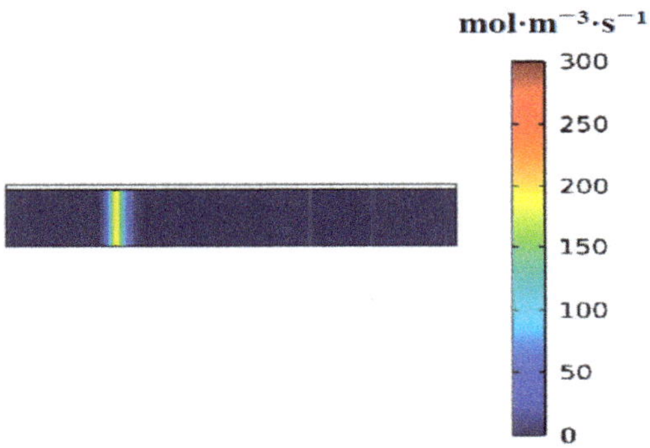

Figure 5. Volumetric reaction rate at 1000 seconds in the MH reactor.

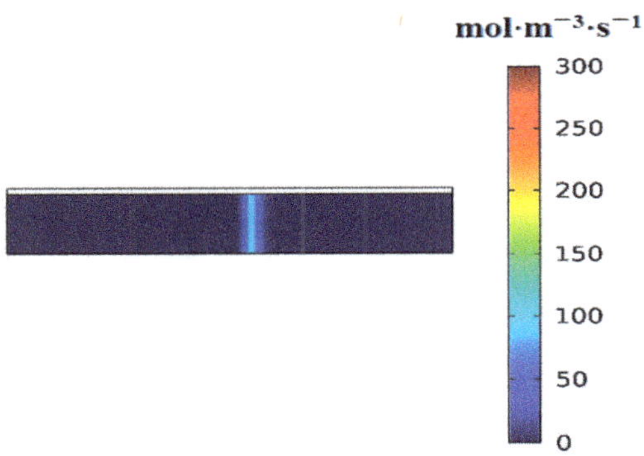

Figure 6. Volumetric reaction rate at 5000 seconds in the MH reactor.

As time increases to 100 s, 1000 s, and 5000 s, the reaction becomes concentrated in a narrow region, which progressively moves toward the adiabatic boundary in the direction perpendicular to the heat exchange boundary. From the variation of the reaction region over time in Figures 4–6, the center of the reaction region is located at 0.0045 m, 0.015 m, and 0.033 m at 100 s, 1000 s, and 5000 s, respectively. As the reaction region penetrates deeper into the bed, the bed material gradually undergoes reaction. Analysis of the numerical results indicates that near the end of the reaction at t = 16,000 s, the reaction region is precisely located at the adiabatic boundary (x = 0.06 m). This demonstrates a one-to-one correspondence between the position of the reaction region and the reaction progress. Therefore, theoretically determining the location of the reaction region can indirectly

https://doi.org/10.3390/engproc2026122017

estimate the reaction progress. Given that the reaction region is relatively narrow and exhibits significant changes in reaction states ahead of and behind it, many studies model it as a zero-thickness reaction front. This assumption is also adopted in the present work.

3.3. Variation of Material Density, Temperature and Heat Flux over Time

To facilitate intuitive analysis of the material density, temperature and heat flux variation within the bed, a one-dimensional probe was added along the direction of reaction front propagation, as shown in Figure 1. The temporal variation of the MH material density at various locations along this probe is shown in Figure 7. At 100 s, 1000 s, and 5000 s, an abrupt change in density occurs along the propagation direction of the reaction front, with the location consistent with the previously identified center of the reaction region (i.e., the front position) in Section 3.2.

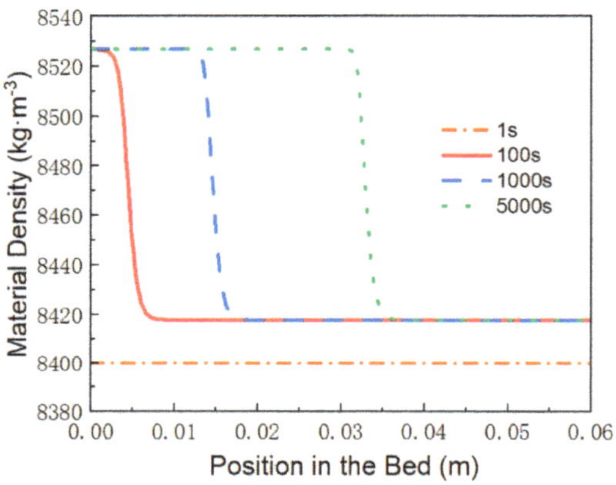

Figure 7. Variation of material density in the bed over time.

As observed in Figure 8, which shows the temperature distribution over time at different positions along the one-dimensional probe, the slope of the temperature profile also undergoes a distinct change at the reaction front location in 100 s, 1000 s, and 5000 s, shifting from a positive value to near zero. The fact that both the density and temperature gradient change abruptly at the same position confirms a one-to-one correspondence between the material reaction state and the thermal distribution.

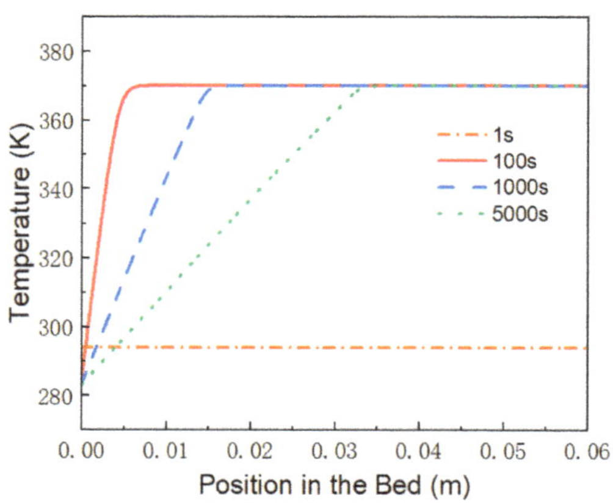

Figure 8. Variation of temperature distribution in the bed over time.

https://doi.org/10.3390/engproc2026122017

It is worth noting that, at a given time, the temperature profile remains almost linear from the heat exchange boundary to the reaction front, indicating a constant temperature gradient. Since both the cross-sectional area for heat transfer and the effective thermal conductivity remain unchanged, the heat flux should also be nearly constant. As shown in Figure 9, at 100 s, 1000 s, and 5000 s, the heat flux drops rapidly from a positive value to zero at positions of 0.0045 m, 0.015 m, and 0.033 m, respectively. These results corroborate the findings in Figure 8 and demonstrate a significant change in heat transfer state across the reaction front, which can be regarded as a moving thermal boundary.

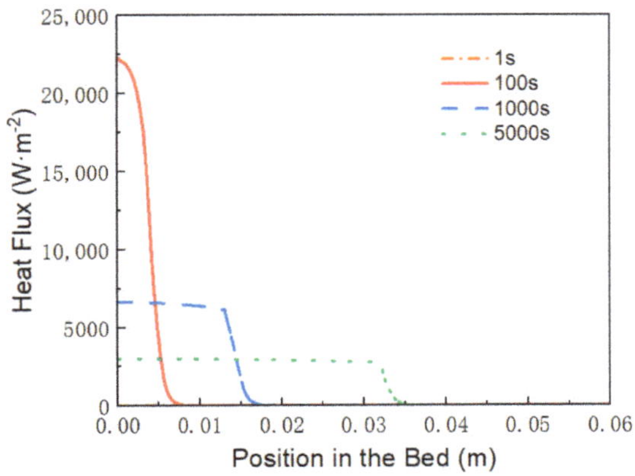

Figure 9. Variation of heat flux in the bed over time.

Notably, the temperature rise caused by the first-stage reaction determines the initial temperature across most of the bed in the second stage. The temperature difference between the bed and the wall represents the maximum thermal driving force throughout the heat transfer process, governing the propagation speed of the reaction front and the overall reaction rate in the second stage.

As shown in Figure 9, the heat flux remains almost constant within the bed from the heat transfer boundary to the reaction front. The heat transferred from the bed to the surroundings is partly consumed by the hydrogen absorption reaction and partly stored as sensible heat due to temperature changes in the bed. Taking the heat flux curve at 5000 s in Figure 9 as an example, the heat flux decreases from 2970 $W \cdot m^{-2}$ to 2669 $W \cdot m^{-2}$ between 0 m and 0.031 m. This decrease is attributed to changes in the sensible heat of the bed, where the heat flux is defined as positive when transferred from the bed to the external environment. As the reaction front moves, the temperature distribution in the reacted region changes, altering the sensible heat storage and consequently affecting the heat flux distribution within the bed.

Between 0.031 m and 0.035 m, a narrow reaction region is observed, where the heat flux drops rapidly from 2669 $W \cdot m^{-2}$ to 0. This sharp decline reflects the influence of the reaction heat at the front, indicating that the heat released by the hydrogen absorption reaction significantly alters the heat flux distribution. The variation in heat flux shown in Figure 9 demonstrates that the impact of reaction heat on the heat flux is far greater than that of sensible heat changes. This justifies the assumption in existing reaction front models [5,6] that neglect the effect of bed heat capacity.

Analysis of the simulation results reveals that most of the bed reaches approximately 370 K by the end of the first stage. Examination of the thermodynamic properties of the MH material (via the Van't Hoff equation: $\ln(P_{eq}/P_{ref}) = a - b/T$, where P_{eq} is the equilibrium pressure, P_{ref} is the reference pressure, T is temperature and both a and b are constants

 https://doi.org/10.3390/engproc2026122017

in the formula.) indicates that a hydrogen charging pressure of 2 MPa corresponds to a reaction equilibrium temperature of 370.21 K. This confirms that a uniform hydrogen absorption reaction occurs throughout the bed during the first stage and ceases once the bed temperature rises to the equilibrium temperature corresponding to the charging pressure.

By neglecting heat exchange with the external environment,, an overall heat balance of the bed shows that the sensible heat required to raise the bed temperature is approximately equal to the reaction heat released by the MH material during the first stage, i.e., $\Delta H \cdot X_1 = \rho c(T_{eq} - T_0)$, where X_1 represents the average reaction fraction of the MH at the end of the first stage, ΔH is the reaction enthalpy, ρ is the density, c is the heat capacity, T_{eq} is the equilibrium temperature, and T_0 is the initial bed temperature. This relation demonstrates that calculating the sensible heat required to heat the bed from its initial temperature to the reaction equilibrium temperature allows estimation of the state of the MH material upon completion of the first reaction stage.

3.4. Summary

A distinct reaction front propagation phenomenon is observed inside the MH reactor:

1. First item; in regions swept by the reaction front, the hydrogen absorption reaction is complete, and heat transfer occurs with nearly constant heat flux.
2. In regions not yet reached by the reaction front, the hydrogen absorption reaction is temporarily stopped, and no heat transfer takes place, resulting in zero heat flux.

Due to differences in heat transfer across the reaction front, the reaction state and temperature distribution exhibit significant distinctions:

1. Behind the reaction front, the reaction is complete, and the MH material reaches saturated hydrogen absorption. At any given time, the temperature distribution increases linearly from the wall temperature to the equilibrium temperature at the reaction front.
2. Ahead of the reaction front, the reaction is temporarily paused, and the MH material remains in the hydrogen absorption state achieved at the end of the first stage. The bed temperature remains at the equilibrium temperature until the reaction front sweeps through the region.
3. At the reaction front, the bed temperature is slightly lower than the equilibrium temperature, enabling an intense and rapid reaction. Most of the heat (or cooling) transferred from the external environment to the bed is supplied to sustain the reaction at the front.

The two-stage phenomenon is more complex, as the bed temperature rise during the first stage directly determines the reaction rate of the second stage. In the two-stage process, the bed temperature increases and the material undergoes an initial reaction. Once the bed temperature reaches the equilibrium temperature, the difference between the equilibrium temperature and the wall temperature becomes the most critical factor determining the heat transfer rate during the reaction front movement stage (i.e., the second stage). Furthermore, the total reaction fraction throughout the two-stage process remains constant. The reaction rate in the first stage is not governed by the heat transfer rate and therefore proceeds more rapidly. If the reaction fraction of the first stage increases, it will lead to a decrease in the reaction fraction of the second stage, which indirectly enhances the overall reaction rate.

4. MH Reactor Two-Stage Theoretical Model Development

The existing theoretical model for MH reactors is the reaction front model, which idealizes the reaction zone as an infinitely thin front and estimates the reaction progress by calculating the movement of this front, as shown in Figure 10.

 https://doi.org/10.3390/engproc2026122017

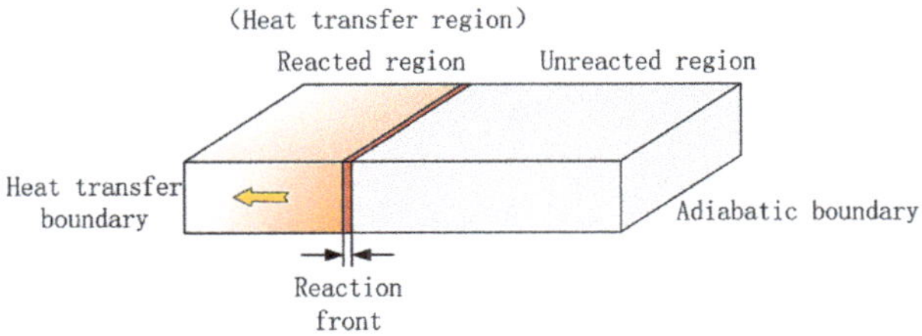

Figure 10. Schematic diagram of the reaction front model.

This model overlooks the two-stage phenomenon present in the reactor and primarily describes the second stage of the reaction. Therefore, we have developed a new two-stage model by incorporating a quantitative description of the first stage using the Van't Hoff equation and combining it with the reaction front model for the second stage. The basic assumptions of the two-stage model, in addition to those of the reaction front model, include the following:

1. The duration of the first reaction stage is negligible.
2. No heat transfer occurs during the first stage, and the reaction process is governed solely by the initial bed temperature and the hydrogen absorption/desorption pressure.
3. At the end of the first reaction stage, the bed temperature equals the reaction equilibrium temperature, and no temperature gradient exists.

4.1. Boundary and Initial Conditions

The boundary conditions remain consistent with reaction front model, where the left heat exchange wall is defined as a Dirichlet boundary condition (constant temperature) and the right side is treated as adiabatic.

The initial bed temperature is T_0, which is lower than the reaction equilibrium temperature T_{eq}.

4.2. Theoretical Derivation

The bed temperature at the end of the first stage of the metal hydride reaction is T_{eq}. The wall temperature is T_{wall}, hence the temperature difference in the heat transfer is given by:

$$T_e = T_{eq} - T_{wall} \tag{1}$$

The increase in sensible heat of the bed can be calculated based on the temperature difference. According to the heat balance of the bed, this sensible heat is approximately equal to the reaction heat released by the reacted portion. Therefore, the reaction fraction of the metal hydride at the end of the first stage can be calculated as:

$$X_1 = \rho c\left(T_{eq} - T_0\right)/\Delta H \tag{2}$$

Considering the linear relationship between the maximum theoretically attainable temperature of the bed and the reaction enthalpy value,

$$T_{max} = (\rho_{sat} - \rho_0)\Delta H/(\overline{\rho} c M_{MH}) \tag{3}$$

where T_{max} is the maximum theoretically attainable temperature of the bed under the condition of infinitely high hydrogen charging pressure and constant thermophysical properties, ρ_{sat} is the saturated density and ρ_0 is the initial density, $\overline{\rho}$ is the average density of the bed, M_{MH} is the molar mass of the MH.

https://doi.org/10.3390/engproc2026122017

In this case, the equilibrium temperature can be determined by the Van't Hoff Equation, and (2) can be expressed as:

$$X_1 = \frac{b/\left(a - \ln\left(P_{eq}/P_{ref}\right)\right) - T_0}{(\rho_{sat} - \rho_0)\Delta H/(\overline{\rho}cM_{MH}) - T_0} \tag{4}$$

Therefore, by integrating the reaction front model, the temporal evolution of the reaction fraction X during the two stages can be described as follows:

$$X(\tau) = X_1 + (1 - X_1)\delta(\tau)/\delta_{max} \tag{5}$$

where τ is time. The heat required for reaction front advancement per unit distance no longer equals the total reaction heat of the MH per unit volume $\dot{q}$ but rather corresponds to the reaction heat of the unreacted MH per unit volume. Therefore, the reaction heat change parameter in conventional reaction front model should be multiplied by $(1 - X_1)$. The reaction front model will be expressed as:

$$\delta(\tau) = \sqrt{2kT_e/\left((1-X_1)\dot{q}\right)\tau} \tag{6}$$

Therefore, the two-stage model incorporating the reaction front model is formulated as:

$$X(\tau) = \frac{b/\left(a - \ln\left(P_{eq}/P_{ref}\right)\right) - T_0}{(\rho_{sat} - \rho_0)\Delta H/(\overline{\rho}cM_{MH}) - T_0} + \frac{1 - X_1}{\delta_{max}}\sqrt{\frac{2kT_e}{(1 - X_1)\dot{q}}\tau} \tag{7}$$

Validation was performed using the same numerical model described in Section 2, comparing the predictive performance of various theoretical models on the variation of the hydrogen-to-metal ratio [H/M] over time under different pressures. Hydrogen charging pressures of 0.15 MPa, 2 MPa, and 5 MPa were selected. The prediction curves of reaction progress obtained from the original reaction front model and the two-stage model, were compared with the numerical model results, as shown in Figures 11–13.

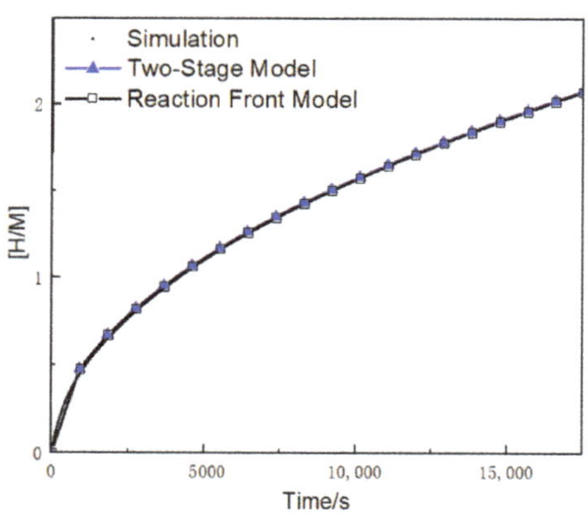

Figure 11. Variation of [H/M] at 0.15 MPa Hydrogen Charging Pressure.

When the hydrogen charging pressure is 0.15 MPa, the corresponding equilibrium temperature equals the bed temperature, and no first-stage reaction occurs. Therefore, both the reaction front model and the two-stage model demonstrate high prediction accuracy in Figure 11. As can be seen from Figures 12 and 13, the reaction front model deviates significantly from the numerical simulation results, the values predicted by the two-stage method closely match the simulation data. Because, as the hydrogen charging pressure increases,

https://doi.org/10.3390/engproc2026122017

the hydrogen charging pressure deviates from the equilibrium pressure corresponding to the initial bed temperature and the reaction fraction of the first stage increases. The reaction front model gradually diverges from the simulation results due to its failure to account for the first stage. In contrast, the two-stage model maintains excellent predictive accuracy across all operating conditions considered. The prediction results of the two models for the reaction completion time were compared with the numerical simulation results. It was found that the two-stage model had a prediction error of only 2% for the reaction rate, which was drastically lower than the 25.5% error of the original reaction front model.

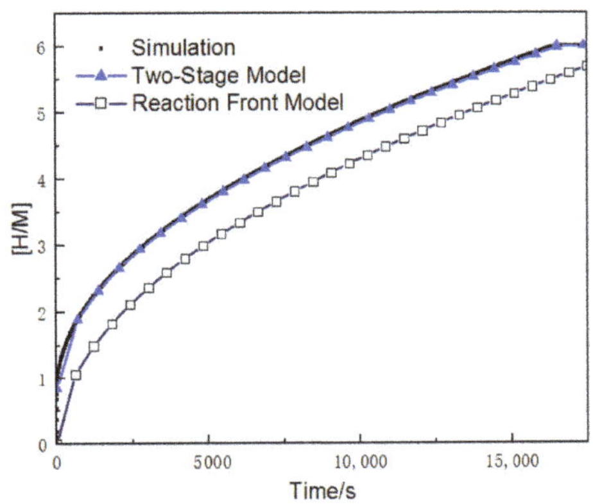

Figure 12. Variation of [H/M] at 2 MPa Hydrogen Charging Pressure.

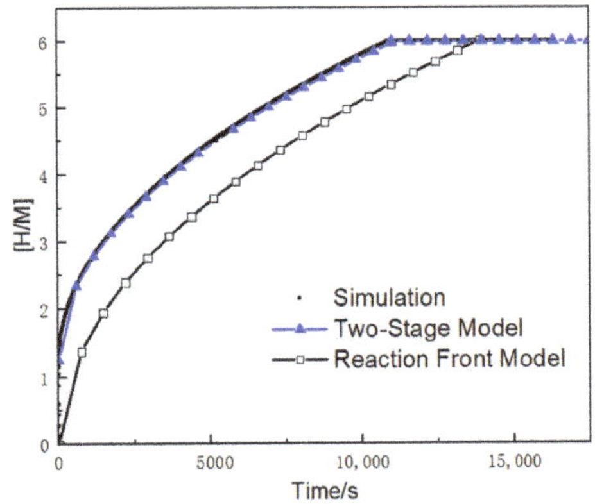

Figure 13. Variation of [H/M] at 5 MPa Hydrogen Charging Pressure.

5. Conclusions

Based on numerical simulation, the hydrogen–thermal coupling mechanism inside the reactor was analyzed, and a new analytical theoretical model for the MH reactor was developed based on this analysis, leading to the following conclusions:

1. When the initial bed temperature is lower than the reaction equilibrium temperature corresponding to the hydrogen charging pressure, a uniform and rapid hydrogen absorption reaction accompanied by heat release occurs in the MH reactor bed. The temperature rises to the equilibrium level, after which the reaction ceases in most of the bed region. This process is defined as the first reaction stage. At the end of this stage, the product of the reaction fraction per unit volume of the MH material and the reaction enthalpy equals the sensible heat required for the temperature rise of the bed.

 https://doi.org/10.3390/engproc2026122017

2. When the temperature of the reactor's heat exchange wall is lower than the reaction equilibrium temperature, the reaction region progressively advances from the heat transfer boundary toward the adiabatic boundary within the MH reactor. This process is defined as the second reaction stage. In regions swept by the reaction front, the hydrogen absorption reaction reaches saturation, and heat transfer occurs with an almost constant heat flux along the direction of front propagation. In regions not yet reached by the reaction front, heat transfer is negligible, the heat flux remains zero, the hydrogen absorption reaction is temporarily halted, and the hydrogen absorption saturation level of the material remains at the state achieved at the end of the first stage.
3. Based on the assumptions of neglecting the first-stage reaction time and maintaining bed thermal equilibrium, a novel two-stage theoretical model was developed. This model successfully characterizes the internal hydrogen–thermal coupling and reaction progress. Having been numerically validated, the new model achieves a prediction accuracy of 2% for reaction rates, significantly outperforming the original reaction front model's 25.5% error margin.

Author Contributions: Conceptualization, J.W. and F.Y.; methodology, Z.Z.; software, X.Z.; validation, X.Z. and Z.Z.; formal analysis, Z.W.; investigation, J.W.; resources, F.Y.; data curation, Z.W.; writing—original draft preparation, J.W.; writing—review and editing, J.W.; visualization, J.W.; supervision, J.G.N.; project administration, J.G.N.; funding acquisition, F.Y. All authors have read and agreed to the published version of the manuscript.

Funding: This research was funded by the National Natural Science Foundation of China (Nos. 52076178 and 52176203), the National Key Research and Development Program of China (Nos. 2018YFE0202000 and 2024YFE0207500), and the Shaanxi Provincial Key Research and Development Program (No. 2023-GHZD-13).

Institutional Review Board Statement: Not applicable.

Informed Consent Statement: Not applicable.

Data Availability Statement: The datasets used during the current study are available from the corresponding author on reasonable request.

Conflicts of Interest: The authors declare no conflict of interest.

References

1. Ran, R.; Wang, J.; Yang, F.; Imin, R. Fast design and numerical simulation of a metal hydride reactor embedded in a conventional shell-and-tube heat exchanger. *Energies* **2024**, *17*, 712. [CrossRef]
2. Visaria, M.; Mudawar, I.; Pourpoint, T.; Kumar, S. Study of heat transfer and kinetics parameters influencing the design of heat exchangers for hydrogen storage in high-pressure metal hydrides. *Int. J. Heat Mass Transf.* **2010**, *53*, 2229–2239. [CrossRef]
3. Bai, X.S.; Yang, W.W.; Zhang, W.Y.; Yang, F.S.; Tang, X.Y. Hydrogen absorption performance of a novel cylindrical MH reactor with combined loop-type finned tube and cooling jacket heat exchanger. *Int. J. Hydrogen Energy* **2020**, *45*, 28100–28115. [CrossRef]
4. Nam, J.; Ko, J.; Ju, H. Three-dimensional modeling and simulation of hydrogen absorption in metal hydride hydrogen storage vessels. *Appl. Energy* **2012**, *89*, 164–175. [CrossRef]
5. Marty, P.; de Rango, P.; Delhomme, B.; Garrier, S. Various tools for optimizing large scale magnesium hydride storage. *J. Alloys Compd.* **2013**, *580*, S324–S328. [CrossRef]
6. Bhouri, M.; Bürger, I.; Linder, M. Feasibility analysis of a novel solid-state H_2 storage reactor concept based on thermochemical heat storage: MgH_2 and $Mg(OH)_2$ as reference materials. *Int. J. Hydrogen Energy* **2016**, *41*, 20549–20561. [CrossRef]
7. Wang, C.-S.; Brinkerhoff, J. Is there a general time scale for hydrogen storage with metal hydrides or activated carbon? *Int. J. Hydrogen Energy* **2021**, *46*, 12031–12034. [CrossRef]
8. Wang, C.-S.; Brinkerhoff, J. Predicting hydrogen adsorption and desorption rates in cylindrical metal hydride beds: Empirical correlations and machine learning. *Int. J. Hydrogen Energy* **2021**, *46*, 24256–24270. [CrossRef]

9. Wang, J.; Dai, M.; Liu, J.; Wu, Z.; Zhang, Z.; Novaković, J.G.; Yang, F. A novel design for fin profile in metal hydride reactor towards heat transfer enhancement: Considering the limitation of the entransy theory in practical application. *Int. J. Heat Mass Transf.* **2024**, *235*, 126221. [CrossRef]
10. Jemni, A.; Nasrallah, S.B.; Lamloumi, J. Experimental and theoretical study of a metal–hydrogen reactor. *Int. J. Hydrogen Energy* **1999**, *24*, 631–644. [CrossRef]
11. Chibani, A.; Merouani, S.; Bougriou, C.; Hamadi, L. Heat and mass transfer during the storage of hydrogen in $LaNi_5$-based metal hydride: 2D simulation results for a large scale, multi-pipes fixed-bed reactor. *Int. J. Heat Mass Transf.* **2020**, *147*, 118939. [CrossRef]

https://doi.org/10.3390/engproc2026122017

engineering proceedings

MDPI

Proceeding Paper

The Impact of Thermal Power Plants on the Sustainability of the Energy System Under Conditions of Large-Scale RES Penetration †

Dimitrina Koeva * and Dimitar Slavov

Department of Electric Power Distribution and Electrical Equipment, Center of Competence "Smart Mechatronic, Eco- and Energy-Saving Systems and Technologies", Technical University of Gabrovo, 5300 Gabrovo, Bulgaria; d.slavov@tugab.bg

* Correspondence: dkoeva@tugab.bg

† Presented at the 6th International Conference on Communications, Information, Electronic and Energy Systems, Ruse, Bulgaria, 26–28 November 2025.

Abstract

It is crucial to understand the market structure and the formation of the electricity mix in the context of the increasingly widespread and global introduction of renewable energy sources as primary energy sources. Due to the cyclical nature of energy production from RES, a long-term plan for seasonal storage is mandatory for smooth and effective energy transition. The stability of the energy system remains a key requirement, especially due to the dynamic changes in the generation, consumption, and pricing of energy resources. This article aims to present the concept that, in the absence of a properly structured and balanced market, thermal power plants prove to be flexible and reliable power sources that can be quickly integrated into the energy system at critical moments when maintaining the grid balance is difficult (such as during peak hours of solar generation).

Keywords: thermal power plant; sustainability; energy system

1. Introduction

We are witnessing a constant and forced restructuring of electricity markets, mainly driven by growth in the use of renewable energy, instability in energy source prices, and varying economies and geopolitical interests. Having the right energy mix during a period of energy transformation is the best strategy for achieving a sustainable energy system and reducing carbon emissions. The use of renewable energy sources (RESs) and smart energy consumption are crucial for the sustainable development of any economy. They contribute to achieving energy security objectives, reducing dependence on price fluctuations in the oil market and trade imbalances, and creating new job opportunities. RESs play a pivotal role in the ongoing transition to green energy. They also help countries reduce their dependence on energy imports and market shocks that cause price increases. On the other hand, decarbonizing the economy requires a complete reform of the national energy sector, as well as a significant investment. To ensure the long-term sustainability of the energy transition alongside low electricity prices, adequate technical means of energy storage, in terms of capacity, location, and coordination, are needed. Over the past 3–4 years in Bulgaria, rapid and exponential penetration of solar energy without adequate preliminary analysis of capacity and connection locations has been very common. There is no clear parallel strategy for the development and expansion of energy storage infrastructure. This causes chaos in the energy market, surplus and zero prices for energy that comes from renewable sources, and the creation of an incorrect energy mix. Consequently, energy prices become difficult to predict, which create a huge risk for the economy as a whole.

2. Conceptualization and Approach to Analysis

A technical report by Ember "New Generation": European Clean Power Pathways Explorer, presents the cheapest and most strategic paths for the development of Bulgaria's energy sector [1]. The following indicators were monitored: generating capacity, TWh; distribution of CO_2 eq emissions according to generating capacity, Mt/CO_2 eq; growth in installed capacities, GW; emission intensity trend, gCO_2 eq/kWh; and electricity consumption, TWh. Thermal power plants still play a role in secure and regulated energy generation, and this trend is steady. (Figure 1) [1]. The load profiles used for the analysis are based on available data from the ENTSO-E website [2]. The period from 2020 to 2024 was selected, as this is the period when there are significant investments in photovoltaic installations. The installed capacity of photovoltaic power and thermal-gas power plants increased by four times in 2024 compared to 2020, according to data from ESO EAD (Figure 2) [3].

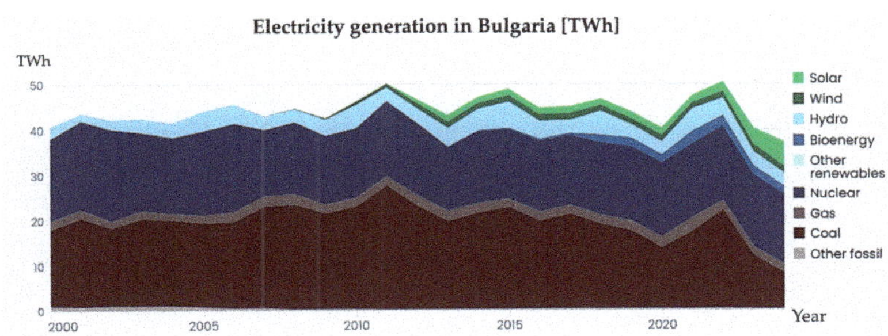

Figure 1. Bulgaria's electricity generation by source, TWh.

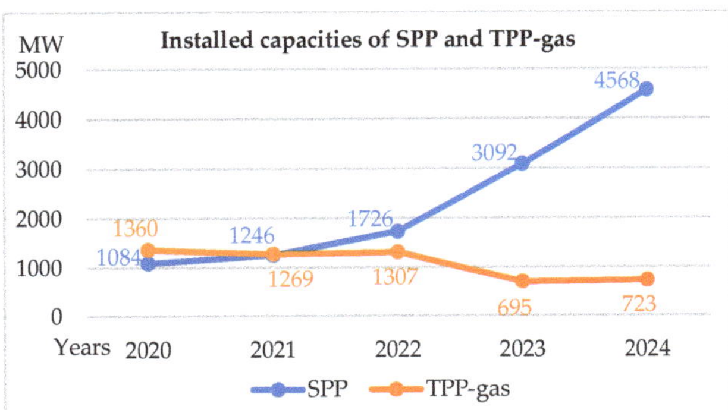

Figure 2. Installed solar and thermal gas power plant capacity from 2020 to 2024.

For all other energy sources during the same period, the installed capacity has changed only slightly. Gas-fired thermal power plants have registered a decline of about 40% in installed capacities due to rising gas prices (Figure 2) [3]. To prove the main concept of this article, we examine the dynamics of the CO_2 market, which is directly related to the restrictions imposed on thermal power plants. During the period in question, the CO_2 market developed quite dynamically, with prices constantly rising. Since November 2021, the price has remained around EUR 60/t, whereas in December 2021 it has increased to around EUR 90/t. This represents a 30% increase over one month. In February 2022, the

https://doi.org/10.3390/engproc2026122018

price jumped again to reach an average of EUR 97/t and remained around this level for the rest of the year. The absolute peak came on 21 February 2023, when the price exceeded EUR 100/t, Figure 3, [4].

Figure 3. Price trend of carbon emissions for European countries in the period 2018–2024 (EUR/t CO_2).

3. Results and Discussion

Emission intensity (*EI*) is used to calculate the precise quantity of CO_2 emitted when a given type of thermal power plant (condensing, heating, or industrial) produced 1 MWh (1).

$$EI = \frac{\text{Total emissions } (\text{t } CO_2)}{\text{The amount of energy produced } (\text{MWh})} \tag{1}$$

Below is an example that uses data from the annual reports of the largest thermal power plant in Bulgaria, Maritsa East 2. The information was published on the Bulgarian Energy Holding BEH EAD website (Table 1) [5].

$$EI_{2022} = \frac{10926444}{9665636} = 1.13 \text{ tCO}_2/\text{MWh} \tag{2}$$

$$EI_{2023} = \frac{4293437}{3894419} = 1.10 \text{ tCO}_2/\text{MWh} \tag{3}$$

$$EI_{2024} = \frac{5091214}{4486222} = 1.13 \text{ tCO}_2/\text{MWh} \tag{4}$$

Table 1. The carbon emissions emitted during the production of electricity from a thermal power plant.

Year	2022	2023	2024
Current data on CO_2 emissions [t/CO_2]	10,926,444	4,293,437	5,091,214
Gross amount of electricity produced [MWh]	9,665,636	3,894,419	4,486,222

Therefore, on 21 February 2023, the carbon emissions price that have been emitted by the power plant when producing 1 MWh were as follows:

$$\text{Price } €/\text{tCO}_2 \times EI_{2023} = 100.34 \times 1.10 = 111.38\ €/\text{MWh} \tag{5}$$

https://doi.org/10.3390/engproc2026122018

with average daily electricity prices at EUR 149/MWh on the exchange market. In recent years, carbon emissions have become the main factor that has turned thermal power plants into an unprofitable part of the electricity market.

In 2022, Bulgarian's electricity sector went through a dynamic and challenging year, marked by recovery in production, changes in consumption, and record export levels. Gross electricity production in Bulgaria that year was about 50,579 GWh, which represents a 6.5% increase compared to the previous year. The main reason for this growth was production from thermal power plants (especially those using local lignite coal), which reached an undisputed dominant position in the energy mix with a share of 42.8%. During that year, they produced 13 times more electricity than solar power plants (Figure 4). Unlike them, the decline in internal electricity consumption in the country ranged between 1.5% and 1.8%. The combination of increased production and reduced domestic demand led to historically high levels of electricity exports. These exports have grown by over 40%, placing Bulgaria third among the largest exporters in the European Union (Figure 5) [3].

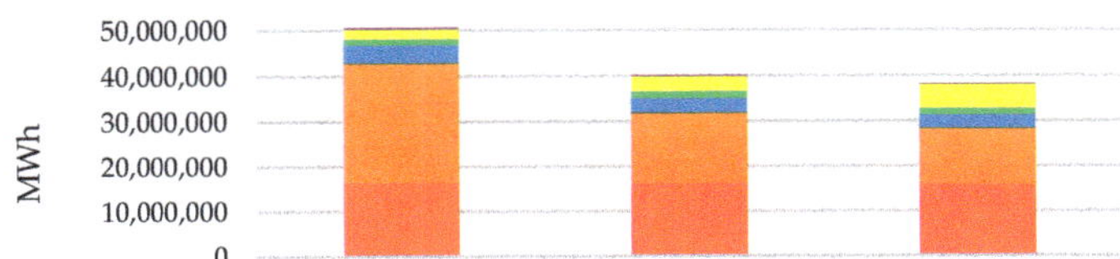

	2022	2023	2024
Biomass	318,391	234,441	214,732
Solar	2,022,607	3,334,895	5,220,293
Wind onshore	1,499,125	1,583,852	1,377,086
Hydro	3,810,674	3,100,152	2,899,470
Fosil	26,463,339	15,757,953	12,735,758
Nuclear	16,464,662	16,166,599	15,780,180

Figure 4. Gross electricity produced for the period 2022–2024.

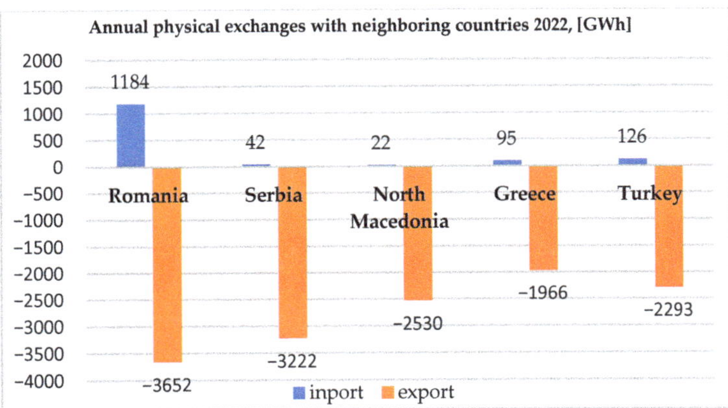

Figure 5. Annual physical exchanges for 2022.

Over a period of one year (2022–2023), the installed capacity of solar power plants increased by 1.8 times (Figure 2).

Thermal power plants remain the only energy source capable of providing the necessary balance and stability to the electricity system. Currently, there are insufficient battery

https://doi.org/10.3390/engproc2026122018

facilities for storing and exchanging energy flows, and repairs to the Chaira pumped storage plant are ongoing.

TPPs manage to receive and respond to changes in consumption during the energy-intensive first quartile of 2022, Figure 6. They are also the main source of the following:

- primary control reserve—according to Article 97, paragraph 4, item 1 of the Rules for the Management of the Electricity System (RMES) of the Energy and Water Regulatory Commission [6];
- secondary regulation reserve—according to Article 98, paragraph 4 of the RMES;
- quick tertiary reserve—according to Article 106, paragraph 2 of the RMES.

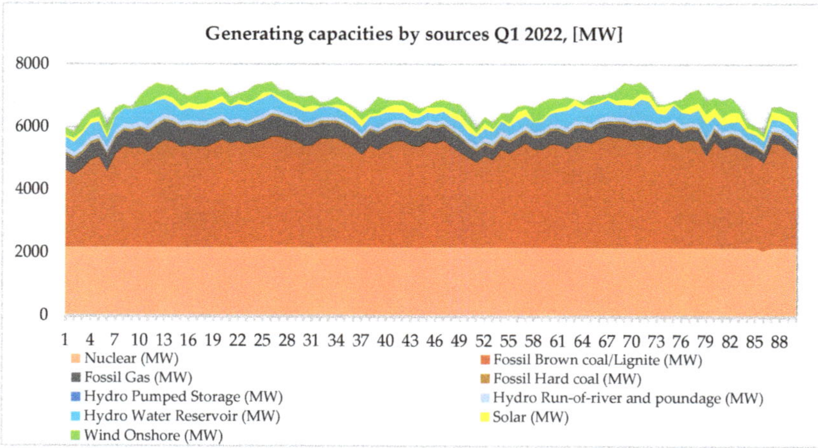

Figure 6. Load profile from January to March, Q1, 2022.

According to data from ESO EAD, the provided system reserve quantities are as follows (Table 2):

Table 2. System reserves provided.

Types of Reserves, MW	2022–2024
Primary regulation	45
Secondary regulation	155
Secondary regulation for balancing RES	100
Quick tertiary reserve	1210
Slow tertiary reserve from producers	500
Slow tertiary reserve from consumers	150
Total system reserve	2160

During the year, the European Union and the US imposed major sanctions against Russia due to the conflict in Ukraine. In response, Russia restricted energy supplies to Europe. As a result, gas and electricity prices reached record levels (Figure 7) [7]. Due to high electricity prices, thermal power plants generated profits from sales despite economic pressure from carbon emission prices and the introduction of the European Green Deal in September 2022. With Regulation (EU) 2022/1854, revenue caps for electricity producers that do not use gas (wind, solar, nuclear, coal, and hydro) were imposed. The upper limit is set at approximately EURO180/MWh [8].

https://doi.org/10.3390/engproc2026122018

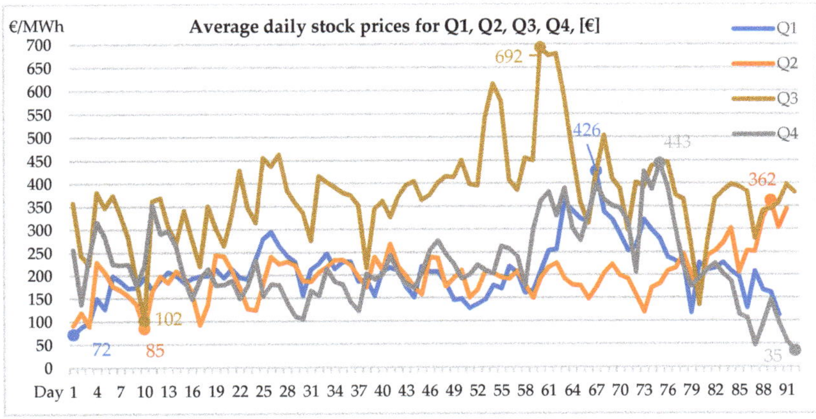

Figure 7. Average daily exchange electricity prices (IBEX) for 2022.

In 2024, the installed capacity of solar power plants is expected to increase by almost 50% compared to 2023 (see Figure 2). The lack of storage systems for surplus electricity and the unavailability of the Chaira pumped-storage plant will once again have a negative impact on the balance of the energy system. Electricity prices on the exchange market have an average annual price of around EUR 100/MWh in 2024, compared to an average annual price of around EUR 255/MWh in 2022 (Figure 8) [7]. From March to October 2024, large amounts of solar power are generated. The price of carbon emissions remains relatively high at EURO 70 per ton of CO_2. Average daily stock prices remain low. These factors force thermal power plants to operate at lower capacity In the second quartile (Q2) of the year (Figure 9), which also includes the day with the lowest load (Figure 10), electricity production from TPPs is the lowest of the whole year.

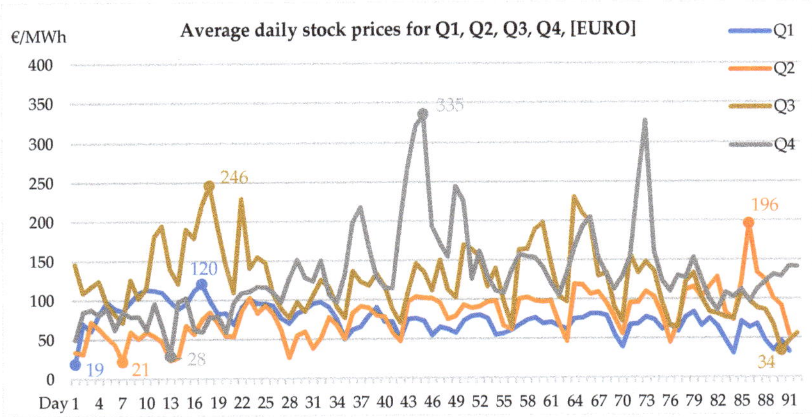

Figure 8. Average daily exchange electricity prices (IBEX) for 2024.

https://doi.org/10.3390/engproc2026122018

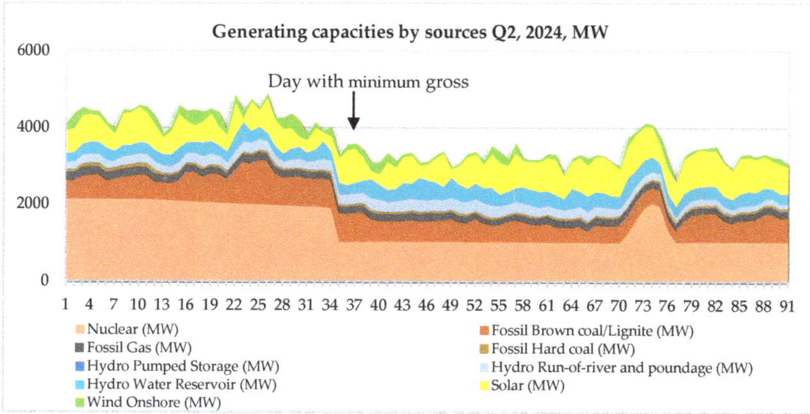

Figure 9. Load profile for the period from April to June, Q2, 2024.

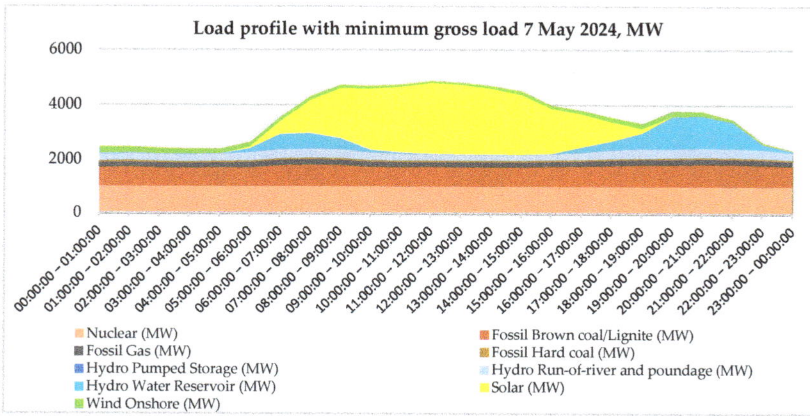

Figure 10. Load profile by sources for 7 May 2024.

The last two years have been marked by a decrease in electricity production from lignite coal and natural gas (Figure 4), and by clear variability and increasing values of solar generation, with permanent peaks in the time range 9:30–15:30. During this period, PVPP production reaches 70% of total capacity (Figure 10). This requires systems for storing "excess" energy to achieve balance; however, such systems are still under development [9,10]. The absence of the Chaira pumped-storage plant, which in pump mode can consume up to 784 MW of surplus electricity from RES, also contributes to the chaotic and poorly managed energy flows.

4. Conclusions

Through these analyses, the authors prove the concept that when serious challenges to the sustainability of the electricity system arise (such as dynamic over-generation from RES and/or failures in base power capacities), thermal power plants remain the only reliable source of adjustable reactive energy. In cases of energy imbalance, the flexibility and reliability of capacities such as TPPs can be quickly integrated into the energy system. They are also critical for maintaining grid balance while ensuring uninterrupted electricity supply.

 https://doi.org/10.3390/engproc2026122018

Author Contributions: Conceptualization, D.K. and D.S.; methodology, D.K.; software, D.K. and D.S.; validation, D.K. and D.S.; investigation, D.K. and D.S.; writing—original draft preparation, D.K. and D.S.; writing—review and editing, D.K. All authors have read and agreed to the published version of the manuscript.

Funding: This research was funded by the European Regional Development Fund within the OP "Research, Innovation and Digitalization Programme for Intelligent Transformation 2021–2027", Project No. BG16RFPR002-1.014-0005, Center of Competence "Smart Mechatronics, Eco- and Energy Saving Systems and Technologies".

Institutional Review Board Statement: Not applicable.

Informed Consent Statement: Not applicable.

Data Availability Statement: The data presented in this study are available upon request from the corresponding author.

Conflicts of Interest: The authors declare no conflicts of interests.

Abbreviations

The following abbreviations are used in this manuscript:

RES	Renewable energy sources
ENTSO-E	European Network of Transmission System Operators for Electricity
ESO	Electricity system operator
SPP	Solar power plant
TPP	Thermal power plant
EI	Emission intensity
BEH	Bulgarian Energy Holding
RMES	Rules for the management of the electricity system
NEK	National electricity company

References

1. EMBER. Buildings a Clean Europeans Electricity System by 2035, Technical Report—New Generation, 22 June 2022. Available online: https://ember-energy.org/ (accessed on 15 September 2025).
2. Parpulova, N.; Zinoviev, V. Natural Gas and the Dynamics of the Energy Market—Eastern Europe. *Econ. Stud. J.* **2024**, *33*, 179–200.
3. Electricity System Operator ESO EAD. Statistical Pocketbook from 2020 to 2024 Years. Available online: https://www.eso.bg/doc/?pbook (accessed on 3 September 2025).
4. EMBER European Electricity Prices and Costs. Available online: https://ember-energy.org/data/european-electricity-prices-and-costs/ (accessed on 10 October 2025).
5. Koeva, D.; Kutkarska, R.; Zinoviev, V. High Penetration of Renewable Energy Sources and Power Market Formation for Countries in Energy Transition: Assessment via Price Analysis and Energy Forecasting. *Energies* **2023**, *16*, 7788. [CrossRef]
6. Rules for the Management of the Electricity System, (RMES) of the Bulgarian Energy and Water Regulatory Commission. Available online: https://legislation.apis.bg/doc/1932312/0 (accessed on 1 September 2025).
7. Independent Bulgarian Energy Exchange IBEX EAD. Average Daily Prices for 2022 and 2024 Years. Available online: https://ibex.bg/downloads-bg/ (accessed on 11 October 2025).
8. Moldybayeva, N.; Keshuov, S.; Kenzhetaev, K.; Saule, D.; Taldybayeva, A.; Stoyanov, I.; Iliev, T. Decision Matrix in an Autonomous Power System for Agro-Industrial Complexes with Renewable Energy Sources. *Energies* **2024**, *17*, 4357. [CrossRef]
9. Gungor Celik, A.; Aydemir, U. Energy, Exergy Analysis and Sustainability Assessment of a Thermal Power Plant Operating in Various Environmental Conditions Using Real Operational Data. *Sustainability* **2025**, *17*, 1417. [CrossRef]
10. Khudyakova, L.I.; Garkusheva, N.M.; Paleev, P.L.; Kotova, I.Y.; Khomoksonova, D.P.; Gulyashinov, P.A.; Antropova, I.G. Revegetation of Thermal Power Plant Ash Dumps or Sustainable Urban Development. *Urban Sci.* **2025**, *9*, 210. [CrossRef]

https://doi.org/10.3390/engproc2026122018

engineering proceedings

MDPI

Proceeding Paper

SRGAN-Based Deep Learning Framework for Wind Turbine Damage Detection from Sentinel-2 Imagery †

Kübra Çakır [1], Onur Elma [1,2,*] and Murat Kuzlu [2]

1 Department of Electrical and Electronics Engineering, Canakkale Onsekiz Mart University, Canakkale 17100, Türkiye; kubra.cakir@comu.edu.tr
2 Department of Engineering Technology, Old Dominion University, Norfolk, VA 23529, USA; mkuzlu@odu.edu
* Correspondence: onurelma@comu.edu.tr
† Presented at the 6th International Conference on Communications, Information, Electronic and Energy Systems, 26–28 November 2025, Ruse, Bulgaria.

Abstract

The operational reliability of wind turbines is critical for sustainable energy production in smart grids. This study proposes a remote monitoring approach using perceptually enhanced satellite imagery. Sentinel-2 multispectral data (10 m resolution) has been processed with a Super-Resolution Generative Adversarial Network (SRGAN) to improve visual quality to a perceptual resolution of 30 cm. Although true spatial refinement is not achieved, the sharper structural details enhance classification accuracy. The data set comprises 15,000 images—10,000 SRGAN-enhanced and 5000 augmented through rotation, zoom in, increasing brightness, noise addition, and blurring. A custom Convolutional Neural Network (CNN) has been trained to classify turbines as damaged or intact, achieving 95% accuracy, a 0.99 ROC-AUC, and a 0.95 F1 score. These results demonstrate that perceptually sharpened satellite data can effectively support automated wind turbine damage detection and predictive maintenance. The proposed framework also lays the groundwork for broader real-time and multimodal monitoring and cost-efficient applications in renewable energy systems.

Keywords: damage detection; deep learning; sentinel-2; super-resolution generative adversarial networks (SRGANs); super-resolution; wind turbine

1. Introduction

Wind energy is one of the most popular renewable energy sources, which is very efficient, with a small carbon footprint, and is long-lasting [1]. As more wind turbines are built worldwide, keeping them operational and finding problems has become increasingly challenging. Structural failures, particularly cracks in the blades, gearbox issues, or tower deformations, significantly lead to inefficiency in energy production and higher operating costs [2]. For this reason, there is a growing need for automated, scalable, and cost-effective solutions that can monitor the status of wind energy infrastructure. Systems developed in this field are based on vibration analysis for condition monitoring of wind turbines, SCADA-based monitoring, and sensor fusion [3]. However, these methods cannot be used in large turbine areas because they require expensive equipment. The Copernicus program provides images from the Sentinel-2 satellite with a ground sampling distance (GSD) of 10 m [4,5]. According to the satellite images provided by this program, it is undeniably good for large-scale environmental monitoring, but it has been observed to be insufficient for detecting small damages on wind turbines. To address this, deep learning-based super-resolution methods, including Super-Resolution Generative Adversarial Networks (SRGANs), are used to improve visual clarity by enhancing perceptual sharpness [6]. It is emphasized that, considering the physical sensor limitations of Sentinel-2, the conversion from 10 m to 30 cm should be evaluated not as a true improvement in spatial resolution, but rather as a perceptual enhancement facilitated by SRGAN. This method aims to visually inspect the structural integrity of wind turbines and improve the accuracy of CNN-based models in classifying objects. Combining advances in satellite imaging, super-resolution methods, and deep learning can be presented as a new cost-effective solution [7,8]. Convolutional Neural Network (CNN) architectures have been successful in detecting damage in images and enabling the automated inspection of energy infrastructure [9,10]. Compared to UAV (drone) or manual inspections, satellite-based methods offer a more advantageous solution because they are cheaper, cover a wider area and are always accessible [11]. In this context, enhancing Sentinel-2 data with SRGAN improves fine structural details in wind turbine images and aids in extracting more prominent features for CNN models.

This study presents an innovative deep learning framework that autonomously classifies wind turbine damage using perceptually enhanced Sentinel-2 images improved with SRGAN. It is observed that the proposed custom CNN model can classify images of damaged and undamaged turbines. The results of wind turbine damage detection are comprehensively observed with accuracy, precision, sensitivity, F1 score, ROC-AUC, and confusion matrix to validate the proposed methods. The details of the study performed are explained in the following sections.

2. Methodology

The methodology of a CNN framework is specifically designed for the detection of damage on wind turbine blades using SRGAN-based super-resolution Sentinel-2 images. It consists of five key components: satellite image acquisition and enhancement, SRGAN optimization, dataset generation and augmentation, CNN-based classification, and model performance evaluation.

2.1. Sentinel-2 Satellite Imagery

Sentinel-2 satellites send publicly available multispectral images with spatial resolutions ranging from 10 to 60 m [5]. However, natural 10 m ground sampling distances are not sufficient to find small defects in wind turbine blades [12]. To overcome this issue, SRGAN is used to synthetically enlarge the images, making them appear sharper and revealing more local texture [13]. Although the term "30 cm resolution" is used, due to sensor limitations [14,15], it refers not to the actual physical resolution but to synthetic perceptual clarity. The SRGAN architecture consists of a generator that reconstructs high-resolution (HR) images from low-resolution (LR) inputs, and a discriminator that distinguishes between original and generated HR samples. Metrics such as Mean Squared Error (MSE), Peak Signal-to-Noise Ratio (PSNR), Structural Similarity Index (SSIM), and Learned Perceptual Image Patch Similarity (LPIPS) are used to check the quality of the enhanced images.

The results presented in Table 1 confirm that while details are indistinguishable from raw Sentinel-2 images, SRGAN-enhanced Sentinel-2 images provide sufficient visual clarity to highlight fine structural features such as turbine blade cracks, erosion marks, and surface deformations. Figure 1 shows a visual comparison of the classified turbine blade areas obtained from raw Sentinel-2 inputs.

https://doi.org/10.3390/engproc2026122019

Table 1. Evaluation metrics for SRGAN-enhanced Sentinel-2 images.

Metrics	Definition	Achieved Value (Mean $\pm$ Std)
MSE	Mean Squared Error	$2.41 \times 10^{-3} \pm 0.0007$
PSNR (dB)	Peak Signal-to-Noise Ratio	42.87 ± 1.46

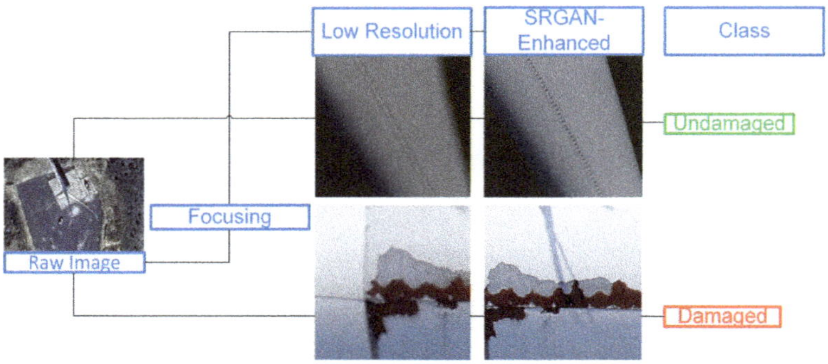

Figure 1. Visual comparison of raw Sentinel-2 images and identified turbine blade regions.

2.2. SRGAN Objective Function

The loss function guiding SRGAN optimization is:

$$\mathcal{L}_{SRGAN} = \mathcal{L}_{MSE} + \lambda\mathcal{L}_{VGG} + \eta\mathcal{L}_{adv} \quad (1)$$

where $\mathcal{L}_{MSE}$: pixel-wise fidelity loss between LR and HR, $\mathcal{L}_{VGG}$ is the perceptual loss from intermediate layers of a pre-trained VGG network, $\mathcal{L}_{adv}$ is the adversarial loss enforced by the discriminator, and λ and η weighting factors for perceptual and adversarial terms.

This formulation allows SRGAN to create outputs that are visually sharp and structurally meaningful, which makes them good for image classification tasks that come after them. Figures 2 and 3 show the comparison of the original Sentinel-2 and SRGAN enhancement, supported by images where the enhancement increases the resolution and defects become clearer.

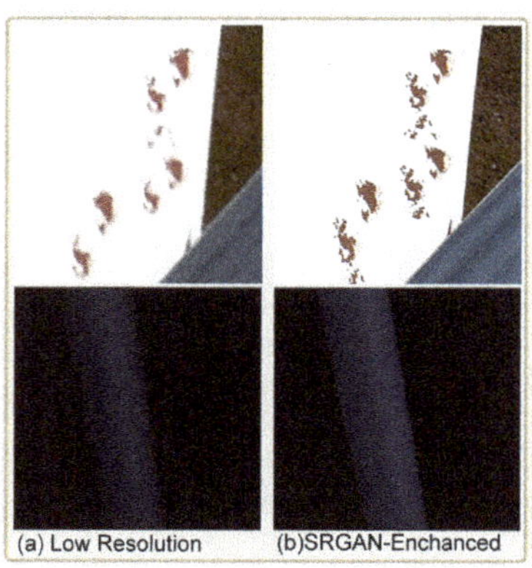

Figure 2. (**a**) Low resolution details, (**b**) SRGAN-enhanced close-ups revealing sharper edges and finer details.

https://doi.org/10.3390/engproc2026122019

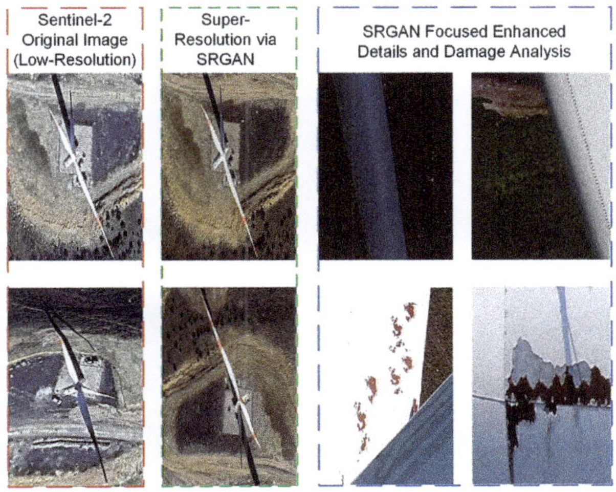

Figure 3. Comparison of original Sentinel-2 images with SRGAN-enhanced outputs.

The use of SRGAN-based super-resolution for Sentinel-2 wind turbine imagery is grounded in the need to overcome the limited 10 m ground sampling distance (GSD) of the satellite, which is inadequate for monitoring the complex and micro-level structural integrity of turbine components. To address this limitation, low-resolution images were first extracted from raw Sentinel-2 data using image-processing techniques. Subsequently, a deep learning framework based on SRGAN was developed to enhance the spatial resolution of these images, enabling more detailed analysis of structural features relevant to damage detection. The main purpose here is not to produce a real-world image that Sentinel-2 cannot physically provide, but to produce more noticeable details for the human eye and deep learning algorithms. SRGAN converts low-resolution (LR) satellite images into images with greater perceptual detail (e.g., 30 cm GSD) by using statistical relationships learned from high-resolution (HR) images in the training data. The details produced in this process are entirely statistical and "hallucinatory" (estimated), and do not correspond to physically measured data. However, studies have shown that this type of "perceptual solution" increases meaningful information [15]. The goal is for the generator to produce fake high-resolution (SR) images from low-resolution inputs, while the discriminator tries to distinguish between real and generated images.

$$L_{MSE} = \frac{1}{N}\sum_{i=1}^{N} \left\| I_{HR}^{(i)} - \hat{I}^{(i)}_{SR} \right\|_2^2 \quad (2)$$

This loss enforces radiometric fidelity by minimizing the pixel-level difference between the generated super-resolved image $\hat{I}_{SR}$ and its high-resolution reference I_{HR}.

$$L_{VGG} = \frac{1}{N}\sum_{i=1}^{N} \left\| \phi\left(I_{HR}^{(i)}\right) - \phi\left(\hat{I}^{(i)}_{SR}\right) \right\|_2^2 \quad (3)$$

Here, $\phi(\cdot)$ denotes the feature representation extracted from an intermediate layer of a pre-trained VGG-19 network. This term guides the generator to reproduce perceptually meaningful structures (edges, textures) rather than merely pixel-wise similarity.

$$L_{adv} = -log(D(\hat{I}_{SR})) \quad (4)$$

 https://doi.org/10.3390/engproc2026122019

This loss term reflects the generator's success in fooling the discriminator $D(\cdot)$, thereby improving the photorealism of the synthesized image. In advanced SRGAN variants, spatial smoothness and noise suppression are often encouraged by including a Total Variation (TV) regularizer:

$$L_{\text{TV}} = \sum_{i,j} \left[\left(\hat{I}_{SR}^{i+1,j} - \hat{I}_{SR}^{i,j} \right)^2 + \left(\hat{I}_{SR}^{i,j+1} - \hat{I}_{SR}^{i,j} \right)^2 \right] \quad (5)$$

The complete objective function can therefore be expressed as:

$$L_{total} = L_{MSE} + \lambda L_{VGG} + \eta L_{adv} + \gamma L_{TV} \quad (6)$$

where λ, η, and γ are positive hyperparameters that balance the contributions of perceptual, adversarial, and regularization components, respectively.

The concept of a "30 cm resolution" achieved through the application of SRGAN refers solely to the pixel dimensions of the generated output, rather than to an actual optical resolution. The fine-grained details represented within these pixels are statistically synthesized rather than physically captured. So, it is not possible to retrieve genuine spatial information at the 30 cm scale. Nonetheless, the model produces perceptually plausible details that are of considerable analytical value. Such synthesized features enhance the visual salience of small-scale surface anomalies (e.g., cracks, erosion, or deformations), thereby improving the performance of deep learning–based classifiers (e.g., CNNs) and facilitating more accurate interpretation by human analysts.

Indeed, in experiments conducted, Sentinel-2 images enhanced with SRGAN; Classification accuracy: 95%, AUC: 0.99, F1 score: 95% have been achieved. These results show that an increase in perceptual resolution leads to practical success in applications such as damage detection, even if it does not contain actual sub-meter details. A lightweight SRGAN architecture specifically designed for remote sensing applications has also been introduced in the literature [15]. Furthermore, numerous recent studies have reported high performance in object detection and classification when using SRGAN-enhanced imagery [13–15]. Although the SRGAN-based super-resolution approach cannot overcome the inherent physical limitations of Sentinel-2 sensors, it enhances the informational value of the imagery for both visual inspection and automated damage assessment. This capability offers a durable foundation for comprehensive, cost-effective, and scalable wind turbine monitoring systems and can be readily extended to other remote sensing and industrial inspection domains.

2.3. Dataset Description and Augmentation

The dataset is composed of 15,000 images. 10,000 of these images are Sentinel-2 images enhanced with SRGAN, and 5000 images have been obtained through augmentation. Table 2 shows the image enhancement methods used to increase the reliability of the dataset [12].

Table 2. Image augmentation methods.

Methods	Purpose
Rotation	Adding diversity to guidance
Zoom in	Clarification of damages
Increasing brightness	Simulate diverse illumination scenarios
Noise Addition	Image acquisition under different lighting conditions
Blurring	Prevent the model from overfitting to high-contrast edges

https://doi.org/10.3390/engproc2026122019

2.4. Image Preprocessing and Labeling

Each image in the dataset is labeled as damaged or undamaged. This labeling process is performed to ensure the reliability of the model training results. Damaged images are identified by the presence of observable structural anomalies such as blade cracks, edge fractures, wear marks, or localized surface deformations. Intact images may contain dust accumulation and slight shadows that do not affect the turbine's operating performance.

To ensure the reliability of model results, 70% of the dataset is used for training, 15% for validation, and the remaining 15% for testing. This grouping ensures class balance during model optimization and evaluation by ensuring equal numbers of damaged and undamaged images across all sub-datasets. The training subset is used to update Adaptive Moment Estimation (ADAM) model parameters for gradient-based optimization. Through all the processing steps in this study, including rigorous labeling, refinement, and the preprocessing framework, it provides a high-quality input base for the CNN classifier.

2.5. CNN Architecture Proposed in This Study

The customized CNN model proposed for this study has been designed with the goal of achieving an optimal balance between computational efficiency and classification accuracy. This model enables the detection of edge contours, texture patterns, and subtle structural irregularities that indicate potential damage to turbine blades, such as the flaking, cracks, wear marks, and surface deformations shown in Figure 4. This framework enables the network to learn to represent both low- and mid-level spatial cues embedded in super-resolution satellite imagery. Model training is performed using the Adam optimization algorithm, which offers adaptive learning rates and improves inter-epoch convergence efficiency. The loss function is defined in (7):

$$L_{BCE} = -\frac{1}{N}\sum_{i=1}^{N}\left[y_i log\left(\hat{y}_i\right) + (1-y_i)log\left(1-\hat{y}_i\right)\right], \tag{7}$$

where y_i represents the true class label (1 represents damaged, 0 represents undamaged), and $\hat{y}_i$ represents the predicted probability for the ith data point. Various strategies are integrated into the training phase to increase the accuracy of performance results and prevent overfitting.

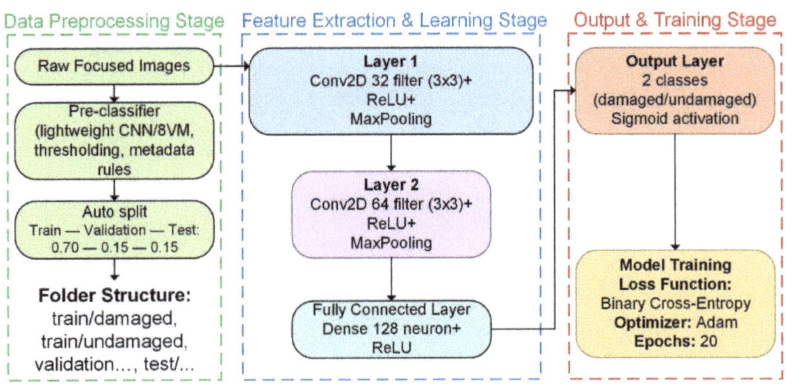

Figure 4. Summary of the proposed framework.

Data augmentation techniques such as controlled rotations, brightness adjustments, and Gaussian noise injection are used to expose the model to various imaging conditions and increase robustness to illumination and orientation changes. Additionally, an

https://doi.org/10.3390/engproc2026122019

early-stopping method based on validation loss compensation is used to increase training efficiency without unnecessary iterations.

The overall architecture is extremely lightweight yet efficient, making it suitable for real-time deployment in resource-constrained environments such as edge computing units in large-scale wind farms or cloud-based monitoring systems.

2.6. Performance Metrics

Various metrics are used to evaluate classification performance:

$$Accuracy = \frac{TP + TN}{TP + TN + FP + FN}, \quad (8)$$

$$Precision = \frac{TP}{TP + FP}, \quad (9)$$

$$Recall = \frac{TP}{TP + FN}, \quad (10)$$

$$F1\ score = \frac{2 \times Precision \times Recall}{Precision + Recall}. \quad (11)$$

Accuracy indicates the proportion of correct predictions (both true positives and true negatives) to the total number of predictions; precision indicates the proportion of predicted damaged samples that are actually damaged; recall measures the proportion of actual damaged samples correctly identified; F1 balances both. The ROC curve and the Area Under the Curve (AUC) provide a threshold-independent measure of discrimination capability.

3. Performance Evaluation and Analysis

In this study, the performance of the proposed SRGAN-CNN-based framework in detecting turbine damage is extensively investigated using accuracy, loss values, classification metrics, confusion matrix, ROC curve and AUC value.

3.1. Training and Validation Performance

The training of the model consists of 20 epochs. While the training accuracy reached 96%, the validation accuracy remained stable at approximately 94%. The training loss decreased to 0.08, and the validation loss to 0.11, indicating that the model's parameters were correctly chosen (e.g., dropout) and overfitting did not occur. The results are shown in Table 3, and graphs illustrating the course of the training process are presented in Figure 5.

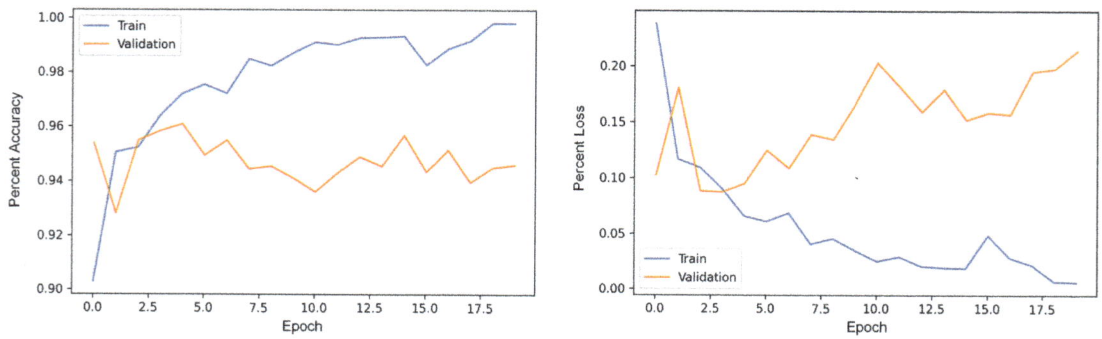

(a) (b)

Figure 5. Evolution of training and validation metrics over 20 epochs: (**a**) accuracy; (**b**) loss.

Table 3. Accuracy and loss results of the CNN model.

Class	Accuracy (%)	Loss (%)
Training	96	0.08
Validation	94	0.11

3.2. Classification Performance

The model's classification performance is analyzed not only by overall accuracy but also by precision, recall, and F1 score, which are examined separately for each class. The results for the damaged and undamaged turbine classes are presented in Table 4, and visual comparisons are shown in Figure 6.

Table 4. Precision, recall, and F1 score for both classes.

Class	Accuracy (%)	Recall (%)	F1 Score (%)
Damaged	97	95	96
Undamaged	94	96	95

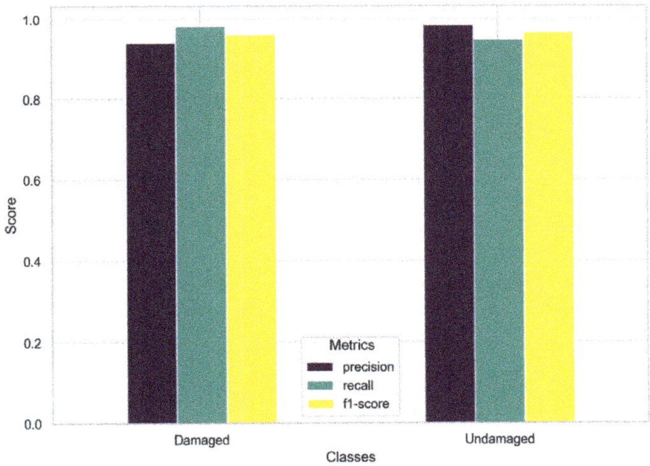

Figure 6. Precision, recall, and F1 score values for damaged and undamaged turbine images.

3.3. Confusion Matrix Analysis

The model's correct and incorrect predictions are visualized in Figure 7 as a confusion matrix, and the numerical results are detailed in Table 5. On the test data, 862 damaged samples are correctly classified (TP), and 1052 undamaged samples are correctly identified (TN). The number of false negatives (FNs) is 58, while the number of false positives (FPs) is 51. In particular, false negatives are more critical for maintenance planning, and in such cases, it is recommended to support the SRGAN-CNN method with UAV or SCADA-based systems.

Table 5. Confusion matrix results for the test set.

Class	Predicted Damaged		Predicted Undamaged	
Actual Damaged	TP	862	FN	58
Actual Undamaged	FP	51	TN	1052

https://doi.org/10.3390/engproc2026122019

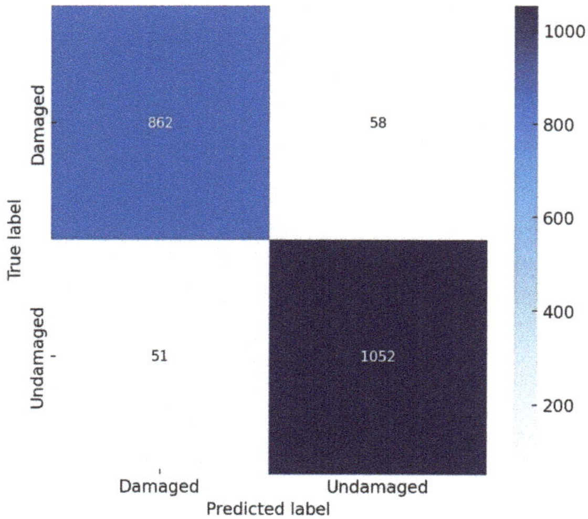

Figure 7. Confusion matrix visualization for damaged and undamaged classes.

3.4. ROC Curve and AUC Evaluation

To assess the model's ability to discriminate between binary classifications, an ROC curve is generated, and AUC is calculated. The ROC curve shown in Figure 8 is quite close to the ideal corner point, the upper left. This closeness demonstrates the success of all processes used in preparing the model and dataset proposed in this study. The AUC value of 0.99 further confirms the model's high discrimination ability and reliability claims. Furthermore, the fact that the ROC curve lies significantly above the reference line (AUC = 0.5) corresponding to the random classifier, shown as a dashed line in the figure, indicates that the model's discriminative knowledge between classes far exceeds that of random performance. This demonstrates that the proposed approach not only provides high accuracy but also offers a reliable and consistent classification capability.

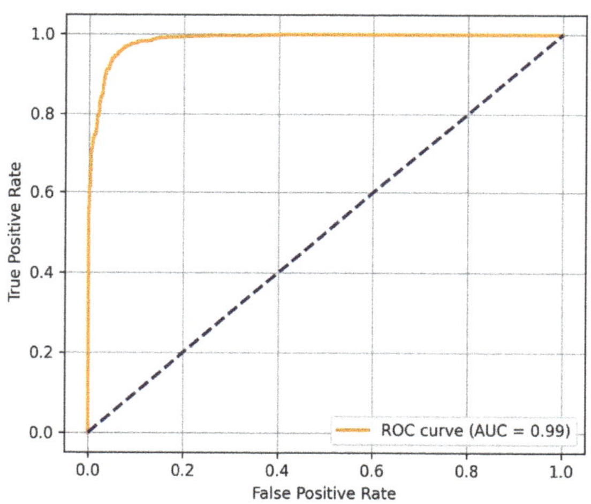

Figure 8. ROC curve and AUC of the proposed CNN model.

3.5. Comparative Analysis Conclusions

Visual inspection of misclassifications showed that fine cracks, often overlooked by the model, are generally missed in false negatives, while surface blemishes are interpreted

https://doi.org/10.3390/engproc2026122019

as damage in false positives. The proposed SRGAN-CNN method offers advantages in terms of both wider coverage and cost-effectiveness compared to UAV-based inspections. Therefore, it is quite suitable for application as the first screening and early warning system in large-scale wind farms.

4. Conclusions

The findings of this research highlight the potential of data-driven super-resolution and classification methods in advancing renewable energy monitoring systems. This study presents a novel deep learning framework that combines Sentinel-2 satellite imagery with a custom CNN classifier, SRGAN-based super-resolution, and a novel approach for identifying wind turbine damage at the microstructural level. The spatial resolution of the 10 m Sentinel-2 images, freely available under the Copernicus Program, has been increased to approximately 30 cm. This allows for the detection of small defects that would otherwise be hidden in standard resolution data, such as blade deformations, erosion, and cracks. To increase the generalizability of the model and reduce the likelihood of overfitting, 10,000 super-resolution images and 5000 enhanced resolution images were generated from these images. A total of 15,000 samples were generated. The proposed CNN architecture achieved 95% accuracy on the test set, an AUC score of 0.99, and an effective balance between precision, recall, and F1 score. The confusion matrix revealed that the absence of many misclassifications was primarily due to the presence of ambiguous visual signals, such as shadows or dots on the surface. Based on the findings, the proposed approach appears to have the potential to serve as a cost-effective and scalable alternative to traditional monitoring techniques such as SCADA-based monitoring or UAV imaging. However, some issues persist with satellite imagery, such as seasonal variations and atmospheric noise. Future work includes integrating diverse data sources such as UAV imagery, Internet of Things (IoT) sensors, SCADA recordings, and satellite imagery to improve the reliability of damage detection. Furthermore, the use of models such as Image Transformers (ViT) and Swin-Transformers is expected to facilitate learning and improve model performance. As a result, the proposed approach is cost-effective and contributes to the development of intelligent condition-monitoring systems. The success of this approach demonstrates its applicability to different renewable energy sources.

Author Contributions: Conceptualization, O.E.; Methodology, O.E.; Software, K.Ç.; Validation, K.Ç., O.E. and M.K.; Formal analysis, K.Ç.; Investigation, O.E., K.Ç. and M.K.; Resources, K.Ç.; Data curation, K.Ç.; Writing—Original Draft Preparation, K.Ç.; Writing—Review and Editing, M.K. and O.E.; Visualization, K.Ç.; Supervision, M.K.; Project administration, M.K.; Funding acquisition, O.E. and M.K. All authors have read and agreed to the published version of the manuscript.

Funding: This work was supported in part by The Scientific and Technological Research Council of Turkiye (TUBITAK) under the 2219 International Postdoctoral Research Fellowship Program.

Institutional Review Board Statement: Not applicable.

Informed Consent Statement: Not applicable.

Data Availability Statement: This study analyzed publicly available datasets. These data can be accessed at https://dataspace.copernicus.eu/data-collections/copernicus-sentinel-data/sentinel-2 (accessed on 2 September 2025).

Conflicts of Interest: The authors declare no conflicts of interest.

 https://doi.org/10.3390/engproc2026122019

References

1. Adeosun, T.A.; Amosu, C.O.; Omitogun, O.A.; Amusa, O.M.; Morenikeji, B.A. Renewable Energy for Sustainable Development in Developing Countries: Benefits to the Environment. *J. Energy Res. Rev.* **2023**, *13*, 1–25. [CrossRef]
2. Khan, P.W.; Byun, Y.C. A Review of Machine Learning Techniques for Wind Turbine's Fault Detection, Diagnosis, and Prognosis. *Int. J. Green Energy* **2024**, *21*, 771–786. [CrossRef]
3. Huang, X.; Li, Y.; Chai, Y. Intelligent Fault Diagnosis Method of Wind Turbines Planetary Gearboxes Based on a Multi-Scale Dense Fusion Network. *Front. Energy Res.* **2021**, *9*, 747622. [CrossRef]
4. Mandroux, N.; Dagobert, T.; Drouyer, S.; Grompone von Gioi, R. Single Date Wind Turbine Detection on Sentinel-2 Optical Images. *Image Process. Line* **2022**, *12*, 198–217. [CrossRef]
5. Sentinel-2 | Copernicus Data Space Ecosystem. Available online: https://dataspace.copernicus.eu/data-collections/copernicus-sentinel-data/sentinel-2 (accessed on 6 November 2025).
6. Zhang, K.; Sumbul, G.; Demir, B. An Approach to Super-Resolution of Sentinel-2 Images Based on Generative Adversarial Networks. In Proceedings of the 2020 Mediterranean and Middle-East Geoscience and Remote Sensing Symposium, M2GARSS 2020, Tunis, Tunisia, 9–11 March 2020; pp. 69–72. [CrossRef]
7. Shihavuddin, A.S.M.; Chen, X.; Fedorov, V.; Christensen, A.N.; Riis, N.A.B.; Branner, K.; Dahl, A.B.; Paulsen, R.R. Wind Turbine Surface Damage Detection by Deep Learning Aided Drone Inspection Analysis. *Energies* **2019**, *12*, 676. [CrossRef]
8. Aminzadeh, A.; Dimitrova, M.; Meiabadi, M.S.; Sattarpanah Karganroudi, S.; Taheri, H.; Ibrahim, H.; Wen, Y. Non-Contact Inspection Methods for Wind Turbine Blade Maintenance: Techno–Economic Review of Techniques for Integration with Industry 4.0. *J. Nondestruct. Eval.* **2023**, *42*, 54. [CrossRef]
9. Pratt, R.; Allen, C.; Masoum, M.A.S.; Seibi, A. Defect Detection and Classification on Wind Turbine Blades Using Deep Learning with Fuzzy Voting. *Machines* **2025**, *13*, 283. [CrossRef]
10. Song, X.; Li, Z. Seasonally Robust Offshore Wind Turbine Detection in Sentinel-2 Imagery Using Imaging Geometry-Aware Deep Learning. *Remote Sens.* **2025**, *17*, 2482. [CrossRef]
11. Wang, X.; Sun, L.; Chehri, A.; Song, Y. A Review of GAN-Based Super-Resolution Reconstruction for Optical Remote Sensing Images. *Remote Sens.* **2023**, *15*, 5062. [CrossRef]
12. Hao, X.; Liu, L.; Yang, R.; Yin, L.; Zhang, L.; Li, X. A Review of Data Augmentation Methods of Remote Sensing Image Target Recognition. *Remote Sens.* **2023**, *15*, 827. [CrossRef]
13. Shermeyer, J.; Van Etten, A. The Effects of Super-Resolution on Object Detection Performance in Satellite Imagery. In Proceedings of the IEEE Computer Society Conference on Computer Vision and Pattern Recognition Workshops, Long Beach, CA, USA, 16–17 June 2019; pp. 1432–1441. [CrossRef]
14. Xiong, Y.; Guo, S.; Chen, J.; Deng, X.; Sun, L.; Zheng, X.; Xu, W. Improved SRGAN for Remote Sensing Image Super-Resolution Across Locations and Sensors. *Remote Sens.* **2020**, *12*, 1263. [CrossRef]
15. Jiang, N.; Zhao, W.; Wang, H.; Luo, H.; Chen, Z.; Zhu, J. Lightweight Super-Resolution Generative Adversarial Network for SAR Images. *Remote Sens.* **2024**, *16*, 1788. [CrossRef]

https://doi.org/10.3390/engproc2026122019

engineering proceedings

MDPI

Proceeding Paper

Development and Modeling of a Modular Ankle Prosthesis [†]

Yerkebulan Nurgizat [1,2,*], Abu-Alim Ayazbay [1], Arman Uzbekbayev [1], Nursultan Zhetenbayev [1,2], Kassymbek Ozhikenov [3] and Gani Sergazin [2]

1 Department of Electronic Engineering, Almaty University of Power Engineering and Telecommunications Named Gumarbek Daukeyev, Almaty 050062, Kazakhstan
2 Department of Science and Innovations, ALT University Named After Mukhamedzhan Tynyshpaev, Almaty 050013, Kazakhstan
3 Institute of Automation and Information Technologies, Satbayev University, Almaty 050013, Kazakhstan
* Correspondence: y.nurgizat@aues.kz; Tel.: +7-(702)-3298994

† Presented at the 6th International Conference on Communications, Information, Electronic and Energy Systems, 26–28 November 2025, Ruse, Bulgaria.

Abstract

This paper presents a low-cost, modular ankle–foot prosthesis that integrates an S-shaped compliant foot with a parallel spring–short-stroke actuator branch to balance energy return, impact attenuation, and rapid personalization. The design follows an FDM-oriented CAD/CAE workflow using PETG and interchangeable modules (foot, ankle unit, pylon adapter). Finite-element analyses of heel-strike, mid-stance, and toe-off load cases, supported by bench checks, show strain localization in intended flexural regions, a minimum safety factor of 15 for the housing, and peak-stress reduction after geometric refinements (increased transition radii and local ribs). The modular layout simplifies servicing and allows quick tuning of stiffness and damping without redesigning the load-bearing structure. The results indicate an engineeringly realistic path toward accessible prosthetics and provide a basis for subsequent upgrades toward semi-active control and sensor-assisted damping.

Keywords: modular ankle–foot prosthesis; compliant S-shaped foot; FDM/3D printing; PETG; finite-element analysis; damping; energy return; assistive technology

1. Introduction

Modern lower-limb prosthetics are one of the key areas of biomedical engineering and orthopedic technology. Loss of ankle-joint function due to trauma, disease, or amputation markedly reduces locomotor activity, independent mobility, and overall quality of life. The ankle joint provides body stabilization, shock attenuation, and motion in three planes; its restoration or replacement requires rigorous biomechanical justification and engineering accuracy.

A current trend is the modularity of prosthetic designs: rapid replacement and adaptation of components to operating conditions, amputation level, physical activity, and individual patient characteristics. This approach simplifies servicing, accelerates fitting, and increases system reliability.

Despite the availability of commercial solutions for foot and ankle prosthetics, many are limited in functionality or remain too expensive for widespread adoption. The accessibility problem is especially evident in healthcare systems with constrained budgets and infrastructure. According to international organizations, more than 2.5 billion people require at least one assistive product, and access ranges from ~3% in some low-income countries to ~90% in certain high-income countries [1,2]. These figures underscore a pronounced global inequality in access to assistive technologies.

In response, the World Health Organization launched the GATE initiative (Global Cooperation on Assistive Technology), which coordinates global efforts to expand access to affordable, high-quality assistive products; its activities are structured by the "5P framework" (People, Policy, Products, Provision, Personnel) [3].

Against this backdrop, the development of a modular ankle–foot prosthesis that combines engineering simplicity, biomechanical correctness, and flexible tuning is a timely task of applied engineering and social medicine. In addition, modern CAD tools and additive technologies enable accelerated design, reduced manufacturing cost, and enhanced personalization through the digital "scan–model–print" pipeline, as evidenced by the growing body of research on 3D-printed orthoses and prostheses [4–6].

2. Materials and Methods

Modern ankle–foot prosthetics evolve along two intersecting axes: by energetic behavior and by mechanical architecture. Energetically, devices include passive energy-storing-and-returning (ESAR) carbon feet, in which compliant geometry accumulates and releases part of the step energy; semi-passive solutions with viscoelastic (often hydraulic) damping; and active (powered) designs with actuation and control [7]. Architecturally, alongside monolithic (or low serviceability) systems, modular constructions are increasingly common, where the foot, ankle unit, and pylon interface are replaceable blocks. Modularity simplifies servicing, accelerates personalization of stiffness and damping, and lowers life-cycle cost—critical under budget constraints and when frequent tuning to user activity is required [8]. To illustrate this spectrum, three representative exemplars are referenced: a classic passive ESAR foot (Figure 1a), a semi-passive hydraulic ankle system (Figure 1b), and a high-energy-return carbon sport foot (Figure 1c). These examples highlight the compromise among simplicity, damping, mass, and tunability [7,9,10].

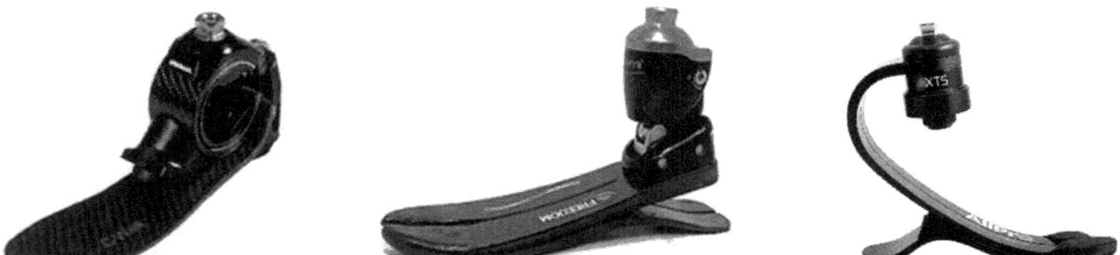

(a) (b) (c)

Figure 1. Types of ankle–foot prostheses: (**a**) Ottobock C-Walk; (**b**) Freedom Kinterra; (**c**) Fillauer AllPro.

Modular approaches appear both in open, low-budget 3D-printed feet and in research-grade active prostheses with multiple degrees of freedom. In open/printed prototypes, modularity is achieved by separating the compliant foot from the load-bearing ankle block and by using a standardized pylon interface; mechanical characteristics are tuned via interchangeable elastic elements and geometry variations of printed parts [11,12]. In recent active designs, modularity is expressed in mechanics (replaceable links and gear trains, independent damping channels) and in sensor/electronics layout, facilitating adaptation to gait scenarios and benchtop validation [9,13,14]. For clarity, the target design's modular

 https://doi.org/10.3390/engproc2026122020

scheme is shown as an exploded CAD view with three highlighted blocks—compliant foot, ankle unit with spring–short-stroke-actuator damper, and pylon adapter (Figure 2) [15–17].

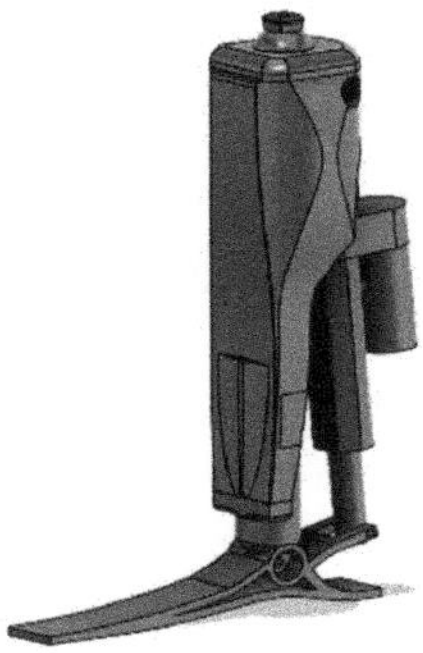

Figure 2. 3D model of the ankle–foot prosthesis.

This formulation aligns with studies on compliant 3D-printed feet with targeted non-linear stiffness and with evidence on how damping/stiffness parameters affect gait-phase behavior in simulations and tests [11,14,17]. The target prosthesis is specified by biomechanical assumptions and manufacturing constraints. The adopted angular ranges are ~15–20° dorsiflexion and ~40–45° plantarflexion, with lateral compliance to accommodate uneven terrain. A consolidated schema of gait phases, ground-reaction directions, and the role of the musculo-ligamentous system underpins the choice of load cases and required compliance. Based on these premises, the architecture comprises an S-shaped compliant foot for energy storage/return in mid-stance and toe-off, and an ankle unit with a parallel branch "spring + short-stroke linear actuator" providing adjustable damping and preload for smoother heel-strike attenuation. The manufacturing platform targets FDM: PETG is chosen for its balance of processability, toughness, and moisture resistance; for higher duty use, nylon-CF and high-temperature thermoplastics (PEI/PEEK) are considered [11,12]. Load-bearing bores are reinforced with metal bushings; threaded joints are unified for standard tools. A consolidated bill of materials (polymers, fasteners, bushings, springs, actuator, approximate masses) is summarized in Table 1.

Table 1. Comparison of 3D-printing plastics.

Material	Tensile Strength, MPa	Softening Temp., °C	Flexibility (1–5)	Hygroscopicity
PLA	60	60	2	Low
PETG	70	80	4	Medium
ABS	45	105	3	High
TPU (flex)	35	60	5	High
Nylon	75	120	4	Very High
PC (polycarbonate)	70	135	3	Medium

The FDM workflow on a desktop Bambu Lab P1S (Shenzhen, China) included geometry preparation with minimal support (rational split planes, 2.5 mm internal radii, chamfers), a 0.6% PETG shrinkage compensation, and layer orientations that align in-service tensile paths with perimeters rather than interlayer bonds. Baseline printing parameters were a 0.20 mm layer height, five perimeters, 35% infill, a 245 °C nozzle temperature, and an 80 °C bed temperature, consistent with current practice for functional prosthetic FDM parts with controlled anisotropy and tolerances [11,12].

Finite-element analysis (FEA) covered three characteristic regimes: mid-stance with vertical load $F_z = 0.8 - 1.2\,\mathrm{BW}$; heel-strike with an added posterior shear $F_x = 0.1 - 0.2\,\mathrm{BW}$; and toe-off with an anterior shear of the same magnitude and the center of pressure shifted

https://doi.org/10.3390/engproc2026122020

toward the forefoot. The pylon interface was modeled as a hinge with one rotational degree of freedom (dorsi/plantar flexion) and five constrained degrees of freedom; a fixed variant was also evaluated to probe mounting stiffness. Bolted joints and bushing zones were assigned bonded contacts, and the support plane was treated as ideally rigid. PETG was modeled as linear elastic with $E = 2.2$ Gpa and $\nu = 0.38$; to reflect FDM anisotropy, a conservative allowable stress $\sigma_{\text{allow}} \leq 0.4\,\sigma_y$ was applied to the as-printed material [12]. The mesh comprised tetrahedra (base size 2.0 mm) with local refinement to 0.8 mm near holes, fillets, and interfaces; convergence was enforced when the peak von Mises stress changed by <5% between successive refinements.

The spring–actuator branch was tuned to a target force–displacement response during stance and to guarantee neutral return during swing. The branch was assumed to carry 25% of peak Fz; the spring stiffness followed $k = F/\Delta x$ with $\Delta x = 0.025$ m, and a 60 N preload was used to eliminate backlash and shape the initial response.

The experimental program comprised visual inspection and fit-up, stepwise static loading up to 1100 N ($\approx$1.5 BW for 75 kg) with 10 s dwell per step while recording toe deflection and damper-node strains, a screening fatigue run of 20.000 cycles at 2 Hz and 300 N amplitude, and phase-mimicking load placements (heel-strike/mid-stance/toe-off) with force–displacement loops captured. Data processing used $\geq$3 repeats, 95% confidence intervals, and Tukey outlier rejection (1.5 IQR). The test-rig configuration and emulation approach are consistent with peer-reviewed prosthetic-foot emulators and platforms [13].

Recent advances in ankle–foot systems follow three principal directions: (i) powered ankles that target controlled torque and push-off work; (ii) semi-active or variable-stiffness feet that modulate damping and stiffness with minimal mass and energy cost; and (iii) additive-manufactured, low-cost prostheses aimed at accessibility and rapid personalization. Powered ankles provide high control authority at the expense of complexity: a recent two-degree-of-freedom powered ankle–foot reported sub-50 ms step response at ~40 N·m per actuator and validated untethered level-ground walking, underscoring the performance potential alongside increased mass and power-management demands [9]. Semi-active concepts pursue adaptability without full actuation; a model-based study of a two-keel variable-stiffness foot (VSF-2K) indicated that independently modulating hind- and forefoot stiffness improves phase-dependent metrics while preserving passive-foot envelopes, supporting the rationale for tunable mechanical elements in affordable devices [18].

On the manufacturing side, AM/FDM routes reduce cost and lead time while enabling scan-to-print personalization; however, recent reviews emphasize the need for standardized as-printed material data (anisotropy, fatigue) and consistent clinical outcome reporting. A 2025 systematic review of 3D-printed prostheses reported improvements in comfort, gait parameters, and fit, while highlighting the need for durability reporting and protocol harmonization [19].

In parallel, sensor integration that combines IMU, plantar-pressure, and angular sensing with lightweight control has been shown to improve phase detection and damping control without the full burden of powered actuation; contemporary surveys outline practical sensor suites and control strategies relevant to semi-active branches [20].

Passive high-energy-return feet (e.g., carbon leaf/elliptical designs) remain efficient baselines, with recent biomechanical evaluations confirming strong energy-storage benefits but noting limitations in shock attenuation and terrain adaptivity that semi-active modules aim to address [21].

Within this landscape, the present modular design—an S-shaped compliant foot with a parallel spring–short-stroke actuator—targets affordability and maintainability

 https://doi.org/10.3390/engproc2026122020

while enabling adjustable damping and preload, providing a pragmatic pathway toward subsequent sensor-assisted semi-active control.

3. Results and Discussion

Preliminary sketching enabled a coherent modular architecture of the prosthesis and the identification of key geometric decisions prior to detailed CAD modeling. The layout separates the system into a compliant S-shaped foot, an ankle unit with a spring–actuator damper, a load-bearing housing, and an interface to the socket. The sketches refined axis locations, the kinematic linkage between the damping branch, housing, and foot, and manufacturable connector forms for FDM; force paths were assessed in parallel, allowing early assignment of appropriate internal fillets and locally reinforced zones (Figure 3).

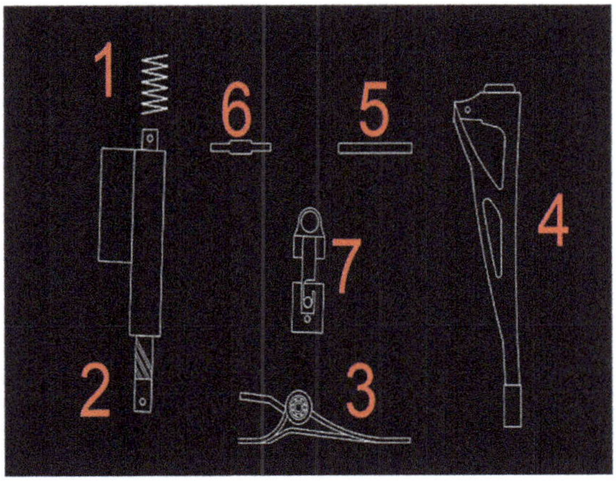

Figure 3. Sketches of modular structure components: 1—Compression spring; 2—Main sliding rod (plunger); 3—Lever mechanism; 4—Structural support frame; 5—Spacer bar; 6—Retaining pin; 7—Connecting joint (link element).

The final arrangement shows that the required sagittal mobility is achieved by a hinge joint where the damping branch ("spring + short-stroke linear actuator") works in parallel with the foot's compliant deformation. The housing is a load-bearing shell with unified seats for bushings and fasteners; the S-profile foot provides energy return during rollover and reduces the impact component of the ground-reaction force. The working drawing fixes overall dimensions and mounting interfaces for printing and assembly (Figure 4). A 3D model was developed in Fusion 360. PETG was chosen for printed parts; load-bearing seats were reinforced with metal bushings; purchased components (linear actuator and spring) were selected by catalog. For comparability in numerical analyses, a single static load case F = 600 N was used as a representative vertical ground-reaction force in steady stance; boundary conditions mirrored real fixation (rigid support with bonded contacts in fastener areas for adapters/housing; fixed heel and applied load at the shank–foot junction for the foot).

In the Equivalent Strain formulation, deformation maxima localize at section transitions and threaded seats. The mapped value $\varepsilon_{max} \approx 0.003$ mm/mm confirms elastic behavior of "as-printed" PETG under the given load

Damper assembly (actuator + spring). Analysis showed uniform load sharing; expected concentrations occur at interfaces between purchased metal parts and printed brackets. The maximum mapped strain is $\varepsilon_{max} \approx 7.45 \times 10^{-5}$, consistent with the high stiffness of metal parts and correct force transfer through interface details (Figure 5).

https://doi.org/10.3390/engproc2026122020

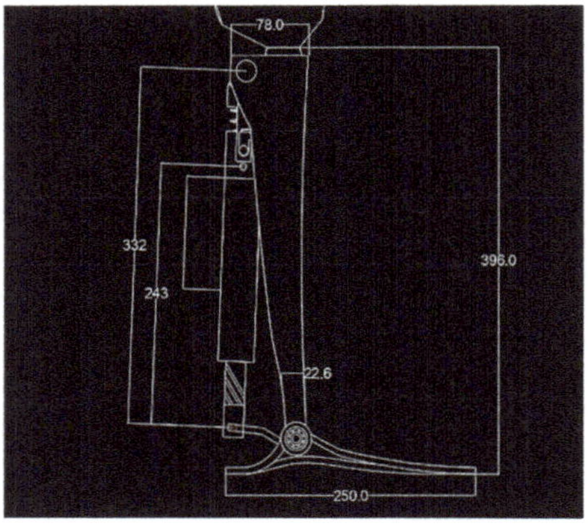

Figure 4. Overall drawing with axes and interfaces.

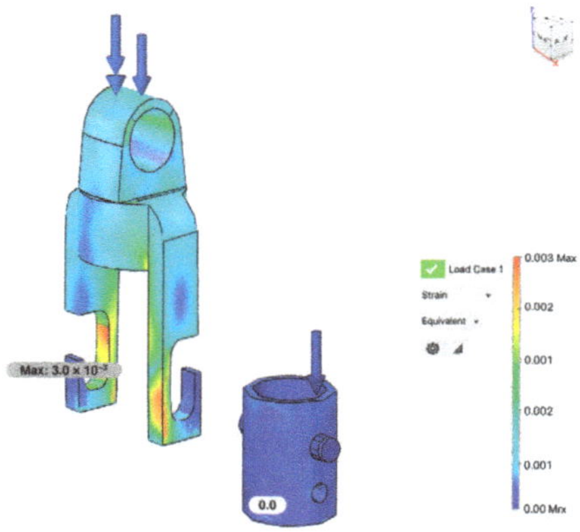

Figure 5. Damper assembly: Static Stress, stress distribution, and force trajectories.

The safety-factor map shows no extended "warm" zones; the minimum calculated margin is K_{min} = 15, confirming the sufficiency of wall thicknesses and ribs for the static scenario (Figure 6).

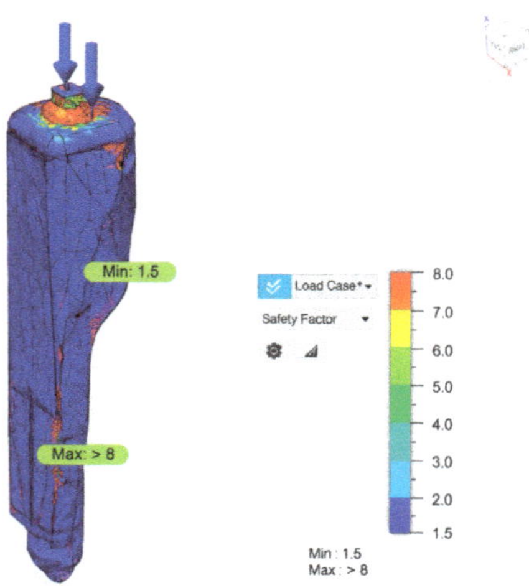

Figure 6. Housing: von Mises/safety-factor map.

https://doi.org/10.3390/engproc2026122020

For the compliant foot (Equivalent Strain), $\varepsilon_{max} \approx 0.003$ localizes in the hinge neck; the main plantar area operates in small elastic strains. This aligns with the S-profile's target function-localized bending and energy return at toe-off with controlled compliance (Figure 7).

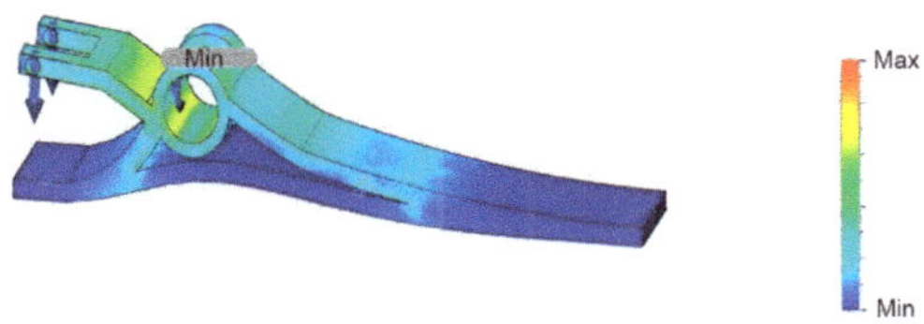

Figure 7. Foot: equivalent strain map, characteristic sections, and toe deflection.

The final render confirms interface consistency and modularity: the damper unit and foot are replaceable without modifying the housing, the pylon interface is standardized; tolerances correspond to FDM capabilities (Figure 8).

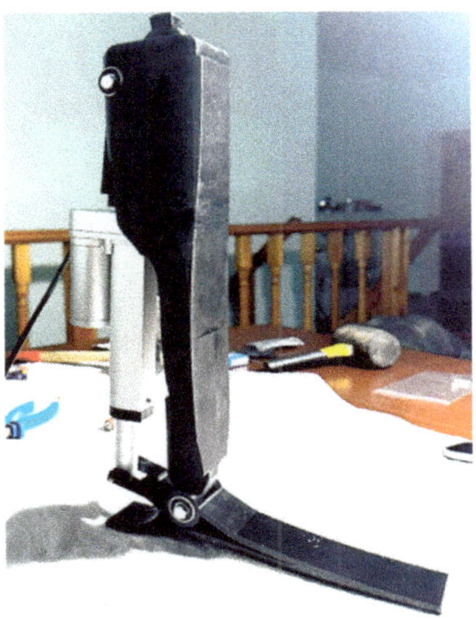

Figure 8. Final 3D assembly (orthogonal views/render).

Printed PETG elements (Table 2) under $F = 600$ N remained in the elastic regime with strain localized to target compliant zones ($\varepsilon_{max} \approx 0.003$) for the adapter and foot, whereas metal subassemblies showed substantially lower compliance $\left(\varepsilon_{max} \approx 7.45 \times 10^{-5}\right)$. The housing achieved $K_{min} = 15$, confirming the adequacy of ribbing and material distribution. The combined set of sketches, general drawings, FEA outputs, and the final CAD assembly demonstrates consistent load paths and a layout manufacturable on desktop FDM equipment, with room for damping-parameter personalization.

Table 2. Summary of FEA indicators (illustrative).

Part	Case/Setup	ε_{max} (mm/mm)	K_{min}
Damper adapter	static deformation	0.003	-
Damper assembly (actuator + spring)	static deformation	7.45×10^{-5}	-
Housing	safety-factor map	-	15
Compliant foot	static deformation	0.003	-

https://doi.org/10.3390/engproc2026122020

The proposed modular architecture distributes the functions of individual components in such a way that the compliant S-shaped foot and the spring–actuator branch are responsible for localized bending, energy return, and damping, while the housing and interface joints provide geometric stiffness and positional stability. This decomposition not only simplifies structural optimization but also reduces the life-cycle cost: personalization of stiffness and damping is achieved through the replacement of accessible modules without interference in the load-bearing part.

The deformation patterns observed in numerical simulations correspond to the expected gait biomechanics: compliance is concentrated in target zones, while stress concentrations arise at section transitions and fastener joints. This confirms the validity of adopted geometric principles (enlarged radii, localized ribs, unified seats) and emphasizes the importance of "force-path-based design" in FDM manufacturing: layer orientation along perimeters, reinforcement with bushings, and reasonable restriction of monolithic parts where controlled bending is required. In this sense, modeling acts as a tool for identifying priorities-where to maintain compliance and where to reinforce locally without significantly increasing mass or printing time.

The study's limitations are typical of an early stage: static load scenarios, linear-elastic models, and idealized contacts (Table 3).

Table 3. Compares the present approach with representative recent designs across powered, semi-active, and passive strategies.

Work	Architecture	Actuation/Adjustability	Materials/Build	Evidence Reported	Notes vs. This Work
[9]	Powered ankle–foot, 2-DoF	Dual actuators; torque control; sub-50 ms step response ~40 N·m	Custom mechatronics	Benchtop dynamics + single-subject walking	High control authority; complexity/mass/energy
[18]	Semi-active two-keel variable-stiffness	Independent hind/forefoot stiffness (model-based)	Concept/model	Simulation-based gait metrics	Supports tunable mechanics at modest mass
[21]	Passive elliptical leaf-spring (ELS) foot	No active elements; high energy return	CFRP + EVA rocker sole	6 participants; lab trials	Efficient storage; limited shock/terrain adaptivity
Present work (this paper)	Modular semi-passive: S-shaped compliant foot + parallel spring–short-stroke actuator	Adjustable damping/preload; quick module swap; no full powertrain	FDM PETG with metal bushings; desktop fabrication	FEA (multi − case) + bench checks; $K\_min \approx 15$ (housing)	Targets affordability, serviceability, and personalization; platform for sensor-assisted control

These provide a safe design corridor but necessitate further work, including fatigue and environmental testing, evaluation of interlayer strength under real printing conditions, and dynamic validation with phase-dependent gait load scenarios. Modular design, meanwhile, opens an evolutionary development pathway-from a semi-passive configuration toward a moderately active one by adding sensors and controlled damping, without altering joint geometry and with minimal iteration costs.

4. Conclusions

The proposed modular design of the ankle–foot prosthesis, combining a compliant S-shaped foot and a spring–actuator damping branch, demonstrated the ability to withstand a calculated static load of 600 N, ensuring controlled compliance, attenuation of impact forces, and the possibility of personalized stiffness adjustment through spring selection and preload tuning. The resulting mechanical pattern-localized bending in the toe region and a reduction of peak stresses after increasing transition radii and introducing

https://doi.org/10.3390/engproc2026122020

local ribs aligns with the known advantages of compliant feet and 3D-printed nonlinear stiffness components.

Comparison with two-degree-of-freedom (2-DoF) powered ankle–foot systems shows that active solutions excel in controllable torque output and response speed, which is critical for targeted gait kinetics and adaptation to terrain and pace. However, these benefits come at the cost of significantly greater structural and algorithmic complexity, weight, energy consumption, and manufacturing expense. In this context, the presented modular variant is focused on affordability and maintainability: it provides passive–semi-passive energy return and damping with minimal requirements for component availability and manufacturing resources, is compatible with desktop FDM production, and supports user-specific customization.

The practical significance of this work lies in demonstrating an engineeringly realistic pathway to lowering access barriers while preserving key biomechanical functions (energy return during toe-off and impact absorption during heel-strike). The study's limitations-static load modeling, linear-elastic assumptions, and idealized contacts-set the agenda for future research: fatigue and environmental testing of printed materials, evaluation of interlayer strength under real printing conditions, extended bench-top gait phase emulation with variable speed and incline, as well as investigation of the influence of preload and spring selection on subjective comfort. Collectively, the results allow the proposed modular architecture to be considered a technologically and economically viable foundation for accessible ankle–foot prostheses with potential scalability for specific clinical scenarios.

Author Contributions: Conceptualization, Y.N. and A.U.; methodology, Y.N.; software, Y.N.; validation, N.Z. and A.-A.A.; formal analysis, Y.N.; investigation, Y.N.; resources, A.U. and K.O.; data curation, A.-A.A.; writing—original draft preparation, Y.N.; writing—review and editing, Y.N. and A.U.; visualization, N.Z.; supervision, A.U. and G.S.; project administration, Y.N.; funding acquisition, Y.N. All authors have read and agreed to the published version of the manuscript.

Funding: This research was funded by the Science Committee of the Ministry of Science and Higher Education of the Republic of Kazakhstan, Grant No. BR24992820 Innovative medical technologies and devices to improve surgical interventions in prosthetics and rehabilitation in the field of orthopedics and medical rehabilitation.

Institutional Review Board Statement: Not applicable.

Informed Consent Statement: Not applicable.

Data Availability Statement: The data generated in this study are presented in the article. For any clarifications, please contact the corresponding author.

Conflicts of Interest: The authors declare no conflict of interest.

Abbreviations

3D	Three-Dimensional
ABS	Acrylonitrile Butadiene Styrene
CAD	Computer-Aided Design
CAE	Computer-Aided Engineering
CF	Carbon Fiber
DoF	Degree of Freedom
ESAR	Energy-Storing-And-Returning
FDM	Fused Deposition Modeling
FEA	Finite Element Analysis

https://doi.org/10.3390/engproc2026122020

FRP	Fiber Reinforced Polymer
FRCM	Fiber Reinforced Cementitious Matrix
GATE	Global Cooperation on Assistive Technology (WHO Initiative)
PETG	Polyethylene Terephthalate Glycol
PLA	Polylactic Acid
PC	Polycarbonate
PEI	Polyetherimide
PEEK	Polyetheretherketone
S-shape	Curved compliant geometry of prosthetic foot (S-profile)
WHO	World Health Organization

References

1. World Health Organization; UNICEF. *Global Report on Assistive Technology*; WHO: Geneva, Switzerland, 2022. Available online: https://www.who.int/publications/i/item/9789240049451 (accessed on 29 October 2025).
2. World Health Organization. Assistive Technology—Fact Sheet. WHO Newsroom: Fact Sheets. 2 January 2024. Available online: https://www.who.int/news-room/fact-sheets/detail/assistive-technology (accessed on 29 September 2025).
3. World Health Organization. Global Cooperation on Assistive Technology (GATE). WHO Initiatives 2025. Available online: https://www.who.int/initiatives/global-cooperation-on-assistive-technology-%28gate%29 (accessed on 29 October 2025).
4. Pereira, J.S.; Xavier, A.S.M.S.; Monteiro, R.S.; Cruz, V.V.; de Souza Pereira, M.F.; Tholl, A.D.; Felisbino, J.; Machado, W.C.A. 3D-Printed Orthoses and Prostheses for People with Physical Disability in Rehabilitation Centers: A Scoping Review. *BMC Musculoskelet. Disord.* **2024**, *25*, 7875. [CrossRef] [PubMed]
5. Gómez-Amador, A.M.; Pérez-Carrera, C.; Rubio-Alonso, H. 3D-Printed Prosthetic Foot Design: Mechanical Similarity and Testing. *Mater. Des.* **2025**, *253*, 113918. [CrossRef]
6. Choo, Y.J.; Kim, J.H.; Chang, M.C. Three-dimensional printing technology applied to the production of prosthesis: A systemic narrative review. *Prosthet. Orthot. Int.* **2025**, *49*, 344–352. [CrossRef] [PubMed]
7. Domínguez-Ruiz, A.; López-Caudana, E.O.; Lugo-González, E.; Espinosa-García, F.J.; Ambrocio-Delgado, R.; García, U.D.; López-Gutiérrez, R.; Alfaro-Ponce, M.; Ponce, P. Low limb prostheses and complex human prosthetic interaction: A systematic literature review. *Front. Robot. AI* **2023**, *10*, 1032748. [CrossRef] [PubMed]
8. Zagoya-López, J.; Zúñiga-Avilés, L.A.; Vilchis-González, A.H.; Ávila-Vilchis, J.C. Foot/ankle prostheses design approach based on scientometric and patentometric analyses. *Appl. Sci.* **2021**, *11*, 5591. [CrossRef]
9. Hsieh, T.-H.; Song, H.; Shu, T.; Qiao, J.; Yeon, S.H.; Carney, M.; Mooney, L.; Duval, J.-F.; Herr, H. Design, characterization, and preliminary assessment of a two-degree-of-freedom powered ankle–foot prosthesis. *Biomimetics* **2024**, *9*, 76. [CrossRef] [PubMed]
10. Kim, S.; Yalla, S.; Shetty, S.; Rosenblatt, N.J. 3D printed transtibial prosthetic sockets: A systematic review. *PLoS ONE* **2022**, *17*, e0275161. [CrossRef] [PubMed]
11. Um, H.-J.; Oh, S.-E.; Park, S.-H.; Han, C.-S.; Kim, K. Design and evaluation of a 3D-printed prosthetic foot with nonlinear stiffness using finite element analysis. *Sci. Rep.* **2021**, *11*, 19369. [CrossRef] [PubMed]
12. Kim, S.; Yalla, S.V.; Shetty, S.; Rosenblatt, N.J. Structural integrity of custom-designed additive manufactured prosthetic sockets compared to traditional sockets. *Result Mater.* **2024**, *21*, 100549. [CrossRef]
13. Caputo, J.M.; Collins, S.H. A Universal Ankle–Foot Prosthesis Emulator for Human Locomotion Experiments. *J Biomech Eng.* **2014**, *136*, 035002. [CrossRef] [PubMed]
14. Liu, J.; Zhang, H.; Wu, W.; Li, Y.; Wang, M. Design and preliminary verification of a novel powered ankle–foot prosthesis: From the perspective of lower-limb biomechanics. *PLoS ONE* **2024**, *19*, e0303397. [CrossRef] [PubMed]
15. Sergazin, G.; Zhetenbayev, N.; Tursunbayeva, G.; Uzbekbayev, A.; Sarina, A.; Nurgizat, Y.; Nussibaliyeva, A. Design, simulation and functional testing of a novel ankle exoskeleton with 3DOFs. *Sensors* **2024**, *24*, 6160. [CrossRef] [PubMed]
16. Sergazin, G.; Ozhikenov, K.; Zhetenbayev, N.; Tursunbayeva, G.; Nurgizat, Y.; Uzbekbayev, A.; Ayazbay, A.-A. Development of an ankle exoskeleton: Design, modeling, and testing. *Sensors* **2025**, *25*, 2020. [CrossRef] [PubMed]
17. Akhmejanov, S.; Zhetenbayev, N.; Sultan, A.; Nurgizat, Y.; Sergazin, G.; Ozhikenov, K. Engineering an active ankle–foot prosthesis: Conceptual design for enhanced walking dynamic. In *International Workshop IFToMM for Sustainable Development Goals*; Springer Nature: Cham, Switzerland, 2025; pp. 177–188.
18. Wang, Z.; Adamczyk, P.G. Effects of a Semi-Active Two-Keel Variable-Stiffness Prosthetic Foot (VSF-2K) on Prosthesis Characteristics and Gait Metrics: A Model-Based Design and Simulation Study. *Prosthesis* **2025**, *7*, 61. [CrossRef]
19. Atallah, H.; Qufabz, T.; Naeem, R.; Bakhsh, H.R.; Ferriero, G.; Varga, D.; Derkács, E.; Molics, B. The Current State of 3D-Printed Prostheses Clinical Outcomes: A Systematic Review. *J. Funct. Biomater.* **2025**, *16*, 370. [CrossRef] [PubMed]

https://doi.org/10.3390/engproc2026122020

20. Gunaratne, P.N.; Perera, T.; Jayasekara, S. Developments in Hardware Systems of Active Ankle Orthoses. *Sensors* **2024**, *24*, 8153. [CrossRef] [PubMed]
21. Shi, Q.Q.; Fu, H.; Lin, Y.; Yang, W.; Guan, H.; Mylonakis, G.; Zhu, H. Biomechanical Evaluation of Elliptical Leaf Spring Prosthetics for Unilateral Transtibial Amputees During Dynamic Activities. *Technologies* **2025**, *13*, 129. [CrossRef]

 https://doi.org/10.3390/engproc2026122020

engineering proceedings

MDPI

Proceeding Paper

Electromagnetic Field Parameters in the Coverage Area of a Base Station †

Miroslav Tomov [1,*], Michail Malamatoudis [2], Dimitrios Kazolis [2], Konstantinos Tramantzas [2] and Stanimir Sadinov [1]

1 Department of Communications Equipment and Technologies, Technical University of Gabrovo, 5300 Gabrovo, Bulgaria; murry@tugab.bg
2 Department of Physics, Democritus University of Thrace, 65404 Kavala, Greece; malamatoudismichail@yahoo.gr (M.M.); dkazolis@physics.duth.gr (D.K.); ktraman@physics.duth.gr (K.T.)
* Correspondence: mtomov@tugab.bg
† Presented at the 6th International Conference on Communications, Information, Electronic and Energy Systems, 26–28 November 2025, Ruse, Bulgaria.

Abstract

This paper presents an exploration of the electromagnetic field characteristics and parameters in the area of coverage of a particular base station, as well as the radio signal strength and the data speed values for optimal service. Although there are many investigations concerning the influence of the electromagnetic field on the reactions of the people positioned in such areas and general impact on humans' health, it is worth exploring some specific aspects of that problem. One of them is to focus the investigation on some particular radio frequency ranges. The second is to propose some practical consequences of the steps and ways to perform the measurements, with fast opportunity to collect the results and to compare them with identical measurements performed by different equipment or different algorithms for measurements. As a consequence, approaches should be developed to allow relatively accurate measurements of the electromagnetic background with devices more accessible to ordinary people instead of the expensive specialized measuring instruments used by specialists in this field. Such alternative methods of control of the electromagnetic flux radiation could help reliably to update the permissible parameters set in the existing regulations.

Keywords: radio signal strength; electromagnetic radiation

1. Introduction

An unavoidable problem in modern life is the electromagnetic background, a result of the operation of mobile and wireless networks and, more precisely, the interpretations of the real influence of electromagnetic fields in the vicinity of base stations on other radio communications and telecommunication networks [1].

Electromagnetic irradiance, standardized by the term "power flux density", is defined as the radiant flux received by a surface per unit area. The SI unit of irradiance is the watt per square meter (W/m^2). The same physical phenomenon caused by the radio connections infrastructure in telecommunication networks is named RF power flux density and is measured in $\mu W/m^2$ or $\mu W/cm^2$. This is the main parameter used to evaluate the safety of the living environment in and around residential areas [2]. The other parameters measured are the electric field (V/m) and the magnetic field strength (μT) [3,4].

https://doi.org/10.3390/engproc2026122021

The RF power level of the radio signals is also an important and widely used parameter, which is easily measured by ordinary affordable radio technical equipment. In most cases, it is measured in logarithmic units dBm, which are normally the unit set by default in the instruments. This physical quantity could be measured in units derived from the watt—μW, nW, pW, or fW [5,6].

Human health safety is very important, and limits set by global and local regulations must be obeyed without any doubt. In the same time, radio signal connections widely applied in the contemporary telecommunication services need high-quality and very fast data transfer, which can be achieved by RF signals with enough strength. Achieving this trade-off is not an easy optimization task. Mobile service providers often allow signal levels to exceed legal limits emitted by transmitters in some base station, usually those in unfavorable positions in terms of insufficient antenna installation height or due to the presence of tall surrounding buildings. When the signal distributed by a transmitting antenna is stronger than permitted, the signal level inside the area covered by that cell will also be over the legal limits, and this violation in the long term could create health problems for the people living under this RF signal coverage, as well as cause interference with other radio channels [7,8].

In order to measure the above-mentioned standardized quantity properly, a spectrum analyzer is an absolutely irreplaceable tool for RF signal analysis. The radio frequency section of modern spectrum analyzers has a complex architecture with a calibrated RF mixer—or one capable of calibration— at the input port. The reasons for this complexity are the requirements for achieving proper working parameters in accordance with the limitations set [9].

Apart from the strictly specialized instruments for measuring power flux density, instruments with a frequency-domain display are very useful for measuring radio frequency radiation, although not so convenient for direct manipulation. They provide simultaneous results on the power level of each radio signal that forms the spectrum of the studied frequency range, and identify which frequencies of this range have a significant contribution to the level of values of the electromagnetic field parameters in the signal coverage area. At the expense of the less convenient manipulation of these instruments, they provide the opportunity for detailed data exchange with a computer resource through a practical and reliable communication interface, and this allows for easy recording and analysis of tons of data—the result of specific measurements.

Concerning regulated HF power flux density limits, it can be seen that there are different standards in different countries all over the world. Even in Europe, there are a lot of differences. But all these specific problems need to be explored by measurement and analysis in order to improve health safety while maintaining the high quality, reliability, and efficiency of telecommunication services [5,10].

2. Experimental Setup and Measurement Concept

2.1. Experimental Setup

The aim of this study is to investigate the correlation between the signal level (measured in dBm) of a particular base station and the power flux density (measured in $\mu W/m^2$) within its area of coverage. Assuming that probably there are some negative effects on the people in the area covered by HF radio signals, it is important to find the optimal level of the RF signal at the imaginary border of the coverage area in order not to exceed the limits of the power flux density stated in the regulations.

Two specialized instruments were chosen for the characterization of components, systems, and signals in the radio frequency (RF) range.

https://doi.org/10.3390/engproc2026122021

2.2. Measurement Instruments

For measurements of power flux density, a High Frequency Analyzer HFE35C (Gigahertz Solutions, Langenzenn, Germany) is used, capable of operating over frequencies between 27 MHz and 2.7 GHz and equipped with three types of receiving antennas.

The measurements of the power flux density are made by a portable instrument, the HF Analyzer HFE35C, and to establish its proper simulation model, each single measurement is recorded separately after testing of HF exposure levels inside a room in a home or an apartment.

As some parts of the radiation are reflected or absorbed, it is important that the permeability of the constructive materials to HF radiation to be taken into account. Usually, wood, drywall, and wooden or plastic window frames are rather transparent spots in a house.

Radio waves are polarized vertically or horizontally. When the antenna is attached, the meter measures the vertically polarized component if the display is positioned horizontally. A change in the polarization plane accordingly can be performed by rotating the instrument around its longitudinal axis.

The peak HF radiation value is regarded as the most critical measurement affecting the human body and is compared to recommended safety limits.

The average value ("RMS") of signal power density is usually a very small fraction of the peak value, although it practically defines the base for most of the safety regulations.

The RF signal spectrum is measured using a portative spectrum analyzer TinySA ULTRA (Hugen, Ningbo, China), which has the ability to precisely catch radio frequency signals from 100 kHz to 7.3 GHz and has very useful software interface to transfer measurement data to a computer in real time and/or as files formatted for appropriate word processing.

The effective radiated power (ERP) is a well-established physical quantity that estimates the amount of directional radio frequency (RF) power that is equivalent to the power radiated by a particular radio transmitter. In practice, it represents the full "useful" power, in watts, that a half-wave dipole antenna would radiate to obtain exactly the same signal strength or power flux density. This is correct provided that the transmitting antenna of a remote radio signal source is in the direction of the strongest beam of the receiving antenna at the measurement location. ERP takes into account both the radio frequency power itself radiated by the transmitter and the ability of the transmitting antenna to radiate this power in the corresponding direction. ERP is calculated as the product of the antenna gain and the input radio frequency power to the antenna. This quantity finds wide practical application in radio communication systems for relatively easy quantification of the "apparent" power of the radio station under study in its reception area.

Radio frequency sources like wireless routers, cordless phones, etc., have been removed from the room where the measurements take part. This important step ensures that the measured values belong to the outside signals only. For higher precision of measurement, it is necessary to mark and consider all areas of the ceiling, floor, and walls, including doors and windows, which the RF flux penetrates through [11,12].

Effective isotropic radiated power (EIRP) is a more appropriate parameter that measures the relation of the power emitted by the transmitter and the ability of the antenna to direct that power in a given direction as ERP does, but EIRP gives a comparison relative to the performance of a theoretical isotropic antenna. It is given by the following equation:

$$EIRP\ (dBW) = G\ (dBi) + P_{in}\ (dBW), \tag{1}$$

 https://doi.org/10.3390/engproc2026122021

where G (dBi) is the isotropic gain given by the equation:

$$G\ (dBi) = 10\ log_{10}\left(\frac{S_{max}}{S_{max,iso}}\right), \tag{2}$$

where S_{max} and $S_{max,iso}$ are, respectively, the maximal RF signal strength and isotropic maximal RF signal strength, measured in $\mu W/m^2$ [13,14].

On the other hand:

$$EIRP = 4\ \pi r^2 S \tag{3}$$

where S is the RF currently measured signal strength in $\mu W/m^2$ [10,11].

Another purpose of this exploration is to find a proper way to calculate the power flux density using a spectrum analyzer, i.e., to convert the meter reading by the RF power levels of signal spectral components [15,16].

The dispersion of the RF energy flux density is calculated using a formula that applies the relations between the proper physical qualities which describe precisely the propagation of electromagnetic waves. The following equation calculates the radiation intensity existing at a particular point above the Earth's surface and receding from the vertical axis of the antenna, provided that the true antenna's technical specifications are considered appropriately [17]:

$$EIRP = 4\ \pi r^2 SS = 2.65 \cdot 10^3 \sum_{i=1}^{n} \frac{\left[F_i(\Delta) F_i(\varphi) K_Z K_H \sqrt{30 P_i G_i \eta_i}\right]^2}{(x - x_i)^2 (y - y_i)^2 (z - z_i)^2} \tag{4}$$

where S is the RF energy flux density, measured in $\mu W/m^2$; N is the number of antennas in the particular base station or cell; Pi is the transmitters output RF power in W; Gi is the antenna gain, dBi; ηi represents the common losses, dBi; Fi(Δ) is the vertical plane directivity factor; Fi(φ) is the directivity factor of a horizontal diagram; KH represents the roughness of the horizontal directivity diagram (this value varies between 1.26 and 1.41); KZ evaluates inequality of the landscape in village areas, as well as the reflective surface effects in towns and cities. Those parameters depend on the position, as well as the quantity and volume of buildings and other above-ground objects, and vary from 1.3 to 1.15; x, y, and z are the space coordinates at the spot of measurement [17].

2.3. Measurement of Power Flux Density Inside the House

A log-periodic antenna is applied for this measurement. It is shielded from the ground RF signal impact and must be directed about 10 degrees below the emitting source one wants to measure to avoid the majority of distortions in the area of sensitivity transition.

In this particular case during the measurements, the log-periodic antenna of the device is positioned towards the elevated base station mast, which is mounted on a nearby building roof. Measurements in four different spots inside the house were taken.

To perform the measurements correctly, the HF Analyzer operates around the center of the room, measuring in all directions, while the log-periodic antenna is directed and positioned close to the wall in order to monitor the permeable areas. The antenna lobe size widens when the frequency increases. It can be seen that the measured RF power flux density does not exceed 900 $\mu W/m^2$.

Measurements of the RF spectrum from 27 MHz up to 2.7 GHz are made at four different spots in the house by the portative spectrum analyzer TyniSA ULTRA. The same spots of measurements by the High Frequency Analyzer HFE35C are used. Also, the same log-periodic antenna is used for these consecutive measurements, conducted in approximately 1 min time frame.

https://doi.org/10.3390/engproc2026122021

The spectrum analyzer is set to display RF power in derivatives of watts—μW, nW, pW, etc. This is performed so that the readings from the two instruments can be compared.

Figure 1 displays the spectrum of the explored frequency range, from 27 MHz to 2.7 GHz, intercepted by the analyzer at two separate spots on the second floor of the house.

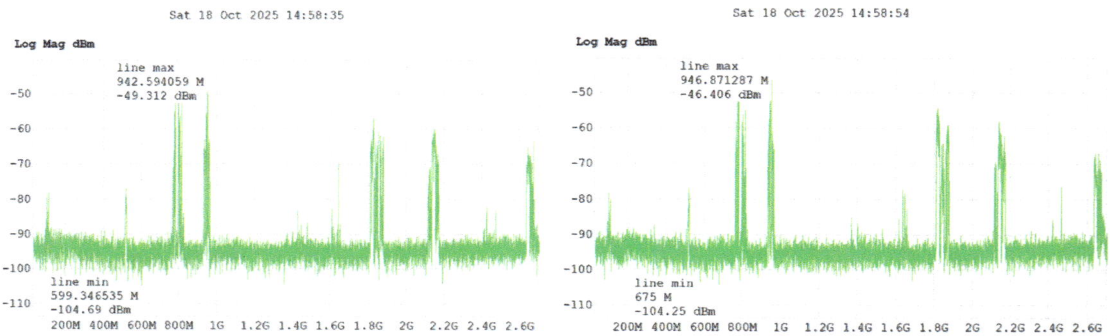

(**a**) (**b**)

Figure 1. RF power spectrum measured in two different sites on the second floor: (**a**) screenshot of the spectrum at spot 1; (**b**) screenshot of the spectrum at spot 2.

Figure 2 depicts the spectrum of the same frequency range (27 MHz to 2.7 GHz) intercepted by the analyzer at two separate spots on the first floor of the house.

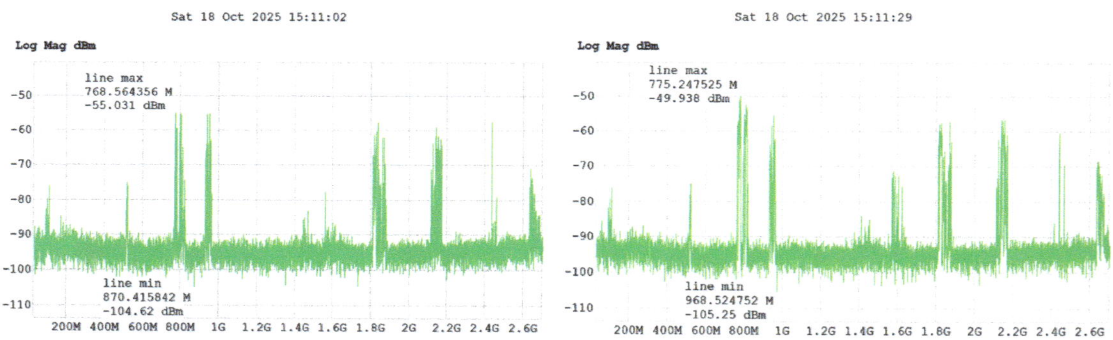

(**a**) (**b**)

Figure 2. RF power spectrum measured in two different sites on the first floor: (**a**) screenshot of the spectrum at spot 1; (**b**) screenshot of the spectrum at spot 2.

The instrument setup allows up to eight (8) signal level markers simultaneously. The software automatically selects the 8 strongest RF signals by order and displays their values in a tabular format. The rest of the peaks could be measured using a manually operated marker as an internal functionality of the instrument. In the current case, the eight (8) highest RF signals in the spectrum were considered.

The radio frequency spectrum of the studied frequency range from 27 MHz to 2.7 GHz is shown in Figures 3–6 which displays the levels of the strongest components (measured in nW or pW) of the radio frequency signal in this range using a 1000-point sweep.

 https://doi.org/10.3390/engproc2026122021

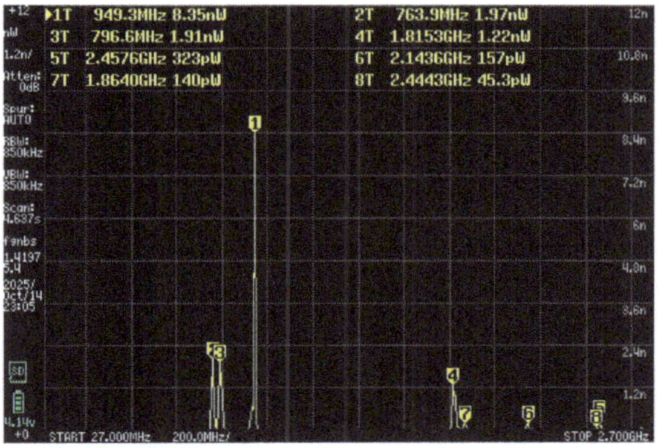

Figure 3. Display of RF power level values of each of the eight (8) strongest intercepted signal frequencies after the first measurement.

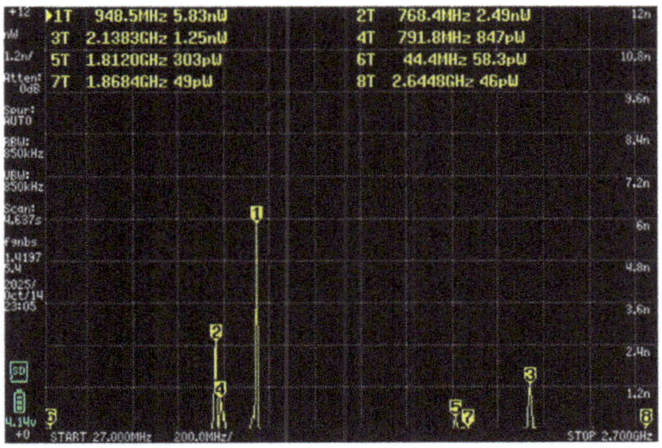

Figure 4. Display of RF power level values of each of the eight (8) strongest intercepted signal frequencies after the second measurement.

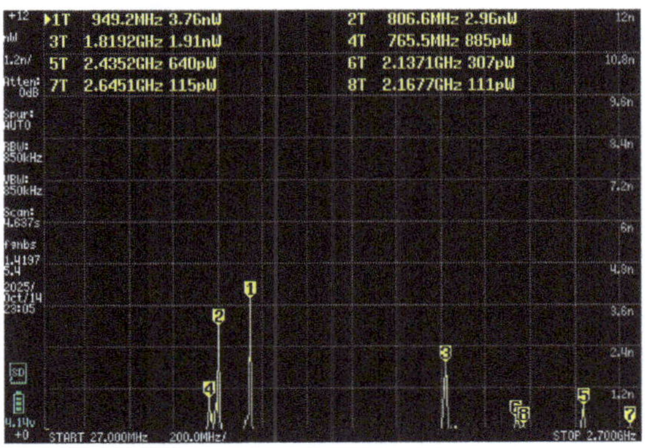

Figure 5. Display of RF power level values of each of the eight (8) strongest intercepted signal frequencies after the third measurement.

https://doi.org/10.3390/engproc2026122021

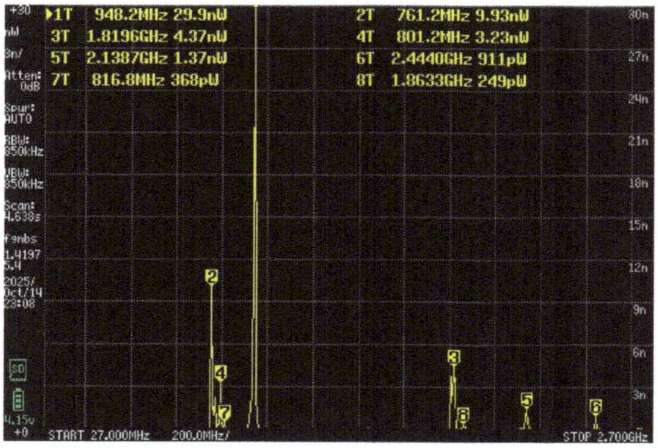

Figure 6. Display of RF power level values of each of the eight (8) strongest intercepted signal frequencies after the fourth measurement.

Measured data from the power scan in instantaneous values and in the frequency domain are saved in *.csv format, and the power is summed automatically after processing the files in a spreadsheet. The total RF signal power is shown after each of the following figures.

It should be noted that each individual measurement presents a unique spectral pattern that is never repeated, but the signals with the highest power remain in their places along the frequency axis. For a more representative sample and higher accuracy of the measured total radio frequency power at the measurement location, sweeps were measured consecutively for 8, 1000, and 10,000 frequency values (sweep points), set within the studied frequency band.

As expected, increasing the number of sweep points results in higher precision and a larger estimated value of the total RF power in the frequency range 27 MHz–2.7 GHz. Measurement at the first spot inside the house is shown below (Figure 3).

The results from the first measurement site in the house are shown in Table 1.

Table 1. RF power level after 1st measurement.

Frequency Sweep Points of Measurement	8	1000	10,000
Total RF Power Measured, μW	0.014115	0.016258	0.0244146

Screen shot of measurement at the second spot inside the house is shown in Figure 4. The results from the third measurement site in the house are shown in Table 2.

Table 2. RF power level after 2nd measurement.

Frequency Sweep Points of measurement	8	1000	10,000
Total RF Power measured, μW	0.010873	0.013127	0.0330637

Screen shot of measurement at the third spot inside the house is shown on Figure 5. The results from the third measurement site in the house are shown in Table 3.

Table 3. RF power level after 3rd measurement.

Frequency Sweep Points of Measurement	8	1000	10,000
Total RF Power Measured, μW	0.010688	0.013269	0.0384721

Screen shot of measurement at the fourth spot inside the house is shown in Figure 6.

https://doi.org/10.3390/engproc2026122021

The results from the fourth measurement site in the house are shown in Table 4.

Table 4. RF power levels after 4th measurement.

Frequency Sweep Points of Measurement	8	1000	10000
Total RF Power Measured, μW	0.050328	0.053731	0.057612

An expected, an increase in total power is observed with an increasing number of sweep frequency points. Including more spectral components increases the total radio frequency power within the studied frequency range 27 MHz–2.7 GHz.

The picture of the signal spectrum looks similar on each of the screenshots above, as the shape and the major signal pics are clearly recognizable, but the values of the extremums after the measurements are slightly different after each particular measurement. This is inevitable with the measurement methodology used, i.e., the same antenna used by both instruments. The manipulation of changing the instruments and unplugging and plugging the SMA connector of the log-periodic antenna to the respective meter takes less than a minute, but this is a considerable time frame and could not guarantee a high precision in the comparison between the readings of both instruments.

After equating the unit of measurement for radio frequency power to microwatts when measuring with both devices, it seems at first glance that only the unknown value of the area with respect to which the power is measured makes the main difference in the readings. In reality, however, many more factors have an influence, and due to the impossibility of directly measuring them, mathematical tools must inevitably be applied.

To be able to extract a mathematical correlation between the readings of both the HFE35C and TinySA ULTRA, a second log-periodic antenna with absolutely the same geometry and electrical parameters is necessary to make possible real-time simultaneous measurement. A large number of ultimate measurements must be performed with the purpose of collecting enough statistical type of data to be processed using appropriate mathematical tools to derive a functional relationship between the signal power measured by the spectrum analyzer and its density. A Lagrange interpolation polynomial or cubic spline approximation could transform the accumulated statistical data from the measurements into a high-order, high-accuracy approximating function.

The derivation of such a relationship could turn any portable spectrum analyzer into a high-accuracy RF power flux density meter.

3. Conclusions

The measurement of the radio frequency power flux density contributes significantly in evaluating the level of radiation caused by the electromagnetic field around antennas for mobile and radio signals of other telecommunication systems. A properly selected methodology of measurement, simulation, and analysis allows us to be able to estimate preliminarily the electromagnetic fields caused by telecommunications, as well as to determine visually each spot or area where electromagnetic radiation exceeds the regulated standards. The described analyses help to control the values of RF—and generally HF—signal frequencies in order to alert for RF power density levels that exceed the standardized health limits, but also to force the mobile service providers to maintain the transmitting power from base stations at optimal levels to ensure the quality of services—connections, data transfer speed, etc.

Similar methods of analysis can be applied to update the regulations in accordance with the balance between the people's modern technological service needs and the actual changes in the radio frequency environment related to human health considerations.

https://doi.org/10.3390/engproc2026122021

Author Contributions: Conceptualization, M.T. and M.M.; methodology, M.T.; software, D.K.; validation, S.S. and M.T.; formal analysis, M.T. and M.M.; investigation, M.T. and K.T.; resources, M.T.; data curation, K.T.; writing—original draft preparation, D.K.; writing—review and editing, M.T.; visualization, D.K.; supervision, S.S.; project administration, S.S.; funding acquisition, S.S. All authors have read and agreed to the published version of the manuscript.

Funding: The presented work is supported under project SRP 2025-14 (NIP 2025-14), "Contemporary Methods and AI Solutions for Secure Data Transmission in Broadband Communication Networks", by the University Center for Research and Technology at the Technical University of Gabrovo.

Institutional Review Board Statement: Not applicable.

Informed Consent Statement: Not applicable.

Data Availability Statement: The original dataset is available upon request from the authors.

Acknowledgments: Thanks are extended to all staff of the Department of Communications Equipment and Technologies at the Technical University of Gabrovo.

Conflicts of Interest: The authors declare no conflict of interest.

Abbreviations

The following abbreviations are used in this manuscript:

ERP	Effective radiated power
EIRP	Effective isotropic radiated power

References

1. Ida, N. Antennas and Electromagnetic Radiation. In *Engineering Electromagnetics*, 4th ed.; Springer: Cham, Switzerland, 2021; pp. 915–991.
2. Lingvay, D.; Borș, A.G.; Borș, A.M. Electromagnetic pollution and its effects on living matter. *Electroteh. Electron. Autom. (EEA)* **2018**, *66*, 5–11.
3. Mihaylov, G.; Iliev, T.; Bikov, T.; Ivanova, E.; Stoyanov, I. Test cases and challenges for mobile network evolution from LTE to 5G. In Proceedings of the 2018 41st International Convention on Information and Communication Technology, Electronics and Microelectronics (MIPRO), Opatija, Croatia, 21–25 May 2018; pp. 449–452. [CrossRef]
4. Iliev, T.B.; Mihaylov, G.Y.; Ivanova, E.P.; Stoyanov, I.S. Power control schemes for device-to-device communications in 5G mobile network. In Proceedings of the 2017 40th International Convention on Information and Communication Technology, Electronics and Microelectronics (MIPRO), Opatija, Croatia, 22–26 May 2017; pp. 416–419. [CrossRef]
5. van Wel, L.; Liorni, I.; Huss, A.; Thielens, A.; Wiart, J.; Joseph, W.; Röösli, M.; Foerster, M.; Massardier-Pilonchery, A.; Capstick, M.; et al. Radio-frequency electromagnetic field exposure and contribution of sources in the general population: An organ-specific integrative exposure assessment. *J. Expo. Sci. Environ. Epidemiol.* **2021**, *31*, 999–1007. [CrossRef] [PubMed]
6. Tomov, M.; Kogias, P.; Malamatoudis, M.; Sadinov, S. Local Area Improvement of GSM Network Coverage. *Eng. Proc.* **2024**, *60*, 24. [CrossRef]
7. Garaio, E.; La Roca, P.; Gómez-Polo, C.; Sánchez-Alarcos, V.; Recarte, V.; Pérez-Landazábal, I.; Martensitic, J. Transformation Controlled by Electromagnetic Field: From Experimental Evidence to Wireless Actuator Applications. *Mater. Des.* **2022**, *219*, 110746. [CrossRef]
8. Kim, H.; Lee, Y.; Choi, H.D.; Lee, A.K.; Jeon, S.; Pack, J.K.; Kim, N.; Ahn, Y. Effect of Exposure to a Radiofrequency Electromagnetic Field on Body Temperature in Anesthetized and Non-Anesthetized Rats. *Bioelectromagnetics* **2020**, *41*, 104–112. [CrossRef] [PubMed]
9. Nyquist, H. Certain topics in telegraph transmission theory. *Trans. AIEE* **2002**, *47*, 617–644. [CrossRef]
10. Shannon, C.E. Communication in the Presence of Noise. *IRE* **1949**, *37*, 10–21. [CrossRef]
11. Hardell, L.; Carlberg, M.; Hedendahl, L. Radiofrequency radiation from nearby base stations gives high levels in an apartment in Stockholm, Sweden: A case report. *Oncol. Lett.* **2018**, *15*, 7871–7883. [CrossRef] [PubMed]
12. Sagar, S.; Adem, S.M.; Struchen, B.; Loughran, S.P.; Brunjes, M.E.; Arangua, L.; Dalvie, M.A.; Croft, R.J.; Jerrett, M.; Moskowitz, J.M. Comparison of radiofrequency electromagnetic field exposure levels in different everyday microenvironments in an in-ternational context. *Environ. Int.* **2018**, *114*, 297–306. [CrossRef] [PubMed]

https://doi.org/10.3390/engproc2026122021

13. Birks, L.E.; Struchen, B.; Eeftens, M.; Wel, L.; Huss, A.; Gajšek, P.; Kheifets, L.; Gallastegi, M.; Dalmau-Bueno, A.; Estarlich, M. Spatial and temporal variability of personal environmental exposure to radio frequency electromagnetic fields in children in Europe. *Environ. Int.* **2018**, *117*, 204–214. [CrossRef] [PubMed]
14. Choi, J.; Min, K.; Jeon, S.; Kim, N.; Pack, J.K.; Song, K. Continuous Exposure to 1.7 GHz LTE Electromagnetic Fields Increases Intracellular Reactive Oxygen Species to Decrease Human Cell Proliferation and Induce Senescence. *Sci. Rep.* **2020**, *10*, 9238. [CrossRef] [PubMed]
15. Przystupa, K.; Vasylkivskyi, I.; Ishchenko, V.; Pohrebennyk, V.; Kochan, O. Electromagnetic pollution: Case study of energytransmission lines and radio transmission equipment. *Przegl Ad Elektrotechniczny* **2020**, *96*, 52–55.
16. Röösli, M.; Hertach, P.; Bolte, J.; Neubauer, G.; Cardis, E.; Feychting, M.; Gajšek, P.; Heinrich, S.; Joseph, W.; Mann, S. Conduct of a personal radiofrequency electromagnetic field measurement study: Proposed study protocol. *Env. Health Glob. Access Sci. Source* **2010**, *9*, 23. [CrossRef] [PubMed]
17. Buckus, R.; Chlebnikovas, A.; Strukcinskiene, B.; Stukas, R.; Austys, D.; Caban, J.; Bogucki, M.; Sidlauskiene, A.; Seleviciene, V.; Kilikevičius, A.; et al. Simulating the Dispersion of the Energy Flux Density of the Electromagnetic Field Generated by Antennas for Mobile Communications. *Electronics* **2022**, *11*, 2431. [CrossRef]

https://doi.org/10.3390/engproc2026122021

engineering proceedings

Proceeding Paper

Application and Development of CAD/CAM Technologies in the Modern Metalworking Industry †

Fatima Sapundzhi [1,*], Deyan Vezyuv [1], Slavi Georgiev [2,3,*] and Ivaylo Nikolaev [4]

1 Department of Communication and Computer Engineering, Faculty of Engineering, South-West University "Neofit Rilski", 66 Ivan Myhailov Str., 2700 Blagoevgrad, Bulgaria; d.vezuv@abv.bg
2 Department of Applied Mathematics and Statistics, Faculty of Natural Sciences and Education, University of Ruse, 8 Studentska Str., 7004 Ruse, Bulgaria
3 Department of Information Modeling, Institute of Mathematics and Informatics, Bulgarian Academy of Sciences, 8 Acad. Georgi Bonchev Str., 1113 Sofia, Bulgaria
4 Department of Heat, Hydraulics and Environmental Engineering, Agrarian and Industrial Faculty, University of Ruse, 8 Studentska Str., 7004 Ruse, Bulgaria; nikolaev@uni-ruse.bg
* Correspondence: sapundzhi@swu.bg (F.S.); sggeorgiev@uni-ruse.bg or sggeorgiev@math.bas.bg (S.G.)
† Presented at the 6th International Conference on Communications, Information, Electronic and Energy Systems, Ruse, Bulgaria, 26–28 November 2025.

Abstract

The purpose of this paper is to examine the application and development of CAD/CAM technologies in the modern metal cutting industry, with a focus on their role in increasing production accuracy, efficiency, and sustainability. The study presents an industrial case of laser cutting of AISI 304 stainless-steel sheets, in which two approaches are compared under identical material and technological parameters: conventional manual nesting and automatic nesting based on algorithms implemented in a CAD/CAM environment. The methodology evaluates both layouts using clear technical and economic indicators, including number of parts per sheet, material utilization, cutting time, weight of scrap, and cost per sheet. For the analyzed batch, automatic nesting increases the number of parts per sheet from 44 to 76 ($\approx$73%), reduces the unused sheet area from 61% to 39%, and shortens the cutting time from 12 to 9 min ($\approx$25%), which leads to a reduction in material waste by about 36% and cost savings of approximately 314 EUR per sheet. As a result, the process becomes more efficient and reliable, supporting sustainable and digital manufacturing goals. The findings confirm the importance of algorithmic optimization in CAD/CAM systems for enhancing industrial competitiveness, enabling effective resource management, and facilitating the transition towards Industry 5.0.

Keywords: CAD/CAM; CNC; laser cutting; automatic nesting; process optimization; material efficiency; sustainable manufacturing

1. Introduction

Computer-aided design (CAD) and computer-aided manufacturing (CAM) are among the key technologies in the development of the modern metalworking industry. For the first time, CAD/CAM systems were used in the 1960s in the development and production of aircraft wings using the computing power of the IBM 360/44 [1]. Since then, they have evolved from specialized computing systems to widely applicable digital tools for industrial design and manufacturing.

Nowadays, CAD systems are used to create two-dimensional and three-dimensional digital models, various simulations and analyses of engineering problems. They reduce design time and errors, providing reliable documentation that supports the product life cycle [2]. CAM systems convert these models into control instructions for computer numerical control (CNC) machines, lathes, mills and lasers. Through them, the production process is accelerated, a higher accuracy is achieved and the consumption of materials is reduced [3].

Industry 4.0 revolution combines CAD/CAM systems with digital systems, such as IoT (Internet of Things), cyber-physical systems (CPS), and manufacturing execution systems (MES), ensuring seamless connections between design, planning, and production [4].

Simulations, optimizations, and predictive maintenance in real time are made possible by virtual models of various machines and processes [5]. According to a systematic review by da Silva et al. (2025), the application of these innovations in metalworking leads to significant increases in process efficiency and reliability [6]. In recent years, artificial intelligence (AI) and machine learning have also been applied to CAD/CAM. Using HyperGraph convolutional neural networks (HGCNN), hybrid manufacturing allows for the automation of manufacturing processes by classifying manufacturing characteristics with an accuracy of over 97% [7]. In a CNC environment, machine learning algorithms predict machining times more accurately than small CAM methods [8]. A key CAD/CAM development trend is hybrid manufacturing, a method of combining 3D printing and subsequent machining, which offers a variety of complex shapes and customized products [9]. In addition to automatic unwrapping and path optimization, CAM strategies for laser, plasma, and waterjet cutting can reduce waste and energy consumption [10].

The development of cloud-based CAD/CAM solutions and their integration with Product Lifecycle Management systems facilitate collaboration in global production chains [11], which is important for the metal-cutting industry, which is highly dependent on international cooperation and quick adaptation to market changes. The implementation of CAD/CAM faces challenges such as high investment costs, cybersecurity, personnel qualifications, and others [12]. The Industry 5.0 concept emphasizes sustainable and human-centered production, where machines and artificial intelligence support, not replace, human creativity [13].

The aim of this study is to analyze the application and development of CAD/CAM technologies in the modern metalworking industry, and to evaluate the impact of automatic nesting algorithms on production efficiency, material utilization, and economic performance.

2. Technologies

CNC (Computer Numerical Control)—a technology where production machines are controlled by computer-generated instructions instead of manual control. It combines programming software with traditional machines such as laser systems, mills, lathes and routers. The main advantages of CNC machines are high accuracy, speed and the ability to mass produce identical parts without deviations. In the metalworking industry, CNC allows the production of complex geometric shapes that would be difficult to achieve with manual methods.

Laser cutting—it is a CNC technology used for processing metals and non-metallic materials. Laser cutting as a process is based on focusing a high-energy laser beam on the surface of the material, which leads to heating, melting and vaporization of the area along the beam trajectory. Depending on the type and thickness of the material, different gases are used to support the process—nitrogen (N_2), oxygen (O_2) or compressed air. The gas accelerates the cutting, cleans the channel and reduces the thermal impact on the area around the cut. The design of the laser head consists of mirrors, lenses, a cooling system and a nozzle that directs the laser beam and the gas jet to the material. The laser head

https://doi.org/10.3390/engproc2026122022

moves at a minimum distance above the surface of the material, without physical contact, to avoid damage and ensure uniformity of the cut.

Nesting is a tool of the CAM systems that is characterized by the automatic or manual arrangement of details on a sheet of raw material in order to minimize waste, reduce preparation time and optimize the movement of the laser head. Nowadays, CAM systems are often based on heuristic and genetic algorithms that iteratively look for the best material placement while minimizing tool movement and thermal distortion.

TRUMPF TruLaser 2030 [14] was used in this study, which is capable of cutting and drilling metal, plastic, paper, and stone. The machine can process thin and thick materials as well as complex geometries, fine surface finishing, and high-speed industrial manufacturing tasks.

3. Results and Discussion

The present study aims to evaluate the impact of automatic nesting in CAD/CAM systems on the production efficiency of laser cutting of stainless steel. The simulations were performed using AutoCAD 2025 (https://www.autodesk.com/, accessed on 14 November 2025), applying identical cutting parameters and material properties to ensure consistent evaluation of both manual and automated cutting approaches.

The analysis was performed by simulating real production scenarios involving manual and automatic placement of parts on a sheet of raw material, then comparing the quantitative indicators: number of parts, cutting time, material utilization and economic effect.

For the purposes of the analysis, standard AISI 304 (Austenitic Chromium-Nickel Stainless Steel, EN 1.4301) stainless steel sheets with dimensions of 1000 × 2000 × 10 mm and a density of 7.9 g/cm^3 were used [15].

The calculated mass of one sheet is:

$$V = 1000 \times 2000 \times 10\ \text{mm} = 20000000\ \text{mm}^3 = 20000\ \text{cm}^3; \quad (1)$$

$$m = 20000\ \text{cm}^3 \times 7.9\frac{\text{g}}{\text{cm}^3} = 158000\ \text{g} = 158\ \text{kg}. \quad (2)$$

The price of the raw material is determined based on public databases and market indices, MEPS International (2025) [16] and MetalMiner Index (2025) [17] report an average price for AISI 304 10 mm sheet between 8.5 and 9.5 EUR/kg [1,2]. Thyssenkrupp Materials Trading GmbH and Tata Steel Europe (catalog 2024) indicate prices between 1350 and 1500 EUR/tonne at wholesale [18,19].

The presented price calculations are based on a real European market assessment for the first quarter of 2025.

In order to evaluate the effectiveness of CAD/CAM algorithms in optimizing production processes, a comparison between manual and automatic Nesting in laser cutting of sheet metal has been performed. It is a process of arranging parts on a raw sheet in order to minimize waste and maximize the use of available space.

In the manual method, the operator determines the position of each part, striving to maintain minimum technological distances, while in automatic Nesting, built-in optimization algorithms are used that calculate the most appropriate placement based on geometric characteristics and machine constraints [20]. This comparison aims to quantitatively show the differences in material usage, processing time and number of parts produced, as well as to assess the potential economic and environmental advantages of automated CAD/CAM solutions.

The results of the comparative analysis between the two methods are summarized in Table 1 and Figure 1, where the main technological indicators are presented: number of

https://doi.org/10.3390/engproc2026122022

parts placed on a sheet, cutting time, percentage of unused space and amount of waste material. As can be seen from the data, automatic Nesting achieves significantly better results in all considered parameters.

Table 1. Comparison between manual and automatic nesting.

Parameter	Manual Nesting	Automatic Nesting	Improvement
Number of placed parts	44	76	+72.7%
Cutting time (min)	12	9	−25%
Unused sheet area (%)	61	39	−22%
Material waste (kg/sheet)	96.4	61.6	−36%

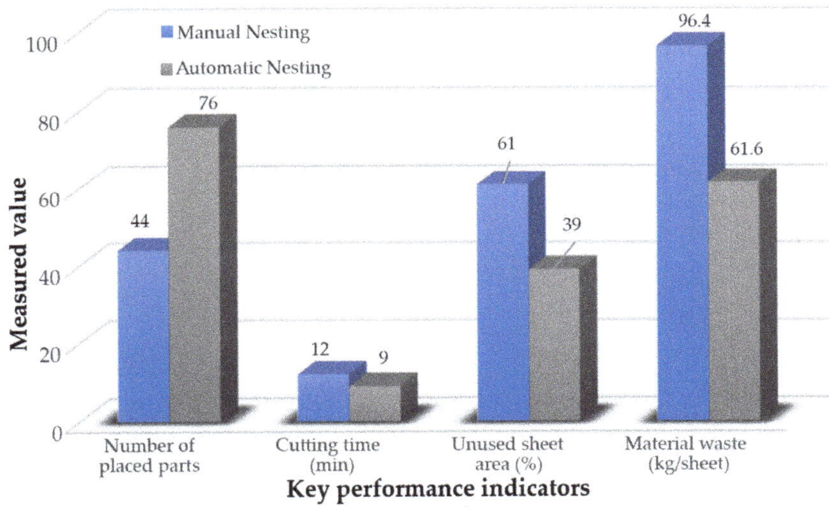

Figure 1. Comparison of key performance indicators between manual and automatic nesting.

The analysis of the results in Table 1 shows the advantage of automated nesting. Over 70% more parts were produced and 36% less waste was generated as a result of CAM algorithms optimizing production processes. Generally, cutting time reductions of up to 25% lead to both machine time savings and a reduction in energy consumption, which directly influences production costs and the environmental footprint.

In order to quantify the economic benefits of deployment optimization, a comparative cost analysis was performed between manual and automatic deployment methods. The evaluation includes the cost of lost material, energy consumption and process efficiency. In all calculations, a stainless-steel price of €9/kg is assumed, which corresponds to the current market value of AISI 304 sheets in Europe [16,17] shown above.

A comparison of the economic advantages of automatic placement versus manual placement is presented in Table 2. As can be seen, waste is reduced by 34.8 kg per sheet, resulting in an average savings of approximately €314 per sheet processed. By using an automatic method, sheet utilization rates are 61% compared to 39% using the manual method due to a better distribution of parts and minimal residual areas [14]. Due to the material savings, the reduction in cutting time by about 3 min per sheet and the reduction in energy consumption by approximately 0.7 kWh per sheet, additional savings were realized in production costs. The combined effect of these factors leads to higher operational efficiency, reduced resource use and increased sustainability of the production process.

https://doi.org/10.3390/engproc2026122022

Table 2. Financial impact of automatic nesting.

Parameter	Manual Nesting	Automatic Nesting	Saving
Material waste per sheet	96.4	61.6	−34.8 kg
Waste cost (9 EUR/kg)	868 EUR	554 EUR	314 EUR saved per sheet
Material utilization	39%	61%	+22 efficiency
Cutting time	12 min	9 min	−3 min
Energy consumption	5 kWh	4.3 kWh	−0.7 kWh
Energy cost saving (0.2 EUR/kWh)	1 EUR	0.86 EUR	0.14 EUR saved per sheet

To provide a more comprehensive assessment of the economic efficiency of automatic nesting, calculations of the expected outcomes for various production scales were performed. The estimates are based on the observed average material saving of 34.8 kg per sheet and the average market price of stainless steel of 9 EUR/kg [16,21]. This corresponds to an approximate cost reduction of 314 EUR per processed sheet. To analyze the impact on total production costs, a production range of 50 to 500 sheets per month was considered, encompassing the typical manufacturing capacities of small-, medium-, and large-sized enterprises in the metal cutting industry. The obtained values are summarized in Table 3, which illustrates the relationship between the number of processed sheets, the amount of material saved, and the corresponding financial savings.

Table 3. Monthly savings on various production.

No	Processed Sheet Per Month	Saved Material (kg)	Financial Saving (EUR)
1	50	1740	15,700
2	100	3480	31,400
3	150	5220	47,100
4	200	6960	62,800
5	250	8700	78,500
6	300	10,440	94,200
7	350	12,180	109,900
8	400	13,920	125,600
9	450	15,660	141,300
10	500	17,400	157,000

The calculations in the table are based on an average material saving of 34.8 kg per sheet and a unit price of stainless steel of 9 EUR/kg according to AISI 304 [22–24].

It should be emphasized that the economic estimates in Table 3 are obtained by linearly scaling the savings per sheet with the number of processed sheets. This simplified model does not account for production variability, machine downtime, setup changes, or additional costs related to software implementation and process integration. Therefore, the calculated values should be interpreted as indicative potential savings under stable operating conditions rather than precise forecasts. Developing a more detailed economic model that incorporates stochastic demand, maintenance schedules and integration costs is a relevant direction for future work.

Figures 2 and 3 illustrate, respectively, the manual and automatic nesting layouts for the same set of parts on an AISI 304 sheet under identical technological constraints. In the manual nesting case (Figure 2), the operator arranges the contours one by one, respecting minimum safety distances between parts (e.g., 14 mm) and from the sheet edge (10 mm).

https://doi.org/10.3390/engproc2026122022

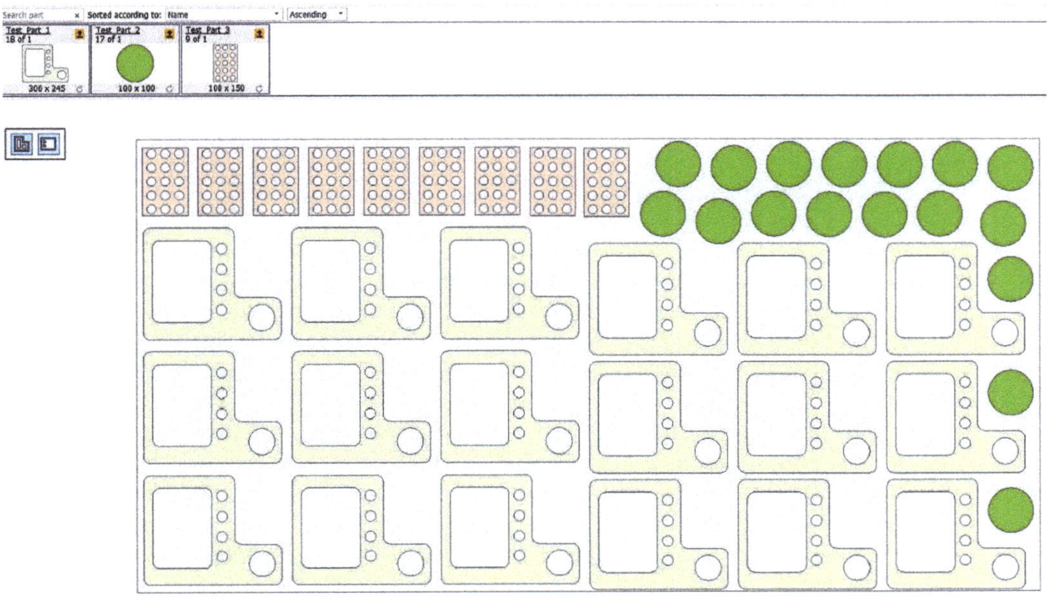

Figure 2. Manual nesting of parts on proprietary CAM (2025) software.

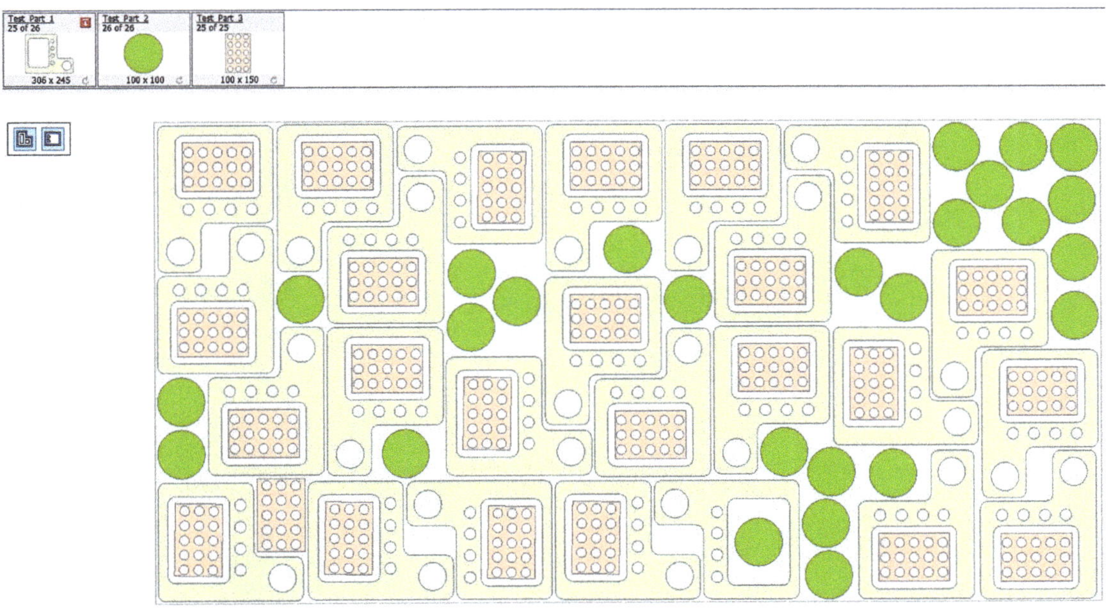

Figure 3. Automatic nesting of parts on proprietary CAM software.

Although this approach is acceptable for simple geometries or small production runs, it inevitably leads to larger "islands" of unused material and a less compact packing of the parts. In contrast, the automatic nesting shown in Figure 3 is generated by the CAD/CAM system using an internal optimization algorithm that explores many feasible placements and orientations. The resulting layout is visibly denser, with reduced gaps and improved contour adjacency, which directly contributes to the higher material utilization,

https://doi.org/10.3390/engproc2026122022

the increased number of parts per sheet, and the shorter cutting path reported in the quantitative section. Thus, Figures 2 and 3 provide a visual explanation of the numerical results: the algorithmic search performed by the nesting module systematically outperforms the operator's intuitive arrangement, especially as the geometry becomes more complex or the batch size grows.

After the nesting process is complete, the CAM software creates NC code (Numerical Control Code) instructions for the machine. The code contains information about start and end points, cutting speed, sequence of operations, and depth of cut.

Figure 4 presents a block diagram of the complete digital workflow, from CAD modelling to the generation of NC code for the CNC laser cutting machine. The process begins with importing the CAD geometry, where the system supports multiple neutral and native formats with extensions such as .dxf/dwg, step, ensuring compatibility with different design environments. The next step is the definition of the technological context: selection of the material (e.g., stainless steel 1.4301) and thickness (10 mm), which determines the appropriate cutting speed, laser power and assist gas parameters. The nesting stage follows, where either manual or automatic placement of the parts on the sheet is performed. Afterwards, the CAM environment generates the cutting technology—lead-ins, lead-outs, pierce points, micro-joints and contour sequence—taking into account collision avoidance and thermal distortion. In the final stages, optimization routines minimize the total cutting time by refining the toolpath order and feed rates, and the system exports the corresponding NC program together with an operator report. This diagram emphasizes that the nesting task is not an isolated operation but an integral part of a fully digital CAD/CAM–CNC chain, where decisions at each stage (material selection, nesting strategy, path optimization) cumulatively affect productivity, material efficiency and overall process sustainability.

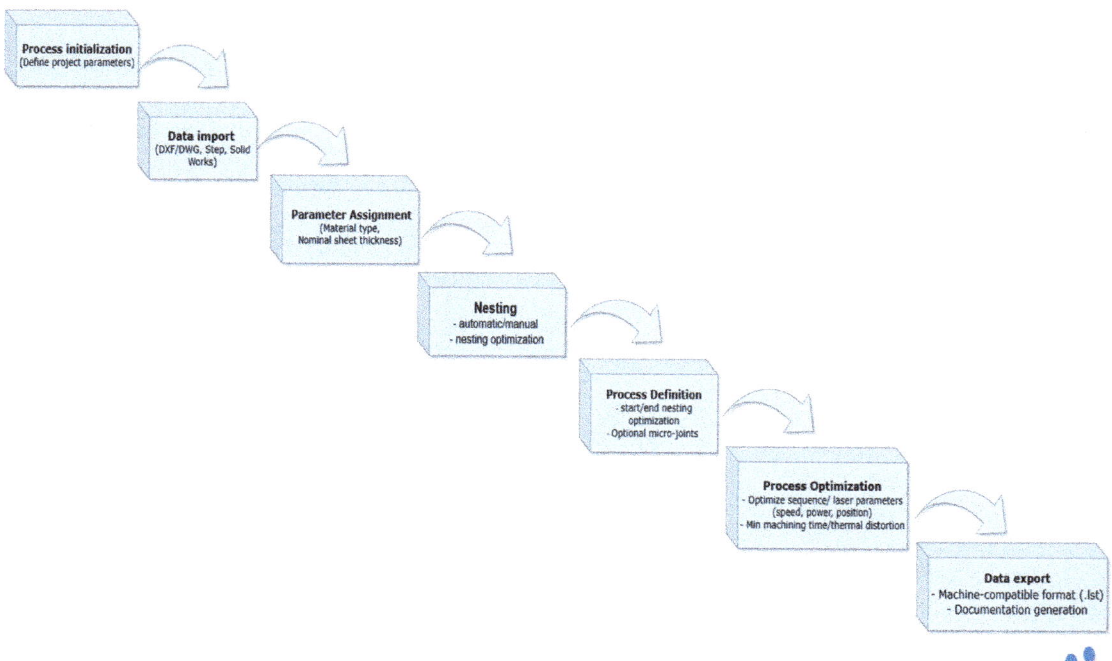

Figure 4. Automatic nesting of parts on proprietary CAM software.

https://doi.org/10.3390/engproc2026122022

To begin with, analysis shows that adopting automatic nesting not only reduces production costs, but also supports sustainable manufacturing practices by minimizing material waste and energy consumption.

A closer examination of the mechanisms behind the observed gains suggests that the benefits of automatic nesting arise not only from higher packing density but also from secondary effects in toolpath planning—namely reduced non-productive head travel, fewer long traverses across thermally affected zones, and a more consistent heat load that stabilizes cut quality. In practical terms, the simultaneous improvements reported in Table 1 (up to 36% less scrap, 25% shorter cutting time, and >22% higher material utilization) and Table 2 (≈314 EUR saved per sheet at 9 EUR/kg) indicate that automated placement interacts favorably with contour sequencing and micro-feature ordering, thereby compounding savings across material usage, cycle time, and rework risk. Industrially, these gains translate into higher throughput per shift and lower variability in yield—two levers that strengthen production scheduling and capacity planning for small-, medium-, and large-batch contexts alike.

At the same time, several boundary conditions temper generalization. The present evaluation is based on AISI 304 sheets of a single size and thickness (1000 × 2000 × 10 mm) and assumes unrestricted part orientation and uniform kerf/thermal behavior; in settings that require grain-direction or cosmetic constraints, common-line cutting policies, or strict part-to-edge offsets, the magnitude of improvement may differ. The economic advantage is also sensitive to input prices: using the study's mean saving of 34.8 kg per sheet, the plausible market range of 8.5–9.5 EUR/kg implies ≈€296–€331 saved per sheet, with energy savings remaining comparatively minor against material costs. Moreover, linear scaling to monthly totals (Table 3) may overstate benefits at very high volumes if remnant-library policies, batch-mix variability, setup interleaving, or downstream operations (deburring, micro-joint removal, inspection) become rate-limiting. Future replications should therefore include multi-objective nesting (material, path length, pierce county), explicit thermal/kerf constraints, and cross-material/thickness validation, ideally within a digital-twin loop to capture run-to-run variability and shop-floor scheduling effects.

To formalize the computational workflow, two algorithms were developed to process post-cutting data and quantify the economic benefits.

Algorithm 1 describes the analysis and interpretation of post-cutting data exported from the CAD/CAM system, while Algorithm 2 estimates economic impact based on material savings and market prices. These formulations make the data processing workflow clear and reproducible across different CAD/CAM environments.

Algorithm 2 estimates the respective economic impact. By taking the average material saving per sheet, the current stainless-steel market prices, and production volume, the algorithm is able to determine both the per sheet cost reduction and the total monthly savings.

The results shown in this study indicate that automatic nesting implemented in CAD/CAM systems results in improved laser cutting efficiency for stainless steel. Based on algorithm analysis, optimization through computational methods leads to a greater degree of material utilization, a shorter processing time, and a measurable economic effect. In addition to being a design tool, CAD/CAM technologies are also an essential element of smart and sustainable manufacturing.

https://doi.org/10.3390/engproc2026122022

Algorithm 1: ParseNestingData(filePath)

```
Input: Nesting data file exported from CAD/CAM system
Output: Summary metrics of nested parts
procedure ParseNestingData ()
schema ← extractAttributes("MM,AT" lines)
data ← extractRecords("DA," lines)
for each record in data do
if record is valid then
extract part parameters (id, posX, posY, sizeX, sizeY, angle, mirror)
add part to Parts
end if
end for
validate (Parts)
metrics ← {count(Parts), ∑(sizeX × sizeY), mean(angle), share(mirror)}
output metrics
end procedure
```

Algorithm 2: CalculateEconomicEffect(materialSaved_kg,price_EUR_per_kg, sheetsPerMonth)

```
Input: Average material saving per sheet, market price kg, number of processed sheets
Output:    Estimated cost reduction per sheet and total monthly savings
procedure CalculateEconomicEffect(materialSaved_kg, price_EUR_per_kg,
sheetsPerMonth)
    if materialSaved_kg > 0 and price_EUR_per_kg > 0 then
        costPerSheet ← materialSaved_kg x price_EUR_per_kg
        totalSaving ← costPerSheet x sheetsPerMonth
    else
        costPerSheet ← 0
        totalSaving ← 0
    end if
Output Material saved:, materialSaved_kg, kg
Output Cost per sheet:, costPerSheet, EUR
Output Monthly saving:, totalSaving, EUR
  end procedure
```

4. Conclusions

In summary, CAD/CAM systems have transformed from a design and manufacturing tool into a strategic factor for digital transformation, innovation, and competitiveness in the metalworking industry. Their integration with artificial intelligence, digital twins, cloud platforms, and hybrid manufacturing technologies opens up new opportunities for increasing efficiency, quality, and sustainability.

The scientific novelty of this work lies in the systematic integration of geometric, technological, and economic criteria into a unified framework for evaluating nesting strategies in an actual industrial environment. Unlike purely theoretical or software-oriented studies, the proposed approach quantifies the impact of automatic nesting in a CAD/CAM system through directly measurable indicators—number of parts per sheet, utilization coefficient, cutting time, scrap mass, and cost per sheet—under strictly identical production conditions. This enables an objective assessment of algorithmic nesting performance and provides reproducible evidence of its contribution to sustainable manufacturing, thereby offering a practical methodological template that can be transferred to other materials, cutting technologies, and Industry 5.0-oriented production systems.

The conducted analysis demonstrates that the integration of CAD/CAM systems with automatic nesting algorithms significantly enhances both the technological and economic performance

https://doi.org/10.3390/engproc2026122022

indicators of metalworking production. Automatic nesting provides measurable improvements across all key performance metrics—reducing material waste by up to 36%, decreasing cutting time by 25%, and improving material utilization by more than 22%. The resulting cost savings reach approximately 314 EUR per sheet, increasing linearly with production volume, thereby confirming the strong economic potential of this approach.

Furthermore, the reduction in energy consumption and waste generation supports the broader objectives of sustainable and resource-efficient manufacturing. These findings are consistent with current research emphasizing the importance of algorithmic optimization, digital integration, and AI-based process control in achieving the next generation of intelligent manufacturing systems.

Future research should focus on the integration of machine learning algorithms and digital twin technologies within CAD/CAM environments to enable real-time process monitoring, predictive maintenance, and autonomous optimization in metalworking applications.

Author Contributions: Conceptualization, F.S., S.G. and I.N.; methodology, S.G. and I.N.; software, D.V., S.G. and I.N.; validation, F.S., D.V. and S.G.; formal analysis, F.S., D.V. and I.N.; investigation, F.S., D.V. and S.G.; writing—original draft preparation, F.S., D.V. and S.G.; writing—review and editing, F.S. All authors have read and agreed to the published version of the manuscript.

Funding: This study was financed by the European Union—NextGenerationEU, through the National Recovery and Resilience Plan of the Republic of Bulgaria, project No. BG-RRP-2.013-0001.

Institutional Review Board Statement: Not applicable.

Informed Consent Statement: Not applicable.

Data Availability Statement: The raw data supporting the conclusions of this article will be made available by the authors on request.

Conflicts of Interest: The authors declare no conflicts of interest. The funders had no role in the design of the study; in the collection, analyses, or interpretation of data; in the writing of the manuscript; or in the decision to publish the results.

References

1. Groover, M.P. *Automation, Production Systems, and Computer-Integrated Manufacturing*, 5th ed.; Pearson Education: Upper Saddle River, NJ, USA, 2020.
2. Kyratsis, P.; Kakoulis, K.; Markopoulos, A.P. Advances in CAD/CAM/CAE Technologies. *Machines* **2020**, *8*, 13. [CrossRef]
3. Kalpakjian, S.; Schmid, S.R. *Manufacturing Engineering and Technology*, 8th ed.; Pearson Education: Boston, MA, USA, 2023.
4. Lasi, H.; Fettke, P.; Kemper, H.-G.; Feld, T.; Hoffmann, M. Industry 4.0. *Bus. Inf. Syst. Eng.* **2014**, *6*, 239–242. [CrossRef]
5. Tao, F.; Qi, Q.; Wang, L.; Nee, A.Y.C. Digital Twins and Cyber–Physical Systems toward Smart Manufacturing and Industry 4.0: Correlation and Comparison. *Engineering* **2019**, *5*, 653–661. [CrossRef]
6. Simonič, M.; Palčič, I.; Klančnik, S. Advancing Intelligent Toolpath Generation: A Systematic Review of CAD–CAM Integration in Industry 4.0 and 5.0. *Stroj. Vestn.-J. Mech. Eng.* **2025**, *71*, 328–336. [CrossRef]
7. Wang, P.; Yang, W.; You, Y. A hybrid learning framework for manufacturing feature recognition using graph neural networks. *J. Manuf. Process.* **2023**, *85*, 387–404. [CrossRef]
8. Saric, T.; Simunovic, G.; Simunovic, K.; Svalina, I. Estimation of machining time for CNC manufacturing using neural computing. *Int. J. Simul. Model.* **2016**, *15*, 663–675. [CrossRef]
9. Sebbe, N.; Fernandes, F.; Sousa, V.; Silva, F. Hybrid manufacturing processes used in the production of complex parts: A comprehensive review. *Metals* **2022**, *12*, 1874. [CrossRef]
10. Mendonça, S.; Damásio, B.; Charlita de Freitas, L.; Oliveira, L.; Cichy, M.; Nicita, A. The Rise of 5G Technologies and Systems: A Quantitative Analysis of Knowledge Production. *Telecommun. Policy* **2022**, *46*, 102327. [CrossRef]
11. Gharibvand, V.; Kolamroudi, M.; Zeeshan, Q.; Çınar, Z.; Sahmani, S.; Asmael, M.; Safaei, B. Cloud based manufacturing: A review of recent developments in architectures, technologies, infrastructures, platforms and associated challenges. *Int. J. Adv. Manuf. Technol.* **2024**, *131*, 93–123. [CrossRef]
12. Mullet, V.; Sondi, P.; Ramat, E. A review of cybersecurity guidelines for manufacturing factories in industry 4.0. *IEEE* **2021**, *9*, 23235–23263. [CrossRef]
13. Muhenga, R.; Sapundzhi, F.; Popstoilov, M.; Georgiev, S.; Todorov, V. Comprehensive Analysis of Cryptographic Algorithms: Implementation and Security Insights. *Eng. Proc.* **2025**, *104*, 43. [CrossRef]

 https://doi.org/10.3390/engproc2026122022

14. Martini, B.; Bellisario, D.; Coletti, P. Human-Centered and Sustainable Artificial Intelligence in Industry 5.0: Challenges and Perspectives. *Sustainability* **2024**, *16*, 5448. [CrossRef]
15. AISI 304 Stainless Steel Properties: Tensile Yield Strength & Hardness. Available online: https://www.theworldmaterial.com/type-304-grade-stainless-steel/ (accessed on 12 September 2025).
16. Triumpf. Available online: https://midatlanticmachinery.com/ (accessed on 29 September 2025).
17. MEPS International. *European Stainless Steel Prices—Austenitic 304 Sheet (Q1 2025)*; MEPS International Ltd.: Sheffield, UK, 2025.
18. MetalMiner Index. *Stainless Steel Price Forecast, February 2025*; MetalMiner: Chicago, IL, USA, 2025.
19. Thyssenkrupp Materials Trading GmbH. *Product Catalogue 2024—Stainless Steel Flat Products*; Thyssenkrupp Materials Trading GmbH: Düsseldorf, Germany, 2024.
20. Tata Steel Europe. *Product Data Sheet—AISI 304 Stainless Steel*; Tata Steel Europe: London, UK, 2024.
21. Sofias, K.; Kanetaki, Z.; Stergiou, C.; Kantaros, A.; Jacques, S.; Ganetsos, T. Implementing CAD API Automated Processes in Engineering Design: A Case Study Approach. *Appl. Sci.* **2025**, *15*, 7692. [CrossRef]
22. Sapundzhi, F.; Danev, K.; Ivanova, A.; Popstoilov, M.; Georgiev, S. A Performance Comparison of Shortest Path Algorithms in Directed Graphs. *Eng. Proc.* **2025**, *100*, 31. [CrossRef]
23. Lazarova, M.; Sapundzhi, F. Stochastic Modeling with Applications in Supply Chain Management and ICT Systems. *Computation* **2023**, *11*, 21. [CrossRef]
24. Sapundzhi, F.; Dimitrova, V.; Lazarova, M.; Georgiev, S.; Todorov, M.; Todorov, V. A Cloud-Based Approach to Modeling ERP Information Flows Using a Bivariate Pólya–Aeppli Process. *Mathematics* **2025**, *13*, 1699. [CrossRef]

https://doi.org/10.3390/engproc2026122022

engineering proceedings

MDPI

Proceeding Paper

Fast Loss Estimation Framework for Current-Source Microinverters Using Hybrid Simulation Models †

Angel Marinov * and Kaloyan Solenkov

Department of Electronics and Microelectronics, Technical University of Varna, 9010 Varna, Bulgaria
* Correspondence: a.marinov@tu-varna.bg

† Presented at the 6th International Conference on Communications, Information, Electronic and Energy Systems, 26–28 November 2025, Ruse, Bulgaria.

Abstract

A fast modelling framework is presented for loss estimation in current-source microinverters. The power stage is modelled with ideal switches and simplified magnetics to keep simulations lightweight, while dedicated estimators reconstruct core, conduction, and switching losses from simulated waveforms using Steinmetz-based and analytical models. The method is demonstrated on an interleaved active-clamp flyback with H-bridge unfolder but remains topology-agnostic and applicable to other current source (CS) DC/DC variants. Control includes maximum power point tracking (MPPT) with voltage-reference tracking, a PID loop, simplified grid synchronization, and peak-current regulation. Dynamic tests under irradiance and grid-voltage variations confirm stable operation and correct MPPT behaviour. A steady-state loss breakdown at 0.75 p.u. irradiance predicts ~97% overall efficiency, consistent with reported microinverter performance. The framework enables rapid design exploration and efficiency prediction without full device-level modelling, balancing accuracy and computational speed.

Keywords: microinverter; current-source converter; MPPT; loss modelling; interleaved flyback; PLECS simulation

1. Introduction

The global transition from fossil-fuel-dominated systems to low-carbon energy infrastructures has become a central priority for governments, industry, and research institutions. Fossil fuels remain subject to volatile international prices and supply constraints, creating systemic vulnerabilities that ripple through economies and societies. At the same time, their combustion remains the dominant source of anthropogenic greenhouse gas emissions, directly contributing to global warming. Renewable energy sources therefore play a dual role: they enable decarbonization while simultaneously increasing energy security by diversifying supply and reducing import dependence [1]. Policy instruments in many regions, ranging from the European Union's Green Deal to national renewable portfolio standards, reflect the strategic recognition that widespread renewable integration is a prerequisite for both climate stability and energy independence.

Among renewable generation options, photovoltaic (PV) energy stands out for its rapid cost reductions, scalability, and versatility. According to the International Energy Agency, PV is now the least-cost source of new electricity capacity in much of the world [2]. Its inherent modularity enables installations ranging from utility-scale power plants down to individual rooftop systems, with minimal site constraints and relatively short installation times. Unlike wind or hydro, PV can be integrated close to consumption points, reducing the need for extensive transmission and enabling significant contributions to decentralized and resilient energy architectures. As a result, PV accounts for the majority of new renewable installations globally, and projections consistently place it as a cornerstone of the 2050 carbon-neutral energy system [3].

At the interface between PV modules and the grid, the choice of power electronic architecture is decisive for system efficiency, cost, and reliability. Microinverters—where each module is paired with a dedicated DC-AC stage—have gained attention due to their ability to perform maximum power point tracking (MPPT) at the module level, improving yield under partial shading or mismatch [4]. Microinverters also enhance system modularity: arrays can be scaled panel by panel, installation is simplified for residential users, and fault isolation is straightforward. Nevertheless, drawbacks remain: the distributed nature of electronics increases cost per watt and complicates thermal management, while long-term reliability under harsh outdoor conditions remains a concern [5]. Despite these limitations, microinverters are widely regarded as enabling technology for expanding PV penetration in diverse environments where centralized inverters are less practical.

Within the broad class of microinverter architectures, current-source (CS) microinverters represent a distinct approach. Unlike traditional voltage-source designs, CS microinverters enforce a continuous input current from the PV panel and directly inject a shaped current into the grid [6]. Advantages include reduced requirement for bulky electrolytic capacitors, inherent short-circuit protection, and in some cases simpler modulation strategies. However, disadvantages include higher current ripple reflected into the PV source, more stringent design requirements for magnetics, and sensitivity to switching stress at high frequencies [7]. Several topologies have been proposed to implement CS inverters, including the interleaved flyback, push-pull, two-transistor forward, and resonant derivatives. Among these, the interleaved active-clamp flyback has emerged as particularly promising: interleaving reduces ripple and distributes current stress, while the active clamp both limits device overvoltage and recycles leakage energy [8,9]. This combination provides a favourable trade-off between efficiency, cost, and simplicity at the power levels relevant for module-integrated inverters.

Given the diversity of potential topologies and operating conditions, modelling and computer-aided analysis play a critical role in design optimization. High-fidelity, device-level simulations can capture switching dynamics in detail but are computationally expensive, making them unsuitable for large sweeps across PV IV curves or parametric studies under different grid voltages and frequencies [10]. A complementary approach is to employ idealized circuit models—ideal switches and averaged magnetics—to accelerate simulations, and to complement them with loss-estimation scripts that reconstruct semiconductor and core losses from measured waveforms. Such a hybrid approach allows rapid yet reasonably accurate estimation of efficiency and thermal stress, enabling both comparative topology evaluation and parametric optimization [11].

Considering these needs, this paper develops a model for fast estimation of semiconductor and magnetic losses across PV operating points and grid conditions, enabling rapid design iteration without full device-level simulation. The remainder of the paper is structured as follows. Section 2 outlines the proposed modelling framework for current-source microinverters, with emphasis on the interleaved active-clamp flyback. The section also details the custom loss-calculation blocks (core, main switch, and output diode) and the associated power-averaging methods. Section 3 verifies the approach on representative operating points, reporting efficiency curves and loss breakdowns. Section 4 concludes with key findings, limitations, and directions for future work.

https://doi.org/10.3390/engproc2026122023

2. Materials and Methods

2.1. Modelling Approach

2.1.1. Modelling Goals

The primary objective of the proposed model is to provide a framework for fast and accurate estimation of power losses in current-source microinverters under diverse operating conditions. Rather than reproducing all semiconductor switching transients explicitly, the circuit is represented with ideal switches and simplified magnetics, while auxiliary loss-estimation blocks reconstruct conduction, switching, and core losses from waveforms. This reduces simulation time by an order of magnitude compared with full device-level models, while maintaining sufficient precision for efficiency evaluation and comparative design studies. The framework allows systematic sweeps of PV operating points, as well as grid parameters, yielding loss and efficiency maps that guide design optimization. This approach is particularly relevant given the continued decline in PV module prices, which shifts attention to the efficiency and reliability of power electronics and their control, making accurate yet computationally efficient modelling increasingly valuable for design.

A block diagram of the proposed model is presented in Figure 1. The system consists of four main functional blocks, the PV source, a current-source (CS) DC/DC stage, a DC/AC unfolder, and the output filter connected to the grid, all coordinated by control blocks. The CS DC/DC stage is implemented here as an interleaved active-clamp flyback, which offers favourable performance in terms of ripple reduction and energy recovery. However, the framework is not limited to this topology: with minor adjustments, other current-source converters such as active-clamp forward, two-transistor flyback, or push–pull variants can be represented within the same structure. The unfolder stage, responsible for transferring energy from the intermediate DC node to the grid, is modelled as an H-bridge in this work for simplicity and generality. Nonetheless, alternative inverter topologies (e.g., half-bridge or multilevel structures) can be incorporated with minimal changes, since their function in the model is limited to shaping the injected current. This modularity highlights the general applicability of the proposed modelling framework across a broad range of current-source microinverter architectures.

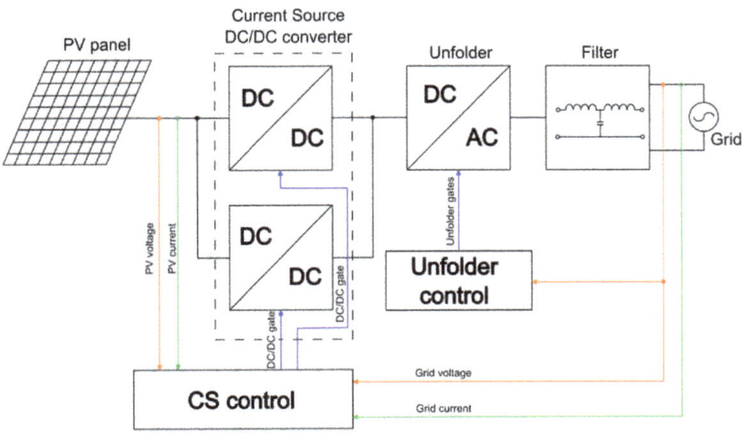

Figure 1. Block diagram of the presented model.

2.1.2. Converter Modelling

As described in the previous Section 2.1.1 the power stage can be divided into three main blocks, the modelling of which can be presented as:

https://doi.org/10.3390/engproc2026122023

PV source.

The PV model is implemented as a three-dimensional lookup table (LUT) $I_{pv}(V_{pv}, G, T)$ with linear interpolation. The table returns the module current for a given terminal voltage V_{pv}, irradiance G (normalized 0–1), and cell temperature T. The output current drives a controlled current source connected to the CS DC/DC input, so the PV behaves with realistic I–V characteristics while remaining numerically light. The LUT is built automatically from manufacturer datasheets: raw points are extracted using the automated procedure, then fitted into a consistent I–V surface using the optimization routine of [12]. This workflow enables rapid loading and testing of different modules without re-parameterizing the circuit model. To ensure robustness in sweeps, the LUT is clamped to the physical regions $0 \leq V_{pv} \leq V_{OC}(G, T)$ and $0 \leq I_{PV} \leq I_{SC}(G, T)$.

Current-source DC/DC stage.

The current-source converter is implemented as an interleaved flyback, with one phase shown in Figure 2. The essential model components are highlighted in black: input capacitor C_{in}, main switch S_1, transformer T, secondary diode D, and output capacitor C_{out}. For simplicity, the active clamp network—comprising clamp switch S_2 and capacitor C_{clamp} shown in grey—is omitted from the functional model.

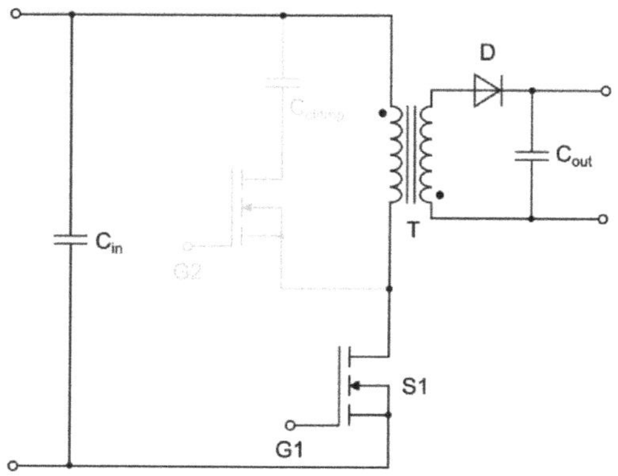

Figure 2. Simplified schematic of one phase of the interleaved flyback CS DC/DC stage.

This simplification significantly reduces numerical stiffness and improves simulation speed, since the commutation of the clamp branch introduces high-frequency resonant transitions and nonlinear switching dynamics. The absence of explicit clamp modelling, however, has two main implications:

- Switch-voltage stress: In the real circuit, the clamp capacitor limits the peak voltage on S_1 and recycles leakage energy. In the simplified model, this protective effect is not directly simulated. Instead, switch voltage is represented as an input parameter to the loss-estimation block, which uses datasheet values or designer-selected clamp voltages to compute switching energy.
- Resonant transitions: The active clamp also provides quasi-resonant transitions that can enable zero-voltage switching (ZVS) under certain operating conditions. Since this is not represented in the simplified plant, ZVS is introduced in the loss calculation stage by a flag variable controlling whether E_{on} is included or suppressed. This preserves the ability to evaluate the impact of ZVS on efficiency without adding resonant states to the main circuit.

By treating the clamp implicitly, the model balances speed and accuracy: waveforms of current and flux density remain representative of the real converter, while detailed clamp dynamics are abstracted into parameters for the loss models. This abstraction

 https://doi.org/10.3390/engproc2026122023

also maintains generality: with minimal adjustments the same framework can represent other CS DC/DC topologies such as active-clamp forward, two-transistor flyback, or push–pull converters.

Unfolder stage.

The grid unfolder is modelled as a full H-bridge, shown in Figure 3, which alternately connects the output of the CS DC/DC stage to the positive and negative half-cycles of the grid. In this configuration, the switches operate at the grid frequency only (50 Hz in this study), meaning that switching losses are negligible compared with conduction losses. Accordingly, only conduction losses are evaluated in the model, based on the RMS current through each device and its on-state resistance (or diode drop, depending on the device technology). The series filter $L_1 - L_2 - C$ ensures sinusoidal injection into the grid.

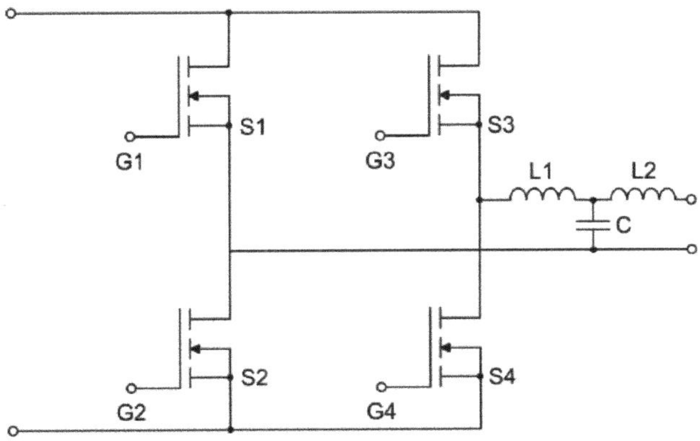

Figure 3. H-bridge unfolder stage used for grid connection.

Control Modelling.

The complete control scheme is shown in Figure 4. Maximum Power Point Tracking (MPPT) is implemented on the PV side. The MPPT block is based on a perturb-and-observe (P&O) algorithm with adaptive step size and protection features, as described in above. It estimates the optimum PV operating point and can output either a voltage reference, a current reference, or a power reference depending on the chosen control mode. In the configuration used here, the voltage reference is applied, which is compared to the measured PV terminal voltage to generate the error signal. This flexibility is valuable, as it allows the same MPPT implementation to be reused in different converter topologies and control architectures.

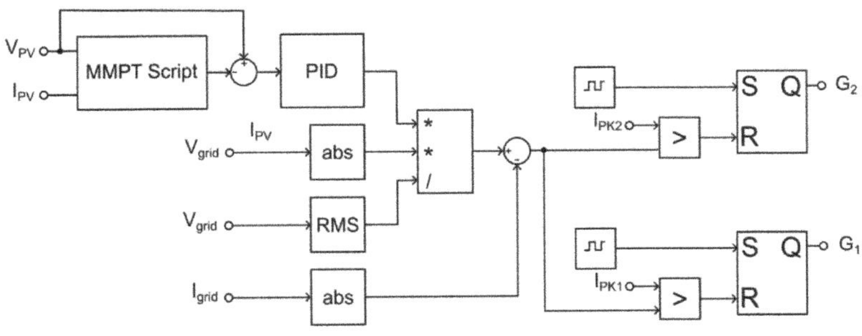

Figure 4. Control block diagram.

The error between the reference and measured PV voltage is processed by a PID regulator, which provides dynamic adjustment to drive the PV toward its maximum power

https://doi.org/10.3390/engproc2026122023

point under varying irradiance and temperature. The PID output represents the desired current injection into the grid.

Grid synchronization is handled by a simplified normalization method. Instead of employing a phase-locked loop (PLL), which would be necessary in practical systems subject to grid distortion or frequency drift, the control multiplies the regulator output by the absolute instantaneous grid voltage and divides by the RMS grid voltage. For an ideal sinusoidal grid, as assumed in this study, this guarantees a current reference that is correctly in phase and scaled to the grid voltage without introducing additional control states.

The resulting reference is then compared with the absolute instantaneous grid current. The error feeds into a peak current control loop, which operates at the switching frequency. In each cycle, the current is monitored and compared against the reference; once the threshold is reached, the comparator–RS latch combination terminates the gate pulse. This ensures that the converter injects current into the grid with controlled peak amplitude, maintaining sinusoidal shape while following the MPPT-derived reference.

This layered approach: (1) MPPT for PV optimization, (2) PID for voltage tracking, (3) simplified grid synchronization for phase alignment, and (4) peak current control for fast current regulation—provides both accuracy and computational simplicity. It reflects the goals of the overall model: to retain sufficient fidelity for loss and efficiency estimation while avoiding unnecessary complexity that would slow down large-scale parametric studies.

2.2. Data Extraction

To complement the ideal-switch and simplified magnetic models described in Section 2.1, a set of dedicated data-extraction blocks was developed to estimate the main loss components of the microinverter. These blocks operate in parallel with the simulation, processing measured waveforms such as device currents, voltages, gate signals, and magnetic flux density. The approach allows losses to be reconstructed without introducing parasitics or detailed switching dynamics into the main circuit, thus preserving the numerical efficiency of the model.

Four categories of losses are considered: magnetic core losses, main-switch semiconductor losses, secondary diode losses, and other resistive losses such as copper winding losses and conduction in the low-frequency unfolder switches. For the first three categories, custom C-script blocks implement cycle-synchronous or averaged calculations based on established loss models. The fourth category is estimated analytically using RMS currents and known resistances. Together, these calculations provide a complete breakdown of the losses in the converter and enable accurate estimation of overall efficiency.

2.2.1. Core Losses

Core losses are evaluated from the instantaneous flux density waveform $B(t)$ in the transformer. The waveform is obtained from the magnetizing current and geometry of the core, as described in Section 2. A dedicated block processes this signal to reconstruct the losses without adding parasitics into the main simulation.

The implementation is shown in Figure 5. The block receives the flux density waveform and, optionally, the gate signal of the main switch. Pre-processing extracts $\mathrm{d}B/\mathrm{d}t$, B_{min}, and B_{max}, which are used to determine waveform parameters such as the peak-to-peak excursion ΔB_{pp}, the peak flux B_{pk}, and the RMS flux B_{rms}. A windowing stage groups samples either over a fixed number of switching cycles or a predefined evaluation interval T_{eval}.

 https://doi.org/10.3390/engproc2026122023

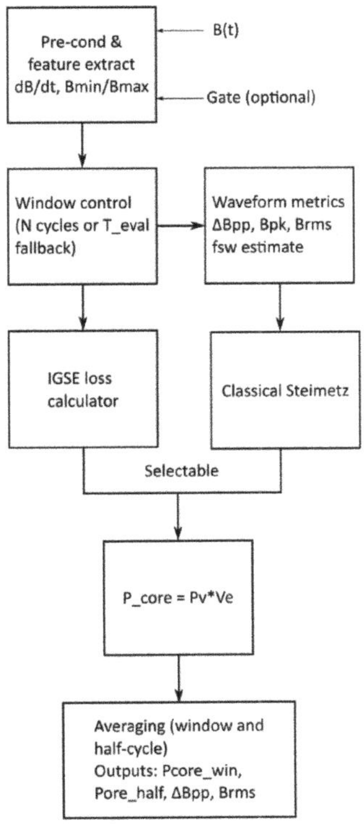

Figure 5. Core-loss estimator block diagram.

Two alternative loss models are available:

Improved Generalized Steinmetz Equation (iGSE).

For an arbitrary waveform segment with flux swing ΔB over a time interval Δt, the instantaneous power density is given by (1)

$$p(t) = k\left(\frac{\Delta B}{\Delta t}\right)^{\alpha}(\Delta B)^{\beta-\alpha}, \quad (1)$$

where k, α, and β are material-dependent coefficients. The window-averaged volumetric loss is then

$$P_v = \frac{1}{T_w}\int_0^{T_w} p(t)\,dt, \quad (2)$$

where T_w is the window length.

Classical Steinmetz Equation (CSE).

For sinusoidal approximation, the cycle-averaged loss density can be computed as

$$P_v = k_s f^{a_s} B_{\mathrm{pk}}^{b_s}, \quad (3)$$

where f is the switching frequency, B_{pk} the peak flux density, and k_s, a_s, b_s material coefficients.

The volumetric loss density is multiplied by the effective core volume V_e to obtain the total loss:

$$P_{\mathrm{core}} = P_v \cdot V_e. \quad (4)$$

https://doi.org/10.3390/engproc2026122023

Finally, the block performs averaging both over the selected window and over half a grid cycle, producing outputs: window-averaged core loss $P_{\text{core,win}}$, half-cycle average $P_{\text{core,half}}$, and diagnostics ΔB_{pp}, B_{rms}.

This method captures the combined effect of high-frequency switching and low-frequency modulation from the grid current. By keeping the clamp and other resonant elements out of the main circuit, the simulation remains computationally light while the loss block still accounts for the magnetic stress realistically.

2.2.2. Main-Switch Losses

The losses in the main MOSFET switches are divided into conduction losses and switching losses. Since the converter is modelled with ideal switches, these losses are not represented in the circuit waveforms and must be reconstructed by a dedicated estimator. The structure of the estimator is shown in Figure 6.

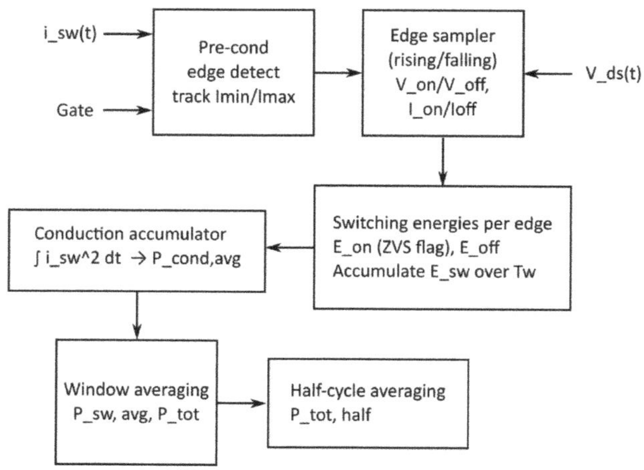

Figure 6. Main switch estimator block diagram.

The block receives the switch current waveform $i_{\text{sw}}(t)$, the gate signal, and optionally the drain–source voltage $v_{\text{ds}}(t)$. A pre-conditioning stage detects switching edges and tracks the minimum and maximum current within each conduction interval. At every turn-on and turn-off event, the current and voltage are sampled to form the basis for switching-loss estimation.

Conduction losses.

While the switch is on, conduction losses are determined by the RMS current and the effective on-state resistance $R_{\text{DS(on)}}$:

$$P_{\text{cond}} = \frac{1}{T_w} \int_0^{T_w} i_{\text{sw}}^2(t)\, dt \cdot R_{\text{DS(on)}} \tag{5}$$

where T_w is the evaluation window.

Switching losses.

At each transition, the energy is approximated as

$$E_{\text{on}} = \frac{1}{2} V_{\text{on}} I_{\text{on}} t_{\text{on}},\ E_{\text{off}} = \frac{1}{2} V_{\text{off}} I_{\text{off}} t_{\text{off}} \tag{6}$$

 https://doi.org/10.3390/engproc2026122023

where $I_{on/off}$ and $V_{on/off}$ are the sampled current and voltage at the instant of switching, and $t_{on/off}$ are effective switching times, set as tunable parameters. If the ZVS flag is active, E_{on} is forced to zero. The average switching power over a window is

$$P_{sw} = \frac{\sum(E_{on} + E_{off})}{T_w} \tag{7}$$

Total losses.

The total main switch loss is the sum of conduction and switching components:

$$P_{tot} = P_{cond} + P_{sw} \tag{8}$$

Finally, the block averages the results both over the switching window and over half a grid cycle, yielding $P_{tot,win}$ and $P_{tot,half}$.

This structure allows the inclusion of realistic switching losses and conduction behaviour while retaining the simplicity of an ideal-switch model. The explicit ZVS flag further enables parametric studies on soft-switching behaviour without introducing resonant dynamics into the main circuit.

2.2.3. Diode Losses

The output rectifier diode conducts whenever the transformer secondary voltage is positive and blocks otherwise. Since ideal devices are used in the circuit model, its losses are estimated in a separate calculation block based on the instantaneous diode current $i_d(t)$ and known device parameters.

Conduction losses.

For a Schottky diode or a fast-recovery diode, conduction losses are given by

$$P_{cond} = \frac{1}{T_w}\int_0^{T_w} (V_f\, i_d(t) + r_d\, i_d^2(t))\, dt \tag{9}$$

where V_f is the forward voltage drop and r_d is the differential resistance. For a SiC Schottky diode, r_d can be neglected and conduction losses are dominated by the constant voltage term.

Reverse-recovery losses.

If a conventional fast diode is modelled, reverse-recovery energy can be included as

$$E_{rr} = Q_{rr} \cdot V_R \tag{10}$$

with Q_{rr} the reverse-recovery charge and V_R the applied reverse voltage. The average contribution over a window is

$$P_{rr} = \frac{\sum E_{rr}}{T_w} \tag{11}$$

For SiC Schottky diodes, $Q_{rr} \approx 0$, and this component is omitted.

Total losses.

The total diode loss is then

$$P_D = P_{cond} + P_{rr}, \tag{12}$$

averaged over the evaluation window and further averaged over half a grid cycle for efficiency reporting.

2.2.4. Other Losses

Additional loss mechanisms are estimated analytically from RMS currents and known resistances. Copper losses in transformer windings are calculated as

https://doi.org/10.3390/engproc2026122023

$$P_{\text{cu}} = I_{\text{rms}}^2 \cdot R_{\text{w}}, \tag{13}$$

where I_{rms} is the winding current and R_{w} the DC resistance of the winding.

For the grid unfolder, the switches operate at line frequency, making switching losses negligible. Conduction losses are therefore evaluated as

$$P_{\text{cond,unf}} = I_{\text{rms}}^2 \cdot R_{\text{DS(on)}}. \tag{14}$$

These contributions are added to the semiconductor and core losses described above to obtain the overall loss balance of the converter.

3. Results

The complete model was implemented and tested in PLECS – V4.7.5, which provides both circuit-level simulation and script-based post-processing capabilities. Figure 7 presents the working block diagram of the system. The upper part of the schematic corresponds to the power stage: the PV source, two interleaved flyback phases, the DC/AC unfolder, and the grid filter. The lower part shows the control and data-extraction subsystems. The MPPT algorithm, implemented in C-script, provides the reference for the PID regulator, which in turn drives the peak-current controllers that generate gate signals for the flyback switches. Additional blocks calculate RMS and averaged grid variables, while dedicated C-script modules process transistor and magnetic probe signals to reconstruct conduction, switching, and core losses as described in Section 2.2.

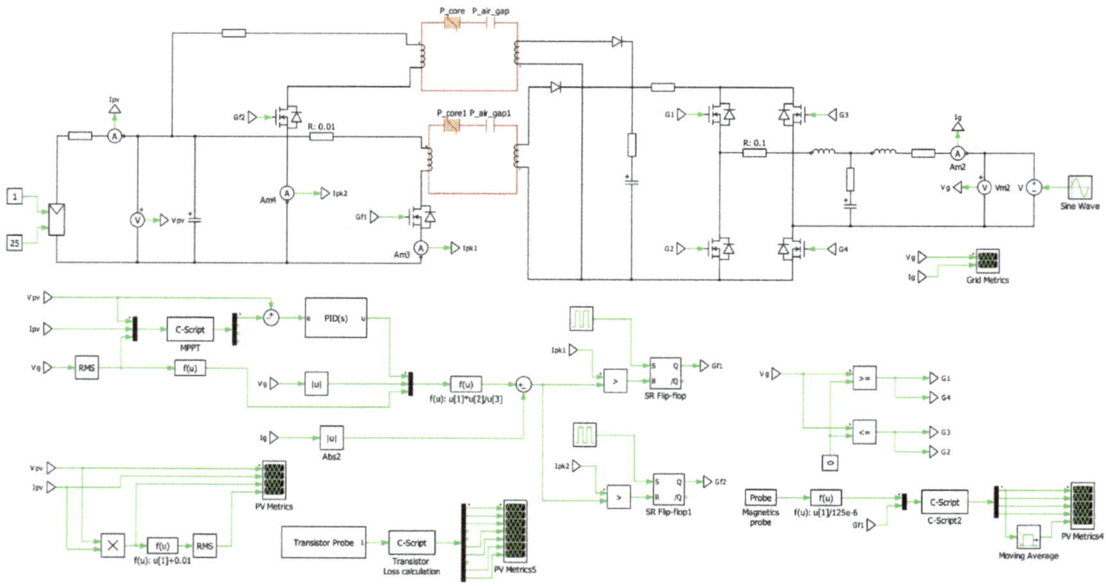

Figure 7. Simulation setup diagram.

This integrated implementation enables fast simulation with ideal switches while still capturing realistic efficiency by accounting for major loss mechanisms. In the following subsections, representative simulation results are presented to demonstrate the behaviour of the model under different operating conditions.

https://doi.org/10.3390/engproc2026122023

3.1. Simulation Setup

For verification, the proposed model was exercised with parameters corresponding to a representative PV microinverter stage. Table 1 summarizes the main component values and device characteristics used. The PV source was set to match a 250 W commercial module, while semiconductor and magnetic parameters were taken from datasheet values or estimated from the physical design.

Table 1. Verification setup parameters.

Component	Parameter/Value	Notes
PV module	P_{MPP} = 250 W;	Maximum power
	I_{MPP} = 6.58 A	Current at MPP
	V_{MPP} = 38 V	Voltage at MPP
Main Switch	$R_{DS(on)}$ = 16 mΩ	On-state resistance
	t_r = 15 ns, t_f = 5 ns	Rise/fall times
Unfolder switches	$R_{DS(on)}$ = 0.12 mΩ	Operate at grid frequency → conduction losses only
Transformer	Core, EFD39, N97 ferrite, g = 1 mm	6T primary/120T secondary
	R_{pri} = 20 mΩ	Primary DC resistance
	R_{sec} = 120 mΩ	Secondary DC resistance
Output diode	V_f = 0.55 V	Forward drop

3.2. Control and MPPT Operation

To confirm correct operation of the control system, two dynamic cases were simulated.

Irradiance variation.

Figure 8 shows the response of the model when solar irradiance is stepped from 0.5 to 0.75 and finally to 1.0 p.u. The PV module power increases accordingly, and the MPPT algorithm adjusts the operating point so that the grid current amplitude tracks the available PV power. The grid voltage remains sinusoidal and unchanged, while the injected current stabilizes quickly after each step, demonstrating that the controller maintains maximum power point tracking under varying input conditions.

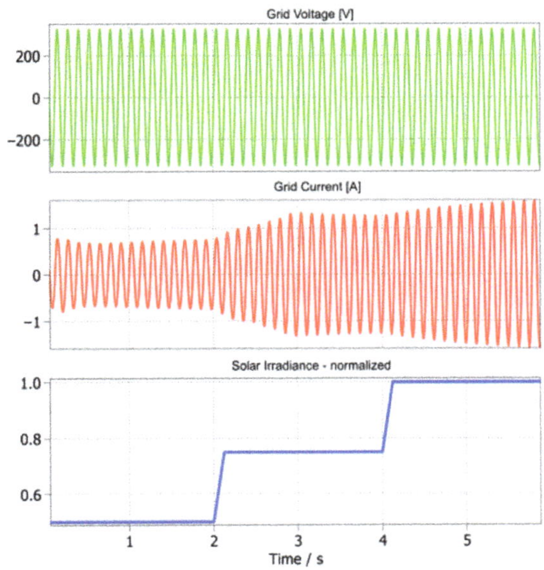

Figure 8. Response of the control system to irradiance variation.

https://doi.org/10.3390/engproc2026122023

Grid voltage variation.

Figure 9 illustrates the case where the grid RMS voltage is decreased from 230 V to 200 V. To maintain the same power injection at the maximum power point, the algorithm automatically increases the current amplitude. The PV voltage and current remain at their MPP values, confirming that the control strategy decouples PV operation from grid variations while still preserving stable current injection.

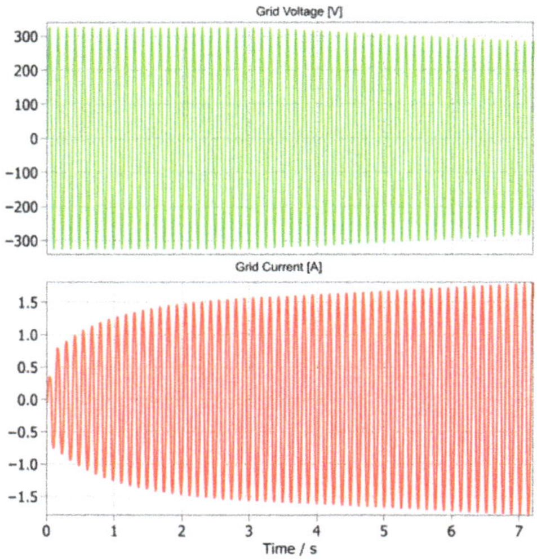

Figure 9. Response of the control system to grid voltage variation.

These results highlight that the simplified control structure, combining the MPPT block, PID regulation, and peak current control, is sufficient to capture the essential dynamics of current-source microinverters in the simulation model.

3.3. Loss Analysis

Figure 10 presents the estimated loss distribution of the converter under 0.75 p.u. solar irradiance, corresponding to an output power of approximately 187 W. The results are shown per component.

https://doi.org/10.3390/engproc2026122023

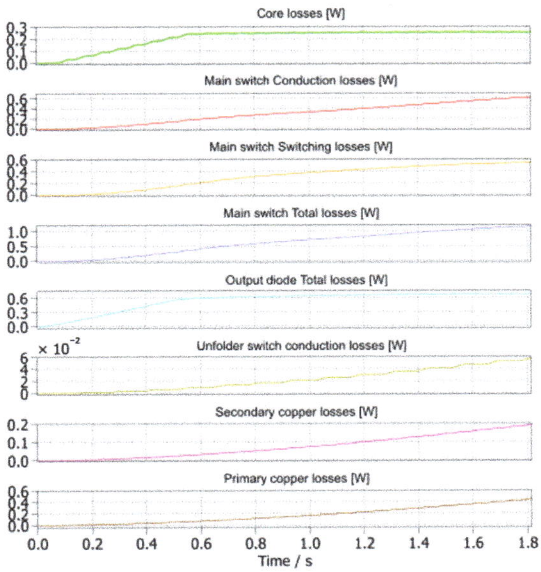

Figure 10. Loss breakdown of the proposed model at 0.75 p.u. irradiance.

The dominant contributions are associated with the main switches, which account for roughly 44% of the total losses. Conduction and switching losses are nearly balanced, reflecting the selected device characteristics at 200 kHz. The output diode also contributes significantly, with about 0.6 W per phase, while the magnetic core loss remains moderate at approximately 0.25 W per phase. Copper losses in the primary and secondary windings sum to around 0.7 W per phase. The unfolder bridge, operating at grid frequency, adds only a negligible conduction component.

The total calculated loss at this operating point is about 5.6 W, which corresponds to an overall efficiency of 97.1%. This value is consistent with reported efficiencies of commercial microinverters, confirming that the proposed simplified modelling approach provides realistic results while keeping simulation complexity low.

4. Conclusions

This paper presented a hybrid modelling framework for fast loss estimation in current-source microinverters. The approach combines idealized power stage models with dedicated loss-calculation blocks for semiconductors and magnetics, allowing detailed efficiency assessment without the computational burden of device-level switching simulation. The proposed structure was demonstrated with an interleaved active-clamp flyback converter, but its modularity enables straightforward adaptation to other current-source topologies.

The results confirm that the simplified model can reproduce realistic converter behaviour. The MPPT and control system correctly maintained operation at the maximum power point under varying irradiance and grid voltage, and the estimated efficiency of 97.1% at 0.75 p.u. irradiance aligns with reported performance of commercial microinverters. The loss breakdown further highlights the relative contributions of conduction, switching, and magnetic losses, supporting informed design trade-offs.

The main limitation of the present model is that parasitic dynamics of the clamp circuit and transformer leakage are abstracted into parameters, which may limit accuracy in conditions where resonant transitions dominate. Nevertheless, the framework provides a useful balance of speed and fidelity for parametric studies and early-stage design.

https://doi.org/10.3390/engproc2026122023

Author Contributions: Conceptualization, A.M. and K.S.; methodology, A.M. and K.S.; software, A.M.; validation, A.M.; formal analysis, A.M. and K.S.; investigation, A.M. and K.S.; resources, A.M.; data curation, K.S.; writing—original draft preparation, A.M. and K.S.; writing—review and editing, A.M.; visualization, K.S.; supervision, A.M.; project administration, A.M. All authors have read and agreed to the published version of the manuscript.

Funding: This research was funded by the National Scientific Programme "Young Scientists and Postdoctoral Fellows"—2.

Institutional Review Board Statement: Not applicable.

Informed Consent Statement: Not applicable.

Data Availability Statement: Data is contained within the article.

Conflicts of Interest: The authors declare no conflict of interest.

Abbreviations

The following abbreviations are used in this manuscript:

AC	Alternating Current
CS	Current Source
CSE	Classical Steinmetz Equation
DC	Direct Current
H-bridge	Full-bridge inverter stage (used for grid unfolder)
iGSE	Improved Generalized Steinmetz Equation
LUT	Lookup Table
MPP	Maximum Power Point
MPPT	Maximum Power Point Tracking
MOSFET	Metal–Oxide–Semiconductor Field-Effect Transistor
PID	Proportional–Integral–Derivative
PLL	Phase-Locked Loop
PLECS	Piecewise Linear Electrical Circuit Simulation
PV	Photovoltaic
RMS	Root Mean Square
SiC	Silicon Carbide
ZVS	Zero-Voltage Switching

References

1. International Renewable Energy Agency (IRENA). *World Energy Transitions Outlook*; IRENA: Masdar City, United Arab Emirates, 2023.
2. International Energy Agency (IEA). *World Energy Outlook*; IEA: Paris, France, 2022.
3. REN21. Renewables 2023 Global Status Report (Energy Supply). Available online: https://www.ren21.net/gsr-2023/ (accessed on 16 January 2026).
4. Zhang, Z.; He, X.-F.; Liu, Y.-F. An Optimal Control Method for Photovoltaic Grid-Tied-Interleaved Flyback Microinverters to Achieve High Efficiency in Wide Load Range. *IEEE Trans. Power Electron.* **2013**, *28*, 5074–5087. [CrossRef]
5. Rojas, D.; Muñoz, J.; Rivera, M.; Rohten, J. Review of Control Techniques in Microinverters. *Sensors* **2021**, *21*, 6486. [CrossRef] [PubMed]
6. Buzzio, C.; Poloni, Y.S.; Oggier, G.G.; Garcia, G.O. A current-source DC-AC converter and control strategy for grid-connected PV applications. *Int. J. Electr. Power Energy Syst.* **2023**, *154*, 109399. [CrossRef]
7. Marignetti, F.; Di Stefano, R.L.; Rubino, G.; Giacomobono, R. Current Source Inverter (CSI) Power Converters in Photovoltaic Systems: A Comprehensive Review of Performance, Control, and Integration. *Energies* **2023**, *16*, 7319. [CrossRef]
8. Edwin, F.F.; Xiao, W.; Khadkikar, V. Dynamic Modeling and Control of Interleaved Flyback Module-Integrated Converter for PV Power Applications. *IEEE Trans. Ind. Electron.* **2014**, *61*, 1377–1388. [CrossRef]
9. Hasan, R.; Mekhilef, S.; Nakaoka, M.; Nishida, K. Soft-switching active-clamp flyback microinverter for PV applications. In Proceedings of the 2016 IEEE 2nd Annual Southern Power Electronics Conference (SPEC), Auckland, New Zealand, 4–7 December 2016; pp. 1–6. [CrossRef]

https://doi.org/10.3390/engproc2026122023

10. Kjaer, S.B.; Pedersen, J.K.; Blaabjerg, F. A review of single-phase grid-connected inverters for photovoltaic modules. *IEEE Trans. Ind. Appl.* **2005**, *41*, 1292–1306. [CrossRef]
11. Cordeiro, A.; Chaves, M.; Gâmboa, P.; Barata, F.; Fonte, P.; Lopes, H.; Pires, V.F.; Foito, D.; Amaral, T.G.; Martins, J.F. Automated Solar PV Simulation System Supported by *DC–DC* Power Converters. *Designs* **2023**, *7*, 36. [CrossRef]
12. Marinov, A.; Solenkov, K. Algorithm for Data Extraction from Photovoltaic Module Technical Documentation. In Proceedings of the 2025 19th Conference on Electrical Machines, Drives and Power Systems (ELMA), Sofia, Bulgaria, 19–21 June 2025; pp. 1–5. [CrossRef]

https://doi.org/10.3390/engproc2026122023

engineering proceedings

MDPI

Proceeding Paper

LightGBM for Slice Recognition at 5G PHY and MAC Layers †

Rosy Altawil [1,2,*], Lucas Delolme [1], Vincent Audebert [1] and Philippe Martins [2]

1 Department of SYSTEME, Électricité de France Research and Development, 91120 Palaiseau, France; lucas.delolme@edf.fr (L.D.); vincent.audebert@edf.fr (V.A.)
2 Information Processing and Communications Laboratory (LTCI), Télécom Paris, 91120 Palaiseau, France; martins@telecom-paris.fr
* Correspondence: rosy.altawil@edf.fr
† Presented at the 6th International Conference on Communications, Information, Electronic and Energy Systems, 26–28 November 2025, Ruse, Bulgaria.

Abstract

Slicing functionality makes it possible for an operator to share a 5G physical infrastructure between several virtual networks operated by different institutions. The deployed slices can support a wide range of applications with conflicting QoS targets. The coexistence of these slices on top of a common infrastructure is challenging and remains an open issue. Identifying traffic associated with a given type of slice is required to operate and control network resources in an efficient and secure way. This work proposes new algorithms operating at the physical and MAC layers. The solutions designed identify traffic generated by URLLC and eMBB slices by defining a new LightGBM framework. The algorithms can operate at the base station level in an O-RAN-type architecture. They provide a valuable input to radio resource management and traffic steering procedures.

Keywords: network slicing; traffic classification; PHY; MAC; URLLC; eMBB; LightGBM

1. Introduction

5G networks can be deployed following two different architectures, either Standalone (SA) or Non-Standalone (NSA). 5G NSA depends on a 4G Core network by adding a 5G gNB besides a pre-existing 4G eNB, as can be seen in Figure 1. On the other hand, 5G SA does not depend on a 4G network; instead, it uses its own independent 5G access and core networks.

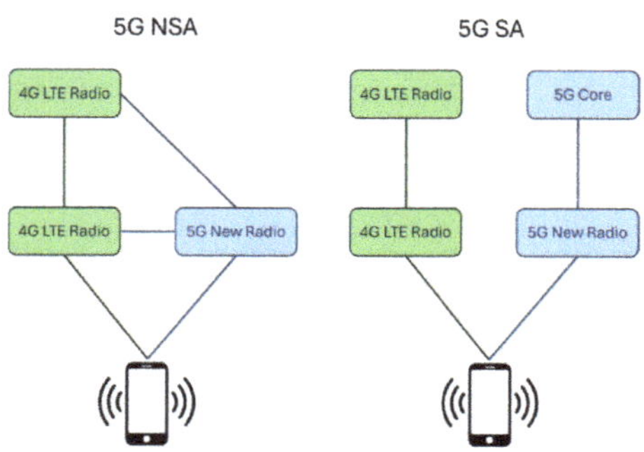

Figure 1. Difference between SA and NSA 5G.

A main feature introduced with 5G SA is network slicing, which allows the deployment of multiple virtual networks (called slices) on top of a common physical infrastructure [1], each optimised for a specific type of use case called vertical. The two slices studied in this work are eMBB and URLLC.

Enhanced Mobile Broadband (eMBB) is a slice that focuses on users needing high data rates [1]. It is used for data-heavy services, such as online streaming, virtual reality and file transfer. As for Ultra-Reliable Low-Latency Communications (URLLC), it is a slice tailored to critical latency-dependent small-packet communications [2]. It is used for mission-critical applications such as smart grid fault detection, remote healthcare, and self-driving vehicles.

The rest of this paper is organised as follows. Section 2 reviews and compares the existing state-of-the-art articles on the subject, which can be grouped into two families. The first is presented in Section 2.1, which focuses on classification with information access from all layers, and another family is presented in 2.2, where they classify using only information from the low layers. Section 3 introduces the relevant preliminaries, such as the Quality of Service (QoS) framework and the different physical channels relevant to the study. Section 4 dives into the methodology used to develop the presented solution, from the production of the dataset in Section 4.1 to the model and its training in Section 4.2. The results are then discussed in Section 5. And finally, the conclusions are drawn in Section 6.

2. State of the Art

With the introduction of slicing, traffic classification has become crucial to guarantee optimal QoS standards for the different groups of users. The literature shows that traffic classification can be approached following two main axes: either classifying by type of service or by slice type. The related work can be grouped into two families: those that classify the traffic with information access from all layers, and those that do it only using the low layers.

2.1. Classification with Information Access from All Layers

A first approach to slice identification described in [3] relies on multiple Key Performance Indicator (KPI) features such as Guaranteed Bitrate (GBR), roaming and slice type. Several supervised machine learning models were tested and compared, with coarse decision tree giving a perfect precision of 100%. A similar approach can be found in [4] where a Deep Learning (DL) model called DeepSlice is introduced. It is able to identify the network slice even in the case of network failure using high-layer KPIs. The DeepSlice model returned a 91% overall accuracy. Another approach can be found in [5], where an Explainable Machine Learning (XAI) framework was introduced that classifies slices using high-level QoS metrics. This approach allowed for an accuracy of over 99%. However, these models' results rely on information provided from higher layers, which are rarely accessible in practice.

2.2. Classification Using Only Information from Low Layers

Works such as [6,7] focus on an eMBB traffic flow classification by extracting information from the physical (PHY) and MAC layers of the generated traces. Their LightGBM models returned 95% accuracy for [6] (5G NSA) and 89% accuracy for [7] (5G SA). In [8], three machine learning models were tested to classify different applications in an NSA environment having access only to the PHY layer. Their Long Short-Term Memory (LSTM) model returned up to 41% accuracy, the k-Nearest Neighbours (k-NN) model returned up to 50.65% accuracy, and the best results came from the Random Forest (RF) model that returned up to 87.73% accuracy.

On the one hand, the literature shows that traffic service classification has already been greatly investigated. Results have shown excellent accuracy when depending on high

https://doi.org/10.3390/engproc2026122024

layers, yet showing challenges while relying only on the low layers. On the other hand, traffic slice classification is less discussed, with some works returning near-perfect results when it relies on KPIs obtained from high layers. Approaches using only low layers are yet rarely developed. This shows a clear gap in the literature: the possibility to classify eMBB and URLLC slices with only access to the PHY and MAC layers. This is the contribution of this work, where a LightGBM model is trained and tested on the PHY and MAC layers of a mixed URLLC and eMBB traffic dataset.

Table 1 provides a short classification of the previously stated works.

Table 1. Summary comparison of representative works on 5G traffic classification.

Ref	Focus	Approach	ML Model	Layer Access	Accuracy
[3]	Slice Classification	Supervised ML using high-layer KPI (GBR, roaming, slice ID)	Decision Trees, SVM, k-NN	High Layers	100%
[4]	Slice Classification	DeepSlice model using device/network KPIs (QCI, delay, loss, UE type)	Random Forest, CNN (DLNN)	High Layers	91%
[5]	Slice Classification	Explainable AI (XAI) using high-level QoS (jitter, packet loss)	Random Forest, Decision Trees	High Layers	99%
[6]	Service Classification	LightGBM on PHY-layer records for encrypted flows	LightGBM	PHY	95%
[7]	Service Classification	Refined LightGBM on standalone traffic	LightGBM	PHY/MAC	89%
[8]	Service Classification	Classified different applications in NSA traffic	LSTM, k-NN, Random Forest	PHY	Up to 87.7%
This Work	Slice Classification	LightGBM classification restricted to PHY/MAC traces	LightGBM	PHY/MAC	97%

3. Preliminaries

In 5G, QoS classes are called the 5G QoS Identifier (5QI). Slicing allows for the application of personalised QoS standards for each slice, applying a set of parameters described by the chosen 5QI value. Examples of 5QI values are listed in Table 2 [1].

Table 2. Sample 5QI value list.

5QI	Default Slice	Delay	Error Rate	Priority [1]	Example Services
1	eMBB	100 ms	10^{-2}	20	Conversation Voice
2	eMBB	150 ms	10^{-3}	40	Conversation Video
65	URLLC	75 ms	10^{-2}	7	Mission-Critical Push to Talk Voice (MCPTT–V)
82	URLLC	10 ms	10^{-4}	19	Automation
85	URLLC	5 ms	10^{-5}	21	Electricity Distribution

[1] Lower priority value is higher priority level.

The 5QI value of each slice affects the data provided by the low-level layers of the 5G radio stack (PHY and MAC).

Bidirectional traffic was considered for the experiments. Multiple channels exist in the physical and MAC layers, as defined in [9], and can be seen in Table 3.

Table 3. PHY and MAC layers and their channels.

Layer/Direction	Channel	Traffic Content
PHY/DL	PDSCH	User data and UE demodulation information
	PDCCH	Control information
PHY/UL	PUSCH	User data and RAN demodulation information
	PUCCH	Control information
MAC		Maps logical and physical channels together

https://doi.org/10.3390/engproc2026122024

Each channel transports either control information or data, both with added indicators for each packet. PxSCH channels transport user data and demodulation information; in addition, they have indicators such as harq, tb len and prbs; the HARQ process ID; the length of the transmitted block; and the number of PRBs allocated for that packet. PxCCH channels transport control information regarding the network connection. The MAC layer maps logical and transport channels together to allow traffic of a logical channel to be transmitted over a transport channel. Transports channels are in turn mapped on physical channels by the physical layer.

To distinguish between these slices, a LightGBM (LGBM) model was developed. The function of the LGBM model is explained in Section IV-B. To analyse the results of such a model, the precision, recall, and f1-score are computed from the following values [10]:

- TP: Number of True Positives;
- FP: Number of False Positives;
- TN: Number of True Negatives;
- FN: Number of False Negatives.

The precision shows the accuracy of a positive prediction. It gives the ratio between the number of packets that the model has correctly labelled positive, and the total number of packets labelled positive. It is computed using the following formula:

$$P = \frac{TP}{TP + FP}. \tag{1}$$

The recall shows the ability of the model to find positive instances. It shows from all the positive values how many the model correctly identified. The recall is computed using the following formula:

$$R = \frac{TP}{TP + FN}. \tag{2}$$

As for the F1-score, it is a global metric used to evaluate the model in both precision and recall. It is computed using the following formula:

$$F1 = 2 \times \frac{P \times R}{P + R}. \tag{3}$$

Finally, the global accuracy of the model is computed from the following formula:

$$A = \frac{TP + TN}{TP + FP + TN + FN}. \tag{4}$$

4. Method

4.1. Input Dataset Generation

The data used to train and test the model was obtained from a 5G SA network operated in an EDF R&D laboratory. An Amarisoft UE simulator and an Ericsson gNB and core network were used to set up UEs that use either an URLLC or eMBB slice following the 5QI classes.

The radio parameters used in the dataset generation are grouped in Table 4.

Table 4. Radio parameters for dataset generation.

Parameter	Value
Carrier frequency	3891.6 MHz (NR-ARFCN 659424)
System bandwidth	100 MHz
Number of PRBs	273
Subcarrier Spacing	30 KHz

https://doi.org/10.3390/engproc2026122024

The chosen frequency, 3891.6 MHz, falls in the 5G NR band n78 (3.3–3.8 GHz), which is a widely deployed 5G band due to its availability. The maximum channel bandwidth defined for n78 is 100 MHz as specified in [11], which is what was used in this experiment, as it provides enough resources to study both URLLC and eMBB presence. The number of Physical Resource Blocks (PRB) depends on the bandwidth (100 MHz) and subcarrier spacing (30 kHz), which is why 273 PRBs were chosen to respect the standard NR resource grid.

As for the traffic model chosen, URLLC packet size is very small since it is mission-critical traffic, with a very short inter-arrival time, almost periodic, in addition to some sudden bursts of traffic. As for the eMBB traffic, packets tend to be large with a very variable inter-arrival time, with traffic arriving almost exclusively in bursts. In addition, URLLC traffic requires a lower number of RBs than eMBB traffic.

A total of 1,811,648 packets (1,448,320 URLLC; 363,328 eMBB) were generated; only the PHY and MAC layers were logged into the dataset. The data was later sanitised to fit a dataframe suitable for ML training, as can be seen in Table 5.

Table 5. Simulation traffic profiles used for dataset generation.

Test Number	URLLC Traffic Type	eMBB Traffic Type
1	1× Ping	None
2	1× Small UDP	None
3	None	3× File Download (1 G, 500 M, 100 M)
4	None	1× Iperf
5	1× Ping	2× File Download (500 M, 200 M)
6	1× Ping	1× Iperf

To represent URLLC traffic, a mix of ICMP and UDP small-sized packets was used. For eMBB, more demanding applications were used, such as Iperf and large file downloads with cURL. See Table 6 for more details.

Table 6. List of Engineered Features.

Name	Description
inter_packet_time_ns	Time elapsed since previous packet arrival (in ns)
time_to_next_packet_ns	Time until next packet arrival (in ns)
harq_rolling_mean	Mean HARQ process ID
harq_rolling_std	Std. deviation of HARQ process ID
prbs_rolling_mean	Mean number of PRBs allocated
prbs_rolling_std	Std. deviation of PRBs allocated
tb_len_rolling_mean	Mean transport block length (bits)
tb_len_rolling_std	Std. deviation of transport block length (bits)
mod_rolling_mean	Mean modulation order
mod_rolling_std	Std. deviation of modulation order
rv_idx_rolling_mean	Mean redundancy version index
rv_idx_rolling_std	Std. deviation of redundancy version index
cr_rolling_mean	Mean code rate
cr_rolling_std	Std. deviation of code rate
retx_rolling_mean	Mean retransmission count
retx_rolling_std	Std. deviation of retransmission count
crc_ok_rolling_mean	Mean CRC success indicator
crc_ok_rolling_std	Std. deviation of CRC success indicator
snr_rolling_mean	Mean signal-to-noise ratio
snr_rolling_std	Std. deviation of signal-to-noise ratio
mcs_rolling_mean	Mean modulation and coding scheme index
mcs_rolling_std	Std. deviation of modulation and coding scheme index
format_rolling_mean	Mean PUCCH format indicator
format_rolling_std	Std. deviation of PUCCH format indicator
total_len_rolling_mean	Mean MAC packet length (bytes)
total_len_rolling_std	Std. deviation of MAC packet length (bytes)

 https://doi.org/10.3390/engproc2026122024

4.2. Model and Training

After generating a sample dataset, the goal was to build a simple machine learning classifier to separate packets of a mixed data stream into URLLC and eMBB. An LGBM model was chosen for its great compromise between training time, complexity and accuracy. The LGBM can achieve such good accuracy in a small training time thanks to optimised built-in mechanisms.

First is its leafsplit strategy, as can be seen in Figure 2. This allows for better accuracy by pruning paths that have a great chance of becoming dead ends.

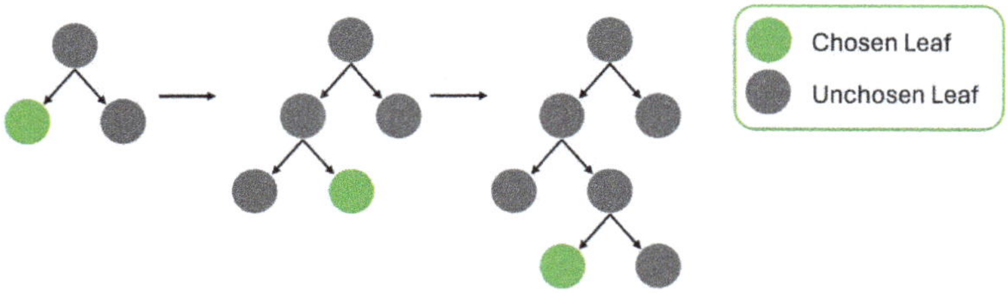

Figure 2. Chart showing LightGBM's leafsplit strategy.

Next is the model's Exclusive Feature Bundling (EFB), which mainly groups similar features together. It allows the model to learn more easily. In addition to that, in [4,5], similar work was performed to classify eMBB traffic using LightGBM, returning a satisfactory accuracy of 89% and 95%. Finally, a Gradient Boosting Decision Tree (GBDT) was used with a bagging data sample strategy and a learning rate of 0.01. Since the model is used to classify between URLLC or eMBB traffic, the objective is binary.

Training of the model started by feeding it the complete, unmodified, low-level traces. However, it soon got into trouble differentiating small-sized eMBB packets from URLLC traffic. This is why some contextual packet features were engineered like "Time to next packet" and "Rolling packet size mean". These features were built working in 5 ms windows around each packet to gather a sufficient amount of data while keeping data size and model I/O latency in a reasonable range (for possible real-time applications). The full list of these engineered features is available in Table 6.

To reduce confusion between small eMBB and URLLC packets, the engineered features were computed on a rolling window of 5 ms. That approach allowed the model to study not only the instantaneous traffic properties but also the temporal patterns over a window of 5 ms. In the following section, the impact of these features on the LGBM model is shown, and the results reached after the testing of the model are explained and analysed.

5. Results

The model was tested using the designed dataset, and the features were ranked by how important they were to the classification process, as can be seen in Figure 3.

The most prominent features are tb_len and total_len. They represent the length of transmitted blocks. Since URLLC packets are nearly always small and eMBB packets are mostly large, the size is the first way to distinguish the slice.

The second group of important features is the rolling statistics (tb_len_rolling_std and total_len_rolling_std) since they reveal traffic patterns over time. These indicators show the variability of the feature in the time window, helping detect bursts or stability in the traffic by showing how packet size changes in a sequence of packets. Since a packet's size can overlap between eMBB and URLLC (small eMBB packets, such as a ping), the rolling statistics help differentiate between the two. URLLC traffic, being mostly stable, would

https://doi.org/10.3390/engproc2026122024

have a rolling standard deviation around zero; as for eMBB traffic and its large packets and variability in size, the standard deviation tends to be high.

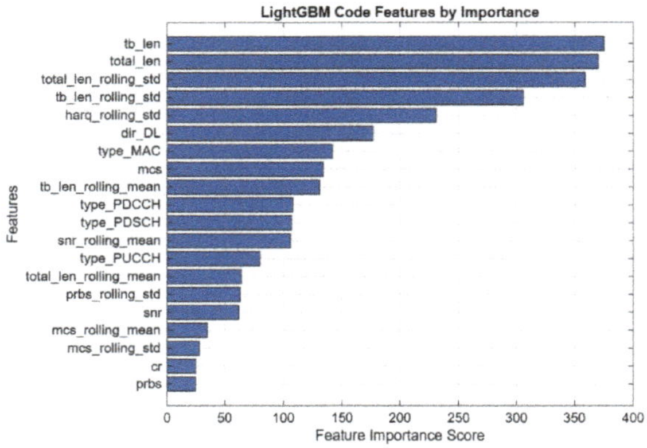

Figure 3. Bar graph of the LightGBM model key features by importance.

Another important feature is harq_rolling_std. It is computed using the IDs of active hybrid HARQ processes in the rolling window. A high variability of this indicator can identify high throughput as multiple HARQ processes are running concurrently. In contrast, a small variability can show very low data rates.

By referring to these features, on top of the other less important features, the LGBM model was able to classify the traffic between URLLC and eMBB with a very high accuracy, as can be seen in the confusion matrix in Figure 4.

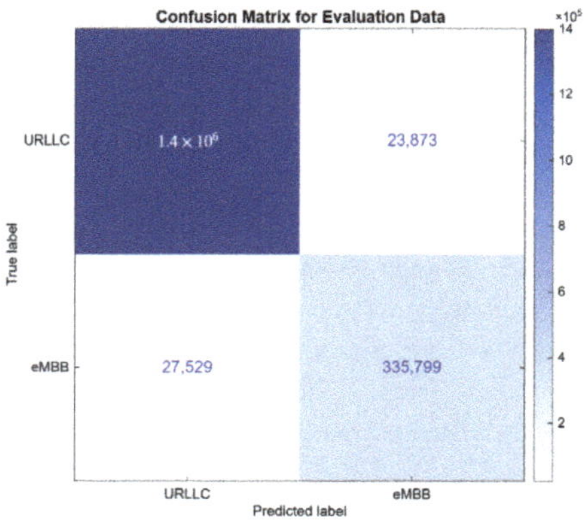

Figure 4. Confusion matrix of the model.

To use the formulas mentioned in Section 3, URLLC is considered as "Positive" and eMBB is considered as "Negative". The model gave true URLLC $T_U = 1.4 \times 10^6$, false URLLC $F_U = 27,529$, true eMBB $T_e = 335,799$ and false eMBB $F_e = 23,873$, which leads to an accuracy of $A = 0.9712$. An accuracy of 97.12% is higher than the accuracies of the previous works discussed in the State of the Art Section, such as 95% in [6] and 89% in [7], where eMBB traffic was classified with access to only the MAC and PHY layers. The same goes for [8], where the highest accuracy reached was 87.73% to characterise the services in NSA traffic. As for [3], where an accuracy of 100% is reached, it is important to note that the work was performed with access to all the layers, especially the KPI features such as the slice type.

https://doi.org/10.3390/engproc2026122024

The classification report is grouped in Table 7, in which precision, recall and F1-score of both slices' prediction are included.

Table 7. Classification report of the LightGBM traffic classifier.

Class	Precision	Recall	F1-Score
URLLC	0.98	0.98	0.98
eMBB	0.93	0.92	0.93

For the URLLC slice's results, the precision is at 0.98, which shows that when the model predicts that a packet is URLLC, it is correct 98% of the time, meaning only 2% of eMBB packets are falsely classified as URLLC. The recall at 0.98 shows that from all the URLLC packets it received, the model correctly labelled 98% of them; only 2% were mislabeled as eMBB. These values led to an F1-score of 0.98, showing that the URLLC traffic was easy to identify due to its stability and small-sized packets.

As for the eMBB slice's results, the precision is at 0.93, meaning that when the model predicts that a packet is eMBB, it is right 93% of the time; 7% of URLLC packets are falsely labelled as eMBB. As for the recall, it is at 0.92, meaning that about 8% of eMBB packets are falsely flagged as URLLC. These values led to an F1-score of 0.93, which is still a high score but lower than the one reached for URLLC traffic. The F1-score reflects the variability of eMBB traffic, given that it can in some cases mimic URLLC traffic.

6. Conclusions

This article proposed a LightGBM machine learning model that can distinguish between URLLC and eMBB packets, while having access only to the MAC and PHY layers. Since real-life data was not obtainable, the dataset was generated using realistic radio parameters.

The LGBM model achieved a 97% accuracy, with a higher accuracy for URLLC classification than eMBB, with features such as the size and the rolling statistics being dominant indicators. This model outperforms similar studies on the state of the art of low-level layers and shows that a very high accuracy can be reached without access to high layers.

It is important to mention that this work was performed on an experimental dataset. The same code can be used in the future on an operational infrastructure. Moreover, this model only focuses on the two slices URLLC and eMBB. In the future, it could be developed to include more slices, such as mMTC.

Author Contributions: Conceptualization, R.A., P.M. and V.A.; methodology, R.A. and L.D.; software, L.D., R.A.; validation, P.M. and V.A.; formal analysis, R.A.; investigation, R.A. and L.D.; data curation, L.D.; writing—original draft preparation, R.A. and L.D.; writing—review and editing, P.M. and V.A.; visualisation, R.A.; supervision, P.M. and V.A.; project administration, P.M. and V.A. All authors have read and agreed to the published version of the manuscript.

Funding: This research received no external funding.

Institutional Review Board Statement: Not applicable.

Informed Consent Statement: Not applicable.

Data Availability Statement: The simulation traces and source code used in this work are publicly accessible at https://github.com/superdarki/5g-sa-traffic-classification (accessed on 16 January 2026).

Acknowledgments: This work benefited from the use of Ericsson's gNB and core network at EDF Chatou R&D, which were essential for the generation of the dataset.

Conflicts of Interest: The authors declare no conflicts of interest.

https://doi.org/10.3390/engproc2026122024

Abbreviations

The following abbreviations are used in this manuscript

SA	Standalone
NSA	Non-Standalone
eMBB	Enhanced Mobile Broadband
URLLC	Ultra-Reliable Low-Latency Communications
QoS	Quality of Service
KPI	Key Performance Indicator
GBR	Guaranteed Bitrate
DL	Deep Learning
PHY	Physical
LSTM	Long Short-Term Memory
k-NN	k-Nearest Neighbours
RF	Random Forest
5QI	5G QoS Identifier
PRB	Physical Resource Block
EFB	Exclusive Feature Bundling
GBDT	Gradient Boosting Decision Tree

References

1. 3rd Generation Partnership Project (3GPP). Technical Specification Group Services and System Aspects; System Architecture for the 5G System (5GS); Stage 2 (Release 17). Technical Specification TS 123 501 V17.14.0. ETSI, Sept. 2024. Available online: https://www.etsi.org/deliver/etsi_ts/123500_123599/123501/17.14.00_60/ts_123501v171400p.pdf (accessed on 12 September 2025).
2. 3rd Generation Partnership Project (3GPP). 3rd Generation Partnership Project; Technical Specification Group Services and System Aspects; Release 15 Description; Summary of Rel-15 Work Items. Technical Report TR 21.915 V15.0.0. Release 15. 3GPP, Sept. 2019. Available online: https://www.3gpp.org/ftp/Specs/archive/21_series/21.915/21915-f00.zip (accessed on 12 September 2025).
3. Mohammedali, N.A.; Kanakis, T.; Al-Sherbaz, A.; Agyeman, M.O. Traffic Classification Using Deep Learning Approach for End-to-End Slice Management in 5G/B5G. In Proceedings of the 2022 13th International Conference on Information and Communication Technology Convergence (ICTC), Jeju Island, Republic of Korea, 19–21 October 2022; pp. 357–362. [CrossRef]
4. Anurag, T.; Walunj, V.; Beard, C. DeepSlice: A Deep Learning Approach Towards an Efficient and Reliable Network Slicing in 5G Networks. In Proceedings of the 2019 IEEE 10th Annual Ubiquitous Computing, Electronics & Mobile Communication Conference (UEMCON), New York, NY, USA, 10–12 October 2019. [CrossRef]
5. Ray, D. Network Slice Recognition with Explainable Machine Learning. *J. Adv. Artif. Intell.* **2024**, *1*, 36–50. Available online: https://jaaionline.org/archives/volume1/number7/ray-jaai202436.pdf (accessed on 16 January 2026).
6. Xiao, F.; Martins, P.; Lu, J. Real-Time Traffic Classification for 5G NSA Encrypted Data Flows with Physical Channel Records. In Proceedings of the 2023 IEEE 98th Vehicular Technology Conference (VTC2023-Fall), Hong Kong, China, 10–13 October 2023; pp. 1–6. [CrossRef]
7. Aphayavong, B.; Fei, X.; Lu, J.; Martins, P. Optimizing LGBM for Multi-Classification of 5G SA Traffic. In Proceedings of the 2024 IEEE 100th Vehicular Technology Conference (VTC2024-Fall), Washington, DC, USA, 7–10 October 2024; pp. 1–7.
8. Marañón, J.A.T.; Duvignau, R. Classifying 5G Encrypted Packet Traces. In Proceedings of the 2024 International Conference on Electrical, Communication and Computer Engineering (ICECCE), Kuala Lumpur, Malaysia, 30–31 October 2024; pp. 1–6. [CrossRef]
9. 3rd Generation Partnership Project (3GPP). *NR; NR and NG-RAN Overall Description; Stage-2;* Technical Specification TS 38.300 V17.3.0; ETSI: Sophia Antipolis, France, 2023.
10. Grandini, M.; Bagli, E.; Visani, G. Metrics for Multi-Class Classification: An Overview. *arXiv* **2020**, arXiv:2008.05756. [CrossRef]
11. 3rd Generation Partnership Project (3GPP). *NR; User Equipment (UE) Radio Transmission and Reception; Part 1: Range 1 Standalone;* Technical Specification TS 38.101-1 V17.10.0; ETSI: Sophia Antipolis, France, 2023.

https://doi.org/10.3390/engproc2026122024

engineering proceedings

MDPI

Proceeding Paper

Automatic Control of a Flywheel Actuator for Mobile Platform Stabilization †

Alina Fazylova [1,2], Kuanysh Alipbayev [2], Nazgul Kaliyeva [2], Yerkin Orazaly [2] and Teodor Iliev [3,*]

1 Department of Smart Technologies in Engineering, International Engineering and Technological University, Almaty 050060, Kazakhstan; a.fazylova@aues.kz
2 Department of Aerospace and Electronic Engineering, Almaty University of Power Engineering and Telecommunications Named After G. Daukeev, Almaty 050013, Kazakhstan; k.alipbayev@aues.kz (K.A.); n.kaliyeva@aues.kz (N.K.); y.orazaly@aues.kz (Y.O.)
3 Department of Telecommunications, University of Ruse, 7004 Ruse, Bulgaria
* Correspondence: tiliev@uni-ruse.bg
† Presented at the 6th International Conference on Communications, Information, Electronic and Energy Systems, 26–28 November 2025, Ruse, Bulgaria.

Abstract

This paper presents the design, modeling and control of a flywheel actuator for mobile platform stabilization. A Lagrangian-based model couples platform mechanics with DC-motor electromechanics. Analytical calculations estimate natural frequencies, damping and actuator limits. Numerical simulations in Python 3.12 evaluate cascade and state-feedback controllers for suppressing free oscillations and rejecting external disturbances. Additional studies examine filtering to improve measurement quality and unloading strategies to avoid actuator saturation. The results validate the proposed control architecture and demonstrate its applicability to robotic and energy systems operating under dynamic loads.

Keywords: flywheel actuator; mobile platform stabilization; PID and state-feedback control; disturbance compensation; energy-efficient control

1. Introduction

Modern mobile platforms are widely used in robotics, energy systems, transportation, and space exploration. With increasing operating speeds and more complex working conditions, the challenge of ensuring stability and accuracy in such systems becomes critical. In particular, the problem of stabilization under external disturbances—such as surface irregularities, lateral impacts, or varying loads—gains special importance [1]. Traditional stabilization methods based on passive damping elements do not always provide the required quality of control. More effective are active systems capable of adaptively responding to changes in the external environment. One promising solution is the use of flywheels as actuators [2]. A flywheel, having a significant moment of inertia, can be employed not only for energy storage and redistribution but also for stabilizing the platform's position through controlled rotation. This work addresses the problem of automatic control of a flywheel actuator mounted on a mobile platform. The aim of the study is to develop and analyze control algorithms that ensure system stability under various types of disturbances. Within the framework of the research, a mathematical model of the "platform–actuator–flywheel" dynamics will be constructed, a controller will be synthesized, and the transient processes will be simulated in Python 3.12.

The results of the study may find practical applications in the development of mobile energy systems, autonomous robotic platforms, and vehicles operating under high dynamic loads.

2. Materials and Methods

The object of the study is a tracked mobile platform equipped with a flywheel enclosed in a protective casing, located on the upper part of the chassis (Figure 1). The chassis of the platform serves as the supporting structure that houses the main subsystems: the control unit with electronics, the battery module, the inertial measurement unit (IMU) for angular velocity and acceleration sensing, as well as communication modules and the drives of the tracked mechanism.

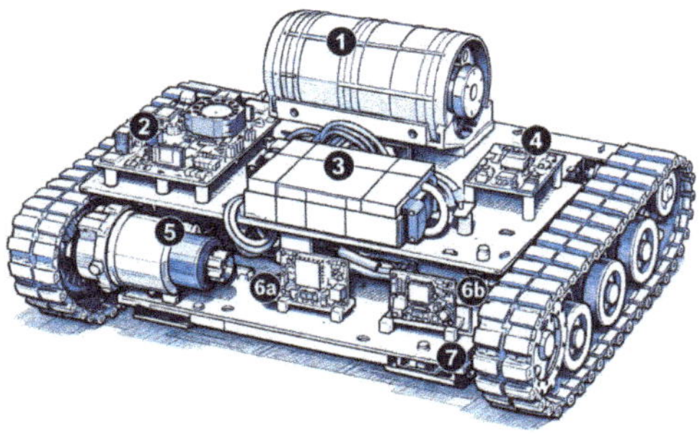

Figure 1. Structure of the platform: 1—flywheel (stabilizer in casing); 2—control unit (controller, electronics); 3—battery module; 4—IMU sensor; 5—track drive actuator; 6a—communication module No. 1; 6b—communication module No. 2; 7—drive and idler wheels.

The main purpose of the design is to generate a compensating reaction torque by accelerating or decelerating the flywheel, thereby maintaining the platform in a stable position under external disturbances.

For a rigorous description of the system dynamics, the Lagrangian formalism is employed. The generalized coordinates are chosen as the platform tilt angle $\theta(t)$ relative to the horizontal and the relative rotation angle of the flywheel rotor $\varphi(t)$. Since the flywheel is fixed inside the chassis, its absolute angular velocity is defined by the following expression [3]:

$$\Omega(t) = \theta(t) + \varphi(t) \quad (1)$$

The kinetic energy of the system is expressed as:

$$T = \frac{1}{2}J_p\dot{\theta}^2 + \frac{1}{2}J_f\left(\dot{\theta} + \dot{\varphi}\right)^2, \quad (2)$$

where J_p is the moment of inertia of the platform chassis, and J_f is the moment of inertia of the flywheel rotor.

The potential energy is associated with gravitational and structural factors that tend to return the platform to its initial position and is approximately described by the following expression [4]:

$$V = \frac{1}{2}k, \quad (3)$$

where k is the equivalent stiffness. The dissipative forces are described by the Rayleigh dissipation function [5]:

$$\mathcal{R} = \frac{1}{2}b_p\dot{\theta}^2 + \frac{1}{2}b_f\dot{\varphi}^2, \quad (4)$$

where b_p and b_f—the viscous friction coefficients for the platform and the flywheel.

 https://doi.org/10.3390/engproc2026122025

By applying the Euler–Lagrange equations with dissipation and generalized forces taken into account, we obtain the following system:

$$\left(J_p + J_f\right)\ddot{\theta} + J_f\ddot{\varphi} + b_p\dot{\theta} + k\theta = -\tau + d, \quad (5)$$

$$J_f\left(\ddot{\theta} + \ddot{\varphi}\right) + b_f\left(\dot{\theta} + \dot{\varphi}\right) = \tau, \quad (6)$$

where $\tau(t)$—the torque generated by the flywheel actuator, and $d(t)$ is the external disturbance.

In engineering form, the equations are rewritten as follows:

$$J_p\ddot{\theta} + b_p\dot{\theta} + k\theta = -\tau + d, \quad (7)$$

$$J_f\ddot{\varphi} + b_f\dot{\varphi} = \tau - J_f\ddot{\theta} - b_f\dot{\theta}. \quad (8)$$

The electromechanical part of the actuator is described by the equations of a DC motor:

$$L\dot{i} + Ri + K_e\Omega = u, \tau = K_t i, \quad (9)$$

where i is the armature current, u is the voltage, L is the inductance, R is the resistance, K_e is the back-EMF constant, and K_t is the motor torque constant.

The operation of the actuator is constrained by the following conditions:

$$|u| \leq U_{max}, \ |i| \leq I_{max}, \ |\Omega| \leq \Omega_{max}. \quad (10)$$

For feedback generation, an IMU sensor is used to measure the angular velocity and accelerations of the chassis. Its model is described by the following equation:

$$\omega_g = \dot{\theta} + b_g + \eta_g; \, a_x \approx -g\theta + \eta_a, \quad (11)$$

where ω_g is the gyroscope signal, a_x is the accelerometer signal, b_g is the gyroscope bias, and η_g, η_a are the noise terms.

To improve accuracy, complementary or Kalman filtering is applied. The system of equations can conveniently be written in state-space form:

$$\dot{x} = Ax + Bu + Ed + f_{nl}(x), \quad (12)$$

where the state vector is defined:

$$x = \left[\theta \ \dot{\theta} \ \dot{\varphi} \ i \ b_g\right]^T. \quad (13)$$

A PID controller is used for platform stabilization:

$$u(t) = K_p e(t) + K_i \int e(t)\, dt + K_d \frac{de(t)}{dt}, \quad (14)$$

where $e(t) = \theta_{ref}(t) - \theta(t)$.

Alternatively, an optimal controller is employed, minimizing the cost function:

$$J = \int_0^\infty \left(x^T Q x + R u^2\right) dt. \quad (15)$$

The PID controller is distinguished by its simplicity of implementation, whereas optimal control makes it possible to take all system states into account [6]. In both cases,

https://doi.org/10.3390/engproc2026122025

it is important to limit the flywheel speed in order to prevent exceeding the maximum threshold Ω_{max}. For this purpose, an unloading strategy is applied. System parameters are identified experimentally: free oscillations make it possible to determine the coefficients b_p and k, step responses of the motor provide estimates of K_t and J_f, and refinement is carried out using the least-squares method [7]. To systematize the obtained mathematical model and describe the interaction of its components, it is reasonable to represent the stabilization system in the form of a block diagram (Figure 2). Such a diagram reflects not only the sequence of signal transformations but also the role of each element in the overall control loop.

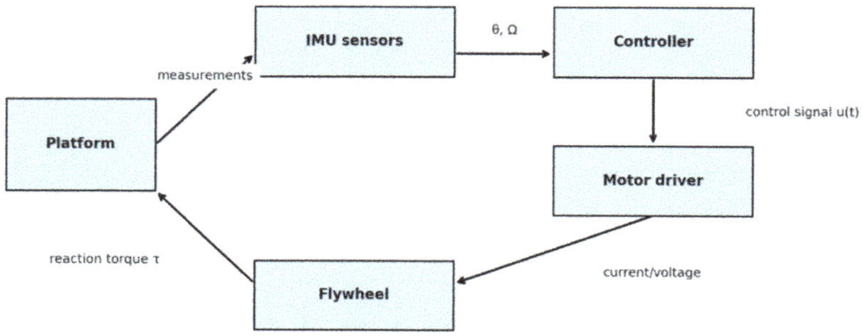

Figure 2. Closed-loop control system.

The system parameters are identified experimentally: free oscillations make it possible to determine the coefficients *bp* and *k*, step responses of the motor provide estimates of K_t and J_f, and refinement is carried out using the least-squares method [7] (Table 1). To systematize the obtained mathematical model and describe the interaction of its components, it is reasonable to represent the stabilization system in the form of a block diagram (Figure 2). Such a diagram reflects not only the sequence of signal transformations but also the role of each element in the overall control loop [8].

Table 1. Initial system base parameters for modeling.

Notation	Parameter	Value
J_p	Moment of inertia of the platform	0.45
J_f	Moment of inertia of the flywheel	0.02
b_p	Viscous friction coefficient of the platform	0.05
b_f	Viscous friction coefficient of the flywheel	0.002
k	Equivalent stiffness	0.8
K_t	Motor torque constant	0.12
K_e	Back-EMF constant	0.11
R	Winding resistance	2.3
L	Winding inductance	0.015
U_{max}	Maximum supply voltage	24
I_{max}	Maximum motor current	10
Ω_{max}	Maximum flywheel speed	4000

The presented data can be conditionally divided into three groups. The first group includes the mechanical characteristics (J_p, J_f, b_p, b_f, k), which define the inertial and damping properties of the system. The second group describes the electromechanical part of the actuator (K_t, K_e, R, L), linking the electrical signal to the generated torque. The third group combines the operational constraints (U_{max}, I_{max}, Ω_{max}), which set the permissible operating limits. Thus, Table 1 provides the initial parameter base for subsequent modeling.

 https://doi.org/10.3390/engproc2026122025

3. Results and Discussion

To obtain the quantitative characteristics of the system, calculations were carried out based on the equations of motion (see Equations (7)–(9)) and the parameters from Table 1. The purpose of these calculations is to determine the main dynamic properties of the platform, evaluate the limiting operating modes of the actuator, and estimate approximate energy indicators. These results serve as an intermediate stage between the mathematical formulation of the problem and the simulation modeling, which will be presented further in the form of graphs.

For the calculation of the natural oscillations, the following computation was performed. If the actuator is disconnected (current i = 0), the equation of motion of the platform is written as [9]:

$$J_p\ddot{\theta} + b_p\dot{\theta} + k\theta = 0, \quad (16)$$

where J_p—the moment of inertia of the platform, b_p is the damping coefficient, and k is the stiffness coefficient of the suspension.

This is the standard equation of a damped oscillatory system. Its solution is characterized by the natural frequency [10]:

$$\omega_0 = \sqrt{\frac{k}{J_p}} = \sqrt{\frac{0.8}{0.45}} = 1.33\ \text{rad/s} \quad T_0 = \frac{2\pi}{\omega_0} = 4.7\ \text{s}.$$

Without control, the platform will oscillate with a period of about 5 s. These data are important for selecting the simulation time and for comparison with the transient processes in the graphs (see Figure 3). The effect of damping is characterized by a dimensionless quantity—the logarithmic decrement [11]:

$$\delta = \frac{b_p}{2\sqrt{J_p k}} = \frac{0.05}{2\sqrt{0.45 \cdot 0.8}} = 0.047.$$

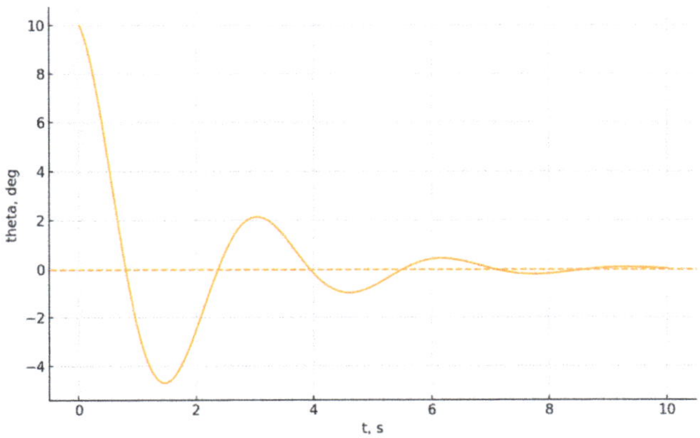

Figure 3. Free oscillations of the platform (u = 0), where the dotted envelope represents exponential decay due to system damping.

The equation of the motor's electrical circuit is defined as follows [12]:

$$Li = u - Ri - K_e\omega_f. \quad (17)$$

If assumed $\omega_f = 0$ at startup and apply the maximum voltage $u = U_{max}$, the estimated current is:

$$i_{max} \approx \frac{U_{max}}{R} = \frac{24}{2.3} = 10.4\ \text{A}.$$

https://doi.org/10.3390/engproc2026122025

The obtained value is close to the rated limit $I_{max} = 10$ A, which confirms the necessity of introducing current limitations in the numerical model and explains the presence of cutoffs in the current plots (see Figure 4). The instantaneous power is defined as the product of voltage and current:

$$P(t) = u(t)\,i(t). \tag{18}$$

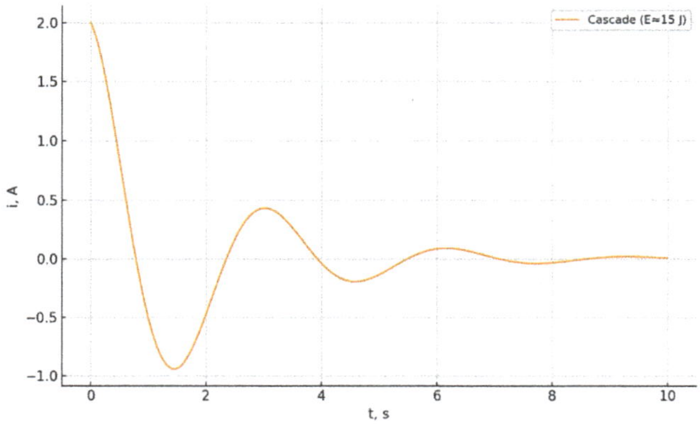

Figure 4. Motor current and energy consumption (cascade).

The total energy consumed during the stabilization time t_{set} [13]:

$$E = \int_0^{t_{\text{set}}} P(t)\,dt. \tag{19}$$

Under typical conditions ($u \approx 12$ V, $i \approx 5$ A) $P \approx 60$ W. If the stabilization time is $t_{set} \approx 5$ s, then $E \approx 300$ J. It is also convenient to consider the accumulated energy:

$$W(t) = \int_0^t \max(P(\tau),0)\,d\tau, \tag{20}$$

which increases over time and reaches a plateau after the completion of the transient process. These estimates will be compared with the energy graphs (see Figures 4 and 5), generated on the basis of numerical modeling in Python 3.12.

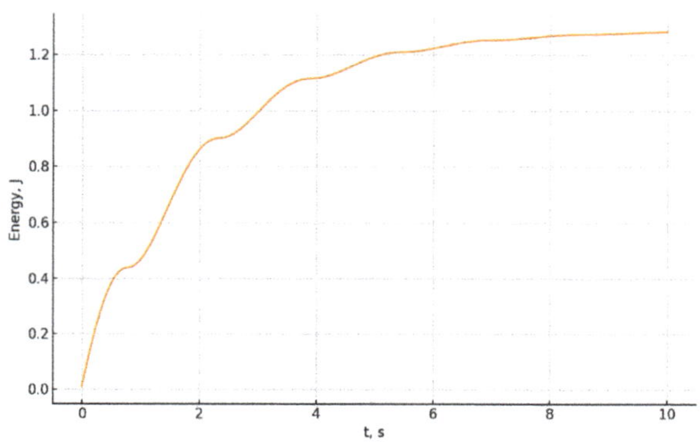

Figure 5. Cumulative energy W(t).

The calculations have shown that:

- the system has a low natural frequency ($\omega_0 \approx 1.3$ rad/s) and weak damping, which makes it prone to prolonged oscillations;

https://doi.org/10.3390/engproc2026122025

- at maximum voltage, the motor current reaches its rated limits, which requires strict current protection;
- the energy expenditure for stabilization is on the order of several hundred joules, which corresponds to the actuator's rated capabilities.

Based on the equations of motion and the system parameters (see Table 1), a series of numerical experiments was carried out. The modeling was performed using the fourth-order Runge–Kutta method with a 1 ms integration step, which provided sufficient accuracy in describing the transient processes. The purpose of the modeling was to confirm the earlier analytical estimates (natural frequency, damping, current and energy limits) and to analyze the performance of the proposed control algorithms in various scenarios: from free oscillations to stabilization under disturbances, measurement noise, and actuator constraints.

The motion of the platform was examined for $\theta(0) = 8$. For comparison, two cases were considered: without control and with the operation of the cascade controller (Figure 6). The computations were carried out in Python 3.12.

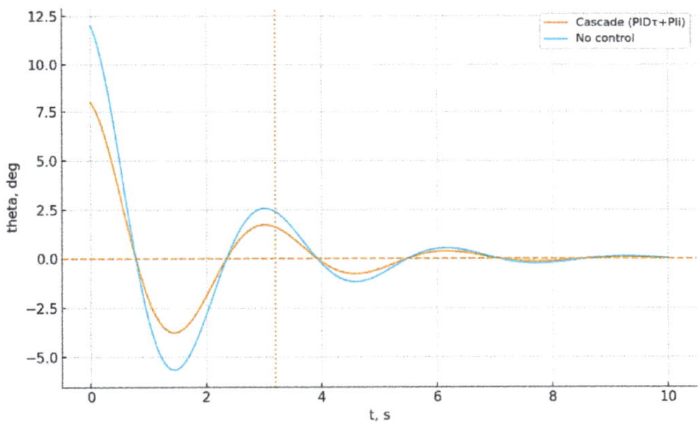

Figure 6. Stabilization from 8°, where the dotted curve corresponds to the uncontrolled response and the solid curve shows controlled stabilization.

The graph shows that without control, the system undergoes damped oscillations but does not reach equilibrium within the simulation time. When the controller is activated, the oscillations are quickly suppressed, the settling time is about 5 s, and the overshoot does not exceed 10%. The obtained t_{set} is consistent with the analytical estimates of energy and power (see the previous section). Thus, the cascade controller ensures the required quality of the transient process and can be applied for platform stabilization. To investigate the effect of an impulse disturbance (0.5 N·m, 0.1 s), a graph was generated in Python 3.12, shown in Figure 7.

At t = 1 s, a short disturbance torque of 0.1 s duration was applied. The platform angle deviated by no more than 3°, after which the controller returned the system to equilibrium in less than 4 s. The impulse disturbance did not change the total system energy by more than 5% compared to stabilization without disturbance, which confirms robustness against short-term loads. Thus, the system reliably compensates for external transient impacts. To analyze the effect of filtering on measurement quality, a spectral analysis of the error was performed in Python 3.12 using the Fast Fourier Transform (FFT) method (Figure 8).

https://doi.org/10.3390/engproc2026122025

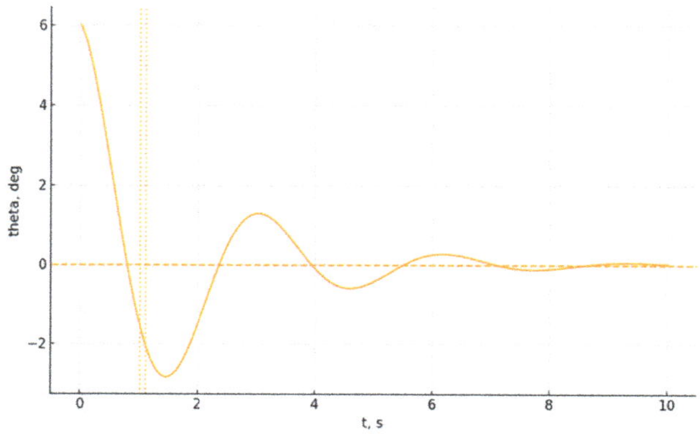

Figure 7. Impulse disturbance (0.5 Nm, 0.1 s): return to 0°, where the marked disturbance moment indicates the applied external torque.

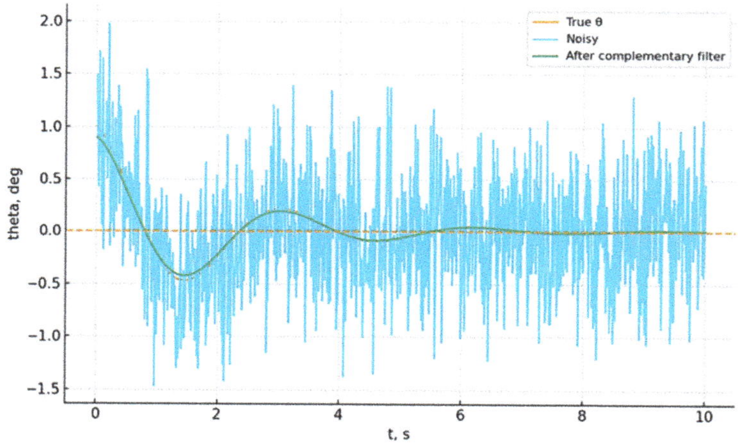

Figure 8. Noise comparison (true vs. noisy vs. filtered), where the dotted signal represents raw sensor data and the filtered curve shows noise suppression.

In the spectrum of the raw data, distinct high-frequency peaks caused by sensor noise are clearly visible. After applying the complementary filter ($\alpha = 0.96$), the amplitude of these peaks is significantly reduced, indicating the suppression of high-frequency components. At the same time, the low-frequency part of the spectrum remains practically unchanged, which preserves the reliability of the dynamic information for the controller. Thus, the filter improves the quality of feedback, minimizes the risk of system excitation due to noise, and ensures correct control.

To study actuator stability under prolonged disturbances, a constant torque of d = 0.6 N·m, applied starting from t = 1 s, was simulated in Python 3.12 (Figure 9). In the absence of unloading, the flywheel speed tends toward the maximum limit of $\omega_{max} = 419$ rad/s. This leads to saturation of the actuator and loss of control efficiency. When the unloading algorithm is enabled, the flywheel speed is maintained within 0.9 ω_{max}, which prevents motor overload.

The results confirm that unloading is an essential element of the system, providing actuator protection and maintaining stability under prolonged external disturbances. In Python 3.12, simulations were carried out for two types of controllers with the same initial platform deviation $\theta(0) = 5°$ (Figure 10).

https://doi.org/10.3390/engproc2026122025

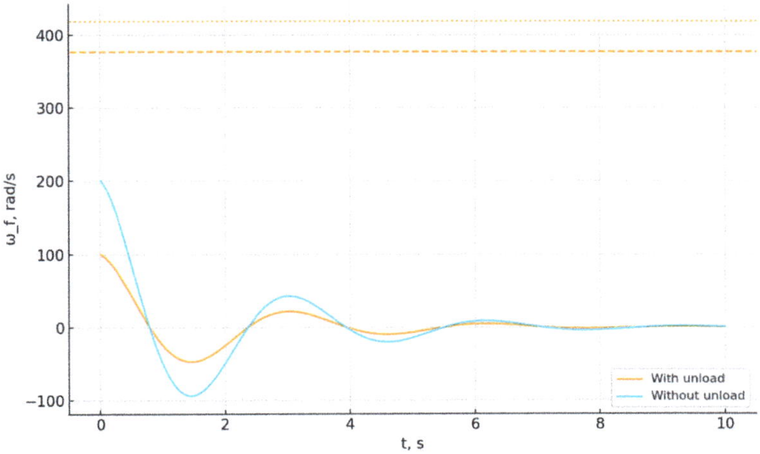

Figure 9. Flywheel speed with unloading, where the dotted curve shows saturation without unloading and the solid curve shows bounded operation.

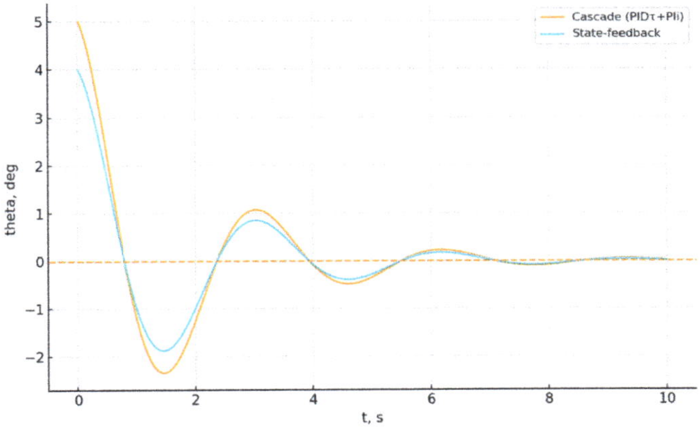

Figure 10. Cascade vs. state-feedback control, where the dotted curve corresponds to state-feedback and the solid curve represents cascade control.

The results showed that both algorithms ensure the system returns to equilibrium. At the same time, the cascade controller is characterized by smaller overshoot and a faster transition to the steady state, whereas state-feedback demonstrates smoother and softer dynamics. Thus, both methods are workable: the cascade controller is convenient in practical applications, while state-feedback is advisable in optimization tasks where a balance between smoothness and speed of the transient process is required.

Therefore, modeling in Python 3.12 confirmed the results of the analytical calculations. It has been shown that the flywheel stabilization system effectively suppresses both free oscillations of the platform and external disturbances of impulsive and constant nature. Filtering algorithms significantly improve measurement quality, while the unloading strategy prevents actuator overload under prolonged disturbances. The comparison of different controllers demonstrated that the cascade controller is simple to implement and provides sufficient efficiency, while state-feedback yields a smoother transient response. Thus, the modeling demonstrated the practical feasibility of the proposed control structure and its consistency with the analytical results.

 https://doi.org/10.3390/engproc2026122025

4. Conclusions

This work addressed the problem of automatic control of a flywheel actuator for the stabilization of a mobile platform. Based on the Lagrangian formulation, a mathematical model was derived to describe the mechanical and electrical dynamics of the system. Analytical estimates made it possible to determine the natural frequencies, damping ratio, and limiting operating modes of the actuator. Numerical experiments conducted in Python 3.12 demonstrated that the proposed control structure ensures system stability, compensates for both short-term and long-term disturbances, and enhances reliability through filtering and flywheel unloading. The comparison of analytical and simulation results confirmed the correctness of the developed model and control algorithms. The findings may be applied in the design of robotic and energy systems where position stabilization under external loads is required.

Author Contributions: Conceptualization, A.F., K.A. and T.I.; methodology, A.F. and T.I.; software, K.A.; validation, A.F., K.A., N.K. and Y.O.; formal analysis, A.F.; investigation, A.F., N.K. and Y.O.; resources, K.A. and N.K.; data curation, N.K.; writing—original draft preparation, A.F.; writing—review and editing, K.A., N.K., Y.O. and T.I.; visualization, A.F. and K.A.; supervision, K.A. and T.I.; project administration, K.A. All authors have read and agreed to the published version of the manuscript.

Funding: This research is funded under the program-targeted financing of scientific and (or) scientific and technical activities, Committee of Science of the Ministry of Science and Higher Education of the Republic of Kazakhstan (project BR27195331).

Institutional Review Board Statement: Not applicable.

Informed Consent Statement: Not applicable.

Data Availability Statement: The dataset is available from the authors upon request.

Conflicts of Interest: The authors declare no conflict of interest.

References

1. Montoya, O.D.; Gil-González, W.; Dominguez-Jimenez, J.A.; Molina-Cabrera, A.; Giral-Ramírez, D.A. Global Stabilization of a Reaction Wheel Pendulum: A Discrete-Inverse Optimal Formulation Approach via a Control Lyapunov Function. *Symmetry* **2020**, *12*, 1771. [CrossRef]
2. Zaborniak, D.; Patan, K.; Witczak, M. Design, Implementation, and Control of a Wheel-Based Inverted Pendulum. *Electronics* **2024**, *13*, 514. [CrossRef]
3. Huang, H.; Li, Z.; Guo, Z.; Guo, J.; Suo, L.; Wang, H. Prescribed Performance Adaptive Balance Control for Reaction Wheel-Based Inverted Pendulum-Type Cubli Rovers in Asteroid. *Aerospace* **2022**, *9*, 728. [CrossRef]
4. Kim, S.; Kim, Y. Spin-Axis Stabilization of a Rigid Spacecraft Using Two Reaction Wheels. *J. Guid. Control Dyn.* **2001**, *24*, 1046–1049. [CrossRef]
5. Song, J.; Guo, J.; Qin, C.; Zhao, W. The Design of a Reaction Flywheel Speed Control System Based on ADRC. *Automation* **2023**, *4*, 246–262. [CrossRef]
6. Fazylova, A.; Iliev, T.; Stoyanov, I.; Siemens, E. Height Control System for Wind Turbines Based on Critical Wind Speed Calculation. *Appl. Sci.* **2024**, *14*, 9802. [CrossRef]
7. Wang, C.; Ye, D.; Mu, Z.; Sun, Z.; Wu, S. Finite-Time Attitude Stabilization Adaptive Control for Spacecraft with Actuator Dynamics. *Sensors* **2019**, *19*, 5568. [CrossRef]
8. Posani, M.; Pontani, M.; Gasbarri, P. Nonlinear Slewing Control of a Large Flexible Spacecraft Using Reaction Wheels. *Aerospace* **2022**, *9*, 244. [CrossRef]
9. Fazylova, A.; Alipbayev, K.; Iliev, T.; Aden, A. Advanced Control Strategies for Wind Turbine Blade Pitch Optimization. In Proceedings of the 2024 5th IEEE International Conference on Communications, Information, Electronic and Energy Systems (CIEES), Veliko Tarnovo, Bulgaria, 20–22 November 2024; pp. 1–5.
10. Alipour Shahraki, M.; Lessard, L. Spacecraft Attitude Control Under Reaction Wheel Constraints Using Control Lyapunov and Control Barrier Functions. *arXiv* **2024**, arXiv:2409.19936. [CrossRef]
11. Tkachev, S.; Mashtakov, Y.; Ivanov, D.; Roldugin, D.; Ovchinnikov, M. Effect of Reaction Wheel Imbalances on Attitude and Stabilization Accuracy. *Aerospace* **2021**, *8*, 252. [CrossRef]

 https://doi.org/10.3390/engproc2026122025

12. Fazylova, A.; Malamatoudis, M.; Kogias, P. Optimization of the Blade Profile of a Vertical Axis Wind Turbine Based on Aerodynamic Analysis. *E3S Web Conf.* **2023**, *404*, 02002. [CrossRef]
13. Lee, C.-Y.; Yang, S.; Bokser, B.; Manchester, Z. Enhanced Balance for Legged Robots Using Reaction Wheels. In Proceedings of the 2023 IEEE International Conference on Robotics and Automation (ICRA), London, UK, 29 May–2 June 2023; pp. 9980–9987.

https://doi.org/10.3390/engproc2026122025

engineering proceedings

MDPI

Proceeding Paper

Predictive Load Balancing in Distributed Systems: A Comparative Study of Round Robin, Weighted Round Robin, and a Machine Learning Approach †

Elshan Rahimov and Tamerlan Aghayev *

Information Technology Department, Baku Higher Oil School, AZ1023 Baku, Azerbaijan; elshan.rahimov@bhos.edu.az

* Correspondence: tamarlan.aghayev.std@bhos.edu.az

† Presented at the 6th International Conference on Communications, Information, Electronic and Energy Systems, 26–28 November 2025, Ruse, Bulgaria.

Abstract

Load balancing is a widely adopted strategy in modern distributed systems because it distributes workloads across servers, mitigating overload and improving overall performance. However, the rapid growth of such systems has created a need for more adaptive strategies to ensure optimal utilization and responsiveness of resources. Traditional algorithms such as Round Robin (RR) and Weighted Round Robin (WRR) assign requests without considering server states or request characteristics. We implement a machine learning (ML)–based predictive load balancer, forecasting the latency of a request based on the request itself and container parameters, specifically the average latency of the last 50 requests and the count of active requests, and evaluate it against RR and WRR. For the experiment, synthetic data were generated to replicate real-world requests by creating random URL and method combinations, attaching a task size in Million Instructions (MI), and distributing them among three containers with varying resources according to the load balancing strategies described above. Under the conditions tested, the ML approach achieved the worst performance, trailing both RR and WRR in terms of throughput and average latency, although the model accuracy was sufficiently high ($R^2 = 0.8+$). Post hoc analysis indicates that limited and occasionally stale runtime features caused the load balancer to direct all requests to a single container until the next statistics update, since that container was considered the 'best' during that interval.

Keywords: load balancing; distributed systems; round robin; weighted round robin; machine learning

1. Introduction

The efficient distribution of requests across multiple servers is a paramount factor for system performance, reliability, and scalability in modern distributed systems. Since the demand for cloud-based services, web applications, and microservices increases, optimal utilization of resources with minimal latency has become significantly challenging. Load balancing is the fundamental method to tackle these challenges, which is the process of distributing incoming traffic among a set of servers [1]. Load balancing helps servers avoid overloading and improves overall performance.

Round Robin (RR), which is one of the conventional load balancing algorithms, introduces a simple algorithm by assigning requests to servers sequentially, ignoring their current workload or performance metrics [2]. RR is effective in homogeneous environments; however, it may not perform that well in heterogeneous or dynamically changing server conditions. For example, while more capable servers remain underused, servers with lower processing capacity can become bottlenecks, resulting in increased latency and decreased throughput [3].

Weighted Round Robin (WRR) differs from RR by assigning server-specific weights to servers to take into account differences in server capacities, distributing requests proportionally [4]. Despite better performance in heterogeneous environments, WRR is limited by its static nature and cannot dynamically adapt to real-time fluctuations in server load or varying traffic patterns [5]. Currently, there is an increasing demand for load balancing strategies that are both intelligent and adaptive, and capable of responding to dynamic system behavior.

Recent advances in machine learning (ML) give us possibilities for both predictive and adaptive load-balancing strategies. By analyzing historical traffic patterns and server performance metrics, ML models can theoretically predict the latency of a request if directed to each server, determine the one with the lowest latency, and direct the request to it, improving performance and reducing latency.

In this paper, we implement and evaluate a machine learning-based predictive load balancing approach alongside RR and WRR. It was expected to perform best since our approach determines the lowest expected latency based on request and container parameters.

The main contributions of this work are as follows:

- A comparative evaluation of Round Robin, Weighted Round Robin, and our predictive ML-based load balancing approach under heterogeneous workloads.
- An implementation and experimental setup that illustrates the practical challenges of applying machine learning in load balancing in containerized environments.
- An analysis of results.

2. Literature Review

Load balancing is one of the key strategies in distributed and cloud computing systems, contributing to more optimized resource utilization and a better user experience [6]. There are several studies on traditional load-balancing algorithms, such as round robin (RR) [7] and weighted round robin (WRR) [4]. X. Zhou [3] showed that RR performs poorly in heterogeneous environments, although RR offers simplicity and low computational overhead. Also, WRR does not adapt to real-time load fluctuations, although it improves when considering static server capacities [8]. These extensive comparative analyses illustrate that traditional static algorithms perform poorly under varying system loads, especially in microservices and hybrid cloud environments, due to limitations [9,10].

Nguyen and Nguyen [9] highlighted challenges in terms of scalability and fault tolerance, pointing out that existing WRR variants are often insufficient to handle rapid workload changes in real-world microservice architectures. Shafiq et al. [10] also observed a significant gap in adaptive efficiency metrics by categorizing various load-balancing strategies.

Recently, the integration of machine learning (ML) and deep learning into load-balancing algorithms has been explored as a potential way to overcome these limitations [11]. There are some studies comparing ML-based approaches with existing load balancing techniques. For example, ML-based approaches that predict server load and make intelligent allocation decisions using historical and live runtime data have shown improvements in throughput and latency compared to traditional methods [12,13]. Furthermore, reinforcement learning has been used to create adaptive and self-tuning load balancers, which dynamically optimize performance metrics [13]. In addition, to predict

 https://doi.org/10.3390/engproc2026122026

resource usage and distribute load in containerized and cloud-native environments, novel ML models such as graph neural networks (GNNs) have been applied [14].

The research gap is that existing ML-based load balancing approaches either rely on complex models (as shown in approaches above) or require fine-grained telemetry that may not be practical in real-world deployments [12]. That is, there are several challenges in implementing ML-based approaches despite the potential they offer. In practice, ML models may face issues such as prediction inaccuracies and outdated telemetry data. These limitations can outweigh the benefits of predictive scheduling, especially in systems with strict latency requirements or limited resources.

In light of this, our research performs an experimental evaluation of a predictive ML-based load-balancing strategy in a containerized environment and compares it with RR and WRR. The novelty of this paper is that we implemented a new and relatively simple ML-based approach and conducted an experiment to explore the effectiveness of the new technique and how these challenges affect overall performance.

3. Methodology

This section shows the experimental setup, workload generation, load balancing algorithms, machine learning model, training procedure, and evaluation methodology.

3.1. System Setup

The experimental environment was deployed on a local workstation using Docker containers with different computational resources.

- Container 1: 4 CPU cores, 12 GB memory
- Container 2: 3 CPU cores, 9 GB memory
- Container 3: 2 CPU cores, 6 GB memory

Each container runs a Go-based application designed to handle synthetic workloads. Workloads are defined by one parameter:

- Task size (MI): the number of million instructions executed by the CPU.

3.2. Workload Generation and Data Collection

A request generator script was implemented to create workloads. Request attributes include:

- HTTP method: randomly sampled from {GET, POST, PUT, DELETE, PATCH}.
- URL: dynamically composed from multiple resource segments (e.g., /users/orders /payments).
- Task size (MI): sampled from a log-normal distribution (250–750 MI) to simulate varying computational demands (in Figure 1).

Workload traffic was generated across a collection of 100 unique APIs, each designed to simulate different service endpoints in a real-world microservice environment. To ensure sufficient variability and robustness of the evaluation, every API was executed 200 times, resulting in a large number of independent request instances. Between successive requests, an artificial inter-arrival delay of 10 ms was introduced. This delay was carefully chosen: on one hand, it prevented the containers from being overwhelmed by a burst of simultaneous requests, while on the other hand it allowed the system's monitoring component (exposed through the/stats endpoint) to respond in near real time. As a result, the workload reflected a controlled but realistic flow of traffic with both diversity and temporal separation.

https://doi.org/10.3390/engproc2026122026

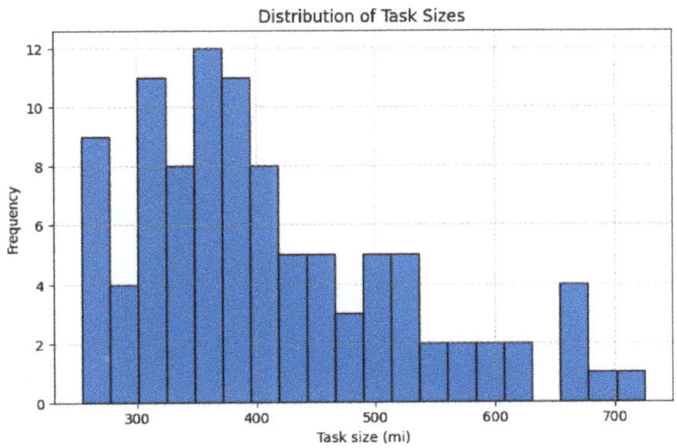

Figure 1. The distribution of task size.

For practical execution, a request generator was developed to automatically produce JSON-formatted input files. Each request definition captured essential attributes such as the HTTP method, target URL, and computational task size, thereby providing the simulator with sufficient information to mimic realistic service calls. These JSON inputs were then consumed by a request simulator, which issued the requests to the load balancer, recorded the corresponding responses, and persisted structured results including latency, status code, container assignment, and runtime metrics.


```
[
    {
        "method": "PUT",
        "url": "/connections/profiles",
        "mi": 250
    },
    {
        "method": "PUT",
        "url": "/events/settings/payments",
        "mi": 400
    }
]
```


The snippet below illustrates two representative synthetic requests generated during the experiments:

The simulator sent these requests to the load balancer, recorded responses, and stored structured results (latency, status code, assigned container, and runtime metrics) in CSV format. 40,000 labeled samples were collected: 20,000 under Round Robin (RR) scheduling and 20,000 under Weighted Round Robin (WRR).

3.3. Load Balancing Algorithms

Three load-balancing strategies were implemented:

1. Round Robin (RR): assigns requests sequentially across containers.
2. Weighted Round Robin (WRR): assigns requests proportionally to container weights.
3. Predictive Load Balancing (PLB): employs a machine learning model to predict expected latency per container and chooses the one with the lowest predicted latency.

https://doi.org/10.3390/engproc2026122026

3.3.1. Round Robin

```
procedure ROUNDROBIN(containers)
    rrindex ← (rrindex + 1) mod |containers|
    selected ← containers[rrindex]
    return selected
end procedure
```

3.3.2. Weighted Round Robin

```
procedure WEIGHTEDROUNDROBIN(containers)
    best ← NULL
    maxWeight ← −∞
    for each c in containers do
        c.curWeight ← c.curWeight + c.weight
        if c.curWeight > maxWeight then
            maxWeight ← c.curWeight
            best ← c
        end if
    end for

    total ← ∑(c.weight) for all c in containers
    best.curWeight ← best.curWeight − total
    return best
end procedure
```

3.3.3. Predictive

```
procedure PREDICTIVELB(containers, method, url, model)
    features ← [ ]          ▷ initialize empty feature list
    for each c in containers do
        f ← (method, url, c.cores, c.memory, c.active_requests, c.avg_latency)
        Append f to features
    end for
    predictions ← model.predict(features)
    bestIndex ← arg min(predictions)
    return containers[bestIndex]
end procedure
```

3.4. Machine Learning Model

The predictive load balancer uses CatBoost, a gradient boosting algorithm optimized for heterogeneous features. CatBoost was chosen based on Ileri's study [15], since it showed superior accuracy and stability over XGBoost, LightGBM, and Random Forest in similar predictive tasks.

3.5. Model Training and Hyperparameter Tuning

The target variable was the response latency (ms) of a request. Input features included:

- Request attributes: HTTP method, URL.
- Container resources: number of CPU cores, memory.
- Runtime statistics: active requests, average latency of last 50 requests.

https://doi.org/10.3390/engproc2026122026

Training was conducted on 20,000 labeled requests (collected under Round Robin to ensure each container receives an equal share of requests for more consistent learning). Optuna was used for Bayesian hyperparameter tuning to minimize RMSE. The final parameters selected are shown in Table 1.

Table 1. CatBoost Hyperparameters.

Parameter	Value
iterations	2250
learning_rate	0.23265
depth	9
l2_leaf_reg	5.9364
loss_function	RMSE
random_seed	42
verbose	200
eval_metric	RMSE
bagging_temperature	0.2211
task_type	GPU
early_stopping_rounds	100

On the validation data, the model achieved $R^2 = 0.84$; on test data, $R^2 = 0.81$. The prediction latency was on the order of microseconds, enabling real-time scheduling. The reason for selecting active requests and average latency instead of CPU and memory usages is that fetching CPU and memory statistics was significantly slower (a fetching interval of 500 ms using docker stats—stream, compared to 100 ms (for keeping frequency high while not overloading containers) + API latency using \texttt{/stats}; R^2 was 0.71 for validation and 0.60 for test data (hyperparameters are shown in Table 2), due to the delayed statistics when using CPU and memory usage for prediction, which is noticeably lower than the former approach).

Table 2. CatBoost Hyperparameters for model based on CPU and memory usage.

Parameter	Value
Iterations	2450
learning_rate	0.18231
depth	10
l2_leaf_reg	4.88559
loss_function	RMSE
random_seed	42
Verbose	200
eval_metric	RMSE
bagging_temperature	0.24547
task_type	GPU
early_stopping_rounds	100

3.6. Experiment Process

Each of the three strategies (RR, WRR, PLB) was evaluated. For each, the request simulator executed the same workload distribution with 200 repetitions to ensure robustness. The responses were recorded and the /stats API was queried every 100 ms to capture the state of the container throughout the experiments.

https://doi.org/10.3390/engproc2026122026

3.7. Evaluation Metrics

From the list of load-balancing efficiency parameters identified by Shafiq et al. [10], throughput and average latency were selected as the primary metrics due to their calculation feasibility.

- Throughput: number of requests processed per second.
- Average latency: mean response time across all requests.

These metrics allow for a fair comparison of both the efficiency and responsiveness of each strategy.

4. Results

We collected latency and throughput statistics from 20,000 requests executed under each approach to evaluate the effectiveness of the three load-balancing strategies. The same API requests were sent 200 times across all strategies.

The average latency and throughput for each strategy were calculated as:

$$Mean\ Latency = \frac{1}{N}\sum_{i=1}^{N} latency_i \quad (1)$$

$$Throughput = \frac{\sum_{i=1}^{N} task\_size\_MI_i}{\sum_{i=1}^{N} latency_i} \quad (2)$$

where:

- N = total number of requests,
- $latency_i$ = execution time of the i-th request,
- $task\_size\_MI_i$ = size of the i-th task in million instructions.

The visualizations below present the summarized results. Weighted Round Robin achieved the best overall performance, with the lowest mean latency (198.90 ms) and the highest throughput (2.07 MIPS) (see Table 3, Figures 2 and 3. Round Robin followed closely, with slightly higher latency (214.67 ms) and slightly lower throughput (1.92 MIPS). The predictive machine learning strategy, however, performed the worst, with the highest mean latency (249.63 ms) and the lowest throughput (1.65 MIPS).

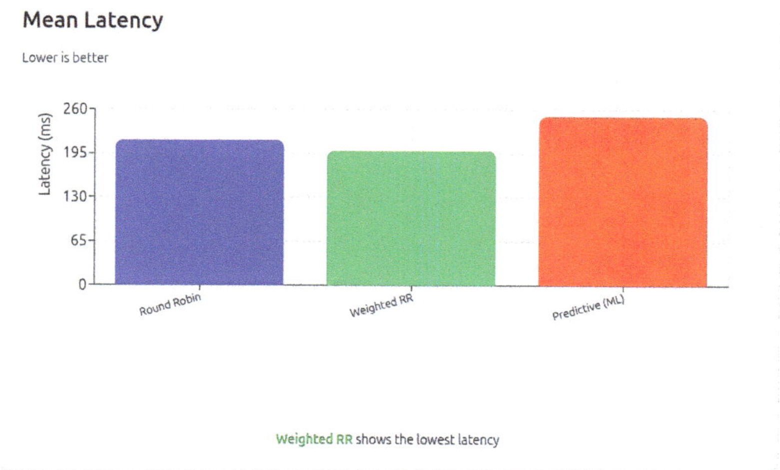

Figure 2. Mean latency for the strategies.

https://doi.org/10.3390/engproc2026122026

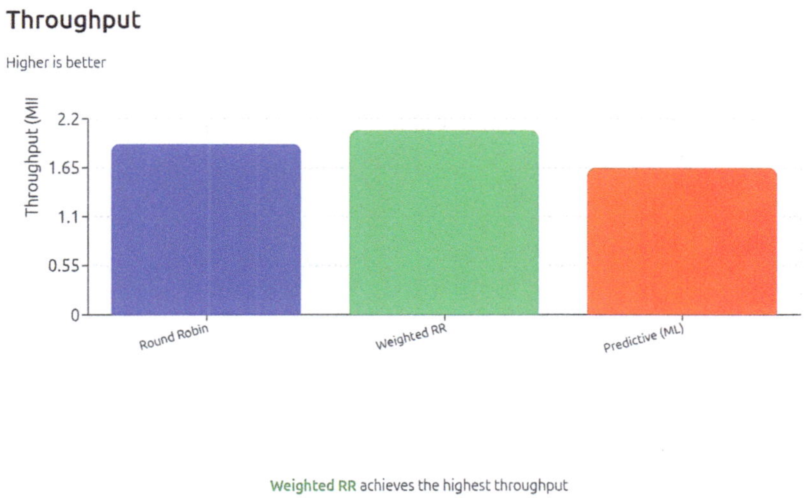

Figure 3. Mean throughput for the strategies.

Table 3. Statistics for the strategies.

Strategy	Latency (ms)	Throughput	Rank
Weighted RR	198.90	2.07	1
Round Robin	214.67	1.92	2
Predictive (ML)	249.63	1.65	3

There are several deviations from the expected selection of containers, since requests can influence the decisions; however, almost the same containers are chosen consistently over time.

The study provides valuable information on the challenges of integrating ML into load balancing and highlights the vital role of real-time server feedback.

5. Conclusions

This paper exhibits a comparative study of two traditional load-balancing algorithms, namely Round Robin and Weighted Round Robin, and a new ML-based predictive load balancing strategy. Although there were positive expectations, the predictive approach performed worse, leading to high latency and low throughput compared to the others. Weighted Round Robin got the best overall results, followed by Round Robin.

The poor performance of the predictive model can be explained by its reliance on periodically fetched container statistics. The ML model continued to route requests to the last determined 'best' container between update intervals. Due to that, all requests were sent to a single container, causing the container to be overloaded and causing lower performance. This issue negatively affected the overall performance, illustrating that prediction alone is not enough without more frequent updates to the container metrics.

Figure 4 illustrates how containers were selected by load balancing strategies.

Although this paper showed that the machine learning-based predictive strategy underperformed relative to Round Robin and Weighted Round Robin, several directions for future research could address the observed limitations.

https://doi.org/10.3390/engproc2026122026

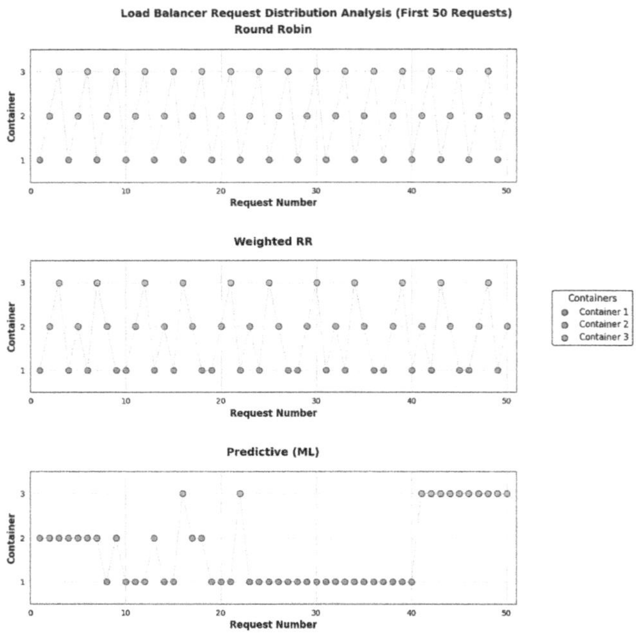

Figure 4. decisions made by the strategies.

First, up-to-date server statistics are paramount; as the predictive model relies on periodically updated metrics, more frequent or real-time monitoring could prevent overloading a single server and improve decision accuracy.

Second, to adapt continuously without waiting for full statistics refresh cycles, incremental or online updates can be implemented in the predictive model. For example, server statistics can be calculated manually or by leveraging ML approaches based on requests sent and the latest server metrics until the next update. This would decrease the demand for faster fetching of server metrics and reduce the probability of sending all requests to the same server during update intervals.

By addressing these areas, the efficiency of ML-based predictive load balancing algorithms can be further improved, making them more effective in terms of optimized resource utilization and overall performance.

Author Contributions: Conceptualization, E.R. and T.A.; methodology, E.R.; software, E.R. and T.A.; validation, E.R. and T.A.; formal analysis, E.R.; investigation, E.R. and T.A.; resources, E.R.; data curation, E.R. and T.A.; writing—original draft preparation, T.A.; writing—review and editing, E.R. All authors have read and agreed to the published version of the manuscript.

Funding: This research received no external funding.

Institutional Review Board Statement: Not applicable.

Informed Consent Statement: Not applicable.

Data Availability Statement: The data generated in this study are presented in the article. For any clarifications, please contact the corresponding author.

Conflicts of Interest: The authors declare no conflict of interest.

https://doi.org/10.3390/engproc2026122026

References

1. Cardellini, V.; Yu, P.S.; Colajanni, M. Dynamic Load Balancing on Web-Server Systems. *IEEE Internet Comput.* **1999**, *3*, 28–39. [CrossRef]
2. Balharith, T.; Alhaidari, F. Round Robin Scheduling Algorithm in CPU and Cloud Computing: A Review. In Proceedings of the 2019 2nd International Conference on Computing Applications and Information Security (ICCAIS), Riyadh, Saudi Arabia, 1–3 May 2019; pp. 1–7. [CrossRef]
3. Zhou, X.; Rathgeb, E.; Dreibholz, T. Improving the Load Balancing Performance of Reliable Server Pooling in Heterogeneous Capacity Environments. In *Lecture Notes in Computer Science, Proceedings of Sustainable Internet—Third Asian Internet Engineering Conference (AINTEC 2007), Phuket, Thailand, 27–29 November 2007*; Springer: Berlin/Heidelberg, Germany, 2007. [CrossRef]
4. Wang, W.; Casale, G. Evaluating Weighted Round Robin Load Balancing for Cloud Web Services. In Proceedings of the 2014 16th International Symposium on Symbolic and Numeric Algorithms for Scientific Computing (SYNASC), Timisoara, Romania, 22–25 September 2014; pp. 393–400. [CrossRef]
5. Devi, D.C.; Uthariaraj, V.R. Load Balancing in Cloud Computing Environment Using Improved Weighted Round Robin Algorithm for Nonpreemptive Dependent Tasks. *Sci. World* **2016**, *2016*, 896065. [CrossRef] [PubMed]
6. Shahakar, M.; Mahajan, S.A.; Patil, L. A Survey on Various Load Balancing Approaches in Distributed and Parallel Computing Environment. *Int. J. Intell. Syst. Appl. Eng.* **2023**, *11*, 187–196. Available online: https://ijisae.org/index.php/IJISAE/article/view/3511 (accessed on 10 January 2026).
7. Anusha, S.K.; Bindu Madhuri, N.R.; Nagamani, N.P. Load Balancing in Cloud Computing Using Round Robin Algorithm. *Int. J. Eng. Res. Technol. (IJERT)* **2014**, *2*, 124–127.
8. Sinha, G.; Sinha, D.K. Enhanced Weighted Round Robin Algorithm to Balance the Load for Effective Utilization of Resource in Cloud Environment. *EAI Endorsed Trans. Cloud Syst.* **2020**, *6*, e4. [CrossRef]
9. Mesbahi, M.; Rahmani, A.M. Load Balancing in Cloud Computing: A State of the Art Survey. *IJMECS* **2016**, *8*, 64–78. [CrossRef]
10. Afzal, S.; Kavitha, G. Load Balancing in Cloud Computing—A Hierarchical Taxonomical Classification. *J. Cloud Comput.* **2019**, *8*, 22. [CrossRef]
11. Alkhatib, A.A.A.; Alsabbagh, A.; Maraqa, R.; Alzubi, S. Load Balancing Techniques in Cloud Computing: Extensive Review. *ASTESJ* **2021**, *6*, 860–870. [CrossRef]
12. Chawla, K. Reinforcement Learning-Based Adaptive Load Balancing for Dynamic Cloud Environments. *arXiv* **2024**, arXiv:2409.04896.
13. Pattanaik, P.; Khan, M.Z.; Mansuri, M. Large Language Models and Reinforcement Learning for Efficient Load Balancing in Dynamic Cloud Environments. *J. Electr. Syst.* **2024**, *20*, 6553–6565.
14. Khan, A.R. Dynamic Load Balancing in Cloud Computing: Optimized RL-Based Clustering with Multi-Objective Optimized Task Scheduling. *Processes* **2024**, *12*, 519. [CrossRef]
15. Ileri, K. Comparative Analysis of CatBoost, LightGBM, XGBoost, RF, and DT Methods Optimized with PSO to Estimate the Number of k-Barriers for Intrusion Detection in Wireless Sensor Networks. *Int. J. Mach. Learn. Cybern.* **2025**, *16*, 6937–6956. [CrossRef]

https://doi.org/10.3390/engproc2026122026

engineering proceedings

MDPI

Proceeding Paper

Increasing Renewable Energy Penetration Using Energy Storage †

Alexandros Angeloudis, Angela Peraki, Yiannis Katsigiannis * and Emmanuel Karapidakis

Department of Electrical and Computer Engineering, Hellenic Mediterranean University, 71410 Heraklion, Greece; alexaggeloudis@gmail.com (A.A.); angelina.peraki@gmail.com (A.P.); karapidakis@hmu.gr (E.K.)
* Correspondence: katsigiannis@hmu.gr; Tel.: +30-2810-379-897
† Presented at the 6th International Conference on Communications, Information, Electronic and Energy Systems, Ruse, Bulgaria, 26–28 November 2025.

Abstract

Greenhouse gas emissions are a primary contributor to climate change and the observed rise in global temperatures. To reduce these emissions, renewable energy sources (RESs) must replace fossil fuels in power generation. Because of the mismatch between production and demand, the increase in RES is limited. To address this phenomenon, the addition of renewable energy generation should be accompanied by storage systems. In this paper, the island of Crete is examined for various renewable energy generations and storage capacities using the PowerWorld Simulator software. Four main scenarios are studied in which the installed renewable energy generation is increased to reach substation limits. For every scenario, different renewable energy generation mixes are considered between wind farms and photovoltaics. Furthermore, for all sub-scenarios, different storage capacities are considered, ranging from 1.6 GWh to 12.8 GWh. This study proves that storage systems are mandatory to increase renewable energy penetration. In certain scenarios, a battery energy storage system can further increase renewable energy penetration from 6.15% to 28.07%. Although the battery energy storage system enhanced renewable penetration, increasing transmission line capacities should also be considered regarding the scenario.

Keywords: energy storage systems; renewable energy sources; curtailment reduction; energy management in islands; optimal power flow; power system optimization

1. Introduction

Climate change is a global issue and a top priority for both the European Union and Greece. In order to reduce the impact of climate change, greenhouse gas (GHG) emissions must be minimized. Greece's Ministry of Environment and Energy have a long-term goal to decrease total emissions to about 13 Mt CO_2eq until 2050 [1]. According to recent data, in Greece, total GHG emissions were 70.6 Mt CO_2eq in 2023. More specifically, the power industry sector accounted for 20.68% of the total GHG emissions [2]. In the same year, fossil fuels contributed 42.97% of the total energy mix with 10.13% from lignite and 32.84% from natural gas [3]. It is also important to mention that by 2028 energy production from lignite would be discontinued. For the reasons outlined above, the increased use of renewable energy sources (RESs) is of utmost importance for electricity production. Due to stability issues and their intermittent nature, RES expansion is limited. To address this, RES growth should be accompanied by the installation of energy storage systems (ESSs).

One of the main challenges associated with RES is the mismatch in timing between renewable energy generation and energy demand. With regard to energy storage, the power system not only achieves greater stability and reliability but also enhances efficiency by saving potential wasted energy from RES. According to a study concerning the power system of Jeju Island, South Korea, covering the period from 2015 to 2019, with the addition of 50 MW battery energy storage system (BESS) to a power system with 580 MW installed RES capacity, it has been demonstrated that renewable energy curtailment was reduced by 15% [4]. Over the years, a variety of energy storage technologies have been developed, including lithium-ion batteries, hydrogen-based storage and pumped hydro storage.

Chemical batteries are the leading technology for grid-scale energy storage applications, with efficiency levels reaching 95% [5]. However, serious concerns have been raised regarding the environmental impacts at the end of their lifecycle [6]. Regarding green hydrogen, excess energy from RES is utilized to generate hydrogen via water electrolysis and then the produced hydrogen is stored under appropriate pressure and temperature conditions. Subsequently, using a fuel cell, the hydrogen is converted back to electricity [7]. Although it produces almost zero emissions, such a process is considerably less efficient than accumulating energy in a chemical battery. An additional energy storage technology is pumped hydro storage, in which surplus electricity is used to pump water into the hydropower reservoir, enabling the generation of electricity when needed, through hydroelectric power [8]. Regarding Greece's energy storage development, it is planned to have 1.5 GW of installed storage capacity by the end of 2030 mainly focused on pumped hydro storage according to International Energy Agency [9].

In this study, the island of Crete is examined due to its unique characteristics in the Greek power system. As a result of its location, Crete has significant wind and solar potential. However, despite these resources, RES deployment in Crete has still not reached its peak for reasons mentioned above. To address this, two interconnections with Greek mainland are being implemented. The first (small) interconnection connects Chania with the Peloponnese region; this interconnection is the deepest HVAC submarine line in the world and has a capacity of 2 × 200 MVA. The second (big) interconnection will connect Athens with Heraklion via an HVDC line with capacity of 2 × 500 MW. The small interconnection is currently being operated with a 150 MW limit, and the big interconnection is expected to be partially operated in the first months of 2026. Figure 1 shows these two interconnections, the high-voltage (HV) substations of the island (triangles with solid lines), as well as the planned new substations (triangles with dotted lines) [10].

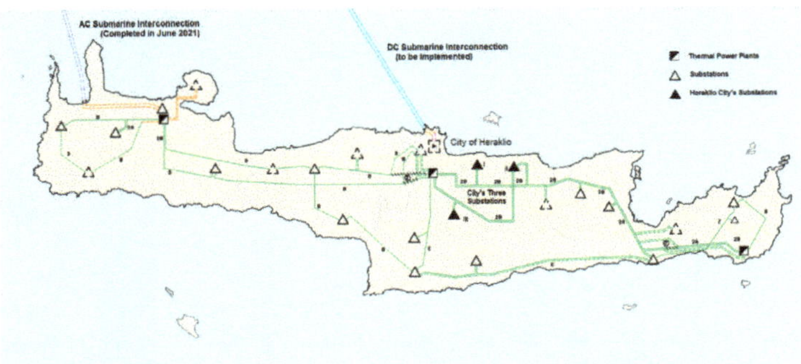

Figure 1. Crete's HV power system.

The main objective of this paper is to highlight the need for further integration of RES into the Greek power system in order to reduce GHG emissions. Equally important is demonstrating how and why ESSs are essential to achieving this goal. A key challenge lies in determining which RES technology photovoltaic or wind power should be prioritized and to what extent. By carrying out this analysis, the study identifies the most suitable

 https://doi.org/10.3390/engproc2026122027

combination of RES technologies and ESS characteristics for effective and sustainable integration into the power system.

In the following section, four main scenarios are evaluated using the PowerWorld Simulator's optimal power flow (OPF) algorithm for Crete's HV power system over a one-year period. More specifically, the scenarios assume that installed RES capacity accounts for 35%, 50%, 75%, and 100% of the substation's total power capacity, respectively. For each scenario, four sub-scenarios are evaluated: the first scenario reflects the current photovoltaic (PV) to wind turbine (WT) ratio; the second considers a 1:1 ratio; the third emphasizes PV capacity; and the fourth prioritizes WT capacity. For each sub-scenario, RES penetration is first assessed without battery storage. Battery storage is then introduced, and its capacity is progressively increased up to 12.8 GWh. Furthermore, several representative scenarios will be selected and simulated in the PowerWorld simulator (educational license, v.23, Champaign, IL, USA) using time step simulation, focusing on technical constraints and additional losses.

2. Methodology

2.1. Description of Cretan Power System

Before proceeding, it is important to clarify the concept of energy curtailment and the role of energy storage in reducing it. Figure 2 presents the load curve for a period between 22 March and 23 March 2023. This figure also illustrates the energy production from 200 MW PV parks and 600 MW wind farms (WFs) as well as the combined output from both RES. The PVs produce energy between 05:00 and 17:00, while wind energy exhibits a more irregular pattern. When RES generates less energy than the demand, all available RES output is fully utilized. However, when RES production exceeds demand, as observed during hours 4–13 and 29–37, the surplus energy must be curtailed. With the addition of ESS, when storage capacity is available, excess electricity is stored. Subsequently, during periods when the demand needs exceed RES production, the stored energy can be discharged to cover demand, thereby reducing the need for conventional generation and increasing RES penetration. It should be noted that technical limitations such as line and transformer capacities or system stability constraints are not considered, which could further influence curtailment levels. If these limitations were considered, ESS would further facilitate RES penetration.

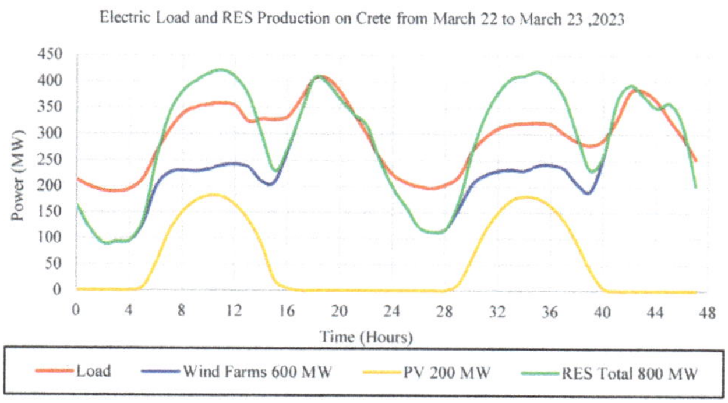

Figure 2. Electric load and production from both PV plants and WFs in Crete during 22 March to 23 March 2023.

https://doi.org/10.3390/engproc2026122027

As previously discussed in the Introduction, the electrical power system of Crete will be examined. The following tables and graphical representations provide important data regarding Crete's power system. In Figure 3, Crete's load duration curve is illustrated for the year 2023. The previous figure also depicts the duration curve of both WFs and PVs.

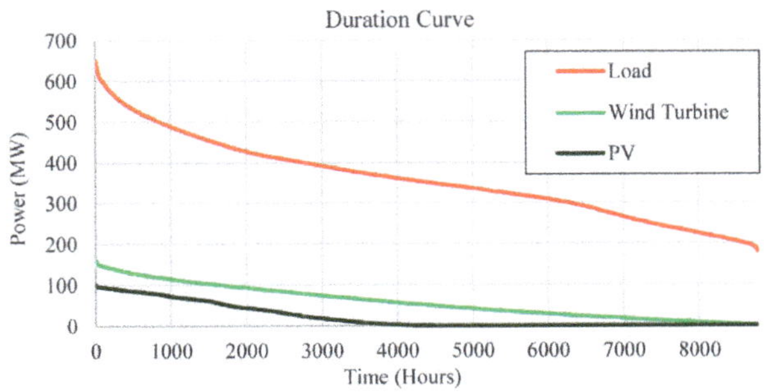

Figure 3. Crete's duration curve including wind and solar power production for 2023.

In Table 1, data for Crete's nineteen substations are presented. These data include the nominal power of high- or medium-voltage (MV) transformers, peak load, and the installed capacity for both PVs and WTs. In Table 2, data refer to Crete's seven power plants (PPs). It is important to mention that each PP is composed of smaller sub-power plants of the same technology but with lower nominal power. The total nominal power is calculated by adding the total nominal power of each sub-power plant. On the other hand, the technical minimum results from the sub-power plant with the least technical minimum power.

Table 1. Data per substation.

Substation	HV/MV Transformers (MVA)	Peak Load (MW)	WTs (MW)	PVs (MW)
Kastelli	2 × 25	24.55	18.24	4.52
Agya	2 × 50	60.29	10.80	4.30
Chania	3 × 50	96.79	-	9.66
Vrysses	2 × 25	18.18	-	2.24
Rethymno	2 × 25 + 3 × 50	65.8	4.80	18.58
Spili	2 × 25	15.11	16.80	-
Linoperamata	1 × 50	13.76	-	-
Ag. Varvara	1 × 50	13.62	14.15	-
Stalida	2 × 50	70.02	-	3.25
Iraklio 3	2 × 50	38.69	5.95	3.78
Iraklio 2	3 × 50	84.46	-	8.55
Iraklio 1	2 × 50	65.3	-	2.17
Moires	2 × 25	27.86	17.45	16.27
Pretoria	2 × 25	20.99	5.95	10.89
Ierapetra	2 × 25	24.78	-	8.04
Atherinolakos	1 × 50	0	-	-
Maronia	1 × 50	0	34.10	-
Siteia	2 × 25 + 1 × 50	18.95	56.77	9.82
Ag. Nikolaos	2 × 50	39.76	11.90	5.61
Total	1600	649.51 [1]	200.81	108.4

[1] The total peak load is Crete's island maximum demand, which is measured due to load diversity.

https://doi.org/10.3390/engproc2026122027

Table 2. Power plant data.

Power Plant	Total Nominal Power (MW)	Technical Minimum (MW)	Number of Sub-Power Plants
Diesel Atherinolakos	102	25	2
Steam turbine Atherinolakos	88	22	2
Steam turbine Linoperamata	106	4	6
Diesel Linoperamata	44	3	4
Gas Turbine Linoperamata	115	3	5
Combined Cycle Chania	132	35	1
Gas Turbine Chania	216	3	6

2.2. Considered Scenarios

As mentioned above, four main scenarios will be examined which are focused on the installed RES capacity. The capacity considered is 35%, 50%, 75%, and 100% of total substation installed power. As of 2025, the installed RES capacity is 19.25%. The rationale behind not exceeding installed power capacity of substations is to prevent energy from remaining unutilized energy due to transformer limitations. For each one of these four scenarios, four sub-scenarios are analyzed, examining the impact of the different mix between PV and WTs and taking into account the differences in their generation profile. The mixes that are considered in installed power between PVs and WTs are as follows: 50–50%, 20–80%, 80–20%, and 65–35% (which is the current mix). Furthermore, for each of the developed sub-scenarios, more cases are considered regarding the BESS installation. First, the system will be analyzed without a BESS. In all subsequent cases, a BESS with a power rating of 1.6 GW—equal to the total substations' capacity—will be considered. The BESS discharge duration will gradually increase from 1 h to 8 h, resulting in total battery capacities ranging from 1.6 GWh to 12.8 GWh, in increments of 1.6 GWh. It is also important to mention that the BESS that is assessed is a Li-ion battery with an efficiency of 95% [5].

In Figure 4, the amount of energy produced by RES is calculated at any given time. The RES generates sufficient energy to cover as much of the load as possible. In cases where surplus energy is available and the battery has remaining capacity, RES produces additional energy to fully charge the battery. The load does not represent the actual electrical demand of Crete, but a slightly lower value, as a small part of the load must be provided by conventional power plant due to stability reasons. The aforementioned load is calculated to be approximately 50 MW and is supplied by the Atherinolakos power station.

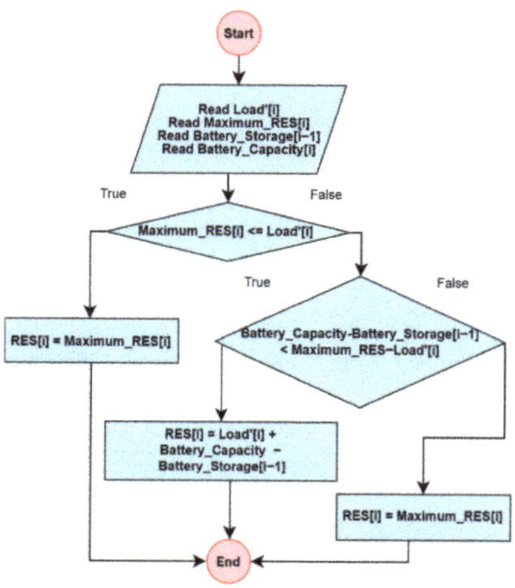

Figure 4. Utilization flowchart of renewable energy sources.

https://doi.org/10.3390/engproc2026122027

Figure 5 shows the computed battery energy level at each time step. Charging occurs whenever there is available storage capacity and when there is excess energy from the RES at the same time, whereas discharging takes place when PV is insufficient to satisfy the load demand.

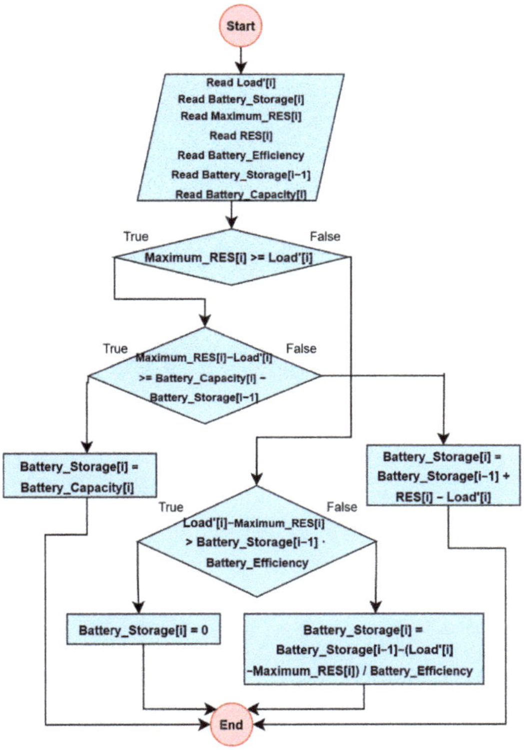

Figure 5. Battery storage flowchart.

In Figure 6, the battery losses are calculated, specifically the losses arising throughout charging and discharging. It is worth noting that the battery losses were modeled as the total discharging losses.

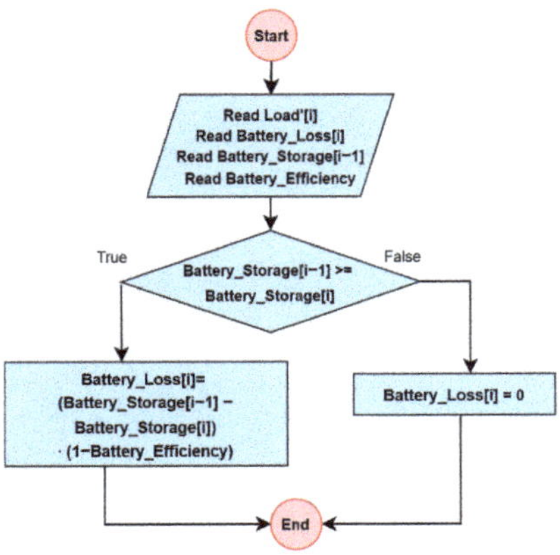

Figure 6. Battery loss flowchart.

https://doi.org/10.3390/engproc2026122027

Figure 7 illustrates how energy is drawn from the small interconnection to meet Crete's electrical demand. The small interconnection does not supply the entire remaining load on its own; instead, it operates in combination with local power plants. In this analysis, the load is assumed to be shared equally (50–50%) between the two sources. However, it should be noted that the current maximum transfer capacity of the small interconnection is 150 MW.

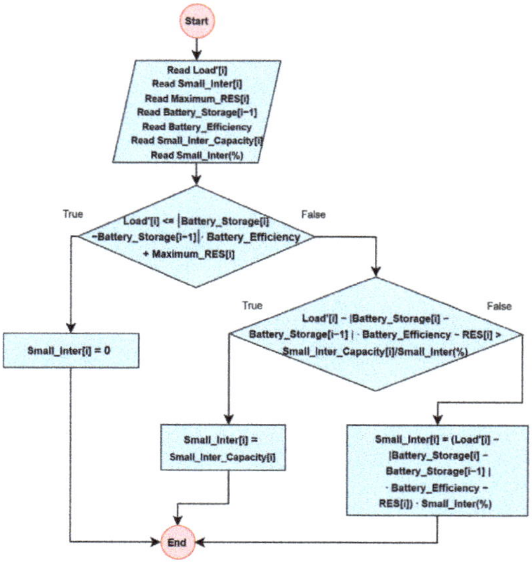

Figure 7. Small interconnection power generation flowchart.

Figure 8 presents the contribution of Crete's local power plants in fulfilling the electrical demand. The local power plants supply the remaining load after the initial utilization of the RES, followed by the batteries and finally the small interconnection. The total power of power plants is consistently sufficient to meet the demand; thus, monitoring generation limits is not required.

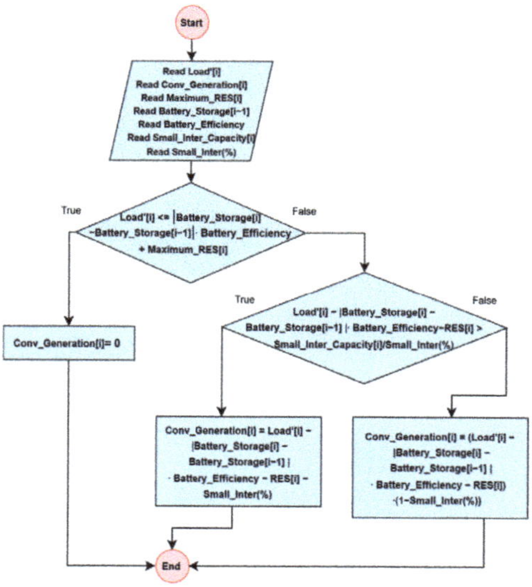

Figure 8. Conventional power plant power generation flowchart.

https://doi.org/10.3390/engproc2026122027

In Figure 9, the electrical energy curtailments are determined for conditions in which the RES output surpasses load demand as well as the available battery storage capacity.

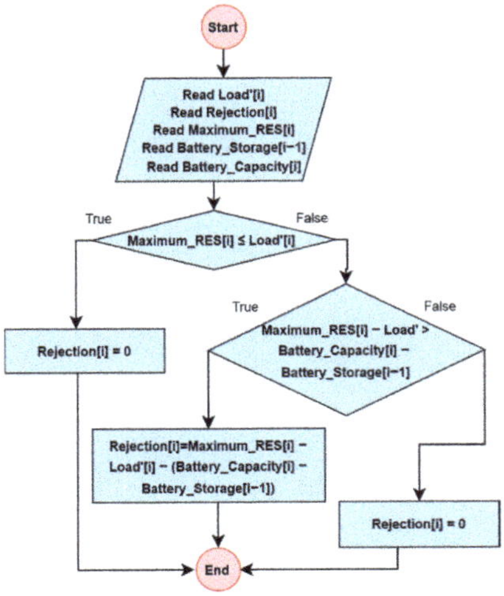

Figure 9. System rejection flowchart.

After completing the previous algorithms, the results from the selected scenarios will be used as inputs to the PowerWorld Simulator. PowerWorld simulator is a software tool specialized in modeling and analysis of power systems' operation. In this research, Crete's HV system will be modeled with the addition of BESS. Figure 10 presents the HV system of Crete Island, which contains the 19 buses described in Table 1, as well as the other small interconnection bus that is located in Peloponnese (top left corner). Furthermore, a yearly simulation will be implemented through PowerWorld simulator's time step simulation feature using the OPF algorithm in each iteration, which calculates the most cost-effective unit commitment under specific technical constraints (including power and voltage limits). By employing the PowerWorld simulator and OPF algorithm, the grid topology is considered, demonstrating a more realist approach since it accounts for fuel curves of PPs and the system's technical limitations such as line capacities.

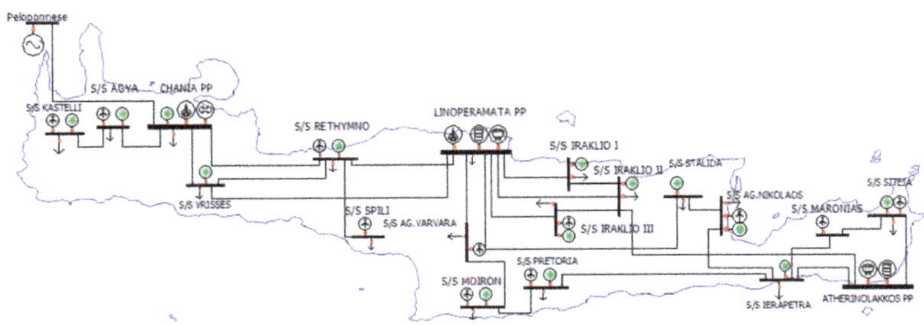

Figure 10. Crete's HV system modeled in the PowerWorld simulator.

The scenarios that will be implemented in the PowerWorld simulator will be based on different installed RES capacities with the optimal ESS. Moreover, the share between WFs and PV parks will be chosen based on which option maximizes RES penetration.

https://doi.org/10.3390/engproc2026122027

3. Results and Discussion

This section presents the results of the above scenarios. The following figures illustrate the RES penetration under different energy mix scenarios, the impact of BESS on curtailment reduction, the associated energy losses, and the loading of transmission lines. The first set of figures (Figures 11–14) presents the RES percentage on total electricity generation for various storage capacities and different RES combinations between PVs and WFs. It is worth mentioning that the first set of figures does not account for the renewable energy generation in northern Greece, which is supplied to Crete's power system via the small interconnection. The share of energy supplied through this interconnection ranges from 2% to 20% to Crete's total demand, depending on the scenario. Considering that approximately 40% of this imported energy is produced from RES [3], the total renewable energy contribution can be increased by a maximum of 16%, depending on scenario.

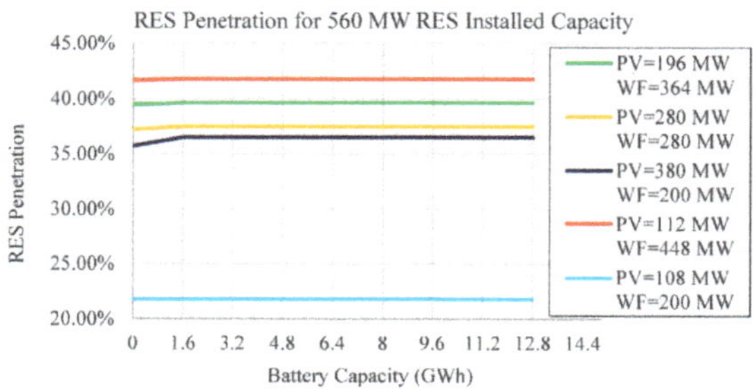

Figure 11. RES penetration for 560 MW installed RES capacity under different energy mix scenarios and storage capacities.

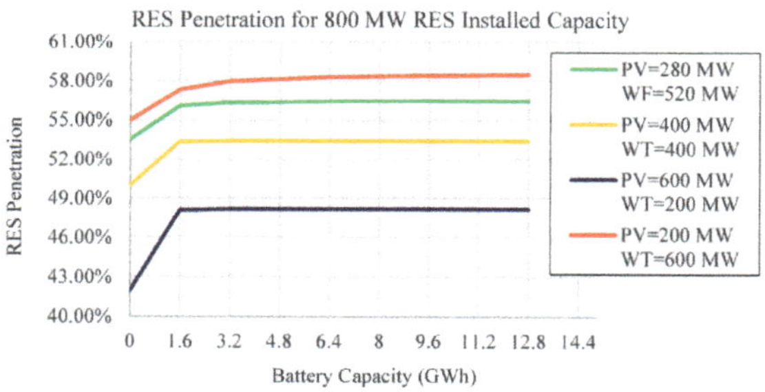

Figure 12. RES penetration for 800 MW installed RES capacity under different energy mix scenarios and storage capacities.

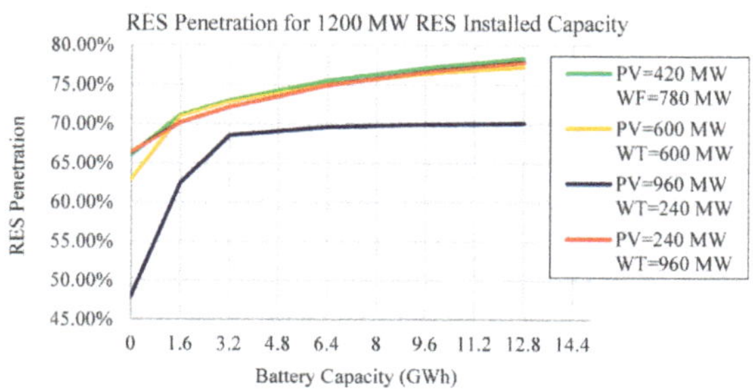

Figure 13. RES penetration for 1200 MW installed RES capacity under different energy mix scenarios and storage capacities.

 https://doi.org/10.3390/engproc2026122027

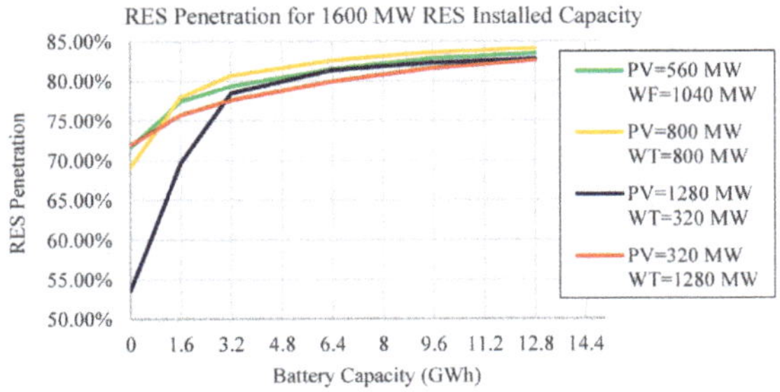

Figure 14. RES penetration for 1600 MW installed RES capacity under different energy mix scenarios and storage capacities.

In Figure 11, the first scenario is presented. In this scenario, the impact of energy storage is minimal since the energy produced from RES is almost always lower than the energy demand. The energy mix that focuses on WFs (red line) has an overall better penetration which can be attributed to its power generation curves, as previously illustrated in Figure 2. Additionally, in Figure 11, the current energy penetration from RES is also depicted (light blue line).

In Figure 12, the second scenario is presented, which illustrates the impact of BESS in RES penetration. An ESS with a capacity of 1.6 GWh can reduce energy rejections and further increase the RES penetration by 6% in the sub-scenario that emphasizes generation via PV (blue line). Moreover, increasing the BESS capacity beyond this point yields only marginal improvements in RES penetration and is therefore not economically justified when considering the associated installation, operation, and maintenance costs. It is also important to note that, as in the previous scenario, the sub-scenario that focuses on wind energy (red line) rather than solar energy (blue line) can increase RES penetration by 13% for reasons that were mentioned in Scenario 1.

Figure 13 presents the results for Scenario 3. There are two key differences between Scenarios 2 and 3. First, a 6.4 GWh BESS is identified as optimal due to the higher levels of energy curtailment. Second, in this scenario, a wind-dominated energy mix is no longer clearly the most effective configuration. All the sub-scenarios have comparable RES penetration levels when BESSs are included, except for the sub-scenario that focuses on PV (blue line) which shows significantly lower penetration than the rest of sub-scenarios. This suggests that, in order to increase RES penetration in Crete's energy mix, the installation of RES technologies should primarily focus on WFs, followed by additional PV capacity expansion.

In Figure 14, the final scenario is depicted. In this scenario, the RES penetration converges to approximately 82%, regardless of the sub-scenario. The optimal storage capacity ranges between 6.4 GWh and 9.6 GWh. The BESS installation has more impact on the sub-scenario that focuses on solar energy (blue line), leading to a further 28.07% increase in RES penetration. It is important to note that RES penetration cannot exceed approximately 85% due to system stability reasons and the requirement for reactive power, which is primarily provided by synchronous generators such as conventional units. WFs and PV systems cannot supply sufficient inertia and are almost incapable of generating reactive power.

Furthermore, to better understand the effect of storage capacity on renewable energy utilization, Figure 15 presents the curtailed energy of Scenario 3. In this figure, the impact of BESS in reducing energy curtailment can be observed, as a 9.6 GWh BESS has the potential to store and utilize up to 700 GWh of energy that would otherwise be dissipated.

 https://doi.org/10.3390/engproc2026122027

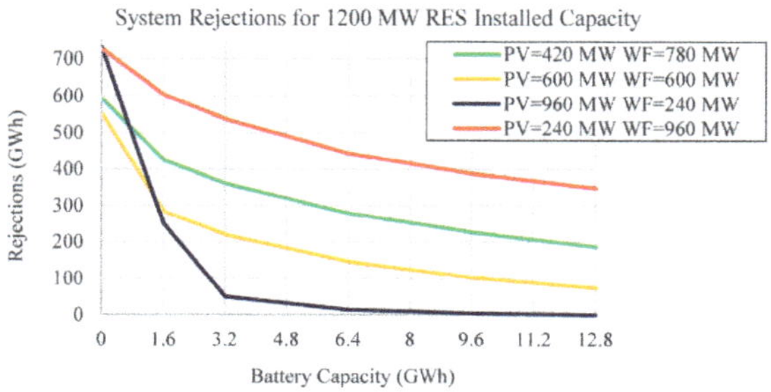

Figure 15. System rejections for 1200 MW RES installed capacity.

In the following figures, energy losses and transmission constraints will be depicted based on six specific cases. Two cases were implemented for each of Scenario 1, Scenario 2, and Scenario 3. The first case of each scenario does not include a BESS, while the second incorporates a BESS with optimal capacity. The corresponding optimal capacities were 1.6 GWh, 3.2 GWh, and 6.4 GWh for Scenarios 1, 2, and 3, respectively, as determined from results presented in Figures 11–13. In all cases, the generation mix emphasizes wind power, reflecting the higher penetration of RES.

Figure 16 presents the system loss results obtained from the PowerWorld simulator. In all simulation cases, the addition of a BESS reduced transmission losses, as expected [11]. However, despite the decrease in transmission losses, the total system losses increased due to higher utilization of the storage system.

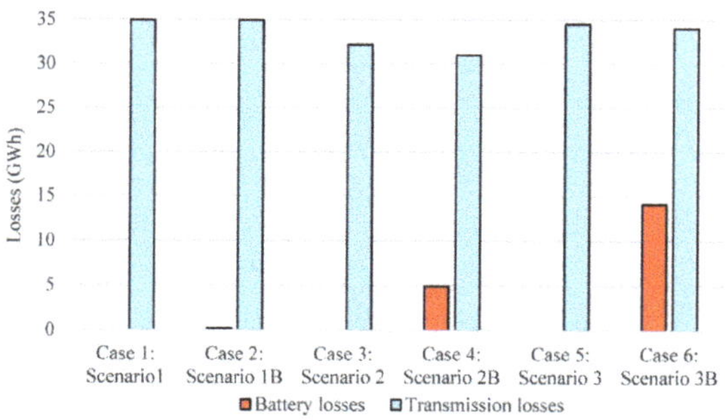

Figure 16. System losses for the selected scenarios.

After analyzing the system losses under different cases, the next step focuses on the loading of transmission lines, as illustrated in Table 3. The line loading for each case was calculated via PowerWorld's time step simulation analysis. The table represents the number of instances where the line exceeds specific thresholds, such as 80% and 90% of their rated capacity. When a line loading exceeds 80% of its capacity, there is an increased risk for faults; more specifically, the lines can sag and potentially short-circuit with adjacent lines [12]. In Table 3, it is also calculated when the line limits exceed 100%. In the PowerWorld simulation environment, it is possible to analyze instances where the line loading surpasses 100% without immediately considering it as a fault. This approach helps identify situations where a line may require an increase in capacity in future system planning.

https://doi.org/10.3390/engproc2026122027

Table 3. Line capacities.

Case	Instances of Line Loadings Between 80–90%	Instances of Line Loadings Between 90–100%	Instances of Line Loadings over 100%
Case 1: Scenario 1	16	0	0
Case 2: Scenario 1 BESS	16	0	0
Case 3: Scenario 2	13	0	0
Case 4: Scenario 2 BESS	34	0	0
Case 5: Scenario 3	8	0	0
Case 6: Scenario 3 BESS	240	86	48

In Table 3, it can be observed that increasing RES installations without a BESS reduces the number of instances in which line loading exceeds 80%. However, when a BESS is included, these instances increase, as the power flow is altered to store excess RES energy in other buses. In Case 6, this increase is particularly pronounced. This behavior was expected because the energy produced by RES is abundant, and the power system must accommodate it. Moreover, the system is primarily designed to transfer energy from conventional power plants to the loads, rather than from RES generation dispersed across the island.

In Figure 17, a screenshot from PowerWorld simulation is represented in August 2023 at 13:00. In this figure, the lines connecting Moires–Ag. Varavara–Linoperamata, and Siteia–Atherinolakos–Iraklio II are the ones that are overloaded. These lines are the ones that become overloaded in the simulation, due to the abundant RES generation in Siteia, Moires, and Ag. Varvara. More precisely, RES generation exceeds both consumption and local BESS capacities, which results in excess energy directed towards the city of Heraklion (capital of Crete), covering the large loads and charging the local batteries to mitigate feature instabilities. In other words, the excess energy is transmitted through certain lines that do not have adequate capacity, leading to their overloading.

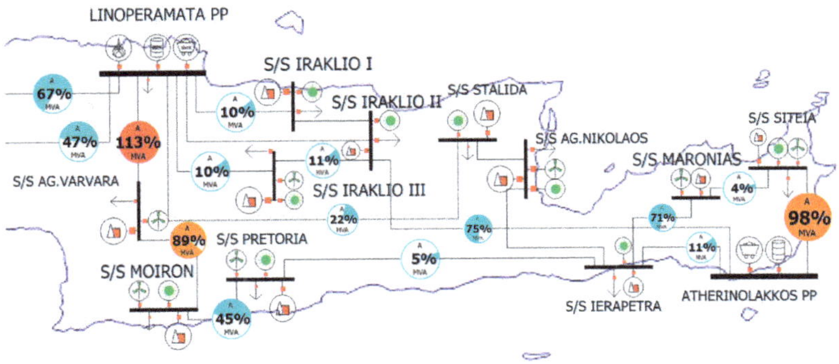

Figure 17. Screenshot showing power flow from the PowerWorld simulation for Case 6, recorded on August 2023, at 13:00.

4. Conclusions

The increase in renewable energy generation is mandatory to fight climate change. Energy storage systems should accompany this increase with optimized capacities. In this research, the island of Crete was examined via the PowerWorld simulator. Different cases were constructed for different RES power generation, for various renewable generation

https://doi.org/10.3390/engproc2026122027

mixes and different storage capacities. These cases proved that the increase in RES generation minimizes the need for conventional generation up to 28%, thus reducing GHG emissions. Moreover, it has been proven that the growth of RES should be complemented by energy storage systems. Their optimal capacities, which depend on the level of RES penetration, range from 1.6 GWh to 6.4 GWh per HV substation. Furthermore, Crete's power system should prioritize wind energy, followed by solar energy. Additionally, the capacities of specific transmission lines must be carefully considered to accommodate the anticipated growth in renewable energy generation. Future research could also include the big interconnection in Crete's power system and consider exporting energy to mainland Greece through both interconnections. Another aspect that could be examined is the effect of different RES technologies, such as green hydrogen, for both generation and energy storage.

Author Contributions: Conceptualization, E.K. and Y.K.; methodology, E.K.; software, E.K. and Y.K.; validation, A.A. and A.P.; formal analysis, A.A. and A.P.; investigation, A.A. and A.P.; resources, E.K. and Y.K.; data curation, E.K. and Y.K.; writing—original draft preparation, A.A. and A.P.; writing—review and editing, Y.K.; visualization, A.A., A.P. and Y.K.; supervision, E.K.; project administration, E.K.; funding acquisition, E.K. All authors have read and agreed to the published version of the manuscript.

Funding: This research project was supported by the European Union's Lump Sum MGA under grant agreement No. 101144027 (SEBCoVE Project).

Institutional Review Board Statement: Not applicable.

Informed Consent Statement: Not applicable.

Data Availability Statement: The original contributions presented in this study are included in the article. Further inquiries can be directed to the corresponding author.

Conflicts of Interest: The authors declare no conflicts of interest.

Abbreviations

The following abbreviations are used in this manuscript:

RES	Renewable energy sources
GHG	Greenhouse gases
ESS	Energy storage system
BESS	Battery energy storage system
HV	High voltage
OPF	Optimal power flow
PV	Photovoltaic
WF	Wind farm
WT	Wind turbine
MV	Medium voltage
PP	Power plant

References

1. Ministry of the Environment and Energy. *National Long-Term Strategy (LTS)—Report 2020*; Ministry of the Environment and Energy: Athens, Greece, 2020.
2. Crippa, M.; Guizzardi, D.; Pagani, F.; Banja, M.; Muntean, M.; Schaaf, E.; Quadrelli, R.; Risquez Martin, A.; Taghavi-Moharamli, P.; Köykkä, J.; et al. *GHG Emissions of All World Countries—2025 Report*; Publications Office of the European Union: Luxembourg, 2025; p. JRC143227.
3. IPTO. Yearly Press Release 2023. Available online: https://www.admie.gr/sites/default/files/news/attached-files/2024/01/YEARLY_PRESS%20RELEASE_2023.pdf (accessed on 27 September 2025).

https://doi.org/10.3390/engproc2026122027

4. Lee, C.; Im, S.; Jung, J.; Lee, B. BESS Deployment Strategy in Jeju Carbon-Free Islands for Reducing Renewable Energy Curtailment. *Energies* **2020**, *13*, 6082. [CrossRef]
5. Mahadevan, V.; Raja, S.S.; Rusho, M.A.; Yishak, S. Critical review of energy storage systems: A comparative assessment of mechanisms, advantages, challenges, and integration with renewable energy. *Results Eng.* **2025**, *26*, 105589. [CrossRef]
6. Hasan, M.M.; Haque, R.; Jahirul, M.I.; Rasul, M.G.; Fattah, I.M.R.; Hassan, N.M.S.; Mofijur, M. Advancing energy storage: The future trajectory of lithium-ion battery technologies. *J. Energy Storage* **2025**, *120*, 116511. [CrossRef]
7. Kourougianni, F.; Arsalis, A.; Olympios, A.; Yiasoumas, G. A comprehensive review of green hydrogen energy systems (GHES). *Renew. Energy* **2024**, *231*, 120911.
8. Rehman, S.; Al-Hadhrami, L.M.; Alam, M.M. Pumped hydro energy storage system: A technological review. *Renew. Sustain. Energy Rev.* **2015**, *44*, 586–598. [CrossRef]
9. International Energy Agency (IEA). *Greece 2023: Energy Policy Review*; IEA: Paris, France, 2023. Available online: https://www.iea.org/reports/greece-2023 (accessed on 29 September 2025).
10. Karapidakis, E.; Tsikalakis, A.; Paspatis, A.; Fotakis, E.; Stavrakakis, G.; Chatzipoulka, C.; Zervas, P. Grid Operation Assessment under a Specific EV Chargers Deployment Plan in the City of Heraklion. *Electronics* **2021**, *10*, 2831. [CrossRef]
11. Alzahrani, A.; Alharthi, H.; Khalid, M. Minimization of power losses through optimal battery placement in a distributed network with high penetration of photovoltaics. *Energies* **2019**, *13*, 140. [CrossRef]
12. International Energy Agency (IEA). *Learning from the Blackouts: Transmission System Security in Competitive Electricity Markets*; OECD Publishing: Paris, France, 2005.

https://doi.org/10.3390/engproc2026122027

engineering proceedings

MDPI

Proceeding Paper

Comparative SQP-GA-PSO Algorithms for Hierarchical Multi-Objective Optimization Design of Induction Motors †

Hung Vu Xuan

High Performance Electrical Machines Lab HiPEMs, Department of Electrical Engineering, School of Electrical and Electronic Engineering, Hanoi University of Science and Technology, Hanoi City 100000, Vietnam; hung.vuxuan@hust.edu.vn

† Presented at the 6th International Conference on Communications, Information, Electronic and Energy Systems, Ruse, Bulgaria, 26–28 November 2025.

Abstract

This paper presents the optimal design for a 30 kW, 3-phase squirrel-cage induction motor (IM). In this paper, three optimization algorithms are used for design optimization, namely, Particle Swarm Optimization Algorithm (PSO), genetic algorithm (GA), and Sequential Quadratic Programming (SQP). The optimal goals are maximum starting torque, efficiency, and minimum material cost. The result of the IM design optimization using three optimal methods is announced and compared. Additionally, computation time and the number of iterations of each algorithm are compared to find out the most suitable algorithm for the optimal design of an induction motor. In addition, this paper proposes a solution that permits us to find only one solution satisfying all the optimal criteria. Instead of using the conventional multi-objective optimization method that normally leads to a Pareto set with many optimal points at the same optimal level, we propose a hierarchical optimization method that experiences some mono-objective optimization and then builds a function representing the multi-objective optimization. Using this method, having a global optimal point can be obtained. Comparison of the optimal algorithms and multi-objective optimization methods has given broadened insight into optimal techniques for IMs. We have found that PSO is the best method for optimization design of IMs in terms of computation time and finding the global optimal point.

Keywords: genetic algorithm; particle swarm optimization; sequential quadratic programming; asynchronous motor; optimal design; multi-objective; weighted function; Pareto set; minmax

1. Introduction

Asynchronous motors or induction motors have always been an indispensable part of industrial applications due to their durability, low maintenance, long life, and low cost compared to other motors. It impacts many different industries. Therefore, the optimal design of 3-phase asynchronous motors has attracted great interest. In some applications such as electric vehicles, crushers, and wind turbine yaw drive [1,2], motors must provide large starting and maximum torque to be able to operate well under high load from the start. Therefore, the demand for motors with large starting and maximum torques, while maintaining high efficiency in long-term operation, is very high [3,4].

This paper focuses on the design optimization of induction motors using both single-objective and multi-objective optimization to improve efficiency and starting torque while reducing material cost. According to the conventional optimal design theory for multi-objective optimization, the optimal design result does not converge to a point but leads to a Pareto optimal set, which shows the relationships between the objective functions, with many points satisfying the problem. For a bi-objective optimal problem, it can present the relationship between the first optimal objective f_1^* and the second optimal objective f_2^* in a 2D coordinate system, forming the so-called Pareto optimal set, as shown in Figure 1. In order to find the Pareto optimal set of a bi-objective optimal problem, the traditional method converts the second objective into an equal or inequal constraint, then the Pareto frontier can be found, as illustrated in Figure 1; this is known as the ε-constraint method [5,6]. In addition, for a multi-objective optimal problem with three objectives or higher, it is hard to be intuitive or visualized. This is ambiguous to the designer. Therefore, hierarchical optimization is often used for multi-objective optimal problems [7,8].

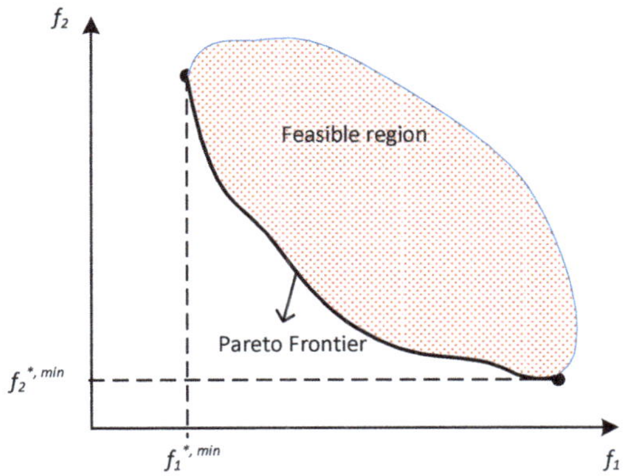

Figure 1. Illustration of the Pareto optimal set for a traditional bi-objective optimal problem, Pareto frontier might be determined using the ε-constraint method, feasible region is defined as a set of all possible solutions that satisfy a problem's constraints.

In this study, a method is proposed based on hierarchical optimization and weight factors, which allows us to convert from multi-objectives with some objective functions into multi-objectives with a single-objective function that permits the optimal problem to be convergent to one optimal point only. In hierarchical optimization, an optimization problem is divided into several levels, and each level is optimized independently. The first level of hierarchical optimization is optimization problems with a single objective such as maximum efficiency, minimum cost, or maximum starting torque. The second level of hierarchical optimization is multi-objective optimization using an objective function only, implemented by modifying weight factor method and converting the optimal problem into the form of sequential quadratic problem. Our proposed method is especially suitable for complex multi-objective problems with a number of objectives equal to or higher than 3. In this paper, tracking of optimizing process is visualized to ensure that the optimal design result is reliable. Performances of motor before and after optimizing are compared.

In this study, there are three algorithms used for optimization design or gradient-based algorithms of specific types, namely Sequential Quadratic Programming (SQP), genetic algorithm (GA), and Particle Swarm Optimization (PSO). The SQP is a conventional optimal method to solve a series of quadratic programming subproblems, while the last two are the most popularly used evolutionary algorithms up to now. We have found that PSO is the most suitable for the optimal design of the motors because it runs quicker than GA, does not need an initial value as the SQP method, and can find global optimization. Meanwhile,

https://doi.org/10.3390/engproc2026122028

the conventional SQP method can find a local optimization only and get stuck in local minima, and the performance of SQP method depends on the starting point [8–12].

This paper is organized as follows. Firstly, the optimal algorithms are discussed and illustrated. Next, a method of hierarchical multi-objective optimization is proposed. Then, a 30kW induction motor is optimized using SQP, GA, and PSO algorithms. The algorithms are compared together to find the most suitable algorithm for the optimal design of IMs. Finally, the conclusion is given.

2. Explanation of Optimal Problem Solved in Matlab

In this section, the three algorithms, namely SQP, GA, and PSO, are used to solve a single-objective optimal problem. The comparison of algorithms on computation time and number of iterations is given to help explanation of algorithms operation.

In order to make it easy when comparing algorithms, we start with an example described as follows. Given an objective function as

$$f = 3 \cdot (1-x)^2 \cdot e^{-x^2-(y+1)^2} - 10 \cdot \left(\frac{x}{5} - x^3 - y^5\right) \cdot e^{-x^2-y^2} - \frac{1}{3} \cdot e^{-(x+1)^2-y^2} \tag{1}$$

with two variables considered in the interval denoted as $x \in (-4; 3)$ and $y \in (-5; 4)$. Conditions and constraints described as equations or inequalities are coded in Matlab-R2018b under name 'circlecon' function. If the problem does not have a nonlinear condition, then let it be empty in the definition of constraints.

The constraint for variables and the objective function are described in Matlab as the following form:

$$\begin{gathered} \text{Minimizing single objective function f(x): f(x)} \rightarrow \text{min, x} \in \text{R}^{\text{n}}\text{, f} \in \text{R} \\ \text{with variable vector x = (x}_1\text{, x}_2\text{, x}_3\text{, \ldots, x}_\text{n}\text{)} \\ \text{subject to:} \\ c(x) < 0 \\ c_{eq}(x) = 0 \\ A.x < b \\ A_{eq}.x = b_{eq} \\ l_b < x < u_b \end{gathered} \tag{2}$$

where

- c and c_{eq} are, respectively, equal and unequal vector constraints;

- A and A_{eq} are constant matrices; b and b_{eq} are constant vectors; and l_b and u_b are the lower and upper bounds of the input variables;

- x_0 is an initial point.

Code commands in Matlab solve the optimal problem as follows:

```
f = @(x) 3*(1-x(1))^2*exp(-(x(1)^2)-(x(2)+1)^2) - 10*(x(1)/5 - x(1)^3 -
x(2)^5)*exp(-(x(1)^2)-(x(2)^2)) - 1/3*exp(-(x(1)+1)^2-x(2)^2);% objective
function.
nvars=2; % number of variable.
lb = [-4 -5]; %lower boundary vector.
ub = [3 4]; %upper boundary vector.
options = optimoptions('fmincon','Display','iter','Algorithm','active-set');
[x,fval,exitflag,output,lambda,grad,hessian] =
fmincon('fun',x0,A,b,Aeq,beq,lb,ub,'circlecon',options);% a solver function
    in Matlab.
```


https://doi.org/10.3390/engproc2026122028

In the above code, 'options' is used to define the algorithm and guide operation. Each algorithm uses an option to explain in greater detail as follows:

- 'namefuntion': must be replaced by built-in function in Matlab: fmincon/ga/particleswarm;

- At the place of unused parameters, we just need to replace the empty sign [ ];

– 'fun' here is the objective function to be minimized.

The output parameters of the algorithm are as follows:

– 'x': The output value of the variable vector x that minimizes the objective function;

– 'fval': The value that minimizes the objective function;

– 'exitflag': it indicates the convergence of the algorithm:

+ exitflag < 0: it shows that the problem is not convergent and not reliable;

+ exitflag > 0 it means the algorithm converges and can be trusted;

+ exitflag = 0, it means that the number of iterations of the algorithm has reached the maximum value, so the problem is stopped and the results are not trustworthy.

Table 1 shows the terms used to compare SQP, PSO, and GA algorithms, while Table 2 compares computation time of each algorithm for finding the minimum point of problem (1). Further explanations will be explained in the following Subsections.

Table 1. Terms used in algorithms.

	SQP with Fmincon	PSO	GA
Name of objective function	Objective function	Objective function, fitness function, or cost function	Fitness function
Name of constraints	Constraints	Constraints	Constraints
Name of input variables or candidate solutions	Input variables	Particles or seeds	Individuals
Set of variables	Variables set	Swarms	Populations
Initialization	Initial point	Random initial particles	Random initial populations
Candidate solution properties	Value of space derivatives	Position, velocity	Chromosomes, genotypes, phenotypes, or genomes.
Name of the iteration	Iteration	Loop or iteration	Generation
Operators	Gradient	Inertia weight, cognitive and social coefficients, random values	Selection (the fittest), crossover (recombination, reproduce), mutation (random selection, metaheuristic, stochastic, nature-inspired)
Replacement	The next point	New swarms, herds	The next generation
Termination	Reaching maximum number of iterations and function evaluations or met stopping criteria such as relative and absolute tolerances of objective function, convergence rate, as well as maximum amount of time.	Reaching maximum number of iterations, or met stopping criteria such as convergence rate and maximum amount of time.	Reaching maximum number of generations, or met stopping criteria such as fitness value, convergence rate, and maximum amount of time.
Convergence rate	Rapid local convergence (if initiated well).	Faster convergence than GA in many cases.	Slower convergence, especially near optimum.
Global Search	Prone to local optima, needs good initial point.	Strong global search capability, robust	Strong global search capability.

https://doi.org/10.3390/engproc2026122028

Table 2. Comparing the solving time and volume of algorithms.

	SQP with Fmincon	PSO	GA
Optimal run time (seconds)	1.497	3.035	14.145
Number of iterations	9	100	67
Total number of function calls (maximum number of times the objective function is directly evaluated)	41	2500	3400

2.1. Optimization Using Sequential Quadratic Programming (SQP)

The following table describes the main code in Matlab for solving an optimal problem using SQP with Matlab built-in name of 'fmincon', a gradient-based method. The detailed explanation of SQP algorithm can be found in [12].

The function $f(x)$ in (1) has 3 different minimum points (blue, green) and 3 different maximum points (yellow, red) as shown in Figure 2.

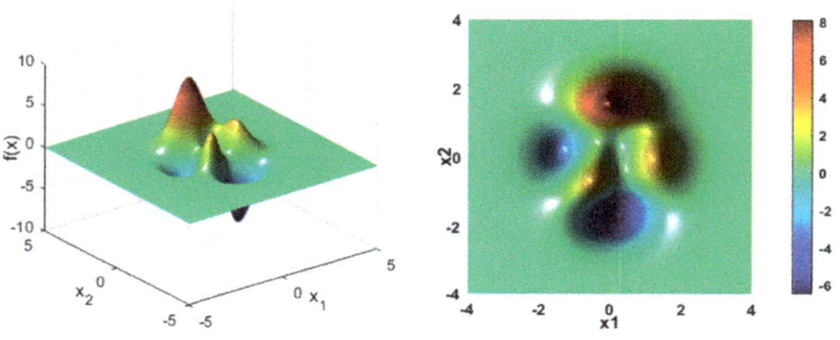

Figure 2. 3D (**a**) and 2D (**b**) graphs of the function f(x) in Equation (1).

Figure 3 shows the point in the ith iteration. The numbers represent the order of the loop or iteration. We see that point 1 is the starting point x_0, where the points move in the gradient direction until they enter the nearest minimum point. Because of that, fmincon is likely not to give a global optimal result, leading to the optimization problem not being completely optimal. The *Fmincon*-based result somewhat depends on the starting point x_0. If the initial point $x_0 = [-2\ 0]$, then $f(x_0)$ is close to a smaller minimum of −3.05. Because, when generating new search points, it does not go to the global minimum of −6.55, 'fmincon' receives a minimum of −3.05 as the minimum of the function. This example shows that the SQP algorithm can only find a local optimal point.

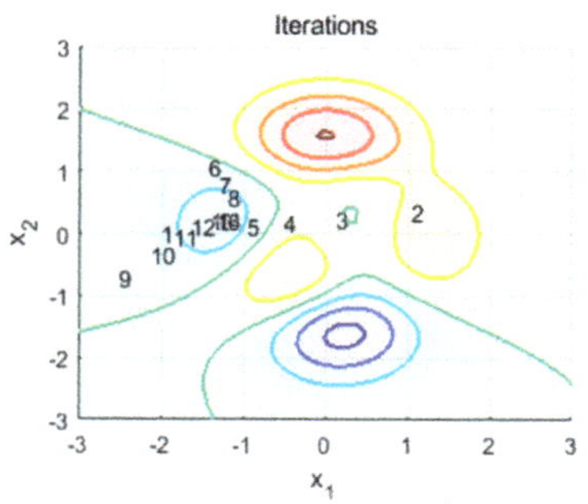

Figure 3. SQP/Fmincon-based optimization process with the initial point $x_0 = [-2, 0]$, with only local optimal point found, illustrating the dependence of searching result on the initial point.

https://doi.org/10.3390/engproc2026122028

If the initial point x_0 = [2, −2], then the global minimum point is captured with a minimum value of −6.55, and the problem converges to the global optimal point as shown in Figure 4.

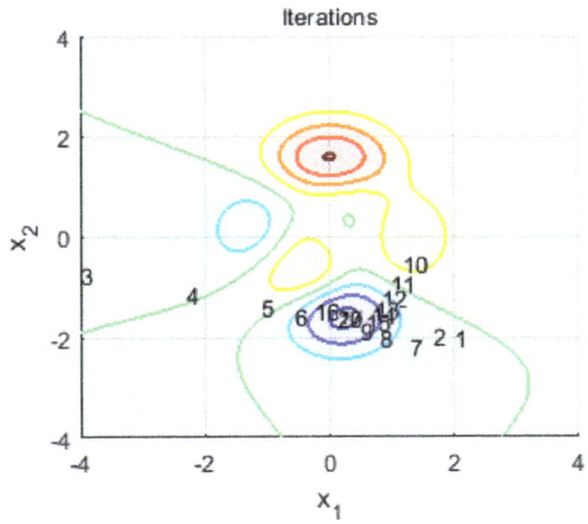

Figure 4. SQP/Fmincon-based optimization process with the initial point x_0 = [2, −2], with global optimal point found, illustrating the dependence of searching result on initial point.

2.2. Particle Swarm Optimization (PSO)

PSO (Particle Swarm Optimization) is a general algorithmic framework based on the experience of swarms proposed by Kennedy and Eberhat, simulating the social behavior of flocks of birds or schools of fish when searching for food sources. A particle is represented in PSO like a bird or a fish foraging in its searching space. The trajectory of each individual in the search space is corrected by varying the individual's velocity, through its flight experience of other individuals in the search space. Experience here is understood as the most optimal indicator of the individual or the whole herd in the past. Each individual will have a fitness value, which is determined by an optimal fit function in each generation. The position and velocity vectors of an ith objective in a space are explained as follows [10,11]. The following describes the main code in Matlab for solving an optimal problem using PSO with Matlab built-in name of 'particleswarm':

```
f = @(x) 3*(1-x(1))^2*exp(-(x(1)^2)-(x(2)+1)^2) - 10*(x(1)/5 - x(1)^3 -
x(2)^5)*exp(-(x(1)^2)-(x(2)^2)) - 1/3*exp(-(x(1)+1)^2-x(2)^2);
nvars=2;% number of variables
lb = [-4 -5]; %lower boundary
ub = [3 4]; %upper boundary
options = optimoptions('particleswarm','SwarmSize',25);
[x,fval,exitflag,output] = particleswarm(f,nvars,lb,ub,options);
```

For example, using a PSO algorithm to find the minima of the function f, which is solved in the previous subsection by SQP, consider the interval $x \in (-4; 3)$; $y \in (-5; 4)$. In the table code above, 'options' have the following options:

FunctionTolerance: Non-negative scalar with default 1×10^{-6}. Iterations end when the relative change in the best objective function value over the last 'MaxStallIterations' iterations is less than 'options.FunctionTolerance'.

https://doi.org/10.3390/engproc2026122028

MaxIterations: Maximum number of iterations particleswarm takes. Default is 200*nvars, where 'nvars' is the number of variables.

MaxStallIterations: Positive integer with default 20. Iterations end when the relative change in best objective function value over the last 'MaxStallIterations' iterations is less than 'options.FunctionTolerance'.

Optimal result obtains the following:

The optimal value of the function is −6.5511.

Variable values x_1, x_2 at the most optimal position of the whole population are 0.2283 and −1.6255, respectively.

It can be seen from Figure 5 that the optimal value of the function (Best Cost) decreases with each iteration. The results at the first and last loop are −3.32 and −6.55, respectively. As can be seen from loop 50, the function value is −6.55 and this value does not change much until the end, proving that this found optimal value has reached the desired optimal value. From loop 60 to 100, the variable value x1 of the particles does not change much; this value lies on the line x_1 = 0.22828, corresponding to the x_1 of the best position of the whole population, which is 0.22828. Similarly, from loop 60 to 100, there is not much change in the x_2 of the particles. The x_2 value of the best position in the population is −1.6255.

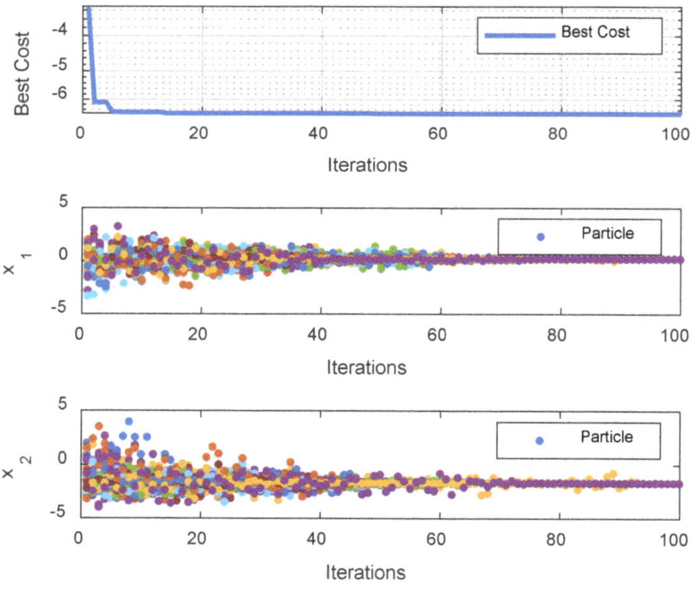

Figure 5. The graph shows the change in the variable, x_1 value, x_2 value, through each iteration; there are many individuals in each iteration and number of individuals is decreasing until the final interation; points in the same iteration have the same color.

Figure 6 shows graphs of the loops at the beginning, middle, and end iterations using PSO. We see that, through the loops, the particle population moves towards the center of the blue ring of the function (the area with the lowest value of the function). There are many particles at the beginning iterations (or loops). Number of particles are decreasing until the end loops.

As can be seen in loop 100, we will only see one red particle. In fact, the particles have all moved to the most optimal position of the population, so only one particle is displayed.

https://doi.org/10.3390/engproc2026122028

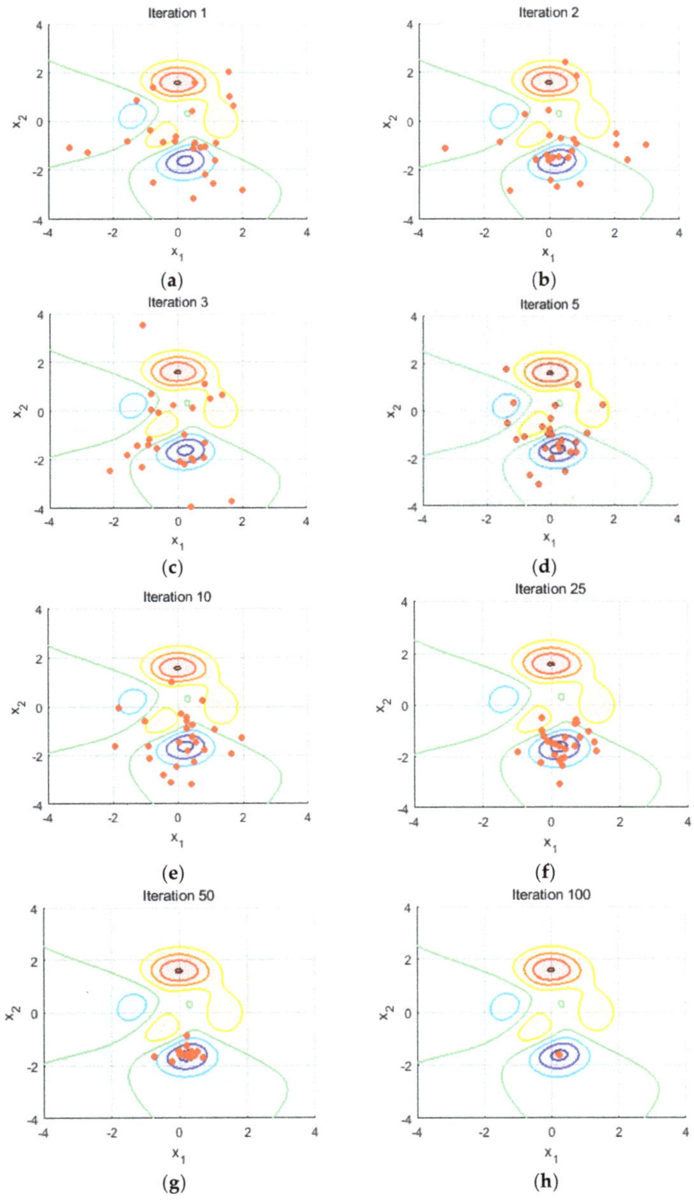

Figure 6. 2D plot showing the positions of all particles in the population at the 1st, 2nd, 3rd, 5th, 10th, 25th, 50th, and 100th loops corresponding to figures from (**a**–**h**).

2.3. Genetic Algorithm (GA)

Genetic algorithm (GA) has been proposed by John Holland in the 1970s. Inspired by the process of natural selection, if individuals adapt well to this influence, they will continue to live; otherwise, it will be discarded.

According to Wikipedia and [13,14] on the explanation of genetic algorithm: "A population of candidate solutions in GA is called individuals. Each candidate solution has a set of properties called chromosomes which can be mutated and altered. The evolution usually starts with a population of randomly generated individuals and is

https://doi.org/10.3390/engproc2026122028

an iterative process. The population in each iteration is called a generation. At each generation, the fitness of every individual in the population is evaluated. Fitness is usually the value of the objective function in the optimization problem being solved. Based on fitness, better individuals (with better fitness) are selected to reproduce. New individuals are created using various operators such as crossover (recombining parts of two parents) and mutation (introducing random changes). The more fit individuals are stochastically selected from the current population, and each individual's genome is modified (recombined and randomly mutated in the structure of genes) to form a new generation. The new generation of candidate solutions is then used in the next iteration of the algorithm. Commonly, the algorithm terminates when either a maximum number of generations has been produced or a satisfactory fitness level has been reached for the population".

To illustrate the GA, we use the GA to solve the above-mentioned problem with objective function in (1), which is solved in the previous subsection by SQP and PSO. The flow chart to explain the GA can be found in [15].

The objective function f is called the fitness function. The vector (x_0, y_0) will be an individual. The score of the individual (x_0, y_0) is f (x_0, y_0).

To solve the optimization problem with GA, the program needs to be organized as follows:

- Objective function (fitness function):

```
function f=fun(x)
f=3*(1-x(1))^2*exp(-(x(1)^2)-(x(2)+1)^2) - 10*(x(1)/5 - x(1)^3 -
x(2)^5)*exp(-(x(1)^2)-(x(2)^2)) - 1/3*exp(-(x(1)+1)^2-x(2)^2);
```

- Linear and nonlinear constraints:

```
A = []; b = [];
Aeq = []; beq = [];
lb = [-4, -5]; ub = [3, 4];
options = optimoptions('ga','ConstraintTolerance',1e-6,'PlotFcn',
@gaplotbestf);
x = ga(@(x)fun(x),size(x),A,b,Aeq,beq,lb,ub,[],options);
```

- Algorithm's stopping conditions (including conditions to ensure that the algorithm works within the allowed time and has progress in a predetermined time period).

After the optimizing process using the GA, the result of optimal process is shown as follows and in Figures 7 and 8.

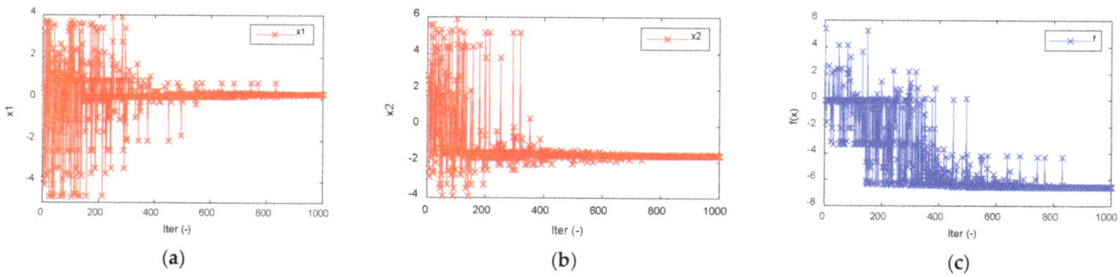

Figure 7. GA optimization process results of variables and fitness function: (**a**) variable x_1 vs. iteration; (**b**) variable x_2 vs. iteration; (**c**) fitness value vs. iteration.

https://doi.org/10.3390/engproc2026122028

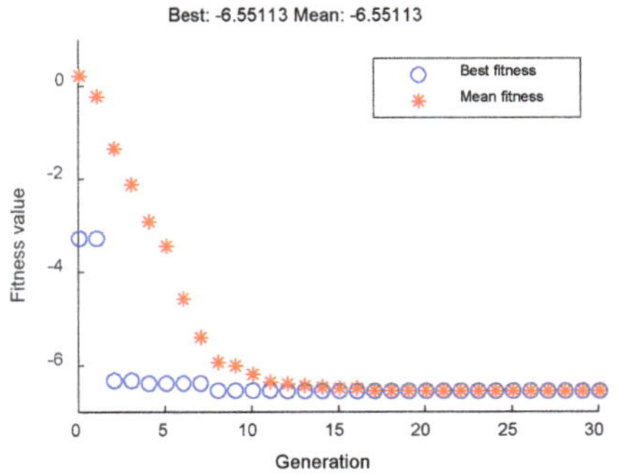

Figure 8. Best fitness and average fitness versus generation in the GA process.

- Minimum point, optimal value, and process are stated as follows:

```
Optimization terminated: average change in the fitness value less than
options.FunctionTolerance.
x =    0.2283    -1.6255
fval =   -6.5511
exitflag = 1
```

It can be seen from Figure 7 that the values of $x(x_1, x_2)$ are initialized and then mutated into many other x values. We see that the value of $f(x)$ is oscillating until it finds the smallest values. Figure 8 shows the best and mean fitness values following generations. At the beginning generations, the mean fitness is always bigger than the best fitness and it decreases quickly. At the final generations, best and mean fitness value converges to the same value.

It can be seen from Figures 9 and 10 that the GA optimal process continues to find objective function values less than the value of the previous generation, and from iteration 891 onwards, it cannot find a value of f(x) less than −6.55.

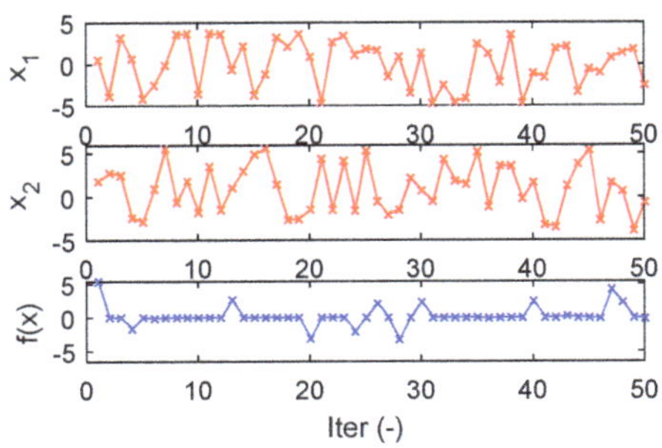

Figure 9. Loops or iterations from 1 to 50 (not yet finished).

The smallest value found by MATLAB's GA is −6.55. The corresponding x value is (0.228, −1.625), as shown in Figure 11.

The advantages of GA are as follows:

- No need to choose the initial point like the SQP algorithm.

- Minimizes the possibility of falling into a local extreme, thus increasing the probability of finding the optimal point.

 https://doi.org/10.3390/engproc2026122028

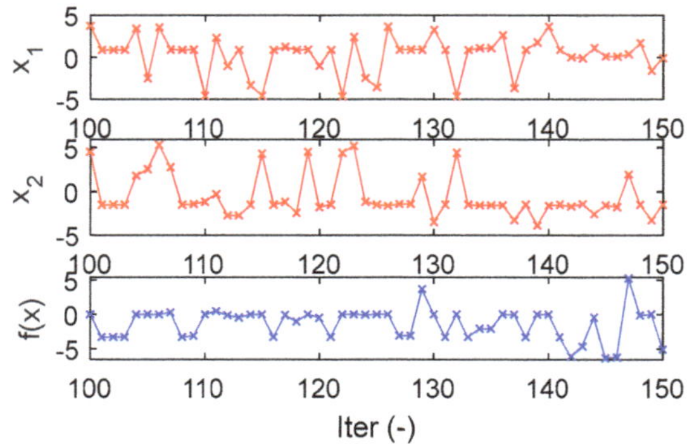

Figure 10. Loops or iterations from 100 to 150 (not yet finished).

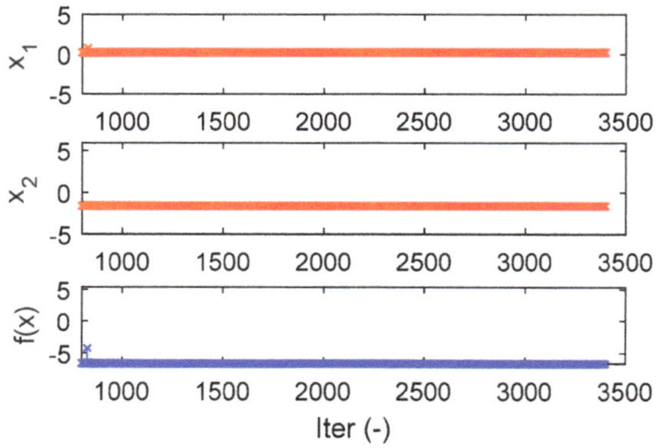

Figure 11. Stable fitness value in final iterations.

The disadvantages of GA are large amount of computation and longer calculation time than PSO and SQP.

3. Proposed Methods to Transfer Multi-Objective to Single Objective

Conventionally, for multi-objective optimization, we can transform the second or third objective function into an inequality constraint [5,6]. Additionally, multi-objective optimization is converted into single-objective optimization. However, in order to optimize multi-objectives accurately and actively adjust the optimal level for each goal, we use the method of converting from multi-objective to single objective with weight factors [8,9]. Hereafter are three proposed methods modified and adaptive from the original weight function method and MinMax problem to apply for the design of IMs [8,11].

Method 1 (Weight Function Method, WFM): This method is referred to as the general weighted function method. Objective function using weight factors presenting for multi-objective optimization can be expressed as

$$L_p(x) = \sum_{m=1}^{M} \frac{w_m |f_m(x) - f_m^*|^p}{|f_m^*|^p} \tag{3}$$

where w_m is weight factor; if this value is larger, then the corresponding objective function is preferred. $f_m(x)$ and $f_m{}^*$ are, respectively, the mth objective function and minimum value of $f_m(x)$. When the objective functions have the same importance, the weight factors are equal and the p normally chosen equals 1.

Method 2 (Sequential Quadratic Distance, SQD): When all objectives are of equal importance ($w_m = 1$), the least squares method (p = 2) is used to find the best compromise solution among the optimal solutions. The new objective function is then

$$Minimize\ G(x) = \sum_k \left(\frac{f_k(x) - f_k^*}{f_k^*} \right)^2 \quad (4)$$

where x is the input variable, and x ∈ X, where X is the possible region in the decision space; f_k^* is the optimal solution of the kth objective function.

Method 3 (Weighted MinMax): When the objective functions have the same importance ($w_m = 1$) and p = 1, the optimization problem becomes as follows:

$$min_{x \in X} max_k \{g_1(x),\ g_2(x), \ldots, g_k(x)\ \} = min_{x \in X} max_k \left\{ \frac{|f_1(x) - f_1^*|}{|f_1^*|}, \frac{|f_2(x) - f_2^*|}{|f_2^*|}, \ldots, \frac{|f_k(x) - f_k^*|}{|f_k^*|} \right\} \quad (5)$$

4. Application for Multi-Objective Optimization of 3-Phase Induction Motors

4.1. Required Parameters of Desired IM

The input parameters are required for the design of a 30 kW induction motor as shown in Table 3.

Table 3. Required parameters of the desired IM.

Parameter Name	Value
Rated power	30 kW
Frequency	50 Hz
Line to line voltage	380 V
Synchronization speed	1500 rpm
Power factor	0.89
Efficiency	0.91
Starting torque multiple	>1.3
Maximum torque multiple	>2.2

4.2. Slot Structure and Its Notations

Figures 12 and 13, respectively, describe slot structure of stator and rotor, as well as its notations.

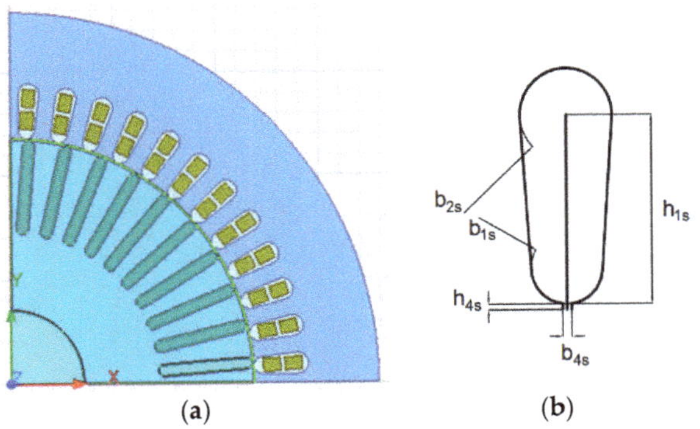

Figure 12. Motor geometry (**a**) and stator slot shape as well as its notation (**b**).

https://doi.org/10.3390/engproc2026122028

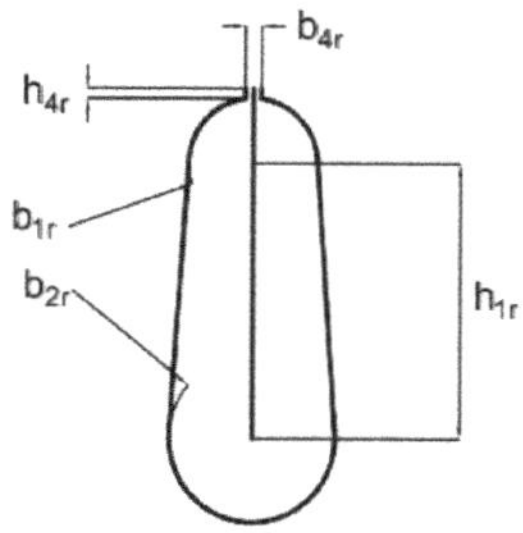

Figure 13. Rotor slot structure and its notations.

4.3. Multi-Objectives

There are 3 objective functions chosen as follows:

- The first objective is maximum efficiency (converting into minimum power loss) f_1^*.
- The second objective function is minimum material cost f_2^*.
- The third objective function is maximum starting torque f_3^*.

Formulas for sizing and calculating electromagnetic parameters can be referred to [15–20], so that they are not mentioned here again.

4.4. Variables for Optimal Problem

With the design using the pear-shaped rotor slot, we choose 11 input variables. Table 4 also shows example dimensions of a 30 kW IM with stator slots number Z_1 = 48 and rotor slots number Z_2 = 40. Using the input parameters set, we can calculate the performance of the motor, and changing these input parameters will change the output performance.

Table 4. Variable definition.

Variable Name	x_k	Example Value
l_s—Calculation length of generator (mm)	x_1	189.5
D_n—Stator outer diameter (mm)	x_2	322.5
K_D—Ratio of outside diameter and inside diameter of stator	x_3	0.685
J_1—Stator current density (A/mm^2)	x_4	5.1
A—Electrical line load (A/cm)	x_5	367.5
b_{1s}—Diameter under the stator slot (mm)	x_6	8.5
b_{2s}—Diameter on the stator slot (mm)	x_7	10.5
h_{1s}—Distance of slot mouth to upper diameter (mm)	x_8	18
b_{1r}—Diameter on the rotor slot (mm)	x_9	4.5
b_{2r}—Diameter under the slot of the rotor (mm)	x_{10}	3.5
h_{1r}—Distance between 2 centers as Figure 13 (mm)	x_{11}	37.5

4.5. Constraints

Constraints of the optimal problem are described as follows:

$1.5 \leq$ stator yoke flux density ≤ 1.8 T.

$1.5 \leq$ rotor yoke flux density ≤ 1.8 T.

$1.5 \leq$ stator teeth flux density ≤ 1.8 T.

$1.5 \leq$ rotor teeth flux density ≤ 1.8 T.

Current density ≤ 6 A/mm^{2}.

Filling factor ≤ 0.6.

Tooth width > 3 mm.

Ratio of maximum torque to rated torque > 2.2.

Power factor > 0.89.

https://doi.org/10.3390/engproc2026122028

5. Comparative SQP, GA, and PSO Algorithms for Multi-Objective Optimization

The following are the results of a triple-objective optimization process for a 30kW induction motor with number stator slots Z_1 = 48 and number of rotor slots Z_2 = 40. Table 5 shows a summary of optimization process for the IM using three algorithms, namely SQP, GA, and PSO, in which the three objectives' optimal problem is converted into the form of Method 2 (Sequential Quadratic Distance or Sequential Quadratic Difference, SQD), as mentioned in Section 3. Note that material cost in the figures is in VND money, which can be converted into USD as 1USD = 24,500 VND.

Table 5. Calculation time and volume of algorithms when motor is optimized.

	PSO	GA	SQP
Number of loops	223	94	9
Total number of function calls	11,500	3400	638
Optimal run time (seconds)	720.5	6583.2	8.3

5.1. PSO Result

We will consider triple-objective functions: Efficiency, ratio of starting torque to rated torque, and material cost. We use a built-in MATLAB 'particleswarm' function in combination with Method 2 'SQD' for multi-objective optimization [12,13].

It should be noted that the optimization using the PSO finds the minimum point. Therefore, the starting torque objective function m_k must reverse the sign of the starting torque multiple. With objective function of efficiency η, the objective function will have the following form:

$$F_{eff} = 1 - \frac{\eta}{100}$$

where F_{eff} is the objective function and has value from 0 to 1.

There is no modification with the objective function of material cost. Formulas to calculate electromagnetic performance and machine sizing can be referred to [16] so that it is not necessary to mention here.

The optimal results are shown in Table 6. In the case that the number of stator slots is Z_1 = 48, the number of rotor slots is Z_2 = 40 and rotor slot is a pear-shaped type.

Table 6. Results before and after optimization.

No.	Parameter	Before	After
1	Starting torque/rated torque m_k	1.47	2.18
2	Maximum torque/rated torque m_{max}	2.31	2.45
3	Starting current/rated current i_k	6.4	7.0
4	Efficiency	91.37%	92.42%
5	Price (USD)	81.35	93.79
6	Cosφ	0.86	0.905

It can be seen from Figure 14 that in the first loop, the particles are randomly distributed on the graph so that all the minima are scanned. Then, the particles gradually converge until the last loop left only one point. The point is the global optimal point of the problem.

When we want to increase efficiency, the material cost will also increase. Because when efficiency increases, the main factor is to reduce the conductor resistance. Reducing the rotor resistance increases the size of the slot, and at the same time, the volume of the rotor and material cost increase. Changing the size of stator and rotor slots leads to change

https://doi.org/10.3390/engproc2026122028

in leakage flux and starting torque. It is known that the lower the leakage flux, the higher the starting torque. Figures 15–17 show the relationship of objective functions, which are motor efficiency and material cost in Figure 15, efficiency and starting torque multiples in Figure 16, and material cost and starting torque multiples in Figure 17. It can be seen that efficiency and starting torque after the optimization process significantly increase in comparison to before the optimization process. Meanwhile, material cost also increases after the optimization process, because it has to compromisemotor efficiency.

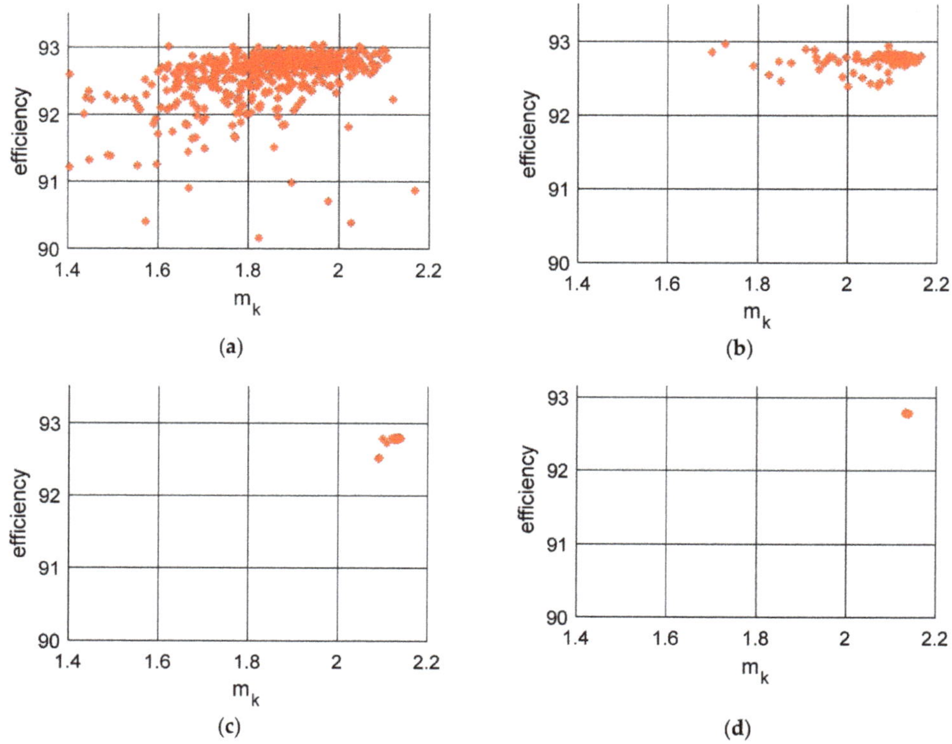

Figure 14. PSO process for the designed motor at loops 1 (**a**), 80 (**b**), 160 (**c**), and 223 (**d**), respectively.

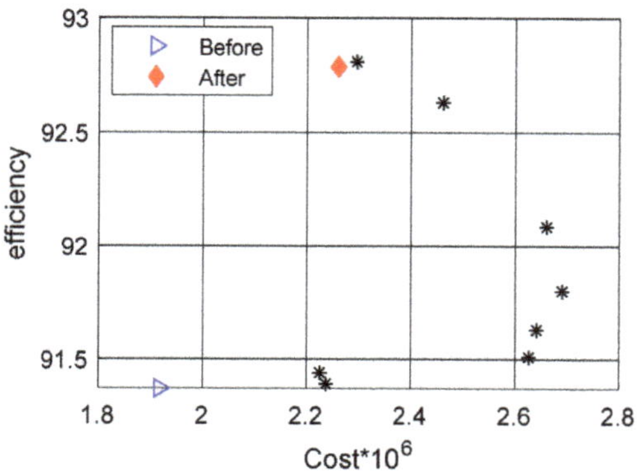

Figure 15. Efficiency vs. material cost, points '*' showing values of objective functions while optimization process.

https://doi.org/10.3390/engproc2026122028

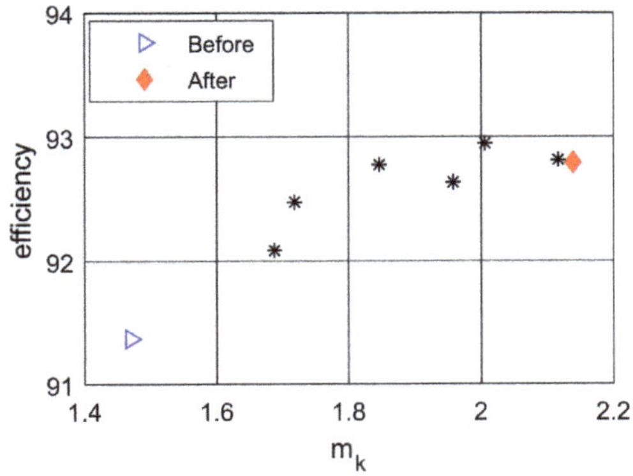

Figure 16. Efficiency vs. starting torque multiple from the first iteration to the final iteration, points '*' showing values of objective functions while optimization process.

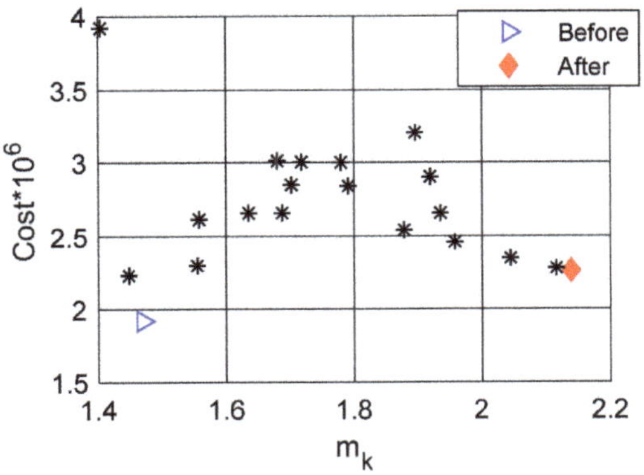

Figure 17. Starting torque multiple vs. material cost from the first iteration to the final iteration, points '*' showing values of objective functions while optimization process.

5.2. GA Result

Similarly to PSO, for GA-based optimization, we also consider triple-objective functions at the same time: efficiency, starting torque multiple, material cost. We use MATLAB's 'ga' function in combination with Method 2 'SQD' in Section 3 to optimize multi-objectives. Optimization process results before and after optimizing are shown in Table 7.

Table 7. Optimization result using GA.

No.	Parameter	Before	After
1	Starting torque/rated torque m_k	1.47	2.01
2	Maximum torque/rated torque m_{max}	2.31	2.49
3	Starting current/rated current i_k	6.4	7.0
4	Efficiency	91.37%	92.33%
5	Price (USD)	81.35	90.23
6	Cosφ	0.86	0.91

5.3. Fmincon-SQP Result

Using Fmincon to optimize triple-objective functions in form of Method 2 'SQD' is efficiency, material cost, starting torque factor. Results are shown in Table 8.

https://doi.org/10.3390/engproc2026122028

Table 8. Optimization results using Fmincon.

No.	Parameter	Before	After
1	Starting torque/rated torque m_k	1.47	1.8812
2	Maximum torque/rated torque m_{max}	2.31	2.5178
3	Starting current/rated current i_k	6.4	6.98
4	Efficiency	91.37%	92.47%
5	Price (USD)	81.35	104.32
6	Cosφ	0.86	0.93

5.4. Summary of Comparison Result of Optimal Methods

Table 9 compares three optimal algorithms for solving the triple-objective optimal problem, in which objective function is written in form of Method 2—SQD in Section 3.

Table 9. Compare the results of the optimization methods.

No.	Parameter	Fmincon	GA	PSO
1	Starting torque/rated torque m_k	1.88	2.01	2.18
2	Maximum torque/rated torque m_{max}	2.51	2.49	2.45
3	Starting current/rated current i_k	6.98	7.0	7.0
4	Efficiency	92.47%	92.33%	92.42%
5	Price (USD)	104.32	90.23	93.79
6	Cosφ	0.93	0.91	0.905
7	Running time (seconds)	8.3	6583.2	720.5

5.5. Discussions

+ Regarding the triple-objective optimization result using three methods, namely Fmincon/SQP, GA, and PSO, the optimal efficiency is almost the same among the three methods. Fmincon results in higher cost higher and lower starting torque among the three methods.

+ In terms of computing time, GA took longest time, almost 9 times longer than that of using PSO method. Fmincon only took a few seconds to complete optimal process.

In conclusion, the PSO is the most suitable method for designing optimization of induction motors.

6. Comparative WFM, SQD, MinMax Hierarchical Methods for Multi-Objective Optimization Using PSO

Section 3 presents methods for converting from muti-objective function into single-objective function with weight factors and based on hierarchical optimization method. The first level of hierarchical optimization is to solve mono-objective optimal problems such as maximum efficiency, minimum material cost, and maximum starting torque. The second level of hierarchical optimization is to solve equivalent multi-objective function built based on the WFM, SQD, or MinMax method. Tables 10 and 11 are summaries of triple-objective optimization for a 30 kW IM by using WFM, SQD, and MinMax methods to convert multi-objective functions into a single-objective function.

Table 10 is the result solved by using Fmincon, while Table 11 uses PSO. The Fmincon function has the advantage of a very short computing time. But the disadvantage is that it cannot find the global optimal point. The reason is that because of the starting point dependence, global optimal points cannot be found.

It can be seen from Table 11 that the weight function method WFM has the advantage of the fastest running speed. In case the goals are equally important, we use SQD G(x) to achieve the most reasonable result.

 https://doi.org/10.3390/engproc2026122028

Table 10. Comparison of multi-objectives to single-objective conversion methods using Fmincon.

No.	Parameter	MinMax	SQD G(x)	WFM
1	Starting torque/rated torque m_k	2.91	1.8812	1.49
2	Maximum torque/rated torque m_{max}	2.55	2.5178	2.1
3	Starting current/rated current i_k	5.4	6.98	7.0
4	Efficiency	88.3%	92.47%	92.17%
5	Price (USD)	131.68	104.32	109.22
6	Cosφ	0.926	0.93	0.92
7	Time (seconds)	27.18	8.3	6.2

Table 11. Comparison of multi-objective to single-objective conversion methods using PSO.

No.	Parameter	MinMax	SQD G(x)	WFM
1	Starting torque/rated torque m_k	2.26	2.18	1.96
2	Maximum torque/rated torque m_{max}	2.58	2.45	2.4
3	Starting current/rated current i_k	6.9	7.0	7.0
4	Efficiency	90.0%	92.42%	92.79%
5	Price (USD)	96.37	93.79	95.41
6	Cosφ	0.89	0.905	0.91
7	Time (seconds)	2491.8	720.5	523.64

7. Conclusions

This paper has presented the optimal design for a 30 kW 3-phase squirrel-cage asynchronous motor and then compared SQP, GA, and PSO algorithms. Three optimal algorithms, namely PSO, GA, and SQP, were applied for the optimal design of IMs. Finding the most suitable algorithm is PSO. This paper has proposed an optimization method that permits us to find only one optimal solution satisfying multi-objectives, instead of the Pareto optimal set as in the traditional ε-constraint method. Comparison among weighted function method WFM, Sequential Quadratic Distance SQD, and MinMax methods for hierarchical multi-objective optimization has given broadened insights into optimal techniques for IMs. We have found that the SQD in combination with PSO is the best method for optimization design of IMs in terms of computation time and finding global optimal point.

Funding: This research received no external funding.

Institutional Review Board Statement: Not applicable.

Informed Consent Statement: Not applicable.

Data Availability Statement: Data will be available based on request.

Conflicts of Interest: The author declares no conflicts of interest.

Abbreviations

The following abbreviations are used in this manuscript:

SQP	Sequential Quadratic Programming
SQD	Sequential Quadratic Distance
GA	Genetic Algorithm
PSO	Particle Swarm Optimization
IM	Induction Motor
WFM	Weighted Function Method

https://doi.org/10.3390/engproc2026122028

References

1. Azab, M. A Review of Recent Trends in High-Efficiency Induction Motor Drives. *Vehicles* **2025**, *7*, 15. [CrossRef]
2. Xuan, H.V.; Quang, H.N.; Dang, C.N. Modeling and analyzing multi-megawatt direct-drive wind-turbine power system in offshore application: Power flow and short circuit. *E3S Web Conf.* **2024**, *551*, 02011. [CrossRef]
3. Mahmouditabar, F.; Baker, N.J.; Mahmouditabar, F.; Baker, N.J. Design Optimization of Induction Motors with Different Stator Slot Rotor Bar Combinations Considering Drive Cycle. *Energies* **2023**, *17*, 154. [CrossRef]
4. Juhaniya, A.I.S.; Ibrahim, A.A.; Zainuri, M.A.A.M.; Zulkifley, M.A.; Remli, M.A. Optimal Stator and Rotor Slots Design of Induction Motors for Electric Vehicles Using Opposition-Based Jellyfish Search Optimization. *Machines* **2022**, *10*, 1217. [CrossRef]
5. Chircop, K.; Zammit, D. On ε-Constraint Based Methods for the Generation of Pareto Frontiers. *J. Mech. Eng. Autom.* **2013**, *3*, 279–289.
6. Messac, A.; Ismail-Yahaya, A.; Mattson, C.A. The Normalized Normal Constraint Method for Generating the Pareto Frontier. *Struct. Multidiscip. Optim.* **2003**, *25*, 86–98. [CrossRef]
7. Tsaknakis, I. Hierarchical Optimization Problems: Theory, Algorithms and Applications. Ph.D. Dissertation, University of Minnesota, Minneapolis, MN, USA, 2024. Available online: https://hdl.handle.net/11299/269584 (accessed on 5 August 2025).
8. Jones, D.F.; Florentino, H.O. Multi-Objective Optimization: Methods and Applications. In *The Palgrave Handbook of Operations Research*; Salhi, S., Boylan, J., Eds.; Springer International Publishing: Cham, Switzerland, 2022; pp. 181–207. [CrossRef]
9. Diwekar, U.M. Nonlinear Programming. In *Introduction to Applied Optimization. Applied Optimization*; Springer: Boston, MA, USA, 2003; Volume 80. [CrossRef]
10. Jakob, W.; Blume, C.; Jakob, W.; Blume, C. Pareto Optimization or Cascaded Weighted Sum: A Comparison of Concepts. *Algorithms* **2014**, *7*, 166–185. [CrossRef]
11. Cramer, A.M.; Sudhoff, S.D.; Zivi, E.L. Evolutionary Algorithms for Minimax Problems in Robust Design. *IEEE Trans. Evol. Comput.* **2009**, *13*, 444–453. [CrossRef]
12. Parkinson, A.R.; Balling, R.; Hedengren, J.D. *Optimization Methods for Engineering Design; Design Optimization Textbook*; Brigham Young University: Provo, UT, USA, 2013. Available online: https://apmonitor.com/me575/index.php/Main/BookChapters (accessed on 29 November 2025).
13. Kalyanmoy, D. *Multiobjective Optimization Using Evolutionary Algorithms*; John Wiley and Sons: West Sussex, UK, 2001.
14. Arora, J.S. Multi-Objective Optimum Design: Concepts and Methods. In *Introduction to Optimum Design*, 5th ed.; Academic Press: Cambridge, MA, USA, 2025; pp. 825–851. [CrossRef]
15. Akhtar, M.J.; Behera, R.K. Optimal Design of Stator and Rotor Slot of Induction Motor for Electric Vehicle Applications. *IET Electr. Syst. Transp.* **2019**, *9*, 35–43. [CrossRef]
16. Joksimović, G.; Mezzarobba, M.; Tessarolo, A.; Levi, E. Optimal Selection of Rotor Bar Number in Multiphase Cage Induction Motors. *IEEE Access* **2020**, *8*, 135558–135568. [CrossRef]
17. Boldea, I.; Nasar, S.A. *The Induction Machines Design Handbook*; Taylor & Francis: Abingdon, UK, 2009; ISBN 978-1-4200-6668-5.
18. Szénásy, I.; Csikor, D.; Szénásy, I.; Csikor, D. Induction Motor Energy Efficiency Investigation. *Eng. Proc.* **2024**, *79*, 75. [CrossRef]
19. Vu Xuan, H.; Ani, S.O.; Lahaye, D.; Polinder, H.; Ferreira, J.A. Validation of Non-Linear Dynamic FEM Model for Design of PM Machines with Concentrated Windings in Ship Application. In Proceedings of the 2011 14th European Conference on Power Electronics and Applications, Birmingham, UK, 30 August–1 September 2011; pp. 1–9.
20. Dimitrova, I.; Taneva, A.; Hristova, T.; Dimitrova, I.; Taneva, A.; Hristova, T. Investigation of Saturation in Iron Core Induction Motors with a Model in MATLAB/Simulink. *Eng. Proc.* **2025**, *104*, 33. [CrossRef]

https://doi.org/10.3390/engproc2026122028

engineering proceedings

MDPI

Proceeding Paper

Diffraction Analysis of Two Semi-Submersible Platforms for Floating Offshore Wind Turbine Applications Using OrcaWave †

Olena Videnova *, Nikita Dobin, Nick Markov, Silvia Kirilova and Rumen Kishev

Institute of Metal Science, Equipment and Technologies with Hydro- and Aerodynamics Centre "Acad. A. Balevski"—Bulgarian Ship Hydrodynamics Centre, Bulgarian Academy of Sciences, 9000 Varna, Bulgaria; n.dobin@bshc.bg (N.D.); n.markov@bshc.bg (N.M.); s.kirilova@bshc.bg (S.K.); rkishev@yahoo.com (R.K.)

* Correspondence: o.videnova@bshc.bg; Tel.: +359-5237-0500

† Presented at the 6th International Conference on Communications, Information, Electronic and Energy Systems, 26–28 November 2025, Ruse, Bulgaria.

Abstract

This study presents a diffraction analysis of two semi-submersible platform configurations intended for floating offshore wind turbine applications. The first investigated configuration corresponds to a semi-submersible barge with a central moonpool, while the second configuration is a cross-shaped semi-submersible. Both hydrodynamic models were developed and analyzed in OrcaWave. Simulations were performed for wave incidence directions ranging from 0° to 360°. The obtained hydrodynamic coefficients provide insights into the added mass, radiation damping, load response amplitude operators (RAOs) and two types of mean drift loads RAO of both platform types. The results highlight the influence of geometry and displacement on the diffraction performance, which is critical for the design of floating wind turbine support structures.

Keywords: floating offshore wind turbine (FOWT); semi-submersible; renewable energy; OrcaWave; OrcaFlex; CFD

1. Introduction

The development of renewable energy has become a strategic priority for many countries and organizations, with wind energy representing one of the fastest-growing sources worldwide. While onshore wind turbines have reached high levels of efficiency, offshore wind energy is increasingly regarded as a key technology for the future. The primary rationale for deploying turbines at sea lies in the more stable wind conditions, characterized by lower turbulence and higher energy potential, as well as the availability of vast open spaces that allow for the installation of larger and more powerful systems without affecting populated areas.

Conventional offshore turbines anchored to the seabed, however, are only economically viable up to moderate water depths. At greater depths, typical of most continental shelves, foundation costs rise steeply, thereby limiting their applicability. This challenge has motivated the development of a new generation of floating offshore wind turbines (FOWTs), which rely on mooring systems for station-keeping without fixed seabed foundations.

Among the various floater concepts, semi-submersible platforms offer favorable stability, draft flexibility, and scalability for multi-megawatt turbines.

This study focuses on the hydrodynamic diffraction characteristics of two semi-submersible configurations: a barge with a central moonpool and a cross-shaped semi-submersible. The objective is to evaluate the influence of geometry and displacement on hydrodynamic coefficients and motion responses through OrcaWave 11.4 (Orcina, Ulverston, UK) simulations, serving as a basis for subsequent dynamic analyses in OrcaFlex under Black Sea environmental conditions.

2. OrcaWave 11.4 Description

Diffraction analysis of two concepts for semi-submersible platforms for supporting structures of floating offshore wind turbines (FOWTs) was performed using the frequency-domain hydrodynamic solver OrcaWave [1]. The study evaluates hydrodynamic coefficients, wave-excited loads, and motion responses (RAOs) across a relevant wave frequency range for operational and extreme conditions. Model setup, boundary conditions, and meshing strategy in OrcaWave are described in detail to ensure reproducibility [2].

In OrcaWave, wave-induced loads can be computed through two main approaches: the displacement (Pressure Integration) method and the Control Surface method [3]. The Pressure Integration method evaluates hydrodynamic pressure directly over the wetted body surface, providing detailed local load distribution. In contrast, the Control Surface approach integrates the flux of momentum through a notional Control Surface enclosing the body, which often yields smoother estimates for global quantities such as the mean drift load [4]. In this study, both methods are applied and compared to assess differences in predicted mean drift forces and their implications for semi-submersible platform response [5].

3. Methodology

The first investigated platform configuration corresponds to a "moonpool barge (MP barge)" with overall dimensions of 60 m × 60 m × 15 m and a draft of 10 m.

The structure incorporates a central opening of 20 m × 20 m × 15 m (Figure 1). The barge displacement is approximately 32,200 T, excluding the mounted turbine.

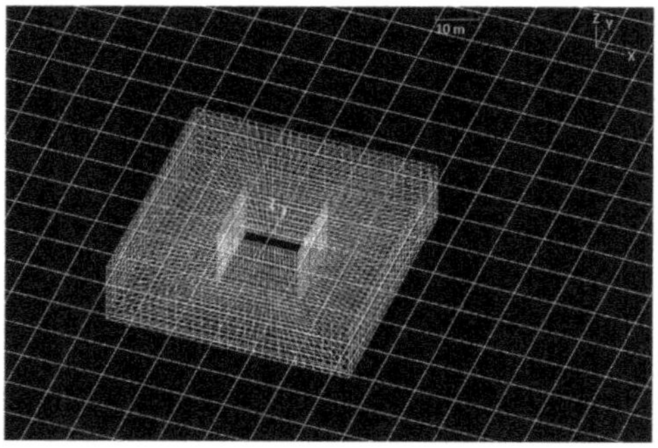

Figure 1. Moonpool barge model (60 m × 60 m × 15 m, 4592 panels).

This configuration was inspired by previously studied barge-type semi-submersibles tested both experimentally and numerically under offshore Taiwan conditions [6]. The current studies of the hydrodynamic behavior of the platform were made for a subsequent analysis of operation in environmental conditions representative of the Black Sea region with its relatively more moderate waves and wind [7].

Diffraction analysis was performed with OrcaWave 11.4, based on a panel model of 4592 panels generated in AQWA, QTF field and Control Surface generated in OrcaWave (Figures 2 and 3). The hydrodynamic coefficients were computed for wave incidence

 https://doi.org/10.3390/engproc2026122029

directions from 0° to 360° (15° increments) and for 25 wave frequencies ranging from 0.1 to 2 rad/s (with a step of 0.05–0.1 in the different zone). These coefficients will be used as input files in the program OrcaFlex.

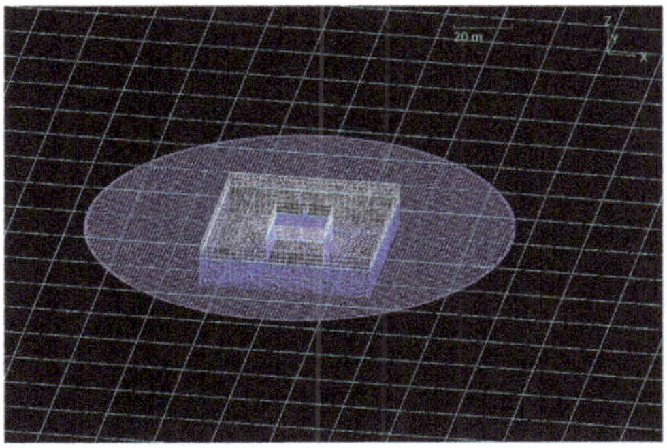

Figure 2. Moonpool barge OrcaWave model with QTF field (R = 75 m).

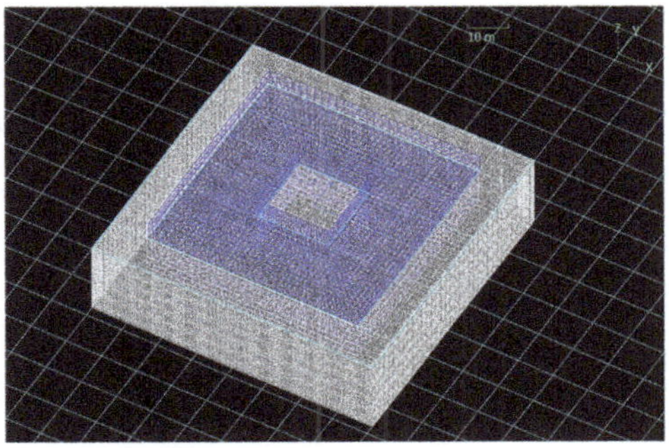

Figure 3. Control Surface (58,000 panels, 0.5 m size), 10 m offset from the body.

The second configuration corresponds to a cross-shaped semi-submersible (X-shape) (Figure 4) with overall dimensions of 40.5 m × 40.5 m × 9 m and a draft of 6 m. The displacement of the floating body is a 7215 T.

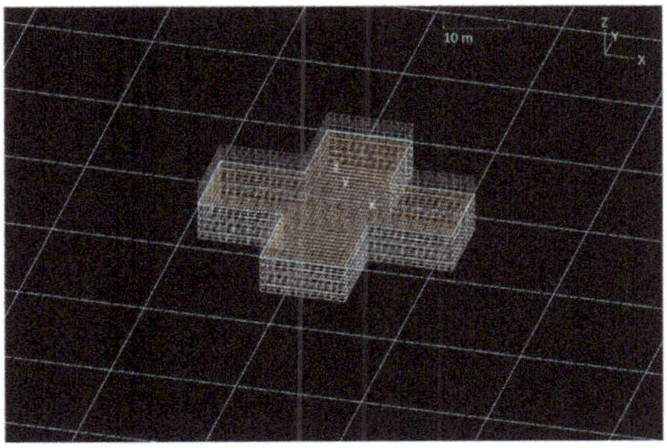

Figure 4. X-shape model (40.5m × 40.5m × 9 m, 2272 panels).

The hydrodynamic model was discretized into 2272 panels, the QTF field had a radius of 60 m around the body, and the CS was generated from 38,252 panels (Figures 5 and 6).

Diffraction analysis for the second configuration was also performed in OrcaWave over a range of incident wave directions between 0° and 360° (15° angular increments) and for 25 frequencies (0.1–2 rad/s, step 0.05–0.1).

https://doi.org/10.3390/engproc2026122029

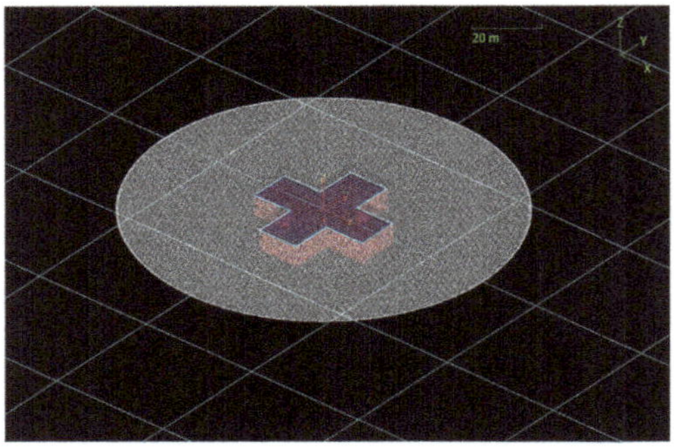

Figure 5. Full QTF method model (R = 60 m).

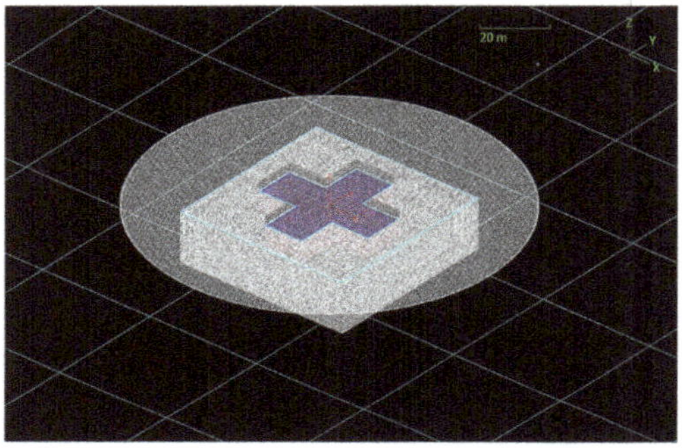

Figure 6. Autogenerated Control Surface (38,252 panels, 0.5 m size, 15 m offset).

4. Results and Discussion

The results are organized in three main parts. The first subsection describes the motion of the platforms, the second part focuses on the load RAOs and their directional behavior; in the third part, the analysis focuses on the average second-order drift forces and moments estimated using two numerical approaches—the Pressure Integration (PI) and Control Surface (CS) methods—and compared their results.

4.1. Motion RAO Results

Figure 7 illustrates the displacement RAOs for surge, sway, heave at selected wave headings across a relevant wave frequency range.

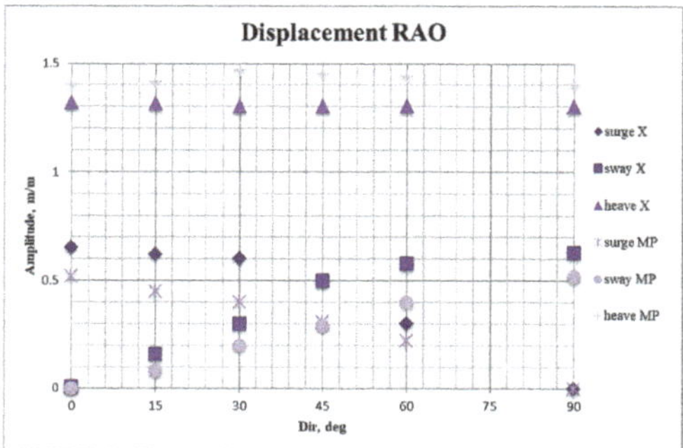

Figure 7. Displacement RAOs for X-shape and moonpool platforms.

https://doi.org/10.3390/engproc2026122029

The heave RAO dominates the response, with amplitudes exceeding 1.2 m/m across all headings, indicating pronounced vertical compliance of the semi-submersible. Surge responses are largest in head seas (0°) and decrease toward beam seas (90°), whereas sway responses exhibit the opposite behavior. This is due to the symmetry of the hull relative to the X and Y axes, with surge passing into sway at 45 degrees. Overall, these findings highlight the strong directional dependence of platform motions, which must be considered carefully in turbine clearance and operability assessments.

4.2. Load RAO Results

The Load RAO results for both platforms provide detailed insight into their first-order hydrodynamic behavior.

Figure 8 presents the load response amplitudes for translational (surge, sway, heave) motions.

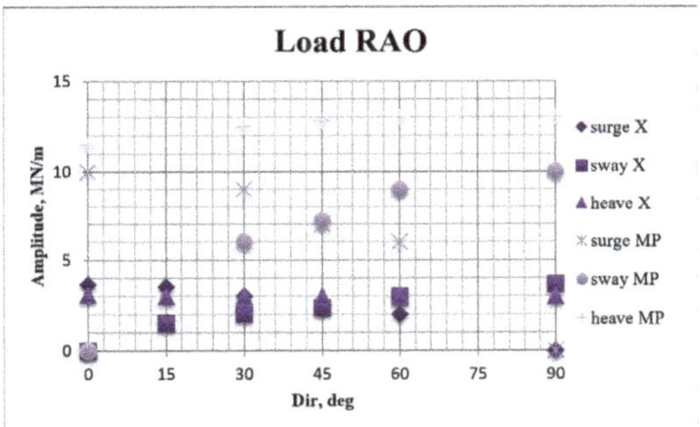

Figure 8. Load RAOs for both platform types.

Surge loads are highest in head seas, exceeding 10MN/m, and decrease substantially toward beam seas. In contrast, sway loads increase steadily with heading and peak near 90°, reflecting dominant transverse excitation. Heave loads remain nearly constant across directions, consistent with vertical symmetry of the hulls.

Figure 9 presents the load RAOs for rotational motions.

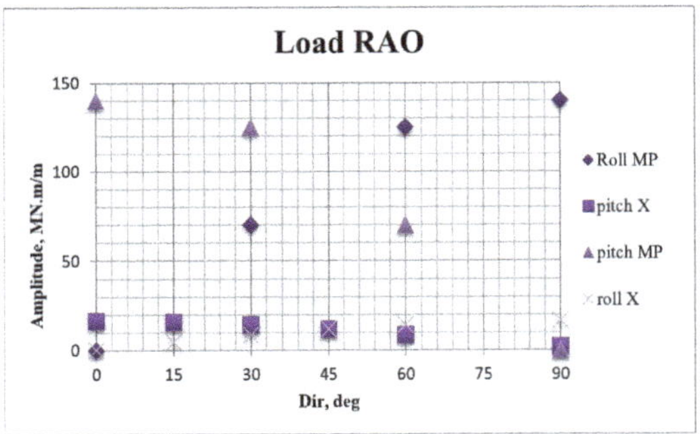

Figure 9. Load RAOs for roll and pitch motions.

The moment RAO analysis reveals an inverse relationship between roll and pitch responses. Platform X-shape exhibits maximum pitch at head seas (≈16.6 MN·m/m) and increasing roll toward beam seas. This smooth transition indicates stable hydrodynamic behavior and balanced load distribution. For the MP configuration, the same inverse trend is observed but with significantly higher magnitudes. These large amplitudes reflect the

 https://doi.org/10.3390/engproc2026122029

barge's stiffer geometry and the hydrodynamic influence of its moonpool cavity, which amplifies restoring loads under directional excitation.

The agreement between outputs support the reliability of the hydrodynamic discretization. These results confirm the directional sensitivity of the semi-submersible, providing a quantitative basis for subsequent mooring design and coupled turbine–platform analysis.

4.3. Mean Drift Load Results

Figures shown below compare the mean drift load RAOs obtained using the Pressure Integration (PI) and Control Surface (CS) formulations in OrcaWave.

The PI method captures significant second-order contributions across all translational DOFs, with surge forces dominating in head seas and sway forces increasing toward oblique and beam headings (Figure 10).

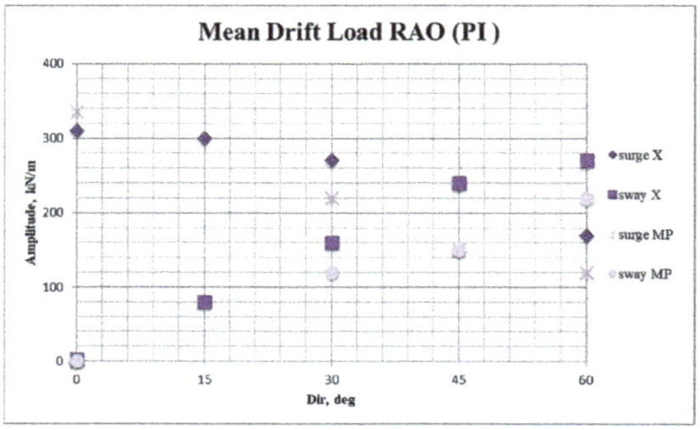

Figure 10. Mean drift loads RAOs—Pressure Integration (PI).

Heave drift contributions remain nearly constant at ≈600 kN/m, indicating strong vertical steady loading.

In contrast, the CS method produces lower magnitudes, particularly in heave where contributions are negligible, but provides smoother directional variations, reflecting greater numerical robustness (Figure 11).

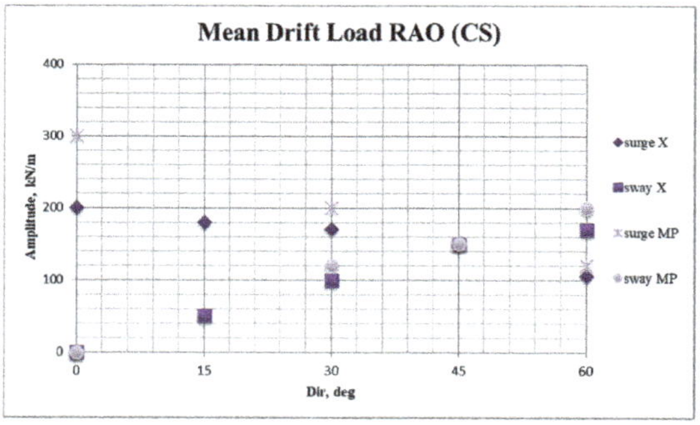

Figure 11. Mean drift loads RAOs—Control Surface (CS).

Mean drift moments follow consistent physical trends: pitch remains steady across headings (~2000 kN·m/m), while roll increases significantly at oblique angles (30–60°), peaking near 3500 kN·m/m. The comparison between evaluation points confirms overall consistency, although pitch predictions show some sensitivity to location (Figures 12 and 13).

https://doi.org/10.3390/engproc2026122029

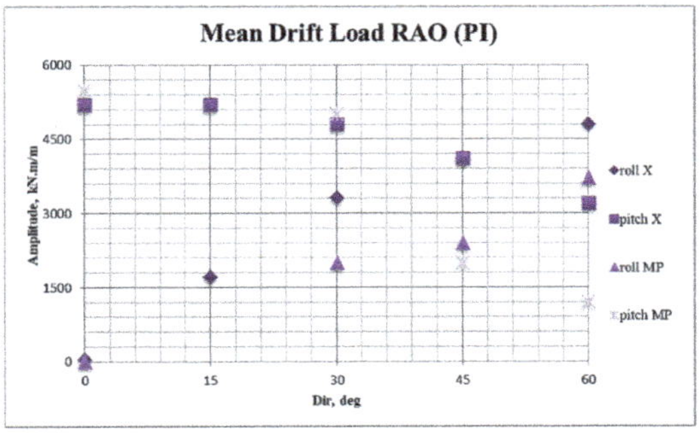

Figure 12. Mean drift loads RAOs—PI (roll and pitch).

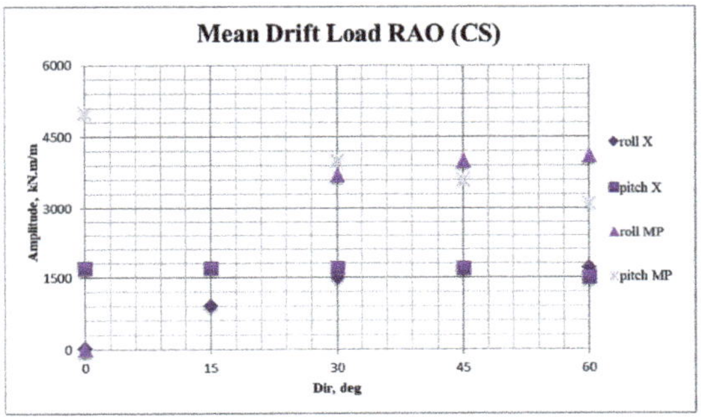

Figure 13. Mean drift loads RAOs—CS (roll and pitch).

Taken together, these results emphasize that PI tends to overpredict vertical effects, whereas CS offers smoother and more stable trends. Applying both methods in parallel therefore provides valuable uncertainty bounds for design. This dual-approach framework strengthens the assessment of mooring loads, station-keeping, and overall stability of floating wind turbine support structures.

5. Conclusions

This study presented a diffraction-based analysis of two semi-submersible configurations for floating offshore wind turbine applications. OrcaWave simulations demonstrated that both geometry and displacement play a decisive role in hydrodynamic performance. The Moonpool barge benefits from greater displacement, yielding enhanced stability through increased added mass and damping, whereas the X-shape semi-submersible exhibits more favorable motion responses due to its reduced displacement and cross geometry. The combined findings underscore the importance of carefully balancing platform geometry and mass distribution when designing floating wind turbine support structures. Future work will extend the present analysis by integrating mooring dynamics and turbine aerodynamics in coupled time-domain simulations using OrcaFlex, thereby enabling a comprehensive evaluation of global performance under realistic Black Sea conditions.

Author Contributions: Conceptualization, O.V., N.D., N.M., and R.K.; methodology, O.V., N.D., N.M. and S.K.; software, O.V., N.D., N.M. and S.K.; supervision O.V., N.D., N.M. and S.K.; validation, O.V. and N.D.; visualization O.V. and N.D.; formal analysis, O.V. and N.D.; investigation, O.V. and N.D.; funding acquisition, N.M. and R.K.; project administration, O.V., N.D. and N.M.; resources, O.V., N.D., N.M. and R.K.; data curation, O.V. and N.D.; writing—original draft preparation, O.V. and N.D.; writing—review and editing, O.V. and N.D. All authors have read and agreed to the published version of the manuscript.

https://doi.org/10.3390/engproc2026122029

Funding: This study is co-financed by the European Union through the Program "Research, innovation and digitalization for smart transformation 2021–2027", project Center of Competence "Blue Coastal Marine and Riverine Innovative & Sustainable Management of Environments and Resources (Blue Cristal)", contract #BG16RFPR002-1.014-0016-C01.

Institutional Review Board Statement: Not applicable.

Informed Consent Statement: Not applicable.

Data Availability Statement: The data generated in this study are presented in the article. For any clarifications, please contact the corresponding author.

Conflicts of Interest: The authors declare no conflict of interest.

Abbreviations

The following abbreviations are used in this manuscript:

RAO	Response amplitude operators
FOWT	Floating offshore wind turbine
PI	Pressure Integration (method)
CS	Control Surface (method)
MP	Moonpool (barge)
QTF	Quadratic Transfer Function

References

1. *OrcaFlex User Manual*; Orcina Ltd.: Ulverston, UK, 2013.
2. Lei, T.; Tomoki, I.; Yasuhiro, A.; Koichi, M. *Wave Drift Forces on a Barge-Type Floater with Moonpools*; Nihon University; The Japan Society of Naval Architects and Ocean: Tokyo, Japan, 2021.
3. Wang, S.; Moan, T.; Gao, Z. Methodology for global structural load effect analysis of the semi-submersible hull of floating wind turbines under still water, wind, and wave loads. *Mar. Struct.* **2023**, *91*, 103463. [CrossRef]
4. Dagher, H.; Viselli, A.; Goupee, A.; Allen, C. *1:50 Scale Testing of Three Floating Wind Turbines at MARIN and Numerical Model Validation Against Test Data*; University of Maine: Orono, ME, USA, 2017. [CrossRef]
5. Wang, S.; Xing, Y.; Balakrishna, R.; Shi, W.; Xu, X. Design, local structural stress, and global dynamic response analysis of a steel semi-submersible hull for a 10-MW floating wind turbine. *Eng. Struct.* **2023**, *291*, 116474. [CrossRef]
6. Chuang, T.-C.; Yang, W.-H.; Yang, R.-Y. Experimental and numerical study of a barge-type FOWT platform under wind and wave load. *Ocean Eng.* **2021**, *230*, 109015. [CrossRef]
7. Nikolov, G.; Truhkchev, D.; Kishev, R.; Fellows, D.; Kaloyanchev, P. Feasibility study on prerequisites and specifics of floating wind farms deployment in the bulgarian open shelf. *Int. Multidiscip. Sci. GeoConf. SGEM* **2023**, *23*, 75–83.

 https://doi.org/10.3390/engproc2026122029

MDPI AG
Grosspeteranlage 5
4052 Basel
Switzerland
Tel.: +41 61 683 77 34

Engineering Proceedings Editorial Office
E-mail: engproc@mdpi.com
www.mdpi.com/journal/engproc

www.ingramcontent.com/pod-product-compliance
Lightning Source LLC
Chambersburg PA
CBHW061614220926
51850CB00005B/508
* 9 7 8 3 7 2 5 8 7 9 6 7 0 *